Library of
Davidson College

Anthropological Realities

Transaction/SOCIETY Texts

Politics in America: The Cutting Edge of Change, edited by Walter Dean Burnham

Social Psychology, edited by Elliot Aronson and Robert Helmreich

Marriages and Families, edited by Helena Z. Lopata

Social Problems in Corporate America, edited by Helen Icken Safa and Gloria Levitas

Sociological Realities: I and II, edited by Irving Louis Horowitz, Mary Symons Strong, and Charles Nanry

Anthropological Realities: Readings in the Science of Culture, edited by Jeanne Guillemin

Anthropological Realities
Readings in the Science of Culture

edited by
Jeanne Guillemin

Transaction Books
New Brunswick (U.S.A.) and London (U.K.)

301.2
A6285

Copyright © 1981 by Transaction, Inc.
New Brunswick, New Jersey 08903

All rights reserved under International and Pan-American Copyright Conventions. No part of this book may be reproduced or transmitted in any form or by any means, electronic or mechanical, including photocopy, recording, or any information storage and retrieval system, without prior permission in writing from the publisher. All inquiries should be addressed to Transaction Books, Rutgers—The State University, New Brunswick, New Jersey 08903.

Library of Congress Catalog Number: 79-66433
ISBN: 0-87855-783-0
Printed in the United States of America

Library of Congress Cataloging in Publication Data
Main entry under title:
Anthropological realities.
   Articles originally appeared in *Society* magazine.
   Bibliography: p.
   1. Ethnology—Addresses, essays, lectures.
I. Guillemin, Jeanne, 1943-   II. Society.
GN325.A56   301.2   79-66433
ISBN: 0-87855-783-0

81-10484

Contents

Preface xi
Introduction xvii

Part I: Anthropologists at Work
1. Fieldwork and Definitions of the Self
   Jeanne Guillemin 6
2. Love Fulani Style
   Paul Riesman 19
3. Kapluna Daughter: Living with Eskimos
   Jean L. Briggs 26

Part II: Myth and Language
4. *Star Wars:* Social Science Fiction
   Conrad Kottak 48
5. "Rapping" in the Black Ghetto
   Thomas Kochman 55
6. Public Drama and Common Values in Two Caribbean Islands
   Roger D. Abrahams 71

Part III: Ritual and Symbol
7. Rebirth in the Airborne
   Melford S. Weiss 98
8. Baseball Magic
   George Gmelch 104
9. The Serpent-Handling Religions of West Virginia
   Nathan L. Gerrard 109

Part IV: Family and Sex Roles
10. Child Training and the Chinese Family
    Margery Wolf 123
11. "I Divorce Thee": Moroccan Marriage and the Law
    Lawrence Rosen 139

12. Future Family
    Margaret Mead 147

Part V: The Survival of Community

13. Status-Seeking in Indian Villages
    David G. Mandelbaum 161
14. Renaissance and the Repression: The Oklahoma Cherokee
    Albert Wahrhaftig and Robert K. Thomas 168
15. Communal Brethren of the Great Plains
    John W. Bennett 178

Part VI: Power and Politics

16. Slaves and Masters in Africa: Three Cases
    Ronald Cohen, John Middleton, and Arthur Tuden 193
17. Algerian Peasant Revolt
    Eric R. Wolf 203
18. ARVN as Faggots: Inverted Warfare in Vietnam
    Charles J. Levy 221

Part VII: Economic Systems and Culture Patterns

19. Capital, Investment, and the Social Structure of a Pastoral Nomad Group in South Persia
    Fredrik Barth 244
20. Bulls and Bears on the Cell Block
    Heather Strange and Joseph McCrory 257
21. The Female Factor in Resettlement
    Lucy M. Cohen 274

Part VIII: Urban Ethnography: People in Cities

22. Nigeria: The Dream Is Unfulfilled
    Leonard Plotnicov 288
23. Mohawks: Round Trip to High Steel
    Ruth Blumenfeld 293
24. Anatomy of a Chicago Slum
    Gerald D. Suttles 297

Part IX: Culture and Poverty

25. The Culture of Poverty
    Oscar Lewis 316
26. The Warrior Dropouts
    Rosalie Wax 321
27. White People's Time, Colored People's Time
    Jules Henry 331

Part X: Development in the Third World

28. Rural Peru: Peasants as Activists
    William Foote Whyte 342
29. Miracle Seeds and Shattered Dreams in Java
    Richard W. Franke 357

30. On Becoming *Bwana* in Kenya·
    Donald Rothchild 366
Part XI: The Ethnic Factor
31. Growing Up Greek American
    Charles C. Moskos, Jr. 387
32. Gypsies: The Hidden Americans
    Anne Sutherland 401
33. The Ethnic Factor in World Politics
    Adbul A. Said and Luiz R. Simmons 415
Part XII: Sociobiology: Back to Basics?
34. What is Sociobiology?
    Edward O. Wilson 434
35. Animal Behavior and Social Anthropology
    S.L. Washburn 444
36. Heredity Versus Culture: A Debate
    Edward O. Wilson and Marvin Harris, with Ann Carroll 459
Part XIII: Anthropology: Ethics and Prospects
37. The Life and Death of Project Camelot
    Irving Louis Horowitz 476
38. As Others See Us
    Nancy Oestreich Lurie 493
39. Science: Forever Incomplete
    Claude Lévi-Strauss 500
Contributors 505

Acknowledgments

Grateful acknowledgment is made to the authors and publishers who granted permission to reprint selections from copyright material.

Jeanne Guillemin, "Fieldwork and Definitions of the Self," abridged from *Urban Renegades: The Cultural Strategy of American Indians*, Columbia University Press, 1975.

Jean L. Briggs, "Kapluna Daughter," from *Women in the Field*, edited by Peggy Golde, Copyright © 1970 Aldine Publishing Co.

Conrad Kottak, *"Star Wars:* Social Science Fiction, *Psychology Today*, February 1978.

Margery Wolf, "Child Training and the Chinese Family," abridged from *Family and Kinship in Chinese Society*, edited by Maurice Freeman, Stanford University Press, 1970.

Eric R. Wolf, "Algerian Peasant Revolt," excerpted from *Peasant Wars of the Twentieth Century*, Harper and Row, 1969.

Fredrik Barth, "Capital, Investment, and the Social Structure of a Pastoral Nomad Group in South Persia," from *Capital, Saving and Credit in Peasant Societies*, edited by E.R. Firth and B.S. Yamey, George Allen and Unwin, Ltd. and the Aldine Publishing Co., 1964.

Gerald D. Suttles, "Anatomy of a Chicago Slum," from *The Social Order of the Slum*, University of Chicago Press, 1968.

Richard W. Franke, "Miracle Seeds and Shattered Dreams in Java," *Natural History*, January 1974. Copyright © The American Museum of Natural History, 1974.

Edward O. Wilson, "What is Sociobiology?" excerpted from *Sociobiology and Human Nature: An Interdisciplinary Critique and Defense*, edited by Michael S. Gregory, Anita Silvers, and Diane Sutch. Copyright © 1978 by Jossey-Bass, Inc.

S.L. Washburn, "Animal Behavior and Social Anthropology," from *Sociobiology and Human Nature: An Interdisciplinary Critique and Defense*, edited by Michael S. Gregory, Anita Silvers, and Diane Sutch. Copyright © 1978 by Jossey-Bass, Inc.

Nancy Oestreich Lurie, "As Others See Us," from *New University Thought*, Vol. 7, 1971.

Preface

The question, What is Anthropology, deserves at least three different answers. The first has to do with the curiosity about foreign people that is a characteristic anthropologists share with others, both past and present. The second response concerns the development of anthropology as a profession with distinct standards for membership and practice. And the third reply describes anthropology as an academic discipline that offers a general perspective on the human condition.

If today's anthropologists were to trace their spiritual ancestors, they would find their origins among the first travelers who ventured past the boundaries of their own societies to meet with people who looked, acted, and spoke in ways that were unfamiliar and, having met with them, recorded their observations. As early as 800 B.C., Greek merchants, trading at Mediterranean ports, were taking notes on the behavior of their foreign customers and handing them on to their associates as an aid in future transactions. Three centuries later Herodotus, the Father of History, while narrating the military struggles of Greece and Persia, livened up his account with a traveler's description of the people of the ancient East—their dress, eating habits, technology, politics, and religion.

In addition to trade and warfare, there were religious incentives for early travel and observation. Starting in 500 A.D., Chinese Buddhist pilgrims began journeying through India and, struck by the strange customs of the villagers they met, wrote down their observations for the historical record. Much more familiar to us are the documents on New World Indians, which were often written by the Jesuit and Franciscan missionaries who accompanied European explorers and traders on their voyages.

The hallmark of these early explorers and travelers in other times and places that makes their reflections of special interest to anthropologists is the clarity of their descriptions. Although in unfamiliar surroundings, their ability to see what was happening around them was untroubled by excessive fear, and it was unmarked by an overwhelming revulsion at the exotic. Granted, most of these first accounts of foreign customs, like later ethnographies, were written by people suffering the discomforts as well as the excitement of travel. Yet, to the degree that they were untouched by the fear of strange people and new experiences, the early chroniclers could perceive and be intrigued by the humanity of the strangers they observed.

Today there are many individuals who travel, live, and work in foreign countries and, as students of culture, record their observations in diaries, journals, and letters. In this era of efficient international travel, the experience of passing the frontiers of another country and becoming subject for some length of time to another national culture and language has become relatively commonplace. Nor is it always necessary to cross an international border to have the sense of being in a foreign country. There are sections of every city in the United States that are transplanted ethnic enclaves or racially segregated communities that are as removed from standard American culture as any culture found outside the national boundaries. In addition, there are a significant number of rural communities, such as Appalachian hamlets and American Indian reservations, where language and custom have evolved in relative isolation from outside influence.

For most of us, the realization that there are foreigners of one kind or another comes in childhood. Up until the time they go to school, most small children think of their immediate family and its customary organization as the whole world, without a question of there being alternatives. Interacting with other children of different backgrounds gives the first clue to the diversity of the many worlds of custom and culture that exist outside the immediate family. The signal event is frequently the first time a school child eats dinner at the home of a friend and discovers, on a very subtle level of perception, that neither the food, its preparation, nor the rules for family eating are "like home." Or the realization may only gradually dawn that neighbors, who are familiar in name and appearance, believe in a different God or no God at all, can be identified as Democrats or Republicans, or have greater or lesser wealth and property.

Then there are the further lessons to be learned listening to how parents and older relatives talk about "them," the outsiders of another race or ethnic group or social class. For adults have a sense of what children do not—that human diversity is also the basis of economic and political competition. In residential neighborhoods, at work, and in legislation, the antagonisms between interest groups are very real and very passionate. A suburban neighborhood mobilizes immediately in defense of property rights when faced with the prospect of a low-income housing project. The integration of minorities into blue and white collar jobs is being accomplished with great difficulty, amid protests of "reverse discrimination." At every level of government, citizen groups by the score claim equity, as if each and all had priority of interest.

The professional origins of anthropology were in a time in the not so distant past when diverse cultures and races could be viewed with much less apprehension. Most of the people first researched by anthropologists were remote from the struggles of industrial society and presented no threat to a reading public that 50 to 75 years ago was entertained by information on exotic groups without having them on the following day move in next door or rally in an antiracist march. There is still that superficial charm about anthropological literature that proves the old adage when it comes to variability in human customs that truth is indeed stranger than fiction. Yet the efforts of anthropologists to popularize cultural relativity, that is, a nonjudgmental approach to the understanding of unfamiliar cultures, were nonetheless aimed against bigotry and racism in all their inhumane potential. During the 1930s Nazi racist doctrines found no more vocal and vigorous opponents than anthropologists.

The early organizers of the profession, most notably Franz Boas in this country and Bronislaw Malinowski and A.R. Radcliffe-Brown in Great Britain, hardly foresaw a future in which the global population, including the descendents of their informants, would increase exponentially and continue to amass in urban areas. What they did have in mind was the retrieval of cultural information from remote groups who they saw as imperiled by contact with Western civilization. The small societies of the Australian outback, the Pacific Islands, Africa, South America, and the rural reservations of North America represented a bygone era, one before technology had disrupted the direct relationship between the community and the national environment.

By incorporating professional societies and securing university doctoral programs for their students, the American and British founders of anthropology sought to weed out the dilettante-describers of exotic cultures and to turn amateur observations into scientific description that would rival both historical documentation and the data of natural science. Licensed to study human beings (from the Greek *anthropos* [man] and *logia* [study]), anthropologists drew on the methods and theories of older disciplines and added to them the requirement that to understand this complex subject, libraries and laboratories would have to be left behind. Thus archaeologists—the most historically oriented anthropologists—had to make their discoveries by systematically exploring the surviving artifacts of extinct societies. Physical anthropologists, the anthropologists with the closest ties to biology and zoology, needed to do actual comparative work with skeletal material of humans and other primates, both living and dead, to unravel the mystery of evolution. For those who sought to understand the common traits of human languages, there was no substitute for going into the field to record native dialects.

More central to the study of man than specialized research in archaeology, physical anthropology, and linguistics has been research on the human community and the development of what anthropologists call the "holistic perspective"—a view of the human community as an integration of collective sentiments and social institutions. Early on, American and British anthropologists found themselves in basic agreement about their primary interest in non-Western, traditional groups, but they differed in their formulations of how and why the small societies they studied maintained their pristine integrity. For several decades, American anthropologists utilized the concept of culture that, devoid of its exclusive association with high civilizations and the fine arts, came to be defined as the total pattern of values and tradition that characterized a community and that was passed on from one generation to the next. Both historical changes in culture complexes and the relationship of the individual personality to group culture were of paramount interest up to the beginning of World War II.

British anthropologists, particularly those who followed the orientation of A.R. Radcliffe-Brown, turned away from historical overview and psychological theory to investigate social structure and institutions as normative orderings of rights and responsibilities within a group. The result was a theoretical emphasis on the functional interrelations of kinship, religious, political, and economic institutions in the corporate community.

To posit too strict a division between the British and American schools would misrepresent the large degree to which the researchers in each camp had to come to grips with cultural rules and social organization in traditional communities. There was also some vital trans-Atlantic communication between a handful of people working in a very new field. In a 1926 letter written to Margaret Mead by a fellow student of "Papa Franz" (Franz Boas), anthropologist Ruth Benedict describes a visit of Bronislaw Malinowski to Columbia University:

> You'd like him a lot. He has the quick imagination and the by-play of mind that makes him a seven-days' joy, and he's discovered as if it were a new religion that acculturation makes so much difference that it hardly matters whether or not the trait is invented on the spot or diffused from some outside source.
>
> . . . . He said, "If only I'd known, Boas was my spiritual father all the time," and "You must tell me what Boas has been teaching for twenty years about

this and that, or I'll be discovering it as if it had never happened to anybody before."

Much less sympathetic than Malinowski to American culture studies, Radcliffe-Brown took the opportunity during the 1920s to spread the good word of structural-functionalism to colleagues and students at the University of Chicago. His influence was felt as much by sociologists concerned with corporate institutions in United States society as by anthropologists dealing with the normative cohesion of small-scale communities.

With time, and especially with the federal funding of university education following World War II, the number of anthropologists who were teaching and doing field research far exceeds the handful who first mapped out the basic principles of method and theory. The membership of the American Anthropological Association, the largest national organization of anthropologists, is currently upwards of 10,000.

As the articles in this volume of readings illustrate so clearly, the desire to leave the familiar behind and explore new terrain still characterizes anthropological methods. There is no substitute for the first-hand experience of going and finding out for oneself how people in a group manage their lives. Yet, as ethnographies have accumulated and historical records have become more precise, there is no reason for an anthropological fieldworker to limit his observations to the "ethnographic present." Historical and cross-cultural comparisons are now more of an imperative in good analysis than ever before.

Nor does a contemporary anthropologist have to be bound to one theoretical school as opposed to another. To make sense of the situation of today's small-scale groups requires emphasis on value systems *and* the functional organization of social institutions. Because even the most remote groups have felt the effects of contact with outside civilization, the emphasis on values must logically account for dual systems. Traditional orientations have not everywhere collapsed when beset by Western civilization. There have been adaptations, adjustments, conflicts, and the sorting out of cultural patterns between "real" and "ideal" lifestyles.

The simplistic functionalist approach to social institutions has been revamped also to take into account the difficulties involved in integrating traditional groups into larger political and economic organizations. The relationship between Third World governments and their tribal and village constituents is not one of perfect harmony, any more than Western colonialism was a peaceful expansion of European dominance. No nation-state represents all its citizens with equal good grace. The legacy of British structural-functionalism, grounded in understanding social roles and networks, reminds us that national governments and large-scale economic corporations as well are not "things" but groups of people whose vested interests, to a greater or lesser extent, may or may not coincide with the interests of citizens and workers.

Despite these larger realities of national governments and international corporations, or rather because of them, anthropology's simple and humane message of cultural relativity is still meaningful. There is, in fact, a new urgency to the plea for respecting not only foreign cultures but also the personal scale of our own lives and interests. The magnitude of international political dramas and global economic forces can only impress us with how little we control our own fates. The technological development of not one but several sophisticated versions of the ultimate nuclear weapon, including one that destroys human lives but leaves buildings intact, adds to our potential dehumanization: we may each be no more significant than a statistic in a computer read-out.

Because its own traditions are so fundamentally humanistic, anthropology affirms the value of human life and social organization, especially when conventional wisdom condones the natural rights of one group over another. We do well to remember that in the evolutionary categories so popular and predominant in nineteenth-century Europe and America, the non-Western, nonwhite people with whom anthropologists chose to spend their time were considered barely human.

* * *

My special thanks for assistance in preparing this volume go to Irving Louis Horowitz, of Rutgers University, whose high editorial standards have been a challenge and an inspiration.

Peter Goldsmith, a former student and fine anthropologist, aided in the collection of bibliographic data. The secretarial staff at Boston College—Lorraine Bone, Alice Close, Shirley Urban, and Bertha Shelkan—did their usual excellent job of manuscript typing, and they have my appreciation for their efficiency and patience. The support of the university in the writing and production of publishable manuscripts also deserves special comment.

There are a good number of people whose moral support contributed enormously to this work—most important of all are those closest to home, my sons Robert Guillemin and John Guillemin. I ask my colleagues and students at Boston College and other friends to accept a collective rather than individualized acknowledgments of thanks. My greatest debt is to an innocent and often beleaguered creature, Bear, to whom this volume is dedicated.

Jeanne Guillemin
Chestnut Hill, Mass.

Introduction

Anthropological Realities has been planned to meet the challenge of bringing the student audience to an understanding of both the exotic nature of anthropology and the complexities of large-scale social change by providing cases of small-scale social organizations without neglecting vital information on, and analysis of, world historical movements. The diversity of cultures represented in this book is wide-ranging, covering the major areas of the world. In addition, attention is given to special subgroups, such as the Canadian Hutterians (Chapter 15), competing urban ethnic groups in the United States (Chapter 24), men as soldiers and prisoners in total institutions (Chapters 7, 18, and 20), and the lives of Latin American women (Chapters 21 and 25). In addition, there are three articles on American culture per se, one by Conrad Kottak on the movie *Star Wars*, another by George Gmelch on the superstitions of baseball players, and a third by the late Margaret Mead on the future of the American family.

The organization of the book in 13 sections stems from the essentials of the discipline—field work methods, myth and language, ritual behavior, and family organization—to increasingly complex subject areas.

Part I of *Anthropological Realities* introduces the reader to the heart of anthropological methods—field work. Although anthropologists, like other social scientists, have the license and at times the intellectual responsibility to use historical resources, statistics, and hard-science laboratory methods, the requirement of long-term interaction with informants is the foundation of the discipline. In a sense, every anthropologist is a witness to his or her informants; the anthropologist is a biographer of the group. The personal nature of this learning experience is documented in the first three essays.

The following two parts cover two areas—Myth and Language and Ritual and Symbol—that are not only the traditional domain of anthropologists but are areas that lie at the most abstract and general level of human behavior. Cross-cultural and now intercultural comparison of traditional myth and communication are among the most accessible of anthropology's information, involving as they do the universals of language and oral tradition. In the same way, universal dependence on ritual and a symbolic ordering of the world make it possible for the reader to put aside the dichotomy between "civilized" and "exotic" and to recognize human trust in familiar patterns of behavior and belief.

Part IV, Family and Sex Roles, deals with kinship and household organization, which are standard areas of anthropological investigation. It does so by moving from the more traditional case material (on Taiwanese families) to a current reevaluation of domestic roles and institutions and the conscious invention of new American family forms. In the same way, the subject of community organization (Part V) proceeds from traditional organization in small societies beset by external pressures to the planned community used as a safeguard against impersonal historical forces—the case of the Hutterians in western Canada.

In Parts VI and VII, material is presented on the two major specialties in social anthropology—politics and economics. The articles on political anthropology cover the institutional organization of power at multiple levels, from the comparative study of slavery in three African societies, to the rural base of colonial revolution in Algeria, and then to state military organization. In this section, two of the articles, on African slavery and on Algeria, provide the historical perspective that is the mainstay of contemporary political anthropology.

Beginning with Part VIII, Urban Ethnography: People in Cities, the thematic scope of the book broadens. The rapid settlement of people from small societies in urban industrial centers is a global phenomenon, more recent in developing countries than in those already industrialized, but nonetheless following the same patterns of adjustment, formation of alliances, and increase in intergroup competition. This section begins with a case study of the new urban migrants in Nigeria and proceeds to a much older but less well-known urban population—the Mohawk Indians—who have sustained their tribal organization in the context of an American metropolis. Finally, the competitive ecology of a Chicago neighborhood, involving blacks, Italians, and Spanish Americans, is discussed.

Culture and poverty (Part IX) pinpoints another global phenomenon—the evolution of basic strategies to cope with economic marginality, strategies that pertain not only to the survival of traditional people but also to their wholesale management by institutions of the state. The principal tenets of the culture of poverty are outlined by the late Oscar Lewis. Following is a biographical narrative by one of Lewis' informants, a young Puerto Rican woman who tells of being relocated from a San Juan slum to a housing project. The other articles deal with observations on minority children and educational programs in two different contexts. The first treats Sioux Indian reservation boys as early drop-outs from boarding school; the second, the problems of black children in white-run institutions.

With the tenth part of this volume, we arrive at an area of growing importance in the field of anthropology—the study of national development and its effect on traditional cultures. The dilemmas of peasants caught between feudalism and nationalism are the subjects of the first two articles. One case is drawn from research in Peru, the other from studies in Java. The third selection treats the difficult and painful coexistence of the black and white sectors in Kenya in the aftermath of national independence. This section gives important coverage also to the role of Third World intellectuals as social critics and activists.

In Part XI, the subject of ethnicity is presented in both its most recent manifestations—as the revival of ethnic identification in older industrialized nations, and as the persistence of ethnic and regional rivalries in new nation-states. Sociologist Charles Moskos plays informant and offers reflections on a Greek-American boyhood, and Anne Sutherland presents an account of the marginal life of American Gypsies. The concluding essay by Abdul Said and Luiz Simmons gives a necessary overview of ethnicity as a factor in world politics, one that will continue to affect national organization and, by extension, international relations.

In the section on sociobiology (Part XII), the most recent subject of debate within anthropology and among some academics outside the field is introduced. The proposal of Harvard biologist Edward O. Wilson that the natural and social sciences combine forces in the search for general laws governing human behavior was first mentioned by him in the final chapter of *Sociobiology: A New Synthesis* (1975). Dr. Wilson concisely sums up his thoughts on this proposed merger for the first time since critics and advocates have reacted to it. Anthropologist S.H. Washburn next takes a turn at discussing the conceptual difficulties in applying the methods of the laboratory sciences to the study of human beings. The final selection, a debate originally aired on Radio Smithsonian, has another anthropologist, Marvin Harris, discussing with Dr. Wilson the issue of "genes versus culture" determinants of social behavior, perhaps the most explosive subject in the sociobiology controversy.

Anthropological Realities concludes with another look at the role of the anthropologist, less as a fieldworker being educated by informants than as a member of a discipline that has been called upon to render good account of itself. The sorting out of moral, intellectual, and professional responsibilities is the theme of this final section. From ambiguities about working for nonacademic employers, especially government officials and agencies, to problems about the application of anthropological information to the solution of pressing human problems, such as poverty and political oppression, anthropologists have to rethink the implications of their various roles. The first article, on Project Camelot, is a discussion by the principal researcher, Irving Louis Horowitz, of what remains the most striking example of international reaction to government sponsorship of social science research. Following this is a response from Nancy Lurie to Native American spokesman Vine Deloria's criticisms of the disinterested anthropologist or the researcher interested only in "pure" scholarship. *Anthropological Realities* closes with a brief, succinct statement by the world's foremost anthropologist—Claude Lévi-Strauss—on the nature and goals of the social sciences, as compared to those of the more advanced sciences. Lévi-Strauss touches briefly on French Structuralism, but his message is summed up when he states that "all problems pertaining *to* humankind are ultimate problems *for* humankind."

Anthropological Realities begins with the most familiar categories in cultural and social anthropology, treating these with maximum emphasis on the forces for change, abroad and within our own society. With each section, the dimensions of analysis expand in order to place research data on people in small societies in the larger context of historical, political, and economic transformations. The volume ends with the theme of professional reassessment. This is appropriate, for it reflects the discipline's response to the changing climate of social science research and writing. The problems surrounding accountability—to scientific goals, to sponsors, to informants, to students, or to ourselves personally—can hardly be solved overnight; the difficult quest for solutions goes on, and from it emerges the high quality of information represented in this collection of readings.

Part I
Anthropologists at Work

Speaking at the University of Chicago in 1937, A.R. Radcliffe-Brown, one of the founders of British social anthropology, asked this important question: "What is the method by which we can discover, analyze, and describe the characteristics of social systems?" The question is a scientific one, having to do with how anthropologists make accurate reports of human behavior. The natural scientist can engineer a controlled series of experiments, for example, using fruit flies to test genetic principles or combining chemical substances to test the laws of chemistry and physics. Accurately observing and recording what people do is a good deal more difficult because it requires acting against a normal and very healthy instinct to mix with and become socially accepted by a group. It also requires acting against another social instinct—the tendency to make quick judgments about the behavior of others, often on the basis of who appears to be the accommodating friend and who the irritating foe.

Given these social instincts, there must be some guarantees of social distance between the researcher and the group being studied. How that distinction is insured varies within the social sciences. A sociologist investigating decision-making in small groups might stand behind a one-way mirror recording the behavior of twelve people who have been asked to act like a jury. How they reach the verdict of guilty or innocent on a fictional case is a process that can be staged over and over again with other volunteer or paid subjects. A social psychologist interested in infant behavior might combine formal observation of parent-child interaction with interviews of each mother and father. Both formal observation and the interview are methods that structure and limit three aspects of investigation: the time spent in research, the size of the social unit, and the personal involvement with subjects. In the social science laboratory, the validity of research rests on standardized procedure and the accumulation of numerous cases of human action and reaction.

Anthropologists are equally interested in accurate reporting, although the way in which they investigate social behavior is very different from the laboratory approach. A clue to the way in which anthropologists work is contained in Radcliffe-Brown's use of the word "discover" in his question about scientific method. Rather than asking individuals to set aside the ordinary routine of their lives and join in a laboratory experiment, the anthropological researcher goes on the assumption that social systems, made up of people who have fixed social relations with each other, are waiting to be discovered. The social system might prove to be an isolated band of hunters and gatherers, a reservation tribe, a farming community, a city neighborhood, migrant workers, or any relatively stable association of individuals. Research is also based on the assumption that, from one generation to another, a group develops set patterns of behavior including language, religious beliefs, a technology, and political organization. This distinct culture sets them apart from other groups and, like the structure of the social system, awaits discovery.

The scientific method of anthropology is based largely on the fact that the principal organizers of the discipline, such as Bronislaw Malinowski, E.E. Evans-Pritchard and Radcliffe-Brown himself, researched remote traditional communities that had little contact with Western society. Both Malinowski and Radcliffe-Brown did their major fieldwork in small island communities where the boundaries of the social system were obvious, and the culture of the groups apparently untouched by modern civilization. The social distance of the researcher was insured by differences in race, language, and custom. Counting on the availability of other such communities for research, Malinowski stipulated that the most elementary conditions for accurate ethnographic work "consist mainly in cutting oneself off from the company of other white men, and remaining in as close contact with the natives as possible, which really can only be achieved by camping right in their villages."

As Malinowski saw it, the goal of fieldwork was to gain a complete picture of tribal life, from cases of kinship interaction and genealogical tables to types of economic transactions and property ownership, to the documentation of the "native mentality" in folklore narratives and magical beliefs. The guarantee that this information would be scientifically accurate rested on the length of time the researcher spent immersed in the daily life of the community. A tourist passing through a remote village could witness a ceremony and ever after declare that the people of such and such a tribe have a single, highly exotic means of treating the common cold.

The ethnographer makes a point of witnessing not just a single event, but recording as many cases of social interaction as he can. In all likelihood, he'll find out that the ceremony the tourist saw had little to do with the curing, but that it had a great deal to do with family relations and the economics of a horticultural society. In the traditions of social anthropology, this kind of factual gathering requires one or two years of balancing participation in community life with observations of customary behavior. The barriers of language and culture can be such that good communication with informants, and therefore accurate reporting, takes months to achieve. On the other hand, the ethnographer, like a good guest, has to know when to leave. Although personal friendships can and often are made in fieldwork, the scientific role of ethnographer presupposes a temporary stay in the community rather than a total commitment to a new lifestyle.

It takes more than just time to guarantee good fieldwork results. In the days of the Western empires, missionaries, traders, and colonial officials spent years associating with native communities, but many categorized such isolated groups as "savage" and "primitive." With some exceptions, the writings of Europeans most familiar with tribal and village communities overseas describe what natives ought to have been instead of what they actually were. Missionaries sent to convert "savages" would have had them to become more civilized Christians. Traders would have had them be more profitable clients. Colonial officials would have preferred them to be more docile and obedient subjects. Being concerned with the "ought" rather than the "is" of any group of informants is a greater obstacle to scientific inquiry than culture differences. Yet the judgment of unfamiliar behavior as peculiar, uncivilized, or evil comes naturally to all of us. We know too that native tribes were often shocked or amused by what seemed to them barbaric European manners and dress. At the heart of anthropology, however, is the suspension of judgments, positive and negative, for the sake of the social science discovery. Malinowski appropriately summed up the ethnographer's credo: "We cannot possibly reach the final Socratic wisdom of knowing ourselves if we never leave the narrow confinement of the customs, beliefs and prejudices into which every man is born. Nothing can teach us a better lesson in this matter of ultimate importance than the habit of mind which allows us to treat the beliefs and values of another man from his point of view."

Although the process and goals of fieldwork are based on a general attitude of tolerance, anthropologists have to deal with very specific problems of method and theory. The essays included in this section on "Anthropologists at Work" represent a spectrum of anthropological notions of fieldwork, its frustrations, its limits, and its immediate and ultimate purposes.

As fieldwork begins, informants have about as much to learn about the anthropologist as the anthropologist does about them. Often the unfamiliarity of the researcher with the language and customs of the community makes for misunderstandings and tensions that are difficult to resolve. While the fieldworker may blunder about in ignorance, informants may be shocked at how an adult, who should know better, can violate fundamental codes of behavior. It is not uncommon for an anthropologist to be looked upon as a kind of child badly in need of socialization and for a community to assign her or him to a conventional role that permits learning. In Jean Brigg's "Kapluna Daughter," we have a vivid illustration of the phases of socialization through which a researcher passes and, in addition, a thoughtful account of how mutual the interpersonal frustrations and, hopefully, the successes of the venture are to both parties.

Even as the fieldworker is intent on recording social behavior, how he or she is being perceived by the community is a question which lingers. The answer to it can only be pieced together by the comments and gestures of informants who openly assess this unfamiliar role of temporary intruder. Many years ago, the category of "European" summed up the crucial differences between anthropologist and natives. In recent times, it is probably just as easy to predict who the anthropologist will be, but the old polarities between white and native have given way to new divisions. Because urban industrialization and nationalism have touched small communities everywhere, informants are now counted as members of a specific economic class, usually lower, and as citizens of a particular nation. Depending on the nation in which they live, their race is another dimension of their social identity that can act as a barrier against communication. A white anthropologist, doing fieldwork in a Rhodesian village or American ghetto, has to contend with the greater society's racism and the politicization of the black and white categories. A fieldwork project on a remote island culture from which one can retreat to the peaceful groves of academe is quite a different venture from the research of national minorities, segregated races, and urban slum-dwellers. Still, no matter where and with whom fieldwork is carried out, the immediate objective is to overcome barriers to communication.

The long-range goal of fieldwork is scientific comparison. If careful notes documenting each day's events are kept, a record of the community's history will accumulate over the course of a year or more and, if thoroughly done, will bear comparison with other similar documents. Sometimes the anthropologist's passion for documentation leads him to write down his every observation. British anthropologist Raymond Firth, author of the classic ethnography *We, The Tikopia*, was once taken to task for including such unhelpful descriptions as "the feet of the native are large" in his thorough coverage of that island community. Nonetheless, the business of the fieldworker is that of an active and observant historian who has but a short while to take in his many impressions of community life. Sometimes the role of historian is amplified by the opportunity to return to the informant community at a later date for another look at how individual lives and the development of the community have proceeded.

The opportunity to do extensive fieldwork in more than one culture brings another dimension of comparison to anthropological research. However far the fieldworker goes in understanding the world from the native's point of view and liberating himself from his own prejudices, there is always the pressing matter of communicating this experience to a wider audience. The professional responsibilities of the anthropologist begin with scientific and intellectual commitment to the standards of the discipline, but they certainly do not end with only anthropologists reading the work of other anthropologists. One of the outstanding achievements of social anthropology in this century has been the education of the general public in the same Socratic wisdom that individual researchers gain in the field. Accurate documentation and comparative analyses have fostered a perspective of cultural relativity, that is, an informed tolerance for diverse human social organization, to the extent that old myths about the less-than-human nature of non-Western, nonwhite peoples have been dispelled. New myths and new prejudices crop up, but the purpose of present anthropological research, as in the past, is ultimately humanistic, to understand the common bonds that link us as human beings to other human beings. Fieldwork is at the beginning of the path to understanding, where researcher and informants, strangers to each other, consent to tolerance.

References

Epstein, A. L. *The Craft of Social Anthropology*. London: Tavistock.
Golde, Peggy. 1970. *Women in the Field*. Chicago: Aldine.
Johnson, John M. 1975. *Doing Field Research*. New York: The Free Press.
Junker, Buford. 1960. *Field Work*, Chicago: University of Chicago Press.
Philip, Bernard S. 1971. *Social Research. Strategy and Tactics*. New York: Macmillan.
Spradley, James P., and David W. McCurdy. 1972. *The Cultural Experience: Ethnography in Complex Society*. Chicago: Science Research Associates.
Wax, Rosalie. 1971. *Doing Fieldwork: Warnings and Advice*. Chicago: University of Chicago Press.

1.
Fieldwork and Definitions of the Self
Jeanne Guillemin

To do responsible fieldwork today, it has become an intellectual duty to extend one's awareness not simply to the people who are the objects of inquiry but to one's self as well—one's self as a limited instrument, a culture-bound personality consciously bent on interacting with a group of strangers. The fact that former researchers were fully social and occasionally fallible beings in the field can only be glimpsed in traditional reports, although wise students always strongly suspect what all professionals know, that the private personality in fieldwork is as much a reality as the more edited public monograph. For myself, the discovery that Franz Boas was nicknamed the Kwakiutl appellative for "fart" or that Malinowski was bothered by the noise of the "damn niggers" was genuinely pleasurable. It was an assurance that the stuff of fieldwork, whatever the objective stance assumed later, was unavoidably a human experience.

The academic value placed on self-awareness is so great and so fundamental to Western notions of learning that a process like participant-observation is insured a future in education. There is perhaps no better way to discover one's own psychological boundaries than to take on the role of stranger in a community. For many years it has been assumed that, for academic purposes, the community or unit of research is an object or thing. The social scientist would work to gain an abstract control of this thing by formulating its reality. Human social organization, being at once too pliant and too intricate, has more often than not eluded theory that would contain it. If a community can be reduced to abstractions at all, it must be given the breadth and dimension of time, so that the researcher, instead of producing a photographic still life, can acknowledge the system and process of its organization. Rather than supporting an imperialistic image of the researcher as capable of abstractly incorporating the community, such an acknowledgment makes fieldwork a coincidence of histories, the investigator's and the group's. The individual fieldworker engages in and even surrenders, to use Kurt Wolff's sensitive phrasing, to the ongoing process of the community until, having artificially intruded, he must artifically withdraw to assess what has been learned.

In my own work among Micmac Indians in Boston and the Maritime Provinces, the fact that I was with people who were "urbanized" or "acculturated," who had a material culture which was not foreign, who lived in physical settings which fit into familiar city and country categories, and who spoke English as well as Micmac, made it unavoidable that I consider a common social structure in which both the Indians and I exist together. Some researchers simply go native and make the community a miniature world. Elliot Liebow in *Tally's Corner* came to terms with the social division, expressed in the metaphor of the chain-link fence, which finally separated him as a White from the total experience of being Black. Yet with the issue of self-involvement in fieldwork, urban research also must deal with the issue of the wider society's political and economic reality, which invariably casts the researcher as the bureaucrat and the community as lower-class "ethnics." In fieldwork interaction, the line between bureaucrats and outsiders is mutually recognized as a border by which two kinds of people maintain their separateness and also a way in which they acknowledge each other's existence.

In using the term "mutually recognized" in conjunction with an idea of interaction, I am speaking as a specialist, like the social worker, the policeman, the housing expert, the volunteer doctor or lawyer, for whom association with people of other than the dominant majority is not necessarily a novelty. For most people, the recognition of what is lower-class behavior (street fighting, wiping one's face on one's sleeve, using ungrammatical English) is distinct from the notion of interaction. To the extent that the middle-class people are "above" lower-class people, they find such behavior painful in a moral sense, the "bad" which defines their "good" manners but which also threatens to contaminate them. To avoid contamination by the poor, the majority seeks, not always successfully, the protection of the exclusively middle-class neighborhood with its "good" schools which serve to protect the children from exposure. The specialist, like a priest in a plague, has a certain immunity born of professionalization which lets him or her handle the poor. Within a well designated and bureaucratically supported role, he or she can approach a considerable number of lower-class people as a superior individual to a mass of inferiors. The asymmetrical relationship of specialist to the poor is based on the assumption that the beneficence and goodness of the former will absorb the inadequacies and problems of the latter by consciously taking account of them.

The urban fieldworker, a curious person (in both senses of the word), is perhaps the only specialist who can resist the existing asymmetrical role relations. The university or funding organization which supports such academic ventures as urban fieldwork usually allows enough independence to let the researcher settle on his own method of approach to the community. In addition, the institution supporting the fieldwork, even if it is a city university, usually has its ties to the urban poor well camouflaged and its physical plant, whether offices or a campus, set up to service a different population. But the urban field-worker is financed, after all, to be innovative, to explore, to bring new information back to an institution in quest of knowledge which it assumes it can incorporate. His role is based on the very antiestablishment idea that, in often unstipulated ways, the inadequacies of the present system require more knowledge and perhaps a new vision of urban people, and he is actually funded to sensitize the dominant society to alternative social organizations, a sensitivity which strains its own organizational values.

Unhindered by more traditional bureaucratic structures, the fieldworker often has a vested interest in gaining some kind of morally superior image of himself and in proving his beneficence through interaction with the poor. For example, the obvious "bad" people who define one's "goodness" are the bureaucratic employees who run the repressive machinery which refuses to give the poor full credit as equal human beings. While reveling in his moral superiority, the researcher will also find occasion to champion individuals in the community against the malfeasance of city bureaucrats and become a leader of the oppressed before returning to his own bureaucratic milieu. He is oblivious to his need to be ultimately correct and right, along with his need for efficiency and direct action, which make academic researchers and city bureaucratic personalities cut from the same cloth.

To be open about a moral stance in a way which is nonimperialistic, one must ask where a morality at a level higher than that of individual gratification exists, where is the new, right way to approach "different others," to discover other-than-bureaucratic ways of relating to urban minorities? The answer perhaps lies in knowing what the personal limits to interclass contact are.

In retrospect, I can see my resistance to dealing with social boundaries existing on several levels. I carried into the field a certain intellectual preference for "cultural relativity," and was prepared to take on the perspective of the Indian community and defend it against my own corporate system. I also had very ambivalent feelings about being a member of the managerial elite. How had I found myself in the company of oppressors when I had no will to oppress? In the field, the subject of my status embarrassed me: I was equally fearful of being catered to as a "superior" and of being put down for my association with "tyrants." During the summer of 1970, when I was living with a family on a reservation in Nova Scotia, a young Micmac who had just come up from the city asked me, "Don't you find this place just wild?" I thought he was referring to a party held several nights before which I had found, in my own terms, "wild." He said, "No, I mean all this," and he gestured to the abandoned cars and the rows of houses in disrepair that we could see outside the window and then to the small, sparsely furnished cabin in which we sat. I nervously replied that I didn't mind (also knowing very well that I did not have to live on a reservation) and I got a knowing smile in return.

In still another way, I would have preferred to have avoided any issue which would mark me as different from the community I was intent on entering. Early in my fieldwork, references to my light hair and skin were a source of frustration to me because they indicated that people were regarding me as a separate object when what I wanted was inclusion in the group. Ironically, I wanted a lack of racism from the Indians which my part of society is incapable of allowing them. The first time I ever went to a Boston country-western bar with a group of Indians, a White stranger came over to the group and asked me to dance. I did not want to ally myself with another White and thought that if I stayed with the Micmac at their table, they would understand my decided preference for their group against my own. Except for the din of the music, there was a dead silence at the table as I refused and I was, once again, conscious of being an object of some interest rather than an insider. I wished sincerely that the incident had never happened; yet, at a later time, several women who were there told me that the whole group wanted to get an idea of whether or not I, as a married woman out alone, would consent to dance with a stranger, as any one of them would have done. In my refusal, I proclaimed myself a more respectable woman than I knew.

Being Categorized

Having informants take guesses about who you are is the first feedback about the self a researcher gets. It was common both on the reservation and in the city for both men and women to size me up as a social worker or a teacher or as someone connected with a government bureaucracy. I never found this flattering and would take care to explain that I had no affiliation with agencies, that I came from an educational institution. For some people, this meant I was not very helpful or worth cultivating. As time went on, I became reconciled to the fact that for them to take me as a middle-class bureaucrat was a very reasonable guess at my identity and that the distinction between a young social worker and woman fieldworker was not as telling as that between them and the Indians.

Another category into which I fitted, although I was very reluctant to see anything but error when this was told to me, was that of the available female. From my point of view, I was on a cerebral mission and preferred to discount my sex as a factor in research. If I had better rapport with women than men in the field, I thought it was due to rigidities in the mens' sex-role typing which placed limits on my otherwise unlimited ability to move as easily among men as among women. It was my duty, or so I thought initially, to overcome *their* limited social categories. In actuality, I was always on the scene as a woman without a man and yet a woman who was resisting the more common bureaucratically-defined category of teacher or social worker. I was moving freely in avoidance of any social responsibilities, institutional or informal.

Occasionally another kind of White person seeks Indian company for "back-to-nature" purposes. There are, for example, businessmen who hire Indian men as hunting guides for a week of shooting and drinking, the hippies who want to get back to basics and camp for a summer on the reservation, the concerned female radicals who begin by wanting to help the poor Indians and wind up living with one for a few months. The informality of my association with the Micmac lent itself to an interpretation of me as this kind of White. I would drink beer and hard liquor, I would joke and appreciate the sexual banter that often went on between men and women, and I was apparently enjoying being with Indians. My behavior, insofar as I was oblivious to my own sex role, could have been perceived as a sign of my availability in a more than spiritual sense. It happened several times that I would take my place among a small group of Micmac without much regard for which people were nearest to me; I just wanted to join in and then not be noticed. On one occasion, in an apartment in Boston, I came into the kitchen where there were about a dozen Micmac, most of them sitting around a formica table. My primary concern was to be part of the group, so I took an empty chair at the table, greeting people and returning greetings as I went. I settled into place, yet after a few minutes I noticed that two women directly across from me were giggling and putting their hands over their mouths to hide their smiles. I was trying to observe the social interaction in the kitchen, but I was also becoming increasingly uncomfortable. It finally dawned on me that the two men sitting on either side of me were facing straight ahead, both sipping at their cans of beer, without either of them saying a word to me or to anyone else. Both of them were single, available men. I had, of course, made a rather aggressive social movement by putting myself between them, especially when, as I realized after sitting down, there were other places to sit. The same move towards men of my own class could have been interpreted as a sexual strategy. Realizing my predicament, I removed myself to a socially more appropriate place in the room, hoping that my *faux pas* would be forgiven.

The most clarification I could give to my role was to call myself a student, a vague designation that carries little meaning at all. The Micmac in recent years have not had much attention from anthropologists or other social scientists. A crew of linguists from a Canadian university had reportedly visited the reservation area in 1970, but for the single purpose of recording language. And there were Indians in both the city and the Maritimes who had met Wilson Wallis during his 1950s research. But for them, and I think for other Micmac, my status as student and as woman contrasted with their general idea of the authoritative academic male studying Indian life.

My presence was handled by the Indian community with greater acumen than Whites would handle it if, for instance, one of them had declared his or her intention of moving into White suburbia. I was an atypical outsider. Even so, a community of widely extended kin networks, of relatively loose family organization, and of considerable geographic mobility could tolerate a stranger; this is a tolerance anthropologists have relied on to a considerable degree. In addition, my chief informants were also my protectors and, whether in a bar or within a family group, assumed the responsibility of getting me through situations where my ineptitude was most obvious. On at least one occasion, burly Boston policemen stomping into a South End bar to stop a fight involving an Indian elicited more panic from me than the scuffle itself. Was there a rear exit? Should I be authoritative and interpret the situation to the officers? Could we just ignore the incident? The reaction of the Micmac with whom I was sitting was complete silence and a quiet appraisal of the policemen's behavior, which in this case was a rather matter-of-fact "Okay, let's break it up" combined with some arm-bending. After the police left with two men—one White, one Micmac—the group, with no verbal reference to the incident, decided to move on and, with a friend on either side of me, I found myself ushered quickly out of the bar. The Indians' exit was defensively calculated and unobtrusive.

At another time, on the reservation, I had enjoyed talking to a relative of the family I stayed with, a young man in his thirties whose life experiences I was interested in and wanted to record. Andrew and Kathy, the parents of the family, had both assumed responsibility for structuring my role as visiting bureaucrat. They understood the intellectual nature of my goals and also sought to protect their kin from complicated sexual involvement with a White stranger. I would accept a ride from Sam, the relative, down to the general store, only to find that one or two of the older children were sent along to help as I bought a roll of film. On other, longer rides around the countryside, with five or six or more people in the car, I would invariably end up in the front seat between Andrew and Kathy, or, if in the back seat, between two women and away from Sam or any other man outside the immediate family. It might have been my status as guest which merited such careful handling; but, on the other hand, when the group in the car was just women and children, I could just as easily land in the back seat with an assortment of children on my lap or take some other woman relative's place in the front seat holding an infant.

At one point, when he had been drinking, Sam began to insist that we go out "for a good time." I wanted to get through the situation with easy good nature and yet still communicate that I was not really available. I said things such as "I have a husband in Boston." Sam replied, "And I have a wife in Montreal, so what the hell. You don't live with your husband either." Sam appeared and reappeared throughout the day, like a recurring and ever more insistent theme. I happened to be returning to the house from a visit next door when I saw Andrew talking to Sam behind some cars in the side yard. I went into the house and a few minutes later Andrew came in. He addressed Kathy with a brief "That's settled," and walked past us both to his armchair in the living room. I had a sense that I had caused trouble, even more than Sam, who doggedly avoided me for the rest of his stay on the reservation. His behavior was not atypical or unusual; the Micmac presume the individual social autonomy of every adult and the natural tendency for men and women who appear single is to have physical relations. In their context, it was my behavior which was strange. I would make my social availability obvious and then qualify it by declaring only cerebral intentions.

In the city, I was less dependent on any one household. There were several families who welcomed my overnight visits and I had my own car to move around in. Nonetheless, there were at least five or six people who felt the obligation to make my presence as an outsider to their group less problematical. All of these were adults who at one time or another had hosted me for two or three days in their apartments and felt consequently that they could do a good job of interpreting my existence to the rest of the community. This responsibility was not always an easy one, for there were several Micmac who were quite hostile and would not even talk to me, even though we might spend hours in the same group together. One man, a construction worker, would glare furiously at me every time we met. I made a point of knowing his nickname and greeting him directly, but to no avail. Finally I asked one of my protective friends if she knew why this man was so unfriendly to me. I was told that he was not like most of the Micmac Indians, who would let people do what they wanted and who did not mind my being around, whatever my reasons. I was not quite satisfied with this answer so I asked one of the teen-age boys I knew for a better assessment. The reply was, "Jeannie, he doesn't know what the hell business you have with Indians and neither do I."

By my persistence in simply hanging around, I found that I was eventually able to talk to people who were initially mistrustful, including the construction worker, and to discover the nature of the way in which I could fail or succeed. I think it is fair to say that all agreed that my presence had to be for personal reasons, either negative or positive. I could not like or dislike a tribe which I did not know, so I must be in the group for reasons of liking or disliking specific persons. If I announced to my first contacts, as I did, that I was writing a paper on the Micmac and wanted to meet many of them, it could be taken, and it usually was, that I was saying: "I like you. I think you know a lot of people and could help me. I intend to be around for a while and I want you to be one of my friends." There were only a limited number of people I had to make that statement to in order to know where and how the Micmac were living and to include myself in their activities. For those to whom I had to be explained second-hand, there was less assurance that I was a friend and there was this mysterious abstraction called a research project which could easily be interpreted as a pretext for doing them harm. If, in explaining me to other people, my initial contacts emphasized my project (as opposed to our friendship), it was to demonstrate that they had a weapon, so to speak, in my persona and wanted others to know it. The notion of a project, as an explanation of me, was only a tie-up to expertise and authority, to a hostile objectivity which could be used against other individual Micmac.

If I had good friends in the group, it also meant that there were people with whom I was likely to be at odds. In one instance, I was visiting the apartment of a woman, Anne, with whom I had spent the whole previous day running various errands in her car. The phone rang and it was another woman I knew who had several grievances against this woman and who, in voicing them, also criticized her as an "apple Indian" (red on the outside, white on the inside), for driving that "White bitch" around all day. Anne hung up and then reported the conversation to me and several other women who were in the kitchen. My first reaction was: "I feel really bad about that. I wish I could talk to her." The subject was changed and I did not have a chance to say any more. Still, I was upset and later in the day I brought the subject up again. I said that I felt I should do something, but I did not know what. When I received no response from my friends, I tried a more retaliatory tack by pointing out that the woman who had called has probably had as many White friends as any Micmac. Immediately Anne and the other women gave their enthusiastic agreement and recounted a list of reasons why the woman had no cause to be so nasty. Anne ended the list by saying, "If she wants to fight, she should get a kick or two in the ass." My initial reaction, to be conciliatory, was in line with my conventional notion of how one handles interpersonal aggression and with my goal in fieldwork to keep as many interactional doors open as possible. To my mind, if I were hostile in return, it would be "war," a total and irrevocable commitment to hostility. For the Indian women, hostility was on a human scale, something which was more or less stirred up, argued back and forth, and then dropped. In this case, I witnessed several more telephone calls in subsequent days between Anne and the woman who had criticized her and two arguments between them which took place at social gatherings. I also saw, in the following weeks, that the woman had not been dismissed as an enemy or treated as a social cipher. Anne and the other women in the apartment had little difficulty after the quarrel subsided in including her and her family in their social life as was done before. That is, they concluded that ever since boarding school days, she had been troublesome and would probably start more quarrels in the future. Some people were like that; it was humanly tolerable to have them around. In contrast, I found it very difficult even to greet this woman, not because she had called me a name but because I had spoken out against her by defending Anne from her attack. Despite her friendliness to me in other, later situations, I could not help but feel that I had committed myself by retaliating rather than maintaining a conciliatory spirit. This is not to say that the Indian women were less principled than I, but that they were more flexible, more adept at contending with variations in human moods and at seeing others as ongoing personalities within the community. Whether a relationship was defined predominantly by contention or by friendship, the goal was, it seemed, to have a relationship. For me, the choice was between a positive relationship, a reflection of my good self, or none at all. Many of the Micmac recognized this and other cultural limits of mine. In small ways, when it was explained to me that "this is the way we eat here" or that there was a "shitpot" in the shed instead of a bathroom or that "Indian boys fight more than they should," I felt the Micmac were trying to bridge the distance between our values by verbal comparisons. The more fundamental differences in habits of interpersonal relationships could not be so easily and adequately accounted for in words, although one of the women had this comment, "You're not so used to nastiness. You shouldn't be hurt."

Being and Acting Alone

Despite my concerted efforts throughout the research to be as convivial as possible, there were real obstacles to my easy inclusion in the community. I did want to be liked and I acted the way I would act with people in my own society. I tried to be accommodating, I tried not to lose my temper, I tried to be supportive. This was my public behavior, the way in which I could act for brief social sorties out and away from my family. What I found myself involved in, both in the city and in the reservation area, were situations of continuous public socializing within which it was almost impossible to sustain the exclusively pleasant stance reserved for parties, dinners, classes, etc. One whole day of being with adults and children meant one whole day of continuous bombardment by voices, faces, ideas and projects picked up and dropped, physical tuggings at my hands, claims being laid to my attention, and, in the background, the constant noise of television or jukebox.

In the midst of all this, I was also trying to gather information like a research instrument, that is, selectively to direct my attention and powers of observation. I could no more help this tendency to be purposeful than I could help my limited idea of sociability, i.e., that one was pleasant only to a few people at a time. It was only about halfway through my fieldwork that I began to see, beyond the genuine irritation which days of constant stimulation could provoke and beyond the pleasure I would get when affection or approval was expressed toward me, that there was a whole and valid organization of human experience among the Micmac. It was based on the understanding that being in the company of other people, as a mixture of pleasure and pain, was a constant assurance of being alive. Visitors came and stayed, relatives moved in and out, children were adopted and grew up, everyone traveled and wrote and telephoned. Within a specific situation, it was the jostling and bumping up against one another which was important, more important than an individual directive or a group's getting a task accomplished. One had to be something that could be bumped up against and to the extent that I was consistently affable and resisted getting into quarrels (as, for example, with Anne's adversary), I was less a part of that reassuring world.

In retrospect, it seems to me that I could have participated more or been more of a social person in Indian terms by making my purposes less explicit or being less action-oriented than I was. If I could have made my project subordinate to battling it out as a social equal among equals, I would have been truly a participant in that community. As it was, my tendency to seek out information, rather than to be at one with the group, set me apart. During my stay in Nova Scotia, Andrew frequently had occasion to tease me, saying: "Relax, relax. You people always ask too many questions. Why don't you listen? The Micmac have been here for thousands of years; we'll be here for many more."

My kind of individuality, I began to think, knew no middle range of sociability. I could dictate any number of bureaucratically-phrased letters,

I could handle such abstractions as nation and government and American people. I had even abstracted a notion of a tribe of Indians and resolved to study them. At the other extreme I existed within the intimacy of my small family. The easy tolerance of a community which continually demands that one be a part of it, giving and receiving human vibrations, is outside my ken. It goes against my ideals of privacy and order and quietude. I began to realize also how much those ideals are based on the assumption that other people are irritants, contact with whom has to be controlled, and how much my family is an extension of myself and therefore a fairly safe bundle of relationships. In theory, I can order human events on an enormous scale, forgetting how illusory the connection is between understanding life and being able to control or direct it.

The fact that I was alone in the field, a lone individual "traveling the fastest," caused comment. This was partly because I was without my husband, but also because I was without anyone. Weren't there people I saw when I wasn't with Indians; didn't I have a large family of sisters and brothers, aunts and uncles, nephews and nieces; didn't I have girlfriends I saw every day; and where were my children? From a Micmac point of view, my other life seemed peculiar. When I was not in the city, I was usually alone or with my immediate family. If I saw other adults it was by invitation or appointment.

Finally, I was prevailed upon to bring my twin boys, then age seven, into Boston for visits with me. Again, this was at a point when the totality of Micmac social organization was becoming evident to me and I felt less interested in detailed fragments of information than in a more complete understanding of their world view. I felt I had to see their world from the perspective of a social being, rather than of an efficient recorder. My children were the most chaotic and warmest part of my life and I had visions of all three of us relaxedly mixing in with whatever small group of Indian people might be together. I had not realized what faithful products of corporation culture we had raised them to be. They are trained to understand everything and quickly verbalize their reactions to new experiences. In fact, they like a new experience because it gives them the opportunity to offer a plethora of those ingenious observations which delight suburban parents and teachers. For example, both children at that time would sit at the same table with me and several other adults and include themselves as serious participants in conversation. But the Indians did not do what White teachers and parents would do. Among the Micmac, the children were either ignored or frowned at, and I bore the burden of attending to their precocious observations. The result of such attention was that I could not continue as an adult talking with the other adults. The Indian men and women in the same situation were handling their children in a very different way. Shouts would frequently be sent out from the kitchen to the next room where the children were playing. These would be messages on the order of, "Dougie, you brat, don't leave your bike on the stairs," or "Mary, goddammit, stop that noise." They had very little to do with tasks and everything to do with both assuring and warning the children that the adults were near. A child walking through the room would be hugged, or pinched, or slapped, or kissed, and then go on its way. Conversation never got so intense, so purposeful, that it could not tolerate this simultaneous flow of physical communication between adults and their children. At last, finding no audience, my children would leave the adults, including me, and I would find myself able to give full attention to grown-up concerns. What I found myself paying close attention to, of course, was a mixture of stories, and jokes, and phone calls, and shouts, and exits, and entrances which defied my intense focus and linear task of information-gathering.

In one instance, near the end of my fieldwork, I brought the boys along to a church meeting house where I had volunteered to sort clothes for a rummage sale. They behaved in what I thought was a good way by exploring the hall, searching through some boxes, and generally assuming that this situation was grist for the mill of their curiosity. There were about seven Indian women there at the time and some ten minutes after we arrived I heard one older lady ask in a perturbed voice, "Whose children are these?" The question seemed rhetorical, as I had greeted her holding both the boys' hands. Perhaps there should be some restraints on their behavior, I thought, and I left my work to speak to them. Then I returned to the job of sorting clothes, more mechanically intent on getting the work done than any of the Indian women. They combined coffee-drinking, cigarette-smoking, trying on some of the donated clothes, and supervising their children with the business of preparing for the sale. I tried to take my cue from them and stopped for a "coffee-break," my understanding of how to handle the polar distinction between work and socializing. As I drank my coffee, I began to get the feeling that the independence I had given my children disconcerted the other women who were keeping closer watch on theirs. The Indian children in turn were a subdued and even helpful presence. My own were rambuctiously playing hide-and-seek among a pile of empty cardboard cartons. I did not mind their noise or their independence as long as I was left free to work, but I wanted to know if others were annoyed. So I asked one of my Micmac friends what, if anything, she would say to my children if they were hers. From where we were sitting, across the room from the twins, she yelled without the slightest hesitation, "Cut it out, you Guillemin kids!" The other Indian women broke into laughter. One, with six children, said, "That sounds just like me, just like a broken record, my kids say." The women all agreed they sounded just the same and I think that they were genuinely relieved that a gesture had been made to account for these children as they did their own.

It was inevitable during fieldwork in a small community, where I felt the power of the group to absorb an individual, that I would have second thoughts about having been educated to value objective verbal assessments of social events more than a relaxed immersion in them. I regretted at times that I could not just for once cease to reflect. In a room full of people and noise or at a bar with Tammy Wynette's "Stand By Your Man" blotting out all talk, I would get a feeling of how good that could be and then I would conscientiously return home and write up the experience as data. The final image in Kubrick's *2001*, that of a fetus with its eyes open, began to seem to me the appropriate symbol of conventional self-awareness devoid of the means to act, for I gradually lost belief in any link between an intellectual understanding of life and the larger goal of our culture: to bring experience so under our control that pain and even death are avoided. I was taught that knowledge is power, but I have come to conclude that, as a society, we have arrogantly tried, with science, to engineer ourselves out of the realities of the human condition into immortality. We began by hoping that machines would release us from drudgery, we systematically eliminated physical hardship by allocating it to the poor, and ended up with a technology which threatens literally to disembody us. Our abstract and depersonalized way of ordering life has allowed us to repress the fact of our human mortality even as it requires that we live with the possibility of global destruction. Nor do we have the power, once we realize the limits of our culture, to easily adapt other ways. There are few of us members of the ruling society who could tolerate permanent membership in a true community, who would not prefer a private combination of psychic pain and physical comfort to a more basic communal mixture.

To use Herodotus' quote, the tendency of all people to "end by preferring their own, so convinced are they that their own usages surpass those of all others," is difficult to criticize. It seems, however, that the implementation of that preference to the social domination of other cultures is a prerogative we must question more seriously each day of our lives. The burden of understanding the limits of our own ways is to observe more than we can act upon, to witness more than we can experience and, ultimately, to acknowledge the validity of other cultures, finishing with the realization that as a society we have really done nothing better, just differently.

2.
Love Fulani Style

Paul Riesman

The Fulani are one of West Africa's largest ethnic groups. They number about six million people—as do the Ibo of Nigeria—and are thus surpassed only by the Hausa and the Yoruba, who number about ten million each. Unlike these other populations and unlike most West African groups, the Fulani are not concentrated in a specific geographic area. Starting out as a pastoral people, they have spread out with their cattle in the steppes and grasslands which lie between the Sahara desert and the more humid areas to the south, where the tsetse fly would kill off the cattle. Small or large minorities of Fulani are found today in every state of West Africa, and their mode of existence ranges from the pure pastoral to the agricultural and to various urban modes of life.

The Fulani described in the article live in a small community in northeastern Upper Volta. They are a pastoral group, though they do not move around continually, and they all cultivate millet, which is a staple of their diet. It should be understood that when I say "the Fulani" I am not referring to the entire ethnic group, but only to the people I know firsthand.

The basic reason I went to the Fulani was to try to find out what it was like to be a Fulani. Before going I did not in the least suppose that I would become one myself, but I did think that the more I adapted to their way of life, the more I conformed to the rules of their society, the more clearly would it be impressed on me what it was like to be a Fulani. I would feel acting on myself the same social forces and constraints that act on a Fulani, though presumably I would react to these forces with different feelings. Conformity, then, was closely bound up with the nature of my work as I perceived it.

In addition, conformity is often an important element in communication. I have always tolerated solitude relatively well; in fact I have often enjoyed being alone and I sometimes feel frustrated when I am prevented from it. On the other hand, if I am with people and yet feel out of touch with them, unable to communicate with them, I feel extremely uncomfortable, sometimes miserable. It is not despair at the impossibility of communication between human beings; it is a more immediate hurt of knowing that you are not recognized as human by them, that you do not appear to them the way you feel to be within yourself.

Together with the pain of non-recognition comes a horrible fear of trappedness. You are trapped in their image of you; your inability to communicate with them makes it impossible for you to break out of this image, and you feel helpless, if not paralyzed. It is this experience, I feel, that is part of the daily life of black people in white American society, but that is another story . . . . However well I may think I understand others, I feel the foundations of my existence crumbling if they do not understand me.

Speaking the Fulani language, then, and conforming to their customs, were all part of my attempt to be recognizably human in a situation that was totally strange to the villagers whom we asked to be our hosts. But now I must contradict myself. Having said that I tried to conform, I must also say that from the very beginning I refused to conform in certain respects. The problem was, what to conform to?

Over the 19 months my wife and I lived with the people of our village it became clear that there was no such thing as Fulani behavior, but rather different comportments that were appropriate to different groups and even individuals in the society, and these comportments varied depending on whom one happened to be with at the time. Gradually, for instance, I formed an idea of Fulani good manners, but this proved to be more useful in dealing with people I didn't know well than with my fellow villagers.

At the beginning, especially, I was a *Tuubaako* (European), and it was to their vague notions of how Europeans behave that the Fulani expected me to conform. My refusal to conform to these notions—some of the villagers had never seen a Tuubaako and many had never seen one close up—confirmed one of their preconceptions inasmuch as the Tuubaakoobe (pl.), in their view, are not governed by ordinary laws and hence can do whatever they want.

The idea of conforming to a set of rules, then, quickly revealed itself as making little sense. What really mattered, it became evident, was a sensitivity to the people I was living with that would disclose to me at any moment how they were feeling, and conformity then meant adjusting my behavior according to my resonance to these feelings. There eventually came a time in my relations with my "together-human beings" when I could no longer plead ignorance, and when whatever I did was assumed to be done because I wanted to do it, and whatever I did not do was thought to be omitted not through oversight but because I actively didn't want to do it.

One question I was asked quite often, particularly by younger people, was, why didn't I go after their women, and why didn't I take another wife? No matter what I answered, they continued to hold that it was because I didn't like them, was not attracted by them. Another idea was that it was because my wife was stronger than me, but it was probably suggested more as a way of teasing me than as a serious answer to the question. The Fulani are polygynous, but everyone is agreed that it is wrong to sleep with another man's wife. Yet every woman older than about fourteen is somebody's wife unless she is a widow or a divorcee. Women, also, are not supposed to commit adultery.

In the evenings after sundown my wife and I would sit out in front of our hut in the village while I made Arabic tea on the hot coals of a wood fire. The young men would gather around—but never the women, except when I played some of the recordings I had made among them on the tape recorder—and we would all drink the tea, passing the warm shot-glasses, sticky with the sugar of spilt tea. When the tea was finished, a group of the young men would often get up and begin to move away together, looking like long-legged night birds in their black, flapping tunics.

"Hey, where are you going?" I would ask.

"We're going to look for women," they would reply with a laugh.

About half of them were married, about half were not, and the women they were going after were invariably married or at least betrothed. As a general rule, however, they never went looking for women among the wives of their close neighbors and relatives, such as their fathers, brothers and children. So while young men from neighboring hamlets were stealing into our village, our young men were hunting about elsewhere; there was always a risk, of course, for you could never be sure that the husband wasn't there, perhaps lying in wait for you with his friends. People sometimes turned up next morning rather badly battered, and quite a few young men got punctures and gashes in their feet and legs from thorns as they made quick getaways into the bush.

How explain such goings on, which apparently violate fundamental moral tenets of the society? To begin with, we may find it helpful to consider Man's view of Woman in Fulani society. A woman cannot be considered without regarding her as beautiful. The more beautiful a woman is the closer she may be said to come to an essential quality of womanhood. Of course, not all women are beautiful, but nearly everyone is felt to have, or to have had, beauty in some measure in her lifetime. Thus our discussion here is not valid for all women in Fulani society at any given moment, but it is valid for nearly all of them at some time in their lives. Though men's attitudes change as they grow older, other qualities desired in women (e.g., being a good mother for the children) never entirely supplant—and sometimes not at all—the desire for beauty. As long as a woman is beautiful she is the object of men's desire. And what men desire they seek to obtain. But the fact of having a woman—in marriage or in any other way—does not automatically prevent her from being desired by others; it just makes obtaining her more difficult.

I hope it is clear that I am not speaking of sexual desire. There is of course a sexual component in this desire, but in listening to Fulani men talk about women it is clear that the feelings are more romantic, in a certain sense; the desire is mingled with a kind of awe in many cases, and to have a beautiful woman is in fact one of the highest goods that the society has to offer—perhaps it is the Good itself. This being the case, however, there is a strong, but not explicitly stated, feeling that women, like all good things in life, should be shared rather than enjoyed by just one person. This attitude, I think, explains in part the normal development of a Fulani marriage. For as much as a year or more, the newly wed couple do not have a house of their own and do not publicly behave in any way that would indicate there was a special relationship between them. A man, of course, has rights over his wife, but these rights are at the same time begrudged by society.

Thus, we can see emerging a covert idea which gives all men a certain claim on beautiful women. The beauty of women moves men to action—even married men—and it makes them go after that beauty. A beautiful woman always has admirers, if not lovers, and the husband of such a woman knows that if he is away, whether on a trip or herding cattle or out looking for women himself, ineluctably his wife will have visitors and that it depends on her wishes alone whether she will go into the bush with them or not.

One of my friends, who had been visiting this girl secretly for several years, was the one to win her hand, but another of my friends was one of the losers. Their attitudes are revealing. The winner was, of course, very happy, though pretending to be nonchalant, but he particularly liked to make fun of the losers. "Go ask your friend J__ what happened," he said with a laugh. I had been completely surprised that J__ had wanted to marry her, for he had never spoken of an interest in her before. He told me that in fact he did not really love her but that he had tried because he thought he had a chance, since the girl's father liked him very much and was opposed to her marrying the suitor who eventually got her.

Perhaps because their role is not an ostensibly active one, Fulani women come to regard themselves much as the men see them. In particular, the half-conscious feeling that a woman's beauty should not be enjoyed by just one man often comes to be shared by the woman in question herself. She realizes that she doesn't have to be content with what she has and seeks to act out in life the transcendence that men see in her. She becomes a prey that can never be captured, the object of a quest that can never be fulfilled.

In practical terms, this means that beautiful women lead unstable lives. They almost never stay married to the person they are first given to by their parents. The man doesn't feel he possesses a woman until she is his wife, no matter how much he may enjoy her favors; as for the woman, not only does she not want to be possessed, but also to the extent that she feels herself to be the object of quest it goes against her very nature to be possessed. Whether married or not, the woman is always free—but in danger of losing her liberty. To the extent that a woman is—or feels—plain or ugly, she will not feel the same freedom (to leave a marriage, for example). On the other hand, she may also be less inclined to experience marriage as possession in the first place.

The reader may have the feeling that this all seems rather familiar and that the Fulani are not so very different from ourselves. Either they really are similar or I have been projecting onto them images and feelings from my own culture. After all, is not female beauty an important force in our cultural life, and is it not usually the man who goes after the woman rather than the reverse in our culture also? And do not our beautiful women (e.g., movie stars) lead similarly unstable lives? I don't have ready answers to these questions. For the time being, however, let me assert my belief that these resemblances are more apparent than real, for while they may bear witness to facts of sexual attraction that are true of men everywhere, the attitudes of the people towards the activities I have been discussing, and their conceptions of what they are doing, are quite different in the two cultures.

How does Man's quest for Woman affect Fulani social structure? It is clear that the practices I have described are in principle forbidden by the society's moral code, while their effect on the women might portend an unstable social order. Is this the case? Does their quest mean that the changes induced by colonization and peace have weakened that code to the point where a majority, if not most, of the people flout it? There is some evidence that the strength of the code has weakened. Old people tell me that divorce, for instance, which is easy now, was more difficult when they were growing up. On the other hand, there is no evidence that the code was not flouted then. It may have been more dangerous for the individual to challenge it then, and hence a smaller proportion of people may have done so, but indirect evidence from stories, sayings about women and discussions with old people about the past, indicate that the attitudes and practices we are discussing have a long history.

This constant challenge to the moral code of the society is not the same thing as a protest against it. First of all, the fact that it is a defiance of the code enhances the value of what is sought in defiance of it. The very fact that Woman is sought in contravention to the official values suggests that something higher is at stake, something "beyond" the routine of "normal" life. This may be part of the nature of Woman herself, as conceived by the Fulani, for it is through her that new life comes into the society. The apparent marginality of women on many occasions in social life may stem not from the fact that she really is considered marginal, but rather from the fact that she belongs to two worlds more obviously than man does, namely the natural world—because of her ability to gestate and bring forth new life—and the social world. And yet, although the quest for Woman seems to suggest the valuing of a good that is beyond the social, to the extent that men and women do participate in the same culture and maintain the same society, this quest heightens the value the Fulani place on their own society as well.

Secondly, this defiance enhances the value of the individual, both for his own sake and as a member of society. By acting against the moral code the individual is demonstrating that he is a free being and that his actions are not automatically determined by social rules and social pressures. But if the individual is free to disobey, then he is free to obey too, and the value of his adherence to the society is thereby enhanced. For, although the Fulani recognize greater or lesser degrees of coercion in social life, it never works with predictable results; if it did, if the person had no choice but to act in a certain way, then for the Fulani the situation would not be a human one. In fact, I believe that such situations do not exist in Fulani society; rather, the maintenance of society is thought to depend on the wills of its members, not on laws, and so, for the Fulani, everything that people do they do because they have chosen to. Acts performed under compulsion, whether of need (e.g., thirst, hunger, bowel relief) or of force, have no value.

Emotional Economy of Abundance

Thus, the defiance of official morality plays itself out in the pursuit of a universally esteemed good and seems, as it were, built into the organization of social life itself. Are there other types of defiance in Fulani society that are less respectable, that call the system into question, for instance, or imply other sets of values? There are instances of deviance, such as refusing to pray, refusing to work, and theft. These acts do not seem to me to be structural, a part of the system, however. One thing that can be said of these three kinds of deviance, however, is that they express a refusal to participate in the system, whereas the defiance of the moral code that we have been studying here is, for the Fulani, the manifestation of an absorbing and zestful participation in the life of the community.

There was a gram of truth in our hosts' notion that the reason I didn't go after their women was that I didn't like them. In reality I found myself strongly moved by them, but I resisted these feelings. Was it only to remain faithful to my wife and to maintain our marriage? This was indeed very important to me, but I believe I would have reacted the same way—only with greater mental torment—had I not been married. For to enter a sexual relationship with someone in that community would have implied for me a deeper involvement in its social life than I felt capable of sustaining.

This sense in the pit of my stomach colors my interpretation of the facts I have presented. Our relationship with the villagers was one of friendship, though it was often described by them as a kind of kinship. It is true, older people all felt like parents to me, people my age were brothers and sisters, and younger people were our children. I was living in an atmosphere of warmth and security that I had never experienced in my own culture, and for which I was not prepared by my upbringing. It was like breathing pure oxygen. But the independence and freedom that I believe the Fulani experience in this atmosphere—I was afraid I could not, for the independence that I am used to from my own life consists in being able to withdraw, separate and differentiate myself from everyone else. I feared that I didn't have the strength that the Fulani do to maintain my sense of self in such a tumult of feelings, for my defense mechanisms were designed for an emotional economy of scarcity rather than abundance.

Fulani culture offers to its members a life that is supremely worth living. The individual is a member of the society from the day he is named (seven days after birth), but his adherence to it feels freely given rather than automatic or compelled, as I believe the example of the quest for Woman shows. What this quest means to them cannot be put into words, except perhaps in their own poetry, for it is by nature both specific and indefinite, limited and infinite. The important thing is that the Good in life is available to them within their culture and it calls from them the fullest expression of their individual personalities as they strive to obtain it.

Many Westerners feel that our culture does not offer anything worth striving for; for myself and others who share this feeling, then, the search is for something to want, rather than for something we know we want. Both kinds of searches have in common that they can never end, for if they did, society would stop. But the place from which the search is begun is different in each case: for many Westerners it begins from a feeling of essential non-relatedness to the rest of the world, while for the Fulani the beginning is in a set of relationships that the person finds himself to be in with other beings.

3.
Kapluna Daughter:
Living with Eskimos

Jean L. Briggs

"It's very cold down there—*very cold*. If I were going to be at Back River this winter, I would like to adopt you and try to keep you alive."

My Eskimo visitor, Uunai, dramatized her words with shivers as we sat drinking tea in the warm nursing station in Gjoa Haven. It was only mid-August, but already the wind that intruded through the cracks in the window frame was bitter, and the gound was white with a dusting of new snow. Last winter's ice, great broken sheets of it, still clogged the harbor, so that the plane I was waiting for was unable to get through to us. I was on my way to spend a year and a half with the Utkuhikhalingmiut, a small group of Eskimos who lived in Chantrey Inlet at the mouth of the Back River on the northern rim of the American continent. They were the most remote group of Eskimos that I could find on the map of the Canadian Arctic, a people who in many ways lived much as they had in the days before *kaplunas* (white men) appeared in the north. They were nomadic; they lived in snowhouses in winter, in tents in summer; and their diet consisted very largely of fish—trout and whitefish—supplemented now and again by a few caribou.

Uunai's words presaged the most important influence on the course of my life at Back River, namely my adoption as a "daughter" in the household of a Utkuhikhalingmiut family. I want to describe an aspect of that relationship here, with the aim of illustrating some of the difficulties that a host community or family may encounter in its hospitable efforts to incorporate a foreigner.

I arrived in Chantrey Inlet at the end of August 1963 on a plane that the

Canadian government sent in once a year to collect the three or four schoolchildren who wished to go to Inuvik. I had with me letters of introduction from the Anglican deacon and his wife in Gjoa Haven. Nakliguhuktuq and Ikayuqtuq were Eskimos from the eastern Arctic who served as missionaries not only to the Anglican Eskimos in Gjoa Haven, but also to the Utkuhikhalingmiut. The letters—written in the syllabic script in which the Utkuhikhalingmiut, like most other Canadian Eskimos, are literate—noted that I would like to live with the Utkuhikhalingmiut for a year or so, learning the Eskimo language and skills: how to scrape skins and sew them, how to catch fish and preserve them or boil the oil out of them for use in lighting and heating the winter iglus. They asked the Eskimos to help me with words and fish and promised that in return I would help them with tea and kerosene. They told the people that I was kind and that they should not be shy and afraid of me—"She's a little bit shy herself"—and assured them that they need not feel (as they often do feel toward kaplunas) that they had to comply with my every wish. They said, finally, that I wished to be adopted into an Eskimo family and to live with them in their iglu as a daughter.

Choosing a Father

I had a number of reasons for wishing to be adopted, and there were several precedents for adoption as well: four other kaplunas of my acquaintance, both scholars and laymen, who had wintered with Eskimos had done so as "sons," sharing the iglus of their Eskimo families. Living in the iglu would be warmer than living alone, I thought (Ikayuqtuq and Nakliguhuktuq agreed); and I thought vaguely that it might be "safer" if one family had specific responsibility for me. The idea had romantic appeal too; I saw it as a fulfillment of a childhood wish to "be" an Eskimo, and I expected no rapport problems, since on two previous trips to the Alaskan Arctic I had identified strongly with the Eskimo villagers with whom I had lived. To be sure, there were also arguments against adoption: I had qualms concerning the loss of an "objective" position in the community, drains on my supplies that would result from contributing to the maintenance of a family household and loss of privacy with resultant difficulties in working. Still, when the moment of decision came, the balance lay in favor of adoption.

There were two suitable fathers among the Utkuhikhalingmiut (that is, two household heads who had wives alive and at home), and these two were both more than eager to adopt me. One, however—an intelligent, vigorous man named Inuttiaq—far outdid the other in the imagination and persistence with which he "courted" me as a daughter. Not only were he and his family extremely solicitous, but he was also a jolly and ingenious language teacher. Most gratifying of all, both he and his wife, Allaq, were astonishingly quick to understand my halting attempts to communicate. There was no question which family I preferred. Fortunately, Inuttiaq also occupied a much more central position among the Utkuhikhalingmiut than did Nilak, the other possible father. He had many more close kin and was also the Anglican lay leader of the group. I was convinced that both anthropology and I would benefit more if I were adopted by Inuttiaq.

Winter

From the moment that the adoption was settled, I was "Inuttiaq's daughter" in the camp. Inuttiaq and his relatives with much amusement drilled me in the use of kin terms appropriate to my position, just as they drilled his three-year-old daughter, who was learning to speak. They took charge of my material welfare and of my education in language and skills. Allaq also to some extent took charge of my daily activities, as it was proper that a mother should. She told me what the day's job for the women of the family was going to be: gathering birch twigs for fuel, scraping caribou hides in preparation for the making of winter clothing or skinning the fish bellies out of which oil was to be boiled. The decision to participate or not was left to me, but if I did join the women—and I usually did—she made sure that my share of the work was well within the limits of my ability and stamina. "We will be walking very far tomorrow to get birch twigs," she would say. "You will be too tired." If I went anyway, it was always silently arranged that my load should be the lightest, and if I wandered out of sight of the other women in my search for birch bushes, someone always followed behind—sent by Allaq, as I discovered months later—to make sure that I didn't get lost.

I felt increasingly comfortable with my family and found their solicitude immensely warming. At the same time, I dreaded the loss of privacy that the winter move into their iglu would bring. Curiously, the effect of the move when it came in October was the opposite of what I had expected. I basked in the protectiveness of Inuttiaq's household; and what solitude I needed I found on the river in the mornings, when I jigged for salmon trout through the ice with Inuttiaq, or, to my surprise, in the iglu itself in the afternoons, when the room was full of visitors and I retired into myself, lulled and shielded by the flow of quiet, incomprehensible speech.

Behaving

The family's continuing graciousness was very seductive. I came to expect the courtesies that I received and even to resent it a bit when they were not forthcoming, though at the same time I told myself that such feelings were shameful. However, as time passed and I became an established presence in the household, I was less and less often accorded special privileges, except insofar as my ineptitude made services necessary. Allaq still mended my skin boots for me and stretched them when they shrank in drying; my stitches were not small enough and my jaws not strong enough. She continued to fillet my fish when it was frozen nearly as hard as wood. But in other respects Allaq, and especially Inuttiaq—who was far less shy than his wife—more and more attempted to assimilate me into a proper adult parent-daughter relationship. I was expected to help with the household work to the best of my ability—to make tea or bannock and to fetch water—and I was expected to obey unquestioningly when Inuttiaq told me to do something or made a decision on my behalf.

Unfortunately, I found it impossible to learn to behave in every respect like an Utkuhikhalingmiut daughter. Inuttiaq lectured me in general terms on the subject of filial obedience, and once in a while I think he tried to shame me into good behavior by offering himself as a model of virtue— volunteering, for example, to make bannock for me if I were slow in making it for him—but to little avail. Sometimes I was genuinely blind and deaf to his lessons, unaccustomed as I was to Utkuhikhalingmiut subtlety. At other times I saw what was wanted but resisted for reasons I will describe in a moment. Inevitably, conflicts, covert but pervasive, developed, both regarding the performance of household chores and regarding the related matter of obedience to Inuttiaq.

Assumptions in Conflict

The causes of the conflicts were three. First was the fact that some feminine skills were hard for me to learn. Overtly my Utkuhikhalingmiut parents were very tolerant of the lack of skill that they rightly attributed to kapluna ignorance and perhaps also to kapluna lack of intelligence, or *ihuma*. However, perhaps because of an assumption that kaplunas were unable to learn, if I was at all slow to understand Allaq's instructions and demonstrations, she easily gave up trying to teach me, preferring instead to continue to serve me. And though she stretched my boots and cut my fish in the most cheerful manner, after a while her added chores may well have been burdensome to her.

A second cause of the conflicts was that some of Inuttiaq's and Allaq's assumptions about the nature of parental and daughterly virtue were at variance with mine; in consequence not only did I have to learn new patterns, I also had to unlearn old ones. Hardest of all to learn was unquestioning obedience to paternal authority. Sometimes I could not help resisting, privately but intensely, when Inuttiaq told me to "make tea," to "go home," "to hurry up" or to "pray." I was irritated even by the fact that after the first weeks of gracious formality had passed he began to address me in the imperative form, which is often used in speaking to women, children and young people. Rationally I know that I should have welcomed this sign of "acceptance," but I could not be pleased. My irritation was due partly to the fact that subordination threatened my accustomed—and highly valued—independence, but it was aggravated by a fear that the restrictions placed on me interfered with my work.

And herein lay the third cause of the conflicts: I found it hard sometimes to be simultaneously a docile and helpful daughter and a conscientious anthropologist. Though Allaq appeared to accept my domestic clumsiness as inevitable, she may have felt less tolerant on the occasions when it was not lack of skill that prevented me from helping her, but anxiety over the pocketful of trouser-smudged, disorganized field notes that cried out to be typed. A number of times, when I could have helped to gut fish or to carry in snow to repair the sleeping platform or floor or could have offered to fetch water or make tea, I sat and wrote instead or sorted vocabulary—tiny slips of paper spread precariously over my sleeping bag and lap. It was sometimes professional anxiety that prompted me to disobey Inuttiaq too; and I am sure that on such occasions, as on others, he must have found my insubordination not only "bad," but completely incomprehensible. My behavior at moving time is an example. My gear, minimal though it was by kapluna standards, placed a severe strain on Inuttiaq when we moved camp. Whereas the sleds of others were loaded to little more than knee height, the load on Inuttiaq's sled was shoulder-high. From his point of view it was only reasonable that he should instruct me to leave my heavy tape recorder and my metal box of field notes on the top of a small knoll, as the Utkuhikhalingmiut cached their own belongings, while we moved downstream, not to return until after the flood season. I, however, questioned whether the water might rise over the knoll, and Inuttiaq's silent scrutiny seemed to say that he considered my inquiry a reflection on his judgment.

I do not mean to create the impression that life in Inuttiaq's household during the first winter was continuous turmoil. There were many days, even weeks, when I, at least, felt the situation to be very peaceful and enjoyable. I was grateful for the warmth of my parents' company and care; it was good to feel that I belonged somewhere, that I was part of a family, even on a make-believe basis. But the rewards of my presence for Inuttiaq and his real family were of different, and probably of a lesser, order. Because Inuttiaq's purchases in Gjoa Haven were supplemented by mine, our household was richer than others in store goods: tea, tobacco, flour, jam, dry milk, raisins and kerosene. But apart from these material benefits, and at first perhaps the novelty (and prestige?) of having a kapluna daughter, it is hard to see what Inuttiaq's family gained in return for the burden they carried. I played "Tavern in the Town" and "Santa Lucia" on my recorder; Inuttiaq enjoyed that and once in a while asked me to play for guests. I helped inefficiently in the mornings to remove the whitefish from the family nets and to drag them home, harnessed with Allaq to the sled. I assisted—erratically, as I have mentioned—with the other domestic chores; and in late winter, when the sun returned and Inuttiaq began again to jig for salmon trout, I usually fished with him. That is all that occurs to me, and a trivial contribution it must have been from my family's point of view.

Satan and Self-Control

It was hard for me to know at the time, however, just what their reactions to me were, because the tensions that existed were nearly all covert. Hostility among Utkuhikhalingmiut is ignored or turned into a joke; at worst it becomes the subject of gossip behind the offender's back. I, too, did my best to smother my annoyance with frustration, but my attempts were not wholly successful. My training in self-control was less perfect than theirs, and at the same time the strains were greater than those I was accustomed to dealing with in my own world. Moreover, the most potentially gratifying of the outlets utilized by the Utkuhikhalingmiut—gossip—was not open to me as an anthropologist. I did my best to learn with the children when they were taught to turn annoyance into amusement, but laughter didn't come easily.

The Utkuhikhalingmiut are acutely sensitive to subtle indications of mood. They heard the coldness in my voice when I said, "I don't understand," noted the length of a solitary walk I took across the tundra or the fact that I went to bed early and read with my back turned to the others. Later, Inuttiaq might give me a lecture—phrased, as always, in the most general terms—about the fate of those who lose their tempers: Satan uses them for firewood. Or he might offer me an especially choice bit of fish—whether to shame me or to appease me I don't know. The contrast between my irritability and the surface equanimity of others gave me many uncomfortable moments, but I persuaded myself that the effects of my lapses were shortlived. When I laughed again and heard others laugh with me, or when they seemed to accept the generous gestures with which I tried to make amends, I was reassured that no damage had been done. I was wrong. But it was only when I returned to Gjoa Haven on my way home a year later that I learned how severe the tensions had become between November and January of that first winter. Then the deacon's wife,

Ikajuqtuq, told me of the report Inuttiaq had made of me in January when he went in to Gjoa Haven to trade: "She is not happy. She gets angry very easily, and I don't think she likes us anymore." Shortly after Inuttiaq's return from Gjoa Haven in January, conflict erupted into the open.

"The Iglus Are Cold"

The two weeks of Inuttiaq's absence in Gjoa Haven had been an especially trying period for me. I had looked forward to them as a much needed interlude in which to type and organize my swelling pile of penciled notes. When Inuttiaq was at home, it was often difficult to maintain the iglu temperature within the range of 27 to 31 degrees at which typing was feasible. If I tried to type during the daylight hours of the morning, when the outdoor work was done, my fingers and carbon paper froze as a result of Inuttiaq's drafty comings and goings at jobs that seemed to necessitate propping the door open. But in the sociable afternoon and evening hours the snow dome dripped in the heat and occasionally deposited lumps of slush into my typewriter, and the iglu steamed so that my work was lost in a wet fog as a result of Inuttiaq's demands for tea, boiled fox, bannock and soup in rapid succession. Many were the frustrated moments when I heartily wished him gone; but it was only when he *was* gone that I discovered how completely our comfort depended on his presence. "When the men are away the iglus are cold," the women said; and it was true. The morning drafts that had plagued me before were nothing compared with the chill that resulted when nobody came and went at all. It was partly, of course, that Inuttiaq had taken with him one of our two primus stoves and one of the two kerosene storm lanterns, which ordinarily heated the iglu. But Allaq's behavior during her husband's absence intensified the cold. She never boiled fish, rarely brewed tea and never lit the lamp to dry clothes—any of which activities would have warmed the iglu. She merely sat in her corner of the sleeping platform, blew on her hands and remarked that the iglu was cold. It was; it was 20 degrees colder than when Inuttiaq was at home. I fretted and fumed in silent frustration and determined that when he came back I would take drastic steps to improve my working conditions.

I broached the subject to Inuttiaq a few days after his return to camp. He listened attentively to my explanation. I told him that I had thought about going to live for a while in the empty wooden building that stood on a peninsula a few miles from camp. The government had built it as a nursing station, but it had never been used except by me as a cache for my useless belongings. It had a kerosene stove, which would make it luxuriously comfortable—unless the stove was as erratic as the one in the similar nursing station in Gjoa Haven, with which I had once had an unfortunate experience. Inuttiaq agreed that the stove was unpredictable. Instead, he suggested that he take me to the nursing station every morning and fetch me again at night, so that I would not freeze. As often before, he reassured me: "Because you are alone here, you are someone to be taken care of." And, as often before, his solicitude warmed me. "Taking me to the nursing station every day will be a lot of work for you," I said. The round trip took an hour and a half by dog sled, not counting the time and effort involved in harnessing and unharnessing the team. He agreed that it would be a lot of work. "Could you perhaps build me a small iglu?" I asked. It would take only an hour or two to build a tiny iglu near our own, which I could use as an "office"; then he need concern himself no further. Lulled by the assurance he had just given me of his desire to take care of me and by the knowledge that the request I made was not time-consuming, I was the more disagreeably startled when he replied with unusual vigor, "I build no iglus. I have to check the nets."

A Daughter's Tent

The rage of frustration seized me. He had not given me the true reason for his refusal. It only took two hours to check the nets every second or third day; on the other days, Inuttiaq did nothing at all except eat, drink, visit and repair an occasional tool. He was offended, but I could not imagine why. Whether Inuttiaq read my face I do not know, but he softened his refusal immediately: "Shall Ipuituq or Tutaq"—he named two of the younger men—"build an iglu for you?" Perhaps it would be demeaning for a man of Inuttiaq's status, a mature householder, to build an iglu for a mere daughter. There was something in Inuttiaq's reaction that I did not understand, and a cautioning voice told me to contain my ethnocentric judgment and my anger. I thought of the small double-walled tent that I had brought with me for emergency use. It was stored in the nursing station. "They say my tent is very warm in winter," I said. Inuttiaq smoked silently. After a while he asked, "Shall they build you an iglu tomorrow?" My voice shook with exasperation: "Who knows?" I turned my head, rummaging—for nothing—in my knapsack until the intensity of my feeling should subside.

Later, when Inuttiaq was smoking his last pipe in bed, I raised the subject again, my manner, I hoped, a successful facsimile of cheerfulness and firmness. "I would like to try the tent and see whether it's warm, as I have heard. We can bring it here, and then if it's not warm, I won't freeze; I'll come indoors." Allaq laughed, Inuttiaq accepted my suggestion, and I relaxed with relief, restored to real cheer by Inuttiaq's offer to fetch the tent from the nursing station the following day—if it stormed—so that he could not go on the trapping trip he had planned.

My cheer was premature. Two days later the tent had still not been fetched, though Inuttiaq had not gone trapping. I decided to walk to the nursing station. I had no intention of fetching the tent myself—it would have been impossible; but I needed a few hours alone, and vaguely I knew that the direction of my walk would be to Inuttiaq a sign, however futile, that I was in earnest about my tent.

But I did not dream that he would respond as charitably as he did. I had just arrived at the nursing station and was searching among my few books for a novel to comfort me in my frustration when I heard the squeak of sled runners on the snow outside and a familiar voice speaking to the dogs: *"Hoooo* [whoa]." Inuttiaq appeared in the doorway. I smiled. He smiled. "Will you want your tent?"

Gratitude and relief erased my anger as Inuttiaq picked up the tent and carried it to the sled. "You were walking," he said, in answer to my thanks. "I felt protective toward you."

It was a truce we had reached, however, not a peace, though I did not realize it at once. Since it was nearly dark when we reached camp, Inuttiaq laid the tent on top of the iglu for the night, to keep it from the dogs. Next morning I went with Inuttiaq to jig for trout up-river, and when we returned I thought that finally the time was ripe for setting up the tent. Not wanting to push Inuttiaq's benevolence too far, and remembering the force of his response to my query about iglu-building, I asked, "Shall I ask Ipuituq to help me put up my tent?" "Yes," said Inuttiaq. There was no warmth in his face; he did not smile, though he did tell me to keep my fur trousers on for warmth while I put up the tent. I obeyed, but the wind had risen while we drank our homecoming tea, so that even in fur trousers tent-raising was not feasible that day or the next.

When the wind died two days later, Inuttiaq and I went fishing again, most companionably. Relations seemed so amicable, in fact, that this time on our return I was emboldened to say directly, without mention of Ipuituq, "I would like to put up my tent."

Naively I thought that Inuttiaq would offer to help. He did not. His face was again unsmiling as he answered, "Put it up."

My anger was triggered again. "By myself?" I inquired rudely.

"Yes," said Inuttiaq, equally rudely.

"Thank you very much." I heard the coldness in my voice but did not try to soften it.

Inuttiaq, expressionless, looked at me for a moment then summoned two young men who were nearby and who came, with a cheer that was in marked contrast to his own manner, to help me set up the tent.

Although Inuttiaq thought it ridiculous anyway to set up a tent in winter, I think now that he was also personally affronted by my request. One clue to his reaction I find in a question that I hardly heard at the time: he had wanted to know, after the tent was up, whether I planned to sleep in it or only to work there, and I think he may have felt that my demand for a tent was a sign that I was dissatisfied with him as a father, with his concern for my welfare.

In any case, his behavior was a curious blend of opposites. He chose the site for my tent with care, correcting my own choice with a more practiced eye to prowling dogs and prevailing wind. He offered advice on heating the tent, and he filled my primus stove so that it would be ready for me to use when my two assistants and I had finished setting up the tent. And when I moved my writing things out of his iglu, he told me that if I liked, I might write instead of going fishing. "If I catch a fish, you will eat," he assured me. But he turned his back on the actual raising of the tent and went home to eat and drink tea.

Never in Anger

On the following day I saw his displeasure in another form. It was Sunday morning and storming; our entrance was buried under drifting snow. Since there could be no church service, Inuttiaq and Allaq had each, separately and in mumbling undertones, read a passage from the Bible. Then Inuttiaq began to read from the prayer book the story of creation, and he asked if I would like to learn. I agreed, the more eagerly because I feared that he had perceived my skepticism toward his religious beliefs and that this was another hidden source of conflict between us. He lectured me at length. The story of creation was followed by the story of Adam and Eve (whose sin was responsible for the division of mankind into kaplunas and Eskimos), and this story was in turn followed by an exposition of proper Christian behavior: the keeping of the Sabbath—and of one's temper. "God is loving," said Inuttiaq, "but only to believers. Satan is angry. People will go to heaven only if they do not get angry or answer back when they are scolded." He told me that one should not be attached to earthly belongings, as I was: "One should devote himself only to God's word." Most striking of all was the way Inuttiaq ended his sermon to me. "Nakliguhuktuq made me king of the Utkuhikhalingmiut," he said. "He wrote that to me. He told me that if people—including you—don't want to believe what I tell them and don't want to learn about Christianity, then I should write to him, and he will come quickly and scold them. If people don't want to believe Nakliguhuktuq either, then . . . a bigger leader, a kapluna, the king in Cambridge Bay [the government center for the central Arctic], will come in a plane with a big and well-made whip and will whip people. It will hurt a lot."

Much of this I had heard before, but this version was more dramatic than previous ones. It made me see more clearly than I had before something of Inuttiaq's view of kaplunas generally. I heard the hostility directed against myself as well, but again he had softened the latter by blending it with warmth, in the manner that I found so confusing. He knew that I believed in God, he said, because I helped people, I gave things to people—not just to one or two, which God doesn't want, but to everybody.

The rest of the winter passed more peacefully, at least on the surface. I spent much of the time working in my tent, and there was no more overt hostility. But I am no longer sure that my peace of mind was justified. In retrospect, it seems possible that the warm and solicitous acts my family continued to perform were neither rewards for improved behavior on my part nor evidence of a generous willingness to accept me in spite of my thorny qualities, but, rather, attempts to extract or blunt some of the thorns. If I knew I was cared for, I might not get angry so easily. I thought I heard similar logic in the admonition Inuttiaq once in a while gave his six-year-old daughter when she sulked: "Stop crying, you are loved." Another possible motive may have been a desire to shame me, by virtuous example, into reforming. Perhaps these kind acts even had the effect of nullifying Inuttiaq's and Allaq's own prickly feelings, permitting them to prove to themselves that—as Inuttiaq once said—they didn't get angry, only I did.

But whatever the interpretation of these incidents, it is clear to me now that there existed more of an undercurrent of tension in my relationship with Inuttiaq and Allaq than I perceived at the time. I began to suspect its presence in the spring, when our iglu melted and I moved—at Inuttiaq's order—back into my own tent; Allaq almost never visited me, as she had done the first days after my arrival in Chantrey Inlet. More important, these winter tensions, I think, added their residue of hostility to a crisis situation that developed at the end of the summer. This introduced a new phase in my relations, not merely with Inuttiaq and Allaq, but with all the other Utkuhikhalingmiut as well—a phase in which I ceased to be treated as an educable child and was instead treated as an incorrigible offender, who had unfortunately to be endured but who could not be incorporated into the social life of the group.

The crisis was brought about by the visit to Chantrey Inlet of a party of kapluna sports fishermen. Every July and August in recent years Chantrey Inlet has been visited by sportsmen from the provinces and from the United States who charter bush planes from private sports airlines and fly up to the Arctic for a week's fishing. Every year the sportsmen ask permission to borrow the Eskimos' canoes, which were given to them by the Canadian government after the famine of 1958 and are indispensable to their economy. In 1958 the disappearance of the caribou herds from the Chantrey Inlet area forced the Eskimos to begin to rely much more completely on fish than they had formerly done. This meant accumulating and storing quantities of fish during seasons when they were plentiful, and to facilitate this, the government introduced fish nets and canoes.

Originally there had been six canoes, one for each of the Utkuhikhalingmiut families, but by the time I arrived in Chantrey Inlet only two of these remained in usable condition.

In Anger

The first parties that came asked, through me, if they might borrow both canoes, and the Utkuhikhalingmiut, who for various reasons rarely, if ever, refuse such requests, acquiesced, at some cost to themselves. They sat stranded on the shore, unable to fish, unable to fetch the occasional bird that they shot on the water, unable to fetch a resupply of sugar for their tea from the cache on the nearby island and worst of all, perhaps, unable to visit the odd strangers who were camped out of sight across the river. Ultimately these kaplunas left and were replaced by another group, which asked to borrow only one canoe. But relief was short-lived; trolling up and down the unfamiliar river in the late twilight, the kaplunas were unfortunate enough to run the canoe on a rock and tear a large hole in the canvas, whereupon they returned the canoe and announced to the men through sign language that since that craft was unusable they were now obliged to borrow the other—Inuttiaq's. When I arrived on the scene, the kaplunas were attaching their outboard to the canoe as Inuttiaq and the other Utkuhikhalingmiut men watched.

I exploded. Unsmilingly and in a cold voice I told the kaplunas' guide some of the hardships that I foresaw if his men damaged the second canoe. Then, armed with the memory that Inuttiaq had earlier, before the arrival of this party of kaplunas, instructed me in vivid language never again to allow anyone to borrow his canoe, I told the kaplunas that the owner of that second canoe did not wish to lend it.

The kapluna guide was not unreasonable; he agreed at once that the loan of the boat was the owner's option: "It's his canoe, after all." Slightly mollified, I turned to Inuttiaq who stood nearby, expressionless like the other Utkuhikhalingmiut. "Do you want me to tell him you don't want to lend your canoe?" I asked in Eskimo. "He will not borrow it if you say you don't want to lend it."

Inuttiaq's expression dismayed me, but I didn't know how to read it. I knew only that it registered strong feeling, as did his voice, which was unusually loud: "Let him have his will!"

"We Wish She Would Leave"

That incident brought to a head months of uneasiness on the part of the Utkuhikhalingmiut concerning my volatility. I had spoken unbidden and in anger; that much the Eskimos knew. The words they couldn't understand, but it didn't matter; the intrusion and the anger itself were inexcusable. The punishment was so subtle a form of ostracism that I would have continued to think that my difficulties were all of my own imagining had I not come into possession of a letter that Allaq's father, Pala, had written to the deacon, Nakliguhuktuq, the day after the kaplunas left. Pala had intended to send it out on the plane that was daily expected to come and pick up the schoolchildren; he had kept it for a time, but then—fearing that when the plane finally came, he would forget the letter—he had given it to me to hold along with my own correspondence. The letter was in syllabics, of course; in an amoral spirit I decided to read it, to test my skill in reading Eskimo. I did not anticipate the contents: "Yiini [that was my name] lied to the kaplunas. She gets angry very easily. She ought not to be here studying Eskimos. She is very annoying; because she scolds and one is tempted to scold her. She gets angry easily. Because she is so annoying, we wish more and more that she would leave."

But it was not until October, when the autumn iglus were built, that the change in the Eskimos' feelings really became apparent. I was not at all sure that Inuttiaq would invite me to move in with his family again as he had done the year before, but I need not have worried; his hostility did not take such a crass form. However, the quality of life in the iglu was in striking contrast with the previous year. Whereas then Inuttiaq's iglu had been the social center of the camp, now family and visitors congregated next door, in Allaq's father's iglu. Inuttiaq and Allaq—the children too—spent the better part of every day at Pala's. Even in the early mornings, when the family awoke, and at night when we were preparing for bed, I was isolated. It was as though I were not there. If I made a remark to Inuttiaq or Allaq, the person addressed responded with his usual smile, but I had to initiate almost all communication. As a rule, if I did not speak, no one spoke to me. If I offered to fetch water or make tea (which I seldom did), my offer was usually accepted, but no one ever asked me to perform these services. The pointedness of this avoidance was driven home one day when we were cooking. I do not recall what was being made or who had initiated the cooking; I think it likely that I had done so, since the primus stood on the floor in front of me, instead of in its usual place near Allaq. Nevertheless, when the pressure began to run down, unnoticed by me, Inuttiaq turned not to me but to Allaq to order her to pump up the primus. And she had to get up and come over to my side of the iglu to pump up the stove! Had he spoken to me, I would only have had to lean over to do it. Too late I realized the dignity inherent in the Utkuhikhalingmiut pattern of authority, in which the woman is obedient to the man. I envied Allaq the satisfaction of knowing that she was appreciated because she did well and docilely what Inuttiaq told her to do.

One day, about a week after we had moved into the autumn iglus, Inuttiaq suggested that when we moved into winter iglus later on, I should be physically walled off to a degree. Often when Utkuhikhalingmiut build their permanent winter iglus, they attach to one side a small chamber, called a *hiqluaq*, in which to store the fish they net. The hiqluaq opens into the interior of the iglu by way of a hole just big enough to crawl through. Inuttiaq's idea was to build such a chamber for me to live in; after I left, he would use it in the orthodox manner, for fish storage.

But in spite of all these tensions, I was still treated with the most impeccable semblance of solicitude. I was amazed that it should be so—that although my company was anathema, nevertheless people still took care to give me plentiful amounts of the foods I liked best, to warn me away from thin ice and to caution me when my nose began to freeze. The Utkuhikhalingmiut saw themselves—and wanted me to see them—as virtuously solicitous, no matter what provocations I might give them to be otherwise. Allaq's sister expressed this ethos of concern explicitly in a letter to Ikayuqtuq in Gjoa Haven: "Because she is the only kapluna here and a woman as well, we have tried to be good to her . . . and though she is sometimes very annoying . . . we still try to help her."

It was at the end of August that the incident with the kapluna fishermen occurred, and it was the end of November before I was finally able to explain myself to the Utkuhikhalingmiut. I had wanted from the beginning, of course, to confront them with an explanation of my behavior, but I had feared that such un-Eskimo directness would only shock them the more. Instead, I had written my version of the story to Ikayuqtuq, had told her about my attempt to protect the Utkuhikhalingmiut from the impositions of the kaplunas and had asked her if she could help to explain my behavior to the Eskimos. My letter went out to Gjoa Haven, along with Pala's, when the school plane came in September. Unfortunately there was no way in which Ikayuqtuq could reply until the strait froze in November, enabling the men to make the long trip out to Gjoa Haven to trade. But when Inuttiaq, accompanied as usual by Allaq's brother, Mannik, finally went out, they brought back from the deacon and his wife a response that surpassed my most sanguine expectations. Inuttiaq reported to his family: "Nakliguhuktuq says that the kaplunas almost shot us when Yiini wasn't there." The exaggeration was characteristic of Inuttiaq's lurid style of fantasy. He turned to me: "Did you write that to Nakliguhuktuq?" I denied it—and later, in Gjoa Haven, Nakliguhuktuq denied having made such a statement to Inuttiaq—but I did confirm the gist of Inuttiaq's report: that I had tried to protect the Eskimos. I described what it was that I had written to Ikayuqtuq, and I explained something of the reasons for my anger at the kaplunas.

Wall of Ice

The effect was magical. The wall of ice that had stood between me and the community suddenly disappeared. I became consultant on the moral qualities of fishing guides; people talked to me voluntarily, offered me vocabulary, included me in their jokes and in their anecdotes of the day's activities; and Inuttiaq informed me that the next day he and I were going fishing. Most heartwarming of all is the memory of an afternoon soon after the men had returned. The iglu was filled with visitors, and the hum of the primus on which tea was brewing mingled with the low voices of Inuttiaq and his guests. I knew every detail of the scene even as I bent over my writing, and I paid no attention until suddenly my mind caught on the sound of my name: "I consider Yiini a member of my family again." Was that what Inuttiaq had said? I looked up, inquiring. "I consider you a family member again," he repeated. His diction was clear, as it was only when he wanted to be sure that I understood. And he called me "daughter," as he had not done since August.

Not that I had suddenly become a wholly acceptable housemate; that could never be. I was not and could never become an Utkuhikhalingmiutaq, nor could I ever be a "daughter" to Inuttiaq and Allaq as they understood that role. Inuttiaq made this quite clear one day about this time when we were both sitting, silently working, in the iglu. "I think you're a leader in your country," he said suddenly. The remark had no obvious context; it must mean, I thought, that he had never reconciled himself to my intractable behavior. There was also the slightly wild look that I caught in his eye when I said I thought that I might someday return to Chantrey Inlet. The look vanished when Allaq explained that I meant to return after I had been to my own country, not merely to Gjoa Haven. "Yes," he said then, "We will adopt you again, or others may want to—Nilaak, perhaps, or Mannik, if he marries." And later, when we were talking about the possibility of other "learners" coming to Chantrey Inlet, Inuttiaq said, "We would be happier to have a woman come than a man—a woman like you, who doesn't want to be a wife. Maybe *you* are the only acceptable kapluna."

But it was the letters that Allaq and Inuttiaq wrote me when I left Chantrey Inlet in January that expressed most vividly and succinctly what it meant to them to have a kapluna daughter. They both said, "I didn't think I'd care when you left, but I did."

Part II
Myth and Language

One of the first and highest hurdles a field worker has to overcome is the barrier of language or dialect that makes communication with informants awkward or at times seemingly impossible. As anyone who has traveled in a foreign country knows, classroom mastery of a new grammar and syntax is a far cry from being able to communicate even the simplest tourist needs: where is the train station, where can I buy stamps, where is Napoleon's Tomb? Since the ethnographer sets himself down in the middle of a group and vows to survive as the "natives" do, his need to communicate successfully is even more pressing, for it determines the sources of food, shelter, and most importantly, access to that necessary antidote to isolation—interested and patient "key" informants.

Because every local community tends to develop its own patterns of speech and in-group vocabulary, even the researcher who is fluent in the standard language of a region or nation has to learn the local dialect or *patois* and become familiar with a variety of patterned communication, from slang and joking to word games and mythic dramas, as well as the unspoken rules of gesture and body movement.

The study of language in the field can procede in one of several directions, each differing from the other in its emphasis on the formal characteristics of speech. Linguistics is the study of the most abstract and systemic features of human languages. Its history in anthropology is a relatively long one, going back at least to Lewis Henry Morgan's nineteenth-century investigation of kinship terminology, and it has been largely untroubled by arguments concerning Western superiority over native customs. The human universal that early anthropologists struck upon quite quickly was the capacity of all human groups to communicate by means of elaborate and complex language systems. By drawing on the records of missionaries and traders and the writings of scholars, and adding to them their own first-hand descriptions of the spoken languages of remote tribes and villages, pioneers like Morgan and later W.H.R. Rivers and Franz Boas gradually refuted the image of the inarticulate savage whose utterances sounded like gibberish to Western ears. Instead, they and others working in anthropological linguistics presented Industrial-Age Europeans and Americans with the apparent paradox of technologically primitive people speaking elegantly constructed sentences.

For Franz Boas, the goal of investigating language cross-culturally was to discover the basis of this common *homo sapiens'* ability to express thought in language and to understand the triple connection between language, how people perceive reality, and the communication of ideas in some evolutionary sense. Alfred Kroeber, one of Boas' first students, took up the last of these concerns and formulated an historical diffusionist approach to language studies, one that focused on the growth and decline of human societies over time and throughout geographic areas. As with culture patterns, the influence of a language spread with expanding or contracting routes of trade, the rise and fall of dominant civilizations, and an increase or decrease in population. Extensive research on North American Indians, which Kroeber avidly supported, confirmed this historical view of peaks and valleys in New World cultures. The comparative study of contemporary Indian languages revealed major linguistic families geographically dispersed through population expansion and migration. Today, the principles of language diffusion seem self-evident, the more so as the languages and technology of industrially advanced societies have become globally accepted.

The more mysterious aspect of language study, the connection between language and reality, has consistently held the attention of anthropological linguists who knew that the different languages of their informants connoted distinct world views, not just different sounds designating a commonly understood reality. In 1929, Edward Sapir introduced an initial formulation of this sense that language itself was a means of structuring a perspective on the world for its speakers. He proposed the following:

> Human beings do not live in the objective world alone, nor alone in the world of social activity as ordinarily understood, but are very much at the mercy of the particular language which has become the medium of expression for their society. It is quite an illusion to imagine that one adjusts to reality essentially without the use of language and that language is merely an incidental means of solving specific problems of communication or reflection. The fact of the matter is that the "real world" is to a large extent built up on the language habits of the group. No two languages are ever sufficiently similar to be

considered as representing the same social reality. The worlds in which different societies live are distinct worlds, not merely the same world with different labels attached.

Sapir and his colleague Benjamin Whorf argued that, far from being just a technique of communication, language leads the speaker to see the world in a certain way without his being consciously aware of how culturally subjective his observations are.

Even a rudimentary attempt to translate from one language to another makes it clear how deeply embedded in words are our fundamental assumptions about the world around us. For example, in research on the Navajo, Clyde Kluckhohn and Dorothea Leighton pinpointed a general cultural orientation—the attitude that "Nature is more powerful than man"—which is directly reflected in the Navajo idiom. While the English speaker says, "I am hungry," and the French speaker says, "J'ai faim" or "I have hunger," the Navajo says "Hunger is killing me" to indicate that hunger is a natural exterior force that assaults the individual. Similarly, what in English is expressed as "I am drowning" becomes in Navajo, "The water is killing me."

The problems with the Sapir-Whorf hypothesis, as with many assertions about language, are twofold. The first has to do with the difficulties in tracking down the relationship between language and external influences on culture. Is the fatalism characteristic of Navajo phrasing expressive of generations of coping with a harsh environment, or does their language actually determine their understanding of reality and immobilize them from overcoming not nature but political and economic oppression?

The Sapir-Whorf hypothesis presents a chicken-and-egg dilemma, but only if we assume that traditional groups like the Navajo remain in static isolation from the larger world. As history would have it, many young Navajo men and women were drawn away from their reservations in World War II and worked in the armed forces or in factories and on farms. Their acculturation to standard American values and behavior profoundly influence the social organization of postwar reservations, and not the least among these influences has been a dramatic increase in bilingualism, that is, fluency in both English and Navajo. The bilingual abilities of many native people whose grandparents were the first anthropological informants thoroughly confound the deterministic implications of Sapir and Whorf's theory. Or we might give it a new phrasing and say that people in rigidly monolingual cultures (and here we would have to include our own) are mainly at the mercy of their own words.

Beginning in the 1950s, anthropological pursuit of a general theory of cognitive processes incorporated ideas from mathematics, physics, economics, and philosophy. The attempts have been many and diverse to probe the "emic" or thoroughly native understanding of a language in order to understand the informant culture.

Despite the subtleties of cross-cultural communication, important generalizations about the relationship between language and behavior have been made. The work of linguist Noam Chomsky has perhaps provided the most important direction of investigation for anthropologists interested in the problem of thought processes. As Chomsky sees language, it is a universal genetically encoded capacity that sets human beings apart from other primates. Every normal child masters a complex set of rules that permit the spontaneous composition of correct sentences. The thought that an individual speaker wants to express takes shape in his mind at what is known as the *deep structure;* the specific rules of the speaker's native tongue transform the thought to an articulate *surface structure,* which is the conventional sentence. In sentences that clearly have a single meaning, such as, "the dog is barking," both speaker and hearer are likely to be in agreement on the meaning of the phrase and its expression. There are many instances, however, in which the deep structure meaning of words is not obvious, and reference has to be made to information beyond the words themselves. Almost any example of modern poetry demonstrates the legitimate potential for ambiguity (or alternate deep structure meanings) in otherwise grammatically correct sentences. In ordinary, nonpoetic parlance, we demand more clarity from each other, although spoken communication, unlike written, is constantly augmented by voice inflection, facial expression, and gestures that help fill information gaps.

Another way to investigate language-reality relations is through the study of institutionalized forms of communication. In the analyses of kinship terminology, myth, oral history, and ethnosemantics, the structural point of view has been mapped out best by French anthropologist-philosopher Claude Lévi-Strauss. Along with Noam Chomsky and others, Lévi-Strauss posits a universal feature of the human brain, the need to impose an order on the world by classifying its features, social and natural, into contrasting categories and then operating in terms of these significant classifications. The use of binary oppositions, such as good and evil, natural and supernatural, pure and impure, old and young, black and white, etc., are found in almost all societies. As a general principle of organization, binary opposition can easily become the basis for conceptualizing the differences between social classes and castes and the symbols of cosmic forces (gods and demons, humans and disembodied spirits). Significant oppositions inevitably find their way into the major myths of a society that, as Lévi-Strauss sees them, give a new format to the conflicts inherent in everyday living. The traditional myth or ritual drama entertains the audience with the possibility that the significant oppositions that order their lives can be resolved, e.g., that sinners can become saints. The plot of the mythic story revolves around the tension between resolving dialectical oppositions and the fact that in people's minds the categories must remain distinct: good and evil, gods and demons, the natural and the supernatural cannot merge or the world would fall into disorder.

Because structural analysis has proven applicable to any body of myth, from the text of Genesis to Greek tragedies, many nonanthropologists have a working familiarity with the ideas of Lévi-Strauss. In a countermovement within the field of anthropology, researchers who began their professional careers with the study of exotic cultures are taking a new look at American popular culture as an expression of the same order of structural opposition as primitive myths and rituals. When anthropologists like Conrad Kottak venture into the world of popular culture, the challenge becomes one of figuring out why national response to a mass media event, in this case *Star Wars*, is so overwhelming and at the same time so unpredictable. Why should yet another "dragon-slayer" like Luke Skywalker charm the public with his adventures in space? The answer lies not only in a structural approach. Beyond binary oppositions, we are a nation plagued with uncertainties about the future of technology and world politics based on weapons of ultimate destruction. That we have mythic traditions at all reveals our need as no different than that of isolated tribes to have heroes, tricksters, devils, and angels take up the burden of our social dilemmas.

The structural approach to myth and drama posits an indirect metaphorical relationship between social fact and spoken word. In quite another, growing area of language study, the object of study goes beyond the words themselves to the social context of language. Called sociolinguistics, this approach focuses on the variability of language use depending on the social identity of speakers and listeners. Even in the United States which has a standard language, English, we know that regional dialects and subcultural languages are prevalent and are frequently used as a means of social identification. Almost any subgroup is likely to develop special styles of communication. All-male and all-female groups tend to speak differently than mixed groups, and, in a few societies, there are separate languages for the sexes. Special languages are also associated with ritual and age-grade groups that initiate their members into secret codes. The vocabularies of modern legal and medical professions are occasionally cited, with wry humor, as examples of secret-society languages designed to confuse hapless clients and patients.

The more linguistic studies are done about contemporary people, the more the effects of social divisions stand out. In formal analysis, languages cannot be ranked one over another. When a society becomes divided, according to ranked castes or classes, however, languages, dialects, and accents are judged according to the economic position of their speakers. In French-speaking Canada, the lower-class, French-speaking habitant and the upper-class, English-speaking member of Parliament are not likely to converse with each other, although the French-Canadian elite is educated to speak English and can therefore conquer the language barrier, if not the barriers to political control. In Indonesia, three different Javanese dialects are spoken; rural farmers use only one, city people and aristocrats are versed in one or two other, more refined levels of discourse.

In populations most directly subject to European colonial pressures, the distinctions between a native language and the language of the ruling class were submerged in the invention of *pidgin* and *creole*—languages drawing on the forms of both. In the United States, one of the most distinctive speech patterns and one that has particular historical depth is that of northern urban and southern rural blacks. Called Black English Vernacular (BEV) by anthropological linguist William Labove, this relatively uniform dialect developed from African and creole languages that were influenced in turn by southern English styles of speech. In his article, "Rappin' in the Black Ghetto," Thomas Kochman examines some of the contemporary forms of BEV, including the institutionalized exchange of insults in "playing the dozens." While mastery of the rules of language is necessary for a child to move toward adult status, wit and the mastery of current idiom are the special province of young people. As Kochman makes clear, inner-city black culture gives extraordinary support to verbal wit as a measure of social prestige.

The final article in this section comes from folklorist Roger Abrahams who provides us with the broadest orientation in language studies. His perspective includes the specific texts of Caribbean songs and the performances at island festivals. Professor Abrahams brings an historical dimension to his description of the Tobago and Nevis societies. As New World cultures in many ways related to American black institutions, their competitive word games and ritual plays have a similar, dual, British and African origin. Like the language forms of people everywhere, these Caribbean forms have changed over time as social circumstances changed, because a tradition is only as viable as people make it. Words, symbols, and mythic figures can lose their power to represent important themes and fall into disuse like outmoded clothes. When larger economic and political realities impinge on ordinary lives, there is a vast resorting to the mundane and mythic vocabularies and an inevitable incorporation of the new. Because no group is immune to impersonal historical forces, the process of adjusting tradition to reality is a continuous one. The single constant is the human need for expression in the imaginative world of play, fable, and drama where everyone—players, narrators, audience—longs for the kind of expression that play, fable, and drama afford—participation in an imaginatively constructed world where words and action give release from the mundane without destroying the familiar.

References

Berlin, B., and P. Kay. 1969. *Basic Color Terms: Their Universality and Evolution.* Berkeley and Los Angeles: University of California Press.
Boas, F. 1966. *Race, Language and Culture.* New York: The Free Press.
Burling, R. 1970. *Man's Many Voices: Language in Its Cultural Context.* New York: Holt, Rinehart & Winston.
Chomsky, N. 1972. *Language and Mind.* New York: Harcourt Brace Jovanovich.
Conklin, H.C. 1955. "Hanunoó Color Categories." *Southwestern Journal of Anthropology* 11: 339-344.
Douglas, Mary. 1966. *Purity and Danger.* London: Routledge & Kegan Paul.
Greenberg, J.H. 1968. *Anthropological Linguistics: An Introduction.* New York: Random House.
Hockett, C.F. 1958. *A Course in Modern Linguistics.* New York: Macmillan.
Hoijer, H. 1954. "The Sapir-Whorf Hypothesis." In *Language in Culture,* edited by H. Hoijer, pp. 92-104. Washington, D.C.: American Anthropological Association.
Kluckhohn, Clyde, and Dorothea Leighton. 1946. *The Navaho.* Cambridge, Mass.: Harvard University Press.
Lee, Dorothy. 1959. *Freedom and Culture.* Englewood Cliffs, N.J.: Prentice-Hall.
Lévi-Strauss, C. 1963. *Structural Anthropology.* C. Jacobson and B. Schoepf, trans. New York: Basic Books.
Lévi Strauss, C. 1966. *The Savage Mind.* Chicago: University of Chicago Press.
Sapir, Edward. 1949. *Selected Writings of Edward Sapir.* David G. Mandelbaum, ed. Berkeley and Los Angeles: University of California Press.

4.
Star Wars: Social Science Fiction
Conrad Kottak

The media event of 1977 was clearly *Star Wars*. Millions of people have seen the George Lucas film, many of them more than once or even scores of times. By last November, *Star Wars* had replaced *Jaws* as the top domestic box-office draw of all time. Good reviews and canny marketing had something to do with it. But other films receive similar treatment and never become hits. How would an anthropologist accustomed to studying nonindustrial cultures explain the huge success of Lucas' space thriller?

For the anthropologist, the "creativity" in any work of art lies in how successfully it brings together cultural themes, motifs, symbols, and meanings that are familiar and significant to the natives. *Star Wars* summarizes and synthesizes the experiences that millions of Americans have shared during the past half century. Like myths, fairy tales, and "new" religions, the film is significant not because it is new, but because it is both old and new—a novel and meaningful blend of preexisting themes.

Star Wars is also a movie for its time. For a decade, the moviemakers have been making films that portray people as helpless and insignificant when confronted by the forces of nature, technology, human imperfection, and various imaginary threats from demons to extraterrestrials. *Star Wars* is a film about reestablishing control. It contains a simple explanation for events that seem beyond our power—the existence of evil. It shows not only that people can solve their own problems, but also that ordinary people can triumph against seemingly impossible odds. As such, the film retells a tale that spans thousands of years and diverse cultures. *Star Wars* is a visual fairy tale, a movie about heroism that invites comparison with epics from all societies.

When Stanley Kubrick's *2001: A Space Odyssey* was released, the United States was fighting an unpopular war in Southeast Asia. Americans felt buffeted by faraway events of shuddering complexity and by institutions lurching out of control. The futures of the nation's young men were in the hands of draft boards and lotteries. Many expressed their frustrations by demonstrating or declaring war on society. Others sought solace in psychedelic drugs and a passive attitude toward life.

Kubrick's film was popular with a more limited segment of American society, particularly college students. The story is about man's rise and eventual escape from the planet, and his rebirth as a Star Child after a space mission to one of Saturn's moons. It all takes place under the influence of a monolith from another world that first appears to man's apelike ancestors and bestows on them the capacity for toolmaking. The aliens' gift becomes a Pandora's box. Technology gets out of hand, as the Frankenstein computer aboard the spaceship to Saturn—Hal 900—turns on the astronauts. The film rebroadcast messages that life was sending: we lack control over our own destinies, and there's not very much that we can do about it.

Most of the big movies released between *2001* and *Star Wars* echoed the message. Our technological advances don't shelter us as much as we think. Neither the luxury liner of *The Poseidon Adventure* nor the glittering skyscraper of *The Towering Inferno* is safe. *The Exorcist* is about spiritual forces out of control, and offers little hope that people can do anything about it. *The Omen* clearly says that evil wins. *Jaws* focuses on capricious natural forces: for no known reason, a shark appears off the northeastern coast of the United States; Quint, an Ahab-like figure, agrees to search out and destroy it, but in the end the shark vanquishes Quint.

The most recent space fantasy, *Close Encounters of the Third Kind*, is already drawing large audiences. Steven Spielberg's powerful and exotic special effects have great appeal, and the film shares some of *Star Wars'* innocence, hope, and childlike sweetness. Still, *Close Encounters*, with its godlike space creatures and theme of awesome technology, has as much in common with the 60s as the 70s. Partly for that reason, it is unlikely to inspire the same enthusiasm as *Star Wars*.

Star Wars came along in time to capitalize on a changing cultural climate. While Luke Skywalker's story was being filmed, Jimmy Carter was cultivating the image of an outsider running for President. Mark Fidrych of the Detroit Tigers was reviving the storybook appeal of a kooky kid making it big in the majors—for love rather than money—and *Rocky* was proving itself the sleeper of the year. Luke Skywalker, who is a bit small for a storm trooper (as Princess Leia remarks), brings to mind the kid shortstop whose key hit in the bottom of the ninth wins for his team in the

World Series. Americans were ready for a quest, and for a hero who was as far as possible from the super-macho football player, the hard-nosed politician, and the revolutionary of the late 60s.

In *The Uses of Enchantment,* Bruno Bettelheim makes a distinction between fairy tales and myths (better termed tragedies) that helps us understand how *Star Wars* contrasts with *2001, The Exorcist,* and, to some extent, *Close Encounters.* Like the myths of Biblical stories and Greco-Roman tragedy, these films confront humans with powerful, capricious, and awesome supernatural entities. Such tales are moralistic and ultimately pessimistic, focusing on the tremendous gap between ordinary mortals and the supernatural. This makes it hard for us, and especially for children, to identify with their characters. Like the once-human heroes of classical mythology, *2001's* astronaut David Bowman is granted immortality. He falls through a Star Gate, is enfolded and nurtured by extraterrestrials and reborn as a Star Child. But Bowman's odyssey says little about the problems and changes we experience in our daily lives.

In contrast, children easily identify with fairy-tale heroes, who receive their rewards right here on earth. As Bettelheim notes, fairy tales use fantasy to suggest what the battle to achieve self-realization is all about. By saying that things will get better, they offer people—especially children—hope. In contrast, tragic myths are cautionary tales that proclaim: this is how things are and will be—and you'd better get used to it.

Mythic tragedies and powerful anthropomorphic gods are found in stratified societies with central governments and sharp contrasts in wealth and power (what anthropologists call "state-organized societies"). Tragedies are charters for oppressive social orders; they tell ordinary people that things must remain beyond their control. Social oppression—a fact of life in a state-organized society—was clear in the 1960s; Americans find it easier to ignore now.

As a visual fairy tale, *Star Wars* appeals most directly to children, and—to use a cliché that happens to be true—to the child in all of us. Bettelheim argues that simple names and plots and anonymous or generic characters give fairy tales an "everyman" quality that makes them universally valid and appealing. *Star Wars* shares these attributes. Its hero's short first name, Luke, is attached to a label—Skywalker—that describes his ambience and activity. Like other fairy tales, it replaces the complexity of everyday life with sharp polarization. Characters are typical, not unique. They are sharply distinguished—black or white, not gray; unambiguously good or evil. Thus their actions and reactions are easy to understand. Supporting figures are also polarized—as helpers or adversaries in the hero's quest; they must be on one side or the other. This is why the *Star Wars* audience responds so noisily when Han Solo comes to Luke's aid at the end. The one loose end is now in place.

The similarities between *Star Wars* and *The Wizard of Oz* are particularly obvious and have been noted by others. *The Wizard of Oz* is the American fairy tale—an important part of growing up in the United States since the turn of the century. American children continue to renew their acquaintance with Dorothy and her companions through the annual telecast of the movie. *Star Wars* is, structurally and psychologically, a similar tale, set in a dazzling futuristic setting, with special effects realized through 70s technology. And although this time the hero is a boy, *Star Wars* shares *The Wizard of Oz*'s appeal to children of both sexes.

Both *Star Wars* and *The Wizard of Oz* begin in fairy-tale time ("Somewhere over the rainbow . . ." and "A long time ago in a galaxy far, far away . . ."). *The Wizard* begins on the gray, arid Kansas prairie; *Star Wars* on the bone-dry planet Tatooine. Both Luke and Dorothy live with an aunt and uncle who farm. Dorothy's aunt and uncle are simple farmers, but in arid Kansas, they also depend on scarce water for their livelihood. The hired hands shown in the black-and-white segments of *The Wizard* become the Scarecrow, Tin Woodman, and Cowardly Lion. In *Star Wars*, Luke's Uncle Owen uses androids to harvest moisture, which he sells. The androids eventually accompany Luke on his adventures.

Since Luke is a boy, the relationship between hero and uncle is primary, whereas the heroine-aunt relationship is stressed in *The Wizard*. In emotional tone, the relationships are inverted: Dorothy's relationship with Auntie Em is warm and loving; Luke's dealings with Uncle Owen are strained and distant. Neither relationship, however, is emotionally intense.

Aunt and uncle are in the films for the same reasons. They represent parents, whom all children, to become self-reliant, must eventually leave. Yet they are only straw parents; the intense emotions that enliven family relationships are disguised in other characters. Clearly identified real parents have no place in such a story. The parent-child separation—whether through the child's removal or through the parents' death—would be too threatening to the child.

Toto and R2D2 are the agents that propel Dorothy and Luke on their adventures. Because Toto runs away, he and Dorothy cannot enter the cyclone shelter with her aunt and uncle, and both are thus transported to Oz. Pursued by Darth Vader's agents, R2D2 reaches Tatooine, bearing documents that give the rebels hope of eventual success. Pursuing R2, Luke is separated from his uncle and aunt; they are killed by Vader's agents. The dog and the droid not only have comparable roles in the two tales, but are also similar in size and sounds (barks and beeps).

Use of the structural method of analysis developed by French anthropologist Claude Lévi-Strauss draws out some of the specific parallels. In numerous studies, Lévi-Strauss has focused on similarities in the themes and relationships portrayed in the myths (tragedies and fairy tales) of widespread cultures. He argues that these similarities rest on, and exemplify, mental properties shared by people everywhere. Structuralism delves beneath native consciousness to uncover a myth's true structure, which consists of its constituent units and their interrelationships. By comparing the principles at work in myths throughout the world, the structural anthropologist hopes to discover universal logical attributes of the human mind. Chief among these, says Lévi-Strauss, is the need to classify.

Although most differences are of degree rather than kind, the mind, says Lévi-Strauss, naturally classifies by absolute opposition. Good and evil, high and low, old and young, white and black, illustrate how all humans convert continuous contrasts into absolute distinctions.

Similarly, Bruno Bettelheim notes that a common fairy-tale device is to divide the child's ambivalent feelings about a parent into two characters. By creating such binary oppositions, fairy tales permit children to maintain their image of a parent as basically good—by externalizing all his or her bad qualities in a separate figure of total evil.

In *Star Wars*, aspects of Luke's father are represented as a good father who is dead (Luke's real father), a good father who is alive, but ambiguously dead by the movie's end (Ben Kenobi), and a father who is totally evil and survives, probably for *Star Wars II* (Darth Vader, whose very name bears a phonetic resemblance to "Dark Father").

In *The Wizard of Oz,* the mother figure is also divided in three: an evil mother whom Dorothy has killed (the Wicked Witch of the East), an evil mother whom Dorothy eventually kills (the Wicked Witch of the West), and a good mother who survives the film (Glinda). The idealized good father and mother—Ben and Glinda—watch over and assist Luke and Dorothy at certain points. But these are incidental; Luke and Dorothy accomplish their major triumphs on their own.

Less obvious is the analogy between Princess Leia and the Wizard. Both represent the child's relationship with the parent of opposite sex. Although Ben Kenobi is called a wizard and looks like Gandalf, Tolkien's Wizard, he is kindly and genuine—not a frightening humbug like Oz. Ben is only part of Luke's father, not the father figure like the Wizard of Oz. The Wizard rejects Dorothy and forces her to demonstrate self-reliance through an act of heroism—capturing the witch's broomstick. The mother figure of Star Wars is well disguised in the wisecracking, rifle-wielding princess, but she remains a likely reward for Luke's heroism. Like other fairy tales, *Star Wars* plays on what Bettelheim calls the Oedipal-period boy's inability to understand that his mother stays with his father voluntarily. Princess Leia is Vader's unwilling captive, threatened with a needle the size of the witch's broomstick.

Just as the father figure compels Dorothy's quest, the princess commits Luke to his adventures with the recording left for Ben Kenobi inside R2D2 containing her plea for help.

In Bettelheim's analysis, male fairy-tale heroes achieve independence by symbolically destroying and replacing their evil fathers. The heroine's self-reliance, however, is revealed in her independence of either parent, as she proves herself ready to establish a home of her own. At the end of her sojourn in Oz, Dorothy discovers that the Wizard is a sham, unworthy of her fear and obedience. Nor can he guide her; they go their separate ways. Glinda arrives to tell Dorothy that she can return to Kansas on her own, by clicking together her ruby slippers and repeating, "There's no place like home."

Incidental characters also link the two films. The tiny, chattering Jawas who capture R2 on Tatooine and who make a living trading metal from robots recall both the Seven Dwarfs, who made a living as mineworkers, and the Munchkins. As disguised humans, Vader's storm troopers parallel the flying-monkey lackeys of the Wicked Witch of the West. The Death Star is the witch's gloomy castle; the grand hall of the rebel headquarters is the Emerald City. There are clear similarities in appearance and behavior between Chewbacca the Wookie and the Cowardly Lion, and between C3PO and the Tin Woodman, but neither match is perfect. C3PO's dangling wires and temporary loss of an arm also recall the Scarecrow's stuffing and momentary body mutilation.

In fairy tales, each helper-companion may be the externalization of a single character trait essential to the adventure's success. Personifications of intelligence, love (heart), and courage accompany Dorothy. Han Solo seems to represent self-interest and greed. Partially modeled on Bogart, John Wayne, and the Lone Ranger, Solo also serves as Luke's materialistic and cynical—but ultimately caring—big brother. He is an agnostic with respect to the Force, falling on a continuum of belief that runs through Luke to Ben Kenobi.

The endings of the two stories are also comparable. Luke, relying on his feelings, his control of the Force, and the voice of an incorporeal Ben Kenobi, destroys the Death Star. A heroic Dorothy returns to Kansas by controlling the magic force in the ruby shoes that Glinda originally instructed her to take from the dead witch. Each hero draws on magic to accomplish a desired objective.

But the parallels are incomplete. The Lucas film, after all, draws on 40 more years of media symbols. In an interview with *Rolling Stone* last year, Lucas admitted his debt to several movies, books, and cartoons, among them James Bond, Buck Rogers, Flash Gordon, Westerns, horror movies, World War II movies, Bogart, and J.R.R. Tolkien. One example of how he has drawn on the past is the resemblance of 3PO and R2D2 to Laurel and Hardy. *Star Wars* is, of course, far more advanced than *The Wizard* in its special effects. Another major difference is that while the film version of *The Wizard* was a finished product, Luke's story awaits completion in a sequel.

The major themes of hope and eventual triumph, however, are common to the two films. With Vietnam and the Nixon era behind us, we are ready again for heroes who are clearly good and villains who are unambiguously evil. We are ready to cheer rebels in just wars against powerful technology and perverted governments. The Death Star is a symbol of people's use of their technology for malicious ends; but the droids R2D2 and C3PO are benevolent servants. The Death Star destroys whole planets, but R2D2 saves the galaxy. Nothing mediates the opposition between humans and technology in *2001*.

Although technology can be used beneficially, *Star Wars* tells us that tools are not enough. To win at anything, we also need to rely on our emotions. *Star Wars* offers no capricious gods or demons, no awe-inspiring extraterrestrials, no cosmic cradlers for an immature humanity. The Force is simultaneously inside and outside us, but it is made up of linked human spirits; by trusting their feelings, people can control it. Despite the spectacle that dazzles us the first time around, *Star Wars* stands apart from other films with space themes. Its significance lies in the fact that it is a simple, down-to-earth tale. *Close Encounters* uses ordinary people to portray extraordinary events. But *Star Wars'* cultural meaning—profound and enduring—results from its use of extraordinary settings to help us deal with the ordinary.

5.
"Rapping" in the Black Ghetto

Thomas Kochman

"Rapping," "shucking," "jiving," "running it down," "gripping," "copping a plea," "signifying" and "sounding" are all part of the black ghetto idiom and describe different kinds of talking. Each has its own distinguishing features of form, style, and function; each is influenced by, and influences, the speaker, setting, and audience; and each sheds light on the black perspective and the black condition—on those orienting values and attitudes that will cause a speaker to speak or perform in his own way within the social context of the black community.

I was first introduced to black idiom in New York City, and, as a professional linguist interested in dialects, I began to compile a lexicon of such expressions. My real involvement, however, came in Chicago, while preparing a course on black idiom at the Center for Inner City Studies, the southside branch of Northeastern Illinois State College.

Here I began to explore the full cultural significance of this kind of verbal behavior. My students and informants within black Chicago, through their knowledge of these terms, and their ability to recognize and categorize the techniques, and to give examples, gave me much reliable data. When I turned for other or better examples to the literature—such as the writings of Malcolm X, Robert Conot, and Iceberg Slim—my students and informants were able to recognize and confirm their authenticity.

An analysis of rapping indicates a number of things.

For instance, it is revealing that one raps to rather than *with* a person supporting the impression that rapping is to be regarded more as a performance than verbal exchange. As with other performances, rapping projects the personality, physical appearance and style of the performer. In each of the examples given, the intrusive "I" of the speaker was instrumental in contributing to the total impression of the rap.

The combination of personality and style is usually best when "asking for some pussy." It is less when "whupping the game" on someone or "running something down."

In "asking for some pussy" for example, where personality and style might be projected through non-verbal means: stance, clothing, walking, looking, one can speak of a "silent rap." The woman is won here without the use of words, or rather, with words being implied that would generally accompany the non-verbal components.

As a lively way of "running it down," the verbal element consists of personality and style plus information. To someone *reading* my example of the gang member's narration, the impression might be that the information would be more influential in directing the listener's response. The youth worker might be expected to say "So that's how the gang got so big," instead of "Man, that gang member is *bad* (strong, brave)" in which instance he would be responding to the personality and style of the rapper. However, if the reader would *listen* to the gang member on tape or could have been present when the gang member spoke he more likely would have reacted more to personality and style as my informants did.

Remember that in attendance with the youth worker were members of the gang who *already knew* how the gang got started (e.g., "Am I right Leroy? You was cribbin' over here then") and for whom the information itself would have little interest. Their attention was held by the way the information was presented.

The verbal element in "whupping the game" on someone, in the preceding example, was an integral part of an overall deception in which information and personality-style were skillfully manipulated for the purpose of controlling the "trick's" response. But again, greater weight must be given to personality-style. In the "murphy game" for example, it was this element which got the trick to trust the hustler and leave his money with him for "safe-keeping."

The function of rapping in each of these forms is *expressive*. By this I mean that the speaker raps to project his personality onto the scene or to evoke a generally favorable response. When rapping is used to "ask for some pussy" or to "whup the game" on someone its function is *directive*. By this I mean that rapping becomes an instrument to manipulate and control people to get them to give up or to do something. The difference between rapping to a "fox" (pretty girl) for the purpose of "getting inside her pants" and rapping to a "lame" to get something from him is operational rather than functional. The latter rap contains a concealed motivation where the former does not.

"Shucking," "shucking it," "shucking and jiving," "S-ing" and "J-ing" or just "jiving," are terms that refer to language behavior practiced by the black when confronting "the Man" (the white man, the establishment, or *any* authority figure), and to another form of language behavior practiced by blacks with each other on the peer group level.

In the South, and later in the North, the black man learned that American society had assigned to him a restrictive role and status. Among whites his behavior had to conform to this imposed station and he was constantly reminded to "keep his place." He learned that it was not acceptable in the presence of white people to show feelings of indignation, frustration, discontent, pride, ambition, or desire; that real feelings had to be concealed behind a mask of innocence, ignorance, childishness, obedience, humility and deference. The terms used by the black to describe the role he played before white folks in the South was "tomming" or "jeffing." Failure to accommodate the white Southerner in this respect was almost certain to invite psychological and often physical brutality. A description related by a black psychiatrist, Alvin F. Poussaint, is typical and revealing:

> Once last year as I was leaving my office in Jackson, Miss., with my Negro secretary, a white policeman yelled, "Hey, boy! Come here!" Somewhat bothered, I retorted: "I'm no boy!" He then rushed at me, inflamed, and stood towering over me, snorting "What d'ja say, boy?" Quickly he frisked me and demanded, "What's your name boy?" Frightened, I replied, "Dr. Poussaint. I'm a physician." He angrily chuckled and hissed, "What's your first name, boy?" When I hesitated he assumed a threatening stance and clenched his fists. As my heart palpitated, I muttered in profound humiliation, "Alvin."
>
> He continued his psychological brutality, bellowing, "Alvin, the next time I call you, you come right away, you hear? You hear?" I hesitated. "You hear me, boy?" My voice trembling with helplessness, but *following my instincts of self-preservation,* I murmured, "Yes, sir." *Now fully satisfied that I had performed and acquiesced to my "boy" status,* he dismissed me with, "Now, boy, go on and get out of here or next time we'll take you for a little ride down to the station house! (Alvin F. Poussaint, "A Negro Psychiatrist Explains the Negro Psyche," *The New York Times Magazine,* August 20, 1967) (emphasis mine).

In the northern cities the black encountered authority figures equivalent to Southern "crackers": policemen, judges, probation officers, truant officers, teachers and "Mr. Charlies" (bosses), and soon learned that the way to get by and avoid difficulty was to shuck. Thus, he learned to accommodate "the Man," to use the total orchestration of speech, intonation, gesture and facial expression for the purpose of producing whatever appearance would be acceptable. It was a technique and ability that was developed from fear, a respect for power, and a will to survive. This type of accommodation is exemplified by the Uncle Tom with his "Yes sir, Mr. Charlie," or "Anything you say, Mr. Charlie."

Through accommodation, many blacks became adept at concealing and controlling their emotions and at assuming a variety of postures. They became competent actors. Many developed a keen perception of what affected, motivated, appeased or satisfied the authority figures with whom they came into contact. Shucking became an effective way for many blacks to stay out of trouble, and for others a useful artifice for avoiding arrest or getting out of trouble when apprehended. Shucking it with a judge, for example, would be to feign repentance in the hope of receiving a lighter or suspended sentence. Robert Conot reports an example of shucking in his book, *Rivers of Blood, Years of Darkness:* Joe was found guilty of possession of narcotics. But he did an excellent job of shucking it with the probation officer.

The probation officer interceded for Joe with the judge: "His own attitude toward the present offense appears to be serious and responsible and it is believed that the defendant is an excellent subject for probation."

Some field illustrations of shucking to get out of trouble came from some seventh grade children from an inner-city school in Chicago. The children were asked to talk their way out of a troublesome situation.

You are cursing at this old man and your mother comes walking down the stairs. She hears you.

To "talk your way out of this":

"I'd tell her that I was studying a scene in school for a play."

What if you were in a store stealing something and the manager caught you?

"I would start stuttering. Then I would say, 'Oh, Oh, I forgot. Here the money is.'"

A literary example of shucking comes from Iceberg Slim's autobiography. Iceberg, a pimp, shucks before "two red-faced Swede rollers (detectives)" who catch him in a motel room with his whore. My italics identify which elements of the passage constitute the shuck.

I put my shaking hands into the pajama pockets... *I hoped I was keeping the fear out of my face. I gave them a wide toothy smile.* They came in and stood in the middle of the room. Their eyes were racing about the room. Stacy was open mouthed in the bed.

I said, *"Yes gentlemen, what can I do for you?"*

Lanky said, "We wanta see your I.D."

I went to the closet and got the phony John Cato Fredrickson I.D. I put it in his palm. I felt cold sweat running down my back. They looked at it, then looked at each other.

Lanky said, "You are in violation of the law. You signed the motel register improperly. Why didn't you sign your full name? What are you trying to hide? What are you doing here in town? It says here you're a

dancer. We don't have a club in town that books entertainers."
I said, *"Officers, my professional name is Johnny Cato. I've got nothing to hide. My full name had always been too long for the marquees. I've fallen into the habit of using the shorter version.*

"My legs went out last year. I don't dance anymore. My wife and I decided to go into business. We are making a tour of this part of the country. We think that in your town we've found the ideal site for a Southern fried children shack. My wife has a secret recipe that should make us rich up here" (Iceberg Slim, *Pimp: The Story of My Life*).

Another example of shucking was related to me by a colleague. A black gang member was coming down the stairway from the club room with seven guns on him and encountered some policemen and detectives coming up the same stairs. If they stopped and frisked him he and others would have been arrested. A paraphrase of his shuck follows: "Man, I gotta get away from up there. There's gonna be some trouble and I don't want no part of it." This shuck worked on the minds of the policemen. It anticipated their questions as to why he was leaving the club room, and why he would be in a hurry. He also gave *them* a reason for wanting to get up to the room fast.

It ought to be mentioned at this point that there was not uniform agreement among my informants in characterizing the above examples as shucking. One informant used shucking only in the sense in which it used among peers, e.g., bull-shitting, and characterized the above examples as jiving or whupping game. Others however, identified the above examples as shucking, and reserved jiving and whupping game for more offensive maneuvers. In fact, one of the apparent features of shucking is that the posture of the black when acting with members of the establishment be a *defensive* one.

Frederick Douglass, in telling of how he taught himself to read, would challenge a white boy with whom he was playing, by saying that he could write as well as he. Whereupon he would write down all the letters he knew. The white boy would then write down more letters than Douglass did. In this way, Douglass eventually learned all the letters of the alphabet. Some of my informants regarded the example as whupping game. Others regarded it as shucking. The former were perhaps focusing on the maneuver rather than the language used. The latter may have felt that any maneuvers designed to learn to read were justifiably defensive. One of my informants said Douglass was "shucking *in order to* whup the game." This latter response seems to be the most revealing. Just as one can rap to whup the game on someone, so one can shuck or jive for the same purpose; that is, assume a guise or posture or perform some action in a certain way that is designed to work on someone's mind to get him to give up something.

"Whupping Game" to Con Whitey

The following examples from Malcolm X illustrate the shucking and jiving in this context though jive is the term used. Today, whupping game might also be the term used to describe the operation. Whites who came at night got a better reception; the several Harlem nightclubs they patronized were geared to entertain and jive (flatter, cajole) the night white crowd to get their money (Malcolm X, *The Autobiography of Malcolm X*).

The maneuvers involved here are clearly designed to obtain some benefit or advantage.

> Freddie got on the stand and went to work on his own shoes. Brush, liquid polish, brush, paste wax, shine rag, lacquer sole dressing . . . step by step, Freddie showed me what to do.
> "But you got to get a whole lot faster. You can't waste time!" Freddie showed me how fast on my own shoes. Then because business was tapering off, he had time to give me a demonstration of how to make the shine rag pop like a firecracker. "Dig the action?" he asked. He did it in slow motion. I got down and tried it on his shoes. I had the principle of it. "Just got to do it, faster," Freddie said. *"It's a jive noise, that's all. Cats tip better, they figure you're knocking yourself out!"* (Malcolm X, *The Autobiography of Malcolm X*)

An eight year old boy whupped the game on me one day this way:

> My colleague and I were sitting in a room listening to a tape. The door to the room was open and outside was a soda machine. Two boys came up in the elevator, stopped at the soda machine, and then came into the room.
> "Do you have a dime for two nickels?" Presumably the soda machine would not accept nickels. I took out the change in my pocket, found a dime and gave it to the boy for two nickels.
> After accepting the dime, he looked at the change in my hand and asked, "Can I have two cents? I need carfare to get home." I gave him the two cents.

At first I assumed the verbal component of the maneuver was the rather weak, transparently false reason for wanting the two cents. Actually, as was pointed out to me later the maneuver began with the first question which was designed to get me to show my money. He could then ask me for something that he knew I had, making my refusal more difficult. He apparently felt that the reason need not be more than plausible because the amount he wanted was small. Were the amount larger, he would no doubt have elaborated on the verbal element of the game. The form of the verbal element could be in the direction of rapping or shucking and jiving. If he were to rap the eight-year old might say, "Man, you know a cat needs to have a little bread to keep the girls in line." Were he to shuck and jive he might make the reason for needing the money more compelling, look hungry, etc.

The function of shucking and jiving as it refers to blacks and "the Man" is designed to work on the mind and emotions of the authority figure for the purpose of getting him to feel a certain way or give up something that will be to the other's advantage. Iceberg showed a "toothy smile" which said to the detective, "I'm glad to see you" and "Would I be glad to see you if I had something to hide?" When the maneuvers seem to be *defensive* most of my informants regarded the language behavior as shucking. When the maneuvers were *offensive* my informants tended to regard the behavior as "whupping the game."

Also significant is that the first form of shucking described, which developed out of accommodation, is becoming less frequently used today by many blacks, because of a new found self-assertiveness and pride, challenging the system. The willingness on the part of many blacks to accept the psychological and physical brutality and general social consequences of not "keeping one's place" is indicative of the changing self-concept of the black man. Ironically, the shocked reaction of some whites to the present militancy of the black is partly due to the fact that the black was so successful at "putting Whitey on" via shucking in the past. This new attitude can be seen from a conversation I recently had with a shoe shine attendant at O'Hare airport in Chicago.

I was having my shoes shined and the black attendant was using a polishing machine instead of the rag that was generally used in the past. I asked whether the machine made his work any easier. He did not answer me until about ten seconds had passed and then responded in a loud voice tht he "never had a job that was easy," that he would give me "one hundred dollars for any easy job" I could offer him, that the machine made his job "faster" but not "easier." I was startled at the response because it was so unexpected and I realized that here was a new "breed of cat" who was not going to shuck for a big tip or ingratiate himself with "Whitey" anymore. A few years ago his response probably would have been different.

The contrast between this "shoe-shine" scene and the one illustrated earlier from Malcolm X's autobiography, when "shucking Whitey" was the common practice, is striking.

Shucking, jiving, shucking and jiving, or S-ing and J-ing, when referring to language behavior practiced by blacks, is descriptive of the talk and gestures that are appropriate to "putting someone on" by creating a false impression. The terms seem to cover a range from simply telling a lie, to bullshitting, to subtly playing with someone's mind. An important difference between this form of shucking and that described earlier is that the same talk and gestures that are deceptive to the "the Man" are often transparent to those members of one's own group who are able practitioners at shucking themselves. As Robert Conot has pointed out, "The Negro who often fools the white officer by 'shucking it' is much less likely to be successful with another Negro...." Also, S-ing and J-ing within the group often has play overtones in which the person being "put on" is aware of the attempts being made and goes along with it for enjoyment or in appreciation of the style.

"Running it down" is the term used by speakers in the ghetto when it is their intention to give information, either by explanation, narrative, or giving advice. In the following literary example, Sweet Mac is "running this Edith broad down" to his friends:

> Edith is the "saved" broad who can't marry out of her religion . . . or do anything else out of her religion for that matter, especially what I wanted her to do. A bogue religion, man! So dig, for the last couple weeks I been quoting the Good Book and all that stuff to her; telling her I am now saved myself, you dig (Woodie King, Jr., "The Game," *Liberator,* August, 1965).

The following citation from Claude Brown uses the term with the additional sense of giving advice:

> If I saw him (Claude's brother) hanging out with cats I knew were weak, who might be using drugs sooner or later, I'd run it down to him.

It seems clear that running it down has simply an informative function, that of telling somebody something that he doesn't already know.

"Gripping" is of fairly recent vintage, used by black high school students in Chicago to refer to the talk and facial expression that accompanies a *partial* loss of face or self-possession, or showing of fear. Its appearance alongside "copping a plea," which refers to a total loss of face, in which one begs one's adversary for mercy, is a significant new perception. In linking it with the street code which acclaims the ability to "look tough and inviolate, fearless, secure, 'cool,' " it suggests that even the slightest weakening of this posture will be held up to ridicule and contempt. There are always contemptuous overtones attached to the use of the term when applied to the others' behavior. One is tempted to link it with the violence and toughness required to survive on the street. The intensity of both seems to be increasing. As one of my informants noted, "Today, you're *lucky* if you end up in the hospital"—that is, are not killed.

Reaction to Fear and Superior Power

Both gripping and copping a plea refer to behavior produced from fear and a respect for superior power. An example of gripping comes from the

record *"Street and Gangland Rhythms"*(Band 4 Dumb Boy). Lennie meets Calvin and asks him what happened to his lip. Calvin says that a boy named Pierre hit him for copying off him in school. Lennie, pretending to be Calvin's brother, goes to confront Pierre. Their dialogue follows:
> *Lennie:* "Hey you! What you hit my little brother for?"
> *Pierre:* "Did he tell you what happen man?"
> *Lennie:* "Yeah, he told me what happened."
> *Pierre:* "But you . . . but you . . . but you should tell your people to teach him to go to school, man." (Pause) I, I know, I know I didn't have a right to hit him."

Pierre, anticipating a fight with Lennie if he continued to justify his hitting of Calvin, tried to avoid it by "gripping" with the last line.

Copping a plea, originally meant "To plead guilty to a lesser charge to save the state the cost of a trial," (with the hope of receiving a lesser or suspended sentence) but is now generally used to mean 'to beg,' 'plead for mercy,' as in the example "Please cop, don't hit me. I give." (*Street and Gangland Rhythms,* Band 1 "Gang Fight"). This change of meaning can be seen from its used by Piri Thomas in *Down These Mean Streets.*

> The night before my hearing, I decided to make a prayer. I had to be on my knees, 'cause if I was gonna cop a plea to God, I couldn't play it cheap.

The function of gripping and copping a plea is obviously to induce pity or to acknowledge the presence of superior strength. In so doing, one evinces noticeable feelings of fear and insecurity which also result in a loss of status among one's peers.

Signifying is the term used to describe the language behavior that, as Abrahams has defined it, attempts to "imply, goad, beg, boast by indirect verbal or gestural means" (Roger D. Abrahams, *Deep Down in the Jungle*). In Chicago it is also used as a synonym to describe language behavior more generally known as "sounding" elsewhere.

Some excellent examples of signifying as well as of other forms of language behavior come from the well known "toast" (narrative form) "The Signifying Monkey and the Lion" which was collected by Abrahams from Negro street corner bards in Philadelphia. In the toast the monkey is trying to get the lion involved in a fight with the elephant:

Now the lion came through the jungle one peaceful day,
When the signifying monkey stopped him, and that is what he started to say:
He said, "Mr. Lion," he said, "A bad-assed mother fucker down your way,"

He said, "Yeah! The way he talks about your folks is a certain shame.
"I even heard him curse when he mentioned your grandmother's name."
The lion's tail shot back like a forty-four
When he went down that jungle in all uproar.

Thus the monkey has goaded the lion into a fight with the elephant by "signifying," that is, indicating that the elephant has been "sounding on" (insulting) the lion. When the lion comes back, thoroughly beaten up, the monkey again "signifies" by making fun of the lion:

. . . lion came back through the jungle more dead than alive,
When the monkey started some more of that signifying jive.
He said, "Damn, Mr. Lion, you went through here yesterday, the jungle run.
Now you come back today, damn near hung."

The monkey, of course, is delivering this taunt from a safe distance away on the limb of a tree when his foot slips and he falls to the ground, at which point,

Like a bolt of lightning, a stripe of white heat,
The lion was on the monkey with all four feet.

In desperation the monkey quickly resorts to "copping a plea":

The monkey looked up with a tear in his eyes,
He said, "Please, Mr. Lion, I apologize."

His "plea" however, fails to move the lion to show any mercy so the monkey tries another verbal ruse, "shucking":

He said, "You lemme get my head out of the sand,
ass out the grass, I'll fight you like a natural man."

In this he is more successful as,

The lion jumped back and squared for a fight.
The motherfucking monkey jumped clear out of sight.

A safe distance away again, the monkey returns to "signifying":

He said, "Yeah, you had me down, you had me at last,
But you left me free, now you can still kiss my ass."

This example illustrates the methods of provocation, goading and taunting artfully practiced by a signifier.

Interestingly, when the *function* of signifying is *directive* the *tactic* employed is *indirection,* i.e., the signifier reports or repeats what someone else has said about the listener; the "report" is couched in plausible language designed to compel belief and arouse feelings of anger and hostility. There is also the implication that if the listener fails to do anything about it—what has to be "done" is usually quite clear—his status will be seriously compromised. Thus the lion is compelled to vindicate the honor of his family by fighting or else leave the impression that he is afraid, and that he is not "king" of the jungle. When used for the purpose of directing action, "signifying" is like "shucking" in also being deceptive and subtle in approach and depending for success on the naivete or gullibility of the person being "put on."

When the function of signifying is to arouse feelings of embarrassment, shame, frustration or futility, to diminish someone's status, the tactic employed is direct in the form of a taunt, as in the example where the monkey is making fun of the lion.

"Sounding" to Relieve Tensions

Sounding is the term which is today most widely known for the game of verbal insult known in the past as "Playing the Dozens," "The Dirty Dozens" or just "The Dozens." Other current names for the game have regional distribution: Signifying or "Sigging" (Chicago), Joning (Washington, D.C.), Screaming (Harrisburg), etc. In Chicago, the term "sounding" would be descriptive of the initial remarks which are designed to sound out the other person to see whether he will play the game. The verbal insult is also subdivided, the term "signifying" applying to insults which are hurled directly at the person and the dozens applying to results hurled at your opponent's family, especially, the mother.

Sounding is often catalyzed by signifying remarks referred to earlier such as "Are you going to let him say that about your mama" to spur an exchange between members of the group. It is begun on a relatively low key and built up by verbal exchanges. The game goes like this:

> One insults a member of another's family; others in the group make disapproving sounds to spur on the coming exchange. The one who has been insulted feels at this point that he must reply with a slur on the protagonist's family which is clever enough to defend his honor (and therefore that of his family). This, of course, leads the other (once again, more due to pressure from the crowd than actual insult) to make further jabs. This can proceed until everyone is bored with the whole affair, until one hits the other (fairly rare), or until some other subject comes up that interrupts the proceedings

(the usual state of affairs) (Roger D. Abrahams, "Playing the Dozens," *Journal of American Folklore*, July-September, 1962).

Mack McCormick describes the dozens as a verbal contest:

> in which the players strive to bury one another with vituperation. In the play, the opponent's mother is especially slandered . . . Then, in turn fathers are identified as queer and syphilitic. Sisters are whores, brothers are defective, cousins are "funny" and the opponent is himself diseased. (Mack McCormick, "The Dirty Dozens," book jacket in the record album *The Unexpurgated Folksongs of Men,* Arhoolie Records).

An example of the "game" collected by one of my students goes:

> Frank looked up and saw Leroy enter the Outpost. Leroy walked past the room where Quinton, "Nap," "Pretty Black," "Cunny," Richard, Haywood, "Bull" and Reese sat playing cards. As Leroy neared the T.V. room, Frank shouted to *him.*
>
> *Frank:* "Hey Leroy, your mama—calling you man."
> Leroy turned and walked toward the room where the sound came from. He stood in the door and looked at Frank
>
> *Leroy:* "Look motherfuckers, I don't play that shit."
>
> *Frank* (signifying): "Man, I told you cats 'bout that mama jive" (as if he were concerned about how Leroy felt).
>
> *Leroy:* "That's all right Frank; you don't have to tell these funky motherfuckers nothing; I'll fuck me up somebody yet."
>
> Frank's face lit up as if he were ready to burst his side laughing. "Cunny" became pissed at Leroy.
>
> *Cunny:* "Leroy, you stupid bastard, you let Frank make a fool of you. He said that 'bout your mama."
>
> *"Pretty Black":* "Aw, fat ass head 'Cunny' shut up."
>
> *"Cunny":* Ain't that some shit. This black slick head motor flicker got nerve 'nough to call somebody 'fathead.' Boy, you so black, you sweat Permalube Oil."

This eased the tension of the group as they burst into loud laughter.

> *"Pretty Black":* "What 'chu laughing 'bout 'Nap,' with your funky mouth smelling like dog shit."

Even Leroy laughed at this.

> *"Nap":* "Your mama motherfucker."
>
> *"Pretty Black":* "Your funky mama too."

"Nap": (strongly) "It takes twelve barrels of water to make a steamboat run; it takes an elephant's dick to make your Grandmammy come; she been elephant fucked, camel fucked and hit side the head with your Grandpappy's nuts."

Reese: "Godorr-damn; go on and rap motherfucker."

Reese began slapping each boy in his hand, giving his positive approval of "Naps" comment. "Pretty Black" in an effort not to be outdone, but directing his verbal play elsewhere stated:

"Pretty Black": "Reese, what you laughing 'bout? You so square, you shit bricked shit."

Frank: "Whoooowee!"

Reese (sounded back): "Square huh, what about your nappy ass hair before it was stewed; that shit was so bad till, when you went to bed at night, it would leave your head and go on the corner and meddle."

The boys slapped each other in the hand and cracked up.

"Pretty Black": "On the streets meddling, bet Dinky didn't offer me no pussy and I turned it down."

Frank: "Reese scared of pussy."

"Pretty Black": "Hell yeah; the greasy mother rather fuck old ugly, funky cock Sue Willie than get a piece of ass from a decent broad."

Frank: "Godorr-damn! Not Sue Willie."

"Pretty Black": "yeah ol meat-beating Reese rather screw that cross-eyed, clapsy bitch, who when she cry, tears rip down her ass."

Haywood: "Don't be so mean, Black"

Reese: "Aw shut up, you half-white bastard."

Frank: "Wait man, Haywood ain't gonna hear much more of that half-white shit; he's a brother too."

Reese: "Brother, my black ass; that white ass landlord gotta be this motherfucker's paw."

"Cunny": "Man, you better stop foolin with Haywood; he's turning red."

Haywood: "Fuck yall. (As he withdrew from the "sig" game.)

Frank: "Yeah, fuck yall; let's go to the stick hall." The group left enroute to the billiard hall (James Maryland, "Signifying at the Outpost," unpublished term paper for the course *Idiom of the Negro Ghettos,* January 1967).

The above example of sounding is an excellent illustration of the "game" as played by 15–17-year-old Negro boys, some of whom have already acquired the verbal skill which for them is often the basis for having a high "rep." Ability with words is apparently as highly valued as physical strength. In the sense that the status of one of the participants in the game is diminished if he has to resort to fighting to answer a verbal attack, verbal ability may be even more highly regarded than physical ability.

The relatively high value placed on verbal ability must be clear to most black boys at early age. Most boys begin their activity in sounding by compiling a repertoire of "one liners." When the game is played the one who has the greatest number of such remarks wins. Here are some examples of "one liners" collected from fifth and sixth grade black boys in Chicago:

Yo mama is so bowlegged, she looks like the bit out of a donut.
Yo mama sent her picture to the lonely hearts club,
  and they sent it back and said "We ain't that lonely!"
Your family is so poor the rats and roaches eat lunch out.
Your house is so small the roaches walk single file.
I walked in your house and your family was running
  around the table. I said, "Why you doin that?" Your
  mama say, "First one drops, we eat."

Real proficiency in the game comes to only a small percentage of those who play it. These players have the special skill in being able to turn around what their opponents have said and attack them with it. Thus, when someone indifferently said "fuck you" to Concho, his retort was immediate and devastating: "Man, you haven't even kissed me yet."

The "best talkers" from this group often become the successful street-corner, barber shop, and pool hall story tellers who deliver the long, rhymed, witty, narrative stories called "toasts." They are, as Roger D. Abrahams has described, the traditional "men of words" and have become on occasion entertainers such as Dick Gregory and Redd Fox, who are virtuosos at repartee, and preachers, whose verbal power has been traditionally esteemed.

The function of the "dozens" or "sounding" is to borrow status from an opponent through an exercise of verbal power. The opponent feels compelled to regain his status by "sounding" back on the speaker or other group member whom he regards as more vulnerable.

The presence of a group seems to be especially important in controlling the game. First of all, one does not "play" with just anyone since the subject matter is concerned with things that in reality one is quite sensitive about. It is precisely *because* "Pretty Black" has a "Black slick head" that makes him vulnerable to "Cunny's" barb, especially now when the Afro-American "natural" hair style is in vogue. Without the control of the group "sounding" will frequently lead to a fight. This was illustrated by a tragic epilogue concerning Haywood, when Haywood was being "sounded' on in the presence of two girls by his best friend (other members of the group were absent), he refused to tolerate it. He went home, got a rifle, came back and shot and killed his friend. In the classroom from about the fourth grade on fights among black boys invariably are caused by someone "sounding" on the other person's mother.

Significantly, the subject matter of sounding is changing with the changing self-concept of the black with regard to those physical characteristics that are characteristically "Negro," and which in the past were vulnerable points in the black psyche: blackness and "nappy" hair. It ought to be said that for many blacks, blackness was always highly esteemed and it might be more accurate to regard the present sentiment of the black community toward skin color as reflecting a shifted attitude for only a *portion* of the black community. This suggests that "sounding" on someone's light skin color is not new. Nevertheless, one can regard the previously favorable attitude toward light skin color and "good hair" as the prevailing one. "Other things being equal, the more closely a woman approached her white counterpart, the more attractive she was considered to be, by both men and women alike. "Good hair" (hair that is long and soft) and light skin were the chief criteria" (Elliot Liebow, *Tally's Corner*).

The dozens has been linked to the over-all psycho-social growth of the black male. McCormick has stated that a "single round of a dozen or so exchanges frees more pent-up aggressions than will a dose of sodium pentothal." The fact that one permits a kind of abuse within the rules of the game and within the confines of the group which would otherwise not be tolerated, is filled with psychological import. It seems also important, however, to view its function from the perspective of the non-participating members of the group. Its function for them may be to incite and prod individual members of the group to combat for the purpose of energizing the elements, of simply relieving the boredom of just "hanging around" and the malaise of living in a static and restrictive environment.

A summary analysis of the different forms of language behavior which have been discussed above permits the following generalizations:

The prestige norms which influence black speech behavior are those which have been successful in manipulating and controlling people and situations. The function of all of the forms of language behavior discussed above, with the exception of "running it down," was to project personalities, assert oneself, or arouse emotion, frequently with the additional purpose of getting the person to give up or do something which will be of some benefit to the speaker. Only running it down has as its primary function to communicate information and often here too, the personality and style of the speaker in the form of rapping is projected along with the information.

The purpose for which language is used suggests that the speaker views the social situations into which he moves as consisting of a series of transactions which require that he be continually ready to take advantage of a person or situation or defend himself against being victimized. He has absorbed what Horton has called "street rationality." As one of Horton's respondents put it: "The good hustler . . . conditions his mind and must never put his guard too far down, to relax, or he'll be taken."

I have carefully avoided limiting the group within the black community of whom the language behavior and perspective of their environment is characteristic. While I have no doubt that it is true of those whom are generally called "street people" I am uncertain of the extent to which it is true of a much larger portion of the black community, especially the male segment. My informants consisted of street people, high school students, and blacks, who by their occupation as community and youth workers, possess what has been described as a "sharp sense of the streets." Yet it is difficult to find a black male in the community who has *not* witnessed or participated in the dozens or heard of signifying, or rapping, or shucking and jiving at some time during his growing up. It would be equally difficult to imagine a high school student in Chicago inner city school not being touched by what is generally regarded as "street culture."

In conclusion, by blending style and verbal power, through rapping, sounding and running it down, the black in the ghetto establishes his personality; through shucking, gripping and copping a plea, he shows his respect for power; through jiving and signifying he stirs up excitement. With all of the above, he hopes to manipulate and control people and situations to give himself a winning edge.

6.
Public Drama and Common Values in Two Caribbean Islands

Roger D. Abrahams

Words, at least in traditional societies, often express far more than feelings or ideas. The way words are used—in tales, riddles, proverbs, and typical modes of address and conversation—can reveal a great deal about the structure and values of a society. And this is especially true of the Negro societies of the New World, where the use of words in various types of traditional word games and public dramatic performances, both planned and impromptu, has been developed into a highly expressive art.

In this article, I want to examine some of the styles of expression common to Negro communities in both the United States and British West Indies. In particular, after a brief look at some North American Negro folkways such as institutionalized boasting contests, I want to show how differences in traditional patterns of public performance on two Caribbean islands—Tobago and Nevis—are closely related to differences in the type of social structure each of these New World communities has evolved.

Human communities have devised only a limited number of ways to organize themselves. Once a pattern is developed in one area of life, that pattern tends to repeat itself in other areas. For example, principles of family organization may be echoed in other structures of government and economics, and the same principles of order may also be seen in the structure of traditional public performances. Folklore, of which such performances are a part, is especially susceptible to analysis in terms of overall cultural patterns. As the expressive and aesthetic dimension of culture in tradition-oriented groups, folklore is made up of items and performances that are self consciously and artistically constructed. And because folk performances are of a totally public nature, and therefore conceived in terms understandable to everyone, the organization behind them is clearly stated. The performance is constructed of conventional materials, and these conventions dictate form, content, roles, and role relationships. Furthermore, because the performance has no written script or guide, the audience must be reminded at each stage where they are in the performance; if they do not know exactly, they will not enjoy or even tolerate the presentation. Conventions provide the kinds of markers that both the performer and audience need to guarantee this constant feeling of orientation. Virtually every scene of a folk play or a folk-tale, for instance, must imply the totality of the composition—where it has been and where it is going. This is why traditional, publicly understood conventions must dominate folk performance.

Impromptu Performances

Because everyone in the community is familiar with the traditional conventions according to which such activities are conducted, the impromptu rhyming competitions, story-telling, and invective contests common among North American Negroes may be regarded as folk performances. In 1958 and 1959, while I was living in a predominantly Negro neighborhood in South Philadelphia, I observed a number of these impromptu performances. After a while, I began to see a pattern in the roles played by the performer, in his relationship to his material and his audience, and in the audience's attitude toward the performer and his enactment.

This pattern centered upon the acclaim given those individuals who were good at using words effectively—individuals whom I came to call "men-of-words." Of note in their performances was the way these narrators became closely identified with the character and actions of the heroes they described. And the audience seemed to identify with the enactment almost as fully as the speaker did. This strong sense of sympathetic involvement and vicarious identification was intensified by the repeated and insistent use of the first-person pronoun "I" by the man-of-words. Eventually, it became clear that these performances were almost always contests between men-of-words, and that such contests were a community-accepted manner of demonstrating masculine strength.

At the time, I assumed that this pattern was probably unique to urban Negro performers in the United States. Since then, field experience in the Southern United States and in the British West Indies has convinced me that this pattern is considerably more wide-spread and may be characteristic of certain performances in most Negro communities of the New World. This similarity becomes clear, for instance, in a casual comparison of blues and calypso singers. Both build their art on personal identification, singing about what they claim to be their own experiences or observations. The calpysonians characteristically perform in a contest situation. And both calypsonians and blues singers can achieve high status in their communities by practicing their art. (It is widely said throughout the West Indies, for instance, that the only man who might beat the Prime Minister in a Trinidadian election is the calypso master, Mighty Sparrow.)

The widespread nature of this performance pattern is even more forcefully demonstrated by the presence of a certain type of verbal contest in every Negro community in which I've done field work. This contest is often called "playing the dozens" or "sounding" in the United States, and in the West Indies it is commonly called "rhyming." This adolescent verbal activity involves invective contests in which one youth will insult a member of another's family—most commonly, his mother—knowing that he will be answered in kind. The first youth will usually frame his insult in rhyme, and describe a sexual feat that he claims to have accomplished himself. This battle is recognized simply as boasting, and though the contestants may become deeply involved in the proceedings, they seldom regard it as anything but a game.

Most of the performance characteristics of the man-of-words tradition can also be observed in this obscene verbal exchange: the constant use of the first-person pronouns, the close identification of speaker with the imaginary situation, the achievement of sexual identity (and peer-group status), and the word-contest structure of the performance.

"Rhyming," unlike more complex verbal traditions, is practiced by most boys, though some are better talkers than others. In combination with teasing and taunting, this "rhyming" type of verbal interplay develops into two kinds of folkloric activities and two kinds of men-of-words: the "good-talking" and the "good-arguing." Banter remains an integral part of the expressive and communicative dimension of everyday life. Almost any extended conversation, especially a contest of wits, can develop into a public entertainment. I have observed such impromptu performances at casual gatherings on the steps or at the pool hall in the big-city atmosphere of South Philadelphia, and at markets, rum shops, and especially on buses and boats in the British West Indies. This kind of activity shows off the person adept at repartee, the good-arguer.

The good-talker, on the other hand, needs a more highly structured situation and more time to exhibit his talents. He commonly employs highly ornate and self-consciously artifical rhetoric; for these effects, he must have a situation in which he can gain the complete attention of his audience. In the United States, the good-talker tends to hold forth at bars or pool halls, at private parties, or at religious meetings. In the West Indies, he may again channel his talents into preaching, but more commonly he holds forth at festivals, such as Carnival or Christmas, or at occasions like wakes or wedding feasts. In both the islands and on the United States mainland, some men-of-words used to specialize in writing love letters for other members of the community.

The most interesting aspect of the widespread existence of such men-of-words among New World Negroes is the different ways in which these men develop their powers in different historical, geographical, and cultural settings. And of equal importance are the ways in which men-of-words fit into the total picture of a community's traditions, institutions, and expressive culture. The rest of this article will be devoted to describing two West Indian groups, the people of Tobago and those of Nevis, in terms of their man-of-words traditions—how these traditions have harmonized with the ethos of their communities, and what recent forces have brought changes in this particular aspect of expressive folklore.

Men-of-Words

In Tobago, there have been numerous traditional occasions for the man-of-words to exhibit his powers: at Bongos (wakes) as story-teller or sermonizer, at Thanksgivings (parties commemorating the end of a trying experience) as speech-maker, and—most notably—as a central performer in a Carnival *mas',* a touring group of masqueraders.

In these Carnival groups, the stylistic traits of the man-of-words performance pattern are harmonized with certain Carnival characteristics. Most of the groups found on Trinidad and Tobago during Carnival have the following traits:

- They represent a community, or—in the cities—a neighborhood;
- The performers play traditional roles, which are designated by traditional costumes and masks, and by certain types of stylized performance consonant with the role;
- The roles are commonly portrayals of power figures, either characters from the underworld (criminals, devils) or impersonations of heroes (military figures, warriors);
- Individual performers commonly take on stage names that are appropriate to the character being played;
- They commonly accumulate groups of followers who dress in similar styles; and
- The performer, while he may perform simply by interacting with the audience, nevertheless finds opportunity for the fullest statement of his

abilities in competition with another performer playing the same type of role. Thus the man-of-words pattern fits easily into this type of Carnival performance.

Commonly a *mas'* is organized around a virtuoso performer: a singer, a dancer, a stick-fighter, or a speechmaker. He may perform alone, and indeed he often does when money-making is the primary motivation. More often, he performs alone one day of Carnival and then with his group the next.

Most of these contests call for the performance of certain set pieces prepared by each virtuoso ahead of time, followed by an improvised "battle." This was the pattern of the Caiso mas', the ancestor of the modern calypso competitions, which took place on both Trinidad and Tobago. The various "chantwells," or mastersingers, would compose songs for the season, and each would try to have his song widely sung. Then, when he met another calypso group, he and his followers would trade songs and the two chantwells would generally engage in a "war"—a contest of invective. As with most of these contests, the "wars" were for the amusement of the crowd. Seldom was either chantwell declared the winner.

Though Tobago has the same types of calypso groups as Trinidad, the Tobagonians have developed at least one, the Speech Band, which seems unique to that island. This type of troupe follows the same general kind of organization as the Trinidadian groups, but exhibits one further characteristic common to the fancy-costume groups: a fascination with exotic hierarchies. The members of a Speech Band form themselves in a very rigid status order, depending primarily on speech-making ability and experience. Each performer assumes an appropriate name, the leader being "King George." When they march, the hierarchical arrangement is fully stated. First comes the "Showboy," a clown figure who clears the way for the group. Then come the apprentices, all called "Robins." Then, in a cluster, come the members of the King's Court—knights such as "Hero, the Conqueror," "Warrior Sealey," and many others. And the King himself is immediately preceded by his sons, "The Prince of Wales" and "The Duke of York."

The King, or more usually his organizer, named "Commander," will determine who speaks and in what order. As the names of the characters suggest, the speeches are properly heroic in tone and diction. They involve a wide range of subjects and themes, but they always rhyme, use inflated rhetoric, and are strongly hyperbolic:

Don't provoke Young Sealey until he get set;
Nothing that I do I never regret.
Stretch forth your fingers to me and let us make a bet.

Words that I tell, you supposed to regret,
For I'm free and faithful, strong as deat'.
Here we are soldiers preparing for war.
Miracles to me are only like a cold drink of water.
These are the miracles, here they are:
Human bones I'll crush to make you t'ousand bags of Gibraltar's flour,
We'll preserve your bones into green pastures' butter.

There are significant differences between Tobago's Speech Band and most of the groups in Trinidad. Most notably, in Speech Band, though the King is the acknowledged master at speech-making, everyone in the group is given an opportunity to perform. This is ensured by "Commander." Furthermore, the unitary focus of the Trinidad groups on the virtuoso is further dissipated on Tobago by making provision for training future warriors—that is, by establishing the role of "Robin" for the younger men.

This diffusion of performance enables communities to feel more fully involved in the contest of wits that occurs on Carnival Tuesday (Mardi Gras on French-speaking islands and in the United States), when one Tobagonian Speech Band encounters another. And even then, the pageantry of the costumes and the involved decorum of enunciating the rules of battle will provide as much dramatic interest as the boasting and cursing contest itself. On Tobago as compared with Trinidad, then, these performances of local men-of-words are rather democratic and not so narrowly focused on the virtuoso abilities of the individual performer. A war-of-words between Tobagonian Speech Bands is really a team affair.

This style of expressive organization, in which dramatic focus is passed from performer to performer, is characteristic of most entertainments on Tobago. Furthermore, this democratic approach to performance has recently become even more pronounced in certain Tobago communities, including Plymouth, the village that I have investigated most extensively. This shift has brought about a number of changes in traditional enactments, including what amounts to a rejection of even the modified focus on virtuoso performance by a man-of-words.

The reasons for this development are complex. Perhaps the most important negative force has been the identification of the virtuoso performance with Trinidad performers, and with the stereotype of the Trinidadian as self-centered and commercially-motivated. Since Trinidad and Tobago achieved independence from Great Britain in 1957, Tobago has sensed that its second-class satellite status, present before nationhood, has become more pronounced. Though the islands are geographically close and have shared a great deal historically and culturally, in many important respects they are different. Trinidad is dominated by urban and semi-urban population centers, and therefore by a predominantly mercantilistic, wage-earning frame of reference. The economy is supported to a great extent by surplus production of goods. Trinidad suffers from a complex cultural situation: Not only have Negroes from many different islands been brought together in what has become a slum environment, but strong resentments have arisen between Negroes and East Indian residents. All of this has created tensions that are exaggerated by additional problems of unemployment and overpopulation.

Life on the Beach

Problems of this sort are not so profound on Tobago, even in Scarborough, the seat of government and the center of population. In towns like Plymouth, because there has been such a steady migration from the town to Trinidad and elsewhere, there is no problem in providing food and employment for anyone who wishes to stay. Though half of the men in Plymouth work in the fields, life really centers on the beach, where the men fish with seines. "Fishening," as they call it, provides them not only with their main source of protein, but also with their major source of money income when the catches are large enough to sell the surplus.

The most important value of beach life is cooperation. There are 13 to 15 seines, but only two nets can be cast at once because of the size of the beach. Therefore the seines are run by a system of "chances"—that is, the fishermen take turns. The two seines that are on their chance continue to be thrown until a reasonable catch is made (which sometimes takes as long as a week). The three to six people who throw the seine are the principals in the catch, but everyone else on the beach at the time will get some fish for his pot that night if the size of the catch permits it. Furthermore, when repairs are to be made on a boat or a seine, those who are best at such things will automatically help, and when a new seine is being "tied," nearly all of the men will do some knitting.

Though there are dissident elements in life in Plymouth, generally the spirit of cooperation reigns. When conflict does arise, it is commonly ascribed to outside influences, which is often substantially correct. When cooperation is threatened, the beach men and their families close ranks and continue their lifeways in a self-conscious and stubborn fashion.

This emphasis on cooperation has ramifications in all aspects of Plymouth life, especially in regard to concepts of family and community, property, and social- and governmental-status arrangements. In regard to the last, there *are* provisions for the achievement of status in Plymouth, and even on the beach. One can become a net owner (who gets 40-75 percent of the take in good catches), or the "captain" of a net team (who gets two "shares"); nevertheless, these positions give no special social distinction. The men on the beach are consciously defensive on such subjects. They insist that anyone, even the Prime Minister, Dr. Eric Williams, when he comes to Plymouth is just another "nyeagar." And this is not a pious platitude. In a number of cases, when men have left Plymouth and achieved some measure of status elsewhere, they have returned to find their outside status of little account in Plymouth.

In one case, a retired policeman was so frustrated by this lack of recognition that he tried to "organize" the men on the beach under his leadership. The men acquiesced, since his activities promised to merely add an element of formal organization to their already orderly existence. However, the government recently attempted to get the men to organize a cooperative to provide more surplus fish at lower prices. Because the ex-policeman was not elected to the presidency of this cooperative, he created an atmosphere that made the fishermen reluctant to join. Consequently, this cooperative fishing enterprise, encouraged and underwritten by the government, is now primarily made up of agricultural workers, shopkeepers, and retired civil servants. An atmosphere of conflict has arisen, and there are strong resentments between the two factions.

But the problem is much greater than just one of factions. Essentially the government, and the cooperative as its agency, are asking the fishermen to break up their beach life and to reject beach values in favor of a fully capitalistic and competitive frame of reference. The fishermen feel that this would not only bring about the destruction of their way of life but would induce, in its place, the attitudes and values of the Trinidadians—whom they regard as thieves and, in personal relationships, dangerous and unpredictable. The people of Plymouth fear the incursion of big-city ways and values.

This reaction to Trinidadian ways seems to have affected public-performance patterns. In the last two decades there has been an unconscious drifting away from single-person performances involving men-of-words or men-of-action, and a contrary impulse emphasizing and elaborating those expressive traditions that are more communal in organization. This is especially observable in the Carnival groups; such virtuoso performances as Kalinda (stick-fight dance), Caiso *mas'*, and Speech Band have virtually disappeared as community-encouraged activities. There are still performing-group members living in Plymouth, but only one man bothers to perform at Carnival.

The virtuosos still bring gasps of admiration when they can be persuaded to perform. But they get no community support in the form of an active following and a set of apprentices—support that, in the past, provided the lifeblood of such performances. Instead, for Carnival, the town informally agrees on a theme for a fancy-costume performance, and the residents spend the two months before Carnival making appropriate costumes. This performance is one in which all may participate. In doing this, the Tobagonians are following a recent trend in Trinidad (and indeed throughout the West Indies), but for very different reasons. Such non-traditional costume groups have proliferated in Trinidad because they can be enjoyed by any audience; there is no problem of understanding their performance, as there is for foreign visitors when they watch many of the traditional virtuoso performers. Also, the virtuoso performances can be played effectively only before small groups, while the costume groups can be seen and appreciated by the multitudes. Since there are few foreign visitors on Tobago, however, and since their Carnival is primarily given for their own amusement, the reasons for change that prevail in Trinidad have little effect there. At least in Plymouth, the change in emphasis seems to have occurred because of the predilection toward community endeavors.

Cooperative Community

This cooperative pattern is repeated in nearly all aspects of Plymouth life. It is reflected in the tendency toward making the family as extended as possible (each person has two godfathers and two godmothers, and everyone in the family refers to them by this quasi-familial relationship); and it is seen in the large number of *susus* (savings groups), sports clubs, and steel-drum bands. But it is most fully seen in the traditional occasions that are still widely observed in the town.

Most dramatically, the cooperative motive arises in times of crisis, such as when a member of the community dies. Immediately, nearly all work stops, and friends and family gather around the immediate survivors. As many as 40 or 50 men will begin getting wood to make the coffin, cutting the wood up, and fashioning a burial device. The same is true of digging the grave; each male friend of the deceased will take his turn with the spade, while the others stand around watching. After the burial, a Bongo (wake) will commonly be held, with the first night devoted to hymn-singing, but subsequent nights given over to games, dances, and riddling. Story-telling, once favored, is now rare, and this perhaps illustrates a further retreat from men-of-words performances. The games are commonly organized on a circular arrangement, their accompanying song is performed in the chanter-response pattern usually associated with African practices, and the song-leader often changes.

Other festival occasions reflect the same communal preoccupation. Any new boat or seine calls for a *fête,* a christening, the appointment of godfathers and godmothers, and so on. Similarly, when someone has returned from a trip or recovered from a sickness, a "Thanksgiving" party is given. Finally, the most important holiday of the year is St. Peter's Day, a fisherman's festival in which not only Plymouthians but fishing folk from all over the island come for games and the blessing of the boats. This festival calls for the same kind of performances as those at the Bongo, except that on St. Peter's Day all the local fishermen and many of their friends from other locales are called upon to improvise a speech or a song for the occasion. St. Peter's Day is the last of the festivals on Tobago that encourage the men-of-words performance.

There is no sense of loss in the passing of these virtuoso traditions, however, because the practices that have replaced them are very harmonious with the traditionally communal orientation of the residents. There is no sense of rejecting the past, a pattern that one does find in a number of other West Indian communities, but rather a selective emphasis upon an *alternative* pattern of traditional performance—the group game or song or dance.

According to Alan Lomax's view on the performance styles of different culture areas, on Tobago we have a reversion to totally African patterns of performance. Lomax contrasts the "integrated African style" of song with that of West European ballad style, which emphasizes the solo performance. Whereas in ballad communities, Lomax asserts, performance is done by individuals who reflect an individualistic and often isolated frame of reference, "it is rare in African performance for one person to sing or dance alone for more than a few seconds," and this echoes a way of life predicated on "disciplined and cooperative action."

There is strong evidence against Lomax's generalization, however. And this contrary evidence is especially strong in the area of verbal ability. Many recent observers have pointed to the importance of individual verbal ability in African groups, and in a variety of situations. John Messenger, for instance, has shown the importance of effective speaking in a Nigerian legal system, and John Blacking has shown how central riddling and other verbal skills are among the Venda Bantu. More recently, Ruth Finnegan has pointed out that among the Limba a story-teller is judged by his ability to use words effectively and is able to gain respect if he can do so. What Ethel M. Albert says of the Arunda therefore seems true of many other African groups:

> ... eloquence is one of the central values of the cultural world view; and the way of life affords frequent opportunity for its exercise. Sensitivity to the variety and complexity of speech behavior is evident in a rich vocabulary for its description and evaluation, and in a constant flow of speech about speech. Argument, debate, and negotiation, as well as elaborate literary forms, are built into the organization of society as means of gaining one's ends, as social status symbols, and as skills enjoyable in themselves.

By pointing this out, I do not mean to criticize Lomax's *approach*—which I believe focuses on crucial matters of style and cultural organization—but simply to point out that certain evidence should qualify his conclusions.

On the other hand, the island cuture of Nevis in the British West Indies is a very good illustration of Lomax's categorical observations. Nevis, which has existed for over 300 years under British domination, has a folklore that is essentially derived from Great Britain. As such, the island has a style of performance and an accompanying ethos that emphasizes solo performance and an image of life as isolated—as full of anxiety and conflict. This does not mean, however, that Negro Nevisians have totally accepted the British way of life and point of view. It simply means that they have espoused British performance patterns because these facets of British culture came closest to embodying the special Nevisian way of seeing and organizing life.

England Plus Africa

Nevis folklore is the result of a syncretic coming together of African and European traditions. In terms of the actual items performed, Nevis folklore is predominantly British. But in terms of structure—of the way in which a performance is organized—Nevis' traditional expression is a development of the man-of-words pattern, with its many African antecedents and analogues.

On Tobago, there has always been a balance between two patterns of performance, the integrated and the virtuoso types, and recent developments away from the latter simply show that a choice is being made. On Nevis too, there has been a drifting away from the man-of-words pattern, but for very different reasons. Whereas on Tobago the situation has developed because of a defensive shoring-up of the sense of community enterprise, on Nevis the only defense is that of individuals retreating into themselves. On Nevis there is very little community activity or feeling.

Nevis has a satellite arrangement with St. Kitts similar to that of Tobago with Trinidad. It is one of the smaller of the British Leeward Islands. With St. Kitts, Antigua, and Barbados, it was one of the "Mother Colonies" in the British Caribbean. Tobago was never regarded as one of the great outposts of European power, never was a highly successful plantation enclave, and therefore has never been fully cultivated and overpopulated. Nevis, on the other hand, settled in 1628, was one of the places in which West Indian sugar fortunes were made, and the island therefore supported a large population of field slaves. The hot-springs system of Nevis was developed into a luxurious spa and became a favorite vacation spot for British visitors and for planters from the other West Indian islands. Add all this to the fact that the first field workers on the island were Scottish-Irish peasants transported for "political" crimes, and the strongly British flavor of the island's traditional expressions is accounted for.

The Scottish-Irish brought their countryside amusements with them, and many of these amusements have been perpetuated by the Negroes who followed. But these customs would not have caught on among the Negroes of Nevis had there not been elements in their situation that made the British entertainments intelligible and appropriate. One appropriate feature was that the British amusements allowed a continuation and an elaboration of a number of African aesthetic traditions, such as the use of topical satire for aggressive purposes and social control and, most important for the concerns of this study, the good-talker type of the man-of-words performance. But the puritanical British vision of the futility of love and any interpersonal involvement was also seized upon by the Nevisian and related to the kinds of distrusts and divisions that are the pitfalls of the matrifocal family organization in decay. This becomes especially evident in sexual involvements. Not only are there many proverbs that argue that man and woman can't live together effectively (unless man uses force), but their songs and dialogues emphasize the same point of view. Perhaps the most dramatic example of this is the widely sung Nevisian adaptation of the English folksong "Johnny's So Long at the Fair." In English versions, it will be recalled, the maiden sings of Johnny, who is late in returning from the fair, and of all the presents that he has promised her. On Nevis, the song becomes a recitation of all of the things that Johnny has already given the maiden.

The ring on my finger is Johnny give me,
The ring on my finger is Johnny give me,
The ring on my finger is Johnny give me,
Johnny alone until morning.

Johnny also gives her shoes, a hat, and a number of other personal items. But after all these are listed, she sings:

Johnny says that he love me, but I do not believe,
Johnny says that he love me, but I do not believe,
Johnny says that he love me, but I do not believe,
Johnny alone until morning.

This divisive and empty vision of personal relationships, in combination with a high degree of economic and social competition, reflects the sense of personal isolation and anomie observable on the island. Furthermore, the island has been in a economically depressed state for nearly a century: The land has been misused, and it is still owned primarily by the planters or the government, which often will not let it be planted. Even in those instances in which a cooperative enterprise that might lead the island out of its spiral of economic stagnation has been suggested, there has been no widespread approval of or action on the plan. On the largest and most populous side of the island, the peasants plant vegetable crops, which are not highly suited to the land and which have a limited market. They are, however, crops that can be vended by individuals in market competition, which fits into the Nevisians' competitive approach to life.

This bankrupt and anomic condition has resulted in many of its residents regarding Nevis as a prison, as opposed to the image of the "tropical paradise" held by most of the visitors and part-time residents from Canada and the United States. Consequently, there has been a series of mass emigrations from Nevis to areas with better employment possibilities. Many Nevisians went to New York and New Haven around World War I, others to the Dominican Republic in the 1930s, and some to Great Britain from 1945-1963. Today, many are going to the American Virgin Islands. Naturally, the ones who leave are the more adventurous, and often the more intelligent. Though the ones who stay behind are often severely tradition-oriented, they are not always the best performers, and on Nevis only a charismatic speaker is capable of winning an audience.

As on Tobago, on Nevis festivals provide the most important occasions for traditional performances. The two most notable Nevisian occasions are Christmas and Tea Meetings. Both provide opportunities for the dramatic exercise of verbal dexterity in a contest situation. But whereas Tobagonians have an alternative of virtuoso or group performances, on Nevis the only type acceptable in this conflict-oriented community is the virtuoso contest. The only group-style performances found there are performed by children in their ring-games, and by small groups of chanting men moving houses or boats. Not only is the man-of-words given an opportunity to display his powers in these festival performances, but almost the only kind of performance an audience will listen to is one in which an individual rises and seizes attention by virtue of his entertainment abilities.

There are a number of occasions in which such contests are an integral part of the festivities. At wedding feasts, for instance, there is commonly a session in which toasts of an obscene, boasting, and comical nature are proposed by a succession of orators. For example,

Here's to the girls that dress in black;
When they dress they never look slack.
When they kiss, they kiss so sweet,
Makes Tommy stand without feet.

The Strolling Players

During the Christmas season, there are many different groups of strolling players who exist primarily to stage just such contests of wit. The most colorful are those who give the old folk dramas. These are of two types: domestic farces, which turn upon ribald seduction and courtship scenes that are primarily enacted in terms of an argument or contest of wits between the man and the woman or between the husband and his rival; and ritual-combat plays, in which the dialogue between the combatants is rendered in elaborate language. The farces, in a sense, elevate the good-arguer to thespian status, while the combat-dramas bring good-talkers onto the stage.

In both categories, there are plays with long histories. Of special note is the "Mummies" play, which is a very full rendering of the British "St. George and The Turk" play. Characteristically, there are a number of word and sword battles between various "champions": St. George and the Turk, St. George and the Black Prince of Paradise, and so on. The orations are not unlike those of the Tobago Speech Band.

Similar plays are given about "Giant Despair and Christian" (taken from *The Pilgrim's Progress*) and "David and Goliath" (stemming ultimately from a play by Hannah More). A recent development on the pattern of serial combat are the "Cowboys and the Indians" plays. In these, a whole set of characters introduce themselves, characters ultimately derived from Street and Smith pulp novels of the 1930s (with a big debt to Hollywood as well). Then two of the cowboys, like "Bing Crosby from the Golden West" and "The Bar Bully," have a showdown. After a number of such confrontations, the Indians introduce themselves one by one (always as "black men"), and there ensues a battle royal between the Indians and the cowboys—a fight not always won by the cowboys.

These troupes, which often know two or three plays, are organized by one man-of-words, who knows all the plays by heart. He teaches the parts to the others by writing out "lessons" for them or by repeating the lines with them. The players change from year to year, but with the organization around the "captain" (the man-of-words) there is no threat of a break in the tradition. The captain usually has a "number-two man" who helps him in putting together the production every year. New troupes are commonly formed when a number-two man goes off on his own. This is an apprentice system similar to that of the Speech Band on Tobago, but there are inherent weaknesses in this arrangement as it has developed on Nevis that have recently led to a breakdown in the performance of these Christmas "sports."

A certain amount of community cooperation is called for in the organization of the troupe. In the past, this was brought about by the importance of the man-of-words. Because of his abilities, he was commonly a highly respected member of the community. But many of the best verbal virtuosos have left in the emigrations, and it has become increasingly difficult for those remaining to attract personnel. Consequently, the position of captain no longer carries such high status. The captains remaining react to this by greater insistence upon being shown proper respect, especially by the younger members of the community who make up the potential additions to the troupe. The young find that they not only have to learn their parts from the captain but that they also have to make repeated proclamations of their respect for him. They react to this by refusing to join him. The only recruits, then, tend to come from the ranks of children of those players who have been with the captain in the past.

The cowboy groups have less difficulty in attracting personnel because of the number of status roles within the play itself, and because the role of the captain has devolved upon a number of players. The young players are eager to graduate to important roles, and the cowboy play, because any number of combats can be added without altering its shape, allows them to do this. One captain of an older play, "The Christmas Bull," found that the only way he could hold his troupe together was to rewrite the play. In the original there was one role for a bull who had a comic combat with an inept local plantation owner, while in the revision eight other bulls were added. Most of the captains are not willing to make such changes. If changes are made, they are generally in the direction of enhancing the part played by the captain, which is already the longest and the most heroic.

The language of most of these plays, especially of the heroic-conflict dramas, is very ornate and hyperbolic. A champion must, after all, excel in both words and deeds. These boasting speeches are not, however, quite so fantastic in style and outrageous in diction as the speeches made during the Tea Meeting.

The Tea Meeting

The Nevis Tea Meeting is a remarkable combination of pageant, mock fertility ritual, variety show, and organized mayhem. The proceedings probably developed out of the fund-raising church events of the 19th century, which are still encountered on a number of other islands in the British West Indies.

For a Tea Meeting, a hall is engaged and a King and Queen and their court are chosen. Costumes are carefully prepared for the royalty and for other performers. The night of the performance, the King and the Queen are called for by a fife and drum ("Big Drum") band. They go to the hall, where the rest of the community has gathered. Then they sit on the stage while members of the audience come up and perform prepared routines—songs, poems, dialogues, speeches, or dances, done by one or two performers, or team songs and dances such as "Japanese Fan Drill" or "Baby Drill." In the middle of the evening, "tea" (cocoa, or some other hot drink) is served, and some ceremonial cakes, fruit, and kisses from the King and Queen are ritualistically auctioned. Then the King, the Queen, and members of the court make elaborate and ironic speeches. These are followed by other acts from the audience, which continue until dawn if the meeting is a good one. In the back sit the scoffers, who throughout the proceedings make loud and often obscene comments about the performers and their routines.

Organizing, or attempting to organize, the proceedings are two chairmen. They are supposed to give a sense of continuity and order to the show, to determine who should perform when, and to decide when the "tea" should be served. One of them usually calls the meeting to order by making a plea for "decorum":

> Ladies and Gentlemen, this afternoon we stand here to accompany this company here, ladies and gentlemen, and I want to here, this afternoon, have decorum. Decorum. Remember the alphabet, ladies and gentlemen: A is for attention, B is for behavior, C is for conduct, and D is for DECORUM. And, ladies and gentlemen, as we march on further, we go to J is for justice and P is for peace that is heaven for the flocks. I ask you to remember those few letters in the alphabet: A, B, C, D, P, and J. Ladies and Gentlemen, I won't procrastinate much more of the valuable time while I ask [the first performer] to provide me with a piece.

As the chairmen continue to make their introductions and to comment upon each act, it becomes clear that they are in fact the main performers. They must not only make these interpolated speeches but must also attempt to outshine the other performers. Most important, each chairman wants to prove himself to be the best speaker at the Tea Meeting. As the Nevisians put it, each wants to be regarded as "the cock with the brightest comb." They preen their feathers by making long, inflated, and macaronic speeches:

> That song remind me of Moses standing on the banks of the Red Sea. It fill my heart with phil-long-losophy, entrong-losophy, joken, and conomaltus. Impro, imperium, prompry, comilatus, allus comigotus, which is to say I come here today without any study. Dea Gratia, by the grace of God, I have tried my best. Time is tempus fugit. That same. I will say a few words about Moses. His life he went into different parts; he spent 40 years in Egypt, 40 years in Medea, and 40 years in the wilderness. I shall now, sum bonum, malcum cum shalltum propendum peerum, desideratum, wobiteratum

attitaratin. I shall now say, 'Veedie, veedie, amrie,' which is to say, 'I came, I saw, and I conquered.' And shall now leave my stand backonawalum, eloquent, precipitie, matic-matic, savong-savong. For I'm well-known for this, a wild cannonball speaker. Who thinks they can come over harder than I? Why if anyone here come from the school, I come from the college. If they're from the college, I'm from the Temple Bar. If they are from the Temple Bar, I am from the House of Parliament. If they are from the House of Parliament, I am from the city of Cairo that is in Egypt.

Speeches of this sort simply proclaim the challenge that the other chairman or some other performer will feel called upon to accept. Meanwhile, each flourish of language causes the emotions of the audience, including those of the hecklers in the back, to rise. As the noise mounts, the chairmen feel a greater need to assert their control, not only by becoming more eloquent but also by becoming louder and, quite often, insulting. In one recent Tea Meeting, the only way one of the chairmen could re-assert control was to grab his wife and begin doing a highly obscene dance. Obscenity, however, is not out of bounds on such occasions.

If you ask most Nevisians, they will tell you they still love Tea Meetings. Recently, however, there have been very few of them. The reasons are primarily the same as those for the demise of the Christmas "sports." The chairmen, like the performing troupes' captains, have all too often become overinvolved in their roles, and the audience, especially the hecklers, sense this fact. There is little attraction in placing oneself in such an assailable and potentially embarrassing position, and so few young men are willing to learn the craft of speechmaking. All of the chairmen are middle-aged or older, and therefore of the age that is becoming less respected and obeyed by the young. The brightest of the young, moreover, continue to leave the island. The competitive atmosphere in which the ceremony developed has now become overripe because of the overwhelming insecurities felt by all; and this is dramatized all too embarrassingly by the chairmen who fail to keep order. Whereas competition used to be the major form of communication and affirmation of community spirit, it now contributes to the breakdown of whatever spirit is left.

Community Break-Down

The breakdown of the traditional practices is, in other words, part of the larger degeneration of the Nevisian community. People on Nevis have retreated into themselves, lashing out at anyone who happens to come too close. In certain cases, members of a family band together in the face of the threat from others in the community, but in other situations it is just the individual who becomes defensive and paranoid.

In presenting Nevisian and Tobagonian man-of-words traditions in terms of their constituent elements and their recent changes, I have tried to show that a variety of non-aesthetic forces may have important repercussions on aesthetic activities. In participlar, I have attempted to point out that these performances represent a model of interpersonal relations in the surrounding community—and that when forces within or outside the community bring about changes in these relations, the changes will naturally be reflected in the community's traditional-performance structure.

The Nevisian Christmas plays are, as has been pointed out, very similar to the performances of the Carnival Speech Bands on Tobago, especially in regard to the boasting rhetoric and the combative scenes presented. But in regard to the model of interpersonal relationships provided by these performances, there are great differences between the two islands. And these differences reflect a real divergence of world view.

The Speech Band on Tobago is organized on a double principle of status. The King is regarded as the finest speech-maker, but the Commander handles the business affairs. He collects the money and arranges with the Commander of the competing groups who should speak first and for how long, and it is these two who must keep order throughout the contest. This dual responsibility, combined with the provision for apprenticeship, draws attention away from the King, who is the main performer. A sense of hierarchical order and decorum is built into such performances, and this very sense of order allows for greater flexibility in regard to the actual speeches made. There are two kinds of speeches made by members of the Speech Band: set pieces written ahead of time, and speeches improvised in reply to pieces given by the other team. The strength of the group, therefore, lies partly in its members' ability to compose and memorize, and partly in their ability to improvise in proper style. The emphasis is always in coordination, even in the contest atmosphere. The result is that this form of institutionalized conflict, because of its emphasis on teamwork, and group effort, is actually a cohesive force in the community.

On Nevis, the freedom to improvise is totally absent in the Christmas plays. One man knows the plays, teaches all of the parts, and takes the most important and most heroic part for himself. It is his show from beginning to end. Such plays call for a high degree of coordination, and this coordination can occur only through community acquiescence to the leadership of the captain, and—to some extent—of his number-two man. It is up to these leaders to see that the players speak their lines properly. The captains' reliance on past compositions to the exclusion of improvisation seems to reflect not so much a traditional orientation in the community as the personal insecurities of the captains themselves, who must fall back on the orders of the past.

The Nevis Tea Meeting, on the other hand, does call for improvisation on the part of the chairmen. But once again, there are significant differences between this technique and that of the Tobagonian Speech Band, for while the Tobagonian speaks both for himself and for his team, the Nevisian man-of-words calls attention only to himself. And not only is there more occasion for improvisation on Tobago, but there is greater range of freedom in regard to topics the speaker may explore. The Tea Meeting chairman, to be sure, must answer the "challenges" given him, and in the same terms as those of the challenge, but most commonly he uses the theme of the other speaker only as an introduction to his own speech. Once the introduction is over, he will fall back on set pieces that he has used in the past. The man-of-words is just as restricted in his speeches as the community is in other aspects of life. The heavy reliance upon performance contests that are fraught with anxiety and tension for the individual performer reflect in a heightened fashion the day-to-day pattern of interpersonal conflict that exists for most members of the peasant groups living on Nevis.

Comparing these two island cultures is instructive in a number of ways. First, it points to the West Indies' tremendous range of response to the plantation system and its decay, and shows that one gauge of diversity and change is to be found in the area of traditional performances. Second, it shows that although a pattern of organization may be observed in a number of communities, it may find very different uses and reflect almost diametrically opposed values. Furthermore, it suggests that such values can be clearly observed operating in the life of a traditional performance, and that such observation can lead to important insights that go far beyond purely folkloristic matters.

I have shown, in a tentative manner, what might be done if we followed Herskovits' suggestion that we work comparatively with folkloristic data in an attempt to assess what is constant about the traditions in a culture area and what the important variables are. Here I have limited myself to one pattern of performance—the man-of-words tradition—and gone into the pattern in detail with reference to only two small islands. A similar study might be made of problems such as the role of the scandal-piece (a libelous composition on local personages and events) in the maintenance of law and social control. And another fruitful study could compare those New World Negro groups that encourage improvisation in their art forms with those that discourage it—a topic ony touched upon here. Such subjects, and others like them, might be used to provide important insights into the value structures of different communities, and into the ways in which changes in these value structures can bring changes in the structure of artistic expression and communication.

Part III
Ritual and Symbol

It is a short step from the analysis of Caribbean festivals to consideration of ritual behavior. The three articles in this section of *Anthropological Realities* address the function of ceremonies and symbols in organizing social perspectives about the world. Of particular importance is the way in which ritually coded behavior permits otherwise fearful subjects—the supernatural, illness and death, physical risks, danger and moral defeat—to be handled satisfactorily. A traditional sequence of events with references to the appropriate symbols is a universal means of calming the individual spirit and reinforcing group morale.

Toward the end of the last century, there was hardly a topic more intriguing to social theorists than how the first human beings developed ritual beliefs and practices. The vantage point from which prominent authors, such as Freud, Durkheim, McLennan, Spencer, and Tylor wrote, rested on several important assumptions. One was that modern Europe had been liberated from the narrow confines of a religious world view. Western man, as evidenced by his superior technology, represented a culminating point in human evolution; his success rested on the victory of scientific logic over irrational superstitions.

In the construction of evolutionary stages in human history, most authors envisioned a prehistory that was populated by the natives described in ethnographic literature. Their customs and beliefs, usually not too well understood or appreciated, were seen as hold-overs from a spiritual dark age that Europeans had successfully overcome. Native preoccupation with dreams, ancestor-worship, and the personification of natural forces were used as evidence of primitive irrationality and contrasted with the logical mind of Western man.

The characterization of technologically primitive groups as backward and shackled by fear and superstition was the most dangerous judgment in the various developmental theories. Many of the non-Europeans categorized as Stone Age or barbarian societies were under one or another colonial jurisdiction whose repressive policies drew on the prejudices of intellectuals. To cite one well-known example, Sir James Frazer in his popular *Golden Bough* volumes (published between 1911 and 1915) maintained that the magic of primitive societies was nothing more than the mistaken application of the most elementary principles of imitation and contagion. What then could be thought of people who kept making the "mistake" of sprinkling water on the ground to bring rainfall or who secretly buried fingernail and hair clippings lest they be used in witchcraft? French professor Lucien Lévy-Bruhl provided the obvious response by introducing the term "pre-logical" to describe primitive mental processes. According to Lévy-Bruhl, the collectively oriented minds of savages were constantly immersed in a mystical, intuitive understanding of reality, and unlike the civilized European, were not capable of logical analysis and the conceptualization of causal influences. The racism inherent in this kind of labeling should not be lost, for it was always the white man who could reason, while those who were brown, black, red, or yellow missed the mark.

Over the years, as anthropological research illuminated the details and order of small-scale, foreign cultures, the image of the superstitious savage has faded. This is not to say that negative stereotypes of racial and ethnic groups do not persist, but one of the important contributions of anthropology to the humanistic sciences has been a defense of the innate intelligence and morality of people at all technological levels, regardless of color or class. The defense is essentially a two-barrelled one: to stress the logic of native ways and to question the exaggerated rationality of Western behavior.

Presentation of the pragmatic skills of traditional people characterized the very earliest ethnographic works. Franz Boas' detailed account of the elaborate Eskimo hunting and fishing technology made a substantial case for their powers of invention and adaptive skills. Boas drove home the point that the direct relationship of natives to the environment, in contrast to an Industrial-Age retreat from nature, had to be taken into consideration in analyzing traditional versus civilized world views. In *The Mind of Primitive Man,* Boas argued for an appreciation of cultural differences in defining reasonable behavior, and he chided his readers with the observation that civilized people were as enslaved by habit and custom as any primitives.

Later, in his essay "Magic, Science, and Religion," Bronislaw Malinowski used much the same strategy to defend Trobriand Island customs.

Directly attacking Lévy-Bruhl's assertions of native mysticism, Malinowski referred to the technological expertise of his informants, and, going one step farther, he defended the logic that prompted their use of magical techniques.

Thus, in his relation to nature and destiny, whether he tries to exploit the first or to dodge the second, primitive man recognizes both natural and supernatural forces and agencies, and he tries to use them both for his benefit. Whenever he has been taught by experience that effort guided by knowledge is of some avail, he never spares the one or ignores the other. He knows that a plant cannot grow by magic alone, or a canoe sail without being properly constructed and managed, or a fight be won without skill and daring. He never relies on magic alone, while, on the contrary, he sometimes dispenses with it completely, as in fire-making and in a number of crafts and pursuits. But he clings to it, whenever he has to recognize the impotence of his knowledge and of his rational technique.

While much of the work in anthropology has reinforced a notion of native rationality, it has taken a good deal of time and effort to explore the continued importance of ritual and religion in the scientifically oriented West. At the time when Frazer and Lévy-Bruhl were writing, belief in the occult, spiritualism, and just plain ordinary monotheism were widespread through Europe's educated classes. Yet there was then, as there is to a degree today, great embarrassment in admitting that one's personal beliefs ran counter to objective science. Although scientific innovations have lengthened human life, made for miracles in transportation and communication, and, for some sectors, eased the conditions of labor, basic anxieties about mortality cannot mechanically be eliminated from the human life cycle. Instead, we compose our lives around familiar habits that normalize our days, making one somewhat like the rest, and we punctuate the yearly calendar with exceptional events—holidays, travel, social events—which are as ritualized as our days. Our times and habits of eating, working, and playing are unconsciously patterned, and, indeed, have to be if we are to avoid the exhausting chore of waking each day to a host of new decisions.

In the article which begins this section, Melford S. Weiss examines a type of ritual that has been given major prominence in ethnographic descriptions. Throughout the life cycle, with the change from childhood to adulthood, the social role of an individual is defined several times over. The child becomes a woman or man, a parent, a person of certain occupational or political rank. These changes in status are often celebrated by what Arnold van Gennep called *rites de passage*. It is an unusual society that does not recognize important life transitions among its members and institutionalize some ceremonial acknowledgment. The rite of passage described by Weiss symbolizes an occupational transition, from ordinary foot-soldier to paratrooper. This change in status, taking place as it does within the rational organization of the military bureaucracy, is celebrated with as much, if not more, ritual than a tribal initiation, and it bears a clear-cut resemblance to van Gennep's traditional model.

Some comparisons between traditional and modern ritual and beliefs are much more difficult to draw. The opposition that we recognize between religion and science has deeply affected Western medicine, resulting in a functional division of body and soul. When something goes wrong with our bodies, we seek the help of a physician. In times of spiritual unrest, we resort to experts in counseling, the psychologist or religious leader. This dichotomy between one and another aspect of the self and the division of expert labor has not been typical of those societies best researched by anthropologists. Nor have the objective causes of disease and death in which we believe always appeared as a significant part of folk medicine. Native understanding of the causes and cures of illness is fundamentally personalistic; that is, some individual causes another to be ill, and another, the source, is called upon to cure the victim. It is not access to miracle drugs but access to supernatural powers that distinguishes the Jívaro sorcerer from the rest of the community.

The repercussions of these two common features of native beliefs, personal intent as a cause of harm and access to the supernatural, have an enormous impact on community relations and world view. As Irving O. Hallowell noted in his essays on the Ojibwa Indians, the crucial question becomes *who* (and not *what*) is responsible. When failing to meet responsibilities towards kinsmen and neighbors can bring about misfortune, there is great pressure on the members of a society to measure up to obligations. The business of sorcerers and witch doctors improves as tensions and stress increase and become indirectly expressed via their powers. Even though magical curers play a special role, they are subject to the same social pressures as the next person and more, for a sorcerer is expected to have all the answers for personal and public disasters, or else he will be accused of villany himself.

In Western society, the rituals of medicine are highly standardized. The doctor's appointment and a patient's admission to a hospital follow prescribed patterns of interaction based on a solemn respect for the physician's knowledge and the belief that the ill and injured must submit to hospital requirements of cleanliness and order. Aside from this public realm of medicine, there is a good deal of medical self-help that individuals take upon themselves to administer instead of paying for professional health care. Most of the over-the-counter drugs that are sold in enormous volume each year have limited curative power. Yet pain-killers, vitamins, lotions, and potions give millions of Americans the comfort of having invoked some chemical force. In the ultimate dilemma of facing incurable disease that cannot be professionally treated, Americans turn also to miracle drugs and treatments, in the hope of finding answers that orthodox medicine cannot give. As Malinowski sagely observed, the use of magic springs not only from human anxiety but from dauntless human optimism.

Americans probably know no greater anxiety than that brought on by competitive performance. A good portion of our gross national product comes from the consumption of items advertised as aids in reducing worries about self-presentation at work and in interaction with the opposite sex. Preparation for a job interview or a big date means reaching for deodorants, skin creams, mouth washes, perfumes, cosmetics, and hair dryers, to mention only a few magical devices available for individual use. When under special pressure, we prove resourceful in investing odd objects and symbols with a magical good luck to tip the scales of fate in a favorable direction. George Gmelch had to go no farther than to American professional baseball players to find a system of magical beliefs that was fully supportive of the thesis that the higher the risks, the greater the reliance on the unscientific.

The final essay on the subject of rituals and symbols turns our attention to the rise of religious sects and the function of group rituals in resolving social pressures. A hundred years ago, the Appalachian serpent-handlers described by Nathan L. Gerrard did not exist. Today this offshoot of southern Protestantism serves the religious needs of a sizeable rural population and has gained a good measure of acceptance in urban areas.

The how and why of new cults and sects is a complex subject, but one that has received substantial attention in anthropology. Since the first missionaries settled among native people, the incorporation and transformation of Christian elements within already-existing belief systems has been commonplace. The literature on nativisitic and revivalistic religions clearly indicates the redefinition of values and goals and the unification of the community that is achieved by faith. From the Ghost Dance of the western plains to the cargo cults of the Pacific islands, the amalgam of Western and non-Western theologies evolved as a defense against extraordinary, often brutal, pressures for social change.

It is no less true today that religion serves to unite dispersed groups, giving purpose to political grievances, as in Northern Ireland and Lebanon, or meaning to the lives of individuals who are otherwise alienated from modern society. American society and Western civilization in general are in an era of tremendous religious activity, demonstrated by new movements within Christianity and the growing popularity of Eastern sects. Part of this activity represents a rejection of science and a loss of faith in technological progress, a retreat from the problems of imposing a moral order on technology that is certain to prove dangerous. The turn of young people in particular toward religion also indicates the need for a structured world view by which to organize a meaningful life. With our heavy cultural investment in scientific rationality, it is easy to underestimate the extent to which religion, ritual, and magic are profoundly rational in accounting for the significant problems of human motivation and the inescapable fact of death. As much as any so-called primitives, the "civilized" peoples require a sense of destiny. More than people living in traditional, small communities, however, we are educated to act and think as individuals who are free in our ability to make choices but who are prey to tremendous isolation from others, unless, of course, we consciously choose to "belong." Religious belief eases one of man's greatest fears, the fear of loneliness, by giving the individual the spiritual context of shared values and symbols. The tension between individuality and the need to belong is as old as the first human community. In its contemporary form, the problem has become one of maintaining individual will while sharing in a moral vision of society. In his classic study, *Escape From Freedom,* Erich Fromm stated the alternatives in a way that merits repeating here:

> ... man, the more he gains freedom in the sense of emerging from the original oneness with man and nature and the more he becomes an "individual," has no choice but to unite himself with the world in the spontaneity of love and productive work or else to seek a kind of security by such ties with the world as destroy his freedom and the integrity of his individual self.

References

Boas, Franz. 1888. *The Central Eskimo,* Washington, D.C.: Annual Reports of the Bureau of American Ethnology.
Boas, Franz. 1963. *The Mind of Primitive Man.* New York: Free Press. (Orig. published 1911).
Durkheim, E. 1961. *The Elementary Forms of the Religious Life.* New York: Collier Books. (Orig. published 1912).
Evans-Pritchard, E.E. 1937. *Witchcraft, Oracles, and Magic among the Azande.* Oxford: Clarendon Press.
Evans-Pritchard, E.E. 1965. *Theories of Primitive Religion.* Oxford: Clarendon Press.
Fortune, Reo F. 1932. *The Sorcerers of Dobu: The Social Anthropology of the Dobu Islanders of the Western Pacific.* London: G. Routledge & Sons, Ltd.
Frazer, J.G. 1911-1915. *The Golden Bough: A Study of Magic and Religion.* 3rd ed. 2 vols. London: Macmillan.
Freud, Sigmund. 1918. *Totem and Taboo; Resemblances Between the Psychic Lives of Savages and Neurotics,* A. Brill, trans. New York: Moffat, Yard and Co. (Orig. published 1912).

Kluckhohn, Clyde. 1944. *Navaho Witchcraft*. Cambridge, Mass.: Peabody Museum of American Ethnology and Archaeology.

Lessa, William Armand, and Evon Z. Vogt. 1972. *Reader in Comparative Religion: An Anthropological Approach*. 3rd ed. New York: Harper & Row.

Lévy-Bruhl, L. 1966. *Primitive Mentality*. L.A. Clare, trans. Boston: Beacon Press. (Orig. published 1923).

Lewis, I.M. 1971. *Ecstatic Religion: An Anthropological Study of Spirit Possession and Shamanism*. Harmondsworth, England: Penguin Books.

Linton, R. 1943. "Nativistic Movements." *American Anthropologist* 45: 230-240.

McLennan, J.F. 1869. "The Worship of Animals and Plants." *The Fortnightly Review* 6: 407-427, 562-582.

McLennan, J.F. 1870. "The Worship of Plants and Animals." *The Fortnightly Review* 7: 194-216.

Mair, L. 1969. *Witchcraft*. New York: McGraw-Hill.

Malinowski, Bronislaw. 1948. *Magic, Science, and Religion*, Boston: Beacon Press.

Miner, H. 1956. "Body Ritual Among the Nacirema." *American Anthropologist* 58: 503-507.

Morgan, L.H. 1963. *Ancient Society*. Cleveland: World Publishing. (Orig. published 1877).

Radin, P. 1957. *Primitive Man as Philosopher*. New York: Dover. (Orig. published 1927).

Spencer, H.L. 1896. *Principles of Sociology*. 3 vols. London: Willams and Norgate. (Orig. published 1876).

Swanson, G.E. 1960. *The Birth of the Gods: The Origin of Primitive Beliefs*. Ann Arbor: University of Michigan Press.

Turner, Victor. 1967. *The Forest of Symbols*. Ithaca, N.Y.: Cornell University Press.

Tylor, E.B. 1873. *Primitive Culture: Researchers into the Development of Mythology, Philosophy, Religion, Language, Art, and Custom*. 2nd ed. 2 vols. London: John Murray.

van Gennep, Arnold. 1960. *The Rites of Passage*. Chicago: University of Chicago Press. (Orig. published 1909).

Wallace, A.F.C. 1966. *Religion: An Anthropological View*. New York: Random House.

Worsley, Peter. 1968. *The Trumpet Shall Sound: A Study of "Cargo" Cuts in Melanesia*. 2nd ed. New York: Schocken Books.

7.
Rebirth in the Airborne
Melford S. Weiss

When an American paratrooper first learns to jump, he does more than step out of an airplane. He steps into a new way of life. Furthermore, his training even takes note of this major transition in his life in a formal ceremonial manner. This training period—marked by pomp and circumstance, superstition and ritual—is what anthropologists refer to as a *rite of passage.*

Rites of passage are universal features of complex as well as simple societies. They mark critical changes in man's life cycle, such as birth, death, and initiation. The paratrooper training program can best be understood as an initiation, a form of entry into an elite group. The process is interwoven with magical and symbolic ritual practices. In one training unit, for example, each time the trainees enter the airplane, the jumpmaster draws a line on the ground in front of the entrance hatch with the toe of his boot. Each prospective jumper then stomps upon the line before entering the airplane in order to ensure a safe landing. Whether or not they actually believe in the practice (many do not) is of decidedly less importance than the fact that this ritual serves to bind the group together.

A paratrooper's training ends in a ceremonial climax. At the close of training it is customary in some military units to reenact the jumping procedure in a fashion symbolic of rebirth. Newly qualified paratroopers are invited to a "prop blast" at the noncommissioned officers' club. There a wooden model of an airplane has been hastily rigged. The new initiates line up in jump formation inside the plane. They jump and land facing the jumpmaster, their instructor. He hands each a loving cup full of "blast juice." This must be quaffed within the count of "1000, 2000, 3000," the time between an actual jump from a plane and the opening of the chute. Failure to drain it to the dregs within the allotted span is called a "malfunction," the term for chute failure. The process must be repeated, perhaps three or four times, till success is achieved. Then the initiate is ritually one with his fellows.

Initiation Rites

Rites of passage vary in different cultures, but according to Arnold Van Gennep a typical rite has three stages: *separation* from the former group or state; *transition* to the new; and, finally, *incorporation*. In birth and death rites, for example, separation is emphasized most: "The Lord giveth, the Lord has taken away." In the case of paratrooper training the transitional phase is most important. The paratrooper rite described here is a composite of training programs of many groups from World War II to the present time.

The paratrooper school is inside a compound surrounded by barbed wire and guarded by sentries. In this compound the trainee is fed, trained, and occasionally entertained. He is allowed to go out in the evening but usually does so in the company of other troopers. Fraternization with the non-paratrooper world is not encouraged, but separation from the former civilian environment is only partial.

The transitional phase usually lasts three weeks. During the last week the candidate makes five practice jumps which mark stages in his progress toward final acceptance. Not all the jumps are equally important—the first and fifth are most significant.

Paratrooper training is officially a secular affair. But certain superstitious practices which are interwoven show that, in the broadest sense, it is also a religious rite. From the beginning of the transition period the trainees are subjected to continuous periods of anxiety. Since they are all volunteers with a strong emotional investment in success, these stresses serve to bind them more closely to one another and to the group they seek to enter. So do the "magical" devices they learn to use to relieve anxiety. These include the wearing of charms and fetishes, such as a girl friend's picture above the heart, a pair of sweat socks worn on a previous successful jump, or a replica of the "trooper wings" placed inside a boot.

Use of "sympathetic magic" is fostered by the paratrooper mythology to which the trainee is exposed during this stage. The following examples of paratrooper tales illustrate elements of both *mana* (a spiritual force independent of persons or spirits which explains success, excellence, and potency when these qualities are not otherwise explainable) and *taboo* (a prohibition based upon the assumption that disastrous consequences can be averted if certain acts are not performed):

He was a jinx and was always present at any accident. I would never jump with him in my line. I once touched him before I was about to jump and pretended to be sick in order to avoid jumping that day. Nobody laughed at me when I told them the real reason.

A master jumper told this story: "When I was a youngster, I felt that should I ever lose my original set of wings I could never jump again. They had a natural magic about them which protected me. When I went home I put them in the bottom drawer of my mother's dresser. I knew they would be safe there!"

Legend maintains that the paratrooper compound is off limits, and one myth relates the unhappy story of the intoxicated soldier from another unit who tried to sneak into the compound and was found next morning with his face severely scratched. The soldier claimed that he was attacked by a small bird and then passed out. But paratroopers claim that the bird was in fact the "screaming eagle," the totemic symbol of the 101st Airborne Division.

During the transition period myth and magic help the trainee to identify with paratroopers in general and share their *esprit de corps*. This becomes a formidable force as airborne units are made up entirely of volunteers. Thus a man becomes a paratrooper by choice and remains one all his military life unless he disobeys a direct order to jump. As in the case of other select military units, paratroopers are bound to one another by pride in a common history and system of training. They consider themselves superior to all other such groups—not only in their military virtues, but in their vices as well. A paratrooper is supposed to be able to outdrink, outbrawl, and outwhore any other member of the armed forces.

The Jumpout Dropout

Systems of initiation depend for their success upon how much the candidate wants to belong to the group. Sometimes, in the case of paratrooper training, he may not want to badly enough. A young man may decide he does not care to spend his active life plunging out of airplanes with nothing but the silkworm's art for support. Since all trainees are volunteers, this is technically no disgrace. All he has to do is request reassignment.

But because of the problem of preserving group morale the dropout is usually eliminated with almost indecent haste. Many instructors feel that to let him hang around will spread the "rot," and other failures or jumping accidents may result. When a would-be dropout says he wants out at the end of a training day, he is more than likely to be called to the orderly room during the next morning's formation. By the time the other trainees return from their midday meal he will have left the training area forever, usually to spend a month's KP duty in some nonelite holding company. For example one dropout said:

> I was scared and I knew it. I dared not let the others know, but I did not think I could hide it very long. We were listening to a master jumper telling us about his first jump and my stomach got queasy and I was sick. I told my sergeant I wanted out. I left the very next day.

If a trainee should quit during the training day, particularly with a public fuss, more brusque tactics may be used. One would-be paratrooper reports:

> I was fed up with this bastard. I made a scene and cursed the Army and shouted that you can shove the paratroopers. I yelled, "I quit." My training NCO rapidly approached me, ripped the patch from my shoulder, and cut the laces of my jump boots.

In some primitive societies those who fail the tests of manhood may be killed outright. The ripping of the patch and the cutting of the laces serves the same function symbolically. It signifies the separation of the dropout from his companions and thus binds the group more closely together, as does the knowledge that the failure is headed for KP or some other nonstatus duty.

As noted before, the transitional phase of paratrooper training has substages. These occur mainly after the first and fifth (last) practice jump. After the first there is no ceremony, but there is a change in the relationship between the trainees and the seasoned paratroopers. As soon as the jumping experience has been shared, the trainee begins to be treated with at least a modicum of respect by his instructors. Conversation in the barracks becomes less guarded. Before any mention of "spilling silk" or "flying a streamer" was avoided. Now jokes about jumping accidents and chute failures are freely bandied about.

The fifth jump is marked by a definite ritual. After the first four the trainee rolls his own chute. After the last he hands it to the platoon sergeant, who rolls it for him and places it in the supply truck. Then the NCO shakes his pupil's hand, congratulates him, and in some cases invites him to use his, the sergeant's, given name. This reversal of roles marks acceptance into the group. The same evening this is confirmed at a party at the enlisted men's club, usually off limits to officers. The paratroopers-to-be, including officer candidates, are invited to join in the drinking and usually do.

The whole transitional period in paratrooper training closely parallels initiation rites in both Western and non-Western societies. During this stage the initiate learns the formulas, gestures, and chants of the brotherhood. These include a paratrooper prayer and a paratrooper song. The latter is a gruesome chant in which the paratrooper verbalizes, jokingly, his fear of sudden and gory death. It is sung to the tune of "The Battle Hymn of the Republic":

Is everybody ready? cried the Sergeant, looking up.
Our hero feebly answered yes, as they stood him up.
He leapt right out into the blast, his static line unhooked.
O he ain't gonna jump no more!

There was blood upon the risers, there were brains upon the chute.
His intestines were a dangling from his paratrooper boots;
They picked him up still in his chute and poured him from his boots;
O he ain't gonna jump no more!

CHORUS: Glory gory what a helluva way to die!
Glory gory what a helluva way to die!
Glory gory what a helluva way to die!
Oh he ain't gonna jump no more!

Wings and a Three-Day Pass

After transition comes incorporation in two stages—an official ceremony and the unofficial "prop blast" described earlier. The official ceremony is a colorful affair in the tradition of most military rituals. It marks the end of the rigorous training and is a welcome climax to weeks of agonizing tension. It takes place the day after the final (fifth) practice jump. The men in the training unit line up in alphabetical order; uniforms are smartly pressed, faces agonizingly clean shaven, and hair close cropped. They stand at attention while the post band plays the national anthem, followed by "Ruffles and Flourishes." The division flag flies just beneath Old Glory.

The men bow their heads as the post chaplain reads from the Bible. After a congratulatory speech the training commandant presents each man with his diploma. The division commandant passes through the ranks, reviews the troops, and pins "wings" to each man's chest. The chaplain delivers the closing benediction. The band continues to play military music as the men now assemble by training platoon and proudly march by the reviewing stand. As the soldiers reach the stand, they are saluted by the senior officers, and the new troopers return the salute. The men are then dismissed and given a three-day pass.

Many features of this ceremony have symbolic significance. The new paratrooper is being initiated into a special brotherhood within the military forces of an American, predominantly Christian, society. The chaplain's benediction gives the ceremony "divine sanction" and links it, however tenuously, with the prevailing Christian religion. The "American heritage" is reflected by the American flag and the national anthem. The polished boots, clean shaves, and close haircuts set up the image of the "clean-cut, all-American boy." The rest of the rite is military, with calculated differences. The marching, the salute, the respect for rank, and the three-day pass remind the paratrooper that he is a member of the armed forces. But the jump-school graduation certificate and the "wings" belong only to paratroopers and serve as permanent marks of that status.

The brotherhood of all troopers is symbolized by the formation itself. While the platoon is the standard military unit, on this one day the men line up in alphabetical order. This wipes out platoon distinctions and incorporates all the men in a pan-paratrooper sodality. Being saluted first by their superiors, against military protocol, shows the "troopers" that they now occupy a coveted status in the military.

Although the training NCOs are not required to attend, they are present throughout the ceremony. At the close they rush to congratulate the new members and welcome them into the brotherhood. The new status of the members has now been recognized and sanctioned by military society With the evening's "prop blast" and its symbolic reenactment of the jumping process, the rite of passage is complete. The initiate is now wholly separated from his past life and "reborn" into a new, select brotherhood and a new way of life.

8.
Baseball Magic

George Gmelch

We find magic wherever the elements of chance and accident, and the emotional play between hope and fear have a wide and extensive range. We do not find magic wherever the pursuit is certain, reliable, and well under the control of rational methods.

Bronislaw Malinowski

Professional baseball is a nearly perfect arena in which to test Malinowski's hypothesis about magic. The great anthropologist was not, of course, talking about sleight of hand but of rituals, taboos and fetishes that men resort to when they want to ensure that things go their own way. Baseball is rife with this sort of magic, but, as we shall see, the players use it in some aspects of the game far more than in others.

Everyone knows that there are three essentials of baseball—hitting, pitching and fielding. The point is, however, that the first two, hitting and pitching, involve a high degree of chance. The pitcher is the player least able to control the outcome of his own efforts. His best pitch may be hit for a bloop single while his worst pitch may be hit directly to one of his fielders for an out. He may limit the opposition to a single hit and lose, or he may give up a dozen hits and win. It is not uncommon for pitchers to perform well and lose, and vice versa; one has only to look at the frequency with which pitchers end a season with poor won-lost percentages but low earned run averages (number of runs given up per game). The opposite is equally true: some pitchers play poorly, giving up many runs, yet win many games. In brief, the pitcher, regardless of how well he performs, is dependent upon the proficiency of his teammates, the inefficiency of the opposition and the supernatural (luck).

But luck, as we all know, comes in two forms, and many fans assume that the pitcher's tough losses (close games in which he gave up very few runs) are eventually balanced out by his "lucky" wins. This is untrue, as a comparison of pitchers' lifetime earned run averages to their overall won-lost records shows. If the player could apply a law of averages to individual performance, there would be much less concern about chance and uncertainty in baseball. Unfortunately, he cannot and does not.

Hitting, too, is a chancy affair. Obviously, skill is required in hitting the ball hard and on a line. Once the ball is hit, however, chance plays a large role in determining where it will go, into a waiting glove or whistling past a falling stab.

With respect to fielding, the player has almost complete control over the outcome. The average fielding percentage takes place on the field. Many baseball fans have observed this behavior never realizing that it may be as important to the pitcher as throwing the ball.

Dennis Grossini, former Detroit farmhand, practiced the following ritual on each pitching day for the first three months of a winning season. First, he arose from bed at exactly 10:00 A.M. and not a minute earlier or later. At 1:00 P.M. he went to the nearest restaurant for two glasses of iced tea and a tuna fish sandwich. Although the afternoon was free, he observed a number of taboos such as no movies, no reading and no candy. In the clubhouse he changed into the sweat shirt and jock he wore during his last winning game, and one hour before the game he chewed a wad of Beechnut chewing tobacco. During the game he touched his letters (the team name on his uniform) after each pitch and straightened his cap after each ball. Before the start of each inning he replaced the pitcher's rosin bag next to the spot where it was the inning before. And after every inning in which he gave up a run he went to the clubhouse to wash his hands. I asked him which part of the ritual was most important. He responded: "You can't really tell what's most important so it all becomes important. I'd be afraid to change anything. As long as I'm winning I do everything the same. Even when I can't wash my hands [this would occur when he must bat] it scares me going back to the mound....I don't feel quite right."

One ritual, unlike those already mentioned, is practiced to improve the power of the baseball bat. It involves sanding the bat until all the varnish is removed, a process requiring several hours of labor, then rubbing rosin into the grain of the bat before finally heating it over a flame. This ritual treatment supposedly increases the distance the ball travels after being struck. Although some North Americans prepare their bats in this fashion it is more popular among Latin Americans. One informant admitted that he was not certain of the effectiveness of the treatment. But, he added, "There may not be a God, but I go to church just the same."

Despite the wide assortment of rituals associated with pitching and hitting, I never observed any ritual related to fielding. In all my 20 interviews only one player, a shortstop with acute fielding problems, reported any ritual even remotely connected to fielding.

Taboo

Mentioning that a no-hitter is in progress and crossing baseball bats are the two most widely observed taboos. It is believed that if the pitcher hears the words "no-hitter" his spell will be broken and the no-hitter lost. As for the crossing of bats, that is sure to bring bad luck; batters are therefore extremely careful not to drop their bats on top of another. Some players elaborate this taboo even further. On one occasion a teammate became quite upset when another player tossed a bat from the batting cage and it came to rest on top of his. Later he explained that the top bat would steal hits from the lower one. For him, then, bats contain a finite number of hits, a kind of baseball "image of limited good." Honus Wagner, a member of baseball's Hall of Fame, believed that each bat was good for only 100 hits and no more. Regardless of the quality of the bat he would discard it after its 100th hit.

Besides observing the traditional taboos just mentioned, players also observe certain personal prohibitions. Personal taboos grow out of exceptionally poor performances, which a player often attributes to some particular behavior or food. During my first season of professional baseball I once ate pancakes before a game in which I struck out four times. Several weeks later I had a repeat performance, again after eating pancakes. The result was a pancake taboo in which from that day on I never ate pancakes during the season. Another personal taboo, born out of similar circumstances, was against holding a baseball during the national anthem.

Taboos are also of many kinds. One athlete was careful never to step on the chalk foul lines or the chalk lines of the batter's box. Another would never put on his cap until the game started and would not wear it at all on the days he did not pitch. Another had a movie taboo in which he refused to watch a movie the day of a game. Often certain uniform numbers become taboo. If a player has a poor spring training or a bad year, he may refuse to wear the same uniform number again. I would not wear double numbers, especially 44 and 22. On several occasions, teammates who were playing poorly requested a change of uniform during the middle of the season. Some players consider it so important that they will wear the wrong size uniform just to avoid a certain number or to obtain a good number.

Again, with respect to fielding, I never saw or heard of any taboos being observed, though of course there were some taboos, like the uniform numbers, that were concerned with overall performance and so included fielding.

Fetishes

These are standard equipment for many baseball players. They include a wide assortment of objects: horsehide covers of old baseballs, coins, bobby pins, protective cups, crucifixes and old bats. Ordinary objects are given this power in a fashion similar to the formation of taboos and rituals. The player during an exceptionally hot batting or pitching streak, especially one in which he has "gotten all the breaks," credits some unusual object, often a new possession, for his good fortune. For example, a player in a slump might find a coin or an odd stone just before he begins a hitting streak. Attributing the improvement in his performance to the new object, it becomes a fetish, embodied with supernatural power. While playing for Spokane, Dodger pitcher Alan Foster forgot his baseball shoes on a road trip and borrowed a pair from a teammate to pitch. That night he pitched a no-hitter and later, needless to say, bought the shoes from his teammate. They became his most prized possession.

Fetishes are taken so seriously by some players that their teammates will not touch them out of fear of offending the owner. I once saw a fight caused by the desecration of a fetish. Before the game, one player stole the fetish, a horsehide baseball cover, out of a teammate's back pocket. The prankster did not return the fetish until after the game, in which the owner of the fetish went hitless, breaking a batting streak. The owner, blaming his inability to hit on the loss of the fetish, lashed out at the thief when the latter tried to return it.

Rube Waddel, an old-time Philadelphia Athletic pitching great, had a hairpin fetish. However, the hairpin he possessed was only powerful as long as he won. Once he lost a game he would look for another hairpin, which had to be found on the street, and he would not pitch until he found another.

The use of fetishes follows the same pattern as ritual and taboo in that they are connected only with hitting or pitching. In nearly all cases the player expressed a specific purpose for carrying a fetish, but never did a player perceive his fetish as having any effect on his fielding.

I have said enough, I think, to show that many of the beliefs and practices of professional baseball players are magical. Any empirical connection between the ritual, taboo and fetishes and the desired event is quite absent. Indeed, in several instances the relationship between the cause and effect, such as eating tuna fish sandwiches to win a ball game, is even more remote than is characteristic of primitive magic. Note, however, that unlike many forms of primitive magic, baseball magic is usually performed to achieve one's own end and not to block someone else's. Hitters do not tap their bats on the plate to hex the pitcher, but to improve their own performance.

Finally, it should be plain that nearly all the magical practices that I participated in, observed or elicited, support Malinowski's hypothesis that magic appears in situations of chance and uncertainty. The large amount of uncertainty in pitching and hitting best explains the elaborate magical practices used for these activities. Conversely, the high success rate in fielding, .975, involving much less uncertainty, offers the best explanation for the absence of magic in this realm.

9.
The Serpent-Handling Religions of West Virginia

Nathan L. Gerrard

... And these signs shall follow them that believe; In my name shall they cast out devils; they shall speak with new tongues; They shall take up serpents; and if they drink any deadly thing, it shall not hurt them; they shall lay hands on the sick, and they shall recover.

Mark 16:17-18

In Southern Appalachia, two dozen or three dozen fundamentalist congregations take this passage literally and "take up serpents." They use copperheads, water moccasins, and rattlesnakes in their religious services.

The serpent-handling ritual was inaugurated between 1900 and 1910, probably by George Went Hensley. Hensley began evangelizing in rural Grasshopper Valley, Tenn., then traveled widely throughout the South, particularly in Kentucky, spreading his religion. He died in Florida at 70— of snakebite. To date, the press has reported about 20 such deaths among the serpent-handlers. One other death was recorded last year, in Kentucky.

For seven years, my wife and I have been studying a number of West Virginia serpent-handlers, primarily in order to discover what effect this unusual form of religious practice has on their lives. Although serpent-handling is outlawed by the state legislatures of Kentucky, Virginia, and Tennessee and by municipal ordinances in North Carolina, it is still legal in West Virginia. One center is the Scrabble Creek Church of All Nations in Fayette County, about 37 miles from Charleston. Another center is the Church of Jesus in Jolo, McDowell County, one of the most poverty-stricken areas of the state. Serpent-handling is also practiced sporadically elsewhere in West Virginia, where it is usually led by visitors from Scrabble Creek or Jolo.

The Jolo church attracts people from both Virginia and Kentucky, in addition to those from West Virginia. Members of the Scrabble Creek church speak with awe of the Jolo services, where people pick up large handfuls of poisonous snakes, fling them to the ground, pick them up again, and thrust them under their shirts or blouses, dancing ecstatically. We attended one church service in Scrabble Creek where visitors from Jolo covered their heads with clusters of snakes and wore them as crowns.

Serpent-handling was introduced to Scrabble Creek in 1941 by a coal miner from Harlan, Ky. The practice really began to take hold in 1946, when the present leader of the Scrabble Creek church, then a member of the Church of God, first took up serpents. The four or five original serpent-handlers in Fayette County met at one another's homes until given the use of an abandoned one-room school house in Big Creek. In 1959, when their number had swelled several times over, they moved to a larger church in Scrabble Creek.

Snakebites, Saints, and Scoffers

During the course of our seven-year study, about a dozen members of the church received snakebites. (My wife and I were present on two of these occasions.) Although there were no deaths, each incident was widely and unfavorably publicized in the area. For their part, the serpent-handlers say the Lord causes a snake to strike in order to refute scoffers' claims that the snakes' fangs have been pulled. They see each recovery from snakebite as a miracle wrought by the Lord—and each death as a sign that the Lord "really had to show the scoffers how dangerous it is to obey His commandments." Since adherents believe that death brings one to the throne of God, some express an eagerness to die when He decides they are ready. Those who have been bitten and who have recovered seem to receive special deference from other members of the church.

The ritual of serpent-handling takes only 15 or 20 minutes in religious sessions that are seldom shorter than four hours. The rest of the service includes singing Christian hymns, ecstatic dancing, testifying, extemporaneous and impassioned sermons, faith-healing, "speaking in tongues," and foot-washing. These latter rituals are a part of the firmly-rooted Holiness movement, which encompasses thousands of churches in the Southern Appalachian region. The Holiness churches started in the 19th century as part of a perfectionist movement.

The social and psychological functions served by the Scrabble Creek church are probably very much the same as those served by the more conventional Holiness churches. Thus, the extreme danger of the Scrabble

Creek rituals probably helps to validate the members' claims to holiness. After all, the claim that one is a living saint is pretentious even in a sacred society—and it is particularly difficult to maintain in a secular society. That the serpent-handler regularly risks his life for his religion is seen as evidence of his saintliness. As the serpent-handler stresses over and over, "I'm afraid of snakes like anybody else, but when God anoints me, I handle them with joy." The fact that he is usually not bitten, or if bitten usually recovers, is cited as further evidence of his claim to holiness.

After we had observed the Scrabble Creek serpent-handlers for some time, we decided to give them psychological tests. We enlisted the aid of Auke Tellegen, department of psychology, University of Minnesota, and three of his clinical associates: James Butcher, William Schofield, and Anne Wirt. They interpreted the Minnesota Multiphasic Personality Inventory that we administered to 50 serpent-handlers (46 were completed) —and also to 90 members of a conventional-denomination church 20 miles from Scrabble Creek. What we wanted to find out was how these two groups differed.

What we found were important personality differences not only between the serpent-handlers and the conventional church members, but also between the older and the younger generations within the conventional group. We believe that these differences are due, ultimately, to differences in social class: The serpent-handlers come from the nonmobile working class (average annual income: $3000), whereas members of the conventional church are upwardly mobile working-class people (average annual income: $5000) with their eyes on the future.

But first, let us consider the similarities between the two groups. Most of the people who live in the south central part of West Virginia, serpent-handlers or not, have similar backgrounds. The area is rural, nonfarm, with only about one-tenth of the population living in settlements of more than 2500. Until recently, the dominant industry was coal-mining, but in the last 15 years mining operations have been drastically curtailed. The result has been widespread unemployment. Scrabble Creek is in that part of Appalachia that has been officially declared a "depressed area"—which means that current unemployment rates there often equal those of the depression.

There are few foreign-born in this part of West Virginia. Most of the residents are of Scottish-Irish or Pennsylvania Dutch descent, and their ancestors came to the New World so long ago that there are no memories of an Old World past.

Generally, public schools in the area are below national standards. Few people over 50 have had more than six or seven years of elementary education.

Religion has always been important here. One or two generations ago, the immediate ancestors of both serpent-handlers and conventional-church members lived in the same mining communities and followed roughly the same religious practices. Today there is much "back-sliding," and the majority seldom attend church regularly. But there is still a great deal of talk about religion, and there are few professed atheists.

Hypochondria and the Holy Spirit

Though the people of both churches are native-born Protestants with fundamentalist religious beliefs, little education, and precarious employment, the two groups seem to handle their common problems in very different ways. One of the first differences we noticed was in the way the older members of both churches responded to illness and old age. Because the members of both churches had been impoverished and medically neglected during childhood and young adulthood, and because they had earned their livelihoods in hazardous and health-destroying ways, they were old before their time. They suffered from a wide variety of physical ailments. Yet while the older members of the conventional church seemed to dwell morbidly on their physical disabilities, the aged serpent-handlers seemed able to cheerfully ignore their ailments.

The serpent-handlers, in fact, went to the opposite extreme. Far from being pessimistic hypochondriacs like the conventional-church members, the serpent-handlers were so intent on placing their fate in God's benevolent hands that they usually failed to take even the normal precautions in caring for their health. Three old serpent-handlers we knew in Scrabble Creek were suffering from serious cardiac conditions. But when the Holy Spirit moved them, they danced ecstatically and violently. And they did this without any apparent harm.

No matter how ill the old serpent-handlers are, unless they are actually prostrate in their beds they manage to attend and enjoy church services lasting four to six hours, two or three times a week. Some have to travel long distances over the mountains to get to church. When the long sessions are over, they appear refreshed rather than weary.

One evening an elderly woman was carried into the serpent-handling church in a wheelchair. She had had a severe stroke and was almost completely paralyzed. Wheeled to the front of the church, she watched everything throughout the long services. During one particularly frenzied singing and dancing session, the fingers of her right hand tapped lightly against the arm of the chair. This was the only movement she was able to make, but obviously she was enjoying the service. When friends leaned over and offered to take her home, she made it clear she was not ready to go. She stayed until the end, and gave the impression of smiling when she was finally wheeled out. Others in the church apparently felt pleased rather than depressed by her presence.

Both old members of the conventional denomination and old serpent-handlers undoubtedly are frequently visited by the thought of death. Both rely on religion for solace, but the serpent-handlers evidently are more successful. The old serpent-handlers are not frightened by the prospect of death. This is true not only of those members who handle poisonous snakes in religious services, but also of the minority who do *not* handle serpents.

One 80-year-old member of the Scrabble Creek church—who did not handle serpents—testified in our presence: "I am not afraid to meet my Maker in Heaven. I am ready. If somebody was to wave a gun in my face, I would not turn away. I am in God's hands."

Another old church member, a serpent-handler, was dying from silicosis. When we visited him in the hospital he appeared serene, although he must have known that he would not live out the week.

The assertion of some modern theologians that whatever meaning and relevance God once may have had has been lost for modern man does not apply to the old serpent-handlers. To them, God is real. In fact, they often see Him during vivid hallucinations. He watches over the faithful. Misfortune and even death do not shake their faith, for misfortune is interpreted, in accordance with God's inscrutable will, as a hidden good.

Surprisingly, the contrast between the optimistic old serpent-handlers and the pessimistic elders of the conventional church all but disappeared when we shifted to the younger members of the two groups. Both groups of young people, on the psychological tests, came out as remarkably well adjusted. They showed none of the neurotic and depressive tendencies of the older conventional-church members. And this cheerful attitude prevailed despite the fact that many of them, at least among the young serpent-handlers, had much to be depressed about.

The young members of the conventional church are much better off, socially and economically, than the young serpent-handlers. The parents of the young conventional-church members can usually provide the luxuries that most young Americans regard as necessities. Many conventional-church youths are active in extracurricular activities in high school or are attending college. The young serpent-handlers, in contrast, are shunned and stigmatized as "snakes." Most young members of the conventional denomination who are in high school intend to go on to college, and they will undoubtedly attain a higher socioeconomic status than their parents have attained. But most of the young serpent-handlers are not attending school. Many are unemployed. None attend or plan to attend college, and they often appear quite depressed about their economic prospects.

The young serpent-handlers spend a great deal of time wandering aimlessly up and down the roads of the hollows, and undoubtedly are bored when not attending church. Their conversation is sometimes marked by humor, with undertones of cynicism and bitterness. We are convinced that what prevents many of them from becoming delinquent or demoralized is their wholehearted participation in religious practices that provide an acceptable outlet for their excess energy, and strengthen their self-esteem by giving them the opportunity to achieve "holiness."

Now, how does all this relate to the class differences between the serpent-handlers and the conventional-church group? The answer is that what allows the serpent-handlers to cope so well with their problems—what allows the older members to rise above the worries of illness and approaching death, and the younger members to remain relatively well-adjusted despite their grim economic prospects—is a certain approach to life that is typical of them as members of the stationary working class. The key to this approach is hedonism.

Hopelessness and Hedonism

The psychological tests showed that the young serpent-handlers, like their elders, were more impulsive and spontaneous than the members of the conventional church. This may account for the strong appeal of the Holiness churches to those members of the stationary working class who prefer religious hedonism to reckless hedonism, with its high incidence of drunkenness and illegitimacy. Religious hedonism is compatible with a puritan morality—and it compensates for its constraints.

The feeling that one cannot plan for the future, expressed in religious terms as "being in God's hands," fosters the widespread conviction among members of the stationary working class that opportunities for pleasure must be exploited immediately. After all, they may never occur again. This attitude is markedly different from that of the upwardly mobile working class, whose members are willing to postpone immediate pleasures for the sake of long-term goals.

Hedonism in the stationary working class is fostered in childhood by parental practices that, while demanding obedience in the home, permit the child license outside the home. Later, during adulthood, this orientation toward enjoying the present and ignoring the future is reinforced by irregular employment and the other insecurities of stationary working-class life. In terms of middle-class values, hedonism is self-defeating. But from a psychiatric point of view, for those who actually have little control of their position in the social and economic structure of modern society, it may very well aid acceptance of the situation. This is particularly true when it takes a religious form of expression. Certainly, hedonism and the associated trait of spontaneity seen in the old sepent-handlers form a very appropriate attitude toward life among old people who can no longer plan for the future.

In addition to being more hedonistic than members of the conventional church, the serpent-handlers are also more exhibitionistic. This exhibitionism and the related need for self-revelation are, of course, directly related to the religious practices of the serpent-handling church. But frankness, both about others and themselves, is typical of stationary working-class people in general. To a large extent, this explains the appeal of the Holiness churches. Ordinarily, their members have little to lose from frankness, since their status pretensions are less than those of the upwardly mobile working class, who are continually trying to present favorable images of themselves.

Because the young members of the conventional denomination are upwardly mobile, they tend to regard their elders as "old-fashioned," "stick-in-the-muds," and "ignorant." Naturally, this lack of respect from their children and grandchildren further depresses the sagging morale of the older conventional-church members. They respond resentfully to the tendency of the young "to think they know more than their elders." The result is a vicious circle of increasing alienation and depression among the older members of the conventional denomination.

Respect for Age

There appears to be much less psychological incompatibility between the old and the young serpent-handlers. This is partly because the old serpent-handlers manage to retain a youthful spontaneity in their approach to life. Then too, the young serpent-handlers do not take a superior attitude toward their elders. They admire their elders for their greater knowledge of the Bible, which both old and young accept as literally true. And they also admire their elders for their handling of serpents. The younger church members, who handle snakes much less often than the older members do, are much more likely to confess an ordinary, everyday fear of snakes—a fear that persists until overcome by strong religious emotion.

Furthermore, the young serpent-handlers do not expect to achieve higher socioeconomic status than their elders. In fact, several young men said they would be satisfied if they could accomplish as much. From the point of view of the stationary working class, many of the older serpent-handlers are quite well-off. They sometimes draw two pensions, one from Social Security and one from the United Mine Workers.

Religious serpent-handling, then—and all the other emotionalism of the Holiness churches that goes with it—serves a definite function in the lives of its adherents. It is a safety valve for many of the frustrations of life in present-day Appalachia. For the old, the serpent-handling religion helps soften the inevitability of poor health, illness, and death. For the young, with their poor educations and poor hopes of finding sound jobs, its promise of holiness is one of the few meaningful goals in a future dominated by the apparent inevitability of lifelong poverty and idleness.

Part IV
Family and Sex Roles

Of all the primates, *homo sapiens* is born the weakest and takes the longest time to grow up. The heavy investment of every society in the organization of the family reflects the basic truth that the care and education of each new generation is no easy matter. The safety of the young is the principal business of the domestic unit, although successful child-rearing is subject to no universal formula beyond acknowledgment of the primary responsibilities of blood relations.

Variability in family organization is important to keep in mind, for, as Americans, we tend to operate rather strictly in terms of the small nuclear family. This household unit of a bread-winning father, housewifely mother and dependent children is depicted as the American norm, and, in the media and social policy, other types of households are treated as being deviant. Or at least this used to be the case. The latest U.S. census reminds us that only a third of the nation's households fit the requirements of the model nuclear family. The remaining two-thirds are characterized by two working parents, extended family, communal living arrangements, or single-parent organizations. Even with the census data, it is difficult to generalize about family and kin relations in this country. There are variations in terms of ethnic groups, social class, and geographic region that are implied in social science research; but family life is still a very private area, perhaps the last refuge of privacy in American life.

In contrast, the American institution of marriage is subject to standard legal conventions. In principle, it is a contract binding two consenting individuals of the opposite sex for life. Whether by religious or civil law, protection of the marriage bond is aimed at stabilizing the institution of the family. Although " 'til death do us part" may be written into the conjugal contract, high divorce and remarriage rates in the United States point to the obvious fact that, while Americans like to be married, they don't necessarily like being married to the same spouse for life. Interpretations of marriage rights and obligations and, therefore, the shape and substance of family life are constantly undergoing change, depending on external pressures and the consent of partners. In *Man and Superman*, playwright George Bernard Shaw remarked concerning the term "marriage" that "the absolute confidence of the public in the stability of the institution's name makes it all the easier to alter its substance."

Learning about marriage and family organization in other cultures places our own combination of legal and private dramas in perspective. Although there are a good many small-scale societies in which the nuclear family is the basis of household organization, anthropologists usually have to deal with larger, extended kinship networks. How marriage and family organization are defined varies with the influence of local descent groups. One of the most fascinating cases in the anthropological literature is that of the Nayar of southwest India. Originally a military caste, the Nayar evolved a strongly matrilineal society based on natolocal residence—that is, men returning from war gravitated back to the place where they were born, and women, their mothers and sisters, never left their birthplace. The marriage ceremony conducted by the Nayer was actually a simple ritual confering adult status on a young woman, who from that time was free to live in her own house and to be courted by a succession of lovers until she became pregnant. When her child was born she selected her favorite suitor to go through a ritual acknowledgment of social paternity, but even then, the raising of the infant was the responsibility of the mother and the matrilineage that included, of course, her male and female relatives. The solidarity of the lineage group was maintained by having its members live in one place and by keeping the outsider "husband" at a distance.

The anthropological study of kinship systems begins with the very origins of the discipline, most notably with the work of Lewis Henry Morgan in this country and W. H. R. Rivers in Great Britain. What anthropologists like Morgan and his contemporaries, Sir Henry Maine and J. F. McLennan, were quick to notice was the extent to which kinship relations were the basis of traditional social organization—past and present. Their versions of social evolution, like the models of religious evolution outlined by developmental theorists, speculated on the transition from family-oriented communities to urban and state centers that were organized on objective, contractual principles.

In the search for meaningful comparisons between traditional and civilized life, anthropologists have had to make somewhat the same choice as in linguistic studies, that is, either to research the formal rules of kinship or to concentrate on the social context within which kinship rules are played out. In tracking down formal rules, for example, a basic question to ask about any kinship system is what groups *may* intermarry, and, if there is evidence of prescribed marriage rules, what groups *should* intermarry. In any group, a young man or woman has to exclude as potential partners those with whom marriage would constitute incest, such as parents, siblings, and perhaps (but not always) those individuals who are classified as close relatives. There usually exists a second category to designate strangers outside the group with whom intermarriage is not approved. In one case in village India kinship rules take on a religious dimension: marriage across caste lines is considered ritually polluting, while marriage between members of different descent groups within the caste is encouraged.

In other groups, an occasional infraction of marriage rules is tolerated; or it may be practical to reclassify the relationship of prospective partners by a reinterpretation of their genealogical relations to each other. The perpetuation of any family group can be looked upon in two ways. The first has been characteristic of British emphasis on descent, and it looks upon the kin group as it recruits members and links groups on the basis of a real or assumed common ancestor. Another approach, introduced by Claude Lévi-Strauss in *The Elementary Structures of Kinship*, stresses the alliances established by exchanging women between and among kinship groups. For example, in what is termed "a generalized exchange system," rules for preferred marriage between a trio of separate residence groups insure a closed circle of communication, provided enough young women from group A are willing to move to group B, and those from group B move to group C, and the women from group C take up their wifely chores in group A. The history of European royal families contains enough familiar examples of political marriages to provide analogy with this kind of anthropological alliance theory. Yet the shift from descent to alliance models, which began in the 1950s, represents a radical twist on an old subject. Robin Fox in his book *Kinship and Marriage* summed up the situation by suggesting that we can look upon "genetic" and "alliance" theorists as two historians interested in European dynasties:

> One historian is primarily interested in the ways in which royal houses perpetuated themselves, arranged their rules of succession, and ensured that the succession did not fail. Marriages were means to this end. The other historian, however, sees the royal houses as units in a series of complex alliances binding together various countries, and these alliances are cemented or "expressed" by royal marriages. One sees marriage as useful in providing royal heirs: the other sees royal heirs as useful in that they can be used in dynastic marriages.

Whichever perspective suits the ethnologist, the bare bones of kinship rules are not by themselves sufficient to understand the full implications of kinship as an organizing principle of behavior. This fact was particularly well brought out in the studies of British social anthropologists during the 1930s and 1940s. The publications of A. R. Radcliffe-Brown and E. E. Evans-Pritchard shifted attention to the social network of kin relations that expanded or contracted under different historical pressures. The Nuer, described by Evans-Pritchard, were able to unite thousands of warriors dispersed throughout the southern Sudan when their territory was threatened by British incursions or unfriendly neighbors. Their unity was insured by their claim to common descent from a single ancestor that made all Nuer kin to each other. Lacking aggression from without, the Nuer put aside the larger lineage affiliation for normal, local-level divisions between kin groups. Description of the moral and practical support gained by kinship ties is standard fare in ethnographic accounts, with reportage now extending to family groups in the very center of Western urban life.

In Margery Wolf's essay on Chinese family organization, our attention is drawn to the extended family as a set of interconnecting, well-defined social roles that, in a dynastic sense, link succeeding generations of kin. The basic problem of any lineage system—how to incorporate the "stranger" who is marrying in—is solved within the Taiwan village patrilineage by structuring the relationship between the new young wife and her mother-in-law, both of whom are relegated to the domestic rather than to the public sphere of family activity. In the raising and education of children, then, the rights and responsibilities of each sex are clearly communicated: the power of ancestral traditions and public roles are vested in men, particularly first-born sons; control of the domicile is in the hands of women, particularly older matrons. The Chinese example details how children of each sex come to recognize authority and arbitrate their roles as siblings, spouses, and eventually as parents.

A sharp delineation of sex roles is also characteristic of traditional Moslem culture, described by Lawrence Rosen in the essay "'I Divorce Thee': Moroccan Marriage and the Law." There, as in the Chinese family, the overt power of men is weighed against the domestic influence of women, and both parties bear the burden of tradition in a world that is rapidly changing. What Rosen's article underscores is the increasing intervention of state law in the private realm of family life at a time when customary expectations of sex role behavior—what spouses owe each other, how husbands and wives should properly act—are under enormous external pressure. Is a country socially and economically backward when its women are sheltered at home? Is it more modern when women leave home for public schooling and jobs? Are the interests of the state, in the last analysis, opposed to the successful raising of children? These and other questions about family organization have yet to be answered either in Third World countries or here in the United States.

Behind the dilemma of changing family organization lies a deeper problem concerning the biological determinants of the human. Many years ago, in 1935, anthropologist Margaret Mead wrote a book, *Sex and Temperament in Three Primitive Societies*, in which she argued that feminine characteristics of passivity and male characteristics of aggression, which we have often assumed to be innate qualities of each sex, are not in fact universal. Depending on the particular society, self-assertion and acquiescence are aspects of style that suit either men or women, if culture so dictates. Does the mother-child bond always necessitate a woman's place being in the home? Does the relative freedom of men from child-rearing obligations permit them economic activities not available to women? Clearly, the relationship of any group to the surrounding environment influences the division of labor between the sexes and among age grades, and this, in turn, affects family life. Big-game hunting as part of the economics of a tribe is invariably the province of men, while gathering wild plants tends to be women's work. Other economic activities, however, from pastoralism to farming and trade, are randomly distributed to and shared by men and women in traditional societies.

The two forces that have rocked traditional notions of family life and sex roles are the spread of industrialization and the expansion of educational institutions. Wage labor at the level of unskilled and semiskilled jobs is available regardless of sex; historically, factory workers have been recruited generally from the lower classes, men, women, and children alike. In many small communities, pressures to take another look at old ways of organizing households and interpreting kin responsibilities come from the recognition that women can work for wages. The second factor, which has yet to have its full effect in developing nations, has brought women into middle-range managerial positions that were once the sole domain of men. The increased visibility of contemporary Western women in white-collar jobs has extended the ambition and competence of many others far beyond the homemaker role. It is fitting that we conclude this section with the comments of Margaret Mead on the transformations of family life that these changes are bringing about. We can look to other cultures for alternative domestic organizations that will ease the friction in working-parent families and increase social acceptance of communal and single-parent lifestyles. Even more important, we have to look upon the family as an institution with a life cycle that is considerably shorter than present life expectancy. A century ago, a married couple could expect to spend the greater part of their adult lives caring for dependent children. With the increased life span not only of Americans but of large portions of the global population, the business of parenting occupies only a half, or perhaps less, of the active adult years. As Dr. Mead reminds us, the institution of the family is as viable as ever; what have increased are the personal options for liberating men and women alike from outmoded social roles.

References

Bateson, Gregory. 1958. *Naven.* Stanford: Stanford University Press.
Evans-Pritchard, E.E. 1940. *The Nuer: A Description of the Modes of Livelihood and Political Institutions of a Nilotic People.* Oxford: Clarendon Press.
Fox, Robin. 1967. *Kinship and Marriage: An Anthropological Perspective.* Harmondsworth: Penguin Books.
Gough, K. 1959. "The Nayars and the Definition of Marriage." *Journal of the Royal Anthropological Institute* 89: 23-34.
Hsu, Francis L.K. 1975. *Iemoto: The Heart of Japan.* New York: John Wiley and Sons.
Kroeber, A. 1909. "Classificatory Systems of Relationship." *Journal of the Royal Anthropological Institute* 39: 77-84.
Lévi-Strauss, C. 1969. *The Elementary Structures of Kinship.* Boston: Beacon Press.
McLennan, J.F. 1865. *Primitive Marriage; An Inquiry into the Origin of the Form of Capture in Marriage Ceremonies.* Edinburgh: Black.
Maine, Sir Henry. 1887. *Ancient Law: Its Connection with the Early History of Society and Its Relation to Modern Ideas.* London: J. Murray. (Orig. published 1861).
Mead, M. 1949. *Coming of Age in Samoa.* New York: New American Library. (Orig. published 1928).
Mead, M. 1959. *Sex and Temperament in Three Primitive Societies.* New York: New American Library. (Orig. published 1935).
Morgan, L.H. 1871. *Systems of Consanguinity and Affinity of the Human Family.* Smithsonian Institution Contributions to Knowledge, vol. 17, article 2. Washington, D.C.: Government Printing Office.
Murdock, G.P. 1949. *Social Structure.* New York: Macmillan.
Radcliffe-Brown, A.R., and C.D. Forde, editors. 1950. *African Systems of Kinship and Marriage.* New York: Oxford University Press.
Rosaldo, M.Z., and L. Lamphere, editors. 1974. *Women, Culture and Society.* Stanford: Stanford University Press.
Schneider, David M. 1968. *American Kinship: A Cultural Account.* Englewood Cliffs, N.J.: Prentice-Hall.
Whiting, B.B., editor. 1963. *Six Cultures: Studies of Child Rearing.* New York: John Wiley and Sons.
Whiting, J.W.M., and I. Child. 1953. *Child Training and Personality: A Cross-Cultural Study.* New Haven: Yale University Press.

10.
Child Training and the Chinese Family
Margery Wolf

The Chinese family has been examined in many contexts—from its place in the eonomy to its role in ancestor worship. Only in passing has it been considered in terms of the family's basic function: the training of future adult members. The accumulation of data about socialization processes is essential to our understanding of human behavior and personality development, but even the researcher whose interests are confined to more specific problems may find that such information yields unexpected insights into areas of culture seemingly unrelated to children. The cooperation, or at least interaction, of the entire domestic group is required to one degree or another in the preparation of the family's children for future responsibilities. Adult attitudes and approaches to the job of socialization suggest a great deal about their attitudes toward one another and their evaluation of their own positions in the family.

Generalizations about the Chinese family in this essay are drawn from the experience of a two-and-a-half-year field study of child-training practices in a small village of Hokkien-speakers in northern Taiwan. The research, designed by my husband, Arthur Wolf, had a dual purpose: to carry out a conventional anthropological village study and to replicate the work of the Six Culture Project. The Six Culture Project, under the direction of its senior members, John W. M. Whiting, Irvin L. Child, and William W. Lambert, sent field teams to six different societies to collect systematic information on child rearing, carefully timed observations of child behavior, child interviews, and comparable ethnographic data. Their methodology included techniques traditional to anthropology as well as those confined until then to psychological laboratories. To their elegant design we added, among other things, some homemade projective tests, informal parent observations and interviews, questionnaires administered in local schools, and, in collaboration with W. W. Lambert, a biochemical analysis of the epinephrine and norepinephrine levels of our sample of 64 children.

In the process of observing and interviewing parents, we found that we were being given information beyond that asked for in our specific questions—information that told us much about the dynamics of the family. A Chinese woman's assumptions about the behavior of close kinsmen, assumptions she may be neither willing nor, in many cases, able to express, were often clearly delineated in her responses to questions about who was responsible for feeding and disciplining her child. Although our questioning was nearly always directed toward adult interactions with the family's children, the responses frequently contained spontaneous information about adult interaction with other adults in the family, a type of information, incidentally, that is extremely difficult to elicit by direct questioning. In a sense, our study of child-training practices produced quite accidentally a projective test of the dynamics of the Chinese family. More simply, it provided another perspective from which to examine the Chinese family and the nature of the interactions of its members.

The village of Peihotien (a fictitious name) is located on the edge of the Taipei basin, a fifteen minute walk from the railroad and a half hour from there by train to the city of Taipei. Although the majority of the families in the village own land, few obtain their sole income from the land. Nearly every family has one member who brings in wages from a job outside the village. Peihotien's proximity to an urban center seems to strengthen rather than to weaken family ties. The market town of Tapu (a fictitious name) has, besides a railway station, several small factories that can and do employ the young people of Peihotien. From Tapu it is only fifteen minutes by train to a small city with many employment opportunities. It is feasible in terms of time and it is economically advantageous for the young men and women of the village to remain a part of their parents' domestic units and commute to employment elsewhere. Few young people, including those without obligations to parents in Peihotien, leave the village to be closer to work opportunities.

Mothers and Fathers

Both the mother and the father of a Taiwanese child share the same broad goals in the training of their son. They want him to become a strong healthy adult who is obedient, respectful, and capable of supporting them in their old age. They want a son who will not embarrass or impoverish them by his excesses, who will maintain if not increase their standing in the community, who will handle relations with outsiders skillfully but at the same time keep them at a polite distance. No matter how alienated man and wife may be from each other, they nonetheless share these common aims in regard to their children. The techniques they use to implement these goals differ considerably and, more importantly, so does the intensity of their desire for any particular result in their sons.

A father's relationship with his son is both affectionate and informal until the boy reaches the age of six or seven. In the evenings the small boy accompanies his father on errands about the village, and falls asleep on his father's lap as the older man chats with neighbors and friends. Although fathers do not play games with their children, they are apt to play with them in the manner that an American adult plays with a kitten or puppy. Fathers of young children are usually fairly well prepared with the sweets or pennies that dry the tears resulting from scraped knees and bumped heads. In return a father expects very little. A toddler is too young to understand what his father wants when he asks the child to bring him a packet of cigarettes, and a four-year-old is too young to understand that he must obey his father's command. The child's disobedience is treated with either amusement or tolerance, depending on his age and his father's mood. If the child's infantile behavior becomes annoying, or if, as so often happens with Chinese children, he falls into a kicking, screaming rage over some small (though conclusive) frustration, he is simply turned over to his mother or older sister with little or no paternal comment.

The age of reason has been established by Taiwanese parents at about six years, coinciding in modern times with the child's beginning school. Since this age is unmarked by any ceremony (other than that of starting school), the father's subsequent change in behavior must seem to the child abrupt, bewildering, and drastic. Social pressure and the father's own understanding of "what is right" force him to create a social distance between himself and his son. The sleepy child no longer finds a haven on his father's lap but is told to go to bed. If he decides to shoot one more marble before complying with his father's request to fetch him cigarettes, he hears his name called in the stern, icy voice of the feared schoolmaster. He may still accompany his father about the village for a while, but the behavior expected of him in his father's presence tends to turn the outing into an ordeal not to be repeated if avoidable. As their interaction becomes more and more formal and their conversation deteriorates into paternal lectures, the father's dignity becomes more impressive and more impregnable.

Taiwanese fathers say that it is only from this aloof distance that they can engender in their sons the proper behavior of a good adult. "You cannot be your son's friend and correct his behavior." A child will not take seriously the friendly suggestions of an obviously loving adult, but he will obey the commands of a stern feared parent. This philosophy, of course, reflects (or is reflected in) the educational techniques of Chinese schools even today. Be it unintentional or simply concomitant, this remoteness also builds the supports necessary to maintain the senior male's position of authority over his adult sons. The weakening powers of an aging father, both mental and physical, provide the all-important social justification for a young man desiring independence and/or control of the family destiny. The increasing indecision and faltering that might be revealed in the camaraderie of an informal relationship can be concealed for a considerably longer time when the son is faced with an austere, aloof figure of authority toward whom society demands he show respect and obedience.

Long before they have learned to fear their father, children are aware of his power in the family. On several occasions I have heard a three- or four-year-old imperiously warn his mother to stop interfering with his (usually dangerous) activity lest he summon his father to beat her. Although the father's wrath may not yet have been directed toward him, the child has observed its effect on his mother or his elder siblings. Children with older siblings may not find their father's change of behavior toward them as abrupt or as unexpected as do first- and second-borns. The mother, intentionally or not, provides considerable assistance to her husband in building his image of authority. The recalcitrant child, or the child who has committed a serious misdeed, may be threatened with all sorts of dire punishments, but if he has reached the "age of reason," or has siblings who are six years of age and older, the threat of paternal punishment is one of the most effective. If the mother's threat is actually carried out and the father beats his son, the strokes may be far lighter than the mother's would have been, since the punishment is administered with cool forethought; but perhaps for the same reason the emotional effect on the child is far stronger.

A male is born into a community and grows up there, learning almost unconsciously the idiosyncrasies of his physical environment and of the temperaments of his neighbors and relatives. By the time he reaches adulthood, there is little in his everyday social world that is so surprising or uncertain that he cannot deal with it automatically. His own peculiarities of temperament or behavior have long been accepted (or rejected) by his neighbors and are hardly worthy of comment. He is a member of a family that considers all non-kin as outsiders and of a community that similarly considers all non-residents. Not so the wife of this man. Growing up in a similar social environment in a distant village, she enters a community of outsiders to live with a family that until the day of her marriage has been classified by her as outsiders. Whereas security and familiarity are givens to her husband, to her they are completely absent and may be for many years to come, if not (in her frightened young eyes) forever. In her first few years of marriage, her own children will seem more a part of this new community than she can ever hope to be. Under these conditions, it is not at all surprising that she should give precedence over the inculcation of respect and respectability in her sons to a different set of values. Her concern in her isolation is more with her own personal well-being than with the vague expectations of the somewhat alien world of her husband and his family. To them, her infant son is the next link in a long chain of descendants carrying their name and their future. To her, he is the source of the first bit of security she has felt since she entered the family. He is her defense against her mother-in-law and her sisters-in-law. His birth, providing an object of shared concern, may change her somewhat ambiguous relationship with her husband into a more satisfactory commitment, but if it does not, the dissatisfactions of that relationship will not matter as much. She may simply endure her present situation and build toward a future family environment that will not be hampered by mothers-in-law or be dependent on husbands. No matter what is involved in her current status, the whole quality of her future life depends on the strength of the ties she develops with her son.

The salient difference between what a Chinese mother and a Chinese father hope for in their relations with their sons can best be described in slightly exaggerated terms. A Chinese father wants respect and obedience even at the price of fear or dislike. If he is to maintain his authority over the household when his sons are themselves adults, he must have their respect if not their admiration, their obedience if not their affection. He is aided in his endeavors by the sanctions of his culture, the example of his neighbors, and the teachings of the schools. A Chinese mother would certainly appreciate her son's respect and obedience, but not at the price of his affection. Her marriage into a family of strangers has forced her to depend entirely on herself in constructing working relationships. The degree to which she can depend on those ties is less related to the sanctions of society, the examples of neighbors, or the teachings in the local school than to the intangibles of action, spontaneous gratitude, and goodwill. Chinese culture extracts from a son the obligation of supporting his mother and showing her a minimum degree of respect; but a woman's experience with social sanctions has usually been that they have operated against her position rather than in any way promoting it. Far more dependable are the ties of affection and gratitude that she weaves in the years of her son's childhood.

Chinese society has given a father both the power and the authority to manage his adult sons. A mother's authority is not so clearly stated, and so she must establish her power in a more subtle fashion. For her, the father's method of withdrawal into formality would be both difficult and dangerous. When her son is six years old, she may expect more of him in terms of obedience and chores, but her menial services to him are still a necessity and will be for some time. These services are often extended considerably longer than is necessary, and are referred to again and again when the child is punished. "Why are you so bad? Do you want me to die? Then who will feed you and take care of you?" Mothers seem to be as convinced as fathers that learning does not take place without physical punishment, but mothers administer beatings in a very different atmosphere. The father's beating is usually preceded by a stern lecture on the expectations of the family and administered with a cool temper; the mother's beating usually grows out of the frustrations of the day and is administered in fury (and often as not interrupted by a relative or neighbor). Once her anger has passed, she may comfort the crying child, explaining why she *had* to punish him, or if he has run away before she managed to strike him, she may just let the whole matter go with a few words of warning when he returns. Impending punishments by a father do not blow over. Paternal punishment of a child or of his siblings occurs just often enough to make it a useful threat, one which mothers employ frequently. As mentioned previously, this threat serves to establish more firmly the father's position of familial superiority, but it also has an interesting side effect on the mother's position. She appears in the role of go-between. Each time she makes the threat and does not carry it out, she becomes the child's go-between rather than the father's, the child's ally rather than the father's. An adult son fuming under the continued dominance of his father is far more likely to recall these "interventions" by his mother than the beatings he received at her hands.

 Village mothers state, as do the fathers, that you must not let a child know you love him or you will not be able to correct his behavior, assuming of course that if you love him you will forgive anything. The open expression of affection toward an older child is considered not only in bad taste but bad for the child. One must not praise children for accomplishments or they will feel they have done well enough and will stop trying to do better. Superficially these dicta do seem to be observed. Upon presenting an essay or school report to his father for his chop (to assure the teacher that it has been seen by the parent), a child who has placed second in the class is admonished to reach first place by next year, and if he has placed first he is warned to do as well the following year or expect a beating. The father may swell with pride as he discusses the matter later with the child's grandmother or mother, but he will show no pleasure in the child's presence. If other adults comment on the achievement, the father counters with deprecating remarks about the child's other, bad, characteristics, concealing his pride from no one, except perhaps the child. The mother's reaction to the child's accomplishment will be somewhat the same, but her pleasure will be less carefully concealed from the child; the extra ten cents to buy sweets or the choice piece of food swiftly stuffed into his mouth before the dish goes on the table will not go unrelated to her pride in him. Like his father, his mother rarely pets or hugs him, but unlike the father, she has many other means available to her for expressing her affection: cooking his favorite dishes, granting privileges, or simply listening to childish prattle about the day's happenings at school. The constant interaction between mother and child provides far more opportunity for the mother to influence her child's attitudes than does the briefer more formal interaction of father and son. Most mothers make good use of their opportunities.

The inferior status of female children is not as pronounced in times of prosperity (the present situation in Taiwan) as it is during periods of economic hardship. Sons are of course preferred, but most families want at least one daughter if they can afford her. In general, the treatment of a girl is not dramatically different from that of her brothers. The attitudes her parents hold toward her, however, are quite different. The expectations and consequent behavior of father and mother toward their son are almost reversed when they deal with their daughter. As an adult the daughter will be nearly irrelevant to her father. Very little of his future prestige or his physical comfort in his declining years will depend on anything she does or does not do. The rigid standards of respect and obedience her brother must adhere to as an adult are of less value in her, since she will be in another household. As long as she does not become wantonly immoral while a member of her father's household, she is a luxury he can enjoy. Fathers who are acting against their natural propensities in the treatment of their sons, find considerable satisfaction in a relaxed informal exchange with their daughters. As long as he maintains the general rules of propriety (i.e., does not openly express his affection for her or allow her publicly to disobey him), he is safe from the criticism of his neighbors. Should she turn out to be a poor wife and daughter-in-law, criticism would not be directed at him, her father, but rather at her mother as the person responsible for her training in the domestic arts. Ultimately, the hardship would fall on the girl herself.

An adult daughter will have no more opportunity to add to her mother's comfort or status than she will to her father's. If she turns out to be an excellent mother and daughter-in-law, she will by definition see less of her mother and relegate her to a position of minor importance in the demands on her time and affection. Publicly, or even privately, the mother will receive little credit for having trained her so well. Should the daughter fall short of adult standards, criticism will eventually be directed at her mother's laxness and incompetence. This potential criticism, however, has little influence on the mother's everyday attitude toward training her daughter. Until one of her sons marries and provides her with a daughter-in-law, the services of her daughter are needed. She can afford to smile on the disobedience and arrogance of her son as on interest accumulating on a loan, but the misbehavior of her daughter threatens daily operating expenses. If she has a family of any size at all, she must have someone to help her wash the vegetables, mind the younger children, hang out the clothes. If the mother does not establish early at least the minimum standards of obedience in her daughter, she will suffer for it several times each day. If some degree of responsibility has not been internalized, the mother will not dare leave the girl in charge of infants and toddlers, send her on errands, or depend on her to have the rice washed in time for dinner.

Taiwanese mothers believe that no children can be expected to understand much during their first six years of life. This is not to say that all training is delayed until their sixth birthday, but rather that not much is expected to result from it until after that age. Nonetheless, by the time they are five, most little girls are doing a few chores regularly and certainly are minding their slightly younger siblings. Before this time, the mother's treatment of her sons and daughters is not noticeably different except in one aspect. The techniques the mother employs throughout are essentially the same, but the intensity of the training for girls is considerably stronger. I doubt that there is any conscious intent involved in this; the girls as potential errand-runners and baby-sitters are kept closer to home and thereby receive a larger dose of the medicine administered. Even in behavior not immediately relevant to their mother's requirements for helpers, girls are found to socialize earlier and better than boys. Their performance on a variety of quantitatively measured variables is usually more consistent with the stated adult values at a considerably earlier age.

The warm intimate relationship that mothers desire with their sons they more frequently achieve with their daughters. As the daughter begins to worry about how she herself will fare at the hands of an unknown husband and mother-in-law, her mother's complaints about the behavior of her husband and his relatives fall on a more sympathetic ear. Her father's indulgence does little to increase his stature in his daughter's eyes, and often serves to damage it, since he is unlikely to defend to her his usually harsher public behavior toward her mother. She may retain a real though slightly cynical affection for her father, but the more frequent interaction plus their increasing similarity of interests and anxieties will involve her sympathies more deeply with her mother. The contrast between her mother's worried fretful questioning of the matchmakers and her father's calmer financial evaluations of a proposed match cements the emotional ties between the women. Her father may be, and often is, even more concerned than his wife about the treatment his daughter will recieve at the hands of her husband's family, but as a man he must pretend to consider it irrelevant, and never having experienced this traumatic change himself, he truly is unaware of many of its more painful aspects. It is on her mother's good judgment that the girl must depend. The tears ritually required of bride and mother when the former leaves the home on her wedding day may fall for different reasons, but they rarely are forced.

As young men sons may fear their fathers, but they nonetheless emulate them, rejecting the open intimacy desired by their mothers in favor of a more manly stance. Even so, the mothers' efforts have not, in most cases, been in vain. As age gradually erodes and reverses the relationship between son and father, that existing between son and mother erodes little and reverses only in the way the mother desires. Should her relationship with her husband be antagonistic, the mother may begin early to isolate him by referring decisions about the household economy to her son rather than to the head of the household. As her son's earning capacity increases and his wages come to her for the purchase of daily requirements, she may also discuss with him the advisability of this or that major purchase or the advantages of joining this or that cooperative loan association. This show of trust and increasing dependence both strengthens their relationship and erases any lingering resentment the young man may have of the punishments received at her hands in his youth. Should, on the other hand, the relationship between husband and wife be a happy one, the wife can act as peacemaker between the older man, fearful of losing his hard-won authority, and the younger, impatient to test his own abilities. She can flatter and in many ways train the younger man by referring to him the minor domestic decisions (decisions she might have made herself without consulting her husband) and by discussing the larger decisions with both men, allowing each to feel that his was the decision acted upon. Eventually, however, the two must meet head-on in conflicts outside her domestic sphere, and the inevitable change in authority will proceed either speedily or gradually, depending on the personalities and abilities of the two men. The external pressures of his world demand that the son treat his aging father with respect, but the internal pressures of his socialization demand that he repay his mother with more than respect.

Grandparents

By the time she is a grandmother, a Chinese woman usually has come to regard her husband's family and community as her own. To her daughter-in-law it is inconceivable that the older woman was ever anything but a representative of the interests of that family. Most women are delighted when their son marries and a daughter-in-law enters their home. Unless the marriage is a love-match, the older woman has chosen the girl herself and investigated her qualities and faults as carefully as possible. Because of the exaggerations of go-betweens, she expects a great deal of her daughter-in-law. The girl's mother, her peers, and her own observations have taught the bride what is expected of a daughter-in-law, and she usually enters her husband's family determined to do her best to fulfill these expectations. For the first few months, or perhaps only weeks, after the marriage, there exists between mother-in-law and daughter-in-law that amiable relationship that in the West is supposed to exist between husband and wife during what is called the honeymoon period. Village women laugh at new mothers-in-law singing the praises of their sons' wives, saying, "We'll wait a while and then see." Indeed, they usually have a very short period to wait. The two women's good feelings quickly sour after a series of disagreements about how to pickle radishes, when to wash clothes, how much to spend on excursions, and when to have the evening meal on the table. Regardless of the merits of her position, the older woman is likely to be the victor in any conflict for a good many years to come.

No matter how antagonistic the young wife may feel toward her mother-in-law or how confident in her own abilities, at the birth of her first child she finds herself in need of the older woman as she will at no other time. The child should be born in its father's home, but if this proves impossible, almost anywhere would be preferable to the natal home of its mother. The young woman's mother is sometimes called to be with her during her first delivery, but even if she should arrive in time to help her daughter during her travail, propriety and her own responsibilities prevent her from staying longer than a day or two. During those first few weeks when the infant seems so fragile to the new mother and each act in its care so fraught with disaster, it is to her mother-in-law that she must turn for reassurance and advice. In the months and years that follow, the young mother may come to regret this early dependence and to resent her mother-in-law's continuing advice, but by then the pattern is set. Even with later births, she will need assistance if not advice, and the two seem to be indivisibly joined in the aging Taiwanese female.

In the first few years of her grandchildren's lives, the grandmother may be regarded by her son as the final authority and the expert on raising children, but as she begins to enjoy the children more, and as her daughter-in-law gains confidence in herself and in the eyes of her husband, the grandmother's position as expert weakens. For many Taiwanese women this shift to the side is graceful and happy, the grandmother finding she takes more pleasure in nurturing and spoiling her grandchildren than in competing with their mother. Depending on her age, the grandmother may at the same time be turning over more and more of the household responsibilities to her daughter-in-law, but more likely she still has quite a few more years of power to control the domestic organization. If, however, the older woman feels really threatened by her daughter-in-law, fearing, for example, that her son may be induced to move to the city for employment or set up a separate household, the tension between the women is felt in all their interactions. The poor grandmother must again take up arms in the battle she thought she had won—the battle for the prime position in the affections of her son. Both grandmother and mother then compete for the children's loyalty and affection, the former to tighten her ties to her son and the latter to build toward her own future security. Both set up incidents in which the adversary appears in the worst possible light to the bedeviled son-husband, and in which, incidentally, the children are given sound practical training in manipulating human relationships. Most of the children in Peihotien could tell us which adult in the family particularly favored him and who favored each of his siblings, parental favoritism being freely discussed by the family in the children's presence. It is not too farfetched to suggest that in those families in which favoritism follows lines of factionalism in the family, the seeds of antagonism between adult brothers are sown.

By the time their first grandchildren have reached the age of reason, most grandfathers are beginning to feel serious threats to their authority in their sons' growing competence and income. By the time the last-born grandchildren reach this age, the grandfather's authority in the family is either completely gone or in a state of sham. Either the old man decides, as did his wife, to forget the forms and enjoy this next generation, or he realizes the futility of assuming the mask of aloof dignity in order to correct behavior. To the children, he is a source of pennies for sweets, an occasional place of solace when the rest of the childhood world turns against them, and a good place for stories when nothing else is doing. The truly aged man no longer able to work at much of anything in the midst of a busy household is a pitiful sight. His physical needs are usually met (although some old men complain that they are not), but busy mothers cannot prevent children from teasing and cannot or will not punish children for disobeying even simple commands an old man might issue. His son sees that all the forms of filiality are observed for the public eye, but his ambivalence toward his aged father often allows for little more. Old women, however, even those who made the lives of their daughters-in-law miserable in earlier years, usually find life considerably more comfortable. Until completely senile or physically incapacitated, they can perform functions in the household that even a revengeful daughter-in-law finds valuable. Sewing, nursing sick children, rocking fussy infants to sleep—these are minor but time-consuming occupations not suitable to old men or half-grown children, but they suit an old woman very well. And when she is beyond even this, if she has trained her son well, his affection will see to it that his wife cares for her with a gentleness that an old man might never experience. The funeral of the father will, nonetheless, be more elaborate than that of the mother.

Sisters-in-law

Rural Taiwanese children, particularly those born early in their mother's child-bearing career, enter a world teeming with adult relatives. Theoretically, these adults should consist of the father's parents, his brothers, and his brothers' wives—adults toward whom and from whom certain behavior is expected by tradition. Father's older brother should be like father only a bit more awesome; father's younger brother should be like father only a little less formal; the wives of both these men should be like second mothers. Actually, few children grow up with a paternal uncle and his family in their home, although many children do have such relatives in their immediate neighborhood. Moreover, few children consider their father's brother's wife in any way similar to their own mother, and very few women would, under any circumstances, consider treating their husband's brother's children in the way they would treat their own children. If the brothers and their wives are on good terms, they do not want to endanger these good relations by disciplining one another's children; and if, as is more common, their relationship is brittle but still operative, nothing could more quickly open (or reopen) hostilities than a fracas between the wives over the misbehavior of a child. During the few years that the two couples are members of the same joint family and during the briefer period in which the family property is divided, all manner of antagonisms and jealousies are raised that will color their relations with one another for many years to come. The exact role played by the wives during these trying years varies with their personalities and with the quality of their relations with other family members, but it is almost never that of peacemaker. It would seem reasonable to expect a daughter-in-law to welcome her husband's younger brother's new wife into the family as an ally against their traditional foe, the mother-in-law, but other factors seem to operate against this. For one thing, the first daughter-in-law and her children have undergone the financial strain and parental tension that exists in a household accumulating the money and negotiating a marriage settlement for a son. Moreover, when this expensive troublesome commodity arrives, she is often given preferential treatment for a period of time or, if nothing else, is the source of much attention and interest. When the household settles down again, the older daughter-in-law is likely to take advantage of the younger's inexperience in the family's routines to shift both duties and blame for errors onto her head, at the same time, of course, shifting the mother-in-law's hostility. This behavior does little to endear older brother's wife to younger brother's wife, and though deposing the mother-in-law might have some advantages for the older daughter-in-law, it would have little for the younger, producing merely an exchange of tyrants. Nevertheless, the sisters-in-law have and work toward, albeit separately, a common goal, that of separate *chia*. Their husbands are fully and emotionally informed of each incident of preferential treatment from the senior generation, the bad habits one man's children are learning from his brother's poorly trained wretches, and the opportunities his children will surely miss because he is forced to make up the deficit in the family budget caused by his brother's insufficient income.

The fact that very few joint families in Peihotien survive the marriage and fatherhood of a second son indicates the success of the sisters-in-law. The relationship between brothers in Taiwanese society is both weak and strained by inconsistent dicta concerning proper behavior toward each other. As children, the elder is required to yield to his younger brother's demands in all things, some of which are outrageous when the younger is still small. If the younger child desires some prize possession of the older and when denied it proceeds to beat the older boy with a stick or rock, the elder has no choice but either to give him the object or to leave the scene with it before adult attention is attracted. If, out of a mixture of pain and frustration, he slaps his younger brother, he can expect punishment for himself and special favor for his little brother. As they grow older and the elder brother is no longer a caretaker but still responsible for his younger brother, the latter continues to hold the strings of power. If elder brother does not like his behavior, in a particular instance, the younger can easily and often does provoke a quarrel, knowing full well that the parents will punish the elder automatically without giving him a chance to explain his actions as an attempt to correct younger brother's aberrant behavior. Younger brothers learn very early and very concretely that older brothers yield to younger brothers, and yet as adults the expectation is exactly the reverse—the younger is expected to yield to his older brother's decisions and guidance, a situation for which he has been poorly prepared. The comparative ease with which sisters-in-law can manipulate the brittle relationship between their husbands is not difficult to understand. Although some students of Chinese society suggest that the wives merely capitalize on the brothers' competition for the parental wealth or property, this seems quite a minor factor in their conflict, since the equality of their shares is clearly prescribed by the culture. Far more explosive is the emotional content of their relationship and the inadequacy of their training, in particular the younger brother's, for their adult roles of dominance and submission. Unless he is extraordinarily tolerant, the elder will retain some degree of resentment over the troubles his younger brother has caused him for so many years, and he may be just a bit heavy-handed in wielding his at last consistently approved authority; unless he is exceptionally adaptable, the younger brother will find his position untenable. If left to themselves, adult brothers might be able to overcome the strains built into their relations with one another, but most men marry before any compromise can be reached and often before the conflict between them has become fully apparent. Their wives are not motivated toward effecting such a compromise. In view of the fact that the brothers are given wives during the same period of time that they are adjusting their adult roles toward one another, it is understandable that the Taiwanese so often place the blame for the break-up of the family on "the narrow hearts of women" rather than on the contradictory demands the society makes upon their husbands.

Taiwanese children are aware almost from birth of the latent or perhaps active hostility between their parents and their father's brothers' families. That these people and their children must be treated with more circumspection than others they learn early and, as we have just seen, painfully. Their paternal cousins, nonetheless, will be their most frequent playmates. It is here, long before they are old enough to conceive of it in the abstract, that they learn the intricacies of kin behavior—the obligations it imposes and the penalties it extracts. As adults these paternal cousins will be the very people to whom a man turns when he needs a peacemaker, emergency funds, a job for his son, an introduction or letter of credit, or sympathetic advice in the quarrels between his brothers and himself. It will be to preserve their goodwill that he punishes his own children harshly for aggression. Yet in his childhood his parents will have ingrained the proper style for their interactions for almost the opposite reasons, reasons ostensibly relevant only to their own generation.

Conclusion

In the preceding pages the Chinese family has been examined in terms of the basic function of families everywhere: the raising of children. The attitudes various family members bring to the job of socialization throw a new light on familiar problems. The husband-wife relationship has been deemed to secondary importance both by the Chinese and by the scholars who study their customs. Insofar as the interaction between husband and wife is not overly charged with either positive or negative emotions, it is indeed a secondary relationship in the context of the family. The wife who does not despise her husband is not likely to raise her children to treat him as an outsider in his own family; the husband who does not reveal an unusual attachment to his wife is not likely to motivate his mother to an anxious competition with the younger woman for the loyalty of his children. When either the personalities or the behavior of husband and wife threaten to intensify the relationship with extra warmth or extra tension, it becomes disruptive to the more important parent-child relationship—in one generation or the next. This disruption, whichever direction it takes, is reflected in the attitudes of various members of the family toward the children of the family.

The brittle relationship between adult brothers is an important facet of Chinese kinship, from its role in the dissolution of joint families to the inherent weakness it brings to the lineages. When such a crucial relationship is also such a fragile one, when the society values a close relationship, and when its fracture causes intense and lasting hostility, it cannot be explained simply in terms of adult problems. A review of child-training practices suggests that the failure of the relationship originates in the inconsistent preparation of the brothers for their adult roles. This background makes credible the sudden disintegration of their relationship when they come into conflict over income and property. Had the younger brother been trained from infancy to submit to the elder, the Chinese joint family might be less of a myth.

The subtly different definitions of filiality that seem to be held by mothers and by fathers, and the strikingly different techniques they use to realize their definitions, say a great deal about the anxieties and the defenses of women in an androcentric society. They also give us a useful basis for comparison between families continuing their descent through the patrilocal form of marriage and those coping with a lack of male heirs by "marrying in" a son-law. The young man who makes an uxorilocal marriage finds himself in a situation quite similar to that of his sister. His rights over his children, like his sister's rights over hers, are not clearly stated, and, again like his sister, he forms ties with them that are individualistic and not dependent on the children's acceptances of cultural mores and values.

It would be satisfying to be able to conclude this paper with an outline for the systematic use of socialization techniques as predictive instruments in the study of the Chinese family. Obviously, that is out of the question. One of the thoughts selected for restatement in this concluding section suggests that the socialization process *reflects* a set of tensions within the family; another argues that child training seems to be the *source* of tension; the third example points out that a particular pattern of socialization is found useful as a basis for comparing two marriage types. There *is* an intimate relationship between the way in which a family trains its children and the dynamics of that family, but the exact nature of that relationship and its predictive value, if any, are yet to be discovered. In time the social sciences may reach a level of sophistication that will allow a quantitative analysis of small groups such as the family. Until that time, those of us interested in things Chinese would do well to cast a speculative eye at the way Chinese are raised. We may find evidence of change, of conflict, or of an error in analysis; at the very least, we will gain further evidence of what the Chinese want of family life.

11.
"I Divorce Thee": Moroccan Marriage and the Law

Lawrence Rosen

Increasingly, many Western countries are changing their divorce laws to allow one spouse to receive a divorce regardless of the other's desires. In this respect, Western laws seem to be approximating the laws of those Moslem countries that allow men the right of divorce on demand.

Unfortunately, like many stereotypes of the nonwestern world, this one too is a mixture of half-truth and complete misunderstanding. It is true that in most Moslem countries men still retain the right to repudiate their spouses unilaterally. But it is equally true that there is a host of social, economic and indeed legal means through which a woman and her family may effectively check her husband's ability to do anything with his seemingly unlimited legal powers. In a modern Islamic nation like Morocco the law codes alone offer only the narrowest view of husband-wife relations in such a society. One must look closely at a number of social and economic factors associated with divorce to get a more sophisticated view.

Moreover, a study of this sort reveals various social and legal problems that are of considerable importance to several aspects of contemporary sociological theory. For if it is indeed true, as we shall argue, that Moroccan society is not composed of a series of fixed groupings whose members relate to one another on the basis of very narrowly defined roles such as "husband" and "wife," then it becomes necessary to consider the situational contexts of these relationships and the ways in which contractual ties and personal manipulations may modify relationships that would seem to be defined simply on the basis of status.

Morocco presents a good example of the interplay of social and legal factors associated with divorce in the contemporary Moslem world. As embodied in the Code of Personal Status adopted two years after national independence in 1956, the Moroccan laws of divorce reflect fewer significant changes from the traditional rules of the Malikite school of Islamic law than do the codes of, say, Algeria, Tunisia or Even Egypt, which were heavily influenced by French and Swiss legal codes. The Moroccan husband's rights of divorce remain very considerable. Indeed, the first time a man repudiates his wife, the courts will not only uphold his right to do so, they will also sanction his power to call her back to his bed and board at any time during a three-month period. If the three months go by without reconciliation—and any pregnancy on the woman's part will be attributed to the husband—the divorce will be declared final. If, however, the husband exercises the right to call his wife back, and then for some reason thinks better of the idea, he can repudiate her a second time. But if he changes his mind again, he must have the wife's consent in order to bring her back. Moreover, the husband will have to give her some gift as a sign of their reconciliation. If, finally, the husband repudiates his wife for a third time, the law will not permit them to take up residence together once again even if both parties desire it. Only after the expiration of the waiting period and the formation and dissolution of a marriage with another man would the woman be eligible to remarry her first husband.

One Moroccan characterized the differences between these three forms of divorce as being similar to the situation of a man who holds a small bird in his hand. To repudiate a woman for the first time would be like releasing the bird with a string attached to one of its legs: provided the bird does not get three months distant the captor can reel it back whenever he chooses. In a second repudiation, however, the bird has been released completely unfettered and will only return to its master if properly enticed. And after a third repudiation the bird will fly away altogether to seek a new and more congenial source of sustenance.

In each of these cases, then, the legal powers of the husband are indeed absolute, but there are several other forms of divorce in which the initiative actually lies with the wife and the officials of the local court. If, for example, a woman can prove to the court that her husband has failed to fulfill one of the defining duties of the marital contract—if, say, he fails to support her or mistreats her excessively—she can petition the court for a judicial decree of separation. In another instance the woman may secure a divorce by getting her husband to agree to accept some form of remuneration for releasing her. Acceptance of such an arrangement by the husband carries with it an inherent and irrevocable repudiation. Clearly such an arrangement places a great deal of power—verging at times on extortion—in the hands of the husband, but the bride and her family may have hedged against such an eventuality when the marital contract itself was drawn up.

At the time a marital contract is agreed upon, representatives for the woman may have certain stipulations written into the document which are intended to strengthen the position of the woman and her family against the husband. Among the most common stipulations not directly concerned with property are, for example, the understanding that the woman need never move more than a specified distance away from her family of origin, or that her husband may never take an additional wife without first granting her a divorce. The woman's family may even stipulate that the marriage will actually be subject to termination at the pleasure of the wife herself. Court officials rationalize this apparent breach of the Koranic law (which grants the power of repudiation to the husband alone) by saying that the woman has actually contracted a situation similar to that in which she gains release from her husband through some form of remuneration. But here the "payment" is with the words the husband himself agreed to have placed in the contract rather than with a sum of money, custody of a child or some other form of consideration.

The most common stipulation found in marital contracts, however, refers to the payment of the brideprice. In Islamic law and custom every marriage requires as its fundamental defining act the payment to the bride or her marital guardian of a sum of money or goods whose value may vary from that of a simple token to any sum agreed upon by the representatives of the bride and groom. However, not all of the brideprice need actually be paid at the time the marriage itself is contracted. Rather, a portion of the brideprice may remain to be paid at the time of any subsequent divorce or at any time the woman herself chooses to demand it. Clearly this condition gives a woman considerable leverage in curbing her husband's right to summarily dismiss her. Any man who has contracted a marriage with this provision in it will think twice before arbitrarily exercising his right of divorce or indeed of provoking his wife in any way that might move her to demand the outstanding portion of her brideprice.

The extent to which a man may find himself obliged to acquiesce in the inclusion of such contractual provisions as these is, for the most part, a function of the relative power of each of the parties concerned, particularly economic power. If a man is attempting to marry up socially or economically, and if at the same time the bride's family suspects that the prospective husband may mistreat his wife or try to make life for her so miserable that she will pay any sum to secure her freedom, the family of the bride may leave part of the brideprice unpaid or require certain other rights for the bride. In some parts of the countryside whole communities customarily use the deferred brideprice clause as a means of insuring some degree of marital stability. There will often be considerable haggling over the terms of a marital contract and the sums involved. The outcome will vary according to such considerations as the intangible prestige value of one's descent, the present market in potential mates and the conflicting motives of various members of both families.

There are several other factors associated with the laws of brideprice payments and divorce that may give women and their families considerable power to modify the husband's legal privileges. In recent years, there has been a substantial increase in brideprices paid in Morocco, particularly by members of the urban upper classes. Where ten years ago a well-to-do man may have paid several hundred dollars as a brideprice, a man of comparable circumstances today may have to spend as much as $1,000. People sometimes speak of this as brideprice competition, and there is little doubt that brideprice payments may be one way to establish social standing in a heterogeneous and highly mobile society lacking in any all-pervasive system of group stratification. But insofar as only the closest friends and relatives will know exactly what sums or conditions are involved, there is reason to suspect that the competition is, in point of fact, not for brideprices per se but for the dowries associated with each brideprice payment.

Upon receipt of a brideprice for his daughter or marital ward, a man will add a substantial sum of his own and use the combined amount to purchase a dowry for the bride. This dowry itself is called, quite significantly, "the furnishings of the household." It is these goods, whether actual furnishings, items of personal jewelry or raw wool, which will be consideed the personal property of the woman and will leave the marriage with her in the event of divorce or widowhood. In addition to their security value these goods, rather than the brideprice itself, are made clearly visible to the entire community as well as to those who later visit the couple's home. Indeed, on the day a bride moves to her husband's home the goods comprising her dowry are paraded around the streets of the city to the accompaniment of oboists and drummers, chanting relatives and screaming children. Poorer families carry the goods in their hands and on their heads while wealthier people will lay out the entire dowry—down to the last fragile teacup—on the beds of several pickup trucks. It is for these goods, which represent both the status of the bride and a real source of her personal security, for which the competition directly expressed in brideprices in being carried on. The mother of the bride is usually the most insistent that her daughter's dowry should be as substantial as possible. She will nag her husband to increase the brideprice demanded, while he, seeking both respite from the nagging and a vehicle for emphasizing his own social standing, will increase the brideprice accordingly.

In addition to setting up an index of relative social status, it is also important to note that the law automatically assumes that all of the "household furnishings" except for the most personal possessions of the husband (such as his clothing and tools) are the sole property of the woman and may be taken away by her when she leaves. Since the woman's family generally doesn't allow the precise content of the dowry itself to be entered into the marriage contract, this legal fiction gives the wife a potentially powerful lever to use against her husband. Indeed, insofar as they can do so without creating an unbearable strain on the marriage itself, Moroccan women frequently try to pressure their husbands into buying them as many things as possible in order to insure themselves against a sudden divorce. Everyone is well aware that the more a man has to lose financially by divorce, the less likely he will be to exercise his legal powers arbitrarily. And if such a divorce means not only the loss of those goods bought during the marriage and any outstanding portion of the brideprice, but also means incurring a whole new set of social and financial debts associated with the collection of a new brideprice, a man will certainly hesitate before making use of his power of instant repudiation. The extent, then, to which a husband may be put at an economic disadvantage by a wife who is herself at a clear legal disadvantage will be a function of the relative power of the persons involved, particularly their respective financial positions.

In addition to the legal prerogatives and economic pressures affecting marital relations, there is a host of ways in which different social ties may be utilized by the parties involved. We have already seen how the bride's mother may cajole and conspire to elicit from her husband the largest dowry possible for her daughter, and how a husband may be reluctant to divorce his wife because of the degree of personal independence he may have to give up in seeking help with a new brideprice from his relatives and acquaintances. Similarly a wife who wants to get her husband to abandon his plan to divorce her may turn to commonly shared friends and relatives, neighbors or some individual "in whose presence her husband feels shame." For example, if a husband and wife are first paternal cousins, which is quite common in Moslem societies, the wife may utilize the position of her father as the husband's uncle rather than simply as his father-in-law to constrain the husband to act as a nephew properly should. Or by galvanizing the opinion of neighbors or threatening a public court action a woman may hope to induce her husband to give her more substantial support, abstain from occasional beatings or spend less of his time at a nearby café. Again the success of her endeavors will vary tremendously with the social, economic and legal positions of all those involved. What remains constant in this system, however, is neither the forms of behavior associated with certain relationships nor the groupings that are crystallized at any given moment to accomplish an ad hoc task but simply the ways in which persons can indeed relate to one another without overstepping "the bounds of permissible leeway" as they pursue their individually and pointedly defined goals.

Mohamed's Case

As an example of the subtle interplay of social, legal and economic factors associated with divorce in Morocco, take the case of a young friend of mine who was experiencing some difficulty with his wife. Mohamed was a clerk in the local administrator's office who had married a girl from his home town of Fez and settled down to live with her in his father's house. Almost from the start, however, his wife and mother began fighting with one another as each tried to maintain the greater degree of influence over Mohamed's actions. The situation created great strains among the members of Mohamed's own family and between all of them and his wife's kinsmen. Mohamed finally decided to move away altogether in the hope that setting up house for himself in a nearby town would solve the basic problem. But his wife continued to nag him and demand his complete attentiveness to her every wish. Mohamed tried go-betweens from his wife's family and from neighbors, but in each case his wife's agreement to behave herself was quickly followed by a renewal of her bossy and nagging attitude. Mohamed was hesitant to divorce her since he would then have to pay a very substantial sum remaining from the brideprice and begin all over again to collect money for a new wife of the standing he deemed appropriate for a man of his background and position. He thought that having children might make her more tractable but was equally afraid that if this did not settle the problem and he still had to divorce her he would then have the additional burden of long-term child support. Quite literally, he said, he could neither live with his wife nor without her. He finally decided that since it was an independent identity of her own and an ability to have a say in her own future that was at the root of his wife's problem the only workable solution was to allow her to finish enough of her education so that she could find some work outside of their home. Although he had the power and even the desire to repudiate his wife forthwith, Mohamed recognized that he was effectively constrained from doing so by the social and financial implications of such an act.

Nonlegal Powers

In more general terms, then, Mohamed's marital difficulties point up several important aspects of the law and practice of divorce in Morocco. Unlike many other societies in the world, in which an individual's actions are almost wholly determined by the ways he is expected to behave towards his various kinds of relatives, in Morocco a person is usually free to manipulate these relatinships in a wide variety of ways. One can play on the different interests of family members, the control one has over the family's property, the aid one can expect from having done favors for non-kinsmen, and indeed the implications of the existing laws to establish a position of relative power vis-à-vis the other people in one's family. Because so many different interests can be brought to bear in the arrangement or dissolution of a marriage, even the strong legal position of a husband may be undercut by the economic and social forces available to his wife and her family.

During the course of a marriage a woman and her family will, therefore, try to balance their social and legal obligations with the demands that can be made on a husband in the hope of giving the wife the greatest degree of security possible under the circumstances. And the husband and his family, in turn, will seek to use their properties and relationships to maintain the husband's ability to exercise his legal powers without incurring a significant loss of money or personal independence. When divorce does occur, then, it is less because of a division of loyalties between one's family and one's spouse than because of the numerous tensions that develop from this constant personal struggle for economic, social or legal superiority.

The Moroccan government is itself aware of the fact that these tensions are at the root of the country's high divorce rate and it has tried to take certain legal steps to ease the situation. The law does, therefore, recognize the woman's right to demand that her husband find living quarters for the couple outside his parent's home and in an area sufficiently well populated with respectable people to enable the woman to call upon the necessary witnesses to substantiate any case she might bring alleging misconduct on the part of her husband. With full recognition that husbands may act without due consideration, in moments of great stress, the law also denies the husband the right to divorce his wife three times all at once. And, recognizing that fear of financial loss is the greatest dissuader of hasty action, the law also requires the husband make a "conciliatory payment" of unspecified amount to his wife upon divorcing her. But insofar as local courts generally fix this sum at roughly one-third of the registered brideprice with a ceiling of less than $100, it is clear that this relatively insignificant sum has not greatly affected divorce rates, though it may have increased the frequency with which a husband and wife use this payment in maneuvering for positions of greater strength in a marital dispute.

Consideration of the laws of divorce alone, then, give only a partial and truncated view of the nature of divorce as it is actually practiced in an Islamic state like Morocco. A woman's legal rights, though limited, can be supplemented with significant economic and social powers. This is so because of the maleability of various relationships each of which contains wide behavioral alternatives that can be developed into divers patterns.

Families Do Not Define Persons

But to say this means that we will have to reconsider certain features of contemporary sociological theory. For it would appear that one's inherent positions in this society do not define the whole person or the whole range of one's possible associations. Rather, one constantly uses both the ideal forms of behavior associated with any inherent position and the wide range of ambiguous behavior permitted within such role relations to establish ties centered on the individual and capable of being developed into a host of distinctive and often ephemeral associations. One cannot, as some present-day students of nonwestern legal processes do, argue with Sir Henry Maine that in such societies "all the relations of Persons are summed up in the relations of Family." The norm of behavior is not so rigidly fixed nor the sanctions on that behavior so narrowly confined that one cannot arrange certain ties with more distant kinsmen or outsiders in such a way as to place one in closer alliance with these persons than with the members of one's own immediate family. And one can also utilize these same contractual ties and manipulated alliances of kinsmen and others to strenghten one's own position in situations where one's legal rights may actually be rather limited.

Although the legal rights of women in many Islamic countries have been substantially increased in recent years, a true picture of the actual relations between husbands and wives—as well as an appreciation of the repercussions any changes in the law might have—requires a careful consideration of the social and economic means through which these legal powers are sustained, amended, or significantly undermined. The Moroccan case thus reflects not only the law and practice of divorce in one modern Islamic state but the dynamic interplay of family law and social structure characteristic of a number of the developing nations.

12.
Future Family

Margaret Mead

There was an article by an eminent psychologist in the *New York Times* recently, saying there wasn't any generation gap, because lots of parents got on with lots of children.

But the generation gap has not got anything to do with parents and children. The generation gap is between all the people born and brought up after World War II and the people who were born before it. It's not at all about children and getting on with parents.

If you happen to be a parent who was born and brought up before World War II, and you happen to have children at the moment, you're on one side of the generation gap and they're on the other. But this is an accident. In about 15 years there'll be parents and children on this side of the generation gap. And all the people on the other side will be at least grandparents.

What we're talking about as the generation gap only happened once. It isn't about parents not getting along with children, or children rebelling or changing styles of morality. It's simply that at the time of World War II the whole world became one, so that there is a complete difference between all young people and all older people.

In New Guinea, you have children who are studying medicine whose parents were cannibals. That's quite a gap. But whether it's more or less of a gap than the gap between a sophisticated cabinet member and his son, that's a question. Or between a professor of physics and his youngest student in college.

We've mixed this gap with conflict between parents and children and professors and college students at present because the oldest members of the new generation—the inhabitants of this new post-World War II world—are just 25 now. Five years ago, the oldest members were only 20, and they were all in college, and none of them were members of the establishment. So that it looked as if this was a battle between students and parents, and students and teachers, and everybody in college. But it wasn't.

Now the oldest are 25, and a lot of them are getting to be members of the faculty. They can't be treated as traitors any more.

At the moment, two things are happening that we have to take into account. One is the fact that we're having a revolt, a new kind of revolt, which is only partly connected with the generation gap. It's particularly characteristic of the Western industrialized society. In the past, most revolutions and revolts and rebellions have been by people who were being done evil to by other people. They were being enslaved, exploited, sent down in mines, treated terribly. It was perfectly clear they were rebelling against bad treatment.

Now, we're have a revolt of all the people that are being done good to. For the first time in history, children—all children, after all, are being done good to by their parents—pupils, students, mental patients, welfare mothers, and even people who are being rehabilitated in Federal prisons, are suggesting they take a share in what's going on.

This is the first time we have had this kind of rebellion, and students are included in it. In the past, the professors knew best, the doctors knew best, the social workers knew best, psychiatrists knew best. There were great numbers of professional people who knew best and did good. Then the beneficiaries were supposed to be appreciative. And they've now become extremely unappreciative. And they're all insisting on getting into the act.

Welfare mothers, after all the taxes we pay, are suggesting that they'd like to have shoes for their children in September, because school begins then and not in November. And some of them are saying that all the children in the family should have shoes; that's better than having to take turns wearing them.

Students get into this particular category too, because they've been done good to for a long time—for several hundred years. There was a period when the students found the professors; they presumably were doing good for the professors, at that point. But the professors soon got control. They've been doing good to the students all over the place; suffering, working for very poor salaries, dedicated and worn out. And now the students are saying "We'd like to take a hand in what's going on." Now, from that point of view, the students and the welfare mothers and the mental patients are all in the same position. This isn't entirely about the generation gap and it isn't only about students.

Whenever there is a period of upheaval in the world, somebody's going to do something to the family. If the family's being very rigorous and puritanical, you loosen it up. And if it's being very loose, you tighten it up.

But you have to change it to really feel you're accomplishing something. If we go back into history we find over and over again, in moments of revolutionary change, that people start talking about the family, and what they're doing to it, and what's wrong with it. They even predict it's going to disappear altogether. It is in fact the only institution we have that doesn't have a hope of disappearing.

No matter how many communes anybody invents, the family always creeps back. You can get rid of it if you live in an enclave and keep everybody else out, and bring the children up to be unfit to live anywhere else. They can go on ignoring the family for several generations. But such communities are not part of the main world.

As one of my sophomore students wrote the other day, when I had asked them to say where they were going to be 15 years from now: "Fifteen years from now it may not be necessary to get married; but nevertheless I expect to live with the father of my children."

And that is, strictly speaking, where we are. Girls are going to live with the fathers of their children—if they can catch them. And on the whole, they're just as interested in catching them as they've been throughout history. But there will be a great deal of discussion, and a great deal of gloom, and a great deal of talk about the family falling to pieces. In fact, we've got more families per capita than we've ever had. We're more married than we've ever been, and we're more married than most people. We've a terribly overmarried society, because we can't think of any other way for anybody to live, except in matrimony, as couples.

It's very, very difficult to lead a life unless you're married. So everybody gets married—and unmarried—and married, but they're all married to somebody most of the time. And so that we have, in a sense, overdepended on marriage in this country. We've vastly overdone it.

At the graveside—you know, when a woman has just lost a husband that she's been happy with 20 years, the first thing people say is, "I do hope she marries again." They don't give her two minutes to grieve before they start marrying her off again. We also have had a form of marriage that is probably one of the most precarious and fragile forms of marriage that people have ever tried. That form—the Nuclear Family—was not named after the Bomb. It was just named after the physical analogy, but calling it the Nuclear Family is very good, because it is just about as dangerous as the bomb.

The Nuclear Family is a family consisting of one adult man and one adult woman, married to each other, and minor children. The presence of any other person in the household is an insult. The only people that can come in are cleaning women and sitters. In-laws become sitters—which means that when they come in, you go out, and you never have to see them. Furthermore, today, mothers are very uncomfortable with adolescent daughters in the house. So they push them out as rapidly as possible. If they're rich, they send them to Barnard, and if they're poor, they get them married, and they work at it, very hard, because there isn't room in the kind of kitchens we've had since 1945 for two women.

We have put on the Nuclear Family an appalling burden, because young couples were expected to move as far from both sets of relatives as they could, and they had to move, a great deal of the time.

Millions and millions of Americans move every year, moving miles from relatives or anybody that they know. We know now that the chances of a post-partum depression for a woman are directly proportional to the distance she is from any female relative or friend. When we put her in a new suburb all by herself, her chances of getting a post-partum depression go way up. There are millions of young families living in such suburbs, knowing nobody, with no friends, no support of any kind.

Furthermore, each spouse is supposed to be all things to the other. They're supposed to be good in bed, and good out of it. Women are supposed to be good cooks, good mothers, good wives, good skiers, good conversationalists, good accountants. Neither person is supposed to find any sustenance from anybody else.

Young people from Europe who wanted to come to the United States had to bring their spouses with them, and leave their parents behind or they'd never have gotten here. In India or Africa, when you have a great mass of very traditional relatives, the thing to do is to take your girl and leave, and go a long way off if you want to live the way you want to live.

So it's a good style of family for change, but it's a hazardous kind of family, nonetheless. And if it is hazardous enough in the city, it's a hundred percent more hazardous in the suburbs. There's a special kind of isolation that occurs in the suburbs. So the attack on the Nuclear Family is, I think, thoroughly justified.

There is a need to have more people around: more people to hold the baby, more people to pitch in in emergencies, more people to help when the child is sick, when the mother is sick, more children for other children to play with so you don't have to spend a thousand dollars sending them to nursery school, more kinds of adults around for the children to pick models from in case father or mother can't do the things they want to do. The communes aim to supply these. Real communes, of course, are more extreme—this country was founded by many forms of communes, and it's been so with them ever since—but the bulk of people don't live in communes. One of the things the communes are emphasizing is a lot of people sharing child-care, sharing bringing up the children again, so the children have more security, and don't have to think every day, "What if something happens to Mommy; what if something happens to Daddy? Will there be anyone at all?" I think we're going to have a trend toward different kinds of living.

It will take quite a little while, because it means building new houses, on the whole—new kinds of apartments, closer together, places where you don't have to drive 15 miles to use somebody else's washing machine when yours breaks, and where people can get together more closely. We won't have this right away—but we're going to have it.

It means places where all the people can live somewhere near young people, and places where young married couples with children will be cherished and cared for and flanked on all sides by people who don't have children at the moment. Maybe they've had them before; maybe they haven't had them yet, maybe they don't want any. But it'll be a place where they, also, can find children, and won't be banished from children as they are at present. If today you don't have children of your own, you hardly ever see any. We banish our old people far away from any children at all, and the only thing we ask them to do is to live on in misery and smile, so their children won't feel guilty.

With the population explosion, the pressure on women to marry is going to be reduced, and the pressure to be mothers is going to be enormously reduced. For the first time in history we're not going to tell a woman that "Your principal glory is to be a wife and a mother."

By dint of telling women that their major job was to be wives and mothers, we told most men their major job was to be breadwinners and very much limited the number of men who could do the things they wanted to do most. We always talk about career women, and the wonderful careers they would have had, if they hadn't had those five children. But nobody looks at fathers and thinks what a life he'd have had if he hadn't had those five children.

He might have been able to paint instead of being a stock broker. Or a musician, instead of running a jewelry store he inherited. When you shut women up in a home and require wifehood and motherhood, you shut men up and require husbandhood and fatherhood at the same time. As we reduce the requirements for motherhood, we reduce the requirements for fatherhood. And we'll release a lot of people to be individuals and to make contributions as individuals, rather than as parents.

This isn't going to happen immediately, but we get a lot of funny forerunners. The members of the Women's Liberation Movement, in its extreme form, walk around saying how well they get on without men. We're quite prepared to have a lot of women get on without men now. It won't do a bit of harm. There're too many women, and if some of them would get on without men it would relieve the pressure.

Twenty years from now, we'll have many fewer families, but children will still be brought up in families because we don't know how to bring them up any other way. The family will be just as safe as it ever was, but everybody won't have to live in it all the time. We'll recognize that the family is the perfect place for children. It is just ideal for children, and doubtfully ideal for anybody else for the whole of their lives—except in very exceptional cases. Of course we'll also recognize that when we used to have the idea of lifelong marriage, the expectation of life was 37. When one spouse died and the other was left with a batch of little children they had to marry somebody else.

Today, the expectation of life is over 30 years after the last child leaves home. In terms of rapid change, it means the rate of change for both husbands and wives is very different than in the past. We may move to an ideal of marriage, which is an ideal of people staying married until the children are grown. At present, they have an ideal of staying together forever, but in fact they get divorced very often. If instead they have as an ideal staying together until the children are grown and not having children until they were ready to do that, not picking out somebody you'd like to spend the weekend with, parenthood will probably become much more solemn, and much more of a commitment. If it doesn't, of course, we're going to have some government putting contraceptives in the drinking water.

Some people are somewhat worried by the present notion of the young that they are not going to get married, but they're going to live "in sin." It's a very funny kind of sin—because you do it with the approval of the dean of women, your minister, and both sets of parents. We used to call it common law marriage—when people are generally known to tradesmen as living together. You could sue people to get part of their property when they died, and all that sort of thing. Well, what young people in general today call an "arrangement" is an absolutely public union.

When I proposed that there be a simple marriage ceremony, which would go with the stated intention of having no children,—they said "No." They're going to experiment with "arrangements"—public, virtuous, publicly proclaimed—and then, later, they're going to get married.

We've been cheating women when, in the last ten years, we wanted women to work. We were very short of cheap labor so we told them they needed to be fulfilled. The last source of educated cheap labor was women. So finally everybody discovered that it is very unfulfilling to stay at home, and a woman, of course, when she has her children, maybe she would stay at home for a few years and then she'd leave to be fulfilled. And the foundations gave money, centers were established to lure her out and get her re-educated.

But of course they weren't going to pay her like men, because after all she was more interested in her home, she wouldn't want to leave her children, and you know art lessons sometimes take up more time than little babies—and so she'd want a job from which she could get home early like being a clerk in a team-teaching outfit, instead of a teacher. Something like that—so she could go home when her children did. And of course she wouldn't want to be very ambitious, because all the strain would be bad; she'd want to keep something for home.

In the last ten years, women have been pretty well beguiled and bedazzled into becoming self-fulfilling, educated cheap labor. And I think it's not surprising if some of them are saying that they think they are exploited, and they don't want to be exploited any more.

At the end of World War II, when they wanted all the women that held jobs to go home so the men could get them back, women who'd done well in Washington were told they were overmature, overexperienced:—"Please go home."

I think we'll be bringing girls up with more sense of themselves as people, and that they're going to be people all the way through. If they choose parenthood, they'll choose it much more as they've chosen vocations, and much less as if it were just something the neighbors are doing.

Part V
The Survival of Community

Current anthropological use of the term "community" covers almost every human group from rural villages to urban neighborhoods, occupational associations, and religious movements. Wherever people today can find and develop a sense of belonging, ethnographers are sure to follow. This sense of belonging is basically what Charles Cooley wrote about many years ago as the "moral order" that prevailed in groups founded on loyalty, freedom, and lawfulness. At work, in volunteer activities, or even within the boundaries of hospitals and prisons, individuals can create a social context that they and others will refer to as a community.

Within the traditions of anthropology, however, the notion of community connoted an elementary social unit created to solve basic survival needs and other secondary requirements, what Malinowski called "cultural imperatives." No group can survive without mastering the fundamentals of food-getting, shelter, and sexual reproduction. Still, just meeting basic needs is never enough; man as a social being with memory and the capacity to envision the future depends on economic, educational, political, and moral systems to order his world. The total function of the community, then, is to manage the resources of the environment and to sustain a cultural organization that accounts for past, present, and future.

As such, and as it was most likely to be found among people isolated from urban centers and state administrations, the community could be seen as a fundamental social organization, a cooperative solution to life's problems.

In his classic handbook, *The Little Community*, Robert Redfield outlined its four principal features. The first of these has to do with a quality of distinctiveness. The boundaries of the group, in a social and geographic sense, should be evident to the observer and apparent in the attitudes of the people in the community. Second, the community is an entity small enough to be understood by personal observation, or at least a large subsection of it should lend itself to field research. A third characteristic of the little community is its homogeneity—a single, enduring tradition governs the lives of community participants. Fourth, the community is self-sufficient, a cradle-to-grave arrangement that provides for all or most of the needs of the people within it.

As Redfield was well aware, the little community he described was an ideal type, rather like an ethnographer's dream in its simplicity and order. Yet the descriptive dimensions pinpointed by Redfield are precisely those that have guided anthropologists in their selection of fieldwork sites, and for good reason. A community with a sense of identity, its own bounded territory, and an inherited tradition of self-sufficiency usually has the integrity and stability to allow successful long-range research.

What has been the fate of such little communities in modern times? Are anthropologists still interested in locating undiscovered tribal hamlets? First of all, the more we learn about small communities, past and present, the more we understand the interdependence of smaller and larger social entities and the virtual nonexistence of a truly self-sufficient community. The interrelations of folk and urban cultures may be direct or indirect, long or short-lived, yet the history of past high civilizations like those of Mesopotamia, Egypt, Peru, Rome, China, and Western Europe vividly illustrate how thoroughly rural settlements could become saturated with the influences of state organization. Conversely, great urban centers depend on trade and commerce with outlying districts; the more expansive the civilization, the more far-reaching the paths of communication. In early Roman times, farmers living outside the city supplied urban residents with food; as the Empire expanded, the word for farmer, "colonus," became generally applicable to people in outposts (colonies) distributed widely over the then-known world. Later, the expansion of Western European empires followed a similar pattern of expansion, contact, and administrative incorporation; in the nineteenth century, with colonies all over the globe, Englishmen could well say that "the sun never sets on the British Empire."

Observers of human behavior in every high civilization have noted the contrasts between rural and urban life; the cosmopolitan and his country cousin have long lived in different worlds and eyed each other with mutual distrust and disdain. It is only in our age of urban industrialism, however, that literature on urban-rural contrasts assumes an evolutionary perspective in which civilization, instead of maintaining a symbiotic relationship with outlying regions, will virtually destroy the traditions and lifeways of the colonies. As nineteenth-century cities in Europe and America grew in size, scholars on both sides of the Atlantic mourned the passage of the small-scale community and its traditional values, and they pondered the new freedoms available to people being liberated from the constraints of custom and drawn into the large-scale industrial economy.

As with theories of religious evolution, the little commuities of Pacific islanders, Australian aborigines, and African tribes served as models of the fundamental and outmoded social unit that Western civilization, on its mission of progress, was leaving in its wake. However, the contrast between the traditional community and modern life was formulated, and one thing was clear: the historical stability of the small group was diminishing in favor of individual options and values. Thus, Lewis Henry Morgan, as part of his interest in kinship, contrasted the small *societas* founded on sacred notions of the family with the state society or *civitas* that was organized on rational, legal, and property-ownership principles. Along the same lines, Sir Henry Maine used historical and cross-cultural legal cases to posit the transformation of kin reciprocities in traditional cultures to contractual agreements binding in high civilizations. For Emile Durkheim and the French comparative sociologists, cases of traditional communal organization offered the sharpest contrast to the individualization of values and work that they saw taking place in turn-of-the-century Europe. Their contemporaries in England and Germany, most notably W. Robertson Smith and Ferdinand Töennies, were detailing similar opposition between urban society and apparently outmoded small communities.

The global expansion of Western institutions and technology has certainly had its effect on community life, but not always in a destructive sense. In the first article in this section, David Mandelbaum describes the impact of technological change on village India as a transformation of caste hierarchies but not as a destruction of either the traditional notion of caste or of village organization. The notion that technological progress inevitably destroys community is obviously too simple a perspective. What needs to be clarified in each case is the extent to which any group faced with economic and political intrusion loses the right to maintain a moral order, for in the ethnographic literature we are consistently faced with the fact that people hold on to the familiar and to known conceptions of loyalty and justice. Progress, when it appears on the horizon, threatens no tradition unless it is attended by new imperatives—that to eat, individuals must leave the land; that to enjoy the privacy of the home, they must surrender to an external political order.

Even under enormous pressures to abandon traditional cultures, many non-Western societies, less resistant than village India, have nonetheless survived contact. The history of American Indian tribes presents many examples of this phenomenon, perhaps none so dramatic as that of the Cherokee. With the early nineteenth-century expansion of the Plantation South westward to the Mississippi, land-holding Indians in Georgia and the Carolinas were seen by their white neighbors as obstacles to economic progress. From around 1820 to 1840, most of the Indians of the Cherokee and Creek nations were removed by the U.S. military to an area beyond the Mississippi. This area eventually became the state of Oklahoma, and, as authors Wahrhaftig and Thomas discovered, Indian communities did survive the trauma of relocation. The obstacles to their survival cannot be underestimated. On the other hand, the stigma of race and social-class barriers fostered the very isolation that permitted the maintenance of Indian language and culture in eastern Oklahoma. The price of cultural survival was and is, therefore, a very high one when the integrity of the group is built on an exclusion from the avenues to economic success and prestige.

The survival of the small community in the context of urban industrialization has not in all cases, been left to random historical circumstances. Conscious of the extent to which a loss of community spelled the lonely despair rather than the freedom of the individual, many people in modern times have speculated on a return to traditions. The last century, if it was a time of tremendous urban growth, also engendered major utopian communities designed to protect their members from the corruptions of progress. Determined to segregate themselves off from the evils of the world, founders of the Oneida, Amana, and other American farm utopias planned well-ordered and self-sufficient communities that would completely serve the moral and physical needs of the men, women, and children within them.

The radical nature of the utopian community lies in the conscious selection of traditions, not necessarily in its orientation toward the agrarian past. Tradition and custom are generally looked on as products of a long social history, and as such, are not subject to the will of any one set of individuals at a particular point in time. The true innovation of the utopian community, of which the Hutterians researched by John Bennett are one of the oldest and most successful examples, was to put human planning ability above historical selection and to rationally impart order to work, worship, leisure, and procreation. Once done, the second problem of utopian communities, whether we speak of Israeli *kibbutzim* or hippie communes, is to convince succeeding generations that retreat from the larger world makes good sense. Most utopian communities have failed in this respect, and even the Canadian Hutterians struggle against the loss of young people and the disintegration of community.

What has helped preserve the Hutterian way of life is a full appreciation of a standardized administration that, despite old-fashioned dress and limited technology, makes them a modern culture and facilitates their dealing with the outside world. Having planned the appointment of leaders and the hierarchical process of decision-making, the founders of the sect provided for off-shoot settlements modelled on the original. This standardized organization bears little resemblance, either in structure or in historical depth, to the primitive groups referred to by Morgan, Durkheim et al. Instead, it partakes of the institutional structure that characterizes modern state and private organizations, namely, the corporate bureaucracy.

Although nineteenth-century theorists accurately perceived the strains that industrial expansion put on traditional communities, there were few persons who understood that the modern *persona* would seek and find identity in the context of bureaucratic institutions—in schools, factories, and offices, and in hospitals, the military, and prisons. The cradle-to-grave needs once met by the little community are now served by a variety of organizations manned by departmental staffs and addressing the needs of specific clients. The creation of a moral order among the working staff or among clients depends on institutional treatment of space and schedule that, more often than not, reinforces individualism. For example, where one works and where one lives are usually two different places, the public space for the working self and the private space for the personal, introspective, and leisure self. Institutional division of time is likewise based on a standardized separation of work hours from private time. How does this dualism of the public and private encourage individualism? It does so by maximizing individual accountability on the job and by giving the widest latitude to individual privacy during off-duty hours, two aspects of work life that have real benefits as well. Still, the people with whom one works may not offer a social context, and after hours an individual may become completely isolated. The ways in which each of us balance the tensions between a group life and the need for privacy remain a problem. What we have illustrated for us in this section are three cases in which participation in the social life of a group has been guaranteed, whether by historical circumstances or by human plans.

References

Bennett, John W. 1969. *Northern Plainsmen; Adaptive Strategy and Agrarian Life*. Chicago: Aldine Publishing Co.

Kanter, Rosabeth M. 1972. *Commitment and Community: Communes and Utopias in Sociological Perspective*. Cambridge, Mass.: Harvard University Press.

Mandelbaum, David G. 1970. *Society in India*. Berkeley and Los Angeles: University of California Press.
Redfield, R. 1955. *The Little Community: Viewpoints for the Study of a Human Whole*. Chicago: University of Chicago Press.
Smith, W.R. 1903. *Kinship and Marriage in Early Arabia*, S. A. Cook, ed. London: A. & C. Black. (Orig. published 1885).
Sjorberg, G. 1955. "The Preindustrial City." *American Journal of Sociology* 60: 438–445.
Stein, Maurice R. 1960. *The Eclipse of Community: An Interpretation of American Studies*. Princeton, N.J.: Princeton University Press.
Steward, J. 1949. "Cultural Causality and Law: A Trial Formulation of the Development of Early Civilizations." *American Anthropologist* 51: 1–27.
White, L.A. 1959. *The Evolution of Culture: The Development of Civilization to the Fall of Rome*. New York: McGraw-Hill.

13.
Status-Seeking in Indian Villages
David G. Mandelbaum

In societies as in people, change may affect only the surface, or go to the heart. Recurrent change (most American elections, for instance) may busily shift around groups and personalities, while altering little or nothing fundamental; but a systemic change alters the basic processes and assumptions of a society.

Trying to analyze the systemic changes in village India today is like trying to find the gift in one of those multi-wrapped Christmas packages. First there is the dynamic, but often thin, layer of modern physical change—new roads, bridges, buildings. Look further and you find the traditional ritual and occupational categories of Indian social life. Is this all? No—the traditional categories, rigid and seemingly unchangeable, actually cover a teeming and continuous competition between the various *jatis*. (A jati, sometimes called a sub-caste, is the family and status grouping which a villager inherits and within which he marries.) Some jatis are trying to rise, others are trying to hold their positions. Is *this* the final picture then—continuing subsurface change behind the static mask? No again— because the shifting around of jatis is only recurrent change. It alters little that is fundamental. In fact, it actually serves as a stabilizing force, by bringing jati rank in line with real economic and social conditions.

What is the ultimate truth then—that there is no systemic change in village India, that the more things seem to change, the more they remain the same? Not that, either. History, and the evidence of the Indian scriptures, show that the social structure of village India was quite different a millennium or more ago—systemic change *has* taken place. Furthermore, there is evidence that modern politics and technology are forcing new systemic changes.

The reigning ideal principle in the villages has been that of social immutability. But the ruling, *actual* principle has been that of social competition among those jatis close in rank. Some observers, focusing on the ideal, find traditional India rigidly stratified and noncompetitive. Others see a contradiction between ideal and reality.

The Hindu ideal is reflected in the scriptural concept of *dharma*, or sacred duty: Each person should fulfill, faithfully and dispassionately, the obligation of his station in life. He should not try to rise, for his station is given to him for the duration of his lifetime as a result of his soul's *karma*, the merit or demerit accumulated by his soul in previous existences.

The popular model for the whole of Hindu society comes from the sacred writings in *Manu* and other scriptural sources. These prescribe that all society is fixed in four categories: *Brahmin*, the priest and scholar; *Kshatriya*, the warrior and ruler; *Vaishya*, the tradesman; and *Shudra*, the laborer and cultivator. (Untouchables are not reckoned as part of caste society.) Each category is fixed in its respective rank, and presumably those in one do not compete with the others.

In real life, the jatis—rather than these broad social categories—are the main units of village society, and the jatis of a locality are supposed to be ranked in some order of ascending status. This implies a fixed structure. Yet there is typically much disagreement about the exact order of rank, especially in the middle ranges, and, as noted, there have been continual attempts by low-ranking jatis to improve their position relative to higher groups. (Similar competition goes on between families and lineages within jatis, but these rivalries are usually suspended when a jati is trying to advance.)

The justification for this apparent flouting of tradition is conveniently provided by a jati's "origin myth." To the members of many jatis, there are two different origin myths—one for society as a whole, the other for their own jati. There is no basic conflict. The myth for society assures them that it is, indeed, a fixed society; and the myth for their own jati assures them that their present lowly position is temporary and undeserved—they really belong higher in the ranking.

A common explanation of their bad luck is that their ancestors—who were divine or noble, or at least of high rank—were temporarily degraded because of some unfortunate occurrence that was really not their fault. Permanent degradation was neither deserved nor intended. Therefore, to really perform their dharma, their sacred duty, lower jatis must struggle to get their proper lofty rank, and to have their right to it acknowledged. The higher jatis feel duty-bound to keep jatis below them in the humble positions to which *their* karma, and local society, assigns them.

The Economics of Social Climbing

Characteristically, a jati's successful social advance in its locality passes through these phases:
• The families of a jati must first acquire the objective conditions for higher status—that is, specifically and primarily, wealth.
• Members of the jati must adopt the cultural practices associated with the higher rank.
• The jati must be able to maneuver successfully against external opposition to its new rank, while at the same time maintaining internal unity.

Wealth, learning how to fit in, overcoming opposition—these dynamics of upward mobility are not much different the world over, although in other societies individuals rather than groups are involved.

To rise, a jati must first have economic power. This is a necessary condition, but not the only one. Wealth must be used properly—that is, the group must use it to engage in purer and more prestigious group rituals.

On the other hand, greater ritual purity is not enough without wealth. A poor jati may go to great trouble to reform jati practices—but if its members remain poor and dependent, they will not have much social leverage.

A whole jati may become rich when some new economic opportunity opens up. For example, the Noniyas of eastern Uttar Pradesh, as William Rowe of Duke University reports, had traditionally been earth-workers and salt-extractors—ritually, a very dubious business with low prestige. Villagers who were still alive a decade ago could recall when the Noniyas were "almost untouchable." But by the end of the 19th century, some Noniyas had already prospered through building and contracting, and they formed an elite that campaigned for higher status. Today, among the 24 jatis in Senapur, their neighbors rank them ninth or tenth.

Once a jati has acquired enough wealth to hope for higher status, its families can try for the second phase—making cultural changes that will help them fit into a higher position, then forcing social acknowledgement of their advance. Gains in wealth and power must be translated into long-term symbols and prerogatives.

There is no absolute congruence between wealth and rank: The wealthiest are not necessarily the highest in ritual position, and members of a ritually high jati may be relatively poor. Not all shifts are possible: It is especially difficult for the very lowest jatis, even if fairly well-to-do, to rise above the untouchable barrier. Still, there is *general* congruence—those with higher ritual positions are, typically, also wealthier and more influential in their locality than those in the lower positions.

Those who want to rise in jati rank tend to dissociate themselves from lowly practices and occupations. Jati occupations considered inescapably debasing include disposal of the dead, handling products of dead animals (particularly of cows), and sweeping and disposing of refuse. As soon as any jatis that perform these tasks can afford to abandon them, they generally do. But it is not so easy to agree on what higher practices or occupations to follow—because there are a number of different models and strategies.

Sacred Thread of the Twice-Born

The rising jatis may seek to move either in a traditional or in a modern direction—or some combination of the two.
- TWICE-BORN. They may seek to be recognized as one of the three top *varnas* (Brahmin, Kshatriya, and Vaishya). These categories are called "twice-born," because, unlike the Shudras and the untouchables, their youths traditionally go through an initiation ceremony in which they are "born again" as full members of their social group. One mark of this rebirth is the right to wear the symbolic "sacred thread."
- MODERN ELITE. They may emulate the modern, educated, elite style and its distinctive modes of occupations, dress, and behavior.

It is common for these two upward paths to be combined, as when a jati association exhorts its members to purify their diet by becoming strict vegetarians, and also advocates college educations for the jati's children.

The Brahmin, Kshatriya, and Vaishya categories offer the three traditional models for the journey upward. The Kshatriya model of warrior and ruler—stressing the virtues of honor, force, secular interests, and power—has often been followed by ambitious jatis. Others have followed the Brahmin model, which stresses purity, piety, priestly interests, and learning. The Vaishya principles of thrift, steadiness, and practical intelligence—as well as purity and piety—have been less often emulated, though they are becoming more attractive in some places where businessmen have acquired more prestige and power.

A rising jati emulates a real group as well as a theoretical model—actual people who exemplify a model and whose conduct can be seen. The ideal principles and the behavior of the real group are never exactly the same. For example, jatis of the Brahmin category are supposed to have a diet at least as pure, ritually, as that of any jati in a locality. In South India this means strict vegetarianism; but in Bengal, Brahmin jatis interpret this canon more liberally—they eat fish. Ambitious villagers also emulate some of the modern ways they see in the conduct of educated officials, in the mass media, and in town and city behavior.

After rising villagers have made some cultural adaptations, the third step of upward mobility—maneuvering to get higher social recognition for their jati—can effectively be made. Ambitious men usually have a clear idea of what they want for their jati; getting it requires long, steady effort. For they must keep pressing against the opposition—against those jatis that feel threatened by their rise, and want to stop it. In their own jati, they must maintain internal unity and dedication.

Success against opposition is usually achieved gradually—beginning with a series of small changes to which others cannot properly object. For instance, members of the rising jati may take jobs that others don't want. (Who cares if earth-workers accept a government contract to dig a canal?) Or they can reform internal jati practices. (How can outsiders protest if widows of the jati are not allowed to remarry?) Once a base of wealth and ritual purity has been built, however, the jati's claims become bolder. In Senapur village, for example, the prospering earth-workers decided to wear the sacred thread, to show that they, too, were of the "twice-born" status. It is at this stage of boldness that rising aspirations and rising resentments collide—usually in a series of physical, legal, and social battles.

To win out, the ambitious jati must mobilize a unified effort—and unity is not easy to come by. Not all groups and families within the same jati reform their practices and amass wealth at the same rate. The most ambitious and energetic members may get to be so far ahead, and so impatient with the stragglers, that they find it hard to admit that they are even jati partners. Disputes break out within the jati itself.

If the more successful members find that they are not getting enough unity and support, they may redefine the boundaries of the group. The more advanced or dissatisfied split off, declaring themselves a separate jati. They may even join up with similar split-offs to form new, more single-minded jatis—and, with fresh unity and vigor, go forth to battle for new status.

All these constant struggles for social advancement seem to imply a revolutionary yeast at work, upsetting old rankings, challenging old superiorities. But in a more fundamental way, the shifting of ranks has actually been a stabilizing force. It tends to bring a jati's ritual rank in line with the realities of its secular, economic power—in short, to bring it up to date; and this is the direction toward which all local social orders in India have gravitated. Thus the acts that seem to—and are intended to—disturb an existing, static order actually maintain the dynamic, adaptive system of jati relations throughout the civilization.

The historical evidence indicates that, despite superficial appearances, the Indian social system has *never* been completely static. Groups have changed positions, new groups have been assimilated, and even revolutionary religious movements—trying to establish a less stratified system—have been repeatedly absorbed and transformed into jatis. All this has been done as recurrent, rather than systemic, alteration.

We know, however, that systemic change has taken place in India in the past. The earliest scriptures, the Vedas, reflect a social order organized by relatively open classes rather than hereditary jatis, and this system was later changed. But clear systemic change did not occur for perhaps a thousand years before the colonial period. Now, though, there is accumulating evidence that India has entered a period of fundamental change and a new kind of society is being developed.

New Pathways to Status

It is too soon to judge precisely which form the new society will take. Since India's independence from England in 1947, political and economic changes in the villages have produced marked social changes. In some ways these changes resemble precolonial conditions when the state might directly intervene in village society. But modern state power has a vastly different base—it does not depend on military conquest and a land-based nobility, but on voting influence, official positions, and such centrally bestowed boons as public works and roads.

There are now new ways to acquire wealth and power. Consequently, some low-ranking groups have bypassed the ruling jatis in their villages and appealed directly to higher political authorities for favors. Some have organized into voting blocs. In these ways, low-ranking jatis can acquire offices, grants, and influence. This implies a shift, not just in the relative positions of jatis, but in the very ways of seeking and obtaining power. This foretells systemic change.

Because of the new methods and substance for success, the older *symbols* of high rank have become less attractive. Thus, those Noniyas who—after long and bitter struggle—had acquired the right to wear the sacred thread now find, to their dismay, that their sons are quite uninterested in wearing the thread. Younger people generally are becoming more interested in acquiring the prestige of higher modern education than the badges of higher varna status.

The organization of jatis is also changing. Ambitious men have found that combining jatis into larger blocs for political strength is a better way of obtaining influence and status than fragmenting the jatis to achieve ritual purity. Many, therefore, urge enlargement and union, and the wiping out of petty, divisive distinctions. The trend is toward fewer, wider, better-organized jatis.

Not that the jatis are being eliminated: Villagers still believe that jati endogamy is basic for their society; that groups are ranked; and that one's own group should try to advance its own status, or if it is near the top, should defend its position. They are not consciously seeking to abolish the jatis—as they see it, in fact, they are simply strengthening their jatis, by working toward fewer and closer groups. But though change will not be rapid (the poorest still find it very difficult to rise), it is definitely under way.

To most Western observers, village India seems a baffling and exotic society—and yet the changes now under way there lead in the same direction as modern changes in nations elsewhere. Everywhere the social and cultural differences between major social groups are decreasing, even though stratification itself persists. There is a general shift away from the traditional, ritual symbols of status to those that reflect modern political or technological realities. Disadvantaged groups at every level of society are entering the political arena as they had never been able to do before.

But every change brings some uncomfortable dislocation. Even a minor shift in jati rank seems, to those villagers who may have been displaced, a major reordering of their world. Only with distance, time, and greater knowledge can we see such changes in proper perspective. The Negro rise in the United States—now, apparently, loaded with fearful portent to so many—may well be another recurrent change, eventually serving to diminish obsolete imbalances and tensions, to adapt old patterns to modern realities.

In broad perspective, the systemic changes, like those taking place in village India now, are themselves—when seen as processes in the development of modern world civilization—only recurrent change.

14.
Renaissance and Repression: The Oklahoma Cherokee

Albert L. Wahrhaftig

Robert K. Thomas

A week in eastern Oklahoma demonstrates to most outsiders that the Cherokee Indians are a populous and lively community: Indians *par excellence*. Still, whites in eastern Oklahoma unanimously declare the Cherokees to be a vanishing breed. Prominent whites say with pride, "we're all a little bit Indian here." They maintain that real Cherokees are about "bred out." Few Cherokees are left who can speak their native tongue, whites insist, and fewer still are learning their language. In twenty years, according to white myth, the Cherokee language and with it the separate and distinctive community that speaks it will fade into memory.

Astonishingly, this pervasive social fiction disguises the presence of one of the largest and most traditional tribes of American Indians. Six rural counties in northeastern Oklahoma contain more than fifty Cherokee settlements with a population of more than 9,500. An additional 2,000 Cherokees live in Indian enclaves in towns and small cities. Anthropologists visiting us in the field, men who thought their previous studies had taught them what a conservative tribe is like, were astonished by Cherokees. Seldom had they seen people who speak so little English, who are so unshakably traditional in outlook.

How can native whites overlook this very identifiable Indian community? The answers, we believe, will give us not only an intriguing insight into the nature of Oklahoma society, but also some general conclusions about the position of other ethnic groups in American society.

This myth of Cherokee assimilation gives sanction to the social system of which Cherokees are a part, and to the position Cherokees have within that system. This image of the vanishing Cherokee in some ways is reminiscent both of the conservative Southern mythology which asserts that "our colored folk are a contented and carefree lot," and of the liberal Northern mythology, which asserts that "Negroes are just like whites except for the color of their skins." The fiction serves to keep Cherokees in place as a docile and exploitable minority population; it gives an official rationale to an existing, historic social system; and it implies that when the Indian Territory, the last Indian refuge, was dissolved, no Indian was betrayed, but all were absorbed into the mainstream.

The roots of modern eastern Oklahoma are in the rural South. Cherokees, and whites, came from the South; Cherokees from Georgia and Tennessee; and whites from Tennessee, Kentucky, Arkansas and southern Illinois.

In the years immediately preceding 1840, Cherokees, forced out of their sacred homelands in Georgia and Tennessee, marched over an infamous "Trail of Tears," and relocated in a new Cherokee Nation in what is now the state of Oklahoma. They created an international wonder: an autonomous Cherokee Nation with its own national constitution, legislature, judiciary, school system, publishing house, international bilingual newspaper, and many other trappings of a prosperous Republic. The Cherokees, who as a people accomplished all this, along with their neighbors, the Creeks, Choctaws, Chicasaws and Seminoles, who followed similar paths, were called the five civilized tribes.

Promising as the Cherokee Nation's future might have seemed, it was plagued by internal controvesy from birth. Bitterness between the traditional Ross Party and the Treaty Party was intense. The Ross Party resisted demands for relocating from the South until its followers were finally corralled by the Army; the Treaty Party believed cooperation with the United States Government was the more prudent course for all Cherokees.

The sons and daughters of the Ross Party kept their ancient villages together. They reestablished these in the hollows and rough "Ozark" country of the Indian territory. Hewing new log cabins and planting new garden spots, they hoped to live unmolested by their opponents. They are today's "fullbloods," that is, traditional and Cherokee-speaking Cherokees. On the other hand, descendants of the Treaty Party, who concentrated in the flat bottomlands and prairies they preferred for farming, are now assimilated and functionally white Americans, though fiercely proud of their Cherokee blood.

The Ross Party was the core of the Cherokee tribes. It was an institution which emerged from the experience of people who lived communally in settlements of kinsmen. The Treaty Party was a composite of individuals splintered from the tribal body. There were of course great differences in life style among nineteenth century Cherokee citizens. The Ross men, often well-educated, directed the Cherokee legislators from backwoods settlements. Treaty Party men were more often plantation owners, merchants, entrepreneurs, and professionals—conventional southern gentlemen. The overriding difference between the two factions, however, was between men who lived for their community and men who lived for themselves.

During the 1880s this difference came to be associated not with party but with blood. Geographically separated and ostracized by Ross men, members of the Treaty Party perforce married among the growing population of opportunistic whites who squatted on Indian land, defying U.S. and Cherokee law. The Treaty Party became known as the "mixed blood" faction of the tribe; the Ross Party as "full bloods." These terms imply that miscegenation caused a change of life style, a reversal of the historic events.

By 1907 when the Cherokee Nation was dissolved by Congressional fiat and the State of Oklahoma was created, the mixed bloods were already socially if not politically, part of the white population of the United States. The Ross Party settlements, now the whole of the functionally Cherokee population, are intact but surrounded by an assimilated population of mixed blood Cherokees integrated with white immigrants.

From the 1890s to 1920s, development of this area was astonishingly rapid. A flood of whites arrived. Land was populated by subsistence farmers, small town trade boomed, commercial farming expanded, railroads were built, timber exhausted, petroleum exploited and token industrialization established.

Already shorn of their nation, fullbloods were stunned and disadvantaged by the overnight expansion and growth. Change was rapid, the class system open. Future distinguished elders of small town society arrived as raggedy tots in the back of one-mule wagons. Not only was social mobility easy, few questions were asked about how the newly rich became rich. Incredible land swindles were commonplace. At the turn of the century, every square inch of eastern Oklahoma was alloted to Cherokees; by the 1930s little acreage remained in Indian possession.

The result of this explosive development was a remarkably stratified society, characterized by highly personal relationships, old time rural political machines, Protestant fundamentalism, reverence of free enterprise, and unscrupulous exploitation; in short, a system typical of the rural south.

Superficially, this society appears to be one with the most resourceful at the top, and the unworthy, who let opportunity slip by, at the bottom. In reality, however, the system consists of ranked ethnic groups, rather than classes. The successful old mixed-blood families, now functionally "white," whose self-identification as "Cherokee" is taken as a claim to the venerable status of "original settlers," dominate. Below them are the prosperous whites who "made something of themselves," and at the bottom, beneath the poor country whites, Cherokee "full bloods."

In primitive tribes, myth is a sacred explanation of the creation of the tribe and of its subsequent history. Myth specifies the holy design within which man was set to live. The fiction of Cherokee assimilation illustrates that modern man still uses myth, though differently. For in Oklahoma, the myth of Cherokee assimilation validates the social conditions men themselves have created, justifying the rightness and inevitability of what was done. As Oklahomans see it, the demise of the Cherokee as a people was tragic, albeit necessary. For only thus were individual Cherokees able to share in the American dream. The Oklahoman conceives of his society as an aggregate of individuals ranked by class, with unlimited opportunity for mobility regardless of individual ancestry. The high class position of the old Cherokee mixed-bloods signifies to the Oklahoman that the job of building Oklahoma was well done. The "responsible" Indians made it. The Cherokees, as a single historic people, died without heirs, and rightfully all those who settled on their estate now share in the distribution of its assets. For the culturally Indian individuals remaining, Oklahoma can only hope that they will do better in the future.

Even as the mythology serves to sanctify their high rank position, it insulates whites from the recognition of the Cherokee as a viable but low ranked ethnic community with unique collective aims and interests. Where a real community exists, Oklahomans see only a residue of low status individuals. The myth, by altering perceptions, becomes self-perpetuating.

Paradoxically, the myth of Cherokee assimilation has also contributed to the survival of the Cherokee as a people. To the extent that Cherokees believed the myth, and many did, it was not only an explanation of how the tribe came into the present but a cohesive force. Since the end of a tribal movement led by Redbird Smith, a half century ago, in response to the final pressures for Oklahoma statehood, Cherokees have seemed inert, hardly a living people. Nevertheless, Cherokee communal life persisted, and is in a surprisingly healthy state. Cherokee settlements remain isolated, and if what goes on in them is not hidden, it is calculatedly inconspicuous. For the freedom from interference that it afforded, Cherokees willingly acceded to the notion that the Cherokees no longer exist.

In addition to sanctioning the form of Oklahoma society, the myth also gives credence to basic social and economic institutions. The economy of the area depends on Cherokees and country whites as an inexpensive and permanent labor market. Cherokees are expected to do low paying manual work without complaint. In 1963, Cherokee median per capita income, approximately $500, was less than half the per capita income of neighboring rural whites. In some areas, Cherokees live in virtual peonage; in others, straw bosses recruit Cherokee laborers for irregular work at low pay. Even though Cherokee communities are relatively hidden, Cherokee labor has become an indispensable part of the local economy. Apparently one would think that daily contact of white workers and bosses with these Cherokee laborers might expose the myth of the well-off assimilated Cherokee. On the contrary, the myth prevails because the humble occupations practiced by Cherokees are seen as evidence that Cherokee character is indeed that which the myth of assimilation predicts.

White Blood Makes Good Indians

Imbedded in the Oklahoma concept of assimilation, is a glaring racism. Typical is the introductory page of a book published in 1938 entitled *A Political History of the Cherokee Nation,* written by Morris Wardell, a professor at the University of Oklahoma.

A selection: "Traders, soldiers, and treaty-makers came among the Cherokees to trade, compel and negotiate. Some of these visitors married Indian women and lived in the Indian villages the remainder of their days. Children born to such unions preferred the open and free life and here grew to manhood and womanhood, never going to the white settlements. This mixture of blood helped to produce strategy and cleverness which made formidable diplomats of many of the Indian leaders."

To white genes go the credit for Sequoyah's genius and John Ross's astuteness, whereas the remaining Cherokee genes contribute qualities that are endearing but less productive. Thus, in a history of the Cherokees published only six years ago, the author, an Oklahoman, says of modern "fullbloods": "They supplement their small income from farms and subsidies from the government with wage work or seasonal jobs in nearby towns or on farms belonging to white men. . . . Paid fair wages, this type of worker usually spends his money as quickly as he makes it on whisky, and on cars, washing machines, and other items that, uncared for, soon fall into necessitous disuse."

Oklahomans divide the contemporary Cherokees into two categories: those who are progressive and those who are not. The page just quoted continues, "this progressive type of Indian will not long remain in the background of the growing and thriving, and comparatively new, State of Oklahoma." That a viable Indian tribe exists is apparently inconceivable.

Either Cherokees are worthy, responsible and assimilating, or they are the dregs; irresponsible, deculturated and racially inferior.

Through mythology, the exploitation of Cherokee labor is redefined into benevolent paternalism. Some patrons have Cherokees deliver their welfare checks to them, deduct from these housing and groceries. Afterwards the remainder is handed over to Cherokee tenants. Unknown to the welfare department, these same Cherokees receive stingy wages for working land and orchards belonging to the patron or to his kin. Patrons consider that they are providing employment and a steady paternal hand for unfortunate people who they contend could never manage themselves. The same ethic enables whites in good conscience to direct vestigal Cherokee tribal affairs; including the disbursement of well over two million dollars in funds left from a tribal land claim settlement.

Politicians Are Victims of Old Fears

It might seem odd that no one seeking to improve his position in the local establishment has ever tried to weaken these relationships. Why has no political figure taken cognizance of those thousands of Cherokee votes, and championed their cause? Instead politicians rely on the inefficient machinery of county patronage to collect Cherokee ballots. Unfortunately no one has yet dared, because fear binds the system. Older whites remember living in fear of a blood bath. The proposal to create Oklahoma meant a new state to whites; to Cherokees it meant the end of their own national existence. Their resistance to statehood was most desperate. Cherokees were a force to be contended with. They were feared as an ominously silent chillingly mysterious people, unpredictable and violent. And Cherokees did organize into secret societies, much akin to the committees of twenty-five delegated in days past to murder collaborators who signed treaties. The reward of public office, politicians feel, does not justify the risk of rekindling that flame. To the extent that Oklahomans are aware of the numbers of Cherokees and the force they might generate, the myth of the assimilated Cherokee is a form of wishful thinking.

Finally, the myth protects the specific relationships of rank and power which determine the stability of the present eastern Oklahoma social system. It does this in the following ways: By preventing recognition by whites and Indians alike of the Cherokees as a permanent community of people whose demands and aspirations must be taken seriously, it allows whites to direct the affairs of the region as they see fit.

By causing Cherokee aspirations to be discounted as romantic and irrelevant, it prevents the emergence of a competitive Cherokee leadership and discourages Cherokees from taking action as a community. For example, by 1904 Cherokees were given what was thought of as an opportunity to develop individualism and responsibility. The U.S. Government divided their communally owned land and each Indian was given his own piece. Thus the efforts of the present day Cherokee Four Mothers Society to piece together individual land holdings, reestablish communal title, and develop cooperative productive enterprises, is smilingly dismissed as an atavistic retreat to "clannishness."

By fostering the notion that Cherokees are an aggregate of disoriented individuals, it allows whites to plan for Cherokees, to control Cherokee resources, and to reinforce their own power by directing programs devoted to Cherokee advancement.

By denying that there is a Cherokee community with which a Cherokee middle class could identify and to which a Cherokee middle class could be responsive, it draws off educated Cherokees into "white" society and leaves an educationally impoverished pool of Cherokees to perpetuate the image of Cherokee incompetence.

The myth prevents scholars, Indian interest organizations, and the like from becoming overly curious about the area. If Cherokees are assimilated and prosperous, as the myth implies, there is neither a problem nor a culture to study. For 40 years no social scientist has completed a major study of any of the five civilized tribes. For 40 years the spread of information which might cast doubt on the myth itself has been successfully impeded.

In all, the myth stabilizes and disguises the Oklahoma social system. The stability of a local social system, such as that of eastern Oklahoma, is heavily influenced by events in the larger society. The past decade of civil rights activity shook Oklahoma. Gradually, Oklahomans are becoming aware that their society is not as virtuous, homogeneous, attractive, and open as they may have supposed. And Oklahomans will now have to deal with the old agrarian social system of Cherokees, hillbillies, mixed-blood Cherokees, and a new urban elite grafted onto the old.

Left behind in the rush of workers to industry and of power to industrialized areas, the Ozark east of Oklahoma is a shell, depopulated, and controlled by newly dominant cities, Tulsa and Oklahoma City. The area, quaint enough to attract tourists, is far too rustic for sophisticated Oklahoma urbanites to take seriously. Local politicians offer weak leadership. Beginning to suspect that the local establishment is no longer all powerful, Cherokees have begun to assert themselves as a tribal community. The Cherokees conceive of themselves as a civilized nation, waiting for the dark days of the foreigners' suppression and exploitation to end. Oklahomans regard Cherokees as an aggregate of disadvantaged people still in the background of an integrated state, a definition which Cherokees do not share. In fact, the Cherokees are flirting with political office and have entered the courts with a hunting rights case. In launching a "Five County Northeast Oklahoma Cherokee Organization," they are gaining recognition as a legitimate community with rights, aspirations, resources and competence.

Consequently, the reappearance of assimilated Cherokees threatens the newly emergent regional power structure. Cherokees and the local establishment have begun jousting on a field of honor extending from county welfare offices (where the welfare-sponsored jobs of suspect members of the "Five County Organizations" are in jeopardy) to annual conventions of the National Congress of American Indians. Besides threatening an already shaky white power structure, the militant Cherokees are challenging the self esteem of the elderly and powerful "assimilated." Curiously, many white Oklahomans do not appear to be alarmed, but pleased, apparently, to relieve the tension that has developed between conflicting images of pretended assimilation and the reality of a workaday world.

The manner in which Oklahomans view their society is the manner in which American sociologists all too often view American society. Great emphasis is placed on class and on individual mobility. And, social description, in these terms, is seen very much as a product of the American ethos.

White Oklahomans consider themselves members of a class-stratified society in which any individual (Negroes excepted) has free access to any class. Descriptions of that system vary according to who is doing the describing. Generally, white Oklahomans conceive their society to be one in which the upper class is made up of prosperous whites and old Cherokee mixed-blood families, or their descendants; next in order is a layer of middle class whites and assimilated Cherokees; then, a lower class of poor, country whites, full-blood Cherokees and Negroes. Young liberals see a two-class system: A middle class of "decent" whites and Cherokees and socially unacceptable class of poor, country whites, Cherokees and Negroes.

How Mythical Is Mobility?

This latter classification suggests that younger people perceive a much more closed system than their elders. Everyone is viewed as part of the same *community*—a word Oklahomans are fond of using. Presumably all groups of people have an equal share in the life of the community. Nationality, the word Oklahomans use to denote ethnic origin, is a principal clue to class position. As evidence of how open their society is, eastern Oklahomans point to Cherokees and poor, country whites (although not yet to Negroes, to whom the system is closed) who occupy respected positions. These are store owners, bureaucrats, and entrepreneurs; Babbitts of the 1960s, though born of traditional Cherokee parents. Always, however, these have been individuals who followed the only approved channel of mobility by scrupulously conforming to standards of behavior defined by those in control of the system.

The classic sociological studies on class in America, such as those by W. Lloyd Warner and Robert Lynd, are essentially static descriptions of the rank position of aggregates of individuals similar to the native Oklahoman's conception of his society. These studies reflect a peculiarly American bias. First, they examine the system that has formed rather than study how the system was formed. Americans are phenomenologists, more concerned with the things they have created than with the lengthy processes whereby these things have developed, more interested in ends than concerned with means.

Secondly, Americans do not stress ethnic considerations. In the American dream all individuals can "make it," regardless of nationality. For sociologists, class is a phenomenon in which individuals have social rank; ethnicity is treated as no more than an important clue in determining that rank. Thus, to be Irish was to be an outcast in nineteenth century Boston; not so today.

Thirdly, Americans, envisioning themselves as a nation of individualists, have assumed that social mobility for the most part rests on individual achievement. Immigrant groups are seen as having migrated into lower class positions in a relatively fixed class system through which individual immigrants rapidly became mobile. By contrast, Oklahoma's rapid entry into the formative American industrial economy caused a class-like structure to form on top of pre-existing ethnic communities.

A more balanced view shows that in the parts of the United States which industrialized earlier and more gradually, whole immigrant communities were successively imported into and butted one another through a social system which was in the process of formation and closure. The ways in which entire ethnic communities achieve mobility are overlooked.

Now it is becoming obvious that this mobility has slowed, even for those ethnic communities (like Poles) already "in the system." For communities which were brought into the system late (like Puerto Ricans) or at its territorial fringe (like Mexican-Americans in the Southwest) the situation is different.

Cherokees maintained technical independence as an autonomous nation until 1907, and in fact held America at arm's length until the 1890s. They provide an example of incorporation of an ethnic group into the industrial system in an area where no earlier group has paved the way. Thus, Cherokees are a "case type" which illustrated the modern dynamics of our system in pure form. Cherokees are now caught in our "historically mature" system of rank ethnic groups—a system which, for some, is rigid and closed, with little chance for individual and less for communal mobility. The total rank-structure of eastern Oklahoma is cemented by the mythology Americans use to obscure and rationalize their privileged position in a closed system.

In their conception of class, American sociologists are often as wedded to myth as are Oklahomans, and the resulting large areas of American social science they have created obediently subscribe to official fictions within the American world view.

Now, successive summers of violence have exploded some of the folk and scientific mythology shrouding the structure of our nation. The *Report of the National Advisory Commission on Civil Disorders* declares: "What white Americans have never fully understood—but what the Negro can never forget—is that white society is deeply implicated in the ghetto. White institutions created it, white institutions maintain it, and white society condones it." Yet throughout this unusually clear report the phenomenon of white racism is barely alluded to, as though it were an "attitude" born by an uninformed populace and unrelated to the core of our national social system. That system, as we see it in operation in Oklahoma, beneath its mythology of assimilation, consists of a structure of ranked ethnic groups, euphemistically called "classes" by American sociologists; a structure which is growing more stable and more rigid. This kind of structure is general in America and, of course, implied in the above quote from the Kerner report. In Oklahoma such a system of relationships has enabled aggressive entrepreneurs to harness and utilize the resources of ethnic communities which are frozen into a low ranked position by the dominant community's control over channels of mobility and by the insistence that the whole complex represents one single community differentiated only by personal capability. Thus, essentially "racist" perceptions and relationships are the "motor" driving the system and are embedded in the very day-to-day relationships of middle class Oklahoma.

15.
Communal Brethren of the Great Plains

John W. Bennett

In all of North America, there is only one sizable group of people who are deliberately, and successfully, defying the trend to a "consumer culture" with its related personal anxieties and general cultural debasement. This group practices strict austerity and limitation of personal property. Commercials do not tempt them, since they own neither TV sets nor radios. Their children are encouraged to play with full-size tractors instead of toys. Their women folk, not enslaved by fashion, make their own uniformly styled clothing. They are the Hutterian Brethren, (*Hutterische Bruder*), a Christian communal sect of 17,000, living mostly in the northern Great Plains of Canada.

The Hutterians (*Hutterites* is a vulgarization of the name) are farmers, organized in colonies of 130 to 150 people on communal farms up to 16,000 acres in size. Their people are contented—few leave permanently for the outside world. Economically they are flourishing as the most successful farmer-adaptors to the ecology of the Great Plains area, and their population doubles about every 15 years. They have been able to support this increase through efficient farming methods and the use of modern equipment and also through frugality and limitation of personal luxuries and conveniences. The combination enables them to save enough money to continually buy land for new colonies.

Hutterians practice total communal property ownership, which they call *community of goods.* This principle originated in the sixteenth century when their ancestors, fleeing into Moravia to avoid persecution in the

Austrian Tyrol, symbolically pooled their possessions in a cloak spread on the ground. Unlike the Amish, also an Anabaptist sect although only partly communal, they do not reject the advantages of modern technology for the community. They buy the most expensive farm machinery, and in their communal kitchens they have the most costly equipment, such as commercial refrigerators and electric meat saws.

But their apartment dwellings (about nine families to a row house) have few modern conveniences save electricity; most lack running water and nearly all lack flush toilets. Decoration is deliberately austere and uniform. The floors are of plain varnished wood; the walls are painted white and at the windows are plain white starched curtains. Furniture is sparse and mostly made in the colony shops. Few individual touches are found—perhaps an oddly-shaped, colorful pincushion or a fine old wall clock refinished by the man of the family and proudly pointed out to visitors.

This uniform austerity and emphasis on communal, rather than personal property and equipment, has a religious and social purpose. The Brethren believe that excessive interest in personal property is a form of idolatry, which comes between man and God. Also owning things different from, or better than, one's neighbors disrupts community morale.

In addition, there are economic reasons. Personal deprivation is the very foundation of their communal prosperity. The lack of plumbing in the family dwellings saves the average colony about $15,000 each year. Communal refrigeration equipment is half as costly as buying refrigerators for each of the 20 families in a colony. Add one carryall station wagon instead of 20 family cars and the savings become even more impressive.

However, as Hutterian leaders are fully aware, it is no simple or easy matter to keep 17,000 people on such a Spartan routine when their colonies, as communes, enjoy prosperity and when the world on the "outside" is affluent. The principles on which this unique society operates are worth consideration by those of us still engaged in the "consumer culture" rat race.

Managed Democracy

The Hutterian system can be called a "managed democracy." Overall policy is made by councils for the *Leut*, or three main branches, of the sect. These meet frequently to set policy and review departures from custom, however trivial. Any changes they sanction are recorded in books called *Gemeinordenungen* and carefully consulted. The power structure operates on two levels; there are the farm enterprise managers and the elders. The elders have considerable charismatic power, especially the chief or "first minister"; the managers have power only over their respective enterprises.

However, all these positions for men (and one for women—the colony's chief cook) are elective.

The basic administrative unit is the colony, which is kept below 150 members for both social and economic reasons. Above this level group decisions become unwieldy, there are not enough responsible positions to go round, and behavior is hard to control, especially among the young— for example, the young men may begin moonlighting for neighboring farmers in order to buy things they are not supposed to have.

Economic reasons are even more weighty. It takes between 8,000 and 16,000 acres to support 150 people, the exact amount depending on local moisture and soil conditions. This is about the largest acreage now available to the Brethren in most parts of the northern Great Plains. So when the colony reaches maximum size the question of splitting up is debated for a year or so and finally voted on by the whole group. This happens every 15 or 20 years. Then the colonists buy more land from 25 to 250 miles away; the land usually costs about $200,000 and is paid for from savings. This is called the "new farm." For a few years they put the new land into production and construct a few necessary buildings. Then lots are cast to see who shall live in the "daughter" colony. Ground rules call for a neat division down the age pyramid, so that the new community becomes, as far as possible, a duplicate of the old. The colonists are quite willing to go— they value the extra responsibility and the dedicated pioneer spirit found in a new colony under more deprived living conditions.

Hutterians are able to save large sums for new land partly by frugal living and partly because of efficient farming methods. The Brethren discovered, sooner than most American and Canadian farmers, that land on this continent has to be continuously productive in order to support an expanding population. Their emphasis on efficiency and technological know-how, so firmly resisted by the Amish, goes back to the founding of their sect. When they fled from Austria, Hutterians soon attracted the favorable attention of Moravian landowners. The lords invited them to act as stewards for their vast estates. They served without salaries in return for protection—a fine bargain for the protectors. Sixteenth century stewards were personnel officers and business managers combined. Thus the Hutterians learned a large number of skills including bookkeeping, farming techniques, and banking. They became construction engineers and surveyors; some set up craft industries and directed the training of apprentices in more than 45 different trades; a few were merchants and physicians.

Hutterian craftsmen made many ingenious gadgets and machines for their own use, and for the entertainment and interest of their masters. A few of these ancient devices still exist in the North American colonies, including several of the famous comb-cutting machines, using precision gears and saws. Hutterians preserve these interests: nearly every colony will have a yarn ball-winder, a sock-knitting machine, a noodle-maker—some of these made at the colony, others factory-made but improved by the colony mechanics. This extends to tools and farm machinery: colonies take pride in building cabs for combines and tractors, hay balestackers, forage wagons, automatic metal saws, and many other things. The Hutterian move toward farm machinery was undoubtedly facilitated by this traditional interest in machines and mechanical gadgets—something the Amish lack.

After being persecuted out of Moravia at the end of the sixteenth century the Hutterians learned another lesson which still stands them in good stead—from the standpoint of communal living. They found out that it does not pay to overproduce and become too wealthy. Catherine the Great invited them into Russia and promised them immunity from military service (which is against their basic beliefs). They settled in the Ukraine and prospered greatly in that rich land. Colonies grew into large villages and some of them departed from the cherished *community of goods*. By 1870, when the Czar removed their immunity from the military draft, the Brethren were ready to move again. They determined to make the next migration a revival of their religious faith and communal traditions.

Eventually the Hutterians accepted the offer of American land agents and moved to the pleasant James valley in the southeastern corner of South Dakota. This was not the last move, nor did it end persecution. Harassment during World War I forced the Brethren to flee to Canada, where most of them remain. But the move did end their dalliance with Mammon. Hutterians, whether in Canada, the Dakotas, Montana, or Washington, do not allow their colonies to become overly large or rich; communities with too much cash on hand will lend it to younger colonies not even their own "daughter" groups.

Hutterian leaders leave nothing to chance in combatting worldly temptations. The executive officers, the managers and ministers, visit back and forth in order to keep an eye on behavior in the various communities. Any laxity—such as clandestine radios, too many electric razors for the men or ornaments on the girls, or too many ornaments on the bureaus—is supposed to be reported to the council. This intercolony surveillance also helps to keep the different groups at about the same living standard. No colony is allowed to lag behind its sisters to the point where jealousy arises and austerity begins to be felt as poverty.

Spending is strictly controlled. Business expenditures of more than $10 must have the consent of the farm manager. Major spending must be approved by the voting council of the adult men. Each family receives a small monthly cash allowance to buy necessities. Many items—such as fabric for clothing, clocks, or pocket knives—are bought and distributed by the elders. So are a few small luxuries, such as special treats of food and refreshment for weddings and religious holidays, including beer and wine. Each colony makes its own wine, and individual families are allowed a gallon a month. Inexpensive gifts are given to children at Christmas; but in general they are encouraged to play with farm equipment instead of toys, which trains them early.

The culture of austerity is also the culture of uniformity. A Hutterian friend explained to me the reason for the special old fashioned clothes they all wear: "It's just that we should all look different from outsiders, but like each other." This conscious uniformity of clothes and possessions is based on the ideal that every man is alike in the sight of God. Differentiation would mean the rise of idolatry and the dissolution of Christian brotherhood.

Silent Struggle in the Heart

The system sounds more severe than it actually is. Hutterian leaders usually show a sensible flexibility in enforcing these rules. The elders will tolerate small infractions so long as they do not spread or become too blatant. In nearly all colonies there are constant small violations of the property rules. Individuals may find some way of making a little extra cash by moonlighting on a neighboring farm or selling a bit of colony produce on the sly. Occasionally items acquired this way are approved as desirable and bought and distributed to everyone. More often the offender is pressured into giving them up. The leaders have good reasons for doing this—whenever a colony breaks up (it happens occasionally) the first symptoms are always individual purchases of consumer goods, especially clothes.

Wisely, the Brethren do not treat the desire for personal property as a deadly sin. They recognize the intractable nature of the human spirit. As one author puts it, every Hutterian experiences a "silent struggle within the heart" when he sees the rich culture of the "outside," which he must reject. The Brethren also acknowledge the difficulty of individual privation in the midst of the collective wealth of the colony. But they glory in the fact that it can be maintained.

The obedience of the Brethren is really remarkable. Group interdependence and surveillance are not enough to account for it. There are other, deeper reasons. One of the weightiest is early social conditioning. Hutterian children are trained from infancy to accept the system and suppress their natural ambitions and material desires. The family raises each child in its two or three room apartment until the age of three. The colony then takes over. From three to six he is in nursery school and then in German school, learning the Hutterian culture and traditions. The teachers may be his own aunts and uncles but kinship makes little difference; through playing out what anthopologists call a "cultural myth" kinfolk are able to ignore their relationship where the needs of the colony are concerned.

A public school teacher comes to each colony to instruct the children in secular education up to the eighth grade level. But these teachers find it difficult to get the students to compete for grades or in artistic work. Only with great difficulty can Hutterian youngsters produce anything really original, since they have been trained to avoid competition or individual differentiation. At 15 they return to their families and take up adult work responsibilities. They are baptized at 20. The insulation of the child from the outside world is almost total up to the age of about 12, since children are taken into town only for important purposes like medical visits. This means that by the time the child does develop an awareness of "the outside," as Hutterians call it, he is already well-socialized in the system.

Temptations of the World

The leaders know that if young people were allowed to attend outside high schools the temptations of the world would undoubtedly prove too much. (This has been tried a few times with the predicted result.) Indeed, if they ever run out of land to support their expanding population (this threatens many areas), the Brethren might find it convenient to send some of their young people to high school in order to ease them out of the community.

Although Hutterian children are almost completely insulated from the outside world, adult Hutterians travel a lot. They visit other colonies and also travel long distances to find good buys on farm machinery and other equipment. They usually try to take along a few women and laborers so everyone has an opportunity to travel.

The people are also shielded from contamination by the mass media. A typical colony will subscribe to one or two newspapers, usually the local sheet and a German language Mennonite publication. Magazines are occasionally picked up from friends in town, but this kind of thing is closely watched. Television sets, radios, and movies are taboo. Every colony has a few young men who have managed to sneak into a theatre once or twice. But outside contacts of this type are not too serious a problem, especially in the more isolated rural areas. It is significant that the colonies in Manitoba, near Winnipeg, have the most trouble with their young people.

In general, the Hutterians control their people and keep morale high through rewards and incentives. Most of them crave responsibility, though they are trained not to show any open sign of ambition. Because the colonies constantly subdivide, plenty of responsible positions become available. These are all elective but the system is subtly rigged to give all the available men a chance. In a study of about 25 interrelated colonies, only 3 percent of the males over 40 had never held one or more managerial jobs.

This satisfying rotation of responsibility may be one reason why so few Hutterians leave the colonies permanently. Total defection is rare. In the *Schmieden Leut,* one of the three branches of the sect, the population rose from 500 to 4,000 between 1900 and 1949. Of those born in this period only 98 men and seven women left the community permanently. Temporary departure is more common—possibly 5 percent of all Hutterian men leave the colonies for about a year.

Culture of Austerity

Commitment to the system is undoubtedly deep. The material deprivation suffered by the Brethren does not disenchant them. The Hutterians are not "poor," by any intelligent standard. Their culture of austerity is the exact opposite of the "culture of poverty" as defined by Oscar Lewis. In the outside world poverty is associated with hopelessness and lack of identification; feelings of alienation are accentuated by contrast with surrounding wealth. In the isolated Hutterian society austerity is consciously planned and sanctioned by religion. It is the basis both of collective economic success and spiritual welfare.

The Hutterian deprivation offers distinct compensations of a spiritual and emotional nature. Instead of running after gadgets the Brethren make their own. Instead of following fashions they refine and improve their traditional models, achieving gentle taste and beauty. True, they pay a certain emotional price for repressing some aspects of their individuality. Fears, anxieties, and little psychosomatic ailments plague them. But they suffer very little true mental illness. (See *Personality in a Communal Society,* 1956, by Bert Kaplan and Thomas Plaut.) They are a remarkably healthy people. Inbreeding has produced a few undesirable genetic results, such as relatively high frequencies of minor bodily deformities, eye troubles, and the like, but it has also increased the intelligence of some of their members—most colonies contain people whose intellectual grasp of technology and economics is impressive, doubly so since they are all self-taught.

It is doubtful whether the Hutterians can provide a model for the reconstruction of personal living in the affluent society. They are a very special and very isolated people. They do, however, furnish certain inspirations. We may learn from them that there is valid satisfaction in cooperative effort and some suppression of individual rights. The Brethren suppress parts of their personalities, but they do so for a noble reason—the welfare and continuity of the group. The art of social living is almost lost in our urbanized society, with its broken families and increasing alienation. Despite the suppressive element in their society the Hutterians are interesting, vigorous human beings—unsophisticated and hickish perhaps, but full of wit and good conversation. They are more than adequate for their world.

Another summation of this unique way of life comes to me in the words of a Hutterian friend: "Some day they (the elders) will let us have radios, and if they do I am going to see to it that we make them ourselves."

Part VI
Power and Politics

We are so used to thinking of politics in terms of elected offices and bureaucratic organizations that other ways of distributing power—through kinship ties, religious roles, or temporary leadership positions—seem slightly less legitimate. Yet the study of non-Western political organization has had to include the rationalized bureaucratic forms of ancient societies—hereditary kingdoms, village councils, acephalous ("headless") tribal organizations, and the substitution of social codes for overt leadership.

To simplify the cross-cultural comparison of political structures, a number of anthropologists, among them Elman Service, Morton Fried, and Marshal Sahlins, have singled out terms that have been used for many years to designate types of societies at the fringes of, or outside of, modern state organizations. According to the work of Elman Service, for example, there are different levels of integregation or complexity that can be recognized in the descriptions we have on traditional and archaic societies. At the least complex level is the small band of hunters and gatherers who are united by bonds of kinship and marriage, with no more complicated arrangement for social order than those family ties and whatever moral and legal sanctions are imposed by the group. At the next level of complexity is the tribe, which consists of a number of bands usually engaged in a nomadic pastoral or horticultural way of life. The political integration of the tribe rests on more than just kin relations, although these are the foundation of social order. Clan associations, ritual societies, age-grade groupings, and clubs of various sorts cut across household and kinship loyalties and provide forums for decision-making above the family level. Like the band, the tribe is basically egalitarian ("communalistic"); yet as circumstances demand, as with external threats to the group, leadership and political organization will emerge as a defensive reaction. The chiefdom, at the next highest developmental level, is both larger than the tribe, and it is organized in a hierarchy of inherited political power. Its economy tends to be more diverse, and it includes pastoral, agricultural, and trade activities. These three political forms—the band, the tribe, and the chiefdom—stand in contrast to the state that, in an archaic sense, is a complex supraorganization in which power and the control of economic resources is explicitly institutionalized along the lines of class or caste and bureaucratic order. An important exclusion from these categories, which in certain historic settings can be read as evolutionary stages, is the peasant community such as the Indian villages described by Mandelbaum. Unlike the band, tribe, and chiefdom, the peasant village is usually seen as a direct outgrowth of the centralized state.

This section of *Anthropological Realities* covers the various levels of political organization, including the derivative peasant community, with an emphasis on the structure of power relations. We go one step further than the conventional categories to consider the development of the modern nation-state in the Third World as it touches the lives of rural villagers. After this, one of our own national institutions of power, the American military, is analyzed for the effects it has on the life of its members.

Whatever unit of social/political organization is being studied, the subject of competition for, and conflict over, limited resources has to be addressed. At the most elementary level, in kinship-centered societies, a relative is a resource, not only in the pragmatic sense of having labor value, but inasmuch as one social personality—the total set of a person's relationships with other kin—complements others. As Radcliffe-Brown noted, the death of one person leaves a social gap and unsettles, even dislocates the relationships of the living. Therefore homicide is an attack on the entire society and especially on the family unit within which the victim's role was most clearly defined.

Property is another resource that comes quickly to mind as a potential source of conflict and competition, although conflict over who owns what is only one of several kinds of disputes concerning "rights over." If one person accuses another of stealing food or failing to deliver livestock as a marriage payment, rightful ownership over things is obviously the issue. If the source of conflict is the failure of a young man to complete his apprenticeship in his mother's brother's household, the issue is one of customary rights of an uncle over the time and labor of his nephew. If a wife is abducted by an aggressive suitor, a challenge is made by a third party to the conjugal rights of the husband, which in most traditional societies are rights of economic partnership as well as sexual access.

In the study of social conflict and political systems, anthropologists find that people quarrel, physically attack each other, and demand political change for much more abstract reasons than lost property or labor. Another factor, the threat to individual honor and the honor of the group, is a much more powerful incentive to action. The deeper issue in violent conflict, warfare, and political action is often the disputed right to a respectable self-image, personal or collective. The person who suffers at the hands of a thief or assailant becomes in the eyes of the community a weak link who jeopardizes the status of the kin group, unless some retaliation is made. The wife who is seduced and the husband who is betrayed threatens the ability of their families to negotiate other marriage contracts (unless, of course, seduction and betrayal have themselves become customary). Generally speaking, the individual who defends his or her own honor is also defending a more abstract notion of group integrity even if, as happens in Western religions, the community is as diffuse as "all good Christians" or saints and angels.

The concept of honor is central to the understanding of political and especially military institutions, for the very reason that it can serve to mobilize individuals to act for the common good, even to risk their lives in defense of the social group. Every political institution codifies its standards of correct behavior, and every military organization supports precise definitions of honorable behavior. The symbols of achievement may be titles only and a special chair, or perhaps feathers, bones, colored ribbons, or pins. Still, such apparently trivial rewards can be invested with great symbolic value. We look to the successful military enterprise in particular as one that guarantees opportunities for increasing personal or group prestige, and much of what we know about primitive warfare suggests a sportive quality to confrontations between opposing groups. It helps considerably when any warriors can claim victory, but there is no real victory; and therefore no real honor, unless the contest has been a fair and balanced one, and this criteria of near equality of resources seems to have been met in many instances.

On the other hand, most social communities above the level of the band have evidenced a more than passing interest in power, and the goals of expansion and conquest are as much a part of non-Western societies as they are of our own. The one great difference may be in levels of military technology; and certainly since the mid-nineteenth century and no less today, the strategies of forging national boundaries have been calculated in terms of access to sophisticated arms.

The expansion of political power raises two vital questions. The first is what class or category of people can effectively impose its will on others. The second is concerned with the degree of functional stability in any institution of social control.

The lead article in this section on politics and power deals with both these questions from an historical perspective. Composed of a trio of case studies on the subject of slavery, it demonstrates how societies can polarize power relationships, creating relatively stable classes of masters and slaves. The passage of the individual slave to freedman status is, as authors Cohen, Middleton, and Tuden illustrate, a telling indication of the flexibility of the total social system. Like his New World counterpart, the African slave was a menial laborer, but the racial difference between black and white that was the foundation of social division in this country did not operate in African systems. Instead, language and tribal or band affiliation marked the slave as an alien, one who had been captured in battle, or who had fallen prey to slave traders. Generally, insofar as a slave could relinquish both and was allowed intermarriage with the dominant population, the total society benefited from the incorporation of acculturated outsiders.

Our second article, by Eric Wolf, deals with another subservient class and its relation to the dominant society. In this case, the role of Algerian peasants as they participated in the liberation of the colony from French rule is analyzed. The historical perspective, which has become a mainstay of political anthropology, reveals the complex effects of colonial settlement on population growth and mobility, rural-urban divisions, and the creation of postcolonial forms of government. European colonial expansion was conducted under a variety of flags, and over the centuries the many colonial possessions were treated as part of the spoils of war and thus passed from one to another national power. Despite the mixture of European settlers that resulted and the importation of cheap labor that was another commonplace, the legacy of colonialism was remarkably standard. It has consisted mainly in a bureaucratic administration, developed as an administrative form during the nineteenth century, and a military force acting as the arm of government. Out of this legacy, new states like Algeria have been formed, each adding important native leadership elements to the process of government.

Whether the change from colonial rule to national independence spells improvement for ordinary folk who live beyond the pale of government power struggles is a separate matter. The prejudices against the peasant villager, who is so frequently the majority constituency in new nations, are so widespread that one might wonder at any government that actively championed his interests. The view among political anthropologists that the peasant is a kind of feudal left-over is reflected in the attitudes that prevail in developing countries. To the radical intellectual of the Third World, no one is more corrupted by a conservative bourgeois attachment to property than is the peasant. To national leaders pressing for economic development, the peasant appears obstinately attached to outmoded agrarianism and the barter economy. Though stereotyped as crafty and shrewd, the peasant is nonetheless always expected to follow and serve the interests of other parties, whatever their political ideologies. In this article by Wolf and in William Foote Whyte's (Part X) article on peasants in Peru, a new look is given to rural villagers as citizens in Third World nation-states.

In the final article in this section, the subject of state organization is presented at the level of the soldier's experience. Unlike the primitive warrior, the member of the modern armed forces is salaried to put his life and honor on the line for his country. In this age of advanced technological warfare, men in combat like those described by Charles Levy have had their lives and labor more devalued than at any other time in history. While national interests are defended in high-level diplomatic talks, and the threat of the ultimate weapon hangs like a cloud over international affairs, the American military has had increasing difficulty in justifying military combat and the rigorous training traditionally demanded of recruits. The demoralized finale to the Vietnam War brought into question, among other things, the capacity of the U.S. military to distribute meaningful rewards, those symbolizing dignity and honor. Since then, the problems identified with warfare and military organizations have multiplied—racism, friction within the ranks, discipline problems, and desertion have been characteristic of all wars but never so blatantly as in Vietnam. One of the most troubling aspects of this latest American military effort was the revelation that the homecoming soldier had a tough struggle for economic survival awaiting him and little in the way of prestige. And for many, they had little emotional stability to help ease that battle.

At the same time, warfare prevails throughout the Third World of developing nations, and it remains an important category of human activity, whether those involved are guerrillas, mercenaries, or government militia. Our presence and that of Western Europe and the Soviet Union is increasingly as the suppliers of arms, while the labor of battle is carried on by people of other nations.

Like military organizations, political systems aim for a fair distribution of dignity and self-respect, although usually on the premise that all citizens are deserving, not just those who can wage war. Every revolution and political upheaval begins with the premise that the old system is robbing people of their rights, and needs to be replaced by a new system that will increase the store of dignity available to its members—or so the rhetoric goes. Though the goals of justice and equity have been taken more seriously by some countries than others, serious economic and political inequities exist in every nation. In addition, there are sufficient documented cases of imprisonment, torture, exile, and mass killings enacted by national governments to engender awe at the power of the state to act against human freedom. We know that governments owe their citizens basic freedoms, yet the point has been reached in comparative politics where the interconnections between large-scale political systems and small-scale human groups are clear, but they do not always demonstrate a vigorous defense of human rights.

In the final sections in *Anthropological Realities*, those on Development in the Third World (X), The Ethnic Factor (XI), and Anthropology: Application and Ethics (XIII), the themes of political dominance and small group organization introduced here will be developed even further into the realm of current national and international affairs.

References

Barth, Fredrik. 1959. *Political Leadership Among Swat Pathans*. London: University of London Athlone Press.
Barton, R.F. 1969. *Ifugao Law*. Berkeley: University of California Press.
Bohannan, Paul, ed. 1967. *Law and Warfare: Studies in the Anthropology of Conflict*. Garden City, New York: The Natural History Press.
Bramson, Leon, and George W. Goethals, eds. 1964. *War: Studies from Psychology, Sociology, Anthropology*. New York: Basic Books.
Chagnon, N. 1968. *Yanomamö: The Fierce People*. New York: Holt, Rinehart & Winston.
Cohen, Ronald, and John Middleton, eds. 1967. *Comparative Political Systems: Studies in the Politics of Pre-Industrial Societies*. Garden City, N.Y.: Natural History Press.
Fallers, Lloyd A. 1965. *Bantu Bureaucracy: A Century of Political Evolution among the Basoga of Uganda*. Chicago: University of Chicago Press.
Fried, M.H. 1967. *The Evolution of Political Society: An Essay in Political Anthropology*. New York: Random House.
Fried, M.H., M. Harris, and R.F. Murphy, eds. 1968. *War: The Anthropology of Armed Conflict and Aggression*. Garden City, N.Y.: The Natural History Press.
Gluckman, Max. 1965. *Politics, Law, and Ritual in Tribal Society*. Chicago: Aldine.
Hoebel, E.A. 1954. *The Law of Primitive Man*. Cambridge: Harvard University Press.
Leach, Edmund. 1954. *Political Systems of Highland Burma*. London: London School of Economics.
Maine, H.S. 1861. *Ancient Law*. London: J. Murray.
Sahlins, M. 1968. *Tribesmen*. Englewood Cliffs, N.J.: Prentice-Hall.
Schapera, Isaac. 1967. *Government and Politics in Tribal Societies*. New York: Schocken Books.
Service, E.R. 1971. *Primitive Social Organization: An Evolutionary Perspective*. 2nd ed. New York: Random House.
Simmel, Georg. 1950. *The Sociology of Georg Simmel*. Kurt Wolff, trans. and ed. Boston: Free Press.
Sumner, W.G. 1960. *Folkways: A Study of the Sociological Importance of Usages, Manners, Customs, Mores, and Morals*. New York: New American Library. (Orig. published 1960).
Wolf, Eric R. 1969. *Peasant Wars of the Twentieth Century*. New York: Harper and Row.

16.
Slaves and Masters in Africa: Three Cases

Ronald Cohen, John Middleton, and Arthur Tuden

Slavery Among the Kanuri

Slaves could be obtained by any one of a number of different methods in Bornu, with some correlation between the type of slave and the way he was recruited. Many slaves of all types, except eunuchs, were born into the role, especially those living in slave settlements. The rule most often followed is that if your father is a slave, so are you; if your mother is a slave and your father not, then you are not a slave, although such a person has lower status in the descent group than others having both parents freeborn.

The method *par excellence* for supplying slaves, especially for the slave trade, was through raids on weak neighbors. Ostensibly such raids were to be carried out on non-Muslim communities only. However, this was not always the case, and there are records of political leaders raiding Muslim villages sometimes within their own borders. The excuse for this practice was generally a political one. The village to be raided was accused of insubordinate political activity, and this was interpreted as a fall from true religious faith which allowed the potential raiders to define the villagers as infidels.

In general, only women and children were taken. Men ran away or were killed defending the settlements. However, men were needed for the trans-Saharan trade and for conversion to eunuchs; in the nineteenth century the trade southward in slaves emphasized adult men so that the reported practice of taking only women and children is probably exaggerated. Captives were led away in chains, with children running free beside their mothers. Political leaders in charge of each raid generally took half to three-fifths of the slaves for themselves and distributed the rest to their chief subordinates who directed the redistribution to their own followers. Judging by the frequency with which such raids are mentioned in the early travelers' accounts, this mode of recruitment must have been extremely common in traditional Bornu society. Every market of any size had attached to it a slave market where male slaves could be purchased for whatever was accepted as the local currency. Often female slaves were sold in separate places, at least those who were to be used as concubines and not field hands. It is important to note that the presence of a market was a constant reminder that the relationship between slave and master was capable of dissolution at any time. Traders from north Africa constantly came to Bornu and other Sudanic states searching for a caravan load of slaves to take back across the desert. Mortality rates among slaves on such trips were extremely high, and this again was widely known among the population. Buyers examined males and females, old and young alike, carefully. The prospective buyer went from slave to slave examining the tongue, teeth, eyes, limbs, and made the slaves cough to find out if they were ruptured. If a slave was found to be faulty within the first three days after a sale, he could be returned to the seller and the price restored.

Recruitment to the role of eunuch involved a special operation from which very few survived. A male captive was castrated surgically and a small stick left in the opening to serve as a passage for urine. Estimates on the survival rate vary from one to five percent but never higher. Yet there was an active export trade in eunuchs who were needed for all the seraglios of the Islamic world as well as in Bornu society where they were used in the household and for a number of political offices in the state.

Finally there are some indications that, depending upon the nature of local administration, certain crimes such as continual petty stealing could result in a man and his paternal relatives being sold into slavery at the discretion of the local political leaders.

In the society as a whole, the connotation of being a slave meant, in effect, having a lower social position than non-slaves at the same social level. However, except for the monarch, positions at all social levels were open to slaves. This creates an extremely different society from that of plantation America. In general, a great deal of the manual work in the fields and in craft production was handled by slaves. Just how much is difficult to say, but certainly it was a highly significant proportion of the labor forces. As a laboring class, slaves wore simple clothing, generally short work shirts, and went hatless to signify their non-Muslim status. This latter quality is still regarded as the primary symbol of the slave status in Bornu although it has lost its non-Muslim connotations.

Aside from work roles, male slaves were also used a wrestlers. Owners would match their slaves who were expert in this sport against one another at harvest time, rewarding winners with robes and other gifts, and often selling losers in the market as punishment. The contests often resulted in the death of one of the contestants.

The major affiliation of Kanuri slaves was to the household since this was, and is, the basic corporate grouping in Bornu society. However, the affiliation—although linked to households (actually the household heads) —was more complicated than this because of the numbers involved and the varying degrees of status among households. The slaves attached to the royal household might be nobles of the realm. Indeed, many of the most important titles of the kingdom were reserved for people of slave status, especially in the nineteenth century when a second dynasty was founded on the remains of the first, and the usurper had to obtain a working administration while the ancient one was still present at least in name. To do this he elevated a number of old slave titles such as *Kachella* (slave military leader), and these came to have extreme importance in his state administration.

The Kachella, like all other slaves of the royal household, were divided into two groups—those of the house and those of the outside—or bush. Of the inside slaves the most important were those eunuchs who were the personal attendants of the monarch. These men formed what amounted to a secretariat for the monarch, and they were important in the succession to the royal office since they were the first to learn of his death. The division into household slaves and outside slaves was also carried on throughout the society. It had more meaning for the noble and wealthy since they could maintain slave settlements whose surplus productivity they controlled. Such settlements were called *Karliyari* or place of slaves, and a number of Bornu towns still bear this name to witness the nature of their origin.

Eunuchs were highly prized among the upper classes. They were used as messengers and go-betweens for women in *purdah* and as political subordinates who helped their master to administer whatever areas he had under his control. In a centralized state, they were the best of all possible followers in matters of reappointment because they did not obligate a superior in any way to appoint or take care of their descendants.

Female slaves were basically of the two same varieties, house slaves or concubines and laborers. The laborers—obtained from markets, born to the status, or captured—were generally from pagan areas to the south of Bornu, especially the Cameroon mountain region. Generally they could be distinguished by their perforated lips, through which they placed large silver discs—a habit considered disgusting and pagan by the Kanuri. Concubines were obtained from the Kanurized offspring of these women or were purchased from Muslims, especially Shuwa nomads from the east who sold their daughters to the Kanuri as concubines. Women captured in raids, from no matter what source, who were considered to be very beautiful were set aside, and the monarch was asked if he wished to have them for his household. If not, they were generally given to other nobles for the same purpose.

Traditionally household slaves were extremely dependent upon and close to their masters. Such slaves sold goods for their owners in the market, managed household affairs, administered the household personnel (including other slaves), and often held slaves of their own. As their masters prospered, so did they. In such a system slaves who met the standards were treated kindly. Those who tried to escape or who were disloyal were put in irons, and continued malfeasance meant that they must be sold, often for the trans-Saharan trek—a horror that must have produced many a second thought on the part of a rebellious slave.

Freeing slaves was not common in Bornu, but it did occur and in a number of ways. Slaves were often sent home when they approached old age. A master would pay transportation costs and often purchase a brother, sister, son, or other relative of their own slave from another owner in order that a family might be reunited for its return home. Again, a man might say to his heirs that upon his death he wished to see a number of his slaves freed. Generally this latter method was used only for household slaves. The most common method, however, was and is through birth and marriage. If a concubine gives birth, she may remain a slave—and by rights her master does not have to marry her—but the child is considered to be free.

The final method of manumission in the twentieth century is to simply opt for it. Since 1936 all slaves have been officially free—they may come and go as they choose.

In conclusion, slavery among the Kanuri was basically a function of the household organization and of warfare and trade. Slaves were a valuable result of warfare and could be used as an export item as well as a locally marketable commodity. The system of household organization and its central position as the most important corporate group in the society meant that slave status within the society was defined fundamentally by the relationship of the slave to the household head.

However, this is not the whole story. Slave status was also a function of sex and age and of the system of *purdah* in marriage which created a need for eunuchs as household servants who could mediate between incarcerated wives and the outside world. The need for large scale productivity and obedience in the economic and political systems also meant that there was a ready market for slaves.

Slavery in Zanzibar

The population of Zanzibar and the Pemba islands toward the end of the last century consisted of three main groups:

- The politically powerful Arabs, perhaps 10,000, lived in the thickly forested, hillier parts of the two islands.
- The Shirazi, about 70,000, were politically independent of the Arabs and lived in the coral areas.
- The third group, the slaves, numbering about 20,000, were from the mainland and were despised by the other two groups. The slaves were held primarily by the Arabs who owned extensive plantations.

Slavery in Zanzibar was of three kinds. The first was temporary enslavement in the islands while waiting to be sold at the central slave market in Zanzibar City. These slaves were kept for a few weeks in barracks, or sometimes on *dhows* in the harbor, were usually chained, and had no direct role in the economy or society of the island. The other two categories were those of slaves actually kept by Arab owners (and a few Shirazi, mainly rulers) in the islands. The owners, if wealthy enough, kept establishments both in the capital, Zanzibar City, and in the countryside in the plantation areas where they lived the life of country squires. The main group of slaves were the field workers; the other, the domestic slaves.

The Arabs on the plantation were relatively few—the owner and his family, a few overseers and guards. On any particular plantation, field slaves were likely to be a great majority of the population. Slaves were permitted to build houses wherever they liked on the master's plantation and to grow food crops. They had three main obligations:

—to weed and pick the cloves, coconut, and other trees which were the property of Arabs only and which provided the main export crops;
—to provide their owners with a proportion of the foodstuffs they grew—a fairly small proportion;
—to sit with the master and his agents and overseers when required and to discuss matters of general interest—the role of country gentleman was an important one for the Arab landowner and slave owner.

Because of the great tribal diversity among slaves, they tended to live and build their huts in small clusters apart from those of other tribal groups on any given plantation. There seems to have been fairly little contact between such tribal groupings. Thus they lived in small isolated groups with little social mobility. There were few women, and therefore relatively few marriages among the slaves.

In general, plantation slavery in Zanzibar seems to have been fairly benign, although there are accounts of great brutality by a minority of Arabs. There are recorded several slave revolts, but most of these were in fact relatively large-scale escapes. Groups of slaves united by tribal affiliation seized Arab *dhows* in Zanzibar harbor and used them to escape, usually with the connivance of sailors or others of the same tribes. Slaves could also always escape to the hinterland of the islands themselves, where they were safe from Arabs—roads did not exist until the turn of the century, after the ending of slavery; but it seems that they were liable to be enslaved by Shirazi, and there is no telling how many escaped in this way. There were a few small communities of runaway slaves living in northern Pemba, but they were small and must have led a precarious existence.

Domestic slaves formed a minority of the slave population and comprised both house servants and concubines. I have met both categories of ex-slaves and talked at length with them about slavery, and, in general, they agree that their lot was far better than that of the plantation slaves. In many cases the house slaves became Muslims, and certainly this made their fate easier. As long as they were obedient, they suffered little cruelty and indignity. They were often given as gifts between Arabs. House slaves tended to come also from certain tribes in the interior which were regarded as superior to others, mainly because they supplied chiefs who allied themselves with the Arab Swahili traders. These were mainly the Maniema of the Congo and the Nyamwezi of central Tanganyika.

Some of the larger Arab households had as many as two or three hundred slaves; these households, of course, would contain many Arabs— both kin of the household head and clients and servants—and each, including the children, had their own personal slave-servants, both male and female. The men were allowed a certain amount of free time in which they could acquire their own wealth; many became artisans, giving part of their income to their masters, who might first set them up in business. Others, especially eunuchs, acted as confidential advisers and messengers, both to members of the royal family and to lesser Arab men of standing; others worked on the local *dhows* as crewmen and occasionally as masters.

Male house slaves were servants of various kinds—cooks, watchmen, eunuchs, guards, porters, and so on. Women slaves were concubines of one kind or another or were married to the men servants if not required as concubines by their owners—this was according to Islamic law on the subject. There were four categories of women found in Arab households in Zanzibar during the period of slavery. First were Arab wives and Arab concubines (there were also a few concubines of European, Circassian, and other origins). Then there were slave women who were used as concubines or married off to men slaves; since slaves could not supply bride-wealth (or bride-price) the owners usually did so, thus establishing a quasi-kin tie with the slaves and their children. And last were women known as *suria*; their status was higher than that of concubines; their children were recognized publically as the free children of slave owners; and on their death, the *suria* women were granted freedom and usually a pension. *Suria* were both Arabs and slaves.

Manumission was almost always made only at the death of the slave owner, as an act of Muslim piety, or for a special Thanksgiving occasion. Perhaps the most famous case was that of Sultan Seyyid Said, who by his last will in 1850 manumitted all his domestic slaves, both men and women, leaving them their personal property and also small sums of money from his own personal estate. But to have freed the field slaves would have destroyed his own family's wealth, and they were not manumitted. In most cases charitable endowment (*waqf*) was made for freed slaves, and many of these *waqf* still exist today. Freed slaves usually became artisans and small traders in Zanzibar City.

Slavery in Zanzibar was a very different institution than it was in West Africa. But it presented several obvious similarities to the plantation slavery of the New World and to slavery at the Cape of Good Hope, in the islands of the Indian Ocean, and in Indonesia. The two obvious factors that were significant were the economic situation and the ethnic distinction between master and slave.

The economy was based on the growing of one or a few cash crops on alien-owned plantations by slave labor; slaves were also used domestically, but this was economically of much less significance. Except on a small scale in Zanzibar City, which was itself very small during the period of slavery—probably never with a total population of more than 20,000—slaves never played a political role, and their use as sacrificial victims (as in parts of West Africa) was unknown.

The other, and associated, factor, was that Arabs and mainland slaves were ethnically and culturally very distinct. (Although the large number of children of African *suria* concubines, who were recognized as legitimate, meant that there was always much racial intermixture in that part of the population called "Arab"; this applied to the royal family as well as to others.) In addition, slaves and Shirazi were ethnically very different.

The slave population, therefore, was sharply distinct from the other elements, a situation unlike that in, for example, West Africa. It followed that slaves were never incorporated into lineages or other groups of the slave-owning community, as had also happened in parts of West Africa. Except for the children of concubines, slaves could not easily be adopted into slave-owning groups; and, as elsewhere, the few who did acquire any considerable political or economic power were usually eunuchs who left no offspring.

That it was mainly an economic institution, however, may also be seen in the fact that "squatting"—which was so clearly based on the farmer slavery—persisted for many years after the abolition of slavery, as long as the clove-based economy, the system of Arab-controlled land holding, and generally recognized ethnic differences between Arab, Shirazi, and mainland Africans, were still accepted as being socially valid.

Ila Slavery (Zambia)

Among the Ila of Rhodesia there were three sources of slaves: raids, payment of debt, and purchase.

Relatively few were obtained from raids. A larger source were those individuals, usually children, who were accepted as payment for debts or fines. But the majority of slaves were purchased from nearby groups culturally similar to the Ila. Cattle, salt, leopard skins, hoes, or grain were the standard media of exchange. Characteristics most eagerly sought by purchasers were youth and absence of deformities.

There were no preferences in sex; both males and females were avidly purchased. Males were used as workers and fighters, while females added cattle to the family herds when they married or, if they did not marry, they produced children for the family and worked in the fields.

The ambiguous and indeterminate positions of Ila slaves are reflected in the terms used to describe them, and the attitudes about them. No elaborate stereotype existed; slaves were represented primarily as people who "didn't know where their ancestors came from" or "women who did not receive property in marriage"—there was no invidious connotation. Direct reference to their being slaves was considered insulting. A joking name, kinship term or spirit name, or the customary term of address for a free person were accepted procedures for addressing slaves.

The relationship between a slave and his owner was clearly not that of superior and subordinate. It was phrased in kinship terms. As soon as slaves were brought to the village, they became part of their owner's kin group. During a communal ritual a kin member informed the ancestral spirits of the slaves' entrance into the group and asked them to recognize and protect the new members. The slave called his owner by a kin term as well, and this genealogical function was adopted and extended to other relatives.

In outward appearance, the treatment and condition of a young slave was indistinguishable from that of the free Ila child. Both free and slave children lived within the village and aided in cattle herding, running errands, and doing minor tasks. Subtle preferences were perhaps shown to actual kinsmen in choice of foods or presents; but impartiality was the general rule, and the fact of slave status or ancestry was minimized.

Slave children were consciously raised as Ila and kinsmen. They underwent the same initiation rites as the free Ila with full ceremonies. During a slave's youth, his owner presented him with cattle from the family herds, further establishing kinship. These animals became the slave's property and represented the nucleus of his private herd. He acquired the same privileges and responsibilities in regard to them and the family herd as direct descendants did. The owner assumed responsibility for his slaves' debts and fines, and fines for slaves and non-slaves were the same.

There were times, however, when the position of a slave was clear, and the fictitious kinship was ignored. At these times young slaves were regarded primarily as property. At the death of an owner, young slaves could be inherited by the creditors of their deceased master or be distributed within the kin group like other property. Older slaves were not inherited in this fashion, but the Ila were vague about the exact age at which a slave was assured of continuity of residence and stability of relations. They did insist, however, that if a slave had lived in one village for a greater portion of his life he was a quasi-kinsman and was not considered property.

The differences between adult slaves and non-slaves was of degree rather than kind. Older slaves were used as labor, thus relieving the owner and his kinsmen of unpleasant tasks. Slaves did most of the work. Further, those slaves (a minority) who did not possess fields of their own, worked exclusively in their owner's fields or herded his cattle. But physical punishment was not common, and the methods used to control slaves were similar to those applied to free men.

Female slaves were absorbed into the kinship system with more difficulty than the males, and their condition reflected the real discrepancies between verbalized and actual kinship affiliation. The *nabutema* (divorced or older unmarried slave women) lived in the center of the village in small huts of inferior quality; they cleared the fields, planted the crops, and gathered wood. If desired, they were assigned to visitors for their sexual pleasure. Of all slaves, they suffered the greatest exploitation.

Slave ancestry presented no definite barrier to inter-marriage with free Ila. Ila free women married male slaves, slave women married free men, and interslave unions took place. However, the most common status for a slave woman was that of a secondary wife (junior wife in a polygynous household). Slave women were sometimes given in marriage to sons or kinsmen of their owner. Thus they served as an extra supply of wives for the kin group.

The children of a marriage between a slave and a free man further served to blur the distinction between slave and non-slave. Slavery, among the Ila, implied a lack of extended kinship affiliations, but second-generation slaves established such affiliations through marriage and residence, since they had more opportunity to establish kinship relations. The Ila summarized this fact by stating that anyone born within a village is a kinsman. Thus, slaves began to incorporate into the Ila kin groups after one generation.

Slave status or ancestry did not hamper the slaves in the Ila economic system for they owned property—including other slaves. Former slaves who had acquired property could establish their own lineage units by purchasing other slaves or by persuading the dissatisfied relatives of a deceased headman to transfer allegiance to them.

Crucial to an understanding of the role of slavery was the fact that slaves contributed cattle to the bride-wealth of their adopted kinsmen, and in return they shared its distribution within the group. (Bride-wealth refers to a payment, or series of them, made by the groom and his kinship unit to the bride's kinship group upon the inception of a marriage.) In addition, upon the death of a headman, slaves or those of slave ancestry inherited a portion of the cattle held in the name of the lineage group. Conversely, the slave's owner, and his immediate kin, were the major recipients of a slave's property after he died. Yet with all these distributions and contributions, the fact remains that the economic activity of the slave was generally restricted to that one section of the total social structure; first-generation slaves did not inherit from or participate in exchanges with any larger kin groups.

Free members of the community maintained multiple ties and relationships through the various kinship groups of their mothers and grandmothers. These relationships, although providing economic aid and support for participants, resulted in conflicting loyalties and responsibilities for non-slaves. As a result, the position of a *musolozhi* (headman) was measurably strengthened by the presence in his village of a number of individuals who "had no other place to go"—that is, primarily, slaves.

Since centralized leadership was lacking, there was a continual struggle among kinship units for political power. Authority was diffused; power did not automatically devolve upon anybody. The authority of the kinship head was based upon the number of dependents he could control, so that a large number of slaves living in a village would be very useful, politically. Since slaves, like kinsmen, were necessary for defense and for support in the constant maneuvering for property and the regulation of village life, a slave who had been unfairly treated could run away from his village, and a neighboring village would accept him gladly. The new owner or the runaway slave himself would reimburse the previous owner, and the slave would be incorporated into the village on a quasi-kinship basis.

It appears that slavery among the Ila did not produce fixed social classes with an unequal distribution of wealth or authority. Those that did exist did not affect the slave permanently, and within a short time slaves were truly incorporated into the kinship system on a basis similar to non-slaves.

17.
Algerian Peasant Revolt

Eric R. Wolf

Six major social and political upheavals, fought with peasant support, have shaken the world of the twentieth century: The Mexican revolution of 1910, the Russian revolutions of 1905 and 1917, the Chinese revolution which metamorphosed through various phases from 1921 onwards, the Vietnamese revolution which has its roots in the Second World War, the Algerian rebellion of 1954 and the Cuban revolution of 1958. All of these were to some extent based on the participation of rural populations. Here I will concentrate on the Algerian Revolution, but first let me make some general comments to set the story in context.

Romantics to the contrary, it is not easy for a peasantry to engage in sustained rebellion. A peasant's work is more often done alone, on his own land, than in conjunction with his fellow's, and his life is geared to an annual routine and to planning for the year to come. Momentary alterations of routine threaten his ability to take up the routine later. At the same time, however, control of land enables him to retreat into subsistence production if adverse conditions affect their market crop.

Moreover, the peasant's interests—especially among poor peasants—often cross-cut class alignments. Rich and poor may be kinfolk, or a peasant may be at one and at the same time owner, renter, sharecropper, laborer for his neighbors and seasonal hand on a nearby plantation. Each different involvement aligns him differently with his fellows and with the outside world. Hence peasants are often merely passive spectators of political struggles or long for the sudden advent of a millennium, without specifying for themselves and their neighbors the many rungs on the staircase to heaven.

If it is true that peasants are slow to rise, then peasant participation in the great rebellions of the twentieth century must obey some special factors that exacerbated the peasant condition. We will not understand that condition unless we keep in mind constantly that it has suffered greatly under the impact of three great crises: the demographic crisis, the ecological crisis and the crisis in power and authority. The demographic crisis is most easily depicted in bare figures, though its root causes remain ill understood. Mexico, for example, had a population of 5.8 million at the beginning of the nineteenth century; in 1910—at the outbreak of the revolution—it had 16.5 million. Vietnam is estimated to have sustained a population of between 6 and 14 million in 1820; it had 30.5 million inhabitants in 1962. Cuba had 550,000 inhabitants in 1800; by 1953 it had 5.8 million. Algeria had an indigenous population of 10.5 million in 1963, representing a fourfold increase since the beginnings of French occupation in the first part of the nineteenth century.

These population increases coincided with a period in history when land and other resources were increasingly converted into commodities—in the capitalist sense of that word. As commodities they were subjected to the demands of a market which bore only a very indirect relation to the needs of the rural populations. Where, in the past, market behavior had been largely subsidiary to the existential problems of subsistence, now existence and its problems became subsidiary to the market. The alienation of peasant resources proceeded directly through outright seizure or through coercive purchase, as in Mexico, Algeria and Cuba; or it took the form— especially in China and Vietnam—of stepped-up capitalization of rent which resulted in the transfer of resources from those unable to keep up to those able to pay. In addition, capitalist mobilization of resources was reinforced through the pressure of taxation and through increased need for industrially produced commodities on the part of the peasantry itself. All together, however, these various pressures disrupted the precarious ecological balance of peasant society. At the same time as commercialization disrupted rural life, it also created new but unstable ecological niches in industry. Increased instability in the rural area was thus accompanied by a still unstable commitment to industrial work.

Finally, both the demographic and the ecological crisis converged in the crisis of authority. The development of the market produced a rapid circulation of the elite, in which the manipulators of the new free-floating resources—labor bosses, merchants, industrial entrepreneurs—challenged the inherited power of the controllers of fixed social resources, the tribal chief, the mandarin, the landed nobleman. Undisputed and stable claims thus yielded to unstable and disputed claims. This rivalry between primarily political and primarily economic power-holders contained its own dialectic. The imposition of the market mechanism entailed a diminution of social responsibilities for all concerned: the economic entrepreneur did not concern himself with the social cost of his activities; while the traditional power-holder was often too limited in his power to offer assistance or was subject to co-optation by his successful rivals. The advent of the market not only produced a crisis in peasant ecology; it deranged the numerous middle-level ties between center and hinter-land, between the urban and the rural sectors. The result was an ever-widening gap between the rulers and the ruled.

Conquest and Colonization

In 1830 an altercation between the Turkish governor of Algeria and the French consul brought French armies to Algiers. At first, France merely established a protectorate, but in 1840 the French government decided on the wholesale conquest and colonization of the entire country—largely in order to divert attention from the growing unpopularity of the regime of Charles X at home. The war was carried on by flying columns with a scorched earth policy of total devastation.

The first effect of the conquest was to deprive the native population of much of their land and to transfer it into the hands of Europeans. Algeria, like most other non-Western areas of the world, had not known the European institution of absolute private property before the advent of the Europeans; rather there existed a complex hierarchy of use rights, with ultimate title to the land being held on the one hand by the bey as ruler and on the other hand by the tribes. In either case, however, the lowliest cultivator could, by investing his labor, maintain his claim to the land and a viable share of its produce; and these rights were heritable.

When in 1863 the French applied Western European concepts of private property in land to Muslim holdings, they destroyed in one blow the entire pyramid of overrights which had guaranteed the livelihood of the cultivator but which had stood in the way of making land a freely circulating commodity. At the same time it threw all land held by Muslims upon the open market and made it available for purchase or seizure by French colonists. The French had already, as successors to the rights of sovereignty, raised taxes and parceled out the bey's best lands to settlers.

The imposition of French norms of private property in land went hand in hand with a program for the dismemberment of the great tribes whose chiefs had been the main supporters and beneficiaries of Turkish rule. The program was so effective that by the time France became involved in World War II the tribe had ceased to exist as a relevant social and political unit within the Algerian polity. When in 1941 the French caretaker government at Vichy took steps to reconstitute the tribes in the interests of improved control, French administrators concurred sadly that the steps taken in 1863 had done their job all too well in ending tribal power once and for all.

The *douars* inhabited by segments of former tribes were not made independent entities in their own right, but organized into larger communes on the French model. Some were communities dominated by Europeans, where the municipal council and mayor were elected by French citizens, and where Muslims were allowed to choose only a fourth of the delegates, even though the Muslim population might constitute the majority; others were mixed communities of Europeans and Muslims headed by a civil administrator and backed by an appointed council of Frenchmen and native chiefs (*caids*); and still others were indigenous communities commanded by a French officer, assisted by a native chief. All Muslims were permitted to use their own customary or Quranic law, but special laws against nonpayment of taxes, political activity against France, public assembly—including pilgrimages and public feasts—without permits, travel without permits, refusal to register births or deaths all singled out the Muslims as a population with special disabilities. The entire edifice of control was capped by making Algeria administratively part of metropolitan France. Assimilation to French cultural norms was set up as an idea, but separation—under conditions of economic, social, political and legal inequality—became the established fact.

Old Bonds Are Broken

The breakup of tribal units and the chiefs' power associated with them, however, produced several unforeseen consequences. It made it impossible for the chiefs to carry out free distributions of grain in time of famine from stores accumulated through gifts and levies paid by their tribal dependents. The law of 1863 also put an end to the distribution of charity by local religious lodges (*zaouias*), drawing supplies from their *habus* properties. These properties had become private lands and were thrown upon the market. Moreover, the new *douars* only rarely renewed the traditional custom of maintaining food reserves in communal silos, which had been supplied by traditional payments. Thus disappeared a set of vital economic defenses, leaving the rural population dependent wholly upon the activities of moneylenders and credit merchants in time of need.

A further paradoxical consequence of tribal fragmentation was the accentuated growth within the *douars* of the councils of tribal notables (*djemaa*). The French recognized these councils in both the mixed and indigenous communes, either granting them considerable autonomy or using them in a consultative capacity, especially in matters of Muslim law. But in the communities dominated by Europeans, theory made no provision for native participation. But here too there also developed a honeycomb of what one French legal expert has called *djemaas occultes* (hidden councils). Both open and hidden councils thereby maintained a tradition of local decision-making and self-management that was to prove of capital importance in aiding the rebel cause in 1954.

French encroachment also produced revolts. The first of these, dating from 1832 to 1847, was led by Abd el Kader. Basing his support on local chiefs in the countryside, the revolt failed; but his distrust of the great families, combined with support of Islam, has caused Algerian nationalists to see in Abd el Kader a forerunner of the populist revolt of the twentieth century. The second revolt, led by a great chieftan, Moqrani, was even shorter lived, 1871-72, and marked the last uprising by a native feudatory. At the same time, however, the prospect of a rebellion in the countryside seems to have haunted numerous Muslim chiefs and merchants sufficiently to cause them to throw in their lot with the French against the rebels. Thus the notables of Constantine on 21 April 1871 addressed themselves to the French authorities in a letter in which, as L. Rinn put it,

> they asked the governor not to confuse them, educated, enlightened people ... who appreciate with gratitude the protection and justice of France, with the "bedouins" or people of the tribes.... [They are] sedentary and literate citizens, who love quiet, peace, tranquility and comfort... the "bedouin" will not renounce their traditional conduct, the customs of their mountains, unless they are subjected to severe and energetic repression which fills them with a dread and terror that causes them to fear for their lives. Only force and violence can conquer their nature.

Force and violence were not long in coming. They took the form of punitive expropriations in favor of European colonists, carried out to make the native population pay for the costs of the rebellion. The expropriations were justified by the Superior Government Council in the following words:

> The expropriation is a punishment capable of leaving a permanent trace; a seizure of property well justified by persistent and repeated return to crime will smite the spirit of the guilty sufficiently by subjecting them to an effective repression with consequences which cannot be wiped out. The real employment of expropriation, that is peace; that is blood and ruins avoided in the future ... political interest, the security of the colony, the civilizing of races who will not come to us until the hope of shaking our domination has disappeared from their minds, a clairvoyant humanity which avoids the disasters of the future by the severity of the present command the maintenance of expropriation and its consequences.

In addition, special punitive levies eight times larger than the annual tax charges were imposed on the rebellious areas and collected through the agency of the chiefs who had remained faithful to the French. The chiefs, said the peasants, "have taken our skin and bones and now they break our bones to eat the marrow." The terrible memory of these years when "justice and truth disappeared," "brother was set against brother" and the chiefs "grew rich through treason" has remained green in Kabyle chants recorded half a century later. It reinforced a permanent ambivalence toward the traditional chiefs and their successors as pro-French intermediaries between the conquerors and the indigenous masses, an ambivalence that was to be of moment in the turmoil leading up to the war of independence.

Envelopment

While the Muslims were thus expropriated and forced to witness the dismemberment of their social framework, Algeria was thrown wide open to European immigration and settlement. The new *colons* were all Frenchmen in name, but only half of them were of direct French origin, drawn mainly from poor, south-central France and—after the French defeat of 1871—from Alsace. The other half was made up primarily of Spaniards and Italians, of Corsicans and Maltese. It was the mixed character of this population which caused the French writer Anatole France to say in 1905 that France had during 70 years fleeced, chased and run to ground the Arabs in order to people Algiers with Italians and Spaniards. At first segregated residentially into separate settlements, they quickly came to make common cause through intermarriage and through common hatred of Arabs. A sense of envelopment and the threat of submersion can be found in the early novels of Albert Camus, himself born and raised in Algeria; and it was this fear which caused the *colons* first to resist any and every effort at reform initiated in metropolitan France, and later to embrace one or another variety of fascism, culminating in their support of the terroristic Organisation de l'Armée Sécrète (OAS) at the end of the war of independence.

The mainstay of *colon* economy, and the mainstay of the Algerian economy as a whole, came to be vineyard cultivation and the production of wine, especially after 1880 when the phylloxera louse destroyed much of French viticulture and France was forced to import much of her wine. Wine exports from Algeria came to form 50 percent of all Algerian exports. The acreage in vineyards more than doubled between 1900 and 1954 at the expense of food crops and pasture. As Michel Launay wrote, "The result is that the vine has displaced and polluted all else: it has chased away the wheat, it has chased away the sheep, it has chased away the forest and the dwarf palm. It has polluted the river where the skins and pips, lees, and refuse are thrown." This was especially true in western Algeria where low rainfall favored the extension of vineyards up to the very limits of the steppe. This area became the center of European rural settlement; nine-tenths of all Algerian vineyards—and thus most of the main cash crop—were in the hands of Europeans. At the same time, vineyard cultivation greatly contributed to social and economic differentiation among the *colons* themselves. Wine production and transport require considerable capital outlays in pressing cellars, vats and other plants and thus favored the ascendancy of the large *colon* over the small who had to rely on him for credit and access to the processing plant. It also placed much of the political control of the colony in the hands of a powerful oligarchy of wine merchants, shippers and bankers.

Many *colons* lost their land and moved to town. By 1954 over three-quarters of a million Europeans, or more than 80 percent of the entire European population, lived in urban centers. Here their occupations mirrored the skewed character of an agrarian country, dependent on one major cash crop, in its relation to an industrial metropolis. Of a total work force of some 300,000 Europeans, 35,000 were skilled workers and 55,000 were listed as unskilled; the remainder worked either in administration or management (close to 50,000) or in services of one kind or another (about 160,000). Most of these were office employees, small traders, caterers and mechanics. Despite these differences, they were as one in defense of their privileges which made the lowest French *colon* the superior of any Arab. Their unity was the product of their common fear of the Muslim majority.

How did that majority react to the changes imposed on it? The revolt of El Moqrani was to be the last major effort at armed resistance until some 80 years later. It was also to be the last major effort, until 1954, of the rural population to take the political initiative. There set in a long period of political inactivity, which only gave way to new political efforts around the time of World War I. Moreover, political activity would be first renewed in the cities, including the cities of France with their newly generated proletariat, before it would spread once again into the rural hinterland. Frantz Fanon, who has analyzed in overly Manichaean terms the conflict between conquerors and conquered, has portrayed their relations as one of continuous and endemic violence. Violence was certainly present during the 83 years between Moqrani's revolt and 1954, but it remained covert rather than overt, quiescent rather than emphatic. This was a period not so much of incubation of the revolution-to-be, but rather of muted changes and adjustments, experiments in social and cultural relations, with attendant advances and retreats. At the same time it was a period marked by shifts in the cognitive and emotional evaluation of different possibilities, rather than by a single-minded ideological rehearsal of things to come.

The Veil

Those Algerians who took any interest in politics and expressed a concern about the relation of Algeria to France oscillated between two main positions; sometimes they held both positions simultaneously, sometimes in quick succession. The defendants of one position called for increased contact with French cultural norms and assimilation to them. Socially, this assimilationism was most congruent with the interests of middle-class professionals of whom there were about 450 in the higher ranks, whose social standing depended on their French education, and who saw in their French degrees a passport to mobility. The other tendency was anti-assimilationist and directed toward an effort to define an Algerian nationality, different from the French and opposed to it. On a behavioral level this tendency manifested itself—even among assimilationists—in an attitude of reserve against foreign encroachment upon the intimate spheres of family life and religion.

Pierre Bourdieu has made the same point in stating that for the Algerians, adherence to traditional forms came to fulfill "essentially a symbolic function; it played the role, objectively, of a language of refusal" and illustrated this point with reference to the traditional custom of veiling of which Frenchmen were especially critical: the veil worn by Muslim women

> is above all a defense of intimacy and a protection against intrusion. And, confusedly, the Europeans have always perceived it as such. By wearing the veil, the Algerian woman creates a situation of non-reciprocity; like a disloyal player, she sees without being seen, without allowing herself to be seen. And it is the entire dominated society which, by means of the veil, refuses reciprocity, which sees, which penetrates, without allowing itself to be seen, regarded, penetrated.

Islam would thus prove to be one of the roots of Algerian nationalism. In the course of the 1920s and 1930s the attitude of refusal and withdrawal would issue in a new and active movement, founded in an attempt to return to the purity of the Quran. The centers of this Islamic revival lay not in the new French towns of the Mediterranean littoral, but in the old Islamic towns of the hinterland, once the seats of active and well-to-do Islamic traders and entrepreneurs, such as Tlemcen, Nedroma, Constantine, Mila, Tebessa, Sidi Okba, Biskra and Ghardaia. With the advent of French rule, many of them receded into the background; Constantine and Tlemcen, for instance, once possessed a thriving textile industry which declined under the impact of French competition. It is no accident, as Morizot has pointed out, that Tlemcen—pivot of a religious exodus to Tunisia in 1911— produced Messali Hadj, the first organizer of a nationalist Algerian party, while Constantine gave rise to Ben Badis, the Algerian protagonist of a revived and militant Islam.

Taught by the Islamic schoolmen of Constantine, Sheikh Abd-el-Hamid Ben Badis was to fuse Algerian religious tradition with the innovating influence of the Islamic reform movement of the early twentieth century. In the context of North Africa, this brought the reformers into direct conflict with local forms of Islam, as practiced in numerous religious lodges. These lodges, and the popular religious fraternities built upon them, had acted strongly in support of Abd el Kader during his resistance against the French and remained anti-French until the turn of the century. Thereafter, however, they had come to an accommodation with the French authorities who consciously supported them as convenient means for keeping the social body of Algeria as divided as possible.

The Badissia, as the reform movement came to be known after the name of its principal figure, was antagonistic to the traditional holy men. Instead it asserted the authority of the reformist schoolmen, the *ulema*, and furthered the creation of numerous orthodox schools (*medersas*) in the hinterland. Beginning in the cities, they nevertheless seeded the hinterland with associations of all kinds, including Islamic boy scouts, under the aegis of their slogan: "Arabic is my language, Algeria is my country, Islam is my religion." Their social support in the countryside was provided in the main by the middle-class peasantry and among the small merchants, entrepreneurs and teachers of the rural towns.

Islam's Role

Such an affiliation of independent peasantry with the new urban world by means of religious associations—new organizational forms within the traditional religious matrix—may also have received reinforcement through the stimulus of economic interests. The Badissia strongly opposed the heterodox religious feasts carried on by the holy men and the expenditures associated with them. These expenditures constitute a major drain on a peasantry, and their abolition by a religious reform movement is a common feature in many parts of the world. In many parts of the Andes and Middle America, for instance, it has underwritten conversions to Protestantism in otherwise traditionally Catholic Indian communities. The Badissia also demanded the restoration of the properties of religious foundations seized by the French. As a notable of Aoubelli said to Michel Launay: "Since at the conquest many Muslims gave their property to the habus to save them from annexation by the French, the claim to a return [of these properties] challenged the whole picture of colonial property." In the words of Jacques Berque, the Badissia created a new and Jacobin Islam.

This Jacobin Islam would have especially strong appeal not only to Islamic traders and entrepreneurs of declining towns in the hinterland, but also to the rural class of middling landowners and numerous small traders, as shown in Launay's investigation of the area of Ain-Temuchent in Oran Province. The agricultural workers and the poor peasants in general clung to their traditional holy men and resisted the reformers. And years later it was this same stratum, the middle peasants, in Ain-Temuchent which furnished support for the uprising of 1954: "The organizers of the insurrection were the small holders, not the little proletarianized small holders but the small holders almost able to make ends meet, well-off in comparison with agricultural workers." Moreover, René Delisle is quite correct when he says that "the insurrection of 1954 and the independence of 1962 are thus, in this respect, only the necessary conclusion of the action initiated in 1930 by the reformist Ulemas, restorers of Islam and of Arab tradition."

New Proletariat

If reformist Islam provided one of the sources of Algerian nationalism, the other source lay in the increasing development of an Algerian semiproletariat. This, in turn, was the product of two major causes: the decay of the traditional pattern of Algerian sharecropping, the *khammesat* (from *khammes,* "a fifth"), coupled with the need—especially strong in central Algeria, among the Berber-speaking Kabyles—to supplement a meager agriculture with some other form of employment.

Under the *khammesat,* the sharecropper received not only tools and seed, but also money advances and food, sums which were then subtracted from the final produce. The new French legal codes, however, allowed sharecroppers to abandon their landlords without previous reimbursement of these costs. While the law thus freed the sharecroppers from a form of traditional bondage, it also hastened the decline of sharecropping and the advent of day labor. Previous conditions of servitude had canceled out the variable effects of good and poor years, by standardizing sharecropper duties and rights. Now workers sought positions as sharecroppers during bad years, in order to guarantee their livelihood, but abandoned their owners with the advent of a promising year. Shortly after the passage of the law the *qaid* of Heumis testified that

> French law having emancipated the sharecropper, the owners in large numbers preferred not to give them work, for fear of losing their advances. The sharecropper no longer finds work because one does not want to engage him in ways other than by the day.

The result was both an increased number of men looking for work as wage laborers and a reduction in the area previously cultivated. Now, said an old Muslim teacher to Launay, "the agricultural worker cannot be sure of anything." One effect of growing wage labor was therefore the creation of a large floating semiproletariat, which was to bear all the stigmata of a growing economic insecurity.

Yet the growing trend toward wage labor possessed still another face.

Increasingly, many areas—but most notably the mountains of Kabylia—began to experience the pressures of population growth on available food resources. French colonization had driven the natives into the barren hinterland, often producing compact and dense settlements in terrain which could not support such numbers. Military pacification and the spread of modern health care further curtailed the Malthusian checks on the population growth. As a result, many Kabyles were forced to seek alternative sources of livelihood outside their mountains.

At the same time, Algerians—and again most especially the Berber-speakers from Kabylia—began to be recruited into the labor force of metropolitan France. World War I witnessed the first massive employment of Algerians in France itself, to replace French laborers called to the colors and now at the front. Between 1915 and 1918 some 76,000 Algerians left to work in French factories. This trend was continued steadily over the years, until in 1950 there were some 600,000 Algerians in the metropolis. This large-scale movement caught up great numbers of Algerians in the forced draft of acculturation. They received their education, as Germaine Tillion has put it, in the "school of the cities." As a result, there developed on French soil a fully fledged Algerian proletariat with strong and enduring ties to the rural Algerian hinterland.

Nationalism and Education

This working-class milieu had two immediate effects. First, it incubated the first modern nationalist Algerian movement, in the formation of the Etoile Nord Africaine in Paris in 1925, in which Messali Hadj became the dominant personality. Left-wing party and trade union activity associated with this experience in urban France provided the migrant workers both with models of organization and with fragments of socialist ideology which they found of use in interpreting the condition of their homeland. It proved doubly significant, moreover, that—upon their return to Algeria—they could do little to give substance to their aspirations through the *colon*-dominated Socialist and Communist unions and parties of the colony. From the first, the logic of the colonial situation forced them to give their support to nationalist parties, first to the Messalist Parti Populaire Algérien, and later to its more militant successors.

The second consequence of the French experience was that it produced among the Algerian workers in the metropole the realization that an adequate French education constituted a passport to entry into the modern technical civilization. Tillion notes that

> twenty-five years later, one meets certain doctors, certain lawyers, certain professors, certain mathematicians or chemists whose brilliant studies have been paid for during these already long distant years by a father or an elder brother out of his laborer's salary. To achieve this result, the illiterate émigré

must have had to deprive himself daily of what in France we call the "vital minimum," and even before he could do that he had to grasp the mechanisms and the values of an alien world, indoctrinate his family, separate his little boy from his mother, and then push him—ardently, patiently, proudly—to the fore.

Both of these trends—the growth of reformist Islam on the one hand, the cityward migration of Algerian workers on the other—were to contribute decisively to the outbreak of the Algerian revolt of 1954. Reformist Islam provided the cultural form for the construction of a new network of social relations between clusters of middle peasants in the countryside and the sons of the urban elite of the hinterland towns. The city ward migration of the Algerian peasantry—most especially that of the Kabyles—not only brought them into contact with industrial and urban patterns of life, but produced a professional class in the course of that migratory experience. Once again networks were forged which linked clusters of peasants in the countryside with spokesmen and representatives in the cities. In studies of prominent Moslems involved in the revolution and its sequel, four features stood out: most were young men, whose formative political experience lay in the years of indecision of the 1930s and 1940s; a disproportionate number, compared to their role in the total population of Algeria, were of Berber origin; many were French-educated; many had served in the French army during World War II. Wholly against the expectations of the French, who had always pursued a policy of keeping the Berbers culturally and politically separate from the Arab population, in order to better divide and rule, the forces generated by a common involvement in processes set up by the French impact itself would bring these disparate groups into fusion.

Death of Assimilationism

Undoubtedly this fusion was speeded up by the events of the period preceding World War II, and the world war itself. As long as there was hope that reform in France could produce greater liberty and autonomy for Muslim Algerians, there also remained some hope that the expectations of both assimilationists and nationalists could be met without the use of force and violence. But as it became increasingly clear—during long years of political prevarication and failure—that no French government capable of instituting reform was likely to emerge, the militant nationalists gained ground, and the tendency toward clandestine operations also gained momentum. To this must be added the impact of domestic trends. Between 1930 and 1954 the number of small Muslim owners decreased by a fifth and the number of day laborers rose by more than a quarter. During World War II and after, harvests were poor, wine production was down and livestock was lost in large numbers.

Even more significant, undoubtedly, were the more proximate causes of a political nature: France suffered a crushing defeat in 1940, revealing her weakness to all who had eyes to see. At the same time, half of the French nation was engaged in fighting the other half in underground operations, sharply raising the level of all-round uncertainty and illegality. The advent of fascism in France strongly supported violence on the part of fascist *colons* against the Algerian population. At the same time, however, Algerians were mobilized in considerable numbers to fight for France, thus both undergoing military training and achieving a level of significant equality with French fellow combatants.

All of this came to a head at Sétif on 1 May 1945. Some 8,000 to 10,000 Muslims had gathered to celebrate the Allied victories in Europe; many came with placards calling for the release from prison of Messali Hadj and for equality between Muslims and Christians. Shots were fired, and a riot ensued which spread to other towns. The riot was fiercely repressed by French air and ground forces and estimates of Muslims killed vary between 8,000 and 45,000, with 15,000 not an unlikely number. There is little doubt, says the Swiss journalist Charles-Henri Favrod, that "it was these events of 1945 which decided the revolution of 1954." French inability and unwillingness to grant concessions in time spelled the end of the assimilationist cause. This is most clearly exemplified in the person of Ferhat Abbas, long a leader of the assimilationists, who decided in April of 1954 that a party that "fights in favor of a 'revolution by law' can no longer advance...."

Militant and subversive movements increasingly developed among the proletarian nationalists. The Parti Populaire Algérien (PPA), driven underground in 1939, developed in 1947 a paramilitary arm in the MTLD—the Mouvement pour le Triomphe des Libertés Démocratiques. Within the MTLD, in turn, there grew up a secret terrorist society called Organisation Spéciale (OS); by 1949 it had 1,900 members. The founder members of the OS became the members of the Comité Révolutionnaire d'Unité et d'Action (CRUA), which unleashed the revolt of 1954. Not all the members of the PPA, however, were to join in the revolt. On the contrary, the struggle for independence against the French was to be accompanied throughout by a deadly struggle between partisans of the revolt and units derived from Messali Hadj's original PPA. This struggle was to prove especially bloody in metropolitan France, where close to a thousand Muslims died in internecine warfare.

The Revolt Begins

The insurrection broke out on the night of 31 October to 1 November 1954 with some three score incidents of attacks on French garrisons and police stations, ambushes and arson. Although widely scattered, most attacks erupted in eastern Algeria, especially in the mountains of the Aurès. The insurgents were few in number, probably no more than 500, with 300 of them concentrated in the Aurès; and they possessed less than 50 obsolete shotguns.

The Aurès was a logical first base for the revolt. Occupied by Berber-speakers, it has long been a zone of dissidence from any central government. Jacques Soustelle, anthropologist, governor-general of Algeria in 1955 and a leading spokesman and conspirator in the movement for an Algérie Française, was to say:

> one sees clearly that the Romans erred in limiting their occupation to the approaches to the mountain, since it remained for centuries the reservoir of uncontrolled forces ready to overflow. Our penetration in the Aurès and Nemenchas has been very weak: we have committed the same error as the Romans, with the same results.

Berber social and political organization resembles an "ordered anarchy"; anthropologists speak of it as unilineal and segmentary. In theory this works as a system of checks and balances as long as the units are more or less stable. Under French rule, however, this ideal balance had been upset. Improved healthy services had removed the checks on population growth and served to increase the pressure of population against available resources. The spread of money economy and the introduction of new needs—for coffee, sugar, ground grain—undermined traditional patterns of self-sufficiency. Land became a commodity, to be bought and sold. After World War I the migration of men to France initiated a system of monetary remissions in which work in the metropolis underwrote the economy of the mountains. All these trends accentuated competion among men and exacerbated opposition between tribal factions. The rebels adroitly exploited these local feuds, finding allies among one or another local fraction in the mountain area and helping them against their enemies. They also formed bandit groups. In the Aurés they established their first military district (Wilaya I), which remained a rebel bastion throughout the war. At the same time, between November 1954 and mid-March 1956, small determined groups of fighters began hit-and-run raids in other parts of Algeria.

With the advent of the revolt, CRUA became the executive committee of the National Liberation Front (Front de Libération Nationale, or FLN), which was to consist of an External Delegation, based in Cairo, and an Internal Delegation, made up of the military leaders of the revolt in Algiers. These military leaders were to head up six military districts, or *wilayas*; a seventh district would comprise metropolitan France. The total organization headed by the military leaders was to be known as the Army of National Liberation (Armée de Libération Nationale, or ALN). At the core of the army were to be the *mujahidin,* fighters for the faith, who were to be the regulars, surrounded by a fringe of civilian guerrillas, *mussabilin,* and *fidayin,* non-uniformed terrorists and saboteurs. The formal table of organization of the army could not hide the fact, however, that the organizational structure of the FLN represented a compromise solution between the interests of civilian and military leaders. This created a strain that was to be compounded during the war by further conflicts between various military leaders, and between those carrying on the guerrilla war inside the country and those who organized armed units outside. Jean Daniel has said that there existed in the FLN not one organizational pyramid, but a multitude of pyramids, and that "the unity of the FLN was never realized except in situations which forced the multiplicity of pyramids to move in the same direction." Ideologically, too, what held the movement together was a common nationalism. Socialist phraseology appeared occasionally in FLN pronouncements but remained vague enough not to become the rallying cry of any one faction against another until after the advent of Algerian independence.

By April 1956 French sources estimated rebel strength at 8,500 fighters and some 21,000 auxiliaries. Possessed of insufficient troop strength, the French were unable to prevent the westward spread of rebel units along the parallel mountain chains of the Atlas, despite repeated commando raids into the hostile interior. By April 1956, however, French units brought to Algeria from France, Germany and French West Africa augmented French forces to about 250,000 men; conscription was soon to add another 200,000. This increased force permitted a change in French tactics from the use of flying columns to the *quadrillage,* or grid system, in which towns and communication centers were held in strength, while mobile units of paratroopers, volunteers and foreign legionnaires probed the hinterland.

This new tactic did not eliminate the ALN, but it did check its activity in the back country. Toward the end of 1956, the ALN therefore mounted an offensive in the urban centers. Terrorist attacks increased in all cities, but especially in Algiers, where 120 acts took place in December alone. As everyone who has seen *The Battle of Algiers* knows, the ALN had successfully infiltrated the Muslim quarter of the city, the Casbah, with its population of 80,000. Here it had recruited some 4,000 men to its ranks, around a core of *lumpenproletariat,* "hooligans with a pure heart," who were given an opportunity to wash themselves clean of past sins. While the shift to urban terrorism had important psychological effects on the urban population, especially among Muslims who were won to the cause of the ALN in proportion to the inability of the French to protect them, the fact is it proved ineffective militarily. Between February and October 1957, the Tenth Paratroop Division commanded by General Jacques Massu effectively destroyed the terrorist organization in Algiers.

The Battle of Algiers

Checked within the country itself, the ALN was thus forced to seek alternative sources of support, which it found in neighboring Tunisia and Morocco. These two neighboring states, which had achieved independence from France in 1956, permitted the ALN to establish training centers on their soil and recruit new forces from among Algerians both within and without Algeria. By the end of 1957 there were more than 60,000 Algerian refugees in Tunis and 40,000 in Morocco. Recruitment by the ALN for this new "external" army grew apace. By the end of 1957, again it numbered 25,000 troops, while the "internal" forces amounted to only 15,000.

Yet this shift in ALN tactics also produced a comparable response from the French. By mid-September 1957 the French had constructed along the Moroccan frontier an elaborate barrier of electrified wire, alarm systems, strong points, mine fields and observation posts. A similar barrier was raised on the Tunisian side, thus effectively sealing off the external armies from the internal zone of operations. In 1958 the French also expanded their military effort inside Algeria. Each of the known ALN bases was cordoned off by a "pacified" zone, and attacks were mounted in turn on each of the separate military districts of the ALN. Communication between the districts was effectively destroyed, while all attempts of the ALN to mount battalion-size counterthrusts proved ineffective.

The rebels were therefore forced back once again upon the small-group tactics with which they had begun the insurrection. French military activity was, moreover, supported by a vast effort at relocating the civilian population, thus separating the rebels from possible sources of support. More than 1.8 million people were moved from their homes between 1955 and 1961, while others fled from the zones of military operation into the already overcrowded cities. Finally, the French counterthrust was capped by the employment of psychological warfare, ranging from mass persuasion and the provision of social services by army personnel to forcible indoctrination and torture.

Who "Won"?

The French effort had several consequences for the nationalist camp. It accentuated feuds among the leadership, especially between the leaders of the revolt outside Algeria and the military chieftains in the field. It isolated the military districts from each other and from outside sources of arms and support, curtailing their fighting capacity and reducing them ultimately to the level of petty principalities, at loggerheads with one another over resources, tactics and strategy. At the same time it left untouched the growing "external army" which grew more important for the nationalist leadership as a bargaining point in any final negotiations for peace in direct proportion to the decline of the internal army in both strength and effectiveness. Thus the end of the war was to find the external army under the leadership of Houari Boumédienne as the only intact and organized body of Algerians.

At the same time, the French effort dialectically produced the forces of its own undoing. As the French proved victorious, the hold of the nationalist cause over the minds of Algerians paradoxically grew apace. Some of the reasons for this were internal. The experience of forcible relocation, flight of refugees to the cities, the destruction of agricultural resources, the annihilation of nomadic groups who could no longer mount their migrations—all these pulverized the social relations of traditional society and produced a fearsome ideological vacuum. The conflict itself further polarized French settlers and Muslims, reinforcing their separate identities, which French efforts at psychological warfare exacerbated rather than reduced. At the same time, the costs of the conflict became ever more burdensome. In addition to loss of life and the stresses attendant upon war, the financial cost of the war to France proved huge: 50 billion new francs and $1.7 million in foreign currency spent on arms and attempts to close budgetary deficits.

But the social and political costs of the war were even higher, for it brought into the open a series of hidden conflicts which severely curtailed France's ability to continue the fight. France had not only gone through the defeat and dislocation of World War II; it had just witnessed defeat at the hands of the Vietminh in Vietnam. People were weary of war, all the more so when conscripts were drafted in metropolitan France to fight in Algeria. At the same time, a new financial and technocratic elite hoped for an expansion of French participation in a European common market, in place of continuing the expensive and fruitless colonial wars. On the other side were ranged the intransigent French *colons* in Algeria, who could countenance no peaceable accommodation with the Muslim majority, and a professional army which had returned from Vietnam grimly determined to install military dominance in Algeria and metropolitan France rather than to accept defeat in another guerrilla war.

These segmental conflicts, however, were but symptoms of a larger long-standing conflict between metropolitan and overseas France. As Herbert Lüthy put it,

The truth of the matter is that the history of the French republic and that of the French colonial empire were impelled by different forces, went their different ways, and seldom met.... The empire was something with which the French people had nothing whatever to do, and its story was that of machinations of high finance, the Church, and the military caste, which tirelessly re-elected overseas the Bastilles which had been overthrown in France.

The Turkish writer Arslan Humbaraci subtitled his book on Algeria "A Revolution That Failed." The most significant facts about postwar Algeria stem from the defeat of the internal rebellion and the survival of the external army. When the French departed, the external army entered Algeria. The exhausted Kabyle rebels were no match for its military and political might. The departure of 900,000 Frenchmen at the same time vacated numerous positions in government and services, which adherents of the rebellion regarded as rightfully their own. Whatever tenuous bonds between professionals, peasantry and workers survived the crushing of the internal rebellion now became further attenuated as the fortified Algerian middle class reaped the rewards of ten years of effort and joined the Algerian elite. Socialist experiments, initiated by Ahmed Ben Bella, involving self-management of nationalized French agricultural holdings and shops, resulted in over-bureaucratization and a grave decline of production. At the same time, Algeria remained dependent for credits on France, granted in return for continuing rights to oil and gas discovered in the Sahara. Ben Bella's attempt to stem the decline by organizing the FLN into a monolithic party of the Communist type proved unable—on any level—to contain the centrifugal forces created by economic decline, continued dependence on France and the rapid "bourgeoisification" of the new Algerian power-holders. In 1965 the army stepped in in order to stabilize the situation.

Under Houari Boumédienne, Algeria continues to proclaim itself "socialist" but emphasizes that its socialism is "Algerian," and not "imported," and relies for much of its definitions of socialism on the Islamic *ulema*. Nationalized shops have been returned to their owners; banks, foreign trade and heavy industry—never nationalized—continue in private hands; and the regime has expressed itself in favor of foreign private investment. Algeria continues to be strongly dependent on French aid, becoming in effect France's closest "client-state." At the core of the society stands a strong army, officered by a strongly nationalist staff. The mood is nationalist Islamic Algerian. It is the Jacobin Islam of Ben Badis which has ultimately proved vitorious.

18.
ARVN as Faggots: Inverted Warfare in Vietnam

Charles J. Levy

In a working class Irish neighborhood of Boston, the community boasts of having the highest proportion of marine enlistees in the country. This claim, repeated to the point of being a cliché, is characteristic of the community's intensely patriotic attitudes. This preoccupation with patriotism became the subject of research three years ago when the study reported in the accompanying article was undertaken. As the marines from the neighborhood began arriving home from Vietnam the following year, the researcher concentrated on getting acquainted with them in order to explore the process of becoming a veteran. Over a period of several years he gradually got to know 60 marine veterans who represented a cross section of the neighborhood to the extent that there are economic and educational variations in such a homogeneous community.

Since the veterans' frame of reference was still the war, it was necessary to reconstruct as far as possible their experiences in Vietnam. The most formal part of this reconstruction was extensive tape-recorded interviews. However, the interviews did not occur until the researcher had established an informal relationship with the men during a year spent on their corners, at their bars and wherever else they "hung." The veterans guided the interviews. Although they were held individually, the interviews produced recurring themes. It was these themes that guided the writing of the essay.

Some of the same themes have reappeared in the veterans' civilian life, particularly in connection with the violence that now characterizes their lives. In its broadest terms, this dependence on violence reflects their having fought an unrequited war. Not only had the war not been won, but the men had been unable to establish a satisfactory working relationship with it. Because they are still trying to achieve the dominance that had been denied them in Vietnam (without any of this necessarily being a conscious process), the war remains alive for them in civilian life. Their threshold for feeling threatened is markedly lower than in the case of men whose civilian life was uninterrupted by the war.

This is not to say that these veterans were nonviolent before their enlistment. But in the past, there were informal rules that limited the amount of damage to the other party. These limits no longer bind them. Another difference, also related to Vietnam, is that this violence is likely to be directed at those who are nominally allies. For example, a group that some veterans rejoined was particularly known for its mutual assistance. But one night there was a fire fight between these veterans. The casualties included one dead. As a consequence, the formerly cohesive group reappeared as two factions, led by veterans, that have been involved in additional combat against each other—resulting in another murder.

The connection with Vietnam may be camouflaged when the victim is a veteran's mother and his weapon is a hurled television set. But the underlying parallels remain, beyond her being a nominal ally. Here, in common with most cases, the violence is spontaneous. For the veterans are still responding to the initiatives of others. And the intentions of these others are still likely to be misperceived. There are times when the continuity with Vietnam is more explicit, as when a veteran destroyed a restaurant in Boston's Chinatown after attacking the waiter who put a hand on his shoulder.

The way in which civilians often view Vietnam from the United States suggests that too much perspective can be just as distorting as too little. For it seems to be popularly believed that the actions of Amercian troops there have resulted from racism and depersonalization of the enemy. But racism would not explain why there has been a high regard for the Viet Cong and North Vietnamese Army (VC/NVA) who are racially indistinguishable from the Army of the Republic of (South) Vietnam (ARVNs) for whom there has been a low regard. Nor would depersonalization of the enemy explain why there was substantial hostility directed against the ARVNs with whom there was personal contact, and little or no hostility toward the more remote VC/NVA.

In the case of American marines, the beginning of an explanation could be found in boot camp. Homosexuality appeared in two contradictory themes of basic training. On the one hand, homosexuals were the enemy. Referring to navy corpsmen in general, and one in particular, a former marine explained:

A lot of them were like prissy. I mean looked on the faggoty-type side. You could tell they were corpsmen. But I mean if that guy was in marine boot camp he'd of got bounced out. Or he'd have so many problems within the system that he fucking wouldn't be able to hack it. He'd go out of his mind. He'd be called "a faggot."

On the other hand, marine recruits were called "faggots" by their drill instructors during boot camp. By compelling these men to accept such labels, the drill instructors achieved on a psychological level the same control that they had on a physical level when, for example, the men were not permitted a bowel movement for the first week of boot camp.

As defined by the boot camp experience, homosexuality was only incidentally a sexual condition. More imporant, it represented a lack of all the aggressive characteristics that were thought to comprise masculinity. The connection between passivity and homosexuality was made vivid to the marines in boot camp inasmuch as they were unable to combat either the label or the activites surrounding it. When a recruit mentioned that he and a friend had been separated in violation of the "buddy system" under which they joined, the drill instructor is reported to have asked. "Do you like Private R?" The next question was, "Do you want to fuck him?"

After sending six men into a small shower room, the drill instructor, in another account, shouted, "Everybody on your back."

> We're all nude. So you fall on top of each other. You get assholes in your face. And then they turn on cold water and they make you run out and stand there.

This ritual, like most others in boot camp, was coupled with violence. As the men left the showers, the drill instructors "beat your fucking head in."

The violence towards trainees was merged with their learning how to do violence, so that "We used to be disgusted with the other services because we considered them unaggressive." Aggression meant learning how to protect not only their lives, but also their masculinity. Accordingly, after boot camp they referred to the Marine Corps as "the crotch," while the other military branches were called "the sister services."

The overreaching lesson of boot camp had been that combat must be on the marines' terms. This point was made by the drill instructors in a way that led one veteran to recall: "You just get shit on all the time if you don't live by their rules. If you don't they'll screw you any way they can." One of these accepted rules involved the rationale for this training, "They have to do it to protect your lives if you're going in combat." Boot camp training was continually linked to Vietnam by such means as reminding the recruits of the date they would be arriving there and by indicating the number of casualties that would result "if you don't take the training seriously."

It was made clear that submission to the drill instructors would provide the recruits with the training that was necessary to in turn make the VC/NVA submit.

Yet, in Vietnam, the marines discovered that the VC/NVA "fight on their fucking terms, not on ours," according to another veteran. Much effort was aimed at getting the VC/NVA to fight on the marine terms. "What we tried to do is fucking chase them around so they don't know what's going on. But it's never that way." The VC/NVA not only refused to fight on the marines' terms, by fighting on their own terms they made the marines' terms inoperable. The link that was established between boot camp and Vietnam reappeared to hinder rather than help morale. For instead of the promised discontinuity between the two settings, the marines vis-à-vis the VC/NVA bore an unexpected similarity to the recruits who were called "girl" by the drill instructors.

The ascendance of the VC/NVA's terms was possible in large part because these terms were unknown to the marines. Even after locating the VC/NVA, their intentions were unclear:

> It depends on where they want to fight. You never know if they want to fight there and get that one company and consider it a day. Or if they want to just really get out of there. You can't tell. Or if they're just sucking you into one big mob scene.

The last of these possibilities, that there were other VC/NVA waiting in ambush, was the governing one. It meant that the marines were never able to assume a correspondence between the VC/NVA they saw and the ones that saw them.

Because the marines were seen in their totality, their intentions were open. Their terms were correspondingly weakened. For the VC/NVA were given an opportunity to develop counter-terms: "They know every map square where they can hold a good defense. Where there's a lot of heavy brush that would be tough for us to move our heavy equipment in."

Some of the problems that arose from trying to prepare men who were still in the United States for Vietnam were inherent to using a low risk artifical setting to anticipate the high risk real one. Training in the United States did not pass for combat in Vietnam: "When they used to send us out we used to go make believe. We set up an ambush and make believe someone walked by. You knew when all this shit was over you got to get to bed. So I mean it's not good." Just as combat in Vietnam does not pass for training in the United States: "You're not sitting there in 'Nam saying to yourself: 'Let me think now, the instructor told me to do it this way.' What the hell!"

The deeper problems that arose had less to do with training for wars in general than with this war in particular. Booby traps caused a majority of deaths in Vietnam. But booby trap training was regarded as a contradiction in terms:

> They show you all the booby traps and stuff. What's good showing you the booby trap. I mean, if you find a booby trap, the odds are good you ain't going to see it 'til after it blows up.

Efforts to simulate a Vietnam in the United States suffered from a more general handicap: "How can you train a person to fight someone that they've been fighting for so long that they haven't done good enough a job to find out anything about them?" Training in the United States, then, was futile for the same principal reason that combat in Vietnam was to be futile for the marines. So the difficulty of anticipating the VC/NVA through training in the United States was at least one authentic reconstruction of the setting to be found in Vietnam. Also the apparent unreality of training in the United States may not have been entirely inappropriate preparation for Vietnam. The above example of marines setting ambushes for other marines was said to be "make believe." But it anticipated the internecine character of the war.

The military techniques of the VC/NVA compelled the marines to violate their own traditions. These traditions were not abstractions. They were reasons for being. They also provided a set of expectations for Vietnam. But after arriving there, it turned out they had no application when "You can't go in and kick ass like you could in other wars." Here is the process of discovery:

> When I first got there, two VC held down the whole platoon just by firing over our heads. Then word was passed out, 'Stay down. Don't waste rounds. They'll just do this for fifteen minutes and leave.' And being a new guy and thinking how the marines are supposed to be so tough, I said, 'Why don't we go get them?' But, of course, they [the experienced marines] knew what they were doing. We probably would've went and got them, there probably would've been booby traps all over the place and we would've probably lost another 20 guys getting two. So we just sit there and stay for 15 minutes, 20 minutes, until they got tired.

When they arrived in Vietnam, these men had belonged to the Marine Corps for about eight months. This is a time to become deeply involved in traditions—even allowing for the intensity of the boot camp experience. The commitment to the traditions of the Marine Corps was largely a result of their coinciding with the traditions of the street corners to which these men had belonged before their enlistment. The interchangeability of the traditions could be seen when the same marine who was "thinking how the marines are supposed to be so tough" later described his Vietnam experience through a street corner analogy: "That's like some guy walking up to you and punching you in the face every night and then before you have time to turn around or put up your hands he's gone."

Oriental Smiles

The previously clear and central distinction between aggressiveness and passivity was lost for the marines when they arrived in Vietnam. They found themselves using aggressive means which had passive results. Meantime, the VC/NVA used passive means which had aggressive results.

The passive aspects of the VC/NVA took a variety of forms. To begin with, the VC/NVA did not fit any of the traditional American notions of what a formidable adversary should look like. They were the wrong size. Sometimes they were the wrong sex. They wore the wrong clothes since the VC and occasionally the NVA lacked uniforms. They even wore the wrong expression: "It's hard to look through an Oriental person. They could probably hate your guts and stab you in the back, but they'll always smile at you." As it turned out, the more passive they appeared, the more difficult it was to defend against their aggression.

The marines heard lectures about Vietnamese men expressing friendship among themselves and with other men through physical contact. But this behavior became all the more inexplicable as a result of the lectures. For if handholding between men was a custom, it meant—as far as the marines were concerned—that these gestures were not aberrations within the Vietnamese society: rather the whole society was an aberration. A marine recalled that

> we had classes before we went over: that's just their way of life. Like them holding their arm on another guy means they're friends. It don't mean— that's what we were told anyways.

Nevertheless, in Vietnam "most of us" believed it did mean they were homosexuals.

The marines needed an explanation that would enable them to relate these male gestures to their own culture, not that of the Vietnamese. This was possible by defining it as homosexuality, since it was a familiar category to marines. By placing the ARVN in it, his behavior ceased to be strange. Equally important, the marines understood what their own behavior ought to be in response:

> I had been in country a year by this time. We were going back to regiment in Danang. We pulled the truck over and the ARVN engineer stopped us at a roadblock. And they bore you to death. They make you sick. They're trying

to be military. So they've got this roadblock up. And they stopped the truck. And the driver is saying "Get out of our way, you little slopes." And they come out and they said, "We have a wounded veteran." We said, "So what?" They said, "He doesn't have one leg. Could you give him a ride up to the hospital?" So everybody's saying, "Let him hop." I was in charge of the detail so I said, "Let him on." I was in the back of the truck. It was a PC three-quarter. So he comes over on his crutches. I said, "Throw your crutches up." So he passed up the crutches. And I grabbed him under the arms and I pick him up and I set him in the seat. The little slope grabbed me by the leg. And I had been in the country long enough to know that most of them are queer. They hold hands and stuff. And this sort of irks most marines and soldiers. And we're told that it's a Vietnamese custom, when you're really friendly you should hold hands. So they try to hold a lot of guys' hands. So they end up getting beat bloody. The guy grabbed my leg. So I got mad. I wasn't in a good mood that morning and I whacked him. And my buddies grabbed his crutches. And I said "Go!" So we took off. We threw his crutches in the rice paddy one time and went about another 150 yards and threw the other crutch and then out he went. He was screaming and crying and begging us. "Out you go." We all had a good laugh about that.

In more important ways, the classification of ARVNs as homosexuals was not based on their presumed sexual activity. The fact that ARVNs were living at bases with their wives contributed to the belief that they were homosexuals. For the presence of wives meant the ARVNs led a soft life. Hence they were not, to use a common marine term, "hard."

In the same way, the fact that ARVNs did not attempt to engage in homosexual activity with the marines was taken as proof that the ARVNs were homosexual. For it was thought that fear, a sign of homosexuality, kept them from making advances: "They wouldn't fool around with us anyway. They wouldn't even look at us the wrong way. 'Cause they knew how good we were, which I thought we were."

A literal interpretation of the war by the marines, among other results, would have made them allies of the ARVNs. But the ARVNs provided the model for a less literal approach that released the marines from whatever obligations remained to define them as allies. It was thought they interpreted the war out of existence: "They don't want nothing to do with the war, but yet it's their war."

The reluctance of ARVNs to engage in combat was treated as interchangeable with fighting on the side of the VC/NVA. A marine who regarded the ARVNs as homosexuals, "every one of them," cited as evidence: "They're just too scared where there is gooks. Where the gooks are, they go in the opposite direction. They don't want to go out and make contact with them at all." A related assumption was expressed by another marine who considered it just as likely they would go in the same direction as the VC/NVA: "I heard if you get a patrol of ARVNs with you, and if they're getting beat, they'll just go right on the opposite side. And they'll shoot at you instead of with you. They kind of get scared."

Unreliable Allies

The marines considered the ARVNs to be so far removed from the war that in the process of preventing their lives from being disrupted they were able to augment them. As one former marine observed "I think they got a good thing going for them because of the black market." Further, this remoteness from the war while in the midst of it often meant that the marines saw themselves being made more vulnerable to attacks from the VC/NVA:

> The ARVNs felt that being in the army was great. They used to wear starched utilities. Everything was so nice. And like the marines were all slobs, because we had our clothes washed in rice paddy water and everything else. Nothing starched. And they looked like they should be in recruiting posters all the time. We had ARVN security and it started to rain. They went in houses—into their buddy's house—until the rain stopped, so they wouldn't get their uniforms wet. And left us out there with no security.

Official ethnology was the response of the Marine Corps to a feeling among the marines that "We didn't like the idea of us fighting for an army of faggots." Specifically,

> You hear the propaganda report, you know, our bullshit like public relations between us and the Vietnamese. Well our public relations give us propaganda material telling us how the Vietnamese are a proud, simple people and courageous. And give us history of the country and how they fought the Chinese and everybody. And the Vietnamese war heroes and all this other shit. To impress upon us the fact that they're really not fucking gutless bastards. But we all knew better and we used to just hate them all the more. The more they tried to justify the Vietnamese the more we didn't like them.

The troops were not in a situation that they thought lent itself to this or any other form of intellectualizing. What did matter was that where the marines were vulnerable to attack from the VC/NVA they became the passive party, and the ARVNs were seen contributing to this vulnerability. In at least one sense, moreover, the marines were more passive vis-à-vis the VC/NVA than the ARVN were. The marines had their passivity imposed upon them by the VC/NVA, while the ARVNs acted passively through their own volition.

At times, the marines worked almost as hard at making themselves the enemy of the ARVNs as they did at making the ARVN their enemy. The first process recreated the theme of boot camp that violence should be done for one group so that they might do violence to a second group. There was a consensus among marines that ARVNs had nothing to fight for: "They didn't give a shit." The marines tried to give them something to fight against by making themselves the foremost enemy of the ARVNs.

As the marines found it increasingly difficult to establish a direct link between means and intended ends, they resorted to these indirect links. The assumption was that a marine offense against the VC/NVA required an offense against the ARVN that would result in an ARVN defense against the marines that would take the form of an ARVN offense against the VC/NVA. The mechanics of this sequence appear in the following episode:

> The marines were in there putting out the fire but unbeknowingst to them, they were stomping to death a three-week-old baby. So this caused uncontrollable laughter among the marines when they found they had accidentally killed a baby. There's nothing else they could do. And they've got to keep up this pretense of being fucking raving maniacs in order to keep the respect of the Montagnards. The gooks think that we're fucking lunatics. And you've got to keep this. As long as they're afraid of us, they won't give you a hard time. If they're afraid you'll shoot them in any minute and you don't find anything wrong in killing. So the guys start laughing. First, it was sort of a nervous laugh and then they just had a fucking grand time.

However, it soon became clear to these marines that an indirect linkage of means and ends was at least as unattainable as a direct one. When they were ambushed soon afterwards, the marine squad leader

> yelled to the commander of the Vietnamese to bring on line assaults. So the four marines get up and they're pumping away. And all the eight gooks just sat there and watched them. And then they withdrew in disorganized retreat. What they do is they ran like hell while the marines were on line shooting. What they [marines] had to do is pull some escape and evasion maneuvers to get away. They were pissed.

In other words, the sequence that materialized consisted of a VC offense that resulted in an ARVN defense that resulted in a marine defense.

In short, one reason the ARVNs became the enemy was that the marines were, after all, bound to them as allies. For the ineffectiveness of the ARVNs in combat meant the task of the marines was that much greater and more dangerous: "Most of the time when they did get into contact they always got their ass kicked. And we usually had to come in and help them out."

The marines were bound to the ARVNs in a more immediate way. They provided the marines with a means of trying to salvage a disrupted frame-of-reference. For the ARVNs were proof that there was, after all, a connection between passivity and homosexuality. The marines were not only able to focus on them as passive targets, they could act against them aggressively.

Locating homosexual ARVNs was a welcome relief from having to cope with an often unrecognizable and always evasive VC/NVA. There were no problems identifying the homosexuality of the readily available ARVNs. The identification was based on criteria that did not require interrogation or scrutiny. The proof was an impression:

> We thought a lot of them were queer, because of the way they act. They were so, I don't know, prissy like, and awkward. And just the way they laughed and looked at you.

This imprecise definition is appropriate considering that "prissy" owes its first two letters to precise.

However, the assaults against assumed homosexuals were in no sense a charade. They were more a form of warfare than an alternative to it. All that kept the beatings from escalating was a lack of resistance. The exceptions illuminated the usual case:

> They'll come up to you and they'll rub your leg and you sucker them. Because as far as we're concerned, they're queer. So the ARVN lieutenant told his men, "The next time a marine hits you, I want you to shoot him." So our lieutenant heard about it and he says, "As soon as you see an ARVN pick up a weapon, first I want you to kill the lieutenant, and then I want you to wipe out all his men." We continued to beat them up and nobody shot anybody.

Meantime, the VC/NVA imposed the ultimate passivity on marines by making them the instruments of their own death. For the VC/NVA were "good at skills that we didn't even know—like booby traps." Most booby traps are arranged to have the victim act as his own executioner. And there is a mockery involved which accounts for the term. It is a trap for the booby. The only aggression permitted the marine was against himself. The more aggressive the marine tried to be, the more susceptible he was to booby traps.

Marines continued to be their own victims when they tried to fight on the terms of the VC/NVA. The marines began using a highly sophisticated mine called the Claymore that they expected to be far more effective than the relatively crude booby traps of the VC/NVA. The Claymore has pellets in the front that are fired by an explosive in the back. However, the VC/NVA were able to carry the Claymore one step further:

> They can sneak right up and turn your Claymore around. And then you start moving around there so you'll hit the Claymore and it's turned around. You'll be the one that gets it.

ARVN as Faggots: Inverted Warfare in Vietnam 231

Booby trapped by their own booby traps. As the marines sought a new means of becoming more aggressive, they were made still more passive.

The invisibility of the VC/NVA and the visibility of the marines were the underlying reasons for the success of one and the failure of the other with booby traps. For there are two conditions that must be met if a booby trap is to operate successfully. First, the hunter must know where his prey will be. Second, the prey must not know where the hunter has been.

There is an interval between planting and detonating a booby trap. The aggressor is removed in both time and space from his aggression. But the marines (and the corner boys before them) were unaccustomed to aggression that was not spontaneous. This was another reason they had both a problem setting booby traps and a propensity for tripping them.

The ambush is closely related to the booby trap. It relies on one's own invisibility and the other's visibility. There are, in addition, elaborate preparations that require deferred aggression. For these reasons, the ambushes prepared by marines were subject to the same problems as the booby traps they set:

> Every night these NVA or VC used to come down and they used to screw up marine ambushes. And they always used to get away. They'd know where the ambush was set up and killer teams were set up. They'd sneak by them when they go into the village to get their rice and what they needed and leave. And then they'd screw them up on the way back. They'd fire on the ambush. And they'd take off up into the mountains. They did this every night. And they [marines] never got any of them.

Hiding entails actively seeking invisibility. It is ordinarily considered a passive act, because it is seen as the avoidance of action. More important, it is seen as the avoidance of being acted upon. But in the context of Vietnam, both these components were redefined when they became the means by which the VC/NVA were able to act aggressively. To speak of a means and end suggests a break that did not exist. Instead, the means and end were part of the same process. When the VC/NVA hid, it was not only a way to avoid disadvantageous encounters with the marines, it was preparation for engaging the marines on advantageous terms:

> A lot of times you don't see them. They suck you into some type of ambush situation where there's a lot of them and a lot of you's. And they've already preregistered the area. Like two weeks before that they'll lie in the same position and fire their weapons for effect.

Not only was the means not entirely passive because it was part of an aggressive end, but the end was not entirely aggressive because it was part of a passive means. That is, the VC/NVA strategy was all the more difficult for the marines to sort out because it was cyclical. The marines found that the VC/NVA "aren't staying and fighting." Instead, "they hit you and run." But the running could not be classified as passive, because in addition to being the last stage of an aggressive act, it was the first stage of the next aggressive act. The confusion that resulted from trying to classify the tactics of the VC/NVA is reflected in the following account where the VC are shuttled between categories of offense and defense:

> The VC was more or less on a defense all the time. Always hiding and coming out at night. But he still had to move around, unless he was in a large group. But he always had to be the aggressor. And he was always under cover and stuff. So when he did come out and you did get in contact with him, he was determined that either he was going to die or he was going to get one of us.

When the VC/NVA hid, it was an aggressive act even if it did not lead to an engagement with the marines. For the marines had an aggressive mission in Vietnam. They were there to eliminate the VC/NVA. A status quo meant failure. The objective of the Marine Corps was summed up by the name given their "search and destroy missions." The VC/NVA could thwart these missions simply by hiding.

> You'd go in there for three days; you'd pull out. And if they were there anyways, they weren't there when we got there. I imagine they must have come back after we left. So those are the most useless operations I ever heard of. If they seen a hole they'd start saying, "Oh, I bet there's weapons down there. I bet there's rice down there." We'd dig it up and there'd be nothing there. We never found nothing. I went on three of those, never found nothing.

The only result of these operations would be "carrying a couple of dead guys back—our own," men who encountered booby traps.

Catching those who hide is a form of aggressiveness except in Vietnam. The contradiction of being permitted by the enemy to take the initiative was described by a former marine: "You catch them when they want you to catch them. They have all their bunkers and everything all set for you."

Traditionally, setting the time and place of battle has been another aggressive characteristic. The marines found themselves helping to set these terms because the VC/NVA "just wait 'til I guess they think they have you at your weakest, then they hit you." Another veteran provides an illustration:

> Usually they'll hit the areas that are most secure. The lines are never checked. There won't be much bother about falling to sleep on watch. The platoon commander didn't care because we were never hit. Everyone gets to not caring.

ARVN as Faggots: Inverted Warfare in Vietnam

Here too the apparent passivity of the VC/NVA was the means to an aggressive act. For they were able to make the camp vulnerable by not attacking it.

The marines had a sense of being objects that comes from being continually visible while those viewing them remain for the most part invisible. But they had not adapted to the dangers that follow from this condition. It was only in retrospect, that the marine veteran just quoted saw that the more secure they felt, the less secure they were in fact. In Vietnam, when the VC/NVA abstained from an attack it was regarded as security not as a forewarning. There was less stress for the marines in facing a disaster that would be observable than in admitting to themselves that they were living with an unseen threat.

Telescoped examples of this dilemma could occur several times a day to the same men. A former marine tells of walking at the head of a patrol along a trail:

> You see a shell case. So you start to step over this way. But you think: "Maybe it was put there on purpose so I'd step over that way." So it really screws your head up. The hell with it. I'd step over this way. And if it blows, it'll blow.

The weakness of the marines was maximized by not only the behavior but more particularly through the attitudes with which they were provided by the VC/NVA. The invisibility of the VC/NVA provided them with a safe view of marines as a prelude to safe action against them: "They could be hiding under a rock or in a tunnel. We could walk right over them so they could see everything you have. What the hell can you do? They're watching you all the time, you never see them."

All this means that the marines were less visible to themselves than they were to the VC/NVA. Until the marines set off a mine or walked into an ambush, they did not usually know where they were in relation to the VC/NVA. In one way or another, "You wait to get hit; wait for them to come to you." But there was more involved than the VC/NVA seeing precisely what dangers the marines were exposed to. For the VC/NVA saw into the operations of the marines as well as the context in which they were held. It amounted to the marines having to rely on the VC/NVA in order to view themselves. The VC made this reliance explicit:

> They talk to us all the time and shit—loud-speakers. In fact they told us one night, before anyone that was with us knew it, that we were going to move up to Phu Bai. Imagine that! They told us over a loud-speaker that they were pulling us out, because they knew if we stayed there that the VC were going to annihilate us. So the squad leader went to the CO and they checked on it and we *were* going to move out about three weeks later. So they knew it before we did. That kind of fucked up your mind a little, you know.

(The announcement by the VC was in English—which served to tell the marines that their language, too, was visible.) Even a formal statement of defeat by the VC/NVA could be made into an aggressive act by them:

> One day eight of them [NVA] turned themselves in. You could see their white flag. They had me walking up. I felt like an asshole. They're fucking clean. New uniforms. Spotless. Their boots were shined. Haircuts. And they're supposed to be living in the mud? They're doing better than we are. And they're walking up. They're clean as a whistle. They had tailored uniforms. So everyone's there wondering: What's going on out there?

In describing the episode, this former marine wonders if "they just sent them out there to turn themselves in to make us look like they were doing good out there." But he dismisses this possibility. It is a reassuring one insofar as it indicates the prisoners were not typical. Yet, to accept this explanation would be an acknowledgement that the NVA were capable of deliberately redefining the terms of war by turning surrender on its head. Further, it would mean that the marines had accommodated the NVA.

Where the marines did succeed in killing, they often discovered that this could not be considered a form of domination, particularly when the victims were civilians. These deaths were both a cause and effect of the marines' passivity. For killing civilians usually meant the marines had lost control. The particular kind of control varied, but every case included a loss of control over the VC/NVA. When the marines were acting in rage, the civilians they killed served as surrogates for elusive VC/NVA. They were acting spontaneously at the time, but afterwards the marines saw their action as a loss of control over themselves:

> You see a guy you're really tight with for a period of months getting killed. We got really pissed off about it. You don't just say, "Well, fuck it." You go like kind of nutty. Anybody that even looked at you the wrong way you'd probably shoot. I think the American fighting man can be the most vicious ever. People don't realize this.

When civilians were killed through mistaken identity, it was a more direct reminder that the VC/NVA were beyond control, to the point of being unidentifiable. The misplaced aggressiveness of these acts sometimes resulted in ridicule, as when a marine shot a village elder one night and was afterwards nicknamed "killer" by his fellow marines. His death was the outcome of a curfew rule that required the shooting of any violators. The curfew was imposed as a means of assuring that the VC/NVA would be identifiable.

Whatever the circumstances, killing civilians weakened the position of the marines. For it meant the villagers became still more dedicated to

ARVN as Faggots: Inverted Warfare in Vietnam   235

the VC/NVA, as seen in the following episode about the death of another elder:

> There's a killer team out one night. They were outside this village. This old man, he was a villager, was going out to do a crap in the rice paddy. And he was killed. That was right at the edge of the village. He was mistaken for a VC. Immediately after that happened the villagers turned VC sympathizers. After that, there was always a build up of VC coming in. Along Highway 1, on the other side of the village, it was always mined. After this happened there was like a triple amount of mines planted in the road. And there was a road going up to the top of the hill. It was never really combed for any mines. Two days later a jeep went over a mine and blew up. That never happened before. But I imagine it was the villagers.

There were other ways in which the marines discovered that killing might not after all be the ultimate measurement of domination after all. For example, the VC/NVA were seen demonstrating a greater control of the situation when they abstained from killing. This realization by the marines made the control of the VC/NVA over them still greater:

> This [NVA soldier] goes "Good morning, marines." A lot of shit they did just to fuck up your head. I mean, they must have had a chance before that to really fucking zap someone. They did this shit just to fucking scare the fuck out of you. Just to let you know that they were on the ball and they weren't fucking around. Everyone fucking flies out of the trenches with their rifles. They're expecting attack. Fucking gook is probably laughing his ass off in the bushes. That's fucked up though.

The marines had finally recognized hiding as a means of killing. But here it was seen as a more subtle form of aggression—a means of killing morale. The VC/NVA directed the attention of marines to the importance of a psychological assault through their constant practice of it. However, the marines were as unable to cope with this sophisticated approach as they were with an apparently unsophisticated agrarian approach to combat.

The marines found that more than themselves was being relegated to passivity. The same thing was happening to the previously inviolate technology that had permitted the United States to maintain an aggressive stance in the world. Here, too, the victim brought on his own undoing, for the aggressiveness of this technology in Vietnam was often self-destructive. The following episode is typical of what could happen when technological superiority was invoked instead of dealing with the VC/NVA on equal terms:

> Say you had 30 gooks in the open. And you were too far away from them. Instead of losing men over them, artillery was the best bet. But we had too

> many restrictions on us. Like when we had to call an artillery mission. They had to get air clearance which is make sure there wasn't any helicopters flying around in the area or any jets, any Phantoms, flying over the area. So by the time we got that clearance then we'd have to get a ground clearance making sure that there wasn't any friendly troops around that area. So by the time the clearance came in, they were walking away. I mean they were just gone.

This failure had much to do with the characteristics of technology that were expedient or tolerated when they appeared in the United States. Its massiveness was inappropriate for the intimacy of combat in Vietnam where no one group was at a great distance from any other group. The bureaucracy attached to the technology was intended to make it manageable, but in the fluidity of this combat the bureaucracy made it all the more unmanageable.

Moreover, the futility of technology was carefully engineered by the VC/NVA. They were skilled at bringing out its limitations. Just as they made the visibility of marines a disadvantage by emphasizing the opposite characteristic among themselves, so they were able to turn technology into a disadvantage by not trying to fight it with technology. Again they stressed an opposite; this time nature. It was a matter of building a strategy out of both their strength and the marines' weaknesses. Americans were unaccustomed to nature being used aggressively. When necessary, the land was used as a weapon:

> In valleys where you're pinned down—a lot of times we've had jets come in over the top of us, when it was hard to hit them any other way. They couldn't come across because of the mountains and stuff. They relax the bombs right over our heads. And you can see the bombs. They'd be going towards us. And we're saying "Ooh, fucking things just don't drop." But they like carried on the momentum of the speed they're going. They go in front of you. They blow up. That takes a lot of skill on an estimate. And a lot of fucking luck. The gooks choose this type of thing because they know that our jets can't come into a valley this way and make it because there's a mountain there and they can't get up. So they set up their defenses so they can shoot down the planes as they're coming in.

The rationale for much of American technology had been the conquest of nature. But in Vietnam, the VC/NVA used nature for the conquest of technology.

Technological futility led to occasional attempts at de-emphasizing technology. But this only made way for problems that were more subtle and therefore less predictable. It brought out the other levels on which American culture was not transferable. These problems were subtle to the Americans, but they were obvious to everyone else. For example, a

ARVN as Faggots: Inverted Warfare in Vietnam 237

program was established to work with the villagers in a manner that minimized technology.

> We had an outfit that was called CAC—Combined Action Company. But cac in Vietnamese means prick. So they had to change it to Combined Action Platoons. They called it CAP. It was a laughing stock of the villages. And the VC played it to the hilt.

The extent to which the ethos of this war disoriented the marines was reflected in their way of trying to cope with it. For they engaged in a classification of the VC/NVA that was in itself disorienting. While the ARVNs represented what the marines feared they were becoming, the VC/NVA represented what the marines would like to have been. It was typically thought that in contrast to the ARVNs, the VC "have a lot of balls." Such metaphors of courage assisted in linking cowardice to a lack of masculinity, which is a short conceptual distance from homosexuality.

Through relating to the VC/NVA, the marines were seeking a way to offset their inability to relate to the terms of the war. Their approval of the VC/NVA was reflected in the narrative of a former marine whose unit had suffered heavy casualties on several occasions, leading to its being known as "the walking dead." Eventually they found themselves at Khe Sanh. The NVA had them surrounded and were again inflicting substantial damage without being damaged. The siege was so thorough that the NVA were tunneling underneath the marine positions. During the excavation, a marine used a stethoscopic device to overhear the conversation of the NVA digging below:

> Scared as everybody was, you had to fucking laugh hearing them swearing and shit. 'Cause they were like us really. I figured the grunts [NVA] were there exactly like us. They didn't like the fucking shit more than we did. They're probably down there swearing about their fucking officers and fucking shit like that. It was funny. We were really laughing.

There was another way in which the marines benefited from thinking of the VC/NVA in personal terms. It made them visible—only to a slight degree—but it was that much of an improvement over invisibility. The contrasting visibility of the marines was indicated when "They'd shoot at you at midnight. You'd light up a smoke and he'd shoot at you." The unseen sniper was made visible insofar as he received a name from the marines: "Bed-Check Charley."

While the personalization of the VC/NVA operated in a way that introduced positive feelings, the impersonalization of the VC/NVA was invoked to prevent negative feelings. The fact that the NVA were trying to kill marines was explained away by one former marine who recalled that "you don't dislike them, because no one NVA ever did anything to you."

In other words, the marines did not suppose that the VC/NVA, on such occasions, were acting personally toward them. Clearly, the same could not be said about the ARVNs. The marines had no trouble relating specific grievances to specific ARVNs. Moreover, they had a sense that homosexuality was more personal than death.

Part VII
Economic Systems and Culture Patterns

Although the youngest of anthropology's subareas, the study of traditional economies has generated a sophisticated body of comparative literature. Its proponents have integrated the technical vocabulary and theories of economists into the analysis of familiar data on primitive groups, with the result that both disciplines are the richer for their efforts.

The economic systems with which anthropologists have the most experience are those on a micro- rather than on a macroinstitutional scale. In addition, the economy of any small group is likely to be embedded in other institutions, particularly kinship and ritual, in ways that bear little relation to the distinction we commonly draw between the rules of finance and economics and those of family and religious life. If the distinctive features of the traditional economy were to be summarized along the lines of the ideal "little community," three primary features would have to be cited. The first concerns the notion of labor, the second, the sharing of resources, and the third, the existence of an exchange system lacking a standardized currency.

In the model traditional community, the skills basic to survival are generally known and used by all the adults in a community. Each person has at hand the means to secure food, shelter, and clothing of a more or less rudimentary kind without relying on neighbors. The division of labor between men and women, a socioeconomic universal, and the practical reliance of the sexes on each other's work temper whatever stereotype of the native as rugged individual might be conjured up from information on technologically primitive groups.

There is some correlation to be found between the political levels of complexity recognized among smaller societies and the complexities that can surround the notion of work. In the most simply organized hunter-gatherer bands, the division of labor between the sexes is most clear. The job of occasional forays for game falls to men, while women are accountable for the usually daily collection of edible plants and insects. In pastoral, horticultural, and agricultural communities, the division of labor is again evident, but the more variety of economic roles available in a society, the less possible it becomes to predict what will distinguish men's from women's work. When the basic responsibilities of securing food and shelter are less than a round-the-clock endeavor, traditional groups tend to develop more specialized roles—the weaver, the potter, the ritual curer—that according to cultural dictates, can become the work of either men or women or of both sexes.

An additional variable in the organization of work is the division of labor by age-grades. In one society, it may be appropriate for young men and women alike to herd cattle and for their grandparents to tend gardens. In another, in which the roles of grandchildren and grandparents are structurally equivalent, the young and the old may be assigned identical minor responsibilities that are suited to their physical strength and social status, while the heavier work and greater prestige is assumed by the intermediate group of adults.

The important point to remember is that the subsistence labor that has to be done in traditional societies is never very far away from the elementary problem of wresting a living from the environment. The distance that modern technology affords us from the immediate effects of natural disasters—from drought, flood, hurricane, earthquake, from diseases that destroy plants and animals—is generally not characteristic of the traditional community. Nor is there likely to be available the tremendous array of occupations on which an urban society relies. To use Durkheim's categories, the primitive society achieves a "mechanical solidarity" based on the principles of religion and kinship but with little specialization of labor. This is opposed to the "organic solidarity" of industrial society in which unity is based on the interdependence of specialized workers who rely on each other's services and products.

The allocation of work responsibilities in primitive societies respects the distinction between the place of work and the family domicile, but with none of the rigidity of our corporate industrial system. Industrialized labor is characterized by clear-cut boundaries between the office-factory workplace and the private home. European industrialization represents, in fact, a breakdown of the medieval model of craftsmanship as a kind of domestic activity, centered in the home.

A second feature of the traditional microeconomy is the tendency to equalize access to services, products, and natural resources. Kinship plays an important part in this process of "leveling." The rights and responsibilities that an individual has as the member of a kin group clearly structure and define work obligations and the consumption of goods and services. Tradition determines that the benefits of an individual's labor is "owed" to the family or lineage or ritual brotherhood instead of accruing simply to that individual worker. In like fashion, the kin group is the source of historical and sacred claims to territory for hunting and gathering, land for gardening, and waterways for fishing.

Shared work responsibilities and inherited communal rights of ownership differ sharply from our culture's individualistic notions of labor and property. In industrial society people are expected to take individual responsibility for their efforts, but not to bring their families to work or share their lives with coworkers. The same holds true for property that, with the exception of husband-wife joint ownership is geared towards individual title-holding. Even in cases where wealth and land is inherited in a family line, an individual is identified as principal inheritor and is given the right to treat his inheritance as a commodity. That is, he is free to sell it at will on the open market and is not bound, as a traditional person would be, to guard its sacred, nontransferable quality.

The third characteristic of the traditional economic system has to do with this very issue of the sacred versus the secular value that is placed on work and things. In the model primitive economy, the worth of human and material resources is not quantified in general, abstract terms of money. Kinship is a sacred bond that insures a closed system of economic transactions; gift-giving, barter, and ritual exchange balance the distribution of resources, and they counteract the centripetal force of competition. Even if a community is stratified into classes, pressures to equalize access create a system of economic redistribution whereby accumulated surplus wealth is apportioned out from a central leader to the rest of the community. The perishable nature of primitive economic goods—foods, wooden carvings, furs, and leather—accelerates the circulation of materials. Even more important, daily, face-to-face interaction diminishes the necessity for an all-purpose, impersonal monetary system. The larger the economic system and the more strangers who must negotiate with other strangers in the market place, the more trust has to be placed in a stable currency and the less trust can be placed in the social guarantees of kinship and personal acquaintance.

Such a purely primitive community, embedded in kinship and shut off from an external market system, is not only a rarity, but a practical impossibility in today's world. Nor are isolated groups who might fit the model without a pragmatic sense of judgment in barter and trade. This fact is lucidly described in the first article in this section, "Capital, Investment, and the Social Structure of a Pastoral Nomad Group," by Fredrik Barth.

The particular group Barth discusses, the Basseri of Southern Iran, provides an excellent example of the limited dimensions of a traditional economy system only partially integrated into local village markets and a money economy. That the Basseri maintain a nonexpanding economy is a function not of their inability to rationally maximize their resources, but of the cultural patterning of kin obligations and the simple fact that any pastoralist or farmer, even those in technologically advanced countries, cannot protect their investments from draught, disease, and inclement weather. While we have long understood the "leveling" of individual resources by demanding relatives as a feature of nonindustrial life, what has been missed often is this other side of the coin—a traditional profit-making mentality. With this kind of analysis, simple polarities between modern and traditional economies begin to break down in favor of qualitative comparisons.

In "Bulls and Bears on the Cell Block," by Heather Strange and Joseph McCrory, we turn to another microeconomic system, with the radical difference that a total institution—one which organizes the entire life of the individual member—not a small community, has nurtured the barter exchange of labor and goods. Isolated from the wider society and from criminal networks, the New Jersey convicts described in this article have created a market system that combines legitimate transactions with illegitimate trade-offs. What is most remarkable in this account and in other descriptions of total institutions are the unwritten codes of behavior that develop into a kind of inmate culture. Despite the turnover in the resident population and the strict routine of institutional life, the human tendency for "cultural elaboration," as Ruth Benedict phrased it, still survives. That is, groups in isolation will flesh out the bare bones of common existence with complex ritual institutions. In the prison setting, the emphasis is appropriately on using scarce economic resources to maximize personal status and alliances. Ironically, men who failed to "beat the system" in the outside world are still playing at the same win-or-lose game, only on a smaller scale.

Thus far, the articles in this section on economics and culture have dealt with the exchange-value of certain things. Will a Basseri tribesman sell his spring lambs for profit? What is it worth to an Eskimo carver to turn a traditional good-luck charm into a work of art? Can a prison inmate negotiate a tape recorder for a fixed number of cigarette cartons. In the final article, Lucy Cohen turns our attention to another kind of commodity —human labor. The study of immigration patterns, hardly a concern of early anthropologists, is at present a growing area of investigation. The isolation of many small communities has broken down not only because of the intrusion of larger economic and state systems, but by virtue of the out-migration of their younger members to more industrialized countries. The Third World migrant and rural peasant form the backbone of the surplus labor supply in virtually every nation of the West. The cash remittance that migrants send to their relatives at home is often the mainstay of the extended family and community life. Women, no less than men, have been participating in migration, but not without changes in household organization and kin obligations. Cohen gives us a concise report of the relatively new and important juxtaposition of Latin American cultural imperatives and the demands of the wage-labor market. As in Margaret Mead's comments on the changing American family, we find that this new division of labor and rationalization of work time deeply affects the traditions of kinship and marriage, and that economics, in fact, is difficult to separate from the general substance of human organization.

References

Belshaw, C.S. 1965. *Traditional Exchange and Modern Markets.* Englewood Cliffs, N.J.: Prentice-Hall.
Bohannan, Paul J. and G. Dalton. 1962. *Markets in Africa.* Evanston, Ill.: Northwestern University Press.
Codere, Helen. 1966. *Fighting with Property.* Seattle: University of Washington Press.
Dalton, G. 1968. "Economic Theory and Primitive Society." In *Economic Anthropology: Readings in Theory and Analysis*, edited by E. E. LeClair and H. K. Schneider, pp. 143-167. New York: Holt, Rinehart & Winston.
Durkheim, E. 1949. *The Division of Labor in Society.* G. Simpson, trans. Glencoe, Ill.: Free Press. (Orig. published 1893).
Firth, R. 1963. *Elements of Social Organization.* Boston: Beacon Press. (Orig. published 1951).
Foster, G.M. 1965. "Peasant Society and the Image of Limited Good." *American Anthropologist* 67: 293-315.
Malinowski, B. 1920. "Kula: The Circulating Exchange of Valuables in the Archipelagoes of Eastern New Guinea." *Man* 51: 97-105.
Mauss, M. 1954. *The Gift: Forms and Functions of Exchange in Archaic Societies.* Glencoe, Ill.: Free Press. (Orig. published 1925).
Nash, M. 1966. *Primitive and Peasant Economic Systems.* San Francisco.
Polanyi, K. 1968. "The Economy as Instituted Process." In *Economic Anthropology: Readings in Theory and Analysis*, edited by E.E. LeClair and H.K. Schneider, pp. 122-143. New York: Holt, Rinehart & Winston.
Sahlins, Marshall. 1972. *Stone-Age Economics.* Chicago: Aldine-Atherton.

19.
Capital, Investment, and the Social Structure of a Pastoral Nomad Group in South Persia

Fredrik Barth

In this essay, I shall present a summary analysis of some aspects of the pastoral nomad economy of the Basseri tribe of Fars, South Persia (Iran). I shall discuss the nature of pastoral capital and its implications for the social structure of the nomads, granted certain cultural premises current among the Basseri. In this discussion I shall draw on material collected in the field during the winter and spring of 1958.

The Basseri are a tribe of 15,000-20,000 pastoral nomads, divided residentially into camps of ten to fifty tents, who migrate between winter pastures in the steppes and deserts of southern Fars and summer pastures in the high mountains 300 miles farther north. A general picture of this tribe has been presented elsewhere, and certain aspects of the prevailing system of land use and migration have been analyzed. In general, the following description may be taken as representative of conditions among the pastoral nomads of the whole South Persian area, a population of about half-a-million nomads.

A pastoral nomadic subsistence is based on assets of two main kinds: domesticated animals, and grazing rights. The recognition by the sedentary authorities of traditional grazing rights vested in distinct tribes is basic to the pastoral adaptation in Fars. Such tribes mostly have centralized political organizations based on chiefs, as do the Basseri, and are further united into large confederacies, which were formerly integrated into the semi-feudal traditional organization of Persia, and which are still recognized by the authorities. The association of every tribe with a corporate estate in the form of shared grazing rights has important implications for the political forms developed in the area. But in this essay I shall concentrate on the internal organization of the tribe, particularly the structure of local camp units. Within camps, all members share equal access to *pastures*; so for my present purposes I shall concentrate my analysis on the other main form of asset, the *herds*, and try to show the connection between features of this form of capital, and the internal structure of camps and of the tribe.

Capital Form

Animals are individually owned private property, and a Basseri household makes its livelihood from the production of the animals owned by its members. A certain minimum of additional property is necessary in a nomadic adaptation, mainly a tent, bedding, saddlebags, ropes, and leather sacks for milk and water, all produced by household members, and clothes, shoes, cooking and eating utensils, obtained from the towns. The total value of such equipment is slight compared to that represented by the animals. Of them the most important producers are sheep, subsidiarily goats, while donkeys are necessary for transport. Every household also has a watchdog.

In South Persia in 1958, the market value of a live adult female sheep was around 80 Tomans (£4). Its product per annum was estimated at:

clarified butter	c. 25 T.
wool	20 T.
lamb: skin	15 T.
total	60 T. or £ 3.

In addition, there were the lambs' meat, buttermilk and curds, to which the nomads could not give a money value of any meaning since these products are not regularly marketed. The corresponding values for goats are somewhat lower, and there is no market for their hides. On the other hand, twinning is much more frequent among them. The main reason why some goats are kept in every herd, however, is to provide goathair for the production of tent cloth.

The productive capital on which the pastoral adaptation is based is thus a large herd of sheep and goats. Of these a 10 percent population of rams and he-goats is sufficient to ensure the fertility of the ewes and she-goats.

Certain features of this form of capital appear to have fundamental implications for the economic and social organization of the nomads:

a. Essentially all productive capital is in consumable form. The livestock may at any time be slaughtered and eaten; and thus the main productive asset of a household may be consumed without the necessity of conversion through a market.

b. *A significant fraction of the income is in the form of capital gains.* Lambs reach maturity in two years, and a female sheep is estimated by the Basseri to have a productive period of about seven years. To maintain the full capital value of the herd, about 15 percent of the lambs must be set aside each year to ensure replacement of stock; the remaining female lambs and a proportionate fraction of male lambs may be regarded as capital gains and give a possible capital increase rate of nearly 40 percent per annum. As in the case of point a., no market mechanism is necessary to effect a conversion from consumable product to productive capital.

c. *There is a continual risk of total or partial loss of capital.* Since all nomadic property is movable, total loss through robbery or warfare is a continual and real danger in the weakly administered areas frequented by the nomads. Furthermore various other disasters may strike the herd: accidents and predatory animals threaten the sheep, particularly when they stray from the main flock, so constant vigilance is required to keep the animals together and protect them; and at times epidemic disease, drought or famine may strike the herds, reducing the total animal population by as much as 50 percent.

d. *The rate of income decreases with increased capital.* This is mainly a consequence of the herding and management techniques known to the Basseri. Unassisted by dogs, a shepherd cannot control a flock larger than about 400 head; the man who owns more animals is forced to divide his flock and entrust other persons with shepherding duties. In fact, since shepherding is a strenuous and exacting occupation, owners of herds larger than about 200 animals already tend to hire a shepherd. A recognized consequence of this is somewhat less careful herding and more frequent losses, as well as a continual pilfering of the produce. The larger the total number of animals, the less effective is the owner's supervision of his shepherds, and the greater is the decrease in the rate of income. Standard shepherding contracts, especially the long-term ones in which there is no supervision, reflect these expectations in their stipulations: *(i) dandune* contract: the shepherd pays 10-15 Tomans per animal per year and takes all produce. At the expiration of the contract period, he returns a flock of the same number and age composition as he originally received; *(ii) nimei* contract: the shepherd pays 30 Tomans per animal per year for a period of 3-5 years. He takes all produce, and at the expiration of the contract returns half the herd as it stands, and keeps the other half.

In addition to these characteristics of the pastoral form of capital, certain other aspects of the economic situation of the Basseri should be described before discussing social implications, namely consumption patterns, borrowing, and investment.

A striking feature of the consumption patterns is the importance of agricultural produce to a nomad household. Wheat is the main staple; rice, dates, sugar and tea are also consumed in large quantities. Together with the considerable needs for cloth and clothing, various equipment, and luxuries, this implies a strong productive specialization and a dependence on market exchanges. A few family budgets in the nomad camp best known to me suggest an average rate of consumption in agricultural and industrial products to a value of more than 3,000 Tomans, or nearly £200, per annum per household of about six persons.

These products are paid for by the marketing of pastoral products, which only among the very poor is augmented by seasonal labour. Marketing and purchases usually take place through the medium of 'village friends'—small peddlers who live in predominantly agricultural villages where they sell industrial goods to the peasants, while supplying nomads with both agricultural and industrial produce. A nomad householder establishes a relation with such a village friend in every area where he spends a long period; during his time there he is provisioned by the peddler, and before his departure he usually settles the accumulated debt by delivery of butter, wool and hides. Though money is rarely used in these transactions, all values are estimated in terms of fluctuating current market prices.

Where the nomad does not have accumulated stores to cover his purchases, he is usually granted a half-year's or one year's credit. While such debts are usually paid for by villagers at a rate of 5 percent per month, nomads are rarely charged more than 20-30 percent per annum, and this is often waived when payment is made. Some nomads' debts run up to 4,000 to 5,000 Tomans.

Though this would appear to represent borrowing for current consumption, such credit serves in fact to conserve the productive asset represented by the herd: payment could be made by delivery of livestock, but by obtaining credit with security in the flock, this loss of productive animals is prevented. With a rate of income on mature sheep of nearly 100 percent per annum (value: 80 T., product: 60 T. plus various foodstuffs), such borrowing is clearly advantageous for the nomad even when full interest is charged; and nomads often succeed in recouping in the course of a year or two in spite of heavy indebtedness.

There are thus outside sources of credit available to members of a nomadic group; likewise, outside investments are open to them. There is, in Fars, an open market in land, and standard land tenancy contracts secure a considerable income for the absentee landowner (one sixth to two thirds of the crop, according to the quality of the land). However, there are difficulties in converting capital in herds into capital in land which partially prevent such investments. Animals may be freely sold, but the market for livestock is severely restricted. The strains of sheep owned by the nomads, though larger and more productive than those of the villagers, are less robust, and experience shows that only some 30 percent survive if kept in one locality through the whole year. Old sheep are of course sold for slaughter to the villages, but they fetch only a small price; animals for breeding and use can only be sold to other nomads. But since fellow nomads have very few sources of income other than their own herds, those who wish to increase their flocks by purchase have relatively limited means and represent only a very small market. The marketing of livestock is thus inevitably a rather slow process.

On the other hand, income from the sale of wool, butter and hides beyond what is required to pay for the household's consumption may freely be accumulated in the form of money, and can be invested in land. The advantages offered by this investment are security, in that the land cannot be lost through epidemics or the negligence of herdsmen, and the fact that income from land is in the form of the very agricultural products which a nomad household requires.

Social Implications

The above sketch of some relatively simple features of the economic situation of the Basseri pastoral nomads highlights factors of relevance to the economic choices faced by nomadic householders. I shall now try to show the social implications which they have for the family development cycle, processes that maintain social homogeneity within the nomad camp, and attitudes and practices with respect to saving and investment.

Family development cycle

A pastoral household requires flocks to subsist as an independent productive unit; among the Basseri at the time of my visit the nomads estimated that a herd of sixty adult sheep/goats was about the minimum required by an elementary family, while the average size of flock was at that time nearly 100 head. But a pastoral adaptation also implies certain labour requirements, and the tasks that are necessary are among the Basseri traditionally divided in such a way as to require the cooperation of at least three persons: a male head of the household, who loads the pack animals and directs the migration, erects the tent, fetches water and wood, and keeps most equipment in repair; a woman who does the cooking and housework, assists in packing and camping, and milks the flock; and a man who herds the animals, driving them to camp to be milked at about 12 a.m. and 5 p.m.

These capital and labor requirements define conditions which a family must satisfy if it is to live as an independent household. It is immediately apparent that an elementary family can only expect to satisfy these conditions with regard to labor force for a limited period of its natural development cycle, i.e., from the time the first son reaches the age of about eight to ten years, till the last son marries; and that it can obtain the necessary capital, if not on credit, then only through inheritance, i.e., normally at the dissolution of the parental household(s). Yet the value placed in Basseri culture on the elementary family as an independent household had called forth certain standardized adjustments, the forms and wider consequences of which may be analysed as social implications of pastoral capital forms and uses, granted the ideal of elementary family households.

The labour requirements of such small households are safeguarded among the Basseri by the formation of cooperative herding units of two to five tents. Since a single shepherd, as noted above, can control a herd of up to 400 head, several households can usually combine their flocks and still remain below this critical number, thus together requiring only one shepherd. Families which are short on personnel establish herding cooperation with families with several adolescent sons, thereby securing the additional labour assistance they need. The increased work involved in shepherding a flock say of 300 instead of 100 is negligible, and so the payments for this service are small: a household which supplies no herdsman for the flock of its cooperative herding unit generally gives the boys from the other tents who perform this duty one or two lambs a year and occasional small presents.

The capital requirements of a newly established family, on the other hand, are obtained by a different pattern, essentially a pattern of anticipatory inheritance. Only sons, subsidiarily collateral agnates or adopted sons, receive a share of their father's flock. This share they are given at the time of their marriage, thereby losing further claims on the estate. Each son receives at the time of his marriage the share which he would have received if his father had died at that moment, with no subsequent adjustments. An example will illustrate this: A man had 200 sheep when the eldest of his three sons married. He first paid the brideprice of 20 sheep, leaving 180; of this estate the groom received his rightful third, or 60 head, leaving 120 for the father and remaining two sons. If the father's flock subsequently increases to 200 again before the next son marries, that son will, assuming the same brideprice, receive 90 sheep at his marriage;

and there is no attempt to correct the disparity between the 60 and 90 sheep received respectively by the first and second son—because, the Basseri argue, his 60 sheep may meanwhile have grown to 600, or have been lost. The marriage of the last son is usually delayed until the parents are old, or one parent dies, so the son can become head of the new household in which the old parent(s) are permitted to live. If the son or only son reaches maturity while the father is still in his prime, the two often divide the flock 'as brothers' and separate.

In a culture where elementary families should live apart in separate tents, the capital forms and management patterns described above thus have clear social implications: certain technical patterns of herding cooperation and inheritance rules are developed, and these again have wider implications. Since the establishment of a household unit depends on the allocation to it of independent productive capital, the separation of men from their fathers and brothers is already completed when they marry—no vested economic or managerial interest ties them to their parental household. They are free to join whichever cooperative herding unit they wish, for personal or economic reasons—the practices prevent the formation of minimal or potential patrilineal nuclei on the basis of shared economic interests.

Social homogeneity

The Basseri constitute a population of striking social homogeneity—apart from the unique position occupied by the quite small chiefly dynasty, which is based on a number of unique features such as private title to lands, political functions, and taxation rights. Nearly all Basseri commoners are independent small herd owners, and this homogeneity of the population has extensive implications for the political organization of the tribe. There is no effective hierarchy of authority in camps or sections, and groups of every size experience great difficulties when trying to reach corporate decisions, unless these are dictated by the tribal chief. This basic social homogeneity may be analysed as the result of a number of processes, to a large extent implicit in the economic features I have outlined. I shall try to show (i) that these features are such as to inhibit the concentration of wealth, and thus the emergence of status differences based on wealth, and furthermore (ii) that they tend to encourage the elimination from the group of persons who deviate significantly in wealth from the average.

(i) A number of different factors tend to inhibit the accumulation of capital in the form of large herds. The continual risk of capital losses has been noted: epidemics, famines, and losses of young animals in case of late frost may all strike as sudden disasters and reduce the herd in a fashion which is unpredictable, and which thus the herd owner cannot anticipate in his stock management. All herds will thus experience intermittent setbacks, sometimes gross reductions.

While this control on herd growth strikes large and small flocks alike, other controls, implicit in Basseri consumption patterns, have increased effects with growing herds. The household with larger herds not only increases its consumption of luxuries and of foodstuffs—that is lambs, as well as tea, sugar, rice, etc. With greater capital in herds, an increasing amount of the wealthy household's labour is also diverted from pastoral production and management to other pursuits: the men require greater leisure, and their efforts are taken up by training and tending horses, hunting, and political activity; the women weave and tie rugs (which are never marketed); and the increased weight of household belongings and larger tents requires more beasts of burden, including camels, which again means a need for a separate camel herder. All these activities and persons depend on the herd without significantly contributing to its care and production; their presence will serve as a brake on the rate of herd increase.

Greater wealth also generally leads to an earlier fragmentation of the household. The pattern of anticipatory inheritance noted above means that the marriage of sons effects a dispersal of the household's capital; furthermore, such a marriage is only possible if the son can be equipped with a share of animals sufficient to support his wife and himself—i.e., about fifty animals or more. The expected marriage age of men is in their twenties; among poor people it may be postponed till the man is as much as thirty-five to permit the necessary accumulation of capital. Wealthy people, on the other hand, have no reason for such delay; and pressure from the boy and the community at large assure a marriage age of eighteen to twenty for the sons of the large herd owners. In other words, within about twenty years of his own marriage, the dispersal of the successful herder's flock commences, giving only a brief period of accumulation for the wealthy, and nearly twice that time for the poorer and less successful. For the wealthy this means also an early loss of the cheap and dependable labour represented by adult, unmarried sons.

Finally, it is common for wealthy herd owners to contract plural marriages; they may after some years take a second, younger wife, and sometimes even a third and fourth. This means a significant increase in the size of household which must be supported by the flock, and the increased consumption will represent a drain on that flock. Furthermore, since plural marriage extends the herd owner's fertile period, it affects the distribution of wealth by inheritance. The elder sons will wish to be married at a time when their father's younger wife is still bearing children—this means that they will receive unduly large shares of their father's estate, since the shares of as-yet unborn half-brothers will not be deducted. In short, the effects of all these different and partly interconnected factors—accidental capital losses, differential consumption rates and the diversion of labour from pastoral production, accelerated division of household and capital, polygyny and increased family size without corresponding reduction of the inheritance shares of elder sons—these all act together to inhibit the concentration of wealth in the form of large herds.

(ii) These factors are not, however, completely effective checks on the accumulation of wealth. Even less are they an effective guarantee against impoverishment, though reduced consumption, postponement of the fragmentation caused by the marriage of sons, etc., will facilitate cases of rehabilitation, just as their obverse hampers accumulation. The homogeneity of the tribe with respect to wealth will not result from these processes alone. But there are other features of the economic situation which also tend to produce homogeneity, though by a different process: there is a distinct tendency and clearly observable frequency of elimination from the tribe of households with unusually great and unusually small capital. This is possible because the Basseri, like other Persian nomads, are but a segment of a larger population where assimilation by sedentarization into peasant villages and urban centres is possible and frequent, and for different reasons sedentarization is the normal result of great capital accumulation, or capital losses.

Firstly in the case of accumulation: factors which tend to reduce the rate of income with increased size of herd have been noted. This means that while the risk of capital losses remains or increases, the increment to a large herd owner's income which results from the addition of further animals to his flocks decreases significantly. Consider, then, the possibilities of alternative investment. In nomadic activities they are nil; but the possibility of investment in agricultural land is always present. I should emphasize that sedentarization is never regarded as an ideal among the nomads; they value their way of life more highly than life in a village. But the economic advantages of land purchase are palpable: the risk of capital loss is eliminated, the profits to an absentee landowner are large, and they are in the form of products useful in a nomadic household. There is thus no feeling that land purchase implies sedentarization—a small plot of land can be let out on tenancy contracts and is merely a source of economic security and useful products. The difficulty in such investment is to convert the capital in animals to money capital by which land may be purchased. As noted, this is a relatively slow process, unless the owner is willing to take a considerable loss; nonetheless, with some patience it may be done, and banking facilities are available in the towns for accumulating savings, though no credit is available to nomads for investment in land.

Once a piece of land has been bought, the wealthy herd owner's money income increases rapidly, since production in marketable goods such as wool, butter and hides continues while expenses for the purchase of agricultural produce are reduced or eliminated. If a herd owner continues to be successful, he will thus accumulate wealth more rapidly, with little promise of profit through further investment in herds, but increasingly in a form which may be directly invested in land. Furthermore, title to land is held in a sedentary legal system where sons upon their marriage have no rights to anticipatory inheritance—which makes it an attractive form of capital from the owner's point of view and prevents a premature dispersal of the wealth.

This gradual process of land accumulation was observed in the field in its various stages. Only towards the very end do informants see sedentarization as its natural end result: they have a house built on their property and become increasingly concerned with the need for management of house and land, they develop a taste for many comforts that can only be satisfied by sedentary residence, etc. Sudden stock losses at this stage seem to be a common precipitating factor which drives them into the village; and even when they are well established as petty landowners they generally erect their old tent in their compound, and reside in it in the summer months.

Cases of sedentarization through capital accumulation and land purchase are by the nature of things relatively rare, and my material for the above description consists mainly of a handful of life histories. Sedentarization through impoverishment, on the other hand, is a constant threat for many and has a high empirical frequency, of the order of one person in every three in the groups of my censuses. Here the process is very simple: accident, sickness or poor management of a small herd leads to losses, and thus to an annual production below what is required for the purchase of food and clothing. But the herd itself is a large food store, and hunger easily drives the nomad to invade this his only productive capital, reducing the pastoral output further, in a vicious circle. The only alternative is to seek additional sources of income. Since shepherding contracts are relatively few (because they are, as we have seen, unprofitable for the herd owner), such sources are mainly found in sedentary society: as seasonal labourer, shepherd for the village flocks, doing local transport with donkeys, etc. To be successful, these activities must give the nomad income both to support his household *and* to increase his flock (thereby constituting a market for rich herd owners who wish to buy land). But frequently such work for a village community disturbs the nomad's migratory cycle, and thus leads only to reduced pastoral production and further animal losses, which makes him all the more dependent on sedentary sources of income. The Basseri feel that once a household's flock falls significantly below the minimal level of sixty adult head, this downward spiral is pretty inevitable and quite rapid; and there is a steady flow of impoverished settlers from every South Persian tribe to the villages and towns of their area.

These features of capital form and management thus tend, in the wider economic situation of the Basseri, to maintain a general economic homogeneity among the nomads, both by inhibiting the concentration of pastoral wealth, and by a constant elimination through sedentarization of the top and the bottom of the economic spectrum. As a consequence, social differentiation based on, or accompanied by, economic differences becomes impossible; and the nomad population becomes characterized by a striking social homogeneity, consisting of independent, economically self-sufficient small herd owners.

Saving and investment

A final implication of these features may be seen in attitudes and practices relating to saving, thrift, and capital accumulation. I have noted the fact that pastoral capital is in a directly consumable form and consists of animals with a short life span. This creates a situation where a certain minimum of thrift is necessary in capital management—the capital can only be maintained through a systematic policy of reserving lambs for the replacement of stock. Whereas in agriculture the distinction between produce and land is clearly apparent, among pastoralists nearly every instance of consumption threatens the productive capital itself, and must be considered and evaluated by the nomad. What is more, many of the factors involved are unknown. Disease may strike so that even a conservative policy of slaughter of lambs and yearlings still result in a reduction of stock. Milking practice is also a field of continual economic choice: not only the question of how many sheep should be left with lambs, but also how many sheep with lambs should be milked, and how much should be left to those lambs. In a good year, near-starvation of lambs gives a greater yield in butter to the nomad and does not appear to have great ill effects; on the other hand, if such lambs are subject to special strain or mild disease, they are lost in much higher frequency than are well-fed, robust lambs. In short, the management of pastoral capital requires a constant awareness of savings and investment policy; it breeds an attitude of continual and thrifty concern for the herd in its practitioners.

The Basseri are very aware of the economics involved in these choices, and discuss such policy at length within the household, though rarely in public, except in the form of gossip about third persons. The basic guiding principle which they adopt comes out in an almost obsessive desire to postpone every incident of consumption—to let each lamb gain weight one more day, or week, or season, to have one more lamb from an old sheep, to make a worn-out pair of shoes last till the next market town, or till arrival in the summer area, or till next spring equinox (the Persian New Year, when it is customary to put on new clothes).

Yet—or perhaps precisely as a correlate of these interests—hospitality is a highly valued virtue. The hospitable man is admired and people speak highly of him whether he is present or absent. Men seek his company and flock to his tent, though without importunity. By their own standards, then, most Basseri are miserly; and a few glaring examples are held up for public ridicule. Thus one of the largest herd owners in the group is popularly known as D.D.T. Khan because, they say, he is such a miser he eats his own lice.

But this failure in good manners (by Basseri canons) caricatured by some and prevalent in most need not be explained only in terms of the special habits of thrift developed as a result of pastoral life. There are also clear social reasons why a pattern of conspicuous consumption and hospitality is not only economically unwise, but also socially and politically unprofitable —in contrast to most of the local societies in the Middle East. These are found in the very features of social structure described in the previous section: the great economic and social homogeneity within Basseri camps. Where wealth differences are small, a policy of social aggrandizement through public consumption of wealth is bound to bring very limited returns. Nearly all the tents of a camp remain independent and self-supporting units; a hospitable man may gain influence in his camp through hospitality, but never to the extent of being able to dominate his camp fellows, or to expect economic support or advantage from them at a later date. On the contrary, the homogeneity itself is valued, and lampoons are sung about anyone who puts on airs and assumes an authoritative manner. For the Basseri commoner, there is little to gain by spendthriftness, and thus few inducements, but many controls, on the practice of hospitality.

Conclusion

The material presented in this brief paper can hardly be drawn together further, since the paper itself is already a summary of select features of the economic and social organization of a pastoral tribe which show a clear relation to certain features of sheep and goat herds as a form of capital. As noted in the introduction, other economic features (e.g., relating to pasture rights and the organization of migrations) have not been discussed, though they appear to have methodologically analogous implications for centralized authority and other features of the political organization of the tribe. In the present essay I have merely attempted to show how certain elementary characteristics of capital in the form of herds are related to a limited range of features of family organization, social homogeneity within camps, and common saving and consumption patterns—granted certain cultural values and conceptions held by the Basseri people. The characteristics of pastoral capital which I have discussed are, I believe, of a type familiar in conventional economic analysis, though here admittedly in a very elementary and rough form. What is interesting, and perhaps surprising, to a social anthropologist is the fact that it should be possible at all to show their social implications by a discussion involving relatively few 'cultural' facts—that the processes by which they are made relevant to social action and features of a local social system seem to implicate few of the other basic premises of Basseri culture. Admittedly, some of these premises are contained in the specific economic definitions and characterizations used; and it would seem a hopeless, and perhaps fundamentally impossible, task to state them all in a manner so that their implications would have the form of a deductive system. But it does seem possible to show how specific social forms are related as a product to simple constellations of determining factors, and thus how partial features of Basseri social structure are directly related to specific characteristics of pastoral capital and other economic facts.

20.
Bulls and Bears on the Cell Block

Heather Strange and Joseph McCrory

A prison is by its nature a total institution. A man who is confined within one exchanges his name for a number as an official identity, a freely selected home for an assigned cell like hundreds of others, a mode of dress and life-style for state-issued clothing and a prescribed regime. Contacts with those outside the walls are severely limited and occur only under the supervision of the prison administration.

Traditionally, prisoners have attempted to circumvent this material and psychological regimentation by forging a "society of captives" based on loyalty to the group and convict solidarity. As the studies by Gresham M. Sykes and Erving Goffman have indicated, an important expression of this ethic has been the practice of generalized reciprocity. Based on a system of shared values and shared deprivation, goods and services are given and received in response to need and the result is the expression of solidarity rather than economic gain. Although it is expected that the exchange between parties will balance out over time, reciprocity is implicit rather than explicit and there is no overt indication that a return is expected. In some cases barter was the mode of exchange—the conditions for exchange were more immediate and A was traded for B more for economic than social reasons.

Both still exist in the contemporary prison, but in the last decade they have been largely supplanted by a greatly expanded system of trade. This more impersonal system of exchange is based not on mutual trust or shared values but on a calculation of the worth of goods and services. It signals not only the diminishing worth of the traditional "con solidarity" but the growth of a marketplace mentality. In contrast to generalized reciprocity the inmate market system does not require regard for the "con" who provides or receives the goods or services. It involves middlemen, sellers and buyers who may not know each other and functions in a businesslike manner with certain idiosyncratic features determined by its location.

To assess the nature of this market system, the reason for its growth and the needs which it serves, data were collected from interviews and written communications with inmates at Trenton and Rahway prisons in New Jersey, from prison notices and memos and previous studies of total institutions. Because the state prison at Rahway exemplifies the typical correctional environment, this article will focus on that institution and explore the aspects of prison life which make an inmate market system both psychologically and economically necessary for most prisoners.

To understand the importance of the market system to most prisoners, it is necessary first to examine the physical setting, daily routine and necessities provided for the inmate by his custodians. Against this background, the psychological value of the system as a means for maintaining some autonomy and its material value as a source of amenities to make prison life more comfortable will become clear.

The Prison

Rahway is a maximum-security prison. Its most imposing feature is a central domed structure which serves as the hub for six spoke-like buildings. A majority of the 1,100 inmates occupy single-man cells in four of these wings.

The top tier of One-Wing contains administrative segregation ("ad seg") where men found guilty of infractions of prison rules are confined according to specified penalties. For example, a man whom the non-inmate Institutional Disciplinary Committee finds guilty of possession of U.S. dollars may be given from three to 15 days lockup with indefinite segregation possible on committee recommendation. "Ad seg" is sealed off from the rest of the wing except for one steel door. There, the men have no contact at any time with the rest of the prison population. A man may be removed to "ad seg" permanently for attempted escape, inciting to riot, possession of narcotics or alcohol or for other offenses. All offenses and possible penalties are listed in a mimeographed notice, "Approved penalties for Disciplinary Court," that was distributed to the prison population during February 1973.

Two-Wing is a dormitory housing approximately 350 men. Inmates who have been able to obtain a classification of "gang minimum," which allows them to work in groups outside of the prison walls under the supervision of an officer, or a classification of "full minimum," allowing them to work in other state institutions in the area, live in the dorms. A man who has detainers against him, has been convicted of a sexual offense or has been placed in "ad seg" is not eligible for either classification. Any other prisoner may petition the non-inmate Classification Committee for consideration.

At the back of the prison a fifth spoke called a "tie to," serves as a corridor leading to a large rectangular structure containing school rooms, drill hall (a recreational area), TV room, library, mess hall, cook house and the officers' dining room. Above the "tie to" is the hospital.

The prison workshops, interdenominational chapel and Five-Wing are behind and separate from the complex described, but they are enclosed within the same tower-dotted walls. Five-Wing, a converted shop, is a one-story structure dormitory that houses all men incarcerated for sexual offenses (C-cases). A man may have committed a sexual offense such as rape yet be housed in another wing if he was convicted of a nonsexual offense such as assault. Known homosexuals are usually housed on the second floor of One-Wing.

The "front house" where the entrance to the prison is located contains administrative offices and a mail room. On Sundays and specified holidays, the front house is jammed with inmates' relatives and friends. Some are lined up in front of the processing center awaiting permission to visit an inmate; others, having had their identities checked against a list of approved visitors, sit on wooden benches or mill about waiting for the name and number of the inmate they are visiting to be announced over the public address system. The visiting room takes up the entire first floor in the area beneath the central dome. It is connected to the front house by another spoke.

A large auditorium is located on the second floor under the dome. Films are shown here periodically. Prior to the Thanksgiving Day riot of 1971, annual variety shows and high school graduation exercises, to which outsiders could be invited, were staged in the auditorium.

The major recreational area for inmates is "the yard." Here, baseball or football teams vie with one another, militant groups practice formations and other men get together to exercise, exchange information or just "hang out."

This is the physical environment for the inmates of Rahway. It is a rigidly compartmentalized compound with each area carefully apportioned for a prescribed use. When a prisoner moves from one area of the institution to another, he goes with a predetermined and approved purpose; any individual's movement within this vast complex is tightly controlled by the prison authorities. An inmate is supposed to be in a particular place—his cell, the yard, the mess hall or a workshop—at a specified time. To go elsewhere, he needs a written pass from an officer. A man caught with a forged pass in his possession is subject to disciplinary court action. Control of prisoner activity is maintained through close adherence to a daily schedule punctuated by bells. Aside from a minor relaxation of the routine on weekends, the daily schedule remains the same day after day, week after week. It illustrates one of the most negative features of prison life: its repetitive boredom.

A Day in the Life ...

Monday through Friday

0600: Since January 1973, lights in each cell are operated by its inhabitant. Prior to that time, lights in the cells were turned on at this hour by an officer from a central switch box.

0630: A bell rings in each wing to officially announce the start of the inmates' day. Immediately following the bell, the wing officer unlocks the individual cell doors and checks that the inmates are still in their cells, a chore which takes approximately 15 minutes. This is the most important check of the day because the few successful escapes from Rahway have usually taken place at night. Although the door is unlocked, an inmate is still prevented from opening his cell door by a brake (a sliding metal bar) controlled from the head of each tier. During this time, most inmates rise, utilize the toilet and wash basin facilities in their cells and dress.

0700: A bell rings in the wing scheduled to go to the mess hall first for all meals during that week. Mess call for each wing is on a weekly rotation basis. The wing officer activates the brakes on each tier, releasing the inmates for breakfast. Neither breakfast nor any other meal is mandatory. An inmate may elect to remain in his cell during meal time if he wishes. Inmates do not march to mess hall, but straggle in bunches. They may be stopped by the officer commanding the "tie to" if the chow line in the mess hall is too long to accommodate arriving men. The wing scheduled to eat last during a particular week may not reach the mess hall until 0745. After breakfast, inmates return to their wings.

0800: A bell announces the call to work. Inmates leave their wing areas by job designation; they pair up through the "tie to" for the purpose of being counted and proceed to their work areas. Inmates enrolled in basic adult education, high school or college level courses attend scheduled classes some weekday mornings, afternoons or evenings depending on the course of study. College level work is offered under the auspices of Mercer Community College which enables a man to work toward an associate degree in arts, sciences, business or community service. Courses below the college level are taught by personnel hired by the prison authorities. Those inmates with no classes or jobs ("idle") remain in their cells until the midday meal. Inmates who go on sick call also remain in their cells. There is no resident physician at the prison but a nurse is always on duty in the hospital. A doctor can be called upon in an emergency and does come to the prison weekday mornings to make rounds of the wings. Inmates with minor ailments are treated in their cells. If more than a cursory examination is required, a sick inmate is given a pass to go to the prison hospital. Should an inmate require surgery, he is sent to the Trenton prison where appropriate medical facilities are located.

1130: Inmates return from their jobs or classes and proceed to their wings where they are locked in by application of the brakes. A count is taken. If the count is correct, a bell is rung.
1200: The lunch bell rings and the routine is the same as the one followed at breakfast.
1300: The work call is the same as the one at 0800, with the exception that the prison band plays marches to send the inmates on their way. Students in some curricula attend classes.
1400: Those on idle or with jobs which do not require work at this hour (mess hall, band, etc.) may go to the yard. If the weather is inclement, the drill hall, which has two basketball courts, ping-pong tables, shuffleboard courts and weight-lifting equipment, may be utilized.
1515: Those in the yard or drill hall must return to their cells.
1530: Most working inmates return to their cells where they are counted. Those working in the mess hall are counted at that location.
1600: A bell announces that the count is correct. Inmates who are not working may now choose to shower or go to the yard. Each wing has its own set of showers. Their use is left to the discretion of the inmate.
1630: Second yard call. Those who stayed in before may go to the yard now.
1700: All inmates return to their cells and mail is distributed.
1730: Supper bell. The same routine as noted for the first meal of the day.
1830: During the summer, optional yard for one hour; in the winter, the drill hall is available for recreation. Inmates whose wing is scheduled for TV proceed to the TV room; men in the wing scheduled for commissary go to pick up goods ordered in writing at an earlier time. Some students have classes scheduled.
2130: All inmates must return to their cells where they are counted for the last time. They are locked in for the night.

Saturday

Mess movements and head counts are the same as during other days. The yard is open from 0900 to 1130 and again from 1300 to 1530. TV and drill hall are the same as other days. The only men working on Saturday are mess hall workers, wing porters and approximately half of the inmates assigned to the regional laundry. For many inmates who have no Saturday work assignments, sleeping late is the favorite pastime. Other men spend their free time doing school assignments, engaging in arts and crafts activities or listening to their radios; a small percentage of the inmates use the yard or drill hall facilities whenever these are available. At 1900, half of the population may go to the movies; the other half attends film showings on Sundays. Movies begin at 1930.

Sunday

0900: Roman Catholic services in the chapel.
1000: Protestant services in the chapel.
Services for other denominations such as Jehovah's Witnesses, Jewish and Muslim affect fewer inmates; they are scheduled at a later hour Sunday or during other days of the week depending on the beliefs of the particular group.
1130: Midday meal is moved up one-half hour to accommodate the visiting schedule.
1145-1600: Three one-hour visiting periods are scheduled. Those who do not receive visits remain in their cells or go out to the yard or the drill hall. The recreation period ends after the last inmates having visitors are searched. No one can move through the "tie to" while the search is in progress in order to keep inmates who had visits from passing contraband to someone not subject to search. The schedule for the rest of the day is the same as that noted for Saturday. Another week has passed. Each inmate has one less week of time to serve.

Sources of Income

As the daily schedule indicates, the average working inmate is on the job for about five hours per day. An inmate does not have to work; he can remain idle. However, a man who remains idle does not receive "work time"—one day deducted from his maximum sentence for each five days worked. If he accepts a job and then refuses to work, an inmate is taken before the Disciplinary Court, which may impose "2 days lockup; up to 60 days loss of commutation time; 6 months idle; plus 30 days loss of privileges" as specified in the February 1973 notice.

Inmates of the Rahway prison who work, as the vast majority do, can be classified into three categories: those who work in state use industries, those who work in the regional laundry and other workers.

State use industries include all shops where shoes, clothing, signs, furniture and other products used by the state are made. Men working in these shops earn from $.85 to $1.05 per day, with a bonus of $.25 per day given for merit. The pay scale in the regional laundry, which services all other state institutions in the area, runs from $.85 to $1.55 per day. One of the highest paid jobs in the regional laundry is "sheet shaking"—removing fecal matter from linen brought in from hospitals.

The category "other workers" includes porters, messhall workers, students, workers in the prison laundry, band members, yard workers, etc. These men earn from $.65 to $.85 per day, according to how their work is classified: unskilled, semiskilled or skilled. The current wage structure at the Trenton prison is similar.

No inmate receives payment in cash. Earnings are applied monthly to each man's account in the Inmate Commissary, which stocks more than 300 commodities. A March 1973 memo addressed to all residents of Rahway elaborated a new policy for establishing prices in the commissary. Attached to it was a listing of commodities available, their cost to the store and the sale price of each. Foodstuffs, numerous brands of cigarettes, cigars and pipe tobacco, a wide variety of toilet articles and miscellaneous items such as stationery, playing cards, can openers, shower shoes and padlocks all were in stock.

Commissary funds also may be used for purchasing specified goods via mail order or may be sent to a prison-approved recipient, such as a spouse, on the outside. The latter option is rarely used. Usually, the inmate must rely on outsiders for the provision of additional funds as well as clothing, special food and other items. Inmates who have no relatives or friends to help in these ways are in the unenviable position of doing without most of the things that could make prison life a bit more bearable. Thus, economic differences between inmates are derived not only from the internal job market, but also from the inputs of outsiders based on statuses which the men held prior to entering the prison.

A Rahway inmate is allowed to spend a maximum of $75 per month in or through the commissary. In terms of wages alone, the highest-paid worker earns less than $50 per month; most earn less than $20. Anything above that amount which is applied to an account must come from the outside. Money orders, but no personal checks or cash, may be sent to an inmate by approved correspondents. However, visitors are permitted to deposit cash at the mail room with an officer who makes out a receipt in triplicate—one copy for the inmate, one for the donor and one to be sent to the commissary for their records. Very few men receive more than $30 per month from outside sources; most get less. Hence, few inmates are able to utilize the maximum commissary allowance.

Each inmate may receive one 15-pound food package per month as well as additional 25-pound packages at Christmas and Easter. Prison officials issue a list of acceptable foodstuffs which includes most cooked foods. Bananas, grapes, nuts in shells, dried fruits, instant and ground coffee, tea and any item in powdered form are forbidden. Dried fruits and grapes are apparently disallowed in an attempt to deny inmates ingredients for making alcoholic beverages collectively known as "hootch"; powdered items are prohibited in order to control the smuggling of drugs.

Although the state provides the basic necessities, a variety of clothing may be ordered by an inmate via mail order or can be sent to him from a store if an order is placed by someone outside the prison. Sweatshirts and sweaters, but no jackets or coats, in specified colors—white or dark—are allowed. Shoes or boots of designated types, even football shoes—as long as the cleats are made of rubber—underwear and handkerchiefs, white sport shirts and bathrobes are among the items which may be received from the outside. Towels are also on the approved list. For those inmates without the funds or the outsiders needed to obtain better quality items the state provides essentials including shoes, underwear, chino pants and "dress" shirts, as well as jeans and blue cotton work shirts for daily wear.

Books are available in the prison library, but both selection and access are limited. Inmates are allowed to visit the small library only when their wing is given library time, usually one evening per week for a two-hour period following dinner. Each man may check out three books for two weeks. Should an inmate miss his assigned time, he must wait until the following week. Inmates are also allowed to receive printed matter from outside the prison. Magazines, newspapers and hardbound books must come directly from a publisher or a bookstore; up to 12 new or used paperback books per month may be sent from any source or brought directly to the prison mail room by an inmate's visitors.

Other goods currently allowed in both the Rahway and Trenton prisons include television sets, radios, tape recorders, typewriters and materials for arts and crafts of specified types. Again, the funds for purchase of these items must come from wages saved or from outside sources.

In addition to these prescribed methods for obtaining goods, illegitimate sources also exist. Thefts from the shops, the kitchens and from other inmates do occur—some with the guards' sanctions. There is a tacit understanding between inmates and guards that inmates who are good workers or who do extra chores such as cleaning or painting after regular duty hours are allowed to take reasonable amounts of food or items from the shops.

A new or inexperienced inmate who enters the prison finds that he and his belongings are vulnerable to the wants, needs, avarice and caprice of others. The streetwise, tough ones show that they know the score and secure a place for themselves; the innocents accept alliances—platonic or otherwise—with men who are tougher and more knowledgeable, either by choice or necessity. In some cases it is simply a mutual need to have someone to "watch my back" and reflects racial, ethnic, generational, or possibly, political loyalty; in other instances it is a voluntary or involuntary sexual liaison. A relationship with one man is preferable to serial sexual assaults by any man who is able and desirous of forcing himself upon a weaker newcomer. Some inmates adhere to a stringent code of sexual behavior and reject any form of homosexuality. They do not differentiate between what they view as a male role or a female role in any relationship—in their parlance, "whether you're pitching or catching, it's still baseball." Sexuality does and will continue to pose a major problem for inmates in all total institutions. But in economic terms, once a new inmate establishes himself as his own man or as someone's friend or "kid," theft of his possessions is rare.

Should the normal functioning of the institution and the social system be disrupted, normal codes of behavior also are disrupted; even "model" prisoners react to the emotionalism of the pressured moment. During the Thanksgiving Day riot at Rahway in 1971, some inmates settled individual grievances against others by direct physical assault. There were also numerous examples of hostility and contempt expressed by some inmates for others through the destruction and theft of property. Men considered to be rats or squealers had all of their belongings destroyed. There were many thefts, particularly from C-cases—men convicted of sexual offenses such as rape or child molestation, who are regarded by many inmates as being at the very bottom of the social pile in terms of status and rank. It is probable that these actions against property were substituted for actions against the property owners. But Gresham M. Sykes's observation that "material possessions are so large a part of the individual's conception of himself that to be stripped of them is to be attacked at the deepest layers of personality" indicates that while the property owners did not suffer physical attack they were subjected to severe psychological punishment as well as economic loss.

The victims of losses during this period of upheaval made claims for replacement of property to the state. At least some of the men are known to have received reimbursement.

When the prison is functioning normally, men have time, boredom and more time. They fill it in a variety of ways depending on their individual interests. But whatever those interests, participation in the inmate market system engages the vast majority of inmates to a greater or lesser degree each day.

Trade with Cigarettes

Tobacco, in the form of cigarettes, has served as an all-purpose currency in a wide variety of total institutions. Cigarettes, as R.A. Radford noted, are "homogeneous, reasonably durable, and of convenient size for the smallest or . . . largest transactions." At Rahway, where actual possession of cash is prohibited, but services and goods beyond those provided by the state are bought and sold among inmates, cigarettes are the primary medium of exchange.

Cigarettes are always available to inmates scheduled to place commissary orders—if they have sufficient funds in their accounts. Prices are relatively stable although subject to the same inflationary tendencies as those in the society outside the walls.

Assuming that an inmate has cigarettes which he doesn't plan to smoke directly, what can he buy with them? The prison market system provides a varied assortment of goods. Food and nonedible items from the inmate commissary are stocked by some inmates who sell them to others in the interim between the days when men may place commissary orders. Such inmates use their cells as stores; they are called "storekeepers" in Trenton, while in Rahway it's the practice to refer to the store by inmate's name (Jack's store). Storekeepers have the same commissary privileges as other inmates. They get business from men who did not place orders for some reason, forgot to buy a needed item or just wished to personally select something from an assortment rather than writing a list and having a guard pack up their goods. It is a chance to exercise choice within a relatively rigid environment. A storekeeper generally sells a $.25 item for one pack of cigarettes, a $.40 item for two packs.

Storekeepers should not be confused with other types of salesmen—merchants in Trenton and peddlers in Rahway. As a Trenton inmate points out: "Merchants will sell anything . . . and the term has a bad meaning. A storekeeper provides a service and makes some profit. A merchant is just out for himself. He's a guy you'd characterize as willing to sell his own mother." In the prison context, the derogatory terms merchant/peddler are applied most frequently to men who sell food stolen from the kitchen or from either the inmates' or officers' dining rooms. Nevertheless, choice foods, especially meat, are always available and always in demand. They are sold individually for a pack or more.

Food sent in the monthly packages from outside, particularly home-cooked dishes, brings periodic income to some men. Others prefer to share with friends, but one Trenton inmate states, "I've seen men who were crime partners hide food packages from one another."

Because dining in the mess hall is optional, men who receive food packages can enjoy the contents in their cells where they heat the food atop radiators or over fires made by burning rolls of toilet tissue. A friend who works in the kitchen may heat it properly or deep freeze it for later use as a favor or for a portion of a special dish. Such services also can be obtained by payment of a pack or two of cigarettes.

One inmate may contract with another to have all of his meals delivered to his cell, paying in advance by the week. They are prepared for him by the other inmate from stolen food or possibly from supplies purchased from men who received food packages. If a man has the resources to support an aversion to dining *en masse*, he might dine on steak or chops from the officers' mess in his cell, watching TV or listening to his radio, while his poorer peers in the mess hall are eating cold cuts or spaghetti.

Alcohol, or hootch as it is called, is relatively cheap at six packs per quart: it is made from anything fermentable, including milk. The major problem is where to set the mash so that it is not discovered. Some men have become as ingenious as the best bootleggers of Prohibition days. Drinkers report horrendous hangovers, but a few hours of escape from the boring routine of prison life are worth the misery.

State-issued underwear, T-shirts or shorts each sell for one pack. Clothing from outside the institution is priced higher than any comparable state-issue item, with good quality shoes or boots being particularly valued by inmates. Clothing which has no state-issue counterpart is also highly valued and appropriately priced. Possession of clothing from the outside allows an inmate to express some individuality and helps him maintain a sense of self-worth. The lack of such goods tends to reinforce feelings of deprivation already inherent in being a prison inmate.

Entertainment media are very highly valued, particularly expensive television sets and radios that offer a selection of AM/FM, short-wave or marine bands. As a status symbol, owning a top quality item in either category is likened by inmates to having a Cadillac outside the walls. Tape recorders are also popular. Because the men are allowed to order any of these things from outside distributors or have them sent by someone outside, prices for used models in terms of cigarettes approximate retail dollar prices.

One means of compensating for lack of funds from friends or relatives outside is for inmates to earn income by making goods or providing services for others. Wooden shelves for the cell (three packs), lamp shades (four packs), desks (as high as two cartons) and clothing racks (three packs) are custom made by the enterprising from stolen state materials. All of these furnishings are classed as contraband by the prison authorities, but many inmates are willing to risk potential problems with officers in order to make their cramped cells more comfortable and to impress their personalities on the drab surroundings.

Guards recognize the social control mechanism available to them from ignoring such infractions. They gain the leverage necessary to enforce or encourage inmate cooperation in keeping a tier orderly and everything functioning smoothly. Troublesome inmates are subject to frequent searches of their cells, confiscation of contraband goods and punishment by the disciplinary court. A man who, by whatever means, can assure order on a tier might even get away with painting his cell (or having it painted for a fee of a couple cartons) a bright, forbidden color without being reported as a rule-breaker.

One Rahway inmate painted his cell a sunny yellow, made a "room-divider" to partition the toilet from the rest of the cell with sheets (stolen from the laundry) dyed orange, and also enjoyed some of the furnishings listed above. He was never taken before the disciplinary court.

Other goods available from fellow inmates include commercial greeting cards, which cost one pack each or custom cards painted to order for three packs each. A wide variety of leather goods—handbags, belts, wallets and cigarette cases, either plain or carved—are made to order by inmates who purchase materials from outside suppliers. Prices vary for these things, as they do for portraits in oils or pastels, according to the talent of the artist or craftsman. Many handcrafted goods and paintings are destined for someone on the outside and payment will most likely be made to someone outside. For example, an inmate orders a leather handbag for his wife from a craftsman whose wife claims it from the prison office. The latter woman mails it to the one for whom it was made and receives payment. The craftsman's wife may then deposit the money to her husband's account in the prison or she may use it herself. The roundabout process is necessary because only an inmate's approved visitors are allowed to receive goods from him.

New books in mint condition can bring up to one-quarter the retail price in cigarettes. Due to the prison's relaxation in correspondence rules, there has been a proliferation of dealers in new books because some inmates are joining numerous book clubs. A few of the men ignore the bills, considering threatened lawsuits from the book clubs laughable. Pornographic books command good prices from the interested, from several packs to several cartons depending on the (imputed) quality of the book. A few years ago, prison officials continued to make some attempts to keep pornographic books out of their institutions, but they have apparently abandoned their efforts as the list of questionable titles has lengthened.

Pornographic photographs are still banned; their introduction into the prison is illicit but profitable for the recipient. Men who own photos rarely sell them. Instead, they rent them to other inmates for up to five packs per night.

Some menial services are available to the man with an abundance of cigarettes because a less fortunate inmate may be willing to perform chores for payment. Recent increases of both wages and the amount of money which can be applied to an inmate's commissary account mean that there are fewer unlucky persons. For example, only one Rahway inmate is known to shine shoes for pay, one pack per pair, and very few men are willing to perform other menial tasks for their peers. One inmate who was assigned as a wing porter did contract to sweep and mop some of the cells on that wing daily for five packs per week per cell, but this is apparently another isolated case. However, a man can arrange to have his clothing carefully laundered and pressed by someone working in the prison laundry for 15 packs per month. Tailoring services can also be secured. Barbers ply their trade for reasonable fees in spite of razors and scissors being forbidden to inmates. And some men gain income by researching legal matters and typing briefs for others.

"Head runners" (wing clerks) sell choice cells to other inmates for cigarettes, being able to arrange transfers as part of their jobs. The amount of payment depends on how difficult it is for a clerk to gain approval for a specific transfer from supervising officers; it is also dependent on how badly an inmate wants a transfer. Members of any prison minority at Rahway—Spanish-speaking inmates, Black Muslims, white inmates in general, etc.—consider a cell to be choice if it is on a tier where others of their group are quartered. Any cell in Three-Wing, the newest wing, is labeled choice because each has a window which the inmate can open and close, unlike the windows in the older wings which are not accessible to inmates. Three-Wing is tiled and is said to be the quietest and cleanest wing in the prison.

Some inmates rent their cells during mess movements to gamblers for card and dice games, taking a percentage of the pot as payment, or to homosexuals for assignations. In either case, men avail themselves of other cells if they think use of their own too risky because a guard might be suspicious. Gambling and overt sexual acts are subject to disciplinary court action.

Good work assignments in the shops and laundries are sold by inmates who can get their civilian boss to request a particular man for a job. Civilian bosses, like guards, can use their powers to reward cooperative men. Or, an inmate may sell a job to another. In order to avoid punishments prescribed for quitting a job, the seller must either convince his boss that he is suffering from illness or injury or get the boss to agree to lay him off for some reason acceptable to the administration.

Borrowing and lending of cigarettes is done informally among friends, but if a man needs "big money"—several cartons—he'll probably have to go to a loan shark. Rahway loan sharks demand repayment of 15 packs for one carton in one month as standard. A man who is considered a bad risk may be given as little time as a week in which to repay borrowed cigarettes at the same interest rate. An inmate who accrues large debts, usually from gambling, which he is unable to pay probably will request that prison officials place him in "ad seg" on the realistic grounds that his life is in danger.

Trade With Dollars

Inmates are not allowed to have cash other than the money assigned to their commissary account. However, some do obtain it from visitors and smuggle it into their cells despite preventive procedures such as strip searches of inmates after contact visits with family or friends.

At Rahway, men are allowed to meet with visitors in a large visiting room during one of three hour-long visits each Sunday afternoon. Because inmates and their visitors sit together on crowded wooden benches resembling church pews with no intervening barriers, these social occasions are called contact visits. Trenton prisoners now enjoy them too, although until 1972 a Trenton inmate was separated from his visitor by a metal partition with windows of bullet-proof glass and forced to converse by telephone. The latter procedure is still used in the Tombs and other Houses of Detention for Men in New York City.

Cash is not particularly difficult for an inmate to obtain from a visitor in spite of watchful guards, but why do both inmate and visitor take the risk if money can be left legally at the mail room? After going through prison processing and waiting in a noisy, crowded room for the visit to be called, chances are that a visitor is experiencing a heightened antiprison feeling so that collaborating with the inmate in a joint effort to beat the system in this small way may be quite pleasurable. However, the inmate needs ingenuity to conceal cash during the strip search so he wants one bill rather than a batch of singles. This sometimes requires planning—asking for cash during one visit, getting it a week or more later. Inmates who receive no visitors but need cash can buy dollars with cigarettes from other inmates—ten smuggled dollars selling for five cartons.

In spite of the widespread use of cigarettes as all-purpose currency, cash is necessary for dealings with those men who divide their lives between the inside and the outside; men whom some inmates want to encourage in economic dealings and whom the prison authorities want to discourage: the guards. An officer who brings goods into the Rahway or Trenton prisons is called "my man" or "my connection." A variety of illicit goods small enough to be hidden on their persons such as drugs, pornographic pictures and liquor are provided for inmates by a few obliging officers. Guards who engage in these transactions demand to be paid in cash, asking $10 or $15 for a pint bottle of cheap scotch or a tab of LSD. There is risk inherent in any transaction between inmate and guard: both are subject to disciplinary action by prison authorities if caught.

The extent of this form of illicit trade is difficult to establish. It seems unlikely that it is very widespread. An inmate who has a good thing going with a guard does not broadcast the fact to his peers for fear of jeopardizing himself and his connection. He may serve as a middleman for trusted inmates without revealing the identity of the involved guard. If so, he gets a small share of the goods or is paid with cigarettes. A guard involved in illegal sales probably deals with only a few, very carefully selected inmates. The wider his sales network, the greater likelihood he has of being caught by an honest officer who might report him or of being ratted on by an inmate trying to curry favor with another officer or a higher prison official.

Changing Values

The general willingness of the average inmate to try to establish rapport with guards is considered despicable by some of the older convicts. Formerly, they say, fraternization would have led to an inmate being considered a possible rat by his peers. But this, like other changes, signals a shift in the orientation and values of relatively new inmates which has fostered the growth of the inmate market system.

Older inmates, mid-thirties or over, men who have done "bits" in one or more "joints" previously, tend to lapse into nostalgic recollections about "the good old days" when they say there was more con solidarity and the haves were generous to the have-nots. At that time, it was considered unpardonable to steal choice foods from the cook house, thus depriving fellow inmates of their fair share at meal time.

Generosity is no longer the norm; hence, the rare generous man has come to be known among oldtimers as "real con."

> *At Trenton*, A guy who is not greedy can understand that not everyone has the connections or mailing list that he has and will share with anyone except grubbers (free-loaders); he's 'real con.' But guys like that are damned hard to find these days.

At Rahway, The maverick who gives indiscriminately to those with less is generally held in high esteem by other inmates; he's referred to as a 'real convict' or 'real con' by some men. There aren't very many.

Another Rahway inmate describes a personal experience,

> The prison issued me a suit of civilian clothes to wear for a court appearance in another state. It must have been twenty years old. The sleeves of the jacket were too short and the waist of the pants was too big. I got a tailor to do some work on it so it looked pretty good. When I tried to pay him for the work he told me, 'No charge to a real con like you, Bobby.' I felt good for the rest of the day.

The "real con" has dimensions which are noneconomic as well. A composite picture based on views expressed by several inmates designates him as a reliable stand-up guy who is respected and trusted by his peers, a man with heart (courage), a man of integrity and dignity who is close-mouthed and has a cool head. He's the one you want covering your back in case there's trouble. Could there ever have been more than a few such men? Assuming that generosity once was the norm, how can one explain the value shift to a general acceptance that anything and everything can be sold? Some men explain it as due to changes in the prison population.

The demographic shift which they believe has taken place has brought more young men and more members of some minority groups, blacks and Spanish-speakers, into the prisons. There is a tendency to view the young as serving relatively short sentences and continuing to be street-oriented rather than con-oriented. They have different ideas, and frequently view themselves as political prisoners victimized by a system of social injustice. Such ideas are radical in the opinion of older conservative inmates. The newcomers even speak a different argot: "I don't even understand what those young (blacks) are saying to each other—and they don't want me to either," states one older, white inmate. Young and old, inmates are further divided along racial and other lines into groups to which members feel primary allegiances. Such memberships may close the generation gap: being a Black Muslim, for example, influences a man's behavior more than does his age. The effect of these changes has been the breakdown of the traditional con-solidarity value that men today believe aligned the inmates against the system that imprisoned them.

Today, instead of a "society of captives" composed of men who share values and behavior patterns to a fairly high degree, there appear to be a number of mutually exclusive groups, each with its own subculture. Although generalized reciprocity tends to characterize behavior within any group, it does not cross group boundaries with much frequency. It is confined by the parameters of mutual trust and loyalty which in today's prison have been considerably narrowed. Trade, however, crosses all boundaries.

The extensive inmate market system performs several important integrating functions for the prison as a whole as well as for the individual inmate. While the market system has expanded to fill the gap produced by waning reciprocal relationships resulting from a breakdown of old values, it has also served to encourage some interaction between members of different groups beyond that imposed on them by work or wing assignments. A common need to buy and to sell may not be as strong a bond as consolidarity but it does keep lines of communication open. For the individual prisoner the system channels goods and services which are of practical value in making the dreary life inside the prison more comfortable and amenable. Moreover, these goods are psychologically valuable to the inmate. Material possessions play a very important role in a man's ability to maintain a positive self-image and to fight the dehumanizing institutionalation process. Owning something not issued to him by the state helps an inmate combat the anonymity of prison life and lets his environment reflect his personality in some way.

Even the act of engaging in the market system, setting a price, determining to buy or sell goods or services can counteract the debilitating repetitiveness of everyday existence by introducing a new element into the inmate's routine. It encourages daily decision-making on the part of most inmates. This skill, so necessary in society outside the walls, could conceivably be lost by a prisoner who for several years fully abdicates responsibility for his existence to a prison regime punctuated by bells and tier brakes which is actively opposed to individual decision-making.

Within the context of life in a total institution this last function of the inmate market system may be most important in terms of the inmate's later adjustment to life outside the walls. Through his participation in trade he continues to exercise choice over a small part of his existence and maintain some autonomy in the economic realm—even if the currency is mainly cigarettes.

21.
The Female Factor in Resettlement
Lucy M. Cohen

The study of the lifeways of immigrants to the urban centers of the United States has been a theme of central interest to social and behavioral scientists, for immigrants are American history. To discover how Latin American immigrants think and feel, and how they act upon problems and the stresses of life, is thus to dwell upon a familiar theme of the American experience.

But there is growing recognition that the period since World War II has brought new immigrants to this country who do not fit the "ideal type" of peasant and immigrant depicted in major works about the settlement and adjustment of earlier newcomers. Passage of the landmark Immigration Act of 1965 reminds us that Americans have now chosen a policy which gives priority to *what immigrants do,* rather than to *who they are.* Skill and occupation, rather than race and ethnic origin, are now the major criteria for admission to the country. For some regions of the world such as Latin America, however, this policy obscures the realities of what it means to enter the United States.

Women Pioneers

Whereas the typical pioneers of immigration in the past have been men, approximately two-thirds of the Central and South American newcomers are women. Moreover, they are not widows or young single persons who venture on long voyages to the promised land. Rather, they are mostly women who established households in their places of origin, and then left children behind under the care of maternal grandmothers or other kin.

Theoretical issues and practical concerns have led students of immigration to consider processes of settlement and adjustment of newcomers. Social scientists have focused much of their research in this area on the study of continuity or discontinuity of cultural traditions, and the impact of new experiences on the newcomers. Latino cultures which are in the midst of change can no longer be single-typed as "indigenous" or "mestizo," or "rural" or "urban," as they have been frequently described. Their cultural world contains interwoven segments of knowledge and meaning drawn from the many ideologies and traditions which are impinging on Latin America.

In recent years various official inquiries into the entry of immigrants and undocumented workers have centered on their effect on the U.S. labor market, with "special concern," as the Domestic Council Committee puts it, that the employment of the alien will not adversely affect wages and working conditions of similarly employed U.S. workers. But the great majority of post-1965 immigrants have entered the United States on the basis of family ties to American residents. It would seem logical, therefore, for policymakers to give attention to the impact of immigration on these families.

Entry and Settlement

Most of these immigrants are of working-class background and have entered the country to improve the family's socio-economic status. They come highly motivated by the belief that self-sacrifice is necessary to attain the desired goal of a better life for their children. Separation from home, however, is not the first major life hurdle which an immigrant has faced. Latinos learn that throughout life there are problems of one kind or another. Success consists in a willingness to face each problem and to overcome it.

Planning for the future and hard work are central values which enable immigrants to master the series of steps involved in entry and settlement. The containment of feeling is also important, particularly for immigrants. Through the practice of *controlarse* (control of the self) and *sobreponerse* (to overcome oneself), Latinos cope with stress-inducing situations. Thus these immigrants do not fit a prevalent stereotype that the peoples of Latin American heritage conform passively to unkind fate. Instead, they contain their feelings, face difficulties, and work hard to master them.

A woman who acts as a leader in migration engages in careful planning, particularly to the caretaking of children left behind and of those brought to this country. The initiative exercised by women as they become the organizers and counselors for other relatives who follow them to this country can be often noted.

Some of the women who are undocumented workers originally entered the country with some time-limited permission, such as a student or a tourist visa. Others crossed the border without any entry documents. Those whose visas have lapsed continue to search for work situations which require their skills or the employers who can sponsor their entry as permanent residents. It is not unusual for men and women who have crossed the border without any papers to get caught by immigration officers and deported. Most of them, however, return to the United States, and some have a history of repeated entries. They, like other Latinos, have active circles of kin and friends to assist and advise them in the United States, at home, and at key border crossing points.

The migration patterns of undocumented workers are different in some respects from those of the immigrants. Women who cross the borders without documents do not usually bring young children with them, since this is considered too grave a risk. Subsequent to entry, such mothers bring their children only when they feel that their job and living situation are stable enough to permit it. The restrictions on immigration, however, have made it increasingly difficult for parents who feel unsettled in their designated visa categories to have their children join them. For example, some mothers on student visas who have children in their countries of origin seriously consider staying in the United States after their visas expire. However, separation from children is difficult for some, particularly since they cannot visit their children at home without the possibility of encountering difficulties in reentering the United States. Moreover, student visas are not easy to obtain.

There are other paths but they are difficult for people with limited means. Relatives in the home country, such as an immigrant's mother, can bring a young child to visit with the parent. However, American consular officers in the countries of origin, fearing that such children will be left with their parents in the United States, require—in some cases—the posting of a bond of $1,000 (at a minimum) to ensure that the child is returned to the country of origin.

Immigrant Households and Children Left Behind

Latino households are flexible units which expand and contract in accordance with the stages of entry and settlement and the life cycle stages of family members. Changes and realignments take place in households and families as evidence of the shifts involved in migration and settlement. Nevertheless, as immigrants settle in the host society, they establish nuclear or extended households composed of blood relatives and kin by marriage, and connected to ties of propinquity in neighborhoods. Information about marital status, children's residence, and their care is crucial to understand the ways in which Latinos reestablish themselves in the host society.

The extended household is characteristic largely of the mothers who are alone with their children and other relatives. This group of mothers includes those who have never married, the separated, the divorced, and the widowed. Both the nuclear and extended families are sources of mutual help in such tasks as child care, the search for jobs, or counseling for problems of illness. The strength of these ties may be noted in the case of single mothers. Single parents, together with their extended kin in the United States and those left behind, have strong bonds of reciprocity. Although the immigrant mothers who are single are the least educated and lowest salaried, they retain economic independence, and among the eligible few seek public assistance.

Almost half of all immigrants have some children 17 and under remaining in their country of origin. Typically, during the initial seven-year cycle of entry immigrants have some of these children with them, and some left behind in the home country. Children tend to be in the phase of later childhood. While partially separated from kin, mothers work had to establish viable living situations, including the official approval of residence which facilitates the entry of spouse or children left behind.

Children in the home country who are in the stages of early and late childhood tend to be cared for, almost exclusively, by the maternal grandmothers. Upon the immigrant mother's departure a child moves to the maternal grandmother's household. This change of residence often means contact with a wide group of maternal kin. Thus the availability of support by their mothers has made it possible for women to lead movements of families and communities of this country. Furthermore, the mother's separation from children in the early and late stages of childhood serves to solidify the child's kinship ties with the maternal line since care is almost exclusively done with this set of kin. Although there are usually not many adolescents left in the home country, those left behind reside with other maternal kin, notably maternal aunts or older married sisters.

Newcomers view separation from children as a phase necessitated by the dire poverty in the home communities and the difficulties in obtaining permission for family groups to enter the United States. Because of their circumstances, immigrants give priority to the entry of older children who have the potential of joining them as workers in the labor force. It is the older adolescents, therefore, who are encouraged to come to the United States as rapidly as possible, in order to expand the total earnings for the family. In the meantime, immigrant parents send regular remittances home which fluctuate according to the type of work but range from a low of $10 to a top amount of $50 a month per household (not per child).

High Commitment to Work

Most of the immigrants enter with the goal of working in order to attain higher levels of living for themselves and their families. They believe that parents ought to sacrifice themselves for their children. Among working-class Latinos there are marked contrasts in educational levels by sex. Most of the men have completed their education at the primary school level, in contrast to the women who tend not to have finished primary school at all. These differences are reflected in the types of work and annual income of the male and female Latino immigrant and accentuated by the structure of the labor force in the United States.

Men and women tend to work in unskilled or semiskilled jobs, but there is greater occupational mobility for men than for women. Furthermore, the Latina who has been previously employed in her home country tends to be underemployed in the United States to a greater extent than men. Women tend to fall in the $4,000 or less annual income category, while men are concentrated in the $4,000-5,999 group.

Most men and women work full time, and of the full-time workers a sizable proportion hold down "moonlighting" jobs as well. Those who work extra time are usually the immigrants with more limited knowledge of English. Women who work overtime regularly are mostly single parents with an extended household. The men have working wives, and are under heavy expenses in purchasing homes.

Reshaping Social Structures

As increasing proportions of Central and South Americans enter the United States, they reshape the character of life in this country, as well as the structure of communities in their home countries. Consequently, the impact of feminine leadership in migration should receive special policy consideration.

One of the most significant present-day trends in immigration is that women play a central role in the international movement of peoples in the Americas. Why have these women, therefore, been neglected in deliberations of Western Hemisphere immigrants policy in the United States? It appears as if Latinas are assumed to enter this country as "dependents" (for example, as spouses or as an immigrant's mother, or as child). Many are not counted in the worker certification programs of the U.S. Department of Labor, and their impact on our economy is not adequately assessed.

Yet women who enter as the relatives of an immigrant and those who lead in resettlement are committed to activity in full-time work soon after their entry. This is highly significant, since they work for a salary to a greater extent than the Latinas left behind and women in the U.S. labor force. Stereotypes of the Latina as a dependent and passively oriented female who does not work outside the home have led us to neglect the reality that she is an active, self-reliant person who no longer stays behind to wait for husbands and brothers to help her with moves to new countries. Feminist leaders in our own nation should pay increasing attention to this immigrant woman's ability to master the tasks of change in our rapidly evolving urban societies.

A second point about the Latina's migration is that she resettles during her active child-raising cycle. To accomplish this she relies heavily on her bonds with maternal kin for child care. For a Latina who enters as an undocumented worker, in particular, the selection of substitute caretakers is essential since she may leave children behind for long periods, or at least until they reach late adolescence. There are no easy solutions for the separation of family groups which takes place during international resettlement. Substitute caretaking, however, is clearly an institutionalized relationship which should receive focal attention as Latino women establish their ascendancy in pioneering immigrant roles.

Part VIII
Urban Ethnography: People in Cities

As illustrated in Lucy Cohen's preceding article on Latin American women, the economies of traditional cultures are increasingly influenced by migration to industrial centers. The effects of this transformation are felt most sharply in the growing numbers of rural folk in urban areas. Explanations for the flow of migrants from country to city range from propositions about the world economy to analyses of individual psychology. When we consider the nineteenth-century influx of migrants, domestic and foreign, into American cities, the larger historical forces that propelled people to industrial centers seem the same as those operating today. In the past, overpopulation of the hinterlands, land reform, religious and political persecution have separately and in combination resulted in large-scale population shifts to urban centers, and the same impersonal forces continue to be the impetus of today's mass migrations.

The city also holds its positive attractions for migrants. Once any group is even partially integrated into the money economy, the prospects of a materially better life usually lie in the direction of urban job opportunities. The more improvements are made in transportation technology, the easier it becomes to justify the investment in a one-way ticket to the city. Since the effects of film, television, radio, and the print media have permeated the most remote corners of the globe, graphic images of modern living are available to virtually everyone. The more available mass media representations of wealth and "the good life" become, the more incentive there is, especially for young people, to consume and display the material symbols of wealth and also to buy freedom from outmoded and often materially poorer ways of living. Once engaged in city life and the wage economy, any migrant finds it difficult to return home, even when the wages are meagre. For many, the choice does not exist, for there is no work available at home. By personal preference or by necessity, migrants willing to labor at the lowest levels of the industrial economy continue to flock to urban centers around the world.

What kind of social environment is the city? The influx of large numbers of people to urban centers has required anthropologists to turn their attention to the study of a very different place to live than the jungle encampment or the rural village. The general characteristics of cities, old and new, are easy to define. We recognize in both archaic and modern cities large concentrations of people in a fixed locale and the transformation of that locale to suit their basic living needs. An economic relationship based on needs for food and raw materials is likely to develop between a cosmopolitan center and the agrarian hinterland, producing a dichotomy of urban-peasant culture. Within the city, significant social divisions arise, for example, between a priestly caste and the secular population, between nobles and commoners, and between an extensive variety of laborers, craftsmen, and merchants.

The cities of different regions and eras have the characteristics of their particular historical age, its civilization, and technology. The ancient religious centers of Mexico and Peru resist classification with the medieval ports of the Mediterranean. Nor can we lump the city of Rome circa 500 A.D. together with, for example, the modern cities of London or Los Angeles. This latter distinction, between the preindustrial and industrial city, is an obvious and important one, and even among present Industrial Age urban centers there are significant differences in geographic size, population density, and, most important of all, recorded patterns of organizational growth and decline.

Manchester, England, for instance, is known as the first modern industrial center, and it traces its urban history back to at least the seventeenth century. Visitors to Manchester today will find no sign of the famous first factories, slums, and poorhouses of Western Europe, although the world's first train station and the little library where Karl Marx and Friedrich Engels wrote their critiques of capitalism do exist still. Today, Manchester is no longer a factory town. Instead, it has become an administrative center for government, for commerce and communications industries that employ thousands of white-collar workers. As a consequence, office buildings and apartment houses have supplanted the old inner-city buildings, and suburban houses have taken the place of peasant cottages.

In contrast, the cities of Third World countries have only in the last

Urban Ethnography: People in Cities   **283**

several decades begun to amass enormous populations in their centers of industry and commerce. In South America and Africa in particular, the virtually overnight increase in rural to urban migration has produced sprawling slums to house the newcomers. These areas of makeshift dwellings, unplanned alley-ways, and piles of refuse are the scene of new cultural contacts among people who have only one thing in common—a need to make a new life from the fabric of familiar and valuable traditions.

The first essay in this section on urban ethnography focuses on the personal aspirations of Nigerian migrants. Complementary to the ambitions of those who leave home are the expectations of kindred left behind. The responsibility of redistributing wealth, such as Barth described among the Basseri, usually still applies to the absentee relative, even though he or she is faced with the higher costs of living in the city. The good son or daughter or parent or cousin must share wages, or risk being emotionally and perhaps even ritually isolated from their families. At the same time, the energies of the migrant are caught up in adjusting to the urban job market. How does one find a job, are government papers needed, what skills and experience are necessary, where does one go for training? The problems are legion, and they are multiplied by language and culture differences between those who control hiring and those who need work. As Plotnicov's article recounts, the first generation to make the transition to urban life is truly caught between loyalties to a familiar rural culture and the requirements of surviving in the city.

One of the universal solutions to urban adjustment has been to use kinship solidarity to recreate traditional ways. While rural-urban loyalties present inevitable conflicts, many Africans have either banded together informally with others from the same village or region, or they have instituted formal brotherhoods based on tribal affiliation and a common language. What cultural ties become in the city is never, of course, a perfect replica of older customs. Instead, there is a selection of some aspects of behavior that suit urban life, and there is the discarding of others. This process of selection is not strictly pragmatic, nor is it geared toward a total assimilation of the group into a more general urban culture. Rather, language, rituals, beliefs, and at times, distinctive traditional dress are maintained to reinforce group solidarity to convey the message of cultural distinction. This conscious and relatively privatized maintenance of custom, however, is usually accompanied by gradual adaption to the modern economy, an adaption that differs according to the occupational niches or black market work that migrants find for themselves.

The Iroquois Indians described by Ruth Blumenfeld in "Mohawks: Round Trip to High Steel" are a case of long-standing adjustment to the urban economy. Because they were among the first Indians to be contacted by Europeans, records of Iroquois culture go back some 300 years. That they have survived into the twentieth century appears at first glance an historical oddity, until we realize that it is the essence of urban life to sustain a plurality of cultures. For many American Indians, the conditions of adaption have included the federal administration of reservations, basically rural enclaves, and easy access to urban centers. The stability of a "home" land base and some government support (which is not guaranteed to Nigerian migrants) is assured tribes like the Mohawk. Furthermore, our systems of transportation, especially the availability of automobiles and cross-country highways, have reduced the relative cost of migration and encouraged travel between country and city. The Mohawk and the hundreds of thousands of other Indians who work in industrial centers do not completely escape the tensions between the traditional and the modern. However, when the technology of transportation and communication becomes as advanced as it is in North America, the dichotomy between rural and urban cultures breaks down: everyone is, in effect, urbanized by an awareness of the larger world and participation in national patterns of labor and consumption.

This does not mean, though, that the American city lacks distinctive features in either its physical layout or the kinds of life styles permitted there. Anthropologists of the American urban scene are required to deal with a middle-range of historical phenomena. That is, the settlement patterns that characterize our cities fall somewhere between the old European cities of Manchester and London and their corollaries on the Continent, and the rapidly growing urban centers in Third World nations. It was only during the last century that small port towns like New York, Boston, Chicago, New Orleans, and Montreal were transformed into international centers of industry and trade, their populations swelled by migrants from overseas and from rural areas within North America. Still, our cities are old enough to have developed stable populations and to suffer from such maladies as physical urban decay and the flight of middle-class families to the suburbs.

As for their being productive social research sites, American cities have long offered several real benefits. First, despite the standardizing influence of large political, economic, and educational institutions, the diversity of cultural groups has persisted. The impersonal anomic quality of the city scene is one aspect of its organization; the other is the congregation of subgroups in racial and ethnic enclaves, in neighborhoods segregated by social class, and in forgotten factory districts and skid-row areas. Second, though diverse urban communities are troubled by dramatic competitive issues, the relative stability of many urban sectors allows long-range research the chance to become immersed in a community. As a third positive feature, there are sufficient historical and statistical data on American urban populations to trace shifting intergroup relationships and trends in population mobility and growth to give the ethnographic study a broad descriptive framework.

Aware of these assets, University of Chicago social scientists (among them "natives" of the city's diverse subgroups) spent much of the 1920s and 1930s studying urban people—elites, immigrants, racial groups, workers and hoboes. While one anthropologist associated with the Chicago school of ethnography, Robert Redfield, formulated the acculturative model of the folk-urban community, two of his colleagues, sociologists Robert E. Park and Ernest W. Burgess, became interested in an ecological approach to the study of urban organization, and they drew parallels between organic and human communities. As they saw it, the migration of a new group to the city could replicate the patterns of accommodation, succession, invasion, and dominance observable in the introduction of a new plant or organism to a favorable natural environment. So it happened that an urban neighborhood could host a series of migrant groups, each replacing the preceding dominant culture. Or, as also happens, the turf of a community might remain in the possession of one group over several generations.

Gerald Suttles' account of urban racial and ethnic rivalries is in the solid tradition of the Chicago ethnographers. The cities of the industrial northeast are not, however, the same as they were 40 years ago. The growth of suburban townships and the exodus of more affluent families from the core city have left the lower classes in almost exclusive possession of residential neighborhoods that boast few of the assets of outlying "bedroom" communities. In the central city, the hierarchy of social classes associated with urban organization has tended to become polarized between the very wealthy who play a major role in directing urban affairs and can afford the best of city or suburban housing and services and those not-so-wealthy people who have no alternative but to put up with decaying neighborhoods and overcrowded schools. Even in cities that are not losing the middle-class homeowner to the suburbs, the dominance of one social class, race, or ethnic group over another is evident in the restriction of subordinate groups to less desirable neighborhoods. Suttles, for example, describes competition between inner-city Italians and blacks for control over a slum area in which no other groups, except Puerto Ricans and Mexicans, have an interest. What we have found is that the organic metaphor of urban life fails to cover the sharp split between those minorities who compete for urban turf and the actual power base of urban government, a base that cannot be reckoned in neighborhood terms.

In contrast to formal segregation, as in the civil creation of Jewish ghettoes in eastern European cities or state supervision of segregated urban blacks in South Africa, lower-class ethnic and racial enclaves in American cities have been maintained by informal prejudices and economic discrimination in schooling, housing, and hiring. Predictably, the culture that sustains itself in isolation, even if that isolation is in the midst of a densely populated area, evolves with a substantial integrity. Yet as more individuals of older urban ghettoes and neighborhoods are affected by city institutions, such as the courts, welfare, and human services, etc., the less possible it becomes for them to survive as politically naive "urban villagers." The problem of political rule and public response is most evident in the Chicago material, but it is a dilemma that lingers behind all accounts of urbanization and modernization. Under what conditions does the freedom implied in urban diversity give way to the institutional management of individual lives? How does traditional custom equip urban migrants to handle civic life and roles, and when does a specific cultural identity become a stigma? With this section on urban ethnography begins an emphasis in this reader on the complexities of social change, not just for the individual, but for entire categories and classes of people who are confronted with large-scale political and economic systems.

References

Banton, M. 1957. *West African City. A Study in Tribal Life in Freetown.* London: Oxford University Press.
Drake, St. Clair, and Horace K.Cayton. 1945. *Black Metropolis: A Study of Negro Life in a Northern City.* New York: Harcourt, Brace and Company.
Fox, Richard G. 1977. *Urban Anthropology. Cities in their Cultural Settings.* Englewood Cliffs, N.J.: Prentice-Hall.
Gans, Herbert. 1962. *The Urban Villagers: Groups and Class in the Life of Italian-Americans.* Glencoe, Ill.: Free Press.
Guillemin, Jeanne. 1975. *Urban Renegades: The Cultural Strategy of American Indians.* New York: Columbia University Press.
Hannerz, Ulf. 1969. *Soulside: Inquiries into Ghetto Culture and Community.* New York: Columbia University Press.
Liebow, Elliot. 1967. *Tally's Corner: A Study of Negro Streetcorner Men.* Boston: Little, Brown and Co.
Little, K. 1965. *West African Urbanization: A Study of Voluntary Associations in Social Change.* Cambridge: Cambridge University Press.
Mayer, P. 1961. *Townsmen or Tribesmen: Conservatism and the Process of Urbanization in a South African City.* Capetown: Oxford University Press.
Margin, W., ed. 1970. *Peasants in Cities: Readings in the Anthropology of Urbanization.* Boston: Houghton Mifflin.
Miller, W.B. 1958. "Lower-Class Culture as a Generating Milieu of Gang Delinquency." *Journal of Social Issues* 14: 5-19.
Park, Robert E. 1952. *Human Communities: The City and Human Ecology.* Glencoe, Ill.: Free Press.

Park, Robert E., Ernest W. Burgess, and Roberick D. McKenzie. 1925. *The City*. Chicago: The University of Chicago Press.
Plotnicov, Leonard. 1967. *Strangers to the City: Urban Man in Jos, Nigeria*. Pittsburgh: University of Pittsburgh Press.
Redfield, R. 1964. *A Village that Choose Progress: Chan Kom Revisited*. Chicago: University of Chicago Press. (Orig. published 1950).
Whyte, William Foote. 1943. *Street Corner Society: The Social Structure of an Italian Slum*. Chicago: University of Chicago Press.
Wirth, Louis. 1928. *The Ghetto*. Chicago: University of Chicago Press.

22.
Nigeria: The Dream Is Unfulfilled

Leonard Plotnicov

The country boy goes to the city. He is looking for fame and fortune—or at least a job. But the farm remains "home"—his family, his roots, and possibly even his heart are there. He swears he will not desert the old people or the old ways: he will send back money; he will write; he will visit; he will renew his ties; and when he has made his fortune he will return to spend the remainder of his life in the bosom of his family.

It seldom works out that way in the industrial nations of the world. And now, even in developing nations of Africa, many people are finding that they can't go home again.

From late 1960 to mid-1962 I did anthropological field work in Jos, a city of over 50,000 in Northern Nigeria. Almost every ethnic group in Nigeria is represented, and in approximately the same proportions as for the nation as a whole. Most of the people I spoke to—those who had come originally from the country—stated emphatically that they felt that the small towns or farms they came from were their "real" homes. They were in the city to make money. Someday they would return.

Their descriptions of these real homes were lyrical and idyllic. The contrast to the city was strong. They did not merely *hope* to return; already retirement houses were being built for them (with money they sent) and they were able to describe the houses and the states of construction in considerable detail.

They were so persuasive and specific that for a long time I believed them—as, undoubtedly, they believed themselves. I believe now that "return home" is merely a widely-held myth—a golden dream that cannot be fulfilled completely and may never be fulfilled at all.

The ties to home are real enough, psychologically and economically. The migrant is entitled to share in the benefits from family land and property, and he is expected to return for important family events and ceremonials, especially funerals. Even if he cannot attend on these occasions, he is expected to help pay their costs, which can be large. Gifts are frequently exchanged, including food stuffs. Immigrants particularly like to receive familiar foods unobtainable in the cities—especially those actually grown on the home farmland.

Why then can't the dream be fulfilled?

One major reason is that the natures and demands of the home ties themselves make friction easy and the accumulation of wealth difficult. Since first loyalty must be to homeland and family, requests for money cannot be easily refused—and they start early. Money that might become investment in a business or savings in a bank is spent instead on traditional gifts to chiefs and elders, gifts or support for relatives (some rather distant), help during illness or for lawsuits, and educational expenses for young male relatives.

The heaviest requests from home fall on those with most apparent success—professionals, traders, clerks, skilled workers. The wealthier of those I spoke to took pride in their ability to meet their obligations, even if it meant financial strain. The poorer complained of "family parasitism" and stated defensively that they preferred to live at a distance. But even they kept writing to the family and tried to meet at least some of the requests.

What happens if a city dweller doesn't send money home? It becomes obvious that he has abandoned his people and the simple rural virtues and been corrupted and seduced by that Babylon, the city. Pleading poverty is not a good defense: anybody who can't make money in the city must obviously be weak in character, dissolute, lazy, spendthrift, incompetent, and generally useless.

Eating Bush Money

Unfortunately the urban people foster the naive beliefs of greenhorn immigrants and old folks at home that city streets are practically paved with gold. Costs are high by rural standards, and wages melt away on essentials—but city dwellers either can't make this clear or don't try. When they come home on visits they almost invariably reinforce the belief that they are doing well. Naturally, they want to impress relatives and "put on the dog" a little. In addition, according to custom they must be generous and distribute money, tobacco, and beer. Stay-at-homes take advantage of the situation to put the squeeze on the city cousin. This form of milking and exploitation is called "eating bush money." If the city dweller ever really hopes to come back he must put up with this, because if he doesn't he will be humbled. To live in the country, one must respect country judgements and standards. Also, in Southern Nigeria, loyalty to home and proof of intention to return must be visibly expressed, by erecting an expensive European-design retirement home. Coming home with dignity is not cheap.

And even the emigré who does return will not find ready acceptance. He has been in alien territory, he has acquired strange customs and viewpoints, he is a threat to the local orthodoxy and the local elite. He can sweeten such a reception usually only at the price of joining that conservative elite himself—defending the old ways, scornful of the outsider, and making the *parvenu* unwelcome.

So only a relative handful actually return. Valdo Pons found a similar situation in Stanleyville, indicating that the same pattern may be present in the Congo. Many men told him that, whatever their feelings, they knew they could not go back to the rustic life to stay:

> ... the village people are ... distrustful and jealous of those who have "followed the Europeans." One may return home to visit, and most ... do so, but to return home permanently is ... courting disaster. "They like you to come back for a few months," one man explained, "but if you stay for good they will poison you."

The changing use of land also makes return very difficult. Southern Nigeria, with government encouragement, has turned more and more to cash crops—palm oil, cocoa, rubber, and bananas for export; palm oil, yams, plantains, rice, maize, and kola nuts for local markets. The larger farms necessary for cash cropping become available precisely because some heirs give up their rights to divided plots and go to the city. They do not, of course, give up their claim to a share of family income from the land.

Home Is Always Elsewhere

Distance does not always make the heart grow fonder; it may foster distrust. Many of my informants complained that they were dunned for money too often—they could not understand exactly what was going on at home, or how their money was being used. They were suspicious that they were not being told everything. One man told me that when he was asked for forty or fifty pounds he sent one or two, "just to keep them quiet." This in turn apparently roused resentment from those at home.

Commonly, the city people complain that their kinsmen—"brothers"—don't repay loans and even cheat them, that they make false reports of family income and "eat" all the profits. Some said that if they left a kinsman in charge of building the retirement house he falsified costs and embezzled funds. Sometimes a wife might be sent back to supervise the remaining construction—but in case of dispute, the house usually remained incomplete.

Perhaps the kinfolk accused were really innocent; but just as they had trouble understanding or believing stories of hardship and poverty in the city, the city dwellers in their turn had trouble believing that crops had been *that* poor, hired labor troubles *that* bad, market prices had fallen *that* far. A city worker could express his displeasure and distrust by withholding money, or by staying away from family ceremonials. But that might cause a country relative to feel that he would be justified in retaliating by cheating.

Disputes are inevitable. What is a fair share? Is it fair to share and share alike on a jointly owned farm when the city "brother" does not work on it?

Some city dwellers try to cover up their grievances, meet only minimal obligations and make only brief appearances at home. Those who do visit often avoid open discussion of disputes, either to keep the visit "pleasant" or to keep up a front before outsiders. But avoidance can be interpreted as guilt—and the longer grievances remain covered, issues are dodged, accusations not challenged, the greater the chances of revenge. In Jos, some old people were pointed out to me who, I was told, were afraid to go home because they might become victims of sorcery; others feared being poisoned. Some retired people intended to go home eventually—but meanwhile they didn't feel well, the climate in Jos was better, and so on. Some even went home, gave up after a while, and came back to Jos.

The reasons given for not returning are many, but most of them mention lack of money—and the shame and fear that causes. "When my business was good, I had planned to go home. . . ."

A retired motor mechanic kept delaying his return—he said he did not have enough money to finish his retirement house. "It's a shameful thing to go home before the building is finished. People'll say, 'What kind of man is this who lives in his father's house and hasn't built his own?'" When after one year I suggested that Jos was really his home because he had lived there longer than on the farm, the real reason came out: "Jos is not my home. I stay here because I fear poison at home. I don't have enough money to satisfy them now. If I go home they'll be expecting me to be rich and give them plenty. Some might have an evil mind if I don't give enough. If I don't satisfy them they'll try by all means to take my life. Those people will come around day after day and I will have to entertain them with plenty of drinks and food. They think that when anybody goes to 'bush' he gets rich—so they want to eat 'bush' money. That's the only reason I stay so long."

Since so few return to the farm to stay and probably even fewer will do so in the future, why is there still a pretense? There are two major reasons:
- Even if the city Nigerian will not go home, he does not want to cut his ties completely. As long as the idea and the hope are maintained, the lines of

communication stay open, relationships and loyalties are observed, and gifts are exchanged (even if the flow is mostly one way).
- "Home is elsewhere." This legend reconciles the immigrant to the loneliness and to the absence of family in the faceless city. Also, if he achieves little success, he has a ready psychological compensation and retreat: he belongs and he has value in a better place—back home.

23.
Mohawks: Round Trip to High Steel

Ruth Blumenfeld

Since 1915, Mohawks from the Caughnawaga Indian Reserve near Montreal have been living in Brooklyn while working on high-iron and high-steel construction jobs in the New York area. In the early days, leaving their wives and children home on the reservation, they stayed only for the duration of each construction project, perhaps moving on to jobs in other cities before returning to Caughnawaga for a few weeks with their families—until the next job. But the Manhattan building boom of the 1920's, with its promise of steady employment and good wages, caused many Mohawks to bring their families to the quiet Brooklyn neighborhood which surrounds the headquarters of Local 361 of the Iron Workers' Union. The Mohawk population of Brooklyn is now about 800.

The men of Caughnawaga were first attracted to high-iron work in 1886 when the Canadian Pacific Railroad bridged the St. Lawrence River with an iron structure. The skill and daring required of the high-ironworker were similar to the traditional requirements of the Iroquois brave who, in older times, often left his village for dangerous jobs in which the rewards were high—whether in wages or booty. Before the French missionaries came the men hunted, fished, and raided neighboring villages. After joining the Jesuit mission colonies, Mohawks frequently accompanied European expeditions as scouts, guides, and navigators. During the eighteenth and nineteenth centuries the Caughnawaga men continued to leave home to work as river pilots, log raftsmen, and "Wild West" troupe performers. In one very famous exploit fifty Mohawks navigated the Nile for the British in a vain attempt to deliver men and supplies to General "Chinese" Gordon's beleaguered garrison at Khartoum.

The Mohawks had never really liked farming (a priest living at

Caughnawaga in the 1870's estimated that only 52 men in a population of 1300 farmed full-time, although most families raised garden plots of beans and corn and kept a few pigs). Since no other enterprises existed on the reservation, they relied on seasonal off-reservation jobs.

When the Canadian Pacific Railroad bridge-building began, dozens of young Indians came daily to watch the construction crews. Their ease and surefootedness on the narrow rails and beams, plus their eagerness to learn construction work, led to their being hired by the builders in some numbers the following season.

A Tepee Grows in Brooklyn

This success encouraged them. They began to travel long distances across Canada and the United States, risking their lives and winning the admiration and respect of the tribe as well as the high wages typical of workers in high-steel. Colonies of Indian construction workers away from the reservation fit in with traditional Iroquois living patterns. On the one hand, the "longhouse"—home—the permanent village, with its continuing security, familiarity, and all the relatives. On the other hand, the "teepee," the temporary home of the immediate family as it traveled.

To the Brooklyn Mohawks, the home reservation of Caughnawaga has continued to be "longhouse," while Brooklyn remains "teepee." For example, no Mohawk has ever been buried in Brooklyn. The bodies of Caughnawaga Indians who lose their lives in construction accidents, or who die of natural causes, are transported to the Canadian reservation for burial. Relatives and close friends of the deceased leave their jobs for several days in order to attend the wake and the funeral at Caughnawaga.

The neighborhood is accustomed to absorbing wave after wave of immigrants. The earliest Dutch and English settlers left their mark in the street-names (Schermerhorn, Jouralemon, Orange, Jay, Livingstone). They were followed by Swedes, Norwegians, Germans, Irish, Italians, Greeks, Syrians, Negroes, and most recently, Puerto Ricans.

In the 1920's and 1930's it was a neighborhood of treeshaded streets, grassy plots, and low rents—a small residential island in a busy industrial area. The ironworkers were within walking distance of the hiring-hall, where they could go not only to find work, but to meet and pass the time with other Mohawks between jobs. And no matter where in the city "the job" might be, transportation to it cost no more than a nickel. A housewife remembers:

> Brooklyn was nice when we first came here—clean and quiet. The location was convenient. We were near stores for shopping, and close to the union headquarters. When the Indians first started moving into Brooklyn, we were taken for Spanish or Italian. After the community had grown some, and

people learned we were Indians, they asked about how people on the reservation lived and did things. But nobody thought we were strange or odd. The Indians were quiet and stayed to themselves.

From the earliest years of the Brooklyn community, the fact that it was never more than a day's trip from the home reservation has had important effects. In the twenties and thirties most of the Indian ironworkers lived in furnished rooms and sent their children back to the reservation to stay with relatives when they reached school age. Not only did the cramped Brooklyn rooms make children inconvenient, but the parochial school at Caughnawaga was free, while those in Brooklyn charged tuition. Since 1930, a free hospital on the reservation has provided a practical reason for the Brooklyn Mohawk women to return to Caughnawaga for the birth of their children. The river at Caughnawaga, with its swimming, boating, and fishing, is perennially attractive during the summer, and accounts for the mass exodus from Brooklyn between June and September.

Other ties bind the Brooklyn Mohawk colony to the home reservation. "The Wigwam," a non-Indian-owned Brooklyn tavern that has catered to Indians since its opening in 1934, is one of the best sources of reservation news. A favorite meeting place for Mohawks, it serves the Canadian ale they like and is decorated with Indian pictures and two crossed rivit-guns topped by a steelworker's helmet. It is one of the first places visited by Indians driving down from Canada, and serves also as a depot for automobiles leaving for Caughnawaga. For the past twenty years, any Mohawk who wanted a ride to the reservation could stop at the tavern on a Friday evening and get a seat in a Mohawk-driven car without any formal arrangements. There are many reasons for the continuing two-way traffic. Many Mohawks return to vote for the Band Council. Others go to consult native curers, to learn how to make some traditional herbal remedy or to purchase it ready-made. Often, dwindling supplies of medicinal herbs are replenished by gathering the wild plants on visits to the reservation.

High-Iron Heroes

Work is a virtue among the Caughnawaga, and to excel on the high scaffold is to prove oneself both as a man and as an Indian. Mohawk boys sit with their fathers and hear marvelous tales of heroism and daring in high ironwork. They hear that there are some jobs in construction work so dangerous that only an Indian can do them. At the traditional wake, after the midnight meal and the departure of the women, the men pass the rest of the night in story-telling. These stories nearly always deal with the daring exploits and adventures of not only the recently deceased, but of other ironworkers dead for many years. Mohawk boys can give detailed accounts of the adventures of Mohawk ironworkers who died long before they were born—just as their ancestors could have told of the exploits of legendary Mohawk warriors long since dead.

Although most the Caughnawaga Mohawks are Roman Catholics, many continue to believe in witchcraft. A few have even "seen" ancient Iroquois deities, such as the Sky God, the evil spirit who takes the form of a baby, "the little people of the bush," and the beautiful maiden with hooves instead of feet.

When the stock market crash of 1929 brought Manhattan's building boom to a sudden halt, the reservation provided a refuge from the depression. The Indians owned homes at Caughnawaga, and received economic aid from governmental agencies there. Some, of course, stayed in Brooklyn, or returned there in hopes of finding work when there was none in Canada. One who stayed was Joe Jocks:

> Things were tight in Brooklyn then. I would get jobs shovelling snow sometimes. One year I played hockey for the Crescent Athletic Club in Brooklyn, before it became the "New York Rangers." I got a steel job and left the club. There were occasional jobs in steel even then.

During the thirties the Mohawk Brooklyn population fluctuated between 50 and 200 because of the ebb and flow of Indians in search of jobs. Some, like John Deer, were newcomers to the city:

> I was eleven years old when my father brought the family to Brooklyn in 1934. We lived on Clinton street for ten dollars a month rent. My father worked on the Tri-Borough bridge and a couple of WPA projects they had going. I really grew up in Brooklyn.

Just before World War II construction began to pick up again, and by 1939 the Mohawk population was back to 200. With the outbreak of war, many Indians built or worked in defense plants. During the forties the population continued to rise and reached a new high around 800 in 1950, where it has remained.

But despite this higher level, and the apparent permanence of the tree-shaded residence, the Mohawks in Brooklyn must be considered as at the turn-around stop on a round-trip journey. Except for Indian women who have married non-Mohawks (thereby forfeiting tribe membership for themselves and children) and for those few who have become US citizens, all the Brooklyn Mohawks plan to return to the reservation on retirement. Meanwhile, many of the old beliefs and practices persist.

In a fundamental sense, though the Caughnawaga Mohawk ironworkers have succeeded in and are a part of the white man's city, they never left home.

24.
Anatomy of a Chicago Slum

Gerald D. Suttles

In its heyday, the Near West Side of Chicago was the stronghold of such men as Al (Scarface) Capone and Frank (The Enforcer) Nitti, and served as the kindergarten for several figures still active in the underworld. For convenience, I will call this part of Chicago the Addams area—after Jane Addams, who founded Hull House there. The name is artificial, since it is never used by the local residents.

The Addams area is one of the oldest slums in Chicago, and researchers have invaded it almost as often as new minority groups have. Like most slums, it remains something of a mystery. In some ways it is easiest to describe the neighborhood by describing how its residents deviate from the public standards of the wider community. The area has, for example, a high delinquency rate, numerous unwed mothers, and several adolescent "gangs." It is tempting to think that the residents are simply people suffering from cultural deprivation, unemployment, and a number of other urban ills. And if the residents insist upon the irrelevance of the standards of the wider community and the primacy of their own, this can be dismissed as sour grapes or an attempt to make of necessity a virtue.

Seen from the inside, however, Addams area residents require discipline and self-restraint in the same way as the wider community does. Conventional norms are not rejected but emphasized differently, or suspended for established reasons. The vast majority of the residents are quite conventional people. At the same time, those who remain in good standing are often exceptionally tolerant of and even encouraging to those who are "deviant."

Certainly the social practices of the residents are not just an inversion of those of the wider society, and the inhabitants would be outraged to hear as much. Nor is the neighborhood a cultural island with its own distinct and imported traditions. The area's internal structure features such commonplace distinctions as age, sex, territoriality, ethnicity, and personal identity. Taken out of context, many of the social arrangements of the Addams area may seem an illusory denial of the beliefs and values of the wider society. But actually the residents are bent on ordering local relations because the beliefs and evaluations of the wider society do not provide adequate guidelines for conduct.

In anthropology, territorial grouping has been a subject of continued interest. Most anthropological studies begin by focusing upon social groupings that can be defined by ther areal distribution. In turn, many of the social units singled out for particular attention—the domestic unit, the homestead, the tribe, and so forth—frequently have locality as one of their principles of organization. And where locality and structural forms do not coincide, anthropologists have regarded this discrepancy as a distinct problem that raises a number of theoretical and methodological issues.

The most obvious reason for focusing on locality groups is that their members cannot simply ignore one another. People who routinely occupy the same place must either develop a moral order that includes all those present or fall into conflict. And because almost all societies create a public morality that exceeds the capabilities of some of its members, territorial groups are always faced with the prospect of people whose public character does not warrant trust. In the United States a very large percentage of our population fails to meet the public standards we set for measuring someone's merit, trustworthiness, and respectability.

Many groups have avoided compromising these ideals of public morality by territorial segregation. More exactly, they have simply retreated and left valuable portions of the inner city to those they distrust. Obviously, this practice has its limits—it tends to aggregate those who are poor, unsuccessful, and disreputable in the same slum neighborhoods. These people must compromise the ideals of public morality or remain permanently estranged from one another.

In slum neighborhoods, territorial aggregation usually comes before any common social framework for assuring orderly relations. After all, ethnic invasion, the encroachment of industry, and economic conditions constantly reshuffle slum residents and relocate them around new neighbors. Since the residents lack obvious grounds for assuming mutual trust, a combination of alternatives seems to offer the most promising course:

- Social relations can be restricted to only the safest ones. Families can withdraw to their households, where they see only close relatives.

Anatomy of a Chicago Slum

Segregation by age, sex, and ethnicity are maneuvers that will prevent at least the most unfair and most likely forms of conflict and exploitation. Remaining close to the household cuts down on the range of anonymity and reduces the number of social relations. The general pattern, then, should be a fan-shaped spatial arrangement, with women and children remaining close by the house while males move progressively outwards, depending on their age.

- Slum residents can assuage at least some of their apprehensions by a close inquiry into one another's personal character and past history. Communication, then, should be of an intimate character and aimed toward producing personal rather than formal relations. In turn, social relations will represent a sort of private compact in which particular loyalties replace impersonal standards of worth.

Neither of these patterns will immediately produce a comprehensive framework within which a large number of slum residents can safely negotiate with one another. The segregation by age, sex, and territorial groups, however, does provide a starting point from which face-to-face relations can grow and reach beyond each small territorial aggregation. The development of personal relations furnishes both a moral formula and a structural bridge between groups. Within each small, localized peer group, continuing face-to-face relations can eventually provide a personalistic order. Once these groups are established, a single personal relation between them can extend the range of such an order. Thus, with the acceptance of age-grading and territorial segregation, it becomes possible for slum neighborhoods to work out a moral order that includes most of their residents.

The Addams area actually consists of four different sections, each occupied predominantly by Negroes, Italians, Puerto Ricans, and Mexicans. And each of these sections falls into a somewhat different stage in its development of a provincial order.

Despite this difference and others, all four ethnic sections share many characteristics and seem headed along the same social progression. The overall pattern is one in which age, sex, ethnic, and territorial units are fitted together like building blocks to create a larger structure. I have termed this pattern "ordered segmentation" to indicate two related features: (1) the orderly relationship between groups; and (2) the order in which groups combine in instances of conflict and opposition. This ordered segmentation is not equally developed in all ethnic sections but, in skeletal outline, it is the common framework within which groups are being formed and social relations are being cultivated.

My own experiences within the Addams area and the presentation of this volume are heavily influenced by the ordered segmentation of the neighborhood. I took up residence in the area in the summer of 1963 and left a little fewer than three years later.

As I acquired friends and close informants, my own ethnicity became a serious problem. A few people worked over my genealogy trying to find some trace that would allot me to a known ethnic group. After close inquiry, one old Italian lady announced with peals of laughter, "Geraldo, you're just an American." She did not mean it as a compliment, and I remember being depressed. In the Addams area, being without ethnicity means there is no one you can appeal to or claim as your own.

Only after a year or more in the Addams area was I able to penetrate the private world of its families, street-corner groups, and insular establishments. These are the groupings within which Addams area residents are least cautious and most likely to expose themselves. In large part my experience with these groups is limited to many adolescent male street-corner groups and my own adult friends, who formed a group of this type.

By far the most striking contrast is between the Negro and the Italian sections. For instance, almost all the Negroes live in public housing; the Italians usually control both their households and commercial establishments. The Negroes have very similar incomes and almost no political power; among the Italians, there *is* some internal differentiation of income and political power. Such differences draw the Italians and Negroes apart and generate radically different styles of life.

In most ways, the Puerto Rican section is the least complex of those in the Addams area. There are no more than 1100 Puerto Ricans in the section and, within broad age ranges, most of them know one another. Until 1965, no named groups had emerged among the Puerto Ricans.

The Mexicans are more numerous, and several named groups have developed among the teenagers. Unlike the Italians, however, the Mexican groups have not survived into adulthood. The Mexicans seem to have much in common with the Italians, and frequently their relationships are congenial. What gives the Mexicans pause is the occasional necessity to divide their loyalties between the Italians and the Negroes.

Although one must not overemphasize the extent of differences between all these ethnic sections, such differences as do occur loom large in the Addams area. The residents are actively looking for differences among themselves. The ethnic sections in the area constitute basic guidelines from which the residents of each section can expect certain forms of reciprocity, and anticipate the dangers that may be in store elsewhere.

The portion of the Addams area now controlled by the Italians is only a residue from the encroachments of the three other ethnic groups. But in total land space, it is the largest of any controlled by a single ethnic group.

In population, it is not exceptionally big, though, and throughout the section an unusually high percentage of Mexicans have been accepted by the Italians as neighbors.

What the Italians lack in numbers, they often make up for by their reputation for using sheer force and for easy access to "influence" or "connections." It is said, for example, that many of the Italians are "Outfit people," and that many more could rely on mobsters if they needed help. Also, it is the general view that the Italians control both the vice and patronage of the First Ward, a political unit that includes the spoils of the Loop—downtown Chicago.

There are some very famous Italians in the Addams area, and they frequently get a spread in the city newspapers. There are many others not nearly so prominent but whose personal histories are still known in the neighborhood. At least five Italian policemen live in the area, and a few more who grew up there are assigned to the local district. The other ethnic groups have not a single resident or ex-resident policeman among them. Most of the precinct captains are also Italian; and, outside the projects, the Italians dominate those jobs provided by public funds. There are a number of Italian businessmen, each of whom controls a few jobs. It is also widely believed that they can "sponsor" a person into many of the industries of the city—the newsstands in the Loop, the city parks, the beauty-culture industry, a large printing company, and a number of clothing firms.

While there is some substance to this belief in Italian power and influence, it is actually quite exaggerated. Many of the Italian political figures seem to have little more than the privilege of announcing decisions that have been made by others. In most of the recent political actions that have affected the area, they have remained mute and docile. When the Medical Center was built and then extended, they said nothing. The Congress and the Dan Ryan Expressways were constructed with the local politicians hardly taking notice. Finally, when the University of Illinois was located at Congress Circle, the politicians, mobsters, and—indeed—all the male residents accepted it without even a show of resistance. In fact, only a group of Italian and Mexican housewives took up arms and sought to save some remnant of the neighborhood.

The Italians' notoriety for being in the rackets and having recourse to strong-arm methods is also a considerable exaggeration, or at least a misinterpretation. The majority of the local Italians are perfectly respectable people and gain nothing from organized crime. Yet, many of the common family names of the area have been sullied by some flagrant past episode by a relative. And in the area, family histories remain a basis for judging individual members and are extended to include all persons who share the same name. In another neighborhood, this information might be lost or ignored as improper; in the Addams area, it is almost impossible to keep family secrets, and they are kept alive in the constant round of rumor and gossip.

The local Italians themselves contribute to their reputation—because on many occasions they find it advantageous to intimate that they have connections with the Outfit. For example, outsiders are often flattered to think that they are in the confidence of someone who knows the underworld. Also, it is far more prestigious to have other people believe that one's background is buried in crime and violence than in public welfare. In America, organized crime has always received a certain respect, even when this respect had to be coerced. A recipient of public welfare is simply dismissed as unimportant. And during the Depression many of the Italians went on welfare.

Behind the Scenes Bargaining

Yet the cohesion and solidarity of the Italians are very limited. They are based primarily on the suspicion that social arrangements are best made by private settlements. This suspicion, in turn, is based on the assumption that recourse to public means can do little more than excite retaliation and vengeance. These same suspicions and doubts undermine the possibilities of a unified and explicit stance by the Italians toward the wider community and political organization. First, very few of them believe that the others will cooperate in joint efforts unless it is to their personal advantage or they are under some dire threat. Second, the Italians simply fear that a united public stand will elicit a similar posture on the part of their adversaries and eliminate the opportunity for private negotiations. Accordingly, the Italians either shun public confrontations or slowly draw away, once so engaged. In retrospect, the spirit of *omerta* seems ineffectual when it confronts the explicit efforts of the wider community. (Literally, *omerta* means a conspiracy between thieves. The Italians use it to mean any private agreement that cannot be safely broached before the general public.)

The inability of the Italians to accept or engage in public appeals leaves them somewhat bewildered by the Negroes' civil-rights movement. By the Italians' standards, the Negroes are "making a federal case" out of something that should be handled by private agreement. Indeed, even those who accept the justice of the Negroes' cause remain perplexed by the Negroes' failure to approach *them* in some informal manner. Throughout the summer of 1964, when demonstrators were most active, the Italians always seemed aggrieved and surprised that the Negroes would "pull such a trick" without warning. The Negroes took this view as a "sham" and felt that the Italians had ample reason to anticipate their demands. To the

Italians this was not the point. Of course, they knew that the Negroes had many long-standing demands and desires. What struck the Italians as unfair about the Negroes' demonstrations was their tactics: sudden public confrontations, without any chance for either side to retreat or compromise with grace.

Ultimately, both the Italians and Negroes did take their differences behind closed doors, and each settled for something less than their public demands. The main bone of contention was a local swimming pool dominated by the Italians and their Mexican guests.

In the background, of course, was the oppressive belief that the benefits of social life make up a fixed quantity and are already being used to the maximum. Thus, even the most liberal Italians assume that any gain to the Negroes must be their loss. On their own part, the Negroes make the same assumption and see no reason why the Italians should give way without a fight. Thus, whatever good intentions exist on either side are overruled by the seeming impracticality or lack of realism.

The forms of social organization in the Italian section are far more extensive and complicated than those of the other ethnic groups. At the top are two groups, the "West Side Bloc" and the "Outfit," which share membership and whose participants are not all from the Addams area. The West Side Bloc is a group of Italian politicians whose constituency is much larger than the Addams area but which includes a definite wing in the area. Generally its members are assumed to belong to or to have connections with the Outfit. A good deal of power is attributed to them within the local neighborhood, city, state, and nation. The Outfit, more widely known as the Syndicate, includes many more people, but it is also assumed to reach beyond the Addams area. Locally, it is usually taken to include almost anyone who runs a tavern or a liquor store, or who relies on state licensing or city employment. A few other businessmen and local toughs are accredited with membership because of their notorious immunity to law enforcement or their reputed control of "favors."

Indirectly, the Outfit extends to a number of adult social-athletic clubs (s.a.c.'s). These clubs invariably have a storefront where the members spend their time in casual conversation or drink, or play cards. A few of their members belong to the Outfit, and a couple of these clubs are said to have a "regular game" for big stakes. Each group is fairly homogeneous in age, but collectively the groups range between the late 20's up to the late 60's.

Below these adult s.a.c.'s are a number of other s.a.c.'s that also have a clubhouse, but whose members are much younger. As a rule, they are somewhat beyond school age, but only a few are married, and practically none have children. To some degree, they are still involved in the extra-familial life that occupies teenagers. Occasionally they have dances, socials, and impromptu parties. On weekends they still roam around together, attending "socials" sponsored by other groups, looking for girls or for some kind of "action." Within each young man's s.a.c., the members' ages cover a narrow range. Together, all the groups range between about 19 and the late 20's. They form a distinct and well-recognized age grade in the neighborhood because of their continuing involvement in those cross-sexual and recreational activities open to unmarried males.

Nevertheless, these young men's s.a.c.'s are somewhat outside the full round of activities that throw teenagers together. A good portion of their time is spent inside their clubhouse out of sight of their rivals or most bodies of social control. Most members are in their 20's and are able to openly enjoy routine forms of entertainment or excitement that the wider community provides and accepts. When they have a dance or party, it is usually restricted to those whom they invite. Being out of school, they are not forced each day to confront persons from beyond their neighborhood. Since many of them have cars, they need not trepass too much on someone else's domain.

These s.a.c.'s are not assumed to have any active role in the Outfit. At most, it is expected that they might be able to gain a few exemptions from law enforcement and an occasional "favor," e.g., a job, a chance to run an illegal errand, a small loan, someone to sign for their clubhouse charter (required by law), and the purchase of stolen goods or of anything else the boys happen to have on hand. It is assumed that they could solicit help from the Outfit if they got into trouble with another group, but very rarely are they drawn into this type of conflict. Almost invariably the opponent is a much younger "street group" that has encroached on what the s.a.c. considers its "rights"—e.g., tried to "crash" one of their parties, insulted them on the streets, made noise nearby, or marked up their clubhouse. Even at these times, their actions seem designed to do little more than rid themselves of a temporary nuisance. Once rid of their tormentors, they usually do not pursue the issue further, and for good reason. To charter such a club requires three cosigners, and these people may withdraw their support if the group becomes too rowdy. Also, they have a landlord to contend with, and he can throw them out for the same reason. Finally, they cannot afford to make too many enemies; they have a piece of property, and it would be only too easy for their adversaries to get back at them. Unlike all the groups described in the other three sections, they have a stake in maintaining something like law and order.

All the remaining Italian groups include members who are of high-school age. While they too call themselves s.a.c.'s, none of them have a storefront. All of them do have an established "hangout," and they correspond to the usual image of a street-corner group.

While the street groups in this section of the area often express admiration for the adult s.a.c.'s, they seldom develop in an unbroken sequence into a full-fledged adult s.a.c. Usually when they grow old enough to rent a storefront they change their name, acquire new members from groups that have been their rivals, and lose a few of their long-term members. Some groups disband entirely, and their members are redistributed among the newly formed s.a.c.'s. Of the 12 young men's and adult s.a.c.'s, only one is said to have maintained the same name from the time it was a street-corner group. Even in this case some members have been added and others lost. Together, then, the Italian street-corner groups make up the population from which future young men's s.a.c.'s are drawn, but only a few street-corner groups form the nucleus of a s.a.c.

Conceptually, the Italian street groups and the older s.a.c.'s form a single unity. In the eyes of the boys, they are somewhat like the steps between grammar school and college. While they may be dropouts, breaks, and amalgamations, they still make up a series of steps through which one can advance with increasing age. Thus, each street group tends to see the adult s.a.c.'s as essentially an older and more perfect version of itself. What may be just as important is their equally strong sense of history. Locally, many of the members in the street groups can trace their group's genealogy back through the Taylor Dukes, the 40 game, the Genna Brothers, and the Capone mob. Actually, there is no clear idea of the exact order of this descent line; some people include groups that others leave out. Moreover, there is no widespread agreement on which specific group is the current successor to this lineage. Nonetheless, there is agreement that the groups on Taylor Street have illustrious progenitors. On some occasions this heritage may be something of a burden, and on others a source of pride. In any case, it is unavoidable, and usually the Italian street group prefaces its own name with the term "Taylor." Among the younger groups this is omitted only when their name is an amalgam made up from a specific street corner or block. Only the adult s.a.c.'s regularly fail to acknowledge in their name the immediate territory within which they are situated.

Direct Line of Succession from the Outfit

Since they see themselves in a direct line of succession to groups reputed to be associated with the Outfit, these street-corner groups might be expected to have a strong criminal orientation. In the Addams area, however, the Italian groups are best known for their fighting prowess, and their official police records show no concentration on the more utilitarian forms of crime. The fact is that, like the other adolescent groups in the area, the Italian boys are not really free to choose their own goals and identities. Territorial arrangements juxtapose them against similar groups manned by Negro and Mexican boys. If the Italian street-corner groups fail to define themselves as fighting groups, their peers in the other ethnic groups are certainly going to assume as much.

There is also considerable rivalry between Italian street-corner groups of roughly the same age. Commonly they suspect each other of using force to establish their precedence. In turn, each group seems to think it must at least put on a tough exterior to avoid being "pushed around." Privately there is a great deal of talk among them about the Outfit and about criminal activities, but it is academic in the sense that there is no strong evidence that their behavior follows suit.

It is intersting that the adult s.a.c.'s that actually have members in the rackets avoid any conspicuous claims about their criminal activities or fighting abilities. Their names, for example, are quite tame, while those of the street groups tend to be rather menacing. And their dances, leisure-time activities, and interrelationships are quite private and unpretentious. Unlike the street groups, they never wear clothing that identifies their group membership. The older men in the s.a.c.'s make no apparent attempt to establish a publicly-known hierarchy among themselves. Other people occasionally attribute more respect to one than another of them, but there seems to be little consensus on this. On their own part, the older groups seem to pay little attention to their relative standing and to be on fairly good terms. During my three years in the area, I never heard of them fighting among themselves.

Unlike the Negro and Mexican ethnic sections, there are no female counterparts to the named Italian street-corner groups. A very few Italian girls belong to two Mexican girls' groups that "hung" in the Mexican section. This, in itself, was exceptional; almost always the minority members in a street group are from a lower-ranking ethnic group. The Italian girls, however, are under certain constraints that may be lacking for those in the other ethnic groups. Naturally, their parents disapprove of such a blatant display of feminine unity. The Italian parents may gain stature by their power and precedence in comparison to the Negro and Mexican adults. Yet what seems far more significant is the general form that boy-girl relationships take among the Italians. On either side, the slightest hint of interest in the other sex is likely to be taken in the most serious way; as either a rank insult or a final commitment. Thus, any explicit alliance between a boys' and girls' group can be interpreted in only one of two ways: (1) all the girls are "laying" for the boys, or (2) they are seriously attached to each other. Neither side seems quite willing to betray so much and, thus, they avoid such explicit alliances.

This dilemma was quite evident on many occasions while I was observing the Italian boys and girls. The girls seemed extraordinarily coy when they were in a "safe" position—with their parents, in church, etc. When alone and on their own they became equally cautious and noncommittal. On public occasions, the boys seemed almost to ignore the girls and even to snub them. On Taylor Street, for instance, an Italian boys' group and an Italian girls' group used to hang about 10 feet from each other. Almost invariably they would stand with their backs to each other, although there were many furtive glances back and forth. During almost two years of observation, I never saw them talk. Later, I was surprised to learn that everyone in each group was quite well-known to the other. For either of them to have acknowledged the other's presence openly, however, would have been too forward. The boys are quite aware of this dilemma and complain that the girls are not free enough to be convenient companions. This, they say, is one reason why they have to go elsewhere to date someone. At the same time, they perpetuate the old system by automatically assuming that the slightest sign of interest by a girl makes her fair game. Out of self-defense, the girls are compelled to keep their distance. On private occasions, of course, there are many Italian boys and girls who sneak off to enjoy what others might consider an entirely conventional boy-girl relationship (petting, necking). In public, though, they studiously ignore each other. Throughout my time in the area I never saw a young Italian couple hold hands or walk together on the sidewalk.

The Barracudas were the first Mexican street-corner group to emerge in the Italian section. They first became a named group in the spring of 1964, and all members were Mexican.

Once established, the Barracudas installed themselves in the northwest corner of Sheridan Park. Virtually every Italian street group in the area makes use of this park, and several have their hangout there. Other people in turn refer to the Italian groups collectively as "the guys from the Park." The park itself is partitioned into a finely graduated series of more or less private enclosures, with the most private hangout going to the reigning group and the least private to the weakest group. The northwest corner of the park is the most exposed of any portion, and this is where the Barracudas installed themselves. Even in this lowly spot, they were much resented by the other groups. To the Italians the park was almost a sacred charge, and the Mexicans' intrusion was a ritual pollution. The Barracudas were harassed, ridiculed, and insulted. On their own part, they became belligerent and vaunted all sorts of outrageous claims about themselves. Soon the situation deteriorated and the Italian groups became extremely harsh with the Barracudas. Since the Barracudas were no match for even some of the younger Italian groups, they removed themselvers to one member's house.

Their new hangout placed them in an anomalous position. Ethnically they were identified as a Mexican group. Yet they were located in a part of the area that had been conceded to the Puerto Ricans. And individually most of them continued to reside in the Italian section. The general result seems to have been that the Barracudas were isolated from any of the other group hierarchies and placed in opposition to every group in the area. Within a year every white group was their enemy, and the Negroes were not their friends. The Barracudas responded in kind and became even more truculent and boastful. More than any group in the area, they openly embraced the stance of a fighting group. They wrote their name all over the neighborhood and even on some of the other groups' hangouts. In the meantime, they made a clubhouse out of a lean-to adjacent to a building on Harrison Street. Inside they installed a shield on which they wrote "hate," "kill," and other violent words. Carrying a weapon became almost routine with them, and eventually they collected a small arsenal. In time they had several small-scale fights with both the Italians from the Park and the Mexicans around Polk and Laflin. In due course, they acquired so many enemies that they could hardly risk leaving the immediate area of their hangout. At the same time, some of them began to go to Eighteenth Street, where they had "connections"—relatives. This only brought them into conflict with other groups in this neighborhood. By the summer of 1965, the Barracudas were as isolated and resentful as ever.

"Incognitos" and the "Pica People"

There are two other groups in the Italian section, the Pica People and the Incognitos. The groups' names are themselves an expression of their isolation. The Incognitos self-consciously avoided comparison with the other groups: They did not hang in the Park, hold socials, or become involved in any of the local sidewalk confrontations. About the same age as the Contenders, the Incognitos were notably different in their exclusion from the local round of praise and recriminations.

"Pica People" is a derisive name meant as an insult for five young men about 19 to 25 years of age. Although these five individuals associate regularly, they claim no group identity and become angry when called the Pica People. Unlike the Incognitos, the Pica People are well-known and often accused of some predatory display. They do not fight for group honor, but there is friction between them and all the other street-corner groups in the Addams area.

It was impossible to determine how these two groups came into existence. (I talked only twice with the Incognitos, who simply said they "grew up together." Local people started calling the Pica People by that name after a movie in which the "Pica People" were sub-humans. I knew some of the members of this group, but they became so angry at any mention of the name that I could not discuss it with them.) What is known of their composition may throw some light on why they were excluded from the structure of the other groups. All informants described the Incognitos as "good guys," still in school and no trouble to anyone. They were not considered college boys but, if asked, most informants said they thought some of them might go to college. Local youth agencies made no attempt to work with them, and the entire neighborhood seemed to feel they were not dangerous. Other street-corner groups in the Italian section did not look down on them, but they did exempt them from the ambitions that brought other groups into opposition.

The Pica People were just the opposite. All members were boastful of their alleged Outfit connections and their ability to intimidate other people. But the Pica People possessed so many personal flaws that they were rather useless to the Outfit. One member was slightly claustrophobic. Another was so weak that even much younger boys pushed him around. A third had an exceedingly unfortunate appearance. Under the circumstances, their pretensions became laughable.

Extremes of Street Corner Groups

The Incognitos and the Pica People seem to represent the extremes of a range in which the street-corner group is considered the normal adolescent gathering. Modest and well-behaved youngsters are excluded as exceptions, as are criminally inclined but unsuccessful young men. Both of these groups feel outside the range considered normal by the local residents and were thereby dissociated from the total group hierarchy.

The social context of the Italian street groups is somewhat different from that of the street groups in the other three ethnic sections. Among the Italians, the major share of coercive power still remains in adult hands. The wider community may not be very pleased with the form *their* power takes, but it is the only case where the corporate power of the adolescents is tempered by that of the adults. Also, since many of the same adults have an active role in distributing some of the benefits that are held in store by the wider community, their power is augmented. Perhaps the most obvious result of the adults' ascendency is that the adolescents do not simply dismiss them or adulthood as unimportant. A more immediate consequence is to give many of the adults the prerogative of exacting considerable obedience from the local adolescents. It is not all uncommon to see an Italian adult upbraid and humble one of the local youths. Not all adults have this privilege; but many do, and their example provides a distinct contrast to the other ethnic groups where similar efforts would be futile.

In the long run, the effectiveness of these coercive controls among the Italians may do little more than confirm their convictions that, outside of natural tendencies, there is no guarantee to moral conduct except economic and numerical strength. Within their own little world, however, such coercive measures constitute a fairly effective system of social control. Personal privacy and anonymity are almost impossible. In turn, each person's known or assumed connections dampen most chances at exploitation because of the fear of unknown consequences. Thus, the opportunities for immorality presented by transient relations and "fair game" are fairly rare. Within these limits, such an authoritarian system of social control will work. Outside their own section, of course, these conditions do not hold; and the Italian boys find themselves free to seize whatever advantages or opportunities present themselves. Among themselves, they are usually only a rowdy and boisterous crowd. With strangers or in other parts of the Addams area, they become particularly arrogant and unscrupulous.

With these qualifications, it appears that well-established adolescent street-corner groups are quite compatible with strong adult authority and influence. In fact, judging from the Italian section, these adolescent street-corner groups seem to be the building blocks out of which the older and more powerful groups have originated. The younger groups continue to replenish the older ones and help maintain the structure within which adults are shown deference.

Moreover, the total age-graded structure of groups in the Italian section relates youngsters to the wider society both instrumentally and conceptually. The Italian street groups see themselves as replacements in an age structure that becomes progressively less provincial. At the upper age level, groups even stop prefacing their name with the term "Taylor"; and a few of their members have a place in the wider society through the Outfit and West Side Bloc. The relationship between these age grades also provides a ladder down which favors and opportunities are distributed. The wider community may hesitate at accepting the legitimacy of these transactions, but they are mostly of a conventional form. The "Outfit" and the "West Side Bloc" have a strong interest in maintaining a degree of social order, and the sorts of wanton violence associated with gangs do not at all fit their taste.

Conclusion

The Addams area is probably a more orderly slum than many others, and it departs sharply from the common image of an atomized and unruly urban rubble. For all its historical uniqueness, the neighborhood does establish the possibility of a moral order within its population. The recurrence of the circumstances that led to its organization is as uncertain as the future of the Addams area itself. In spite of all these uncertainties, the Addams area shows that slum residents are intent upon finding a moral order and are sometimes successful in doing so.

Part IX
Culture and Poverty

With the spread of urban industrialization, many traditional people from remote islands and rural hinterlands have become absorbed into the world economy at the lowest social and economic levels. In terms of material wealth, they appear as the "have-nots," populating urban slums and undeveloped agricultural areas. In terms of political power, they are likely to be citizens without a voice—migrants, aliens, illiterates.

The poor of any nation not only have problems; they are usually thought of *as* a problem. They provide cheap labor for industry, but they also exist as living proof that the state has failed to represent the interests of all its citizens. They may be politically powerless, but their very alienation from government can nurture radical movements that threaten the status quo. In most industrialized nations, the vulnerability of the poor to economic depression can impose heavy welfare and social assistance responsibilities on government. In the newer nations that supply raw materials for industry, the refusal of ruling powers to acknowledge such responsibilities —a "let them eat cake" attitude—can demoralize the poor while dehumanizing the objectives of government.

In the United States, during the 1960s, the Kennedy-Johnson administrations spearheaded "war on poverty" programs aimed at solving economic and political inequalities. At the same time, funding for domestic social science research increased and drew the attention of anthropology to field opportunities among racial and ethnic minorities in this country. Anthropologists, however, arrived at the war on poverty scene equipped with categories, theories, and a methodology developed outside the realm of practical problem-solving. Even previous contact with the Bureau of Indian Affairs and with African colonial administrations had not pushed anthropology far from the pure as opposed to the applied science model. As far as most fieldworkers in exotic climes could see, there were no problems with the small communities they investigated. Any difficulties that did exist seemed to arise out of the foibles of bureaucratic officials; fieldworkers seldom passed up an opportunity to identify with the natives against local administrators, while at the same time avoiding leadership and official positions. In contrast, the goal of social reform in the 1960s was to convert the human service sectors of government to democratic instruments for curing social ills. What this entailed was the increased participation of poor people and minority groups in formulating the direction of programs. In part, anthropological research took on the function of understanding and voicing the outlook of socially marginal groups in order to improve the responsiveness of national policy to their situation.

In this liberal era, the most important theory to be generated by the anthropological perspective came from the late Oscar Lewis, author of our first selection. The idea behind a general "culture of poverty" model originated with research among impoverished and largely illiterate workers in Mexico City, the conclusions of which were easily generalized to include the American poor. Lewis contended that social and economic deprivation tends to produce a standard subculture that cuts across regional, rural-urban, and even national boundaries. In his Introduction to *The Children of Sanchez,* the author briefly catalogues the essential economic, social, and psychological features of the culture of poverty:

> The economic traits which are most characteristic of the culture of poverty include the constant struggle for survival, unemployment and underemployment, low wages, a miscellany of unskilled occupations, child labor, the absence of savings, a chronic shortage of cash, the absence of food reserves in the home, the pattern of frequent buying of small quantities of food many times a day as the need arises, the pawning of personal goods, borrowing from local money lenders at usurious rates of interest, spontaneous informal credit devices *(tandas)* organized by neighbors, and the use of second-hand clothing and furniture.
>
> Some of the social and psychological characteristics include living in crowded quarters, a lack of privacy, gregariousness, a high incidence of alcoholism, frequent resort to violence in the settlement of quarrels, frequent use of physical violence in the training of children, wife beating, early initiation into sex, free unions or consensual marriages, a relatively high incidence of the abandonment of mothers and children, a trend toward mother-centered families and a much greater knowledge of maternal relatives, the predominance of the nuclear family, a strong predisposition to authoritarianism, and a great emphasis upon family solidarity, an ideal only rarely achieved. Other traits include a strong present time orientation with relatively little ability to defer gratification and plan for the future, a sense of resignation and fatalism based upon the realities of their difficult life situation, a belief in male superiority which reaches its crystallization in

machismo or the cult of masculinity, a corresponding martyr complex among women and finally, a high tolerance for psychological pathology of all sorts.

As his writings in this section indicate, Dr. Lewis identified these general features with the unconscious covert quality of the "inner core" of culture, a concept generated by American acculturation studies. All groups denied the social and material advantages of society did not necessarily have a culture of poverty. Only those who accepted the constraints of poverty as an immutable natural order, along the lines of language and world view, fell into this cultural category. Groups that consciously perceived alternatives for change and mobilized in trade unions, in revitalized religions, or political action movements could not properly be described as having a culture of poverty. Action against poverty, then, had to be distinguished from a passive acceptance of its culture.

The central controversy which the culture of poverty theory provoked was directly related to problems of implementing social change. If its negative aspects—physical brutality, fatalism, unstable family life, and authoritarianism—are only the direct responses of the poor to economic marginality, then the social remedy is, of course, to improve the target group's economy. If, however, these negative traits are integrated into a complex of cultural values, tinkering with the economic situation would not solve problems overnight; it might take generations for a group to adjust to better conditions and for the results of programs to be felt. Needless to say, waiting generations for results has little appeal to a four- or eight-year White House administration.

In partial refutation of the culture of poverty model, Elliot Liebow and others argue that the poor in urban settings maintain a dual value system. The "good life" that is highly prized by the dominant society is also appreciated by the poor who would like the opportunity to work and earn money, to live in stable households and enjoy a measure of respectability. Being denied opportunities, they live instead according to the demands of poverty, adjusting their behavior and expectations to real-life circumstances: minimal education and training, erratic employment opportunities, low-paying jobs, and poor health and housing conditions. The problems of the poor lie not in their inability to cope with reality but in the institutions that consistently exclude them from full participation.

The methodology that Lewis used in his research was another bone of contention. Though his informants might be bound unconsciously to their culture of poverty world view, Lewis found them capable of telling in their own words the stories of their lives, how they felt about their families, and the better lives they envisioned. The passage included in this section, "Even the Saints Cry," illustrates Oscar Lewis' use of the first-hand narrative as a technique in anthropological inquiry. In relinquishing the role of objective analyst, and becoming essentially a translator of culture, Lewis invited the criticisms of other anthropologists who were more interested in social structure and process than life history narratives. Still, the approach has several virtues, depending on the political climate and the mood of the general public. At a time when minorities were just beginning to make themselves heard nationally, Lewis' work permitted the reality of the poor to be communicated in the first person without much intervention from the social scientist. In addition, millions of readers throughout the nation were able to identify with the personal events described in informants' narratives. Books like *Five Families, The Children of Sanchez,* and *La Vida,* picked up on the American public's unquenchable taste for family drama and the personal struggle against adversity.

From the war on poverty to the present, educational credentials have been advocated as a means of release from the oppression of poverty. Without a high school diploma or, in many fields, a college degree and graduate work, the prospects for employment can be grim. Yet the dropout rate among lower-class racial and ethnic groups is much higher than it is for the upper classes. As in the culture of poverty debate, the question becomes one of locating the problem in the behavior of the people or in the institutions of oppression. Do we blame the victims or resocialize the teachers? The fieldwork investigation of Sioux Indian schooling conducted by Rosalie Wax provides a qualitative analysis of high dropout rates among reservation tribal youth. The conflict between the conventional values of educational officials and traditional Sioux culture parallels information available on other socially marginal groups: the bureaucratic definition of the "good student" usually has little to do with local cultural definitions of good behavior, and instead of working with the lower-class community, educational personnel unwittingly cooperate in keeping the dropout rate at a maximum.

The situation of urban people is usually compounded by multiple institutional restraints. In the third selection in this section, one of the most creative commentators on American culture, Jules Henry, reflects on the education of children in a large housing project in the city of St. Louis. Far from sustaining easily a dual value system, the men, women, and children of the Pruitt-Igoe project are well aware of their low status, and they suffer the disorganization that results from extreme poverty. The price of poverty is indeed high, insofar as young children are shunted between crowded, physically inadequate public housing and equally crowded, understaffed schools.

One of the most valuable results of anthropological research on minority groups has been the fuller understanding of how institutions like schools, housing projects, welfare offices, and the like impose a particular bureaucratic framework on the lives of the poor. As sociologist Georg

Simmel noted many years ago, to be poor in the modern world means to be a public person, one whose life is open to the scrutiny of government. This is clearly the case for America's poor. It is almost surely to become the case for the poor in industrializing nations as state administration of problem people increases in volume.

We would do well to remember that just as there are poor people who, in their drive to change social conditions gain a measure of dignity, there are in other countries groups whose poverty is quantitatively and qualitatively different than in this country. Poverty as a factor in social organization has to be measured against the standards of living characteristic of the region and the national society, for the underprivileged of any nation are known and know themselves by comparison with an observable elite. While the social and economic gaps between rich and poor vary from nation to nation, the common jeopardy for the poor is fatalism, the loss of hope that can characterize an individual's world view. In societies where personal worth is measured only in terms of material wealth, the poor are accorded the least sense of social dignity.

While the discipline of anthropology has a tremendous vested interest in the distinctiveness and variety of many cultures and therefore resists sweeping generalizations, focus on the global issue of poverty represents a necessary coming-to-grips with what we have been witnessing for a long time: the homogenizing impact of the industrial economy on human organization.

References

Coser, L.A. 1965. "The Sociology of Poverty." *Social Problems* 13:140–148.
Coles, Robert. 1970. *Uprooted Children: The Early Life of Migrant Farm Workers.* Pittsburgh: University of Pittsburgh Press.
Henry, Jules. 1963. *Culture Against Man.* New York: Random House.
Lewis, O. 1959. *Five Families.* New York: Basic Books.
Lewis, O. 1961. *The Children of Sanchez.* New York: Random House.
Lewis, O. 1966. *La Vida: A Puerto Rican Family and the Culture of Poverty—San Juan and New York.* New York: Random House.
Liebow, Elliot. 1967. *"Tally's Corner": A Study of Negro Streetcorner Men.* Boston: Little, Brown.
Moynihan, D.P. 1965. *The Negro Family: The Case for National Action.* Washington, D.C.: U.S. Government Printing Office.
Parker, S., editor. 1973. "Poverty and Culture." In *To See Ourselves: Anthropology and Modern Social Issues,* edited by Thomas Weaver. Glenview, Ill.: Scott, Foresman.
Parker, S. and R. Kleiner. 1970. "The Culture of Poverty: An Adjustive Dimension." *American Anthropologist* 72: 516–527.
Schulz, David A. 1969. *Coming Up Black: Patterns of Ghetto Socialization.* Englewood Cliffs, N.J.: Prentice-Hall.
Valentine, Charles. 1968. *Culture and Poverty: Critique and Counter-Proposals.* Chicago: University of Chicago Press.

25.
The Culture of Poverty
Oscar Lewis

I want to take this opportunity to clear up some possible misunderstanding concerning the idea of a "culture of poverty." I would distinguish sharply between impoverishment and the culture of poverty. Not all people who are poor necessarily live in or develop a culture of poverty. For example, middle class people who become impoverished do not automatically become members of the culture of poverty, even though they may have to live in the slums for a while. Similarly, the Jews who lived in poverty in eastern Europe did not develop a culture of poverty because their tradition of literacy and their religion gave them a sense of identification with Jews all over the world. It gave them a sense of belonging to a community which was united by a common heritage and common religious beliefs.

In the introduction to *The Children of Sanchez*, I listed approximately fifty traits which constitute what I call the culture of poverty. Although poverty is only one of the many traits which, in my judgment, go together, I have used it to name the total system because I consider it terribly important. However, the other traits, and especially the psychological and ideological ones, are also important and I should like to elaborate on this a bit.

The Helpless and the Homeless

The people in the culture of poverty have a strong feeling of marginality, of helplessness, of dependency, of not belonging. They are like aliens in their own country, convinced that the existing institutions do not serve their interests and needs. Along with this feeling of powerlessness is a widespread feeling of inferiority, of personal unworthiness. This is true of the slum dwellers of Mexico City, who do not constitute a distinct ethnic or racial group and do not suffer from racial discrimination. In the United States the culture of poverty of the Negroes has the additional disadvantage of racial discrimination.

People with a culture of poverty have very little sense of history. They are a marginal people who know only their own troubles, their own local conditions, their own neighborhood, their own way of life. Usually, they have neither the knowledge, the vision nor the ideology to see the similarities between their problems and those of others like themselves elsewhere in the world. In other words, they are not class conscious, although they are very sensitive indeed to status distinctions. When the poor become class conscious or members of trade union organizations, or when they adopt an internationalist outlook on the world they are, in my view, no longer part of the culture of poverty although they may still be desperately poor.

Is it All Bad?

The idea of a culture of poverty that cuts across different societies enables us to see that many of the problems we think of as distinctively our own or distinctively Negro problems (or that of any other special racial or ethnic group), also exist in countries where there are no ethnic groups involved. It also suggests that the elimination of physical poverty as such may not be enough to eliminate the culture of poverty which is a whole way of life. One can speak readily about wiping out poverty; but to wipe out a culture or subculture is quite a different matter, for it raises the basic question of our respect for cultural differences.

Middle class people, and this certainly includes most social scientists, tend to concentrate on the negative aspects of the culture of poverty; they tend to have negative feelings about traits such as an emphasis on the present and a neglect of the future, or on concrete as against abstract orientations. I do not intend to idealize or romanticize the culture of poverty. As someone has said, "It is easier to praise poverty than to live it." However, we must not overlook some of the positive aspects that may flow from these traits. Living immersed in the present may develop a capacity for spontaneity, for the enjoyment of the sensual, the indulgence of impulse, which is too often blunted in our middle class future-oriented man. Perhaps it is this reality of the moment that middle class existentialist writers are so desperately trying to recapture, but which the culture of poverty experiences as a natural, everyday phenomena. The frequent use of violence certainly provides a ready outlet for hostility, so that people in the culture of poverty suffer less from repression than does the middle class.

In this connection, I should also like to take exception to the trend in some studies to identify the lower class almost exclusively with vice, crime and juvenile delinquency, as if most poor people were thieves, beggars, ruffians, murderers or prostitutes. Certainly, in my own experience in Mexico, I found most of the poor decent, upright, courageous and lovable human beings. I believe it was the novelist Fielding who wrote, "The sufferings of the poor are indeed less observed than their misdeeds."

It is interesting that much the same ambivalence in the evaluation of the poor is reflected in proverbs and in literature. On the *positive* side, the following serve as typical:

"Blessed be ye poor: for yours is the kingdom of God." (*Luke,* 6:20).

"The poor are the protegés of the Gods." (Menander, *The Lady of Leucas,* c. 330 B.C.)

"It is life near the bone, where it is sweetest." (H.D. Thoreau, *Walden,* Ch. 18.)

"The poor man alone,
When he hears the poor moan
From a morsel a morsel will give."
(Thomas Holcraft, *Gaffer Gray.*)

"Yes! in the poor man's garden grow
Far more than herbs and flowers,
Kind thoughts, contentment, peace of mind,
And joy for weary hours."
(Mary Howitt, *The Poor Man's Garden.*)

"Poverty! Thou source of human art,
Thou great inspirer of the poet's song!"
(Edward Moore, *Hymn to Poverty.*)

"Few, save the poor, feel for the poor."
(Letitia Elizabeth Landon, *The Poor.*)

"Happier he, the peasant, far,
From the pangs of passion free,
That breathes the keen yet wholesome air
of ragged penury."
(Thomas Gray, *Ode on The Pleasure Arising from Vicissitude.*)

"O happy unown'd youths! Your limbs can bear
The scorching dog-star and the winter's air.
While the rich infant, nurs'd with care and pain,

Thirsts with each heat and coughs with every rain."
(John Gay. *Trivia.* Bk. II, I. 145.)

"My friends are poor but honest."
(*All's Well That Ends Well*, I, iii. 201.)

The following illustrate the *negative* elements in some of the stereotypes of poverty:

"All the days of the poor are evil."
(*Babylonian Talmud*, Kethubot, 110b.)

"He must have a great deal of godliness who can find any satisfaction in being poor."
(Cervantes, *Don Quixote*, Pt. II, Ch. 44.)

"Poverty is no disgrace to a man, but it is confoundedly inconvenient."
(Sydney Smith, *His Wit and Wisdom* (1900), p. 89.)

"The resolutions of a poor man are weak."
(Doolittle, *Chinese Vocabulary II*, 494 (1872.))

"What can a poor man do but love and pray?"
(Hartley Coleridge, *Sonnets*—No. 30.)

"If you've really been poor, you remain poor at heart all your life."
(W. Somerset Maugham, Introduction to Arnold Bennett, *The Old Wives Tale*, in *Ten Novels.*)

"The life of the poor is the curse of the heart."
(*Ecclesiasticus*, 38:19.)

"There is no virtue that poverty destroyeth not."
(John Florio. *First Fruits*, Fo. 32.)

"Poverty makes some humble, but more malignant."
(Bulwer-Lytton. *Eugene Aram.* Bk. 1, Ch. 7.)

"The devil wipes his tail with the poor man's pride."
(John Ray. *English Proverbs.* 21.)

"The poor, inur'd to drudgery and distress,
Act without aim, think little, and feel less.
And nowhere, but in feign'd Arcadian scenes,
Taste happiness, or know what pleasure means."
(William Cowper. *Hope* I. 7.)

In short, some see the poor as virtuous, upright, serene, independent, honest, secure, kind, simple and happy, while others see them as evil, mean, violent, sordid and criminal.

Most people in the United States find it difficult to think of poverty as a stable, persistent, ever present phenomenon, because our expanding economy and the specially favorable circumstances of our history have led to an optimism which makes us think that poverty is transitory. As a matter of fact, the culture of poverty in the United States is indeed of *relatively* limited scope; but as Michael Harrington and others show, it is probably more widespread than has been generally recognized.

Poverty Here and Abroad

In considering what can be done about the culture of poverty, we must make a sharp distinction between those countries in which it involves a relatively small segment of the population, and those in which it constitutes a very large section. Obviously, the solutions will have to differ in these two areas. In the United States, the major solution proposed by planners and social workers for dealing with what are called "multiple problem families," the "undeserving poor," and the "hard core of poverty," is slowly to raise their level of living and eventually incorporate them into the middle class. And, wherever possible, there is some reliance upon psychiatric treatment in an effort to imbue these "shiftless, lazy, unambitious people" with the higher middle class aspirations.

In the undeveloped countries, where great masses of people share in the culture of poverty, I doubt that social work solutions are feasible. Nor can psychiatrists begin to cope with the magnitude of the problem. They have all they can do to deal with the growing middle class.

In the United States, delinquency, vice and violence represent the major threats to the middle class from the culture of poverty. In our country there is no threat of revolution. In the less developed countries of the world, however, the people who live in the culture of poverty may one day become organized into political movements that seek fundamental revolutionary changes and that is one reason why their existence poses terribly urgent problems.

If my brief outline of the basic psychological aspects of the culture of poverty is essentially sound, then it may be more important to offer the poor of the world's countries a genuinely revolutionary ideology rather than the promise of material goods or a quick rise in the standards of living.

It is conceivable that some countries can eliminate the culture of poverty (at least in the early stages of their industrial revolution) without at first eliminating impoverishment, by changing the value systems and attitudes of the people so they no longer feel helpless and homeless—so they begin to feel that they are living in their own country, with their institutions, their government and their leadership.

26.
The Warrior Dropouts
Rosalie Wax

Scattered over the prairie on the Pine Ridge reservation of South Dakota, loosely grouped into bands along the creeks and roads, live thousands of Sioux Indians. Most live in cabins, some in tents, a few in houses; most lack the conventional utilities—running water, electricity, telephone, and gas. None has a street address. They are called "country Indians" and most speak the Lakota language. They are very poor, the most impoverished people on the reservation.

For four years I have been studying the problems of the high school dropouts among these Oglala Sioux. In many ways these Indian youths are very different from slum school dropouts—Negro, Mexican-American, rural white—just as in each group individuals differ widely one from another. Yet no one who has any familiarity with their problems can avoid being struck by certain parallels, both between groups and individuals.

In slum schools and Pine Ridge schools scholastic achievement is low, and the dropout rate is high; the children's primary loyalties go to friends and peers, not schools or educators; and all of them are confronted by teachers who see them as inadequately prepared, uncultured offspring of alien and ignorant folk. They are classified as "culturally deprived." All such schools serve as the custodial, constabulary, and reformative arm of one element of society directed against another.

Otherwise well-informed people, including educators themselves, assume on the basis of spurious evidence that dropouts dislike and voluntarily reject school, that they all leave it for much the same reasons, and that they are really much alike. But dropouts leave high school under strikingly different situations and for quite different reasons.

Many explicitly state that they do not wish to leave and are really "pushouts" or "kickouts" rather than "dropouts." As a Sioux youth in our sample put it, "I quit, but I never did *want* to quit!" Perhaps the fact that educators consider all dropouts to be similar tells us more about educators and their schools than about dropouts.

On the Reservation

The process that alienates many country Indian boys from the high schools they are obliged to attend begins early in childhood and reflects the basic Sioux social structure. Sioux boys are reared to be physically reckless and impetuous. One that does not perform an occasional brash act may be accepted as "quiet" or "bashful," but he is not considered a desirable son, brother, or sweetheart. Sioux boys are reared to be proud and feisty and are expected to resent public censure. They have some obligations to relatives, but the major social controls after infancy are exerted by their fellows— their "peer group."

From about the age of seven or eight, they spend almost the entire day without adult supervision, running or riding about with friends of their age and returning home only for food and sleep. Even we (my husband, Dr. Murray L. Wax, and I), who had lived with Indian families from other tribal groups, were startled when we heard a responsible and respected Sioux matron dismiss a lad of six or seven for the entire day with the statement, "Go play with Larry and John." Similarly, at a ceremonial gathering in a strange community with hundreds of people, boys of nine or ten often take off and stay away until late at night as a matter of course. Elders pay little attention. There is much prairie and many creeks for roaming and playing in ways that bother nobody. The only delinquencies we have heard Sioux elders complain about are chasing stock, teasing bulls, or occasionally some petty theft.

Among Sioux males this kind of peer-group raising leads to a highly efficient yet unverbalized system of intra-group discipline and powerful intra-group loyalties and dependencies. During our seven-month stay in a reservation community, we were impressed by how rarely the children quarreled with one another. This behavior was not imposed by elders but by the children themselves.

For example, our office contained some items very attractive to them, especially a typewriter. We were astonished to see how quietly they handled this prize that only one could enjoy at a time. A well-defined status system existed so that a child using the typewriter at once gave way and left the machine if one higher in the hierarchy appeared. A half-dozen of these shifts might take place within an hour; yet, all this occurred without a blow or often even a word.

Sioux boys have intense loyalties and dependencies. They almost never tattle on each other. But when forced to live with strangers, they tend to become inarticulate, psychologically disorganized, or withdrawn.

With most children the peer group reaches the zenith of its power in school. In middle class neighborhoods, independent children can usually seek and secure support from parents, teachers, or adult society as a whole. But when, as in an urban slum or Indian reservation, the teachers stay aloof from parents, and parents feel that teachers are a breed apart, the peer group may become so powerful that the children literally take over the school. Then group activities are carried on in class—jokes, notes, intrigues, teasing, mock-combat, comic book reading, courtship—all without the teacher's knowledge and often without grossly interfering with the learning process.

Competent and experienced teachers can come to terms with the peer group and manage to teach a fair amount of reading, writing, and arithmetic. But teachers who are incompetent, overwhelmed by large classes, or sometimes merely inexperienced may be faced with groups of children who refuse even to listen.

We marveled at the variety and efficiency of the devices developed by Indian children to frustrate formal learning—unanimous inattention, refusal to go to the board, writing on the board in letters less than an inch high, inarticulate responses, and whispered or pantomime teasing of victims called on to recite. In some seventh and eighth grade classes there was a withdrawal so uncompromising that no voice could be heard for hours except the teacher's, plaintively asking questions or giving instructions.

Most Sioux children insist they like school, and most Sioux parents corroborate this. Once the power and depth of their social life within the school is appreciated, it is not difficult to see why they like it. Indeed, the only unpleasant aspects of school for them are the disciplinary regulations (which they soon learn to tolerate or evade), an occasional "mean" teacher, bullies, or feuds with members of other groups. Significantly, we found that notorious truants had usually been rejected by classmates and also had no older relatives in school to protect them from bullies. But the child who has a few friends or an older brother or sister to stand by him, or who "really likes to play basketball," almost always finds school agreeable.

Day School Graduates

By the time he has finished eighth grade, the country Indian boy has many fine qualities: zest for life, curiosity, pride, physical courage, sensibility to human relationships, experience with the elemental facts of life, and intense group loyalty and integrity. His experiences in day school have done nothing to diminish or tarnish his ideal—the physically reckless and impetuous youth, who is admired by all.

But, on the other hand, the country Indian boy is almost completely lacking in the traits most highly valued by the school authorities: a narrow and absolute respect for "regulations," "government property," routine, discipline, and diligence. He is also deficient in other skills apparently essential to rapid and easy passage through high school and boarding school—especially the abilities to make short-term superficial social adjustments with strangers. Nor can he easily adjust to a system which demands, on the one hand, that he study competitively as an individual, and, on the other, that he live in barrack-type dormitories where this kind of study is impossible.

Finally, his English is inadequate for high school work. Despite eight or more years of formal training in reading and writing, many day school graduates cannot converse fluently in English even among themselves. In contrast, most of the students with whom they will compete in higher schools have spoken English since childhood.

To leave home and the familiar and pleasant day school for boarding life at the distant and formidable high school is a prospect both fascinating and frightening. To many young country Indians the agency town of Pine Ridge is a center of sophistication. It has blocks of Indian Bureau homes with lawns and fences, a barber shop, big grocery stores, churches, gas stations, a drive-in confectionary, and even a restaurant with a juke box. While older siblings or cousins may have reported that at high school "they make you study harder," that "they just make you move every minute," or that the "mixed-bloods" or "children of bureau employees" are "mean" or "snotty," there are the compensatory highlights of movies, basketball games, and the social (white man's) dances.

For the young men there is the chance to play high school basketball, baseball, or football; for the young women there is the increased distance from over-watchful, conservative parents. For both, there is the freedom, taken or not, to hitchhike to White Clay, with its beer joints, bowling hall, and archaic aura of Western wickedness. If, then, a young man's close friends or relatives decide to go to high school, he will usually want to go too rather than remain at home, circumscribed, "living off his folks." Also, every year, more elders coax, tease, bribe, or otherwise pressure the young men into "making a try" because "nowadays only high school graduates get the good jobs."

The Student Body: Town Indians, Country Indians

The student body of the Oglala Community High School is very varied. First, there are the children of the town dwellers, who range from well-paid white and Indian government employees who live in neat government housing developments to desperately poor people who live in tar-paper shacks. Second, there is the large number of institutionalized children who have been attending the Oglala Community School as boarders for the greater part of their lives. Some are orphans, others come from isolated sections of the reservation where there are no day schools, others come from different tribal areas.

But these town dwellers and boarders share an advantage—for them entry into high school is little more than a shift from eighth to ninth grade. They possess an intimate knowledge of their classmates and a great deal of local know-how. In marked contrast, the country Indian freshman enters an alien environment. Not only is he ignorant of how to buck the rules, he doesn't even know the rules. Nor does he know anybody to put him wise.

Many country Indians drop out of high school before they have any clear idea what high school is all about. In our sample, 35 percent dropped out before the end of the ninth grade and many of these left during the first semester. Our first interviews with them were tantalizingly contradictory—about half the young men seemed to have found high school so painful they could scarcely talk about it; the other half were also laconic, but insisted that they had liked school. In time, those who had found school unbearable confided that they had left school because they were lonely or because they were abused by more experienced boarders. Only rarely did they mention that they had trouble with their studies.

The following statement, made by a mild and pleasant boy, conveys some idea of the agony of loneliness, embarrassment, and inadequacy that a country Indian newcomer may suffer when he enters high school:

> At day school it was kind of easy for me. But high school was really hard, and I can't figure out even simple questions that they ask me.... Besides I'm so quiet [modest and unaggressive] that the boys really took advantage of me. They borrow money from me every Sunday night and they don't even care to pay it back.... I can't talk English very good, and I'm really bashful and shy, and I get scared when I talk to white people. I usually just stay quiet in the [day school] classroom, and the teachers will leave me alone. But at boarding school they wanted me to get up and talk or say something.... I quit and I never went back.... I can't seem to get along with different people, and I'm so shy I can't even make friends.... [Translated from Lakota by interviewer.]

Most of the newcomers seem to have a difficult time getting along with the experienced boarders and claim that the latter not only strip them of essentials like soap, paper, and underwear, but also take the treasured gifts of proud and encouraging relatives, wrist watches and transistor radios.

> Some of the kids—especially the boarders—are really mean. All they want to do is steal—and they don't want to study. They'll steal your school work off

you and they'll copy it.... Sometimes they'll break into our suitcase. Or if we have money in our pockets they'll take off our overalls and search our pockets and get our money.... So finally I just came home. If I could be a day scholar I think I'll stay in. But if they want me to board I don't want to go back. I think I'll just quit.

Interviews with the dropouts who asserted that school was "all right"— and that they had not wished to quit—suggest that many had been almost as wretched during their first weeks at high school as the bashful young men who quit because they "couldn't make friends." But they managed to find some friends and, with this peer support and protection, they were able to cope with and (probably) strike back at other boarders. In any case, the painful and degrading aspects of school became endurable. As one lad put it: "Once you *learn* to be a boarder, it's not so bad."

But for these young men, an essential part of having friends was "raising Cain"—that is, engaging in daring and defiant deeds forbidden by the school authorities. The spirit of these escapades is difficult to portray to members of a society where most people no longer seem capable of thinking about the modern equivalents of Tom Sawyer, Huckleberry Finn, or Kim, except as juvenile delinquents. We ourselves, burdened by sober professional interest in dropouts, at first found it hard to recognize that these able and engaging young men were taking pride and joy in doing exactly what the school authorities thought most reprehensible; and they were not confessing, but boasting, although their stunts had propelled them out of school.

For instance, this story from one bright lad of 15 who had run away from high school. Shortly after entering ninth grade he and his friends had appropriated a government car. (The usual pattern in such adventures is to drive off the reservation until the gas gives out.) For this offense (according to the respondent) they were restricted for the rest of the term—they were forbidden to leave the high school campus or attend any of the school recreational events, games, dances, or movies. (In effect, this meant doing nothing but going to class, performing work chores, and sitting in the dormitory.) Even then our respondent seems to have kept up with his class work and did not play hookey except in reading class:

> It was after we stole that car Mrs. Bluger [pseudonym for reading teacher] would keep asking who stole the car in class. So I just quit going there .... One night we were the only ones up in the older boys' dorm. We said, "Hell with this noise. We're not going to be the only ones here." So we snuck out and went over to the dining hall. I pried this one window open about this far and then it started to crack, so I let it go .... We heard someone so we took off. It was show that night I think. [Motion picture was being shown in school auditorium] ... All the rest of the guys was sneaking in and getting something. So I said I was going to get my share too. We had a case of apples

and a case of oranges. Then I think it was the night watchman was coming, so we run around and hid behind those steps. He shined that light on us. So I thought right then I was going to keep on going. That was around Christmas time. We walked back to Oglala [about 15 miles] and we were eating this stuff all the way back.

This young man implied that after this escapade he simply did not have the nerve to try to return to the high school. He insisted, however, that he would like to try another high school:

I'd like to finish [high school] and get a good job some place. If I don't I'll probably just be a bum around here or something.

Young Men Who Stay in School

Roughly half the young Sioux who leave high school very early claim they left because they were unable to conform to school regulations. What happens to the country boys who remain? Do they "shape-up" and obey the regulations? Do they, even, come to "believe" in them? We found that most of these older and more experienced youths were, if anything, even *more* inclined to boast of triumphs over the rules than the younger fellows who had left. Indeed, all but one assured us that they were adept at hookey, and food and car stealing, and that they had frequent surreptitious beer parties and other outlaw enjoyments. We do not know whether they (especially the star athletes) actually disobey the school regulations as frequently and flagrantly as they claim. But there can be no doubt that most Sioux young men above 12 wish to be regarded as hellions in school. For them, it would be unmanly to have any other attitude.

An eleventh grader in good standing explained his private technique for playing hookey and added proudly: "They never caught me yet." A twelfth grader and first-string basketball player told how he and some other students "stole" a jeep from the high school machine shop and drove it all over town. When asked why, he patiently explained: "To see if we can get away with it. It's for the enjoyment . . . to see if we can take the car without getting caught." Another senior told our male staff worker: "You can always get out and booze it up."

The impulse to boast of the virile achievements of youth seems to maintain itself into middle and even into old age. Country Indians with college training zestfully told how they and a group of proctors had stolen large amounts of food from the high school kitchen and were never apprehended, or how they and their friends drank three fifths of whiskey in one night and did not pass out.

Clearly, the activities school administrators and teachers denounce as immature and delinquent are regarded as part of youthful daring, excitement, manly honor, and contests of skill and wits by the Sioux young men and many of their elders.

They are also, we suspect, an integral part of the world of competitive sports. "I like to play basketball" was one of the most frequent responses of young men to the question "What do you like most about school?" Indeed, several ninth and tenth graders stated that the opportunity to play basketball was the main reason they kept going to school.

One eighth grader who had run away several times stated:

> When I was in the seventh grade I made the B team of the basketball squad. And I made the A team when I was in the eighth grade. So I stayed and finished school without running away anymore.

The unselfconscious devotion and ardor with which many of these young men participate in sports must be witnessed to be appreciated even mildly. They cannot communicate their joy and pride in words, though one 17-year-old member of the team that won the state championship tried, by telling how a team member wearing a war bonnet "led us onto the playing floor and this really gave them a cheer."

Unfortunately, we have seen little evidence that school administrators and teachers recognize the opportunity to use sports as a bridge to school.

By the eleventh and twelfth grades many country Indians have left the reservation or gone into the armed services, and it is not always easy to tell which are actual dropouts. However, we did reach some. Their reasons for dropping out varied. One pled boredom: "I was just sitting there doing anything to pass the time." Another said he didn't know what made him quit: "I just didn't fit in anymore. ... I just wasn't like the other guys anymore." Another refused to attend a class in which he felt the teacher had insulted Indians. When the principal told him that he must attend this class or be "restricted," he left. Significantly, his best friend dropped out with him, even though he was on the way to becoming a first-class basketball player.

Different as they appear at first, these statements have a common undertone: They are the expressions not of immature delinquents, but of relatively mature young men who find the atmosphere of the high school stultifying and childish.

The Dilemma of Sioux Youth

Any intense cross-cultural study is likely to reveal as many tragi-comic situations as social scientific insights. Thus, on the Pine Ridge reservation, a majority of the young men arrive at adolescence valuing *élan*, bravery, generosity, passion, and luck, and admiring outstanding talent in athletics, singing, and dancing. While capable of wider relations and reciprocities, they function at their social best as members of small groups of peers or relatives. Yet to obtain even modest employment in the greater society, they must graduate from high school. And in order to graduate from high school, they are told that they must develop exactly opposite qualities to those they possess: a respect for humdrum diligence and routine, for "discipline" (in the sense of not smoking in toilets, not cutting classes, and not getting drunk), and for government property. In addition, they are expected to compete scholastically on a highly privatized and individualistic level, while living in large dormitories, surrounded by strangers who make privacy of any type impossible.

If we were dealing with the schools of a generation or two ago, then the situation might be bettered by democratization—involving the Sioux parents in control of the schools. This system of local control was not perfect, but it worked pretty well. Today the problem is more complicated and tricky; educators have bcome professionalized, and educational systems have become complex bureaucracies, inextricably involved with universities, education associations, foundations, and federal crash programs. Even suburban middle class parents, some of whom are highly educated and sophisticated, find it difficult to cope with the bureaucratic barriers and mazes of the schools their children attend. It is difficult to see how Sioux parents could accomplish much unless, in some way, their own school system were kept artificially small and isolated and accessible to their understanding and control.

Working Class Youth

How does our study of the Sioux relate to the problems of city dropouts? A specific comparison of the Sioux dropouts with dropouts from the urban working class—Negroes, Puerto Ricans, or whites—would, no doubt, reveal many salient differences in cultural background and world view. Nevertheless, investigations so far undertaken suggest that the attitudes held by these peoples *toward education and the schools* are startlingly similar.

Both Sioux and working class parents wish their children to continue in school because they believe that graduating from high school is a guarantee of employment. Though some teachers would not believe it, many working class dropouts, like the Sioux dropouts, express a generally favorable attitude toward school, stating that teachers are generally fair and that the worst thing about dropping out of school is missing one's friends. Most important, many working class dropouts assert that they were pushed out of school and frequently add that the push was fairly direct. The Sioux boys put the matter more delicately, implying that the school authorities would not really welcome them back.

These similarities should not be seized on as evidence that all disprivileged children are alike and that they will respond as one to the single, ideal, educational policy. What it does mean is that the schools and their administrators are so monotonously alike that the boy brought up in a minority social or ethnic community can only look at and react to them in the same way. Despite their differences, they are all in much the same boat as they face the great monolith of middle-class society and its one-track education escalator.

An even more important—if often unrecognized—point is that not only does the school pose a dilemma for the working-class or Sioux, Negro, or Puerto Rican boy—he also poses one for the school. In many traditional or ethnic cultures boys are encouraged to be virile adolescents and become "real men." But our schools try to deprive youth of adolescence—and they demand that high school students behave like "mature people"—which, in our culture often seems to mean in a pretty dull, conformist fashion.

Those who submit and succeed in school can often fit into the bureaucratic requirements of employers, but they are also likely to lack independence of thought and creativity. The dropouts are failures—they have failed to become what the school demands. But the school has failed also—failed to offer what the boys from even the most "deprived" and "under-developed" peoples take as a matter of course—the opportunity to become whole men.

S. M. Miller and Ira E. Harrison, studying working class youth, assert that individuals who do poorly in school are handicapped or disfavored for the remainder of their lives, because "the schools have become the occupational gatekeepers" and "the level of education affects the kind and level of job that can be attained." On the other hand, the investigations of Edgar Z. Friedenberg and Jules Henry suggest that the youths who perform creditably in high school according to the views of the authorities are disfavored in that they emerge from this experience as permanently crippled persons or human beings.

In a curious way our researches among the Sioux may be viewed as supporting both of these contentions, for they suggest that some young people leave high school because they are too vital and independent to submit to a dehumanizing situation.

27.
White People's Time, Colored People's Time

Jules Henry

Among the children of the very poor survival must take precedence over every other consideration. But current motivational theory tends to downgrade immediate and physical motives. It turns its eagle vision instead, like a rising young executive, on "goal-striving," "status-seeking," and "planning." By such elite and middle-class standards the poor must be said to have little or no motivation.

Under a grant from the National Institute of Mental Health we have been studying a large St. Louis housing development inhabited almost exclusively by very poor Negroes. We middle-class observers have noted the pronounced tendency of the tenants toward "random-like" and unrealistic behavior. Their attitudes toward space, time, objects, and persons lack our patterns or organization, lack our predictability—even sometimes seem to lack sense ... to us. How do they seem to the project dwellers themselves? After more than a year of field work with about fifty families we have the strong impression that they are well aware of the differences.

For instance, they make a strong distinction between C.P. (colored people's) time and W.P. (white people's) time. According to C.P. time a scheduled event may occur at any moment over a wide spread of hours—or perhaps not at all. They believe, however, that in the highly organized world of the whites it occurs when scheduled.

The housing project is so isolated from the social and economic life of the city and the white community that the occupational classes of the census bureau scarcely apply to it. The tenants work as domestics, or in the nooks and cracks of our economy; employment is uncertain, pay is poor, resources are scarce. Yet unemployed men talk of jobs they do not have, and the women in this "City of Women" speak of husbands dead, fled, or who never existed.

Illusion is thus a way of life. Young and old spend money they do not have for expensive clothes and cars. People with no power and status brag of influence and position and concentrate on getting the better of each other. The illusion of middle-class success settles invisibly over them. Thus a white school teacher working with Negro children remarks that they are not interested in solid accomplishment but only in showing off. Obviously such short-cutting must interfere with learning and with facing school and life realistically.

Casting out the poor and the Negro from white society has resulted in a social life so saturated by illusion that the fancy soon becomes the only possible achievement.

Disorganization and a life of dreams fit into the social dynamic of the school room to create educational under-achievement.

The children of disorganization cannot create classroom organization; and the teacher can only work with those who have somehow managed to acquire enough of the necessary motivation. Often we have seen a harassed teacher working with a very few children in a class and trying to ignore the disorder and uproar the others are creating. Here are some notes made in one such sixth grade classroom, with both Negro and white children:

> The teacher was leaning over Paul's desk helping him with arithmetic. Irv and Mike were watching. Alice was talking to Jane and Joan to Edith. Nearby Alan, Ed, and Tom were pushing and shoving. Tom got out of his seat, made a wad of notebook paper and tossed it into the air several times. Tom and Ed suddenly slammed their desks shut, got up, and walked out noisily, Lila and Alice followed. Alan grinned at the observer, waved his hand, and said, "Hi." The teacher took no notice ....

This process of *partial withdrawal*—whereby the teacher simply withdrew to those few students she could handle—may occur anywhere an individual tries to cope with a disturbed environment; I have also seen it in mental hospitals. It reflects not so much the relationship between authority and client but the total social situation.

In school pupils have the choice of building status either with their teacher or their friends; to many, reputation among friends may be much more important. The pressure of peer-groups is very strong, and self-destructive status choice can occur in any such conflict between the demands of authority figures and the demands of the group. What usually tips the balance toward teacher and self-preservation is a measure of hope in the future. Disorganization can tip the balance the other way.

This is especially true if the disorganization has unique attractions for the children. In integrated classrooms, the approval of white students may become so attractive to Negro children that they gladly risk official displeasure, punishment, or failure. In coeducational classes, attracting the attention and getting the approval of the opposite sex can become much more important than "teacher's dirty looks." All such "split" situations introduce disturbing and competing elements. Students can make status choices that ruin their whole future lives.

Very, very poor children, both by feeling and understanding, lack the structure on which conventional education can build. Their background does not have the elements of order necessary to achieve. Their homes are crowded, full of disturbance, physically and personally disorganized; they do not operate on schedules that pay much attention to school concepts of time. They lack both belief in achievement and fear of no achievement.

When thirty to fifty such children are a class supposed to be run by one teacher, disorganization must result. From it the teacher in sheer self-defense may select only those elements suited to her task—she will teach those considered teachable and let the others go. But even the children most willing and able to learn are under tremendous pressure from their classmates to give up and join them. By pleasing the teacher they can buy success in a vague and distant future only at the probable expense of making their present life lonely, unhappy, and even dangerous.

The poor motivation of the low-achiever is not therefore a demon somehow arising from and locked up inside himself but one effect of a whole sea of pressure and pain which has surrounded him since birth; and in which he himself seldom knows why he gasps.

The Missing Ingredient

But why all this disorder, illusion, and destruction? Does it come about because, as some moralists believe, the poor lack an essential fiber, so that they tack and waver in the wind against which *we* advance?

This view is actually not far wrong. The poor do lack a fundamental vitamin that we others absorb with the smell of food, with the promise of gifts at Christmas, with plans for graduation. *They lack the essential strength of hope.*

Hope is not a simple nutrient. It goes straight to the heart of organization and makes it work.

Among lower animals organization occurs largely through in-born genetic factors. With man, things are not so direct, and the word "culture" has been chosen to designate the complex learnings that determine his behavior.

But "culture" varies between societies and even between groups within societies. For the middle and upper classes in our society, achievement and security are major determinants. They organize behavior—or our behavior is organized around them. They act as carrots; the fear of their opposites—failure and insecurity—acts as a goad. When people do not see success and failure as we do, their behavior will appear to us random and purposeless; and we disapprove of it. But those who cannot *hope* for achievement or security can have no concept of the organization of behavior through time toward goals.

The culture of the middle-class itself has been superficially charted. How, for instance, does the middle-class handle *hope, time,* and the *self?* Achievement depends on hope—and hope rests on time. Some *time* in the future we hope to achieve something. Even to say "Billy has stopped wetting the bed" means that desired change has occurred through time: Billy used to wet the bed but does so no longer.

But the parent with no hope can have only partial understanding of his child's having stopped bed-wetting. He can have no fruitful conception of the conscious movement through time toward desired goals. Relative to large social goals, his actions are undirected.

Flight From Death

Though the poor have little hope for life, they do not wish to die. According to comparative suicide rates they have less taste for final voluntary quietus than any other class. Therefore, they concentrate on those factors that keep them alive—now—that make direct, obvious, and strong contributions to present life. The culture of the very poor is a *flight from death.*

In this setting, the very disregard of common methods of looking at things and objects—such as how to arrange a house—can become institutionalized, a way of life. Such disregard in objects we call disorder; in behavior we call it randomness.

Martin Heidegger in *Being and Time* relates the perception of self to existence through time. When people think of themselves they seem to say, he argues, *"That* is the way I was, *this* is how I am now, and in the *future,* I hope to be something else." These perceptions of self have past, present, and future; and it is from them, he believes, that we conceive time. They presuppose change during time—movement from what used to be toward what will be. Self must therefore exist at least partly as a function of time; it must include organization through time.

But what happens to a person who has no expectations or hopes for himself or his children? His behavior, having neither background nor direction, is disorganized. What is left of him in the irreducible ash—the *survival self*—the flight from death.

The survival self has no real sublimation or higher displacement—nothing but physical life—in a very limited but very intense form. The survival self must concentrate on those experiences which give it continual and vivid reassurance that it is alive—heightened perhaps and smoothed by drugs or alcohol. It must, literally, keep *feeling* its life. Sociologists of middle-class background contemptuously refer to this state as "hedonism" —living for pleasure. It is not—it is flight from death.

The famous second law of thermodynamics states, in paraphrase, that disorder within an isolated system can only increase. Life is not pure physics; but there is a useful parallel. Consider a middle-class neighborhood or suburb. It is not an isolated system. Its members go out into the community, and the community comes in at the door and the mind. The resources of the community are known to and used by it, and it is subject to steady cultural and economic stimulation—which it in turn affects. The interaction brings adjustment and regulation; the disorder or randomness— "entropy" in the language of physics—is low.

The slum or lower-class housing project does not have access to these sources of support and stimulation. A paradox—or vicious circle—exists: because of their disorganization and lack of hope the very poor cannot or do not get to the major sources of economic and cultural stimulation; and their disorganization and hopelessness came in the first place from lack of access to these resources. Cut off from hope, stimulation, and change, the poor neighborhood is an isolated human thermodynamic system, and its disorganization can only increase.

Many middle-class selves are also in flight from death; but they are trained to look at life through the lens of achievement, sustained by hope and expectation, and they can fly along this path—perhaps even to greater achievement. This sustenance is not available to the great majority from the slum and housing project.

Our conclusion then must be that hope is a boundary: it separates the free from the slave, the determined from the drifting—and the very poorest from almost all those above it. A corollary conclusion—even more surprising—follows: *time, space, and objects really exist for us only when we have hope.*

Short of reforming his world, how can we stimulate the slum child to greater school achievement? Certainly it will not be enough to merely improve teaching methods and curricula. We must improve the school as a social system.

Some proposals are in order:

Building up perceptions

Children whose central milieu involves so much disorganization and disorder cannot master mathematics, or any other discipline involving order and direction. I would urge that these children be given pre-school training in which the basic perceptions that other children acquire without apparent effort be deliberately taught. For instance, a child must learn fundamental shapes and categories—insideness and outsideness, roundness, straightness, flexibility, rigidity, transparency, opacity, motion in a straight line, motion in a circle, rocking motion, and many other basic perceptions. A child should have this perceptual competence before he starts school.

Calming Down

Poor children often come to school unfed, after wretched nights torn by screaming, fighting, bed-wetting; often they cannot sleep because of cold and rats. They come to class hungry, sleepy, and emotionally upset. To start routine schoolwork effectively at once is impossible. I propose that teachers be specially trained—as they are in the Youth Development Project of the greater Kansas City Mental Health Foundation—to deal with such children, and that they *breakfast with them* in school. The school should, of course, furnish the food, perhaps out of government surplus. School breakfast would accomplish two things: it would feed hungry children, otherwise unable to concentrate adequately on their work; and it would bring teacher and pupil together in an informal and friendly atmosphere, associated with satisfaction, before the strain of classroom constriction and peer-group pressures dictate that teacher become an enemy. It is essential, therefore, that the teacher be present. A program like this suggested by me in Kansas City brought about immediate and sharp improvement in attendance, behavior, and in schoolwork. The more the teachers know about the emotional management of these children, the better.

Expansion of participation

The frequently proclaimed immediate goal of instruction—more personalized attention—is especially important with low-achievers. This can be done by reducing class size, or by increasing the number of teachers. The extra teachers, if not as highly qualified as the regulars, should nevertheless be trained and familiar with the lessons. They can be substitutes, teachers in training, or even members of the domestic counterpart of the Peace Corps whenever that is established. They should be able to help with routine tasks, with keeping order—and with seeing to it that each child has more time, attention, care, and opportunity to learn.

Very poor children need hope in order to achieve. So do those who work with them.

Part X
Development in the Third World

For approximately the first half of this century, anthropologists worked in a world structured by colonial relations; large countries maintained strategic strongholds in exotic areas, and, in peace and war, competed for dominance in commerce. In the years following World War II, anthropologists and the people they study have been vitally affected by the transformation of former colonies into independent nations. This independence has not transposed the relationship between Western nations and the Third World nations of Latin America, Africa, and Asia. Less industrialized countries are still in many ways at the beck and call of technologically advanced nations that consume their raw materials at an avaricious pace and back their governments with stable currency. The power of stronger nations over weaker ones continues indirectly through ideological propaganda, foreign aid programs, economic agreements, the influence of multinational corporations, and contracts for military hardware. The emergence of the Soviet Union as a major industrial power completes the triad of world blocs with a different ideological and economic model of nationalism than that put forth by the West.

The observation that Third World nations are very much influenced by industrialized countries cannot discount the organizational changes taking place within newly independent states. The principal inheritance of the former colonies has been the notion of progress. Each new nation has set for itself an agenda for reaching a higher level of self-sufficiency, both politically and economically. Developments that took several centuries in Western Europe are slated to take place in small fractions of that time by consciously planning a sequence of reforms.

Implicit in any agenda for progress is, of course, at least a partial denial of traditional politics and economics. The folk traditions of a new country can and often do become the basis for a national heritage; the arts and crafts of tribes and villages are displayed in the museums of capital cities as proof of a distinctive cultural past. But traditional kin-oriented approaches to politics stand in opposition to the rational bureaucratization of government and native rule. Whatever else it may imply, it entails a resolution of old and new rules of political behavior. In the same way, and to an even greater degree, the development agenda demands a rationalization of human labor and land use. The natural cycle of the seasons that shapes the work of the hunter-gather, the pasturalist, and the peasant are irrelevant to the efficient running of a factory. Even the transition from subsistence to large-scale farming requires an extended work day, a reorganization of labor, and a full-year schedule of land management.

The obstacles to political and economic change in new nations are several. To leaders in the central government and often to officials from more advanced countries, native cultural resistance appears as a major drawback. The traditional personality suffers not simply from a fundamental reliance on kinship but from the converse—a lack of individuation. We have come to think of modern man in terms of his adaptability to Western notions of production, that is, the extent to which he embraces the goals of progress. At the same time, the programs for development that are foisted on rural folk by their upper-class city cousins are a mixed bag of national ideology, unrehearsed scenarios for ecological disruption, and a radical restructuring of power relations.

Is the population targeted for national reform hindered by its traditional culture? In "Rural Peru: Peasants as Activists," William Foote Whyte presents a well-documented study that refutes any simplistic polarization between modern and traditional openness to change. In Peru's feudal *hacienda* system, the peasant farmer is caught between traditional obligations to landlords and integration in the expanding plantation economy. In such a case, neither the rhetoric of reformers nor the enthusiasm of guerilla revolutionaries makes as much sense as the immediate practical goal of seeking better control of land use. There are no guarantees of success. As in the earlier account of Algerian peasants by Eric Wolf, the active involvement of villagers in social change is documented, with the same large question mark hanging over the label "progress."

In our second selection, Richard W. Franke's account of agrarian reform in Java, focus is on the use of modern technology and planning to increase the national food supply and thus the self-sufficiency of this new nation. The implementation of such a reform, as direct in its aims as it sounds, cannot be separated from the national political climate. The plan may take into consideration maximum yield with minimum soil depletion and an equitable distribution of resources for labor invested. But rational planning can be blown to the winds if and when economic programs are subject to political jealousies. As in Professor Whyte's article on Peru, an account is given of the role of an educated class as a radical political faction. In Java, however, we find that ideologically motivated students worked hand-in-hand with rural people. Paradoxically, the national agricultural movement floundered because of conservative influences on the national, not the local village level.

Progress is only one of the legacies of Western colonialism. The Western administrators who were sent to man colonial outposts brought their own brand of European culture with them. A more conservative lot than their compatriots at home, colonial administrators protected their positions at the top of the dominance hierarchy while encouraging certain favored natives to become go-betweens educated in Western values and customs. Decades, and in some areas of the world, centuries of contact have redefined the native symbols of authority and status, giving an elite value to Western clothes, languages, and education.

The tension between subjecting natives to European rule and converting them to Western civilization varied from one historical phase to another and among the different European nations. Inasmuch as an individual administrator was given leeway to work out his own type of relationship with the native population, there was a greater or lesser investment of personal energy in cultivating protégés and socializing informally with village headmen and tribal chiefs or, for that matter, with native women.

Although Spain, France, and England, to cite three major examples, had basically different approaches to native rule, racism ultimately pervaded all sectors of colonial administration. The more complex the colonial bureaucracy, the more necessary it was to educate at least part of the native population to insure good communication between Europeans and their subjects. Someone had to explain the role of governor and district commissioner, the principle of a head tax, and the presence of a foreign military. The Christian missionaries who journeyed to colonial outposts often assumed part of the task of education, so that their schools provided administrators with apt translators, clever assistants, and puppet chiefs. Despite Christian conversion, the general social attitude that natives were less than human conflicted sorely with the rewards and distinctions meted out by European officials: the intermediary might acquire wealth and titles, but he was never valuable as a person, only useful. Full consciousness of this conflict was achieved only with the rise of a native intellectual class that was able to reflect on its compromise by Western education, yet also touched with rage at exclusion from white neighborhoods, clubs, occupations, and last but hardly least, from white positions of power. In addition, in each bid for national independence, educated natives pointed to Western humanism and the democratic foundations of European states to reinforce their protests against colonial oppression.

The transition from colonial to national government permitted native elites of several kinds—traditional, religious, military, and educated—to take over the reins of government. It did not necessarily mean that people of European descent vanished from the landscape. In his essay on class and race relations in Kenya, Donald Rothchild has selected an issue of growing concern in African politics: the presence of a native white minority within a nonwhite majority. In the late nineteenth and early twentieth centuries, the temperate climate of the Kenyan highlands attracted English settlers, and like the Boers and English of South Africa, they came to stay. Unlike the whites in South Africa, the former "Bwana" rulers of Kenya preserve their position as a social aristocracy, not as political rulers of blacks. Their assertion that they too are natives of Africa underscores the need for peaceful coexistence. As black Africans perceive the problem, the old social barrier of racism remains to be broken down, despite the passing of colonialism.

After independence, nations of the Third World have come under enormous pressure to stabilize their governments, even at the cost of internal violence and the suppressing of human rights. To maintain vital economic relations with industrialized nations, the relatively undeveloped countries of the world must give minimal guarantees that organizationally they are capable of meeting economic contracts and using development funding with an efficiency that will do credit to the donor government. Visiting officials and representatives of large corporations cannot possibly be confronted on their arrival by competing political factions or an unexpected turnover in high-level leadership without questioning the worth of negotiations.

By the same token, economic dependence on the United States, West Germany, Japan, or Russia tends to conservatize the political structure of developing nations; from the highest national office to the district manager of an agricultural reform program, the highest rewards accrue to those who stay in office, no matter how they manage. That the price of dependence on industrialized nations is a high one has not been lost on many national groups, particularly those in African and Middle Eastern states, though autonomy from corrupting outside influences requires a stable and cohesive government as much as dependence. With few exceptions, the role of the military in new nations is central, much more than we would recognize in our own country. Along with a civil service modeled on the defunct colonial administration, it is the overt or covert source of government stability in many new countries. As with the civil service, military organization bespeaks no political ideology, any more than programs for economic development necessarily address human needs. The prevailing emphasis in the Third World is instead on practical solutions.

What happens to the "little people" in whom anthropologists have been so long interested when we find that human rights take a back seat to national development? The question remains to be answered, in part because there are many situations on which no information has been forthcoming. We do know, though, that despite the global multiplication of nation-states, the lines of influence between the powerful and the weak are essentially unchanged. The general impact of the mass media, some reports by anthropologists themselves, and the concerted efforts of groups like Amnesty International to gather information have turned flagrant violations of human rights—a nation's dirty linen—into matters of international censorship. We have made the interesting and important discovery that nations, like individuals, will act to save face, and this may prove a saving grace for millions of people caught in the gears of progress and development.

References

Casanova, Pablo G. 1965. "Internal Colonialism and National Development." In *Studies in International Comparative Development* 1, 4: 27-37.
Davis, Shelton. 1977. *Victims of the Miracle.* Cambridge: Cambridge University Press.
Herskovits, M.J. 1945. "The Processes of Cultural Change." In *The Science of Man in the World Crisis,* edited by Ralph Linton, pp. 143-70. New York: Columbia University Press.
Horowitz, Irving Louis. 1972. *The Three Worlds of Development.* New York: Oxford University Press.
Geertz, Clifford. 1963. *Agricultural Involution.* Berkeley and Los Angeles: University of California Press.
Inkeles, Alex, and David H. Smith. 1974. *Becoming Modern.* Cambridge: Harvard University Press.
McClelland, D., and D. Winter. 1969. *Motivating Economic Achievement.* New York: The Free Press.
Varese, Stefano. 1972. *The Forest Indians in the Present Political Situation of Peru.* Copenhagen: International Work Group for Indigenous Affairs.
Wilson, G., and M. Wilson. 1968. *The Analysis of Social Change Based on Observation in Central Africa.* Cambridge: Cambridge University Press. (Orig. published 1945).
Wilson, Peter J. 1974. *Oscar: An Inquiry into the Nature of Sanity.* New York: Random House.
Worsley, Peter. 1968. *The Trumpet Shall Sound: A Study of "Cargo" Cults in Melanesia.* 2nd ed. New York: Schocken Books.

28.
Rural Peru: Peasants as Activists
William Foote Whyte

The guerillas' presence tends to alter the situation in which peasants, sharecroppers, squatters, peons and Indians live. These people are condemned to an existence which follows the same unchanging routine from year to year, from decade to decade, from generation to generation, until it assumes in their minds the proportions of an immutable natural order.

Carlos Romeo

The writer of those lines is a follower of Fidel Castro and a theoretician of the revolutionary potential of the peoples of Latin America. My point in citing him is that his sentiments about the rural peasantry sum up the feelings of an extraordinarily wide range of observers of the Latin American scene, whatever their political views or goals.

For revolutionaries or reformers, for Fidelistas or rhetoricians of the Alliance for Progress, the peasants are enmired in "an immutable natural order." They are seen as an ignorant lot, tradition-bound and incapable of change even when that change might substantially improve their earthly condition. As such they cannot be brought to share in their country's wealth without the intervention of more enlightened outsiders who will point the way.

Of course reformers and revolutionaries have radically different notions of what form their intervention should take. The former, generally speaking, embrace a theory of community development according to which strategies have to be devised so that the peasantry will be "involved" in discussions of possible changes and their traditional conservatism overcome through the "participation process." Revolutionaries tend to assume —sometimes at the cost of their lives—that the agents of change will be their own guerilla bands operating in the countryside where they will serve as catalysts of the dormant revolutionary impulses of the peasants.

I would argue the contrary proposition, that far from being dull pawns in an immutable natural order, the peasants are caught up in constant processes of change, and that many of these changes are initiated by themselves without benefit of outside guidance. I will try to demonstrate this proposition from studies of the Peruvian countryside, but I believe that this general conclusion would apply throughout Latin America and, indeed, in most of the Third World. It should be borne in mind, however, that I am not arguing against outside intervention, whether by reformists or revolutionaries. I am simply suggesting that before any self-appointed agents do intervene, they would do well to find out where the ball is and in what direction it is rolling. Then they will be able to give it a well-directed push, rather than falling flat on their faces, as so many "development projects" have done, or being killed, as so many guerillas have been.

For the purposes of this argument, there is one segment of Peruvian rural society that presents the toughest challenge to my contention. This is the sierra hacienda or large landed estate, which would seem to offer peasants a minimum of opportunity to change their lot. Here, if anywhere, one would assume that change could come only from the outside, and that it would probably have to be effected by violent force.

The Sierra Hacienda

In Peru the word "hacienda" is used to refer to two quite different types of social and economic units. In the coastal hacienda (sometimes referred to in English as "plantation"), workers generally live in houses built by the company, are paid regular wages, and their children have access to at least elementary schooling. Many of the haciendas are unionized. Many of them also can best be described as agro-industrial complexes, since they run from cultivation to manufacture (paper, chemicals, rum, for example). Many of the commercial haciendas are operated at a high level of technology and agricultural sciences, with agronomists serving either as managers or consultants.

The traditional sierra hacienda is drastically different. It has been likened to the feudal manor because of the extreme domination exercised by the hacendado over the peasants. The owner or renter of the hacienda retains the best lands for himself while each peasant family, in return for the right to occupy and cultivate a small plot of land, generally in the most undesirable areas, is required to provide from three to six man-days of work a week, either on the hacendado's lands or on projects for which he hires out his labor and for which he himself pockets the wages. Furthermore, the women of the peasant families usually have obligations in the household of the hacendado. In general, the hacendado has good connections with the political and economic power figures in his area; the peasants traditionally have lacked these connections and are subjected to various forms of exploitation and denial of opportunity. Because he normally received only a token payment—perhaps a penny or two a day, plus a supply of coca to chew on—he was unable to accumulate capital to become a landowner himself. In fact, the only major difference between the traditional Peruvian hacienda and the manor at the height of the middle ages is that the Peruvian peasant is free to leave the land. If he does, however, he loses any claim to the land he has cultivated and on which he built his home. This is the situation that has prevailed through much of the Peruvian sierra, where over half of the population lives. We are therefore talking about a situation of extreme inequality of power and resources, where it is natural to raise the question as to whether any basic change is possible without outside intervention or violent revolution. Let us examine several cases in the light of this question.

Twenty years ago the Yanamarca Valley, north of Jauja in the central highlands, was almost entirely made up of haciendas. In the past two decades, five communities have emerged out of serfdom, and the only two remaining haciendas in the area are organized and operated in a manner far different from the traditional style.

I shall tell the story in terms of one community, whose history seems broadly representative of the process of liberation throughout the valley. To maintain the anonymity of the principal actors, I shall use pseudonymns for personal names and call the community "Pueblito," but the facts are carefully documented by our associates carrying out the field work.

The liberation of Pueblito began in 1952. The first initiative came from Arturo Sánchez, a young man from the highlands who had gone to Lima for a medical education and had become involved in APRA Party activities. As a student leader, he had to go underground when General Manuel Odría took over the government in 1948 and began his repression of APRA (Popular American Revolutionary Alliance) which he regarded as a leftist organization because it was then actively seeking the support of workers and peasants. Some time later, Sánchez turned up in Pueblito, settled down to work the land, and married a Pueblito girl.

Organizing Peasants

Sánchez' first organizational step centered on a project for establishing a school in Pueblito. Although Peruvian legislation requires the hacendado to provide some schooling for the peasants, most landlords in the past have ignored this obligation altogether, or have complied in a token fashion, providing one dilapidated room and an occasional teacher. Like many other landlords, José Marimba sought to discourage the school project, arguing with the peasants that school would be of no value to their children. Under Sánchez' leadership, however, the peasants succeeded in interesting the Ministry of Education in their project, so that there was a beginning of a school even against the landlord's opposition.

As the peasants began to organize themselves around the school project, Marimba got into difficulties on another front. In the first place, he had won control of the land only in a bitter court battle. His father had divided several haciendas and a power plant in Jauja among his children, with Pueblito going to one of José's sisters. At great expense to himself, Marimba carried through litigation that won him Pueblito in exchange for other properties that he gave up. Marimba thus started his operation of Pueblito in somewhat tight financial straits. This was unfortunate for Marimba, since he was a man of expensive tastes. From 1942 to 1952 he had secured large loans from the Agricultural Development Bank, ostensibly to improve Pueblito, but he had spent most of his money on international travel and gracious living in Jauja and Lima.

Until 1952, Marimba spent very little time in Pueblito, leaving everything in the hands of an administrator. When the bank began to press for repayments on its loans, Marimba turned his concentrated attention on Pueblito and sought to squeeze more work out of the people. When some men proved unresponsive to his urgings, he expelled them from the land. The first time he did this, there was no overt response from the other peasants. Therefore, some time later, when he found two of the community leaders not applying themselves as diligently as he wished, he promptly ordered them and their families to leave the property at once. At this point, all the peasants rallied around and vowed that if these two men were to be thrown out, Marimba would have to throw them all out. At the same time, they flatly refused to do any further work for him. Marimba appealed to the authorities in Jauja, but this did not break the unity of the community.

When the peasant challenge came, José Marimba found himself in a deteriorating position. The legal struggle for Pueblito against his brothers and sisters had been expensive and had destroyed family solidarity. While the Marimba family had held unquestioned social and political preeminence in Juaja in the days of his father, José now found himself in acrimonious competition for prestige and influence with a rising businessman-farmer who actually worked in his various enterprises. Furthermore, José's arrogant manner had made him unpopular with both his peers and his social inferiors.

Marimba's response to the peasant challenge was typical of the old order in rural Peru. In Jauja and Huancayo, the departmental (state) capital, he lavishly entertained members of the local and national elite—thus further depleting his resources. As the Bank pressed for repayment of the loan, he sought to cultivate the officials of the Huancayo office, two recent graduates of the Agrarian University. He urged on them the following arguments: "We are friends," "We are gentlemen," "We are fellow white men."

When the officials persisted in their unfriendly, ungentlemanly and unwhite demands, José went to Lima to call on the president of the bank, whom he considered to be a friend of the family. The president went through the motions of telephoning Huancayo and asking information on the case. When the Huancayo officials submitted a written report that documented in detail Marimba's incompetent and irresponsible management of Pueblito, the bank president took no further action, and the Huancayo office renewed its pressures on the landlord.

By the time of the strike against Marimba, the community leaders had already been in touch with lawyers in Jauja and with union leaders in Jauja and Huancayo. Through these contacts they learned that the title of José Marimba to Pueblito was in doubt and that another family claimed to own the property. On the advice of their lawyer they made a deal with the other claimant to buy Pueblito from him. At the same time, they made a deal with the Agricultural Development Bank to take over the mortgage on which Marimba had been defaulting.

Marimba has not given up yet. At this writing, he is still fighting in the courts to get Pueblito back, but now that the peasants have the bank, lawyers, union leaders and relatives and friends of the other presumed former owner on their side, it seems hardly likely that Marimba will ever make a comeback. Meanwhile, Pueblito is developing as an independent community. The villagers have started building new homes and vigorously developing their economy.

Change Comes to the Convención Valley

Until 1881, the Convención Valley was entirely divided into haciendas, there being no towns or other commercial settlements. At that time, an hacendado turned over one-third of his estate to build an independent town. The town became Quillabamba, the present provincial capital and now the most important city in the 60-mile-long valley.

Due to its geographical isolation and adverse health conditions, the valley was sparsely settled until the 1940s. Construction of a railroad into the valley in 1933 and the eradication of malaria in the late 1940s led to a flood of immigration from the mountains. Even so, labor was so scarce that the hacendados had to offer peasants substantially more land for their own family cultivation than was customary in the sierra.

Typically, however, the hacendados retained the bottom-lands along the river for their own use, giving the peasants the steep slopes. While the bottomlands were much superior for crops traditionally grown in the area, it turned out, ironically, that the slopes were better for the cultivation of coffee, a fact which was not lost on the peasants on the hillsides who first went into coffee cultivation. By the time the hacendados began converting to coffee, it had already become a mainstay of the peasant economy.

The peasant movement into coffee coincided with a continuous and spectacular rise in its price in the valley. If we give the 1945 price an index number of 100, by 1954 the index had risen to 1,221. In the 15 years up to 1960, coffee shipped out of the valley rose almost sevenfold, from 583,000 to 3,820,000 kilos.

Until the advent of coffee, the hacendados controlled peasant access to markets, themselves handling the sales of such peasant production as reached the market along with their own output. As the coffee boom developed, *rescatistas* or middlemen entered the local scene. They were not interested in land reform, but they were interested in buying coffee. And since the peasants owned the bulk of the coffee, the rescatistas naturally went directly to the peasants. This development led to the creation of key contacts for the peasants in Quillabamba and other market towns, as local merchants built storage facilities and entered into the business of buying and selling coffee. As coffee production grew, the peasants were also creating town merchants whose interests were allied with theirs.

The hacendados recognized that the peasants' rising stake in coffee constituted a threat to their economic and political position in the valley. Some of them now tried to maneuver the peasants out, reclaiming the slopes of the mountainsides so as to extend their own coffee cultivation into more suitable areas. Coffee also became the focus of a clash in time commitments. At harvest time coffee offers less flexibility to farmers than do crops such as corn and potatoes. Coffee ripens all at once and must be picked when it is ready. This meant that just at the time when the hacendado had his greatest need for labor, the peasants had the greatest need to apply their labor to their own land. Furthermore, it meant that the peasants had much more to lose in maintaining the traditional obligations of the hacienda system. This naturally accentuated the conflict between peasants and landowners.

To protect themselves against being pushed off the land and to support their demands for limits of their labor obligations, Convención Valley peasants began to unionize. At the outset, unionization was an entirely indigenous movement, all the leaders being peasants from the valley. The peasants had some support from the merchants in the towns and, beginning in 1951, they extended their ties into Cuzco, getting lawyers to represent them in grievances that they pressed before the Ministry of Labor. The union federation grew slowly until 1960, at which time unions on several haciendas carried out a two-month "sympathy strike" on the grounds that fellow workers on another hacienda were being mistreated. At that, the hacendados began pressing their congressmen in Lima to get the national government to intervene in support of their position. Instead of sending armed forces, however, the government dispatched an investigator to look into the situation. To the surprise and indignation of the hacendados, the investigator recommended that the *condiciones* or traditional labor obligations should be abolished, a solution that would have consolidated peasant control of the lands they were cultivating and deprived the hacendados of most of their labor. To be sure, the report was shelved in the Ministry of Labor, but the fact remains that the government did not intervene on the side of the hacendados. This was a major victory for the peasant union and their movement began advancing rapidly throughout other areas of the valley.

Their gains now began to attract outsiders. Most prominent of these was Hugo Blanco, a native of Cuzco who could speak Quechua and had received his university education in Argentina. His father-in-law, a Cuzco lawyer, had represented the peasants on one hacienda in their protests to the Ministry of Labor office in Cuzco, so Blanco was already thoroughly familiar with the background of the situation. In 1960 he went in to settle on the hacienda his father-in-law had represented.

Blanco proved to be a charismatic figure. He was soon elected to represent his hacienda union in the peasant federation, and he moved on from this victory to become an effective organizer of new unions, particularly in the northern section of the valley.

A self-confessed Trotskyite, Blanco believed that it would be necessary to go beyond unionization to lead the peasants in forcibly taking over the lands—thus providing an initial base for the revolution that might come to Peru. As soon as he had established his power base through organizing new union locals, Blanco ran for the headship of the peasant federation. This precipitated a split in the movement. The older leaders who had started the unions were interested in land, not revolution. They were committed to more traditional trade-union methods and to an extension of the political influence of their movement.

Blanco received a majority of the votes in a hotly disputed election. But the leaders of some 20 peasant unions, including most of the early union leaders, claimed fraud and walked out of the meeting. They quickly consolidated the local units they controlled into a new confederation, thereby dividing the union movement in the valley into two organizations.

At the time of the disputed election, an order for the arrest of Blanco was issued by the police authorities of the valley. The peasant leader then went into hiding for a period of nine months, during which time there were sporadic outbreaks of violence against police and military officials, for which Blanco and his supporters were held responsible. At the end of 1962, Blanco was captured and placed in prison, where he is now serving a 24-year term.

Despite the split between the Blanco faction and the older leaders of the union movement, and despite the brief rise and fall of another rival union allied with APRA, the position of the peasants in relation to the hacendados was steadily strengthened.

Early in 1962, just prior to the disputed election, the union leaders ordered a strike against all the hacendados in the valley—there was to be no work for any hacendado nor any payment of rental in return for the land occupied by the peasants. By early 1963 all of the peasants in the valley and both federations were supporting this policy. It is not necessary here to give details on the governmental decisions that consolidated the peasant victory. Let me simply note that the first presidential decree recognizing the peasant victory was issued under the conservative government of Manuel Prado; some months later the military junta, in power from 1962 to 1963, recognized the de facto control of the lands by the peasants.

While the strength of the peasant mobilization is impressive, we must also recognize the weaknesses of the hacendados of the Convención Valley. There are indications, for example, that they did not enjoy the kind of political and public relations position enjoyed by large landowners in other parts of Peru. In fact, at the height of the conflict, *La Prensa,* the newspaper owned by the then Prime Minister Pedro Beltrán, published on its front page a feature story about a certain Señor Romaineville, the largest hacendado in the Convención Valley. The article was distinctly unflattering. It reported that Romaineville had not set foot on his property in at least 12 years and portrayed him as the archetype of the exploitative absentee landlord. Furthermore, when the showdown came, there were 10,000 peasants on the voting lists, and few of them were any longer controlled by the hacendados.

The Spread of Unionization

The establishment of peasant ownership ended one stage of revolution in the Convención Valley but it was only a beginning of another. In the several years following the peasant victory, schools have been built so fast and in so many areas of the valley that neither the Ministry of Education nor the government community development agency, *Cooperación Popular,* has been able to keep up with the demand for teachers or building materials that could not be locally manufactured. The valley also seems to be throbbing with an increased level of economic activities.

During the period when a unionization movement was transforming the Convención Valley, unionization spread also into other parts of rural Cuzco. On many an hacienda, the hacendado found himself in the unprecedented position of having to sit down and negotiate with representatives elected by his peasants and with a leader of the peasant federation from Cuzco, if he wanted to get his crop planted or harvested. In the early months of the Belaúnde administration (begun in late July of 1963), it seemed that unionization of the peasants was not only gaining ground rapidly but was also leading to forcible demands for peasant ownership. These were described by hacendados as "invasions" of their lands and by the peasants as "recovering the rights that have been stolen from us." At this point, under pressure from the congress, which was dominated by a curious coalition of the formerly leftist APRA and the party of their old oppressor General Odria, Belaúnde had to put in a tough Minister of the Interior, who ordered a roundup of leaders of the peasant federation in Cuzco, thus stripping the federation of its top officers.

While this repressive move practically destroyed the peasant federation as a formal organization, it is important to note that conditions on the countryside did not revert to the status quo before unionization. Hacienda Chawaytiri, which was included in our study area, is a case in point. There the organized peasants had been able to negotiate a marked reduction of the days worked per month and a threefold increase in the cash payments, together with other equally sweeping changes in the conditions of work. When the union was no longer in formal existence, the peasants nevertheless reported that the administrator and his representatives supervised them in a much more humane manner than had been customary before unionization. Furthermore, when the hacendado announced he was going to cut the daily payment by two-thirds, the campesinos declined to report for work. The work relationship was reestablished only when the hacendado agreed to reestablish the three soles daily rate (the sol then being worth about 3.7 cents).

Moreover, a field worker who studied the hacienda in 1965 reported that relations between the peasants and the hacendado or his representatives remained in the post-strike pattern. The administrator had not resumed the use of physical force as a form of discipline. He did not even shout at the peasants any more. In fact, some of the campesinos commented, "You know, he is really a nice fellow, when you get to know him." Previously, the *mandón* (a campesino who served as straw boss under the administrator) had done nothing but transmit and enforce the orders of the hacendado or the administrator. In 1965 he was taking quite a different stance. Our field worker observed him one day with the other campesinos sitting around and waiting for the rain to stop. The administrator came along and asked why the men were not working. The mandón replied. "Times have changed. It is not right to make the men work in the fields in the rain." The administrator did not press the point.

These cases of peasant mobilization should not be confused with the guerrilla movements that broke out in areas of rural Peru in 1965–66. The guerrilla leaders were middle-class intellectuals who had little or no contact with the peasants before they launched their violent attack upon the authority of the government. They hoped that once they had raised the flag of revolution the peasants would flock to their side, fight with them, shelter them and feed them.

Guerrilla Violence

Take, for example, the career of Luis de la Puente Uceda. He was a young lawyer who had once been a fanatical member of APRA. As APRA seemed to be turning to the right, he turned to the left, abandoned the party, and became a disciple of Fidel Castro. In 1965, he entered the Convención Valley with an armed force variously estimated at between 100 and 300 men—both estimates probably being high.

The strategy of taking a force into the mountains to start the revolution was explicitly based upon the Castro model, yet the Peruvian revolutionists failed to take into account several important differences between their situation and that facing Castro at the time he launched his movement. When Castro took to the hills, Cuba was under a repressive dictatorship, and it seemed to most people that a violent revolution offered the only hope of change. Peru in 1965 was under a democratically elected government, with a president who had been talking about land reform and rural development. While de la Puente and his supporters could argue that this kind of talk was just a sham and that no basic changes would take place without a revolution, it was by no means clear to all Peruvians, even to Peruvians on the left, that a violent attack on the government offered the only hope for bringing about basic changes.

While Castro did his fighting first in the hills, he maintained close contacts with secret supporters in the towns and cities, so that his movement had strong urban links. The Convención Valley was exceedingly isolated from urban Peru, being connected only to Cuzco, and that by a railroad that could be closely controlled by the authorities.

Why did de la Puente choose the Convención Valley for his uprising? While I am not aware of any public statements of his on this question, I suspect there were two fundamental reasons: the much publicized militancy of the peasants, and the nature of the terrain which made the valley a good place to hide. If these were indeed the factors convincing to de la Puente, he was fundamentally in error on both points.

The peasants had in truth demonstrated their militancy, but they had won what they were after: control of the land. De la Puente was offering them enormous risks in exchange for possible gains that seemed vague and uncertain. His men found few potential revolutionaries in the valley.

The rugged terrain of the Convención Valley did in fact provide a good place to hide, but once there it was exceedingly difficult to get out. In effect, there were only two ways in or out, both along the river. The rugged mountains offered no ground-cover for fugitives. As soon as the government learned of the guerrilla activities, the army proceeded to bottle up both ends of the valley and then sent in patrols to root out the guerrillas.

The guerrillas had expected to live off food provided by sympathetic peasants, but voluntary contributions turned out to be sparse indeed. To keep alive, then, the guerrillas had to resort to forcible seizures of food—as did Che Guervara later in Bolivia—further alienating the peasants.

The final scene of the drama occurred after de la Puente had retreated to the Mesa Pelada, a desolate plain above the valley. A peasant woman informed a military patrol of the location of the guerrilla group. De la Puente and the last six men remaining with him were shot dead in the resulting encounter.

If change in rural Peru is as widespread as I claim it to be, how do we account for the fact that so many Latin American intellectuals, whether radicals or reformers, persist in seeing the countryside as an area of social and economic stagnation? They do this by applying the exception principle. Whenever a case of change comes to their attention—and the Convención Valley movement has received wide public attention in Peru—they explain it away as an exceptional situation that has risen out of peculiar conditions. But they do not then go on to ask whether there may not be other instances of change, not so well publicized. For example, the transformation of the Yanamarca Valley was completely unknown in intellectual circles in Lima until our field workers happened upon this less dramatic peasant movement. The unionization movement throughout rural Cuzco was indeed publicly noticed at the time, but it seems to have been forgotten soon after the government roundup of union leaders. It was as if intellectuals assumed that the Cuzco haciendas had returned to the status quo ante, which was definitely not the case.

Underlying the application of the exception principle is the intellectual's inclination to view reality through moralistic and ideological filters. The moralistic filter is supplied by the concept of "exploitation." The Peruvian constitution, the United Nations Declaration of the Rights of Man, and any number of other such statements of principle, decree that no man shall be forced to work for another or to work without adequate compensation. When in hacienda Chawaytiri the *condición* of work-day obligations is cut by more than a third and when the daily payment is raised by 200 percent, intellectual reformers or revolutionaries see no change at all because the Indians are still being exploited.

The ideological filter is the intellectual's mental model of the way major structural changes take place. If revolutionary, he has an image of a dramatic nationwide confrontation of reactionary, and radical forces, culminating in a radical capture of power in the capital city. The community and area level changes I have described clearly have no place in this model, and so they are not allowed to disturb the myth of the passive peasant.

When faced with the realities of events in the Yanamarca Valley, one Peruvian social scientist made this comment: "You can't say that those communities have become independent. They continue to be under the domination of the national oligarchy, and that oligarchy continues to be under the domination of Yankee imperialism." By that logic, no change will take place until the millenium.

While the approach presented here differs from that of the ideological revolutionaries, it is important to recognize that it differs in an equally fundamental way from the usual line of community-development theorizing. While the radical ideologists are fixated on the concept of power, the community developers avoid the power issue altogether. For them the secret of change and progress in the countryside is "participation." If the peasants can be involved in solving the problems of their community together, progress will result. Furthermore, community development theorists tend to treat the community as if it existed in a vacuum, thus neglecting the crucially important relations it has with the outside world.

Power is a central issue in our approach, but I am undertaking to dispel the mysticism that tends to becloud the power issue in ideological argument. By getting down to cases, I seek to show how power is exercised and how shifts in power actually take place.

What explains the changes I have described in the Yanamarca and Convención Valleys and in rural Cuzco? In order to provide a systematic explanation, we need to think in terms of the transformation of the structure of power.

The hacendado is at the apex of the triangle. Peasants are clustered at the bottom of each side of the triangle. The absence of a line connecting them depicts their unorganized state. The hacendado deals with peasants and their families strictly on an individual basis, holding out special favors for those "loyal" to him and threatening dire penalties for those who are not submissive. The hacendado himself has strong horizontal ties—family, social and political connections with people at roughly the same status in the society. The hacendado also has links upward in the society with important politicians and judges, with bank officials and other figures of economic significance. The peasants do not have these ties. To gain favors from any of these superior power figures, they must go through the hacendado himself, which means that he is in a position of monopoly, both political and economic.

How do the peasants break this monopoly? They do it basically in two ways: by closing the base of the triangle and by establishing upward ties in the society, independent of the hacendado.

We have seen that the peasants may close the base of the triangle through coordinated efforts to found a school on the hacienda, through organizing against repressive landlords or through an extensive unionization movement as in the Convención Valley. The peasants' upward ties can be forged with the Ministry of Education, with the Ministry of Labor or with the Agricultural Development Bank. In the case of the peasants of the Convención Valley, upward ties were not established until the advent of coffee created middlemen in the towns whose interests were allied with those of the peasant growers.

Part of the drama was played by lawyers in the courts. When the peasants laid claim to the land or stopped working for the hacendado, he would typically appeal to the political authorities to get the police or troops sent in. Sometimes this worked, but sometimes it did not. If he was unsuccessful in the direct appeal for force, he would go to court to get a legal order requiring the peasants to comply with his interpretation of their obligations. In that event, the peasants would get their own lawyer (for various reasons, there is a buyers' market for legal services in rural Peru) and he would sue the owner on their behalf for 30 years of back pay. The legal justification for this claim is clear, for the Peruvian constitution outlaws the traditional hacendado-peasant relationship, in which the peasant is forced to work without wages (other than a token payment) in order to cultivate a plot of land. Where the hacendado's power is unchallenged, this constitutional provision remains a dead letter, as does the law requiring him to provide a school, but when the peasants can organize themselves to make the challenge, they create a very awkward situation for the hacendado, his lawyer and the courts, since they are claiming rights that are unequivocally guaranteed them.

There are also forces at work that tend to make the old ways increasingly unsatisfactory to the hacendado. The traditional style of farm management does not yield increasing economic returns over the years. The hacendado does not care to spend much time on his hacienda where the cost of living is relatively low. He is a city-oriented man, and with each passing generation this orientation becomes more pronounced. The hacendado and his family are committed to the "good things" of modern urban living, from education to entertainment and travel, and the price of those "good things" is constantly increasing.

When the hacienda no longer yields the income necessary to maintain the status and style of life to which he has become accustomed, what can the hacendado do? He has just three alternatives:

1. He can try to squeeze more work out of the campesinos.
2. He can sell the hacienda and invest the money in something else.
3. He can invest money in the hacienda to reorganize it in terms of "modern" scientific agriculture and "modern" farm management methods.

As José Marimba's experience suggests, the first strategy is more likely to yield increased peasant resistance than increased farm output. If he decides upon the second strategy, to whom can he sell? For reasons that should be abundantly clear by now, the demand for land on the part of current and potential hacendados does not begin to meet the supply of purchasable haciendas. Poor as they are, the peasants are emotionally attached to the land and are likely to be willing to pay the hacendado more for it then any other potential purchaser. If the hacendado sells out to them, the transformation of hacienda into community is thereby accomplished.

We are just beginning to find hacendados who have successfully pursued the third strategy. It is too early to make any definitive statements, but so far we are inclined to assume that very few current sierra hacendados have the will, ability, knowledge and psychological orientation required to transform their properties into "modern" farm enterprises. And those few who successfully carry out the third strategy thereby build a social system that is drastically different from the traditional hacienda.

The Need for Revolution

What does this approach tell us about the probability of a violent social revolution in Peru? On the one hand, it knocks one of the props out from under the argument for the inevitability of violence: a violent revolution is inevitable, it is said, because those holding power will not yield it voluntarily. José Marimba, the hacendado of Pueblito, did not yield power voluntarily, but he lost it nevertheless. And so it was with the other hacendados in the Yanamarca and Convención Valleys.

On the other hand, nothing written here provides grounds for optimism to those who would like to prevent a violent revolution in Peru. I have demonstrated that sweeping changes in social structure have come about in certain rural areas, but generalizations from these cases must be made with the following reservations in mind:

First, I have carried the cases only to the point of the power shift and slightly beyond it. It must not be assumed that after overthrowing the hacendados the campesinos live happily ever after. They continue to face very serious economic and political problems, which I shall not discuss here, as we are just beginning to study postindependence developments.

Second, in the countryside, avoidance of a revolutionary situation probably depends upon the geographical extent and the rapidity of movements such as those examined here. Neither the data we have nor the behavioral science theories available permit us to make any predictions as to the probability that widespread changes will come fast enough to relieve the severe tensions now prevalent throughout rural Peru.

Third, until Fidel Castro, it was generally assumed that revolutions started in cities. The smashing defeats of those who tried to apply his rural model in Peru and Bolivia suggest that students of revolution would be well advised not to neglect the urban front. And I have ventured no statements about the state of Peruvian cities.

Finally, the present military government of Peru is committed to preventing a violent revolution through carrying out its own model of revolution, imposed from the top down. If and when the Agrarian Reform Law promulgated in June of 1969 is fully implemented, it will mean a transformation of the countryside far more extensive and drastic than any change we have yet observed in Peru. Indeed, the government's efforts to carry out a peaceful revolution without popular participation are being closely watched by politicians, military men and social scientists throughout Latin America. We hope to study this next stage of the development of Peru, but that story must await some future report.

29.
Miracle Seeds and Shattered Dreams in Java

Richard W. Franke

Culturally, politically, and economically, Java is Indonesia's most important island. It is also one of the world's richest agricultural regions. Streams, carrying an abundance of soil rich in nutrients, flow from the more than thirty active volcanoes along Java's central ridge. From time to time the volcanoes erupt, spewing out lava that eventually turns to fertile soil in the warm and humid valleys and on the coastal plains.

For hundreds of years Javanese farmers have ditched, terraced, plowed, planted, and weeded this marvelous confluence of natural elements to produce the rice on which their lives depend. So rich is the soil, so dependable the water supply, so excellent the climate, that for centuries the population has increased, and the land has supported not only farmers and their families but also princely dynasties, courts, traders, armies, and eventually even the industrial development of Java's recent colonial rulers, the Dutch.

But the outcome of the island's history has not been a happy one for Java's peasants. By the turn of the twentieth century, the strains of population growth and the expropriation of rice lands by Dutch sugar interests had begun to produce the paradox so common in the underdeveloped world today—increased profits for the wealthy few and a declining standard of living for the mass of producers. Throughout the depression of the 1930s, the Japanese occupation during World War II, the war for independence from the Dutch in the 1940s, and to the present day, this decline has continued. It has brought the people of Java to the verge of famine and created ever worsening conditions for the vast majority of the island's 80 million inhabitants.

With an annual per capita income of less than $80 in 1969, Javanese peasants are among the poorest in the world. Nutritional standards are declining at an alarming rate. In 1960 the average Javanese consumed 1,946 calories per day, 200 short of United Nations minimum recommendations. By 1967 consumption had dropped to 1,730 calories. Protein intake is declining as well. Minimum adult recommendations call for 55 grams of protein per person daily. In 1960 the Javanese consumed 38.2; by 1967 this had fallen to an average of 33.4, meaning that millions of the poorest farmers and laborers subsist at even lower levels.

In Javanese villages and in the sprawling urban slums of the island's largest cities, the results of this undernourishment are obvious even to the casual observer. Children stare dully, unable to focus properly. Many persons have reddish hair and distended bellies, both signs of various stages of malnutrition. High rates of influenza, dysentery, tuberculosis, and more recently, outbreaks of cholera constantly plague a population physically too weak to resist disease. Cuts and burns heal with exasperating slowness, adding to the risk of infection. Even the body size of Javanese has been declining over the past fifty years, a result of the worsening diet. Java, it would seem, has received far too little help from the wealthy nations of the world.

Yet this island has been the object of one of the most elaborate food production schemes of the past two decades. Between 1967 and 1972 the government of Indonesia and its Western allies spent well over $100 million, mostly on Java, in an attempt to produce nationally 15.4 million tons of rice—the amount needed for self-sufficiency—by 1973. By the 1972 harvest, however, the program was clearly failing; the 12.2 million tons produced in that year were at least 2.1 million short of the need. With international food supplies at their lowest levels in years, the Indonesian government was able to purchase only 1.5 million tons abroad, leaving a 600,000 ton deficit, which in turn increased local rice prices by 30 percent in just a few months.

To make matters worse, the government has almost ignored soybean production, which has undergone an absolute decline, causing protein intake to drop even below the disastrous levels of 1967. In the countryside of Java and in the urban slums, this will mean a further decline in nutrition for an already badly undernourished people.

How has this tragedy come about? Why have all these millions in expenditures failed to stem further impoverishment among the majority of Javanese? The answers lie in the blindness of development theorists to the social and political realities of Java and in the nature of aid programs from the wealthy nations—programs based on these faulty theories.

The program that was to have overcome the food shortage on Java is called the Green Revolution. The product of more than two decades of scientific research, the program is part of a broad and optimistic experiment occurring in several developing countries. Under the auspices of the Rockefeller Foundation, a seed research laboratory was established in Mexico City in 1944. Within several years, technicians had produced new varieties of corn and wheat with yield potentials far above those of local Mexican varieties.

By 1962 the Ford and Rockefeller Foundations united to establish the International Rice Research Institute at Los Banos, the Philippines, hoping the successes with wheat and corn could be duplicated with rice.

Sooner than expected, a genetic cross was achieved between a variety of rice from Indonesia and one from Taiwan. The result was a strain, IR-8, capable of doubling the yields of most local Asian rices. So profitable did the germ plasm from the new seeds seem that experts eagerly fostered their dissemination across the fields of southern Asia. By 1968, India, Pakistan, Thailand, the Philippines, Taiwan, South Vietnam, and Indonesia had begun large-scale planting of IR-8 and associated varieties of "miracle seeds."

With such a technological boon in hand, agricultural development planners began to revise their outlook on the development process. They now began to view as simpler, and more strictly economic, problems they had once seen as the results of psychological barriers, set up by "traditional" peasants unaccustomed to the idea of innovation, and institutional barriers, such as the outmoded labor and tenancy arrangements. If the new seeds could offer tremendous production increases at the level of the family farm, then perhaps all that was necessary to achieve their acceptance was the assurance that individual planters would earn a high rate of profit.

Such a position is represented in the highly influential study by Chicago economist Theodore Schultz, *Transforming Traditional Agriculture*. In looking for ways to lower production costs to farmer-producers, thus increasing the profits from the farming enterprise, Schultz argues that if outside lending institutions can provide finances that will lower risk and if outside research and development organizations can pay for and even execute trials and experiments, then nothing should stand in the way of widespread acceptance of the new technology.

Economic planners were quick to take the cue from Schultz's proposals. During the 1960s, development programs and the discussions that surrounded them emphasized the construction of dams, irrigation works, harbors, markets, and roads. They advocated the provision of loans for fertilizer, pesticides, and above all, for new seeds.

With this new philosophy, the miracle of the Green Revolution should have been easily transmitted from the laboratory of the geneticist to become the major force for development in much of the impoverished world. Or so it seemed. The recent history of agricultural development programs on Java, however, reveals how poorly the theory and the seeds have fared.

Interest in agricultural development in Indonesia dates from the early 1950s. Reacting with a first flush of nationalism against the half-hearted agricultural extension system of the Dutch, the head of the national extension service proposed a way of intensifying contact between farmers and technicians. In each administrative unit, made up of about 15 villages, a five-acre farming plot was set aside where both farmers and technicians could experiment with different planting and growing techniques. Practical and imaginative in its conception, the program failed primarily for lack of government funds.

By 1959 planners had fashioned a new program. This experiment, known as the "paddy center," consisted of large areas of almost 2,500 acres each, served by a central facility for credit, fertilizer, seed distribution, and education. The program began to show signs of failure by 1962–63, chiefly because rice produced in these centers had to be sold to the government, and the government kept its price lower than the open market price. Farmers resented the loans, while planners felt that they were too easily available and were undermining the farmers' "sense of responsibility."

As the government continued to introduce new but ineffectual programs, some Javanese farmers took the initiative for change into their own hands. Under pressure from a growing movement of peasant and workers' associations, the government was forced to pass a series of land reform acts, beginning in 1960. Within months, however, the makeup of local land reform committees was so embroiled in politics that other kinds of agricultural programs were also likely to become engulfed. By 1964, tensions between landowners and the landless had become so great that violent confrontations were frequently reported from the countryside.

With the peasants becoming involved in politics, an elite group within Indonesia's upper-class university system made their own plans. In 1963 some idealistic students and teachers at the College of Agriculture of the University of Indonesia, noting that their history of service to farmers and food production was somewhat less than illustrious, came up with the idea of personally aiding the farmers. The students planned to go into the villages, live with the farmers, teach and learn from them, and take their experiences back to a following group of students who would do the same.

The first year of the program was a heady success. Starting out in an area not far from the university, twelve students lived in three villages, worked in the fields with the farmers, offered suggestions for improved cultivation techniques, listened to farmers' points of view, and interceded with local government and private institutions on the farmers' behalf as only elite students—and perhaps radical political organizations—would dare to do at the time. Per acre yields rose 50 percent over regular plots, from 1,984 to 2,866 pounds per acre (before processing), and this happened before the introduction of the miracle seeds from Los Banos.

With only their own ideas, enthusiasm, and dedication, Indonesian students and farmers were doing with locally bred improved seeds what experts and advisers from outside were later to claim required the services of aid organizations, private foundations, and multinational corporations.

By the next rainy season, enthusiastic administrators from the Department of Agriculture had taken over the program from the university. More than 400 senior students from nine different schools lived and worked with farmers in more than 200 villages, amounting to 27,000 acres of paddy land. Despite difficulties in supplying some villages on time and some decrease in talent and enthusiasm due to the program's rapid expansion, another kind of success was achieved.

Students won the confidence of farmers as the government had never done. The potential of their actions showed itself in one village where local officials had stolen fertilizer intended for the project. The students responded by sending a well-documented letter to the officials threatening that if the fertilizer was not made available to the farmers, copies of the letter would find their way to even higher officials. The fertilizer came.

As the program expanded, it did not just involve greater numbers of students and farmers and larger amounts of land. Peasant leagues and radical political movements were growing in east and central Java, and the new program to increase rice production became entangled in the web of Indonesian politics. What the students at Indonesia's top agricultural college were discovering in their first few seasons with the farmers, Indonesia's Communist party had begun to learn and teach years earlier.

In 1953 the party had called for its workers to live in the villages and study the social and economic conditions there, working at the same time to win the confidence of smallholders and farm laborers. The program's slogan was the "three togethers": eat together, live together, work together; and organize to help small farmers and farm laborers overcome their fear of action. By these methods the party hoped to surmount what it considered the major obstacle to Indonesia's economic development—social and political control by a powerful ruling group.

At the same time the party was giving the farmers technological advice. In addition to attacking the powerful bureaucracy as "feudal remnants" and "imperialist forces," radical leaders urged farmers to adopt the "five principles": plow deeply, plant closely, use more fertilizer, improve seedlings, and improve irrigation.

The Communist party and student activists came to regard technology and strong political organizations for the poor as joint necessities in any attempt to bring about a more efficient use of resources on Java, both natural and human. Unlike most Western theorists, they rejected a simplified view of technology alone as the means to greater food production.

Javanese politics gave them precious little time, however, to test their theory. In September, 1965, as 1,200 students were starting the program for the rainy season, the long-smoldering struggle between landowner and landless, between Moslem storekeeper-religious official and Javanese Buddhist-Hindu farmer, between the Indonesian army and the Communist party, finally broke out into the open and ripped apart the fragile coalition that Indonesia's first president, Dr. Sukarno, had vainly tried to patch together. The army won.

During much of the rainy season of 1965–66 Indonesian society was embroiled in a protracted slaughter of known or suspected Communists. On Java alone, between 200,000 and one million persons were killed and radical peasant and workers' organizations destroyed. Little was done that year to increase the production of food.

By the dry season of 1966, the slaughter had come to an end in most areas. Despite the enormous social dislocations, the government expanded the area planted in rice from 27,000 to 415,000 acres, and this occurred in the first dry season that had ever been made a target of the rice production increase idea.

Dry season planting, however, was not the only innovation. At the invitation of the new military regime, American and West European advisors, most of whom had been thrown out of the country in 1963–64, now returned in large numbers to help put together a new development effort in Indonesia. In June, 1967, the government contracted with CIBA (Chemical Industries of Basel, Switzerland) to have this giant multinational corporation provide the technical apparatus for an experimental project to increase rice production in a small area in south Sulawesi (Celebes), to the northeast of Java.

Although no evaluation of the project was made, contracting with Western corporations continued at a rapid pace. By the rainy season of 1969–70, the West German companies Hoechst and A.H.T., the Japanese Mitsubishi, and a new, unknown company called Coopa were also offering the new agricultural technology, which for the first time included the miracle seeds from Los Banos. Together these companies provided fertilizer, miracle seeds, pesticides, and management advice for 2,470,000 acres, more than 20 percent of the entire wet-rice land of Indonesia.

Even from the start this massive program ran into difficulties. The new pesticides, untried on Indonesian fields, killed not only the harmful rice stem borer and various grasshoppers, as they were intended to do, but also the fish in the irrigation canals, an important source of protein in the peasant diet. One critic of the program asserted privately that one of the German companies was spraying onto the fields and into the canals the very chemical that had previously killed millions of fish in the Rhine, but the government never investigated this charge. Above and beyond all the stories and complaints, one fact was evident: farmers were not repaying the loans they had been granted.

Complaints continued. Students reported that in many areas the packages of fertilizers, seeds, and pesticides were not arriving. Then in the latter part of 1969, just about the middle of the 1969-70 planting season, the nature of Coopa, the mysterious corporation, became clear. Reporters for *Indonesia Raya*, a major muckracking newspaper in Jakarta, discovered a company letter dated in Vaduz, Liechtenstein, on the same day as the day of its arrival in Indonesia. Company officials had claimed registration was in Italy, but this was only part of the problem for, as the paper reasoned, "even the most modern airplane in the world cannot carry a letter from Liechtenstein to Indonesia in less than one day." When further evidence came in, the only question remaining was which generals secretly owned the company? At a cost of more than 150 million rupiahs (equal to $400,000 at the time), Coopa failed to deliver the technology for which it has contracted, and when evidence began to link the company's operations with members of President Sukarno's personal staff, the President announced that the entire affair would be handled out of court. The development planners' idyllic rate of profit seemed to have become highly elusive.

Scandal ridden as it was, the total program of multinational corporation agriculture rolled on into the dry season of 1970 before the real reaction came. Continuing reports of unsatisfactory harvests were added to stories of inefficiency and corruption. Even in the best agricultural areas, harvests had fallen off from 2½ tons per acre in 1965 to 2 tons per acre in 1968-69; in many regions crops were almost entirely lost because pesticides and fertilizers never arrived. Some government offices reported harvests of as little as from 220 to 882 pounds per acres, and a major famine occurred on the north coast of Java, involving 100,000 persons.

Various international lending institutions, including foreign embassies, commissioned private studies of the program, and all agreed that no matter how perfect it looked on paper, something was not working. That that "something" was intimately related to the destruction of peasant and student political power and the rise of a bureaucratic military state was apparently outside the realm of development theory. The example of the students who once forced the government to deliver fertilizer was lost in the midst of theories that saw political action from below as insignificant, perhaps even threatening, in comparison to the power of technology.

Since the program was failing, something new had to be tried. By the rainy season of 1970–71, American and Indonesian planners launched a new program, incorporating many features of the pre-1965 experiments. First, interest rates on farmer loans were reduced from 3 to 1 percent. Secondly, the program was not packaged: a farmer could choose his own fertilizer and pesticide dosages without endangering his chance of getting seeds or a preharvest cost-of-living loan. Aerial spraying of pesticides, a major source of farmer opposition to the foreign companies program, was discontinued altogether. Finally, to insure that the rate of profit would not be disturbed by price instability, the United States provided surplus rice that could be alternately injected into, or withdrawn from, regional markets. Farmers, it was hoped, would finally begin to see a profit from their harvests. The new plan, however, was doomed to failure by factors at the village level.

Like the national society of which they are a part, Javanese villages are highly stratified, with access to production resources distributed most unequally among different groups. A village along the north coastal plain of central Java illustrates this problem well. Excellent soil, good irrigation, nearby transportation, milling facilities, markets, and a long history of farmer acquaintance with new technology through their experience with the sugar factories should have made this a perfect place for a Green Revolution success story. Most farmers, however, cultivate plots of less than one acre, too small to support their families. They are forced, therefore, to supplement their farming with outside jobs. Since not enough jobs are available, many of the farming households ought to go bankrupt, but they do not. In the village a group of large landowners, government officers, and town employees command capital for the small farmers. The capital takes the form of loans against the future labor of poor farmers, a form of debt-bondage in which the farmers must give up their option for outside jobs and be permanently on call to their patrons.

The mechanism is simple. During the preharvest period, smallholder families may run out of cash or food. If unable to find work outside the village agricultural economy, they are forced to attach themselves to a wealthy family by asking for a loan. Since they have nothing to offer in repayment—their next harvest will be no more effective in bringing them even a minimum of subsistence (much less a surplus) than was the last—they become permanently indebted, accepting a 30 to 50 percent cut under the market wage for farm labor and giving up the opportunity for future labor arrangements outside the village.

In such a situation, miracle seeds might seem highly beneficial. In addition to improving everyone's production of food, raising the standard of living, releasing the central government from its dependence on food imports, and lowering food prices, the productivity increases of from 50 to

100 percent on local farming plots of smallholders might eventually offer them the opportunity to reassert their independence from the lenders. That, however, is just the problem.

The wealthier families have clearly perceived the danger of too much technical progress of this sort, and during the rainy season of 1970–71 and the dry season of 1971, they used various means of preventing the smallholders from gaining access to the loans or to the technology. In some cases meetings to publicize government loans were never called, but notice of bank loans was passed along lines of kinship and neighborhood, thus kept within the circles of the village elite. In some cases subtle hints were delivered to small farmers; not much is needed to convince a family on the brink of starvation that they are better off with the security of the wealthy patron than striking out on their own even if the chances of success seem to be high. Failure to a family farm is not quite like bankruptcy for a modern business; there are no courts to handle starvation proceedings.

By the end of the dry season in September, 1971, the new technology was being utilized only on about 40 percent of the available paddy land, representing only 20 percent of the 151 households in the village. Poor families were totally absent from the list of participants. For them the promise of economic development meant only an increase in the wealth and lending potential of their patrons, and an opportunity for more of their class compatriots to fall into permanent debt and servitude.

In other parts of Java, the relationship between the social classes has deteriorated beyond the increased debt-labor bondage. In south-central Java, wealthy households are using the increased productivity of their fields to actually buy up paddy land from poorer families, driving the latter into the already jobless urban areas. In west Java, a region where landholding differences are even more extreme, some wealthy farmers have even begun buying Japanese-made rice-field tractors and home milling facilities, thus pushing an even greater number of landless and smallholding households out of the remnants of the rural labor market. The very possibility of technological success is creating a human disaster. For the poor, the Green Revolution in Java offers only the choice between servitude and homelessness.

What will the development theorists say about all this? Their answer lies in their actions: the programs continue as before with no substantial changes. The technology advocates, the rate-of-profit theorists, the military dictators, and the large landowners are attempting to produce enough food for the people of Java. They are failing. Their optimistic plans and programs have created only increased human suffering and promise more of the same. Perhaps solutions will come, not from the development experts, but from the small farmers and landless laborers of Java.

30.
On Becoming *Bwana* in Kenya
Donald Rothchild

> At present, in Kenya, Europeans are masters and Africans servants. The vast majority of Europeans in Africa believe that relationship to be an integral part of the natural order of human society. They not only believe that but feel passionately about it as no one in this country does about any political topic.
>
> Norman Leys, 1931

> But those who still want to succumb to that decadent Bwana Mkubwa mentality can pack up and go. The ships are always ready.
>
> President Jomo Kenyatta, 1969

For the African nationalist, the struggle for racial equality was inseparable from the conflict over political and economic independence. The European or Asian seeking special privileges in the post-*uhuru* (freedom) period based on his racial identity rather than his contribution to nation-building was warned that his presence in the country was not determined solely by his contribution to the economy. Those non-Africans exuding a *bwana mkubwa* (big boss) complex were regarded as dispensable. In this case, symbolic rewards were given a higher priority than material rewards, reflecting deep African feelings on this sensitive issue.

A Structure of Privilege

European privilege in Kenya followed naturally from the British government's decision to use white settlers for developmental purposes. These immigrants could press the administration for concessions on land, labor, taxes, education, segregation and whatever else they desired.

Vulnerability as well as sympathy for settler claims were apparent in Commissioner Sir Charles Eliot's remarks at the turn of the century to the effect that "you cannot invite people to dinner and then lock the dining-room door."

As a consequence of settler demands, a structure of privilege emerged during colonial times which was largely coextensive with racial identity. There were exceptions, of course—poor Europeans, a number of less prosperous and even pauperized Asians and, especially in the terminal stages of colonialism, an emerging class of privileged Africans. However, the dominant Europeans achieved a favored status in most spheres of activity, leaving an indispensable middle sector for Asian clerks, entrepreneurs, artisans and technicians—the adjuncts of the imperialist structure. Albert Memmi's picture of the contrasting privileges of the colonizers and the colonized applies aptly to Kenya. He writes that

> every act of the colonizer's daily life places him in a relationship with the colonized, and with each act his fundamental advantage is demonstrated. If he is in trouble with the law, the police and even justice will be more lenient toward him. If he needs assistance from the government, it will not be difficult; red tape will be cut; a window will be reserved for him where there is a shorter line so he will have a shorter wait.

On such issues as fingerprinting, trial by jury, residence in the fertile highlands and the franchise, the European community took pains to secure special rights for itself.

European dominance in the world of commerce and industry led to the establishment of an inequitable structure which survived the transfer of power. As recently as 1964 the colonial structure was still reflected in the statistics on the distribution of earnings. Whereas 99 percent of African male employees in private commerce and industry earned under £480 per annum and 78 percent of Asian males earned less than £720, the figures for European male employees were as follows: 6 percent earned up to £599; 19 percent, £600 to £1,199; 31 percent, £1,200 to £1,799; 23 percent, £1,800 to £2,399; and 21 percent, £2,400 and over. Approximately 170,000 Africans earned an annual wage bill in private industry and commerce of £21m.; by contrast some 28,999 Asians earned £15m., and 10,000 Europeans earned £15m. In addition to this advantage in wages, European (and Asian) employees also received favored treatment in recruitment, promotion, housing and leave policies.

The manner in which the European settlers secured a privileged position for themselves on land, labor and taxation matters further points up the spillover from political to economic hegemony. Official and unofficial European domination of the administrative and legislative organs of the territory guaranteed a sympathetic hearing for settler demands. This is not to say that conflicts between administrators or between civil servants and settlers were insignificant, but only that settlers received a more exhaustive, and, frequently, a more understanding hearing than Africans and Asians.

Soon after establishing control over the East Africa protectorate in 1895, British policy-makers began efforts to develop the territory through permanent settlement. In order to allure settlers, protectorate officials offered the possibility of owning or leasing large land holdings in the cool, "uninhabited" highlands. The Crown Lands Ordinance, 1902, authorized the commissioner to sell up to 1,000 acres to a single applicant on a 99-year-leasehold basis; larger concessions could be secured by approaching the Foreign Office and later the Colonial Office directly. Under the terms of the Crown Lands Ordinance, 1915, as subsequently issued, leaseholds could be granted on large holdings for a 999-year period; rental costs were set at low levels, and there were no longer to be any restrictions on accumulations or transfers of paid-up land—except with regard to sale to non-Europeans.

From this time until the East Africa Royal Commission 1953–1955 Report, official policy accorded the European community "a privileged position" in the highlands, allowing members of this group, and only members of this group, the right to acquire and occupy land in this area. The highlands had become the tribal reserve of the Europeans. To heighten inequalities further, the Europeans were allowed to acquire vast holdings. M.P.K. Sorrenson estimates that by the end of 1915, 4,500,000 acres in the highlands had been alienated to some 1,000 Europeans. The larger estates included the East Africa Syndicate, 320,000 acres; F.R. Lingham, E.S. and Mrs. Grogan, 132,862 acres; Lord and Lady Delamere, 115,627 acres; G. and R.B. Cole and Viscountess Cole, 72,850 acres, and so forth. But only a small part of this agricultural or pastoral land was placed under intensive cultivation. Out of a total occupied area of 4,420,573 in 1925, a mere 392,628 acres (9 percent) was estimated to have been put to full use.

The special position of the European settlers in acquiring the most arable land was buttressed by the administration's assurances on the accessibility of an adequate labor supply. In colonial societies such as Kenya, landed estates could operate only where low-cost labor was readily available. "It is no use 'opening up' for white plantations sparsely peopled regions, however fertile," Sir Frederick D. Lugard argued in 1926, "if there is no labor for their development." Since the government looked to white settlement as the means of development, it inevitably found itself left with no alternative but to frame a labor policy supportive of settler interests. To be sure, such a policy was explained in terms of African welfare. What this meant was that the government was to play an active role in shaping the relations between the African workers and the dominant white employers, organizing the economic relations in the territory in such a manner as to foster the privileged position of the European residents.

The structure of European settler privilege in colonial Kenya was also bolstered by a variety of direct and indirect subsidies. A number of observers criticized the apparent tendency to run railway branch lines and roads through European-settled areas rather than through the densely populated reserves. Moreover the tariff and taxation systems heavily favored European interests. On the surface, such a conclusion would seem to be controverted by the colonial administration's breakdown of taxes paid by the racial communities. Sir Edward Grigg noted in 1926 that Kenya Europeans contributed £444,789, or £35 10 shs. per person; Goans (Indians from formerly Portuguese Goa) £53,423, or £20 17 shs. per person; Indians £165,813, or £6 4 shs. per person; and Africans £999,849, or 7 shs. 3d. per person. But the statistics on Europeans seem inflated by the inclusion of nontax revenues and payments for services rendered.

In addition, a closer examination of the tax structure reveals a disproportionate African contribution to the general welfare. Customs duties had a dual function: providing a substantial proportion of territorial revenues as well as giving protection to European wheat growers and millers. The burden of the 30 percent wheat duty of 1922 fell heavily upon the African consumer. And import duties were noticeably uneven in their effect. They were shouldered by middle-class Europeans and Asians, and, over time, by an increasing number of Africans, not by the well-to-do European farming class. It was only when European and Asian customs payments fell 42 percent and 27 percent respectively in the 1926–1931 period, that a reassessment of the tax structure became inevitable—but even then the dominant community was long able to prevent the introduction of an income tax.

The other major source of territorial revenue, the hut and poll tax, fell directly upon the shoulders of the African community. The African contribution of direct taxes in 1931 far outweighed those of all other communities. From the African standpoint these burdens were considered to be excessive in nature, in part because the 12-shs. charge was a significant proportion of earned income and in part because an owner of multiple huts was liable for an additional tax on each of his dwellings.

Finally, the colony's educational policy was supportive of an edifice of European political, economic and social advantage. Education became a primary means of maintaining a highly differentiated structure, developing propensities which enabled the dominant community to compete advantageously for positions of importance. In European eyes, the important consideration was to secure full control over the financing of schools so that members of their community could regulate standards as they felt necessary. Thus education was to remain racially compartmentalized, with vastly greater sums being spent to educate European than non-European children.

Underlying this dual approach was an awareness of the dangers of equal opportunity. The structure of European privilege rested upon this community's continued dominance of skills and capital. Since equal educational opportunity would raise doubts about the European's future indispensability, it was opposed largely on the grounds of African unsuitability for formal study. The District Commissioner of South Nyeri outlined his fears of educational programs intended to train African clerks:

> Consolidation should be ... our keynote for the next few years, lest we fall into the error of forcing progress beyond the limits to which the native mind is capable. Already there are signs that some are bewildered by the great changes which have taken place. The older men cannot understand them and are naturally a little suspicious, the younger generation are apt [to] abuse the freedom and privileges which are being extended to them.

From European Privilege to Arrogance

It is only a short step from privilege to arrogance. A transference quickly occurred from the real world of European political, economic and social dominance to the fantasy world of egoism and automatic high status.

There is abundant evidence of the non-African's sense of his own superiority. The European did not hesitate to proclaim his inherent right to prevail. While working to instill western values and norms, he tended at the same time to be disdainful of the acculturated African—the very person who reached out to acquire the techniques of European civilization. In 1936, for example, one district officer wrote as follows about the Kikuyu Independent Schools Association:

> In a dream, caused by a sort of mental indigestion and an exaggerated sense of tribal importance, these people can see themselves on at least the same footing as Europeans in the course of the next generation. Their astonishing self-assurance leads them to believe that they are fully competent to accomplish all this by "paddling their own canoe." In their ignorant impatience they completely overlook the many important things, not easily or quickly acquired, which are so necessary for the conversion of the primitive individual into a competent citizen of a civilized state .... It is well known that Africans are incapable as yet of maintaining by their unified efforts any sort of large movement organized on European lines by themselves.

If the administrators spoke guardedly of their superiority and right to rule, the settlers openly proclaimed their innate qualifications. European superiority was regarded as "a natural fact, made daily and hourly obvious, and not a piece of arrogant snobbery." The settlers repeatedly based their claims to hegemony upon their connection with an allegedly superior civilization. In an opening address to the Electors Union in 1949, for example, a European spokesmen asserted as follows:

> We as the more fortunate members of this country have had the good fortune to spring from a race which has traditions of justice and government by law and we, therefore, have a particular responsibility in this country to the other races. We have assumed and quite rightly, the role of leadership in this country. We have been largely instrumental in the development of the country and in establishing a sound economy.

But a right to leadership which rests on cultural superiority is vulnerable to challenge from those educated in the ways of the same European civilization. They feared that education would lead to dissatisfaction—even agitation. Hence white racial arrogance sometimes found expression in resistance to social modernization for Africans. This resistance went contrary to the oft pronounced justification of the Europeans as the "trustees" who would lead the Africans to the treasures of western civilization. In some instances they acted like museum keepers who wished to have time stand still for the African cultures.

At the same time many European residents showed antipathy toward the educated African, they also viewed the traditional African with less than full admiration. Africans were oftentimes described as lazy, lacking in mechanical aptitude, untruthful, gullible, smelly and "low in the scale of civilization." As summarized by a not atypical administrative officer, "... the African in the mass is still a primitive creature"; his salvation lies "in Christianity and the better ideals of his own original ethical code."

Yet the two themes of distrust for the educated and disdain for the uneducated are not without a common basis. The Europeans, desirous of continued status enhancement, seemed anxious to exclude the indigenous inhabitants from a crucial role in the affairs of their land. They sought to assure European hegemony by perpetuating a myth of African inferiority. Moreover, a racially stratified society was flattering to the self-esteem of the dominant community—provided that the European remained on the top. The Europeans' self-confidence was enhanced by the Africans' lack of acquaintance with the tools and techniques of western civilization.

Racial superiority, then, involved a world of illusion where status attached automatically to those most closely associated with European civilization. This automatic status gave the European emigrant a psychological uplift denied him in the increasingly egalitarian country of his birth. Regardless of class or national origin, the European gained strength from his relationship with the apparently submissive African.

This search for a world of unequals was pronounced among the backward-looking members of the gentry who looked upon Kenya as an escape from the onrushing democratic, rational and industrial tendencies of modern-day European life. From the outset it was official policy to encourage "English gentlemen of position and money to interest themselves in the Protectorate," and, following Lord Delamere's example, a number of retired military officers and persons associated with the British aristocracy did come to settle in the highlands. They brought the pastimes of the British upper classes—horse-racing, cricket, fox-hunting, private clubs—even wife swapping—to the Kenya frontier. They also brought parliament, university and bureaucracy. As a consequence of all this, European life in Kenya assumed an aristocratic tone. But if the tone was aristocratic, the social structure was, in reality, largely middle and lower class. The great majority of settlers were not the rich and highborn members of Lord Delamere's "gin palace" set but of much more ordinary origins.

More significant than the presence of a gentry class among the settlers was the general demand on the part of Europeans for deference. In Kenya, deference was the right of an elite race, not merely an elite aristocratic class. In this sense, all white men in the tropics were aristocrats, entitled to respect simply as a consequence of their racial identity. As long as the black man remained obedient, trusting and subservient ("knew his place"), he was likely to be treated in a patronizing manner. Should he step out of line and threaten the racially stratified order by securing a formal education or middle-level employment, he was regarded with considerable scorn and hostility. When working for the Nairobi City Council in 1951 as a sanitary inspector, the future parliamentary minister Tom Mboya was described to a superior as cheeky and disrespectful for volunteering to test a European woman's bottle of milk.

As long as the African majority accepted unequal status, the dominant minority adopted a paternalistic approach to regulating the affairs of the territory. Officials and non-officials both insisted on retaining unchallenged political and administrative authority in their own hands, and they dismissed any Asian or African claims to meaningful participation in the policy-making process. Yet within this white-dominance structure, an air of benevolent sentiment could be discerned. Europeans spoke of their role as one of "leading the African towards a better life" (i.e., a western way of life). Africans were gradually assimilated to some extent into the cultural mores and practices of the dominant element. Where the indigenous populations resisted such assimilationist advances (for example, in the female circumcision controversy), the Europeans responded with missionary fervor to break Kikuyu resistance. A similar settler reaction emerged when the "Mau Mau" movement began to fight against these encroachments on indigenous culture. "The rebels simply do not *want* western institutions and western methods," bemoaned one observer. "Kenyatta ... for all his sophistication and western training, wanted to turn his back on imported ideas—back to the tribe, the ancestral spirits, to the Gods of the Kikuyu."

To most Europeans, the lifting of the Africans to "civilized standards" was a task for centuries to come. In Kenya, they had "found a population of various tribes, who had existed for aeons of time ... in a state of primitive and unchanging savagery." It was their mission to rectify this situation— slowly and along lines that furthered their own interests as residents on the East African scene. From the African standpoint, this amounted to psychological and economic exploitation at one and the same time, and they struck back against such racial arrogance first during the early nationalist movements and later as they gained political power.

Asian Arrogance

Asian arrogance differed from its European counterpart in both kind and degree. Although a number of Asians did secure great wealth over the years, the average Asian employee earned considerably less than most European employees in the territory. Unable to gain access to important political and administrative positions, the Asians could not participate in a meaningful way in the policymaking functions of colonial Kenya. The result of this was a generally disadvantageous position. A dominant white minority discriminated against them in such areas as urban residence, political representation, immigration, education, farm land rights, the administration of justice, commercial opportunities and many others.

Kenya's Asian leaders, recognizing that their main disadvantages stemmed from their inability to influence the administrative and policy-forming process, pressed colonial authorities to allow for increased political participation on the part of spokesmen for this community. The protracted battle over the extent of Indian participation in the legislative and executive councils as well as over the principle of the common voting roll is indicative of their struggle to gain access to the political center. That the Europeans were able to bring enough influence to bear to rebuff these initiatives demonstrates the nature of their hegemony over the general structure of Kenya life during colonial times.

But even though the Asians lacked political, economic and social opportunities in certain spheres of activity, it does not follow that deprivation ensured feelings of solidarity with the members of the host community. In fact, the Asians exhibited a special kind of racial-cultural arrogance of their own. Eminently proud of their cultural and racial backgrounds, they stood aloof from the African masses and came to accept a middle place for themselves within Kenya's white-dominance system.

After commenting that "the Asians had come to believe in the myth of white superiority," Yash P. Ghai notes that,

> The pyramidical racial structure was sometimes taken too much for granted; it was proper and inevitable that in the order of things, the white men should be at the helm. Rather as corollary of this attitude, and, partly as a rationalisation of the better economic, social and political status of the Asians compared with that of the Africans, the Asians began to believe that the Africans were inferior to themselves. If the African got less wages than the Asian, if he had to live with the whole family in one small room—"the boys" quarters—if he had to work miles or lift heavy weights, the Asian conscience was untroubled because the African was different, he was inferior; he was used to these things; he did not want and certainly would not know what to do with modern conveniences and gadgets.

Although it would be wrong to equate the Asians' cultural exclusivity with racial arrogance, feelings of superiority and disdain toward Africans did become manifest among them from time to time. This exaggerated conviction of their own importance frequently surfaced in commercial relations where the middle-class Asians all too often took advantage of their African customers by overpricing, mislabeling, selling inferior goods, misweighting and so forth. The former Deputy Speaker, Dr. F.R.S. de Souza, reports that when he complained to a shopkeeper over getting kerosene which consisted of half kerosene and half water, the businessman replied: "why didn't you tell me it was for you?"

My 1967 survey of Asian businessmen seemed to indicate that they felt quite confident of being able to turn in a better performance under equal circumstances than their counterparts in the other racial communities. In part, this high self-esteem can be explained by the Asians' long record of success in the face of various discriminatory practices. The Asian businessman viewed his European competitor as having secured a favored status because of his access to finance and his connections with overseas agencies. A significant number of respondents stressed the advantage European businessmen possessed as a consequence of their "monopoly" of overseas accounts. This feeling doubtlessly reflected widespread Asian feelings about European domination of the import trade and their exclusive control over a number of local agencies.

Contrariwise, the Asian businessman tended to be disdainful of his African competitor. In speaking of Africans very few of these respondents mentioned such praiseworthy characteristics as diligence, integrity, intelligence or ability. Instead they emphasized the important role of governmental support in facilitating the emergence of an African business class:

> They get all local agencies. They can [secure] some support from other Africans. Government gives first preference to them.

If the Europeans' privileged status was essentially a holdover from the white-dominance system of colonial times and if the Africans' newly emerging position in the business world was primarily the result of governmental efforts, what advantages did the Asians see themselves as having? They answered that their good fortune lay largely in their own industriousness and business acumen.

The Asian respondent made no mention of government encouragement during colonial or postcolonial times. Instead most of his success was attributed to individual or communal achievement. For him the Asian was clearly a superior competitor. Europeans "monopolized the consumer goods"; Africans were accorded preferential treatment by the government. Supremely confident of his ability, the typical Asian businessman seemed to enhance his self-esteem by deriding his non-Asian competitors. Such attitudes smacked of the colonial mentality and naturally grated on African sensibilities.

African Resentment

Kenya nationalists were never free of constant reminders of non-African privilege. Marked differences in such areas as housing, transportation, judicial patterns, employment opportunities, education, land acquisition, representation and voting rights, all formed a structure of life which even after independence assured maximum opportunities to the expatriate noncitizen rather than the African citizen. Although Africans were fully aware of the Europeans' and Asians' contribution of skill and capital, they questioned the indispensability of some of the expatriates. Moreover, they bristled angrily when the continuation of privilege led to disrespect or to expressions of racial arrogance.

In 1967, the Africans surveyed by this author were quite explicit about Europeans' and Asians' sense of their own superiority—83 percent of the Africans replied that Europeans as a whole think they are better than Africans; and 89 percent of the Africans said that Asians in Kenya felt superior to them.

Those most prone to suspect Europeans and Asians of racial arrogance are the older, less educated, female Luhyas and Luos—those who generally remained at the greatest distance from European and Asian peoples and life-styles. By contrast, the younger, better educated, Kikuyu and Embu/Meru male respondents tended to be more optimistic about the possibility of interracial cooperation.

The African view of the non-Africans' sense of superiority distinguished, somewhat unconsciously, between missionary arrogance and an isolationist arrogance. In a missionary sense, the guests, disdainful of African values and practices, sought to transform the African cultural heritage in their own likeness. In an isolationist sense, they sought to withdraw themselves from the surrounding environment. This effort to maintain social distance, the reverse side of the same coin of arrogance, was deeply resented by Africans. When describing the difficulties of integrating the elite Nairobi School, one observer presented the following description of intergroup relations:

> The students of African origin are treated with contempt and arrogance by *some* of their Asian and European opposite numbers, and even the teachers.
>
> The Asian students have not overcome their instinct of communal exclusiveness. The European students have yet to be convinced that in independent Kenya their old excessive privileges and their unearned pre-eminence of that glorious imperialist past are today out of question.
>
> As for the Africans it is only the few snobs and upstarts who have access to the 'polite white community' provided they are ready to bow compliantly as helpless underlings to the dominance of their self-assertive "petty-masters," and do so with prompt docility.

Although resentment of privilege is virtually universal, it intensifies noticeably when privilege is identified with racial exclusiveness. Africans came into close contact with the luxuries of western society soon after Europeans settled in Kenya. They observed what seemed an alluring world of opulence but were barred from meaningful participation in this new way of life. Not surprisingly, such proximity to affluence often bred envy. Africans envied the large cars and fancy bicycles used by non-Africans. They spoke bitterly of enormous European land holdings left largely uncultivated "while thousands of Africans were starving of hunger in their own country."

But the reaction to privilege was by no means limited to envy alone. In the period prior to independence, Africans smarted over their lack of employment and promotion possibilities, their humiliating treatment on the job, their exclusion from the highlands, the restrictions on their right to raise such cash crops as coffee, their lack of participation in the policymaking process and their comparatively heavy tax burden. Many of their grievances over employment and business opportunities carried over in postcolonial times. Accusing safari lodge owners of discriminating against tour drivers and other employees, for example, J. M. Kariuki, an Assistant Minister for Tourism and Wildlife, spoke of these businessmen as "radicals of 20th century slavery and bearing a colonial attitude towards Africans."

Other expressions of resentment over African working conditions, promotion opportunities, discrimination in housing and so forth are commonplace. Clearly much of the strength behind the African nationalist demand for corrective equity lay in a desire to compensate for the systematic discriminations of the past. Thus one of the author's African survey respondents, describing Asians and Europeans as "[blood] suckers or parasites," answered that these people, even if citizens, should not be given equal chances with Africans because "they've exploited us enough and this is now our chance." Others emphasized the need to give first chances to Africans in order to overcome the imbalances of opportunity inherited from the past.

The African community's continuing bitterness even after independence over alleged racial arrogance on the part of out-group members is pointed up by three specific sources of irritation: the refusal to share essential skills, the failure of non-Africans to attend public rallies, and the persistence of private social clubs. Africans have long suspected Asians, and to a lesser extent Europeans, of safeguarding their positions by keeping information about modern techniques and practices to themselves. There are numerous accounts of Africans assigned to tedious jobs which block off possible advancement because no new skills are imparted. Other reports note instances of Asian artisans speaking Hindi when African apprentices approach. Such suspicions show up dramatically in the author's survey of African attitudes—32 percent thought that Europeans dislike having Africans "learn anything that will help them to get good jobs," and 78 percent felt the same way about Asians. Surprisingly, the younger, better educated, higher income males were the least suspicious of European intentions in terms of African access to knowledge. Uneasiness over the willingness of non-Africans to share their skills persists to the present time, particularly regarding Asians holding down lower and middle-level jobs. In this sense, anti-Asian feeling may be more a reflection of class than ethnic considerations; the Europeans, who remain momentarily beyond competition, are less suspect than the great body of Asians who are under severe pressures in the market place.

African leaders frequently expressed their displeasure over the non-Africans' failure to attend public rallies. They looked upon such nonattendance as an affront to the new African government, a manifestation of a lingering colonial mentality among Europeans and Asians, a sign of racial arrogance and disrespect. For the District Commissioner for Mombasa, Eliud Njenga, it was a discourtesy for Mombasa Asians not to turn up for a rally addressed by President Kenyatta.

> When your own spiritual leaders are coming there are big celebrations. You should all do as much, or more, when you are expecting the Head of the country where you eat and drink.

This statement was endorsed by Sammy Maina, KANU's Nairobi branch organizing secretary, who said in a press statement that "it is more than obvious that Asians hardly attend political rallies, leave alone welcoming the President at his country-wide tours."

African misgivings about the exclusiveness of private social clubs, particularly in postindependence times, are not without substance. Europeans regarded their clubs as sanctuaries, safe places where they could isolate themselves from Africa and Africans. The Africans were fully alert to the significance of the club's role in acting as a vortex of racial exclusivity. When independence came, they moved swiftly to alter the basis of club life in the country. Circular No. 2 of the Ministry of Home Affairs advised all clubs to change any constitutional provisions which might bar membership to persons on the grounds of race, color or creed. The only result was that some of the clubs yielded half-heartedly to this advice, admitting a small number of prominent Africans to their membership. African indignation over the continuance of such exclusive social centers remained evident after independence. The Kiambu Liquor Licensing Court, for example, refused to renew a club's liquor license on the grounds of racially discriminatory membership fees. Other practices suspected of being used to preserve the essentially European nature of these clubs were the need to be introduced by committee members, voting on membership by secret ballot, unavailability of membership forms and absent or uncooperative administrative personnel. Unlike the situation in neighboring Tanzania where the fashionable Dar es Salaam Club was taken over by the state in 1964, Kenya's social clubs stayed firmly in private hands after independence. But if the financial costs of such an arrangement were low, the cost in terms of African suspicion and anger was considerable.

New Dignity

In brief, then, Africans were psychologically hurt by what they perceived as evidences of the "conquerors' arrogance"— their sense of superiority, their determination to perpetuate their dominance and uniqueness, and their failure to identify with African goals and aspirations. The emotions arising from this psychological hurt, as Susan Wood perceptively notes, are "the most powerful single source of the impetus and direction of African nationalism." For Kenya Africans, *uhuru* symbolized much more than political and economic self-determination. It also symbolized the beginning of genuine interracial equality and the emergence for black people of the possibility of creative individuality in an African-ordered world. Africans would force all but the tenaciously prejudiced to regard them as men and no longer "as sykes and baboons." And this new dignity would apply, hopefully, to their customs as well as to their persons—a central point of conflict in colonial Kenya.

Africans responded in various ways to the psychological hurt of European and Asian arrogance. On the one hand, they accommodated themselves to the outsiders' power. When, at times, the "inferiorized group" did accept specious European claims to superiority, the result was devastating in terms of self-confidence and self-respect. In a period of transculturation and uncertain values, the indigenous culture was no longer able to fulfill its main task of "mak[ing] self-esteem possible." In order to overcome any remaining traces of the *bwana mkubwa* complex, President Kenyatta and others have urged a new African assertiveness. Advising the *wananchi* (common man) to reject abuse from arrogant non-Africans, he asserted that,

> you should know that you are the *bwana mkubwa* of this country. Many of you still have the colonial mentality, but from now on you must know that you are human beings like other people. Do not let anyone look down on you.

On the other hand, other Africans refused from the beginning to accommodate themselves to foreign power and reacted aggressively toward any European and Asian pretensions of superiority. Such rejection during colonial times took the forms of isolation or open protest and rebellion. The Kikuyu struggle on the land and female circumcision questions, culminating in the "Mau Mau" emergency, was indicative of this refusal to submit to a European-structured world.

With the advent of independence, African protest and rebellion gave way to African power. President Kenyatta told a Mombasa rally that his government had achieved greater development in six years than the colonial power had achieved in 60 years. In another sense, African power meant an insistence upon respect, and, if necessary, upon the use of punitive measures to deal with abusive and arrogant Europeans and Asians.

For the African majority, growth as self-respecting citizens required a certainty of their own intrinsic worth. The sin of arrogance lay in its assault upon self-esteem. No matter how many roads, hospitals or bridges the colonialists constructed, colonialism remained an aggression upon Africa so long as it depersonalized African peoples and robbed them of confidence in their abilities, in their values and in themselves as men and women. Independence was indispensable to African fulfillment, precisely because self-rule restored pride.

Naturally political independence was only a stage toward full emancipation. The European and Asian presence remained fully in view, raising doubts in African minds over the genuineness of their new freedom. Torn between conflicting desires for development and full Africanization, the

Kenya government moved pragmatically toward a balancing of these goals. But on one issue there could be no negotiation or compromise—any manifestations in an independent Kenya of non-African pretensions to superiority. African self-esteem, given an uplift by the successful independence drive, could not accept the violence of racial insult.

The attack on arrogance represented an increase of humanity for the guests as well as the hosts. It liberated them from old colonial attitudes, affording them an opportunity to look out upon the world around them in a freer and less structured manner. As they came to Africanize their perspectives on life, they gained a new compassion and understanding for those in their midst. They grew; they discovered a new identity. Such a broadening of vistas did surface with greater and greater frequency after the trauma of *uhuru* became accepted. One Asian wholesaler stated forthrightly that he felt his African employees were "as good as our own people." Such indications of confidence in African ability came most frequently from the employers who had worked closely with outsiders, those who had emerged from the isolation of racial life in pre-independence times. Decolonization therefore meant an expanded humanism for the non-African as well as the African—at least for those who remained in Kenya and willingly identified with African goals and aspirations.

Part XI
The Ethnic Factor

Although many of the cultures researched by anthropologists evolved independent of urban populations and high civilizations, past historic phases of isolation have been succeeded by our present centralized, competitive era of global communication. Put briefly, there are more people on the planet Earth than ever before, and they tend to bump into each other with greater frequency. The increase in urban populations and the post-World War II spread of nationalism have generated new processes for drawing social boundaries and defining group membership. But national identity alone has proved too general a category for identification. Instead, historical connections with specific subnational factions have surfaced as a significant part of public selfhood.

Of central importance in the quest for a consciously promoted public identity has been the revival of ethnicity. Taken from the Greek *ethnos*, referring to people of common descent, language, and history, today's ethnic groups can be distinguished by characteristics of race, religion, language, culture, or nationality, either singly or in combination. What is more important than the characteristics per se is the social significance they are given. In Rhodesia and South Africa, racial antagonisms and differences in language and culture divide whites and blacks. In Northern Ireland, not race nor language but religious affiliation sets Catholics at odds with Protestants. In these and many other countries, the conscious claim to ethnic identity as a political stance has dramatically affected the politics of national and local governments. In old and new nations, East and West, alliances based on ethnicity rather than political ideology represent a new approach to large-scale state organization.

In the United States, the success of Alex Haley's *Roots* in book and televised forms has focused attention on a phenomenon that has been gaining momentum for at least a dozen years. The "new ethnicity" of this decade has people of all ages exploring their geneologies and reclaiming the culture of immigrant ancestors. Probably no one would be more surprised than those same ancestors were they to witness the reinvestment of pride in "old country" customs. After arriving in this country, most of our immigrant forebears were under great pressures to shed any aspects of behavior that set them apart as foreigners in a nation based on a single, dominant English heritage. The prejudices against Micks, Wops, Kikes, Krauts, and Polacks were felt where it hurt most, in hiring and promotions; and the threat of economic marginality added impetus to the process of cultural assimilation. In the two World Wars, first and second generation Americans, English-speaking and educated enough to earn wages, proved how loyal they were by serving in the armed forces; ethnic identities were submerged in patriotic fervor and in the belief that America was the land of opportunity, which, for many, it has been.

How does it happen now that the popular mind has turned toward ethnicity and away from a broader identification with the American character? To phrase the question in another way, we can ask, "What are the foundations of national patriotism?" Writing in the first decade of this century, William Graham Sumner forthrightly stated the functional basis of patriotic feeling:

> When the great modern states took form and assumed control of societal interests, group sentiment was produced in connection with those states. Men responded willingly to a demand for support and help from an institution which could and did serve interests. The state drew to itself the loyalty which had been given to men (lords), and it became the object of that group vanity and antagonism which had been ethnocentric. For the modern man patriotism has become one of first of duties and one of the noblest of sentiments. It is what he owes to the state for what the state does for him, and the state is, for the modern man, a cluster of civic institutions from which he draws security and conditions of welfare.

That Americans feel a loss of confidence in the nation's capacity to guarantee their security and social welfare is one explanation of the "new ethnicity." Cycles of economic depression and unceasing inflation have weakened confidence in national economic policy. In addition, the troubled ending of the Vietnam War and the entire Watergate interlude severely undermined faith in American political organization. It is no wonder, then, that the ethnic revival in the United States has its stronghold among lower-class sectors that are highly vulnerable to economic slowdowns, overrecruited in times of national war, and otherwise underrepresented in national politics. For many people, the reclaiming of a positive ethnic identity is both a retreat from the unpromising larger realities of government, and a denial of demeaning and unsavory ethnic stereotypes.

In the public promotion of ethnicity, there is more often than not some form of political strategy. Writing in war-torn Britain some 40 years ago, novelist E. M. Forster commented that the comforts of selecting a genealogy are considerable, i.e., forebears of doubtful racial or social origins can be stuffed into the closet while dead relations of proper background are proudly put on display. The organized ethnic group, like the individual, composes a positivistic history linking purity of ancestry to the significant accomplishments of a pantheon of heroes. Thus, ethnic history can be used to justify the present-day aims of the group and validate its claims for public support.

Though governments are not ultimate guarantees against economic depression or political corruption, the weight of Western national, state, and municipal bureaucracies has over the last several decades shifted more and more to human services and provisions for disadvantaged groups. In public rituals—the St. Patrick's or Columbus Day parade, the Lithuanian or German neighborhood fair, the dedication of a war memorial to Private Grenowski—ethnic organizations vie with each other for the attention of elected politicians and administrators. As several well-known political figures have learned to their regret, there is no greater faux pas than the ethnic slur. At the same time, ethnicity can operate as a legitimate claim for political attention, and it may also reflect the loss of real opportunities for power in politics and the economy, a placebo the working class is encouraged to take.

The nature of competition between ethnic groups takes its form from the history of population settlement and the development of social hierarchies. In this country, the phrase "new ethnicity" cannot be divorced from the history of all sorts of immigration, including the importation of African slaves, and from the national stratification of race and class that results in rivalries between lower-class urban blacks and their white, European-descended neighbors. The political organization of today's ethnic groups comes right on the heels of government response to the black civil rights movement. In attempts to secure funds for job programs, housing, and education, local-level antagonisms cannot help but reflect racial divisions and the common deprivation of lower-class communities, white and black and other "colors."

To contrast our own organization with that of our North American neighbors, the national development of Canada has produced an entirely different set of ethnic relations. Eastern Canada was originally settled in the seventeenth century by French peasant farmers governed by a small group of land-owners. It was only at the start of the nineteenth century that

English rule was finally imposed on the politically subject but relatively numerous French population. Migration from the British Isles gradually increased the proportion of English-speaking settlers but Western Canada also proved attractive to non-English-speaking migrants from continental Europe—Germans, Scandinavians, Russians, and others—who established ethnic communities that have kept much of their cultural heritage intact. The result is what sociologist John Porter has aptly described as the "vertical mosaic," a country of ethnic plurality controlled by an English political elite.

The flow of migrant people over national borders still has an effect on national political organization when aliens establish themselves as permanent residents. As sources of cheap labor, numerous enclaves of Pakistanis and East Indians have settled in Great Britain; Algerians and Tunisians have in a parallel fashion migrated to France. A less stable population of Spanish and Italian workers journey to northern European countries to earn money for an eventual retirement in their native villages. These and other international migrants become what Nancy Gonzalez has called "neoteric societies," integrated into the national economy at the lowest occupational levels but still socially and politically marginal.

In Charles Moskos' autobiographical account, "Growing Up Greek American," we have a case of another kind of integration, the happy coincidence of traditional customs with the norms of the dominant society. As social scientist playing informant, Moskos gives his account of what many first generation Americans have experienced: the support network of the traditional group, the struggle of migrants to establish a measure of economic security, and the gradual Americanization of the younger generation.

In other instances, an ethnic population can be economically successful but maintain itself socially and politically aloof from the dominant society. This happens most frequently when a marginal group begins to monopolize trade and commercial finance. Chinese groups in Southeast Asia and both the Chinese and East Indians in East Africa and the Caribbean have carved out economic niches in the different nations in which they live, often without claiming the political representation that reflects their numbers or wealth. This type of marginality makes for a different kind of vulnerability. The destruction of Jews in Nazi camps and the recent deportation of Asians from Uganda are two of many historical cases in which the scapegoat role has been attached to an "alien" population. Gypsies, who were also a target of Nazi genocide, are perhaps the oldest example of the marginal ethnic group that knows no national sentiment as powerful as its own tribal customs. As Anne Sutherland's article on Gypsies in America vividly describes, their strategy over many generations and in passage through many countries has been to work at the economic fringes of the larger society and defensively resist assimilation.

Among the newer, less developed nations of the world, the problem is still one of integration—how to make one nation indivisible. What economic and political decisions do national leaders make to encourage or enforce the unity of diverse ethnic minorities and to keep them from provoking civil war? Will urbanization prove to be a unifying force? Will aggression from neighboring states provide a catalyst for national unity? On the subject of ethnicity, Abdul Said and Luiz Simmons argue that the decline of the symbols and ideology of the nation-state is more than a passing phenomenon, that for better or worse, ethnicity will remain a divisive element.

Positive and negative reactions to ethnic-based activities also have to be assessed. As the West passes through a phase of national devolution and decentralization, we tend to equate ethnic politics with a return to more humane forms of problem-solving. It is not yet certain that in the United States all kinds of interest groups can express themselves politically without fear of reprisal—ethnics, women's liberationists, "Right-to-Lifers," homosexuals. There are sufficient reports from around the world to remind us that the modern state has the power of organization and technology to persecute and destroy whole populations that appear threatening.

Information that filters out of Chile, Uganda, Indonesia, Brazil, and other nations indicates that diversity is not, in fact, tolerated. Even when human rights are the letter of the law, the ambitions of those in office can override the notion of civil liberty. Even without these contemporary reminders, we can consider our own genocidal wars against southern and Plains Indians or the diabolical persecutions that took place in Nazi Germany and Stalinist Russia in order to realize with what seeming rationality the interests of the nation can be put before those of humanity.

In the field of world politics, the anthropologist cannot help but be aware of the role of ethnic subgroups. The discipline itself has long been involved with just those marginal and "alien" groups that are most likely found in the lowest political order. By past and present research, we have tended to put our confidence in the ethnic community that manages its internal affairs and competes on an equal footing with other subgroups; yet we have also understood that democracy needs to be guaranteed precisely because political imbalances happen all the time. The morality of state affairs is quite a different matter than cultural diversity. Still our ordinary sense of decency tells us that people should be allowed behavioral options and not be coerced to relinquish important traditions. Good government requires a vision that is greater and more universally humane than the narrow interests of an ethnic group, and also it avoids buying national progress at the price of human suffering.

References

Bennett, John W., editor. 1975. *The New Ethnicity: Essays in Comparative Sociology*. New York: Basic Books.
Glazer, Nathan, and Daniel P. Moynihan. 1963. *Beyond the Melting Pot*. Cambridge, Mass.: M.I.T. Press.
Glazer, Nathan, and Daniel P. Moynihan. 1975. *Ethnicity: Theory and Experience*. Cambridge, Mass.: Harvard University Press.
Hughes, E.C. 1943. *French Canada in Transition*. Chicago: University of Chicago.
Ianni, Francis A.J. 1974. *Black Mafia: Ethnic Succession in Organized Crime*. New York: Simon and Schuster.
Kuper, Leo. 1975. *Race, Class, and Power: Ideology and Revolutionary Change in Plural Societies*. Chicago: Aldine.
Porter, John. 1965. *The Vertical Mosaic: An Analysis of Social Class and Power in Canada*. Toronto: University of Toronto Press.
Shibutani, T., and Kim Kwan. 1965. *Ethnic Stratification*. New York: Macmillan.
Sumner, W.G. 1960. *Folkways: A Study of the Sociological Importance of Usages, Manners, Customs, Mores, and Morals*. New York: New American Library. (Orig. published 1906).
Sutherland, Anne. 1975. *Gypsies: The Hidden Americans*. London: Tavistock Publications.
van den Berghe, Pierre. 1970. *Race and Ethnicity: Essays in Comparative Sociology*. New York: Basic Books.
Wagley, C., and M. Harris. 1958. *Minorities in the New World: Six Case Studies*. New York: Columbia University Press.

31.
Growing Up Greek American
Charles C. Moskos, Jr.

The vagaries of Balkan history intertwine with my family origins. My parents were born Ottoman subjects of Greek ethnic stock in what is today Albania.

During the Ottoman period Argyrocastro, in northern Epirus (my father's birthplace in 1898), was a regional center of moderate importance in the western reaches of the empire. In the decades following the dismemberment of the Ottoman Empire, Argyrocastro was to be left with a negligible hinterland and declined into a backwater town. But during my father's youth Argyrocastro, with a population of about 12,000, was considered an urban paragon for that part of the world. Along with commercial establishments of all kinds, the town possessed schools, newspapers, and even a telegraph line. Automobiles were not unknown.

The villages surrounding Argyrocastro were predominantly Greek Orthodox. In the town itself, however, Albanian Muslims outnumbered Greek Christians by about three to one. Christians dominated the commerce of the city, but Muslims owned most of the real estate. Many of the Christians spoke Albanian, but they identified with their coreligionists in "liberated Greece" across the border to the south. Such sectarian cum national demographics were the paramount social facts of my father's upbringing.

For a period during 1914 Argyrocastro was the nominal capital of the "autonomous government of northern Epirus," which sought to distance itself from the newly created Albanian state in anticipation of eventual union with Greece. History was not to be kind to the Hellenes; the entire region of northern Epirus was destined to remain outside the Greek nation.

False hopes were raised in the winter of 1940–41 when the Greek army thrust back an invading Italian force and occupied most of southern Albania. (My memory as a six-year-old of the Greek liberation of Argyrocastro is more vivid—owing to the impact of my father's exultant elation—than that of Pearl Harbor Day a year later.) Control of northern Epirus was to come under, variously, the kingdom of Italy, the monarchial regime of the Albanian chieftain Zog, fascist Italy, nazi Germany, and the rigidly communist state of Enver Hoxha. Although my parents always identified as Greek, it was an anomaly that my family could never harken to a Greek homeland.

Father's Family

All sides of the Moskos family were Greek Orthodox and identified as Greek. Yet my father's mother, Helen, spoke only Albanian, and it was Albanian which was the language of the home. My father's father John was bilingual, speaking both Greek and Albanian fluently. Owing to the beneficence of Epirotic philanthropists, who made their fortunes and residences abroad, a free Greek school system had been established in the towns of Epirus even though the region was Ottoman. My father had eight years of formal schooling which gave him a sound background in arithmetic, reading and writing Greek, and a smattering of French. Greek history and patriotic songs were also taught in school, but with the understanding that such seditious learning be kept under wraps outside the classroom to avoid antagonizing the Turks. Remarkably for that time period and locale, girls also attended the free Greek schools, a privilege not accorded girls in the Muslim schools of Argyrocastro or, for that matter, Greek girls in most of "liberated Greece" either. Thus my father's three sisters, unlike their mother, were literate.

My father's father was a shoemaker, as was his father before him. This was the same trade his sons—my father and my two uncles—would follow as shoe repairmen in the United States. (Yet when the generations-long Moskos tradition of cobbling was to disappear with his American-born sons, there was neither regret nor nostalgia on my father's part.) My father's first and only job in Argyrocastro, however, was not in shoemaking. At age fifteen he obtained employment in the Greek-managed telegraph office. But in 1916, when Italy occupied northern Epirus, the Greek-speaking telegraph employees were abruptly replaced by an Italian staff. My father was now eighteen years old and without a job or a future. His own father's marginal shoemaking business could not afford another hand. His two older brothers and a maternal uncle were already in Chicago. The decision to emigrate to America was inevitable.

An agent in Argyrocastro arranged for passage and an Italian passport.

The ticket was purchased with the severance pay my father received from the departing Greek management at the telegraph office. First it was a stagecoach to a port on the Adriatic, then by local ships to Naples via Corfu and Patras. At Naples he boarded the Italian ocean liner *Caserta*. The crossing was stormy; but anxiety was not with waves, but with the German submarines lurking underneath. In December 1916 my father—who was born under Ottoman rule, who spoke Albanian as his first tongue, who was ethnically Greek, who was presumably recorded as an Italian immigrant, and who was to become an American citizen—arrived at Ellis Island.

But to arrive at Ellis Island was not the same as to be admitted to the United States. All arrivals first had to pass a physical examination, a requirement many did not anticipate. Denial of entry was signified by the examiner placing a chalked "X" on one's back. The fear of U-boats during the crossing was nothing compared to the stark terror of that cursed "X." A compatriot of my father, a man who had been his companion all the way from Argyrocastro, was one of the unfortunates. Rather than admit complete defeat, he changed his destination to South America. My father was never to know whether his fellow *argyrocastritis* ever found a new home. My father, happily, passed the examination in routine fashion.

After being processed through Ellis Island my father took a train to Chicago. The next day he was shining shoes in his brothers' stand. In America only a few months, my father decided he needed a more suitable first name. His baptismal name—Photios—had too alien a ring to American ears. Slips with appropriately American-sounding first names were placed in a hat. "Charles" was drawn, and this was the name under which he became a U.S. citizen in 1925.

My father's uncle Constantine and two older brothers, Evangelos and Spiros, had preceded my father to America by several years. Good men, from my father's viewpoint they were nevertheless forever mired in old country provincialism. Learning only the rudiments of English, they found their companionship among fellow Epirots in Chicago. The larger Greek-American community, much less purely American life, were beyond their ken. Evangelos, the oldest brother, has assumed the mantle of family head in the traditional style.(My grandparents in Argyrocastro had died in the 1918 influenza epidemic.) At times my father would chafe under Evangelos's heavy patriarchal hand. There was the time when Evangelos forbade the purchase of a suit, cut to the latest fashions of 1919 America, which had caught my father's eye. In disgust, my father ran off to Wichita, Kansas. He stayed there several months, shining shoes, until a chastened Evangelos brought him back to Chicago. But my father had made his point—he would not be a bumpkin in Chicago. Yet whether out of fear or respect, my father would never deign to smoke in front of Evangelos.

In 1919 the three Moskos brothers opened up their first shop with shoe repair services as well as a shoeshine stand. In the mid-1920s Evangelos and Spiros, feeling that they had accumulated enough money, returned to Albania. They left the shop in my father's hands. All my father's business activities in Chicago were located in the near North Side, the area immortalized in Zorbaugh's *The Gold Coast and the Slum*. Whatever the sociological cachet of the area, the work hours were excruciatingly long. My father worked the proverbial "Greek half-day," i.e., twelve hours daily. Sundays offered a respite when the shop was open for only four hours.

Upon returning to Argyrocastro my uncle Spiros invested his earnings wisely in a tannery. He rebuilt the family home—with running water, no less—and enjoyed the role of comfortable burgher until the Second World War. Evangelos, on the other hand, found his American savings insufficient to sustain an appropriate life-style. In 1927 he returned illegally—having neglected to acquire American citizenship during his first sojourn—for a second try. My father turned the shop over to Evangelos and set up his own place of business. The net of the Immigration Service eventually fell on Evangelos, who was turned in by a fellow Greek with whom he had argued, and deported in 1930. My father's efforts to bribe the immigration officers in his brother's behalf were unavailing.

In 1929 my father opened up a shoe repair shop in the art deco Michigan Square Building, one of the last large buildings to go up in Chicago before the depression. The building fronted on prestigious Michigan Avenue and the landlord allowed a shoe repair store on the back side of the building facing Rush Street. It was my father's intention and accomplishment that the Michigan Square store would not be an ordinary immigrant's hole-in-the-wall shop. Its well-appointed fixtures included an elevated shoeshine stand made of marble and semi-enclosed booths for "while-you-wait" service. In addition to my father, there were another shoe repairman, a hatter, a clothes presser, and two shoeshiners. Except for some of the shoeshiners who were black, all the employees were Greeks. During the depression and the war my father made a good though not munificent living. He was now solidly ensconced in the lower middle class. His working hours also became more reasonable. My father's week at the shop was down to a mere sixty hours: ten hours a day with Sundays completely off!

My father's maternal uncle, Constantine Zisos, was the first of the family to arrive in America. Coming to Chicago about 1905, he worked continuously at only one place—the Armour packinghouse. After twenty-five years of labor at Armour, he was summarily laid off in 1930. Speaking only a few words of English and without the wherewithal to earn a living, Constantine became his nephew's charge. My father paid his uncle's modest living expenses and used him as a factotum in the shoe repair shop.

My granduncle suffered a stroke in 1935 which led to his moving into our home. He lived with us as a semi-invalid until his death ten years later. It was a cardinal tenet of our family lore that Armour had nefariously and with malice aforethought discharged my granduncle just to remove him from pension eligibility.

My granduncle's plight was to become vivid again almost fifty years after he had been laid off by Armour (almost three-quarters of a century after he first started working for Armour). A Northwestern University student with the Armour surname had come to see me to complain about a "C" he received in one of my courses. Usually a soft touch to grade pleaders, I idly asked him if he were of *the* Armours. Yes, he offered, his great-grandfather was the founder of the famous packinghouse. I caught my breath! Could it be? Had the fates delivered the scion of the family that had done my family wrong? Was my granduncle—the man from whom my own baptismal name derived—finally to get vengeance through the instrument of a course grade in introductory sociology?

Trying to conceal my agitation, I asked if he did not know that in these days of grade inflation a "C" meant his course work had no redeeming value. Getting more voluble, did he not know that in the spirit of his forebearers this was a ruthless world? Finally losing control, who was he to expect that judgement ought be tempered with mercy? Not knowing what was causing this torrent of abuse, he fled my office. Only in America!

Like most Greek immigrants, my father had originally intended to make his fortune and then return home to lead a leisured and respected life. Again like most of his fellow immigrants, circumstances did not work out the way originally planned. Although life in America could be hard, it did have its compensations. My father partook of the amusement parks and Lake Michigan cruises of 1920s Chicago. Introduced to baseball by black shoeshiners, he became a Cubs fan. He liked American dancing and was an habitué of the great ballrooms of that era, the Aragon and Trianon. He enjoyed big city life.

My father became active in the AHEPA, a lodge whose membership consisted largely of other Greek small businessmen. A nationwide fraternity, the AHEPA was modeled after the Masonic orders. It sought to transcend homeland regionalisms among the Greek immigrant community, to foster Americanism among its members, and to work for the acceptance of Greeks by the larger American society. In addition to the programmatic and assimilationist AHEPA, the Greek immigrant scene was characterized by a multitude or organizations whose constituency came from one particular region in the old country. It as at an affair sponsored by one such organization that my father met Rita Shukas. She was to become his wife and my mother.

Mother's Family

My mother's father, Harry Shukas, was born in 1887 in the village of Chatista in northern Epirus, a day's walk from Argyrocastro. Chatista was an entirely Greek-speaking village and, unlike the Moskos side of the family, the Shukas's were never exposed to the Albanian language. The dance at which my future parents met was sponsored by the Chicago diaspora of Chatista. By the 1930s there were more *chatastanoi* in Chicago than were left in the old country. Thus, although my parents met and married in America, theirs was an Epirotic union.

Around the turn of the century Chastista was a village of some four hundred souls. Many of the men wrested a living by making barrels and being itinerant carpenters. Most of the villagers supplemented their incomes by grazing animals as well. Harry Shukas's father was a shepherd but also served a term as *muktar,* or village headman. My great-grandfather died a violent death, murdered by an Albanian Muslim in a revenge killing. Despite the backwardness of the village, it did possess a primary school supported by local assessments and Greek Epirotic philanthropy. My grandfather completed that school with six years of education.

At age fourteen, like many of the young men of the village, Harry Shukas went to Constantinople to seek his fortune. He stayed there eight years, working in stores owned by relatives. My grandfather would later wax elegiac over the Constantinople of his youth. He readily adapted to urban ways and took pleasure in the cosmopolitan character of the city. Quick-witted and now in command of Turkish, he saw himself becoming an established merchant in his own right. But my grandfather's optimism for a future in Constantinople was cut short by the Young Turk revolt of 1908. With the old Ottoman order teetering, my grandfather was prescient enough to see that the new Turkish nationalism would soon turn against the non-Turkish minorities, especially including the Greek merchant community. When the new government changed to draft law to include—for the first time—non-Muslim men, this was cause enough for my grandfather to make a hurried departure from Constantinople. He had decided to go to America.

First, however, Harry Shukas returned to Chatista to marry a comely village girl, Alexandra Soulios. My grandmother's physiognomy was definitely Oriental, revealing some Mongol ancestry somewhere in the family lineage. Her father was a small merchant who rotated between Chatista and Constantinople. He was pleased to give his daughter's hand to the ambitious young man who seemed to have a bright future wherever he went. One step ahead of the Turkish draft, my grandfather left for the

United States in 1910. His new bride, already pregnant with my mother, remained behind.

The archetypical quality of my grandfather's move from village to Constantinople to these shores was memorably evoked in the 1963 movie *America, America*. Watching Elia Kazan's film treatment of *his* uncle's odyssey, I knew it was my grandfather's story too.

My grandfather's destination in America was Chicago, where some fellow *chatistanoi* had already settled. He first worked as a busboy. Soon he moved on to waiting tables at downtown Loop hotels. (My grandfather always appreciated the generous tip and, later in his life, when he was on the giving side, he responded in kind. One ought be a "sport," as he phrased it.) By 1913 he had saved enough money to open, with a partner, a short order restaurant and ice cream parlor in Maywood, a nearby Chicago suburb. In 1915, only five years after his arrival in America, Harry Shukas set up his own Parkview Sweet Shop facing Garfield Park on Chicago's West Side. With its walnut booths and marble-topped soda fountain, the store was an original edition of the classic sweet shop. My grandfather was to stay with that store until his retirement four decades later.

For the first couple of years the sweet shop barely broke even. In 1917 my grandfather received his draft notice. With his army entry imminent, he was desperate. He would lose the store. Fortunately, and to his everlasting gratitude, a fellow *chatistanos* volunteered to manage the store during my grandfather's army stint. While in the service he was stationed at Camp Grant near Chicago and never left the state of Illinois. The army, contrary to its reputation, perfectly matched my grandfather's talents to an appropriate job—operating the post canteen. He claimed never to have held a rifle in his hands.

In 1917 my grandfather sent for his wife and the daughter he had never seen. With the money in hand, Alexandra Shukas and her seven-year-old daughter walked the several days it took to cross the Albanian border. They then made their way to the Greek port of Patras where passage was secured for America. The two women arrived in Chicago in 1918 with no inkling that my grandfather—now in the army—would not be able to meet them. Although my grandmother was to spend close a half-century in this country, she never really learned English. In America, however, owing to her husband's tutoring, she did become literate in Greek. She was to become a charming mixture of Balkan provincialism and Chicago savvy. Always an indifferent housekeeper, my grandmother served well—despite her lack of facility in English—behind the cash register in the family store.

In the 1920s my grandfather's business prospered. The Shukas family filled out with the arrival of two sons, Tom and Peter. My grandfather bought the building the store was in and moved his family into the flat above it. That flat was within reaching distance of the Lake Street elevated train, and the family grew up with the rumbling vibrations of the "L." In 1927 Harry Shukas went into partnership with a German-American friend, Schwanke, and they built a magnificent block-long apartment building. The building was lost in the depression, thus dashing my grandfather's hopes to make it really big. Schwanke tried to persuade my disconsolate grandfather to pick up the pieces and go to Oklahoma with him to try their luck in the oil fields. My grandfather thought it better to stay with the Lake Street sweet shop which at least offered a familiar living. What would a Greek know from Oklahoma oil? (Schwanke did go to Oklahoma and did strike it rich!)

Coming to America at a young age, my mother's English was unaccented and in manners she did not appear to be foreign born. Yet she was raised in the conventional style of the Greek-American middle-class standards of her time. Somewhat pampered by her father, my mother took piano lessons and possessed a nice wardrobe. But my grandfather's intentions did not include continued schooling for my mother; she dropped out before finishing high school. Her parents assumed that the proper roles for a young lady were limited to dutiful daughter, competent housewife, and devoted mother. Rita Shukas was to live up to all these expectations, but she was always a woman of her own mind. She did not work outside the home anytime in her life.

Youth in Chicago

My parents were married in 1933. Their courtship was romantic dating in the American manner. The wedding, however, was old country. My father's best man, a leading confectioner in the Chicago Greek community and a prominent member of AHEPA, saw to it that the Greek Orthodox bishop of Chicago performed the nuptials. After a series of apartment rentals, my parents bought their own two-flat. All our Chicago residences were on the West Side within walking distance of my grandparents. I was born in 1934 and my brother, Harry, in 1936.

Neither of my parents could be described as intellectually inclined. I doubt if either had ever read a book in their lifetimes. My mother had a penchant for crime magazines. My father was an avid reader of newspapers in both Greek and English. Yet it was expected that their sons would do well in school and surely go on to college. Had they had daughters instead, the academic expectations would have been the same. Although I have never been able to pin it down precisely, my parents passed something on which fostered learning. Perhaps it was their belief that there was more to life than making money, or the respect they had for the opinions of their children. Perhaps it was a sense of her own educational deficiencies that led my mother to project high academic achievement onto her sons.

It was my mother's presumption that one would get a better education in a Catholic parochial school than in the public system; I therefore started school at Our Lady of Angels. (This was the school that suffered a tragic fire in 1958 in which ninety-five children and nuns perished.) Even though I was the only non-Catholic in any of my classes, the good sisters never proselytized—probably on the assumption that Greek Orthodox was close enough. I was treated with affection and learned my three R's and a lot of religion as well.

A flaw in my character was apparent as early as my days at Our Lady of Angels. As recalled to me by my brother, on Fridays it was my custom to take the meat out of my luncheon sandwich and eat it surreptitiously before entering the school grounds. During the lunch hour I could then publicly join my schoolmates in eating a meatless sandwich. In this way I ate my bologna, but kept in the good graces of my peers—if not of Him above.

My Chicago neighborhood was lower middle class and overwhelmingly Catholic, predominantly Italian and Irish. Ours was the only Greek family around. It was certainly true that ethnic categories were the dominant social reality of my young consciousness. It was also the consciousness of everybody else I knew. After all, everybody—except the Indians—had to come from somewhere before America. Perhaps because I was always short for my age, I was pressed on occasion to prove my scrapiness, this being when I was taunted with the epithet "Dirty Greek." Yet such taunts seemed to be generated more by a spirit of schoolboy macho than any real maliciousness. Besides, it was a cardinal tenet in my family upbringing that Greeks were better than "Americans"—which referred, depending on the context, to all non-Greeks or to Protestant Anglo-Saxon groups which were a kind of remote and generalized "other." Not only did we Greeks have a tradition going back to classical Hellas, but even in the United States was it not self-evident that we were more likely to advance, less likely to get into trouble, and had a family life superior to the Americans themselves?

But there was a defensive side to our ethnic smugness—a hyperawareness of every Greek who could somehow be singled out for his or her achievements. To grow up Greek in the 1930s and 1940s meant that household names included the gambler Nick ("The Greek") Dandolos and the wrestler George ("The Golden Greek") Londos as well as Dimitri Metropoulos, the renowned conductor. We were alert to the careers of obscure politicians like Dean Alfange of New York, or even more obscure film personalities like George Colouris and Katina Paxinou. There was even the rumor that the baseball star Bob Lemon—née Lemonides—was Greek. This was in the era before the advent of Greek-American celebrities, sports personages, and political figures on the national scene.

To be Greek American in Chicago meant a local identification with one of the Greek Orthodox churches in the city. Our own church was the Assumption on the West Side supported mainly by Greek small businessmen. Saint Andrew on the North Side was regarded as the church of "rich Greeks." Holy Trinity was the more traditional immigrant church in the old Greektown near the Loop. (My present church, Saint Demetrios, is located in Chicago's new Greektown on the Northwest Side.) Saints Constantine and Helen on the South Side was noted for its magnificent edifice capped by a dome resembling that of the glory of Greek Orthodoxy—Saint Sophia in Constantinople.

Decades later, when the neighborhood changed, Saints Constantine and Helen became Islamic following its purchase by the Black Muslims, who made it their showpiece mosque. I always thought that there was something historically correct for a vacated Greek church to become Muslim rather than be turned over to another Christian body. The transformation of the old "Saint Connie's" from Orthodox to Islamic, like that of the original Saint Sophia, seemed to recapitulate in the American context the Ottoman heritage in Greek life.

Politics

Politics—either Greek of American— was a conversational staple in the family circle. The monarchist versus republican schism which characterized Greek political life since the turn of the century was also to cleave the Greek-American community up through World War II. My own family was staunchly on the republican side. A small communist group existed in the Chicago Greek community, some of whom were family acquaintances. I remember these communists as engaging individuals, but also noticed that my parents and grandfather treated them with amused condescension. Although as a boy I was certainly aware of Greek politics, they were not— excepting the irredentist Epirotic cause—all that salient. It was my family's political view of America which naturally had the most meaning for me.

The politics of my family were rightist and consonant with the small shopkeepers we were. My grandfather was a conventional Republican through the 1920s. But following the loss of his apartment building in the depression, he voted for Roosevelt in 1932—the only Democratic vote he ever cast. He veered toward a radical right and isolationist position in the period before World War II, finding himself attracted to the Townsend Plan, Father Coughlin, Charles Lindbergh, and Colonel McCormick of the *Chicago Tribune*. Both my grandfather and mother were viscerally anti-FDR. Even Eleanor Roosevelt was viewed as a failed woman because her children were improperly raised. My father was somewhat closer to the mainstream. A Republican by habit, he could vote for Democratic candidates easily enough. In later years my father became extremely enamored of Spiro Agnew, as much for the former vice-president's political philosophy as for his Greek background.

All my family—down to the present generation—has consistently held conservative social views. Advancement was seen in individual terms, not through organized collective action. Social altruism in a liberal sense was an alien concept. Responsibilities extended to self and family. If everybody took care of his own, there would be no social problems. With diligence, some innate talent, and a little luck, the American Dream could be realized. An added ingredient would be the esteem accorded by the Greek-American community. One's goals ought be for a better life, not a better world.

Youth in Albuquerque

In 1945 our family moved to Albuquerque, New Mexico, to find a better climate for my hay fever. My father tried his hand in the restaurant and bar business, but soon decided to keep to his old trade. He opened up Albuquerque's finest shoe repair shop which he operated until his retirement. Albuquerque was selected for our new home because of the presence of a Greek community with its own church. The Greek population, large for a Rocky Mountain city, was the legacy of an AHEPA tubercular sanitorium which had attracted Greeks from around the country to Albuquerque. The sanitorium had closed by the time we arrived, its failure being locally attributed to the excessive demands and Greek idiosyncracies of its patients.

The focal point of the Albuquerque Greek community was Saint George's Church. The older male generation, immigrants mainly running restaurants and bars, found election to the church board and AHEPA offices a means of acquiring some recognition and status in a familiar environment. The older women, almost all housewives, took part in the female auxiliaries. The younger American-born generation belonged to church youth groups; most served in the choir or as altar boys. Efforts to maintain a Greek language school were more sporadic. Social life centered on namedays, baptisms, and major religious holidays, especially the Holy Week liturgies. Extravagant formal weddings to which the whole Greek community was invited were major events. The community would be periodically rent by disputes arising out of bruised egos and personality clashes. Such disputes became especially acrimonious when the qualifications of the priest—whom we seemed to have changed every couple of years—were brought into question.

The Greek community was extremely alert to any straying from proper bounds. The rare divorce was always cause for much clucking. One of the more memorable scandals was a young woman who gave birth to a child out of wedlock. Suitably penitent, she sought readmission to the church youth group. Despite the pleas of the priest and the choir directress to show a little Christian forbearance, we self-righteously refused to accept her back. If there were a generation gap in those days, the forces of prudery were strongest on the youth side.

In the late 1940s and early 1950s I knew every member of the several-hundred-strong Greek community in Albuquerque. It ranged from the old bachelors who frequented the pool halls near the railroad station through the main body of small businessmen to a few individuals who through real estate investment had become quite well to do. Few of them had anything in common with the pristine Hellenes in classical Greece whom one read about. Rather, they were more Byzantine, more complicated, more like the forceful characters in a Harry Mark Petrakis novel.

There was George Ades, probably the first Greek in New Mexico. A Zorba-like figure, Ades had run away from a crime back East—a murder in a gambling fight, it was rumored—and settled in New Mexico in territorial days. He married into an old-line New Mexico family—descended from the *conquistadores*—and learned to speak Spanish himself. There was Theo Karvelas, compact and bald, who was unique in that he was the only adult immigrant in Albuquerque to possess an American high school diploma, acquired in night school back in Pittsburgh. Karvelas, the intellectual of the Greek community, was a major influence in my own life. There was Father Peter Remoundos, a bear of a man, who tempered religious solemnity with perceptive wit. In what was the most appropriate eulogy I ever heard, Father Remoundos captured the essence of Greek Americana by pronouncing a local chef "an artisan with the ladle and the knife."

Ethnic Contours

Looking back to those immigrant Greeks—in Chicago, Albuquerque, and elsewhere—one wonders whatever happened to the mold that produced them. We shall never see their likes again. Certainly the American-born generation has made its mark, has acquired security and even comfort in American society. But maybe it has come too easy. When we measure ourselves against our progenitors, are we not more bland or—God forbid—more plastic?

Even though the Greek community was a vital part of my growing up, it by no means defined its totality. I was an active student politico in junior and senior high school. Albuquerque was divided into two basic ethnic groups, the Anglos and the Spanish (the term Mexican was pejorative and

Chicano had not yet come into fashion). A Greek was obviously neither. What successes I had in high school politics could be largely attributed to the fact that I could make appeals to both groups. My closest friends were non-Greeks, boys who like myself fell between the *pachucos* (Spanish toughs) and stompers (Anglo toughs) on the one hand and the country club set on the other. My youth in Albuquerque was a family-centered Greekness overlaid by an *American Graffiti* existence of drive-ins, unrealized sexual fantasies, and teenage mischief.

Ethnic contours have been the basic terrain of my family's maps of social reality. Whether in the context of Christian versus Muslim in the old country, or the multitude of hyphenated Americans in Chicago, or the Anglo-Spanish cleavage in New Mexico, group consciousness—natural rather than false, I would argue—was certainly ethnically derived. While it is plausible to argue that ethnic differences reflect root economic realities, it is equally defensible to hold that class differences are outcomes of primordial affiliations. Both positions are probably true. Even to become Americanized—as American-born Greeks have become—seems to speak both to a partial absorption into class-based groups *and* an evolving ethnic adaptation which will still be discernible from the broader American culture.

Adulthood and Family

The fates have smiled on the years since high school. Always good in academics, I received generous scholarships, along with paying jobs, which enabled me to receive a B.A. from one of America's most elite private universities (Princeton) and a Ph.D. from one of the country's great public universities (UCLA). My professional career has been intrinsically rewarding, and sometimes I wonder how one can earn such a good living for doing what is pleasure. My political and personal philosophy have come to correspond with my petty bourgeois roots and present circumstance. I was exceedingly fortunate to marry a modern woman who knows how to handle a traditional man. My wife Ilca, German born, has to my embarrassment and pride even learned to speak Greek better than her husband.

I returned to the Chicago area—whose Greek community has been replenished by large numbers of new immigrants—when I took a position at Northwestern University. Mueh of my family life has been a pleasant déjà vu. I was married by the priest who baptized me. In the ideal Greek fashion my *coumbaros,* or best man, was the son of my parents' *coumbaros.* Like my parents before me, my wife and I speak in Greek when we talk code in front of the children. My father lives with us and wears his years well.

There have been losses too. My mother died too early at age forty-three and was never to see her sons grow to maturity. My brother is managing editor of the *Albuquerque Tribune*. My uncles in Albania died in penury, a condition in which my father's sisters continue to live. My grandparents Shukas lived into ripe old age, staying close to and, finally, moving in with my uncle, a pharmacist, and his family. Much of my father's time is spent attending the funerals—a reminder that we must all make that crossing over the Styx—of his rapidly diminishing cohort of friends. Wars took their toll. My uncle, Peter Shukas, was killed in World War II, and later my cousin and godson, James Shukas, was to die in Vietnam.

All in all, it seems fair to say that if the family did well in America, America did well by it.

32.
Gypsies: The Hidden Americans

Anne Sutherland

Approximately every twenty years someone predicts that the Gypsies are a dying culture and laments that the old ways have gone and that the future is bleak for the Gypsy. Usually, these predictions are based on events that make traditional occupations difficult or impossible, and the cultural repercussions of the economic situation are felt to be far-reaching. First it was education that would bring the end of Gypsies, then the radio, and now television. What next?

Some have pointed out that the children are wearing American-style clothes, and that the men are no longer wearing earrings and a red bandanna on their heads; such observers have mistakenly interpreted differences in clothes by age group, sex, or country as evidence of assimilation. Some listen too closely to the vanity of the old men who assert convincingly that they are the last Gypsy king.

Certainly changes in life style, dress, occupations, and customs have taken place among the Gypsies. Economic adaptability, combined with the inflexibility of certain basic rules, is the Gypsy's *forte,* and the consequence of flexibility is often change. A man, who began life by trading horses or hammering copper, might then move on to trading used cars or hammering car fenders or repairing copper boilers and drills; women tell fortunes when and where they can, but when they cannot, they move into farm labor or welfare with their families. Most of them do a little of everything. Just as for most hunting and gathering people, it is not so much one particular skill that is important as the ability to extract a living somehow or other from the natural environment, so for the Gypsies what counts is the versatility that can use for its own ends whatever is available in the human and technological environment in which they find themselves. This versatility has changed relatively little.

Gypsies have faced dramatic technological changes since they left India and began wending their way into Western Europe. To most anthropologists, technological change without social change seems inconceivable; yet the descriptions of the most basic economic and social behavior from the earliest accounts to the present day, from Russia, Greece, North Africa, and Western Europe, to North and South America, are easily recognizable as "Gypsy." There are great differences, of course, but these are attributable just as often to tribal differnces as to changes over time. No doubt individuals, and even large groups of Gypsies, have become assimilated throughout history, often through coercion. One of the most famous and apparently successful attempts to integrate the Gypsies into the wider society was when they were made serfs in Rumania between the fifteenth and nineteenth centuries. Even this drastic measure failed to some extent, for the Rom in America are probably descendants of those serfs.

The American Rom

The Rom in America are fully aware that changes have taken place among them. There is little an old person likes more than to talk of the good old days, the days of "life on the road" when "we didn't need no doctors or no schools." Of course, they fail to add that they still spend almost the entire summer traveling (just as when they camped) and on average travel 42 percent of the time; the young families over 50 percent of the time. Mobility is a major method of problem solving and of social control, and as long as there is conflict there will be mobility. They also fail to mention that in those days their occupations did not require even a minimum of literacy but which they now find very useful for dealing with the welfare system.

Social change has taken place among the American Rom. There has been an increase in the proportion of endogamous marriages, that is, marriages contracted within the *vitsa* or within related *vitsi* relative to those contracted with unrelated *vitsi*. There has also been an increase in conflict for resources, and this has brought about a new emphasis on territoriality. The most economically viable *kumpania* is the one that has become more restricted to one *familia* or one *vitsa*. These tendencies are associated with an increase in the population density of the Rom in the United States, which means a relative saturation of their resources, that is, exploiting non-Gypsies by means of certain occupations. The biggest problem for the Rom has been the illegalization of fortune-telling, which has not ended fortune-telling but has made it less viable an occupation for large groups and correspondingly more suitable for a smaller tightly controlled group (like the *familia*) that can operate with police protection in one place. In some areas, this is predetermined by the authorities, who may give licenses only to one family. Conflict over territory is related to conflict over marriage bonds by *Xanamik*, who are in competition with each other, and marriages between related persons has increased.

Future demographic and economic pressures combined with the increase in conflict in certain areas may bring a tendency toward more strict patrilineal recruiting in the *vitsa* and away from the expressed cognatic principle of recruitment in order to restrict the size of the *vitsa* given the relative scarcity of resources. What has already happened in this area of social relations is the very rapid division of the *vitsi* along sibling lines into *familiyi* branches that eventually become new *vitsi*. But an assimilation of the Rom into the wider society seems unlikely, and if this is so, the question that arises is: how have they remained socially distinct?

There are many examples in the literature of ethnic groups or subcultures that live within a wider culture, face tremendous pressures to assimilate, but have resisted this course. The Mapuche Indians of Chile, for example, in recent times have effected a successful adaptation to reservation life within their traditional social framework. Although they have had to change considerably in order to cope with new economic conditions, they have been able to do so in such a way as to retain their social integrity. There are, however, ethnic groups that have a long history of interaction with a wider culture whose values and social institutions they reject. The Anabaptist groups in North America—the Hutterites, Mennonites, and the Amish—like the Rom, are very aware of outside pressures that threaten their existence, and also like the Rom, have suffered persecution for hundreds of years because of their way of life. Moreover, they have to cope with internal social pressures, either as a result of external conditions or demographic growth, which they resolve by periodic migration. Because of these pressures, the most important issue that these Anabaptist groups face is the continuous maintenance of social boundaries between themselves and the wider culture.

The study of ethnic groups should concentrate on the analysis of social boundaries and how they are maintained. For groups that do not live in isolation, boundary maintenance is neither a simple nor a static issue. In fact, the very continuity of the ethnic unit depends on boundary maintenance. The study of social boundaries should be centered on an analysis of how the categories (ethnic labels) of a group are interconnected with their actions. One ethnic group or subculture in American society, the Amish, have certain interesting similarities with the Rom. Both the Amish and the Rom are discrete societies that nevertheless interact in many ways with persons from American society. The groups are perhaps extreme cases among minority groups both because they are such separate cultural groups and because they have worked out very effective methods of boundary maintenance over a long period of time.

The Rom have many similarities with the Amish in the question of boundary maintenance. As an ethnic group, the Rom represent a somewhat exceptional case for two reasons. Not only do the Rom have a fairly separate social organization, and therefore could be considered a culture in its own right, but they also have been labeled a pariah group because of the attitude of the host population toward them. Fredrik Barth has stated that:

> These [pariah groups] are groups actively rejected by the host population because of behavior or characteristics positively condemned though often useful in some specific, practical way. European pariah groups of recent centuries (executioners, dealers in horseflesh and leather, collectors of night soil, gypsies, etc.) exemplify most features: as breakers of basic taboos they were rejected by the larger society. Their identity imposed a definition of social situations that gave very little scope for interaction with persons in the majority population, and simultaneously as an imperative status represented an inescapable disability that prevented them from assuming the normal statuses involved in other definitions of the situation of interaction. Despite these formidable barriers, such groups do not seem to have developed the internal complexity that would lead us to regard them as full-fledged ethnic groups; only the culturally foreign gypsies clearly constitute such a group. Classifying the Gypsies as a pariah group has been useful for understanding their social processes and structure. At best, it has resulted in partial ethnography, which can often be very misleading.

It is interesting to look at the question of boundary maintenance once one has a more thorough understanding of social processes. For the Rom, the maintenance of boundaries between themselves and the *gaje* (non-Gypsies) is a continuous, almost daily, concern. It is based on two factors: (a) social contact with *gaje* is limited to specific kinds of relationships, namely economic exploitation and political manipulation for advantages. Purely social relations and genuine friendship are virtually impossible because of the second factor; and (b) a whole symbolic system and set of rules for behavior (*romania*) that place the *gaje* outside social, moral, and religious boundaries in a multiplicity of ways, the most important being the *marime* status. The relationship between these two oppositions: Rom/ *gaje* and *romania/marime* is the key to their maintenance of a distinct way of life.

The Rom are also aware that they live within a society that generally despises them and erects its own boundaries against them. Because they are always trying to improve their economic position by manipulating *gaje,* not only to earn a living but to gain political advantage over other Rom, they must often counter the prejudices and erroneous labels that are given to them. On the other hand, their sense of moral superiority is not threatened by their position in American society or by the attitudes of *gaje* toward them, and their separateness, which they covet, is actually protected and enhanced. Therefore, while on the one hand, they often find it useful to counter *gaje* attitudes, these same attitudes help to maintain the boundaries and reinforce Rom ideas about the foolishness of the *gaje*.

Boundary maintenance is also contingent on their ability to adjust to change. The Rom have developed an economic system that allows great flexibility and a moral system that is very inflexible. They can adapt to numerous cultural, technological, and economic changes while maintaining very rigid ideas of *romania* and *marime* (inside and outside) enforced by the authority of the elders. This combination of economic adaptability and moral or ideological solidarity is common to all Gyspy groups.

Solidarity and Leadership

One of the most apparent characteristics of the Rom is that they are almost constantly involved in conflict with each other, a factor that masks their equally intense solidarity as a group. Although their expressions of solidarity may be less obvious than their expressions of conflict, the solidarity of the Rom is proportionally as intense as the degree of infighting.

Solidarity is perhaps best manifest when death or a serious illness occurs. The death of an adult male or female is treated as a loss to the whole group as well as a personal loss to relatives. Mourning by cognatic relatives, friends, and Rom from the area is extremely intense. As one man explained it, "When there is a death or an illness, all Gypsies get together, whether they have to walk, sell everything, no matter what. It's a sign of respect. You can't understand how strong we are about sickness, about operations and the rest." On one occasion a family, upon being told of the death of a relative 500 miles away, dropped what they were doing and left within fifteen minutes for the funeral.

Death is not the only time when the Rom come together as a group. Any serious trouble, such as an arrest, will unite everyone in a collective effort to help. If necessary, fines, bail, lawyer's fees, and bribes will be paid by a collection in the *kumpania*. This cooperation is more than a method of self-protection as a group against outsiders, it is also a measure of the value that is placed on group membership. Imprisonment, like death, means the loss of a member of the group. To go to jail is to have to live among the *gaje* and to be denied the fellowship of one's own people. Jail is a *marime* place in the sense that it requires separation from the Rom.

The Rom say that *marime* means being rejected from the Rom as a group and being dirty or polluted. For the moment, it is the sense of rejection that is most relevant. When a person is declared *marime* publicly, whether by a group of people (such as families in the *kumpania*) or more formally in a *kris romani* (trial), he is immediately denied commensality with other Rom. Anything he wears, touches, or uses personally is polluted (*marime*) for other Rom, and he is generally avoided in person as his *marime* condition can be passed on to others. *Marime* in the sense of rejected from social intercourse with other Rom is the ultimate punishment in the society just as death is the ultimate punishment in other societies. For the period it lasts, *marime* is a social death.

Marime is a very effective punishment for several reasons. First, almost all social interaction among the Rom involves eating together. To be denied commensality is to be barred from the most enjoyable and important social contact. Second, a *marime* sentence always includes the family of the *marime* person so that an individual must consider the consequences of his actions for his family as well as for himself. Third, *marime* forces a person to associate with the *gaje* in a way that he would not normally do. Finally, *marime* means a loss of respect and status in the group (even when reinstated) and contains the stigma of uncleanliness and moral defilement.

Marime is the public rejection of a Rom by his society; however, even voluntary separation or separation imposed from outside is associated with *marime*. Jail is a *marime* place because it means a long separation from the group and association with *gaje*. Relatives will make great sacrifices to protect each other from jail. When they do not, it is always because the individual has committed some offense that is difficult to punish, and it is convenient to let the *gaje* do it for them. Voluntary exile from the group is also a *marime* crime. This rarely happens because of a conscious choice to leave the group. More often it is because a sexual offense has occurred and the person involved leaves rather than face the consequences. Suicide is also viewed as extremely shocking and incomprehensible and may result in a *marime* sentence on the family of the suicide victim. The point that is important here is that the same intense emotion that is expressed against a person who has been declared *marime,* emotion that includes the horror of pollution, is also expressed in support of a person who is threatened with loss of physical or social life whether it be by illness or from American laws.

Part of the painfulness of being denied contact with one's own people, whether it be in a jail, a hospital, or a job, is that of being alone. To be among a group of Rom is the natural everyday context within which a person lives, learns, and expresses his personality; to be among a group of *gaje* is to be alone. Wherever he travels or lives, a Rom is rarely alone. More often he is surrounded by large numbers of relatives and friends. Only when he is rejected by the community or chooses to be by himself is the individual alone. Loneliness is perhaps the rarest condition an individual experiences in his lifetime.

As might be expected, visiting and gossip are major pastimes and it is rare to enter a home that does not have visitors or to find a group of Rom anywhere who are not discussing the recent events in their own or in other *kumpaniyi*. Just as the Nuer love to talk about cattle, the Rom love to talk about each other. Of course the frequent marriages, baptisms, parties, feasts, and funerals are always occasions for visiting and gossip.

Besides being a major pastime, gossip is also a major form of social control. It is the primary means of pressuring an individual. Once word gets around that some people consider another person's actions to be *marime*, others will not wish to risk contamination and will avoid him. Consequently, no individual can afford to ignore anyone's statements concerning his reputation no matter how unfounded in fact they may be. Gossip can make or break a person's reputation, and when it occurs it must be fought immediately. To ignore gossip would be tantamount to admitting guilt. This does not mean there are no curbs on gossiping. One man in Barvale was declared *marime* for six months for malicious gossiping.

Naturally, visiting and gossip take place among Rom who are living in close proximity, that is in the same or a nearby *kumpania*. People in nearby *kumpaniyi* are constantly in touch with each other and maintain an intense system of communication among themselves. They generally know what is happening, what is being talked about, and where people are. During travels, more distant relatives and *vitsi* members are contacted, and every traveler to an area brings news about people in the area he just left. Since there are always people coming and going from the *kumpania*, contact is maintained with many areas of North America. This enhances their sense of solidarity as a people since without communication, they could not maintain their social and moral system.

Of course, not all Rom meet each other in travels, and sometimes it is important to contact relatives or friends who are far away. For example, when there is a serious illness or death, relatives must come to the side of the stricken person. For these emergencies, the Rom have an amazing system of communication that makes it possible for one person to contact any other in a very short time. Even if the person has deliberately gone into hiding, he can often eventually be found. Although letter and telegraph are often used, the telephone is the main instrument of communication and it has been a great boon to communications in the last thirty years.

The communication system works through the *kumpania* and *vitsa* units. Every *kumpania* leader has a list of key telephone numbers of other *kumpania* and *vitsa* leaders. They must have the number since it could be listed under any name. If they do not have a number for someone in the *vitsa* they want to contact, they can contact someone in the *kumpania* where he is likely to be and get a message to him. Since people are constantly on the move, and numbers go out of date quickly, a list of non-Gypsy telephone numbers is also required.

Gossip, visiting, and other forms of communication are informal expressions of solidarity and means of social control. The formal system includes, (a) a code of tradition and rules called *romania*, (b) a legal body that makes decisions and enforces the rules (*diwano* and *kris romani*), and (c) punishment by fine or *marime* to enforce the legal decisions. *Romania* is the highest authority of the Rom, is accepted by all those who consider themselves Rom, and is given a kind of sacredness demanding obedience. *Romania* is a set of moral codes and rules of behavior known by all but interpreted primarily by elders. Disagreement about proper behavior takes the form of denying accusations or presenting contradictory statements of fact; the moral rules themselves are not usually questioned. Occasionally, they may be changed. A meeting of *vitsa* heads from all over the country was once held in Los Angeles to discuss new rules for elopement, settlement of brideprice, and informing. *Romania* is an all-inclusive, obscure concept and is very difficult to define, but in a single context it is usually quite clear. *Romania* includes traditions, customs, ideal behavior, morals, beliefs, rituals, and attitudes. In practice, the force of *romania* is the general consensus of opinion on a particular question.

When a consensus of opinion cannot be reached, then the interpretation of *romania* must be taken to a final decision-making body, the *kris romani*, which is said to be composed of a man and wife from each *vitsa* in the vicinity (which may be a very large area comprising five or six states) led by one or more judges. It is said that the *vitsi* assemble in a chosen place to hear both sides of the case and make a decision. Their decision is final and a man pledges to accept it before the *kris* convenes. Not to accept the decision would be to deny *romania*.

Punishment itself is rejection from *romania*. Punishment is to become *marime*, to be denied physical contact and social intercourse with one's own people, to be forced to live among the *gaje*, and to be polluted. *Romania* is social life; *marime* is social death.

Secular and Mystical Authority

An individual becomes increasingly more powerful with old age, a large *familia* following, a good reputation, and the establishment of effectiveness with *gaje* authorities in the *kumpania*. If a man has a strong and aggressive wife, is wealthy, and shows an ability and desire to help other Rom who come to him for aid, then he may become a leader, a *rom baro* or "big man."

The sexual division of authority is more difficult to define than it first appears. In general, the authority of the men is based on secular, political knowledge, such as manipulating *gaje* officials, using "strong men" to scare or coerce opponents, and speaking and arguing well, especially in a *kris*. The authority of women is based on their knowledge of the *mule* (spirits of the dead), medicines, and their innate ability to pollute (*marime*) a man. Men may appear dominant in many instances, but fear of mystical reprisals is not taken lightly by the Rom. The distinction between the power of men and the power of women is illustrated in the belief that death, the final authority, is a man, but a woman can scare him away by cursing him and threatening to lift her skirts over him to make him *marime*.

The division of male secular and female mystical authority has parallels in many other societies so it is not surprising to find it among the Rom. However, a simple opposition of secular and mystical authority would be very misleading of Rom politics. Whatever the basis of their authority, the effect is that old women have a great deal of influence and secular power. There are many examples of old women who become the ruling force in a *kumpania* and control access to economic resources and *gaje* authorities. Not only do women occasionally run a *kumpania*, but an old widow will undoubtedly be the ruling force in her *familia* and perform all the duties of a *familia* head normally performed by men. There is no difference in potential power of a *phuro* and *phuri*, but since widows are more common than widowers, this can have a great effect even on a male-headed *kumpania*.

More than sex, age is the crucial factor in authority. Power and old age diminish sexual separation. Powerful old men and women can sit and talk with each other. Old people have more knowledge and authority than young people. The older one becomes, the more one knows about *romania*. Knowledge of *romania* is a great source of power, for *romania* is an absolute and final authority. Since an individual generally only learns about behavior as the situation arises—for example, a woman knows nothing about procedure at birth until she herself has a baby—it is only the very old who can claim to know everything about life, beliefs, customs, and expected behavior. In their persons, they embody the force of *romania*.

As men and women get older, more and more respect and authority is given to them. In *Romanes*, respect and authority are expressed by the word *pakiv* (or *dav pakiv*), which means to "obey, respect, esteem, or honor." This concept is connected with the terms normally used for leaders who are *rom baro* ("big man") and *romni bari* ("big woman"). To be *baro*, means to be obeyed and respected and, by implication, to be old.

Although old age is essential for authority, not every *phuro* (old man) or *phuri* (old woman) becomes a *rom baro* or *rom bari*. The difference is that a *rom baro* heads his *kumpania* or his *vitsa* and *kumpania* whereas the eldest patriarch (*phuro*) or matriarch (*phuri*) has authority over a limited number of families who are their descendants.

The *rom baro* has authority that goes beyond his own *familia* whether it is his *kumpania* or his *vitsa* and *kumpania*. At the same time a *rom baro* has the same duties to his *familia* as any other head of *familia (phuro)*, and in any *kumpania* there may be several *phuro* or *phuri* whose word is law for their kin. In most cases, there is only one *rom baro* for a *kumpania*.

Roles of the Rom Baro

Some of the duties of a *rom baro* to his *vitsa* or *kumpania* are the same as the duties of a *phuro* to his *familia*. The role of the *phuro* is very important because he has strong control over his *familia* and may be a contender for *kumpania* leadership. Basically, the *phuro* or *phuri* is responsible for handling only problems that arise in his *familia*, although he may enlist the aid of the *rom baro*. These include marital and legal problems, contracts for summer work, and arrangements for ritual feasts. The difference between a *rom baro* and a *phuro* is basically (a) realm of authority, which is correlated with (b) amount of authority. For example, the strength of Stevan's authority was greatest as *phuro* for his own *familia*, less as *rom baro* for the five Kashtare *familiyi* in Barvale, less again as *rom baro* for the *kumpania* as a whole, least for his *vitsa*, and nonexistent for his *natsia*. It must be stressed that it would be very difficult for a *phuro* to become *rom baro* without the following of a large *familia* that congregates under his authority. For this reason, one of the first tactics of a leader is to bring as many relatives as possible into his *kumpania*, smooth over difficulties for them, and help them to get set up economically. In return, they can usually be relied upon to give support for his leadership. On the other hand, he is also anxious to keep out nonrelatives who will not support him and whose loyalty is to their own *phuro*. This is one reason why a *kumpania* generally tends towards consolidation under one leader and one *vitsa* until some event occurs to shift the balance of power.

Basically the duties of a *rom baro* fall into two major sections: (a) to handle all internal problems that arise in the *kumpania* or in the *vitsa*. These include disagreements in work, marriage, family relations, trials, funerals, etc.; and (b) to handle all affairs with *gaje* authorities in the *kumpania*, help anyone who is in trouble with American law, arrange work contracts, establish relations with the authorities that are advantageous to the goals of the Rom community, and deal effectively with outside pressures to conform to American society.

A Rom who can claim to have influence with non-gypsies who are themselves in a position of authority (police, social workers, judges, district attorneys, lawyers, politicians, civil servants, etc.) can use this influence or threat of influence to coerce other Rom. Other Rom fear his ability to get them arrested or harassed by these authorities. Often this influence is highly exaggerated, but sometimes it is based on fact, such as when bribing does take place. A more subtle approach is to gain knowledge of the laws and manipulate them for one's own political advantage. Both these methods are used to handle internal as well as external problems. The law may be used to get a daughter returned from a *Xanamik* by claiming she has been kidnapped or claiming that statutory rape has taken place. A fight may be stopped or a brideprice returned by taking out a warrant for someone's arrest and then dropping the charges when the money is paid. Finally, there is always the threat of getting someone cut off welfare. All these methods of coercion require a knowledge of law, police, and welfare procedures. They represent one way in which *gaje* support the internal political system by enforcing rules which the Rom themselves have difficulty in enforcing.

Influence with police or welfare authorities is not only used as a form of social control but is also used to help people in the *kumpania*. Through trial and error, the *kumpania* has built up a body of knowledge and experience with social workers so that they know exactly which story and type of behavior reveals as little as possible about themselves yet still establishes their eligibility for welfare. They also know which stories the social worker is not likely to accept (even if they are true).

Problems over school attendance and medical examination, psychological examination, and employment (or adult education) for men, are also handled or advised by the *rom baro* or *phuro*, who has experience and knowledge in these matters. Any problem that he handles for a family enhances his reputation for being effective at dealing with the *gaje* and reinforces his leadership.

Building up influence with *gaje* authorities is a major criterion for getting control of the *kumpania*. But a leader must also have influence with his own people. He must have a large family and *vitsa* following in the *kumpania*, be well-respected, give impressive speeches, be large and strong, and have lots of grandchildren. When he fulfills these conditons, he must then be clever and crafty enough to enlist the support of *gaje* authorities, smooth the path for his people with them, and be effective in getting them out of trouble. He is the bridge between the Rom and the *gaje*.

Symbols of Leadership

The term for leader, *rom baro* or "big man" does not refer only to size in the sense of greatness, power, or authority, but also to physical attributes.

To be large, tall, big in frame, fat, and have a large head are all physical ideals in general, but particularly for a *rom baro*. In general, when speaking of the power of a *rom baro*, people refer to the man's size as if to prove their point.

A large head is particularly important, and this can be enhanced by wearing a large hat, usually a stetson, and having large mustaches. When recounting the greatness of ancestors, the largeness of a mustache is often included in the description. The head and hat are important symbols of authority and prestige. Just as a woman must remove her jewelry (her symbols of prestige) at a *pomana* (a death feast), a man cannot wear a hat. Along with a large and impressive stetson hat, the rest of the Western clothing is a favorite outfit of authoritative men.

A very important factor in leadership is wealth. Wealth is displayed in specific ways, primarily in the gold jewelry that the wife wears, but also in a large and expensive car. Ownership of property is also being stressed recently. Some important leaders boast of owning property although very few other Rom are interested in property as it was detrimental to their mobility. Wealth is also shown by generosity, and a leader who is generous is highly respected by all. A man who is wealthy is almost certain to have authority and prestige, but it is possible to make a show of wealth to compensate for the lack of it. Finally, other symbols of power are needed as proof of influence with *gaje* officials. These may be calling cards, letters from *gaje* officials or any evidence of having worked for them, such as a check from the police department.

Conflict

Most Rom feel that conflict is on the increase. "Gypsies used to live together, all the tribes [*natsiyi*] around a campfire. They traveled together and got along. Now they fight a lot and don't associate [with other *natsiyi*] so much." The general feeling is that fighting between *natsiyi* has increased, and this was one reason given for keeping other *natsiyi* out of the *kumpania*. Whenever possible, blame for a fight is shifted to members of other *natsiyi* or distantly related *vitsi* within the *kumpania*. Similarly, support and aid is generally for the more closely related persons. The increase in conflict is also the reason given for preferring endogamous marriages over marriages between unrelated *vitsi*. In general, a distrust of distantly related or unrelated Rom is prevalent.

In cases of conflict, problems in a *kumpania* are solved by transferring blame to an outsider, who must leave the *kumpania*; problems that arise outside the *kumpania* must be resolved by a higher authority, the *kris romani*. *Gaje* authorities are used to support the leaders of a *kumpania* and to stop or create trouble as the situation demands. The political relationships between *gaje* and *kumpania* leaders take a defined and consistent pattern for resolving conflict. The same pattern was observed for economic relations between leaders and *gaje*. However, an understanding of this pattern does not tell us what the issues and internal factors really are for Rom society. These internal factors are the kin and affinal relationships, the broader social categories (*vitsa, natsia*), and other concepts, such as *marime*, which are crucial to an understanding of political relations and conflict. It appears that support in time of conflict is given first to one's *familia*, then to one's *vitsa*, and finally to members of the *kumpania*. Relations between members of different *natsiyi* are generally hostile.

Gypsies Versus Other Ethnics

The history of the Gypsies is, in a sense, the documentation of the survival of a group of people who have lived as outcasts in another society; thus from the point of view of many cultures, they are a pariah group. This status in the wider culture in which they live has had an important effect on their own social organization and, at the very least, has reinforced the rigid boundary between Gypsy and non-Gypsy. In the U.S., where the very existence of the Gypsies is unknown or doubted by most non-Gypsies, they have not had to face so harshly as in Europe the consequences of being considered a pariah group. However, although no society develops in isolation, ethnic groups, and the Gypsies in particular, are by definition part of a wider social unit so for them the question of boundary maintenance between themselves and the wider society is primary, and a major concern of their social organization will be a response to this problem.

But although the Gypsies share with other ethnic groups the problems of determining inclusion and exclusion from the group, of determining the set of rules governing interethnic social encounters, and of identifying another person as a fellow member, there are important differences between the Gypsies and other ethnic groups in America. The major ethnic groups in America are integrated into American culture to the extent that (a) an important part of their identity includes being American as opposed to another nationality, and (b) they participate in a major aspect of structure; for example, stratification in America is partly based on ethnic relations between black and white Americans. The Gypsies are less integrated into American society both in terms of structure and group identity. Second, and probably related, is that they have a more complex internal social organization than other ethnic groups, although at the same time it is oriented to the problems of living in an alien culture and to maintaining a strong distinction between themselves and others. This may be because historically they have had more time to come to terms with the problem of adaptation without assimilation than have other minority groups in America, and their mechanisms for doing so are highly developed.

Against these adaptive advantages, the Gypsies have more serious disadvantages than other ethnic groups. Blacks and Chicanos have suffered from discrimination in the educational system, but the Gypsies have hardly participated at all. Illiteracy may be useful in some instances for maintaining isolation, but as Gypsies become more known in America, particularly in welfare and police departments, they are at a serious disadvantage in their relations with such bureaucracies. Once Gypsies are officially recognized, they are in danger of being unable to cope with American bureaucracy, and not everyone will be able to adopt the time-honored solution of moving on to greener pastures. Related to this problem is the increasing demographic pressure among Gypsies in America and in the world generally. The fight for territories is intense precisely because, within their economic framework, making a living is becoming increasingly difficult. To combat this problem, some Gypsies, like other ethnic groups, have organized themselves politically into pressure groups. These groups are most vocal in England and France where demographic pressures are greatest. In the U.S., the movement is embryonic and as yet marginal, but destined to grow as the numbers of Gypsies grow and as the economic situation worsens.

33
The Ethnic Factor in World Politics
Abdul A. Said and Luiz R. Simmons

A revived sense of ethnic identity has grown in the last few decades and ethnic politics has emerged as a significant factor in the international political system. In recent years the antagonisms of indigenous ethnic communities in Cyprus, Iraq, Malaysia, Guyana, Uganda, and Canada (to name but a few states) have wrought important changes in the international relations of nation-states. There is an increasing tendency of ethnic peoples to think fundamentally in terms of the ethnic group and to demand separate political status for the group that is global in scope, and this is effectively challenging the political demography of Africa, Europe, and the Americas, as well as Asia. The ethnic conflicts of Ireland, the bloody struggle of Biafra and the secession of Bangladesh, the unsettling race riots in the United States, and the transformation of ethnic discontents into ethnic nationalism have placed their mark on the domestic and international politics of nations in persistent and conspicuous emanations.

Yet both traditionalists and behavioralists continue to rely upon the nation-state as the analytical tool for understanding international politics. According to this framework for analysis, states are political systems exhibiting community, consensus, and a monopoly on the means of violence. The incidence of the state of war is a direct consequence of the lack of community and consensus between and among nation-states. War and the lesser tensions and hostilities are consequences of the improvident transactions of total identities, that is, nation-states. That few such total identities appear to exist in international politics has not changed foci of analysis or our perceptions of the international system.

Out of an estimated 164 disturbances of significant violence involving states between 1958 and May 1966, a mere 15 were military conflicts involving two or more states. Most significant violence that has taken place since 1945 has found its cause in ethnic, tribal, and racial disputes that have often exerted a spill-over effect in international politics.

The ethnology of the planet is often a subject of inquiry limited to anthropologists and sociologists. The political scientist has not been as diligent in approaching the study of these societies as he might have been because the focus of international relations since 1945 changed from nation-state to the possibilities of world federalism, regionalism, and multilateralism. Coincident with this development was the introduction of popular scholarly literature emphasizing the detribalization of multiracial states, the disappearance of ethnic loyalites (particularly in the postindustrial United States), and finally the emergence of transnational subcultures. In sum, the vanishing ethnic did indeed vanish, but only from the minds of students of international relations as theories of nation builders and supranationalism rose in attention and influence.

Nation Versus States

Why then statistically has much of the present serious violence involving states been the consequence of the unresolved differences of these vanishing ethnics? Why do the ethnics persist? What accounts for their sensational impact on international politics in the past five years? There are perhaps as many as 862 ethnic groups (nations) living within the nation-states of the world. What future impact will they have as and if the nation-state continues to be a declining form of economic and political association?

Raymond Aron has noted recently that ethnic conflict will replace class conflict in the latter third of the twentieth century. This is because the legitimacy of the modern state is struggling to overcome an international challenge to its supremacy rooted in the internal contradictions between the nation and the state. This contradiction becomes fully visible when loyalty to the state and loyalty to one's nation conflict. In this conflict are forged the incandescent passions of secession, civil war, and the unconscionable talent of some ethnic nations to completely destroy others. The state can be defined in terms of territory, population, and government; its formation can be predicted in contemporary international relations since it signifies the victory of positivism in the political affairs of men. A state is generally recognized when it exerts political control over a specific geographical area. Sovereignty is not a derivative of natural or divine law. Control is accompanied by international recognition in the transactions among nations. Loss of control is invariably a precursor to loss of recognition. The history of exile governments is not a happy one. The state is a positivist contraption, both artifice and artifacer of the nineteenth-century fruition of the positivist approach to human affairs. But the nation is a conscious expression of people's shared sense of peoplehood, reflecting what Kurt Lewin has described as the "interdependence of fate." The political self-consciousness of nations is a product of the nineteenth century. Ernest Barker has stated the issue with enviable precision:

> The self-consciousness of nations is a product of the nineteenth century. This is a matter of first importance. Nations were already there; they had indeed been there for centuries. But it is not the things which are simple "there" that matter in human life. What really and finally matters is the thing which is apprehended as an idea, and as an idea, is vested with emotion until it becomes a cause and a spring of action. In the world of action apprehended ideas are alone electrical; and a nation must be an idea as well as a fact before it can become a dynamic force.

We are entering a new era where state-nationalism as it has been known for the past few hundred years is undergoing serious, and perhaps fatal, stress. It may seem presumptuous to talk of the end of the nation-state in an era characterized by references to rising nationalism, but history is made of such contradictions. After the successful defense of monarchy, the defeated parliamentarians of the New Left were, in fact, destined to be vindicated within two generations. In our era, the secession of Bangladesh, the Kurdish independence movement, or the struggle in Northern Ireland mark a fundamental shift in international politics.

The proliferation of new states after World War II has obscured the problem of scale and underscores the absurdity of describing the People's Republic of China and the Bahamas as nation-states. The real international system consists of no more than twenty or thirty national and transnational actors who have any significant impact, and the top five actors have over half of the world's human and natural resources. The nation-state as a unit of analysis makes differences of degree so vast as to constitute differences in kind. Ethnic groups, on the other hand, are more clearly defined and therefore constitute a real as opposed to a juridical construct for analysis.

The dominant causal agent behind the international political system that is beginning to emerge is the technological revolution in communication that permits previously isolated ethnic groups to become more visible and in certain cases interact across national boundaries. Perhaps mass communication, instead of unifying, is paradoxically differentiating mankind into progressively smaller communities.

The new international system is both more parochial and simultaneously less geographic. Ethnic groups find more affinity along lines other than the national boundaries of traditional nation-states. The human need for a sense of community is gradually dissolving the bonds of geography that unite diverse groups within states. Community in this sense is the community of the ethnic group or of communes, citizens who find their interests coinciding outside the political context of a nation-state. What this means in practical terms is that a given community may rejoice at victories other than those of its state, since the defeat of its state will be a victory for its vision of community. The internal struggle within each state seeks its analogue in external politics. The domestic dispute requires the creation of a foreign-policy dispute. The case of the Kurds of Iraq serves as a good illustration. Mustafa Barazani, the Kurdish leader, rejoices at Iran's and Israel's victories, since the defeat of Arab Iraq will be a victory for the Kurdish community.

We have entered the age of international politics of ethnicity. In such an environment—where distance as a barrier to national and transnational culture groups is a diminishing consideration and relationship becomes paramount—man relies less and less upon the nation-state as an agent for fulfillment. A politics of ethnicism is beginning to dominate the behavior of divergent and anthropomorphically different cultures, which will impact widely upon the respective nation-states and demand new theoretical models explaining interaction. Ethnicism confutes the viability of a national ethic and suggests the use and importance to the understanding of international relations of ethnic groups, and the invalidation of concepts of national interest such as status and faith, that become dominant neologisms in explaining politics among nations.

The domestication of international politics is no doubt a disturbing trend for the decision-makers who must plot the course of the modern state. Many governments now predicate their internal legitimacy—the maintenance of which is the first priority of all governments and to which other goals are secondary—on the performance of external policies. That is, there is an increasing trend by many governments to justify domestic policies by reference to foreign commitments and antagonisms. The conflict politics among states of the future will often be a response to the politics of ethnic dissociation.

The present phenomenon of ethnic conflicts cannot be adequately analyzed within the context of traditional concepts of international relations. Concepts of balance of power, bipolarity, or even polycentrism as loci of conflict obscure the fact that, as Andrew Greeley has observed, "the conflicts that have occupied most men over the past two or three decades and which have led to the most horrendous outpouring of blood have had precious little to do with this ideological division . . . . In a world of the jet engine, nuclear energy, the computer and the regionalized organization, the principal conflicts are not ideological but tribal. Those differences among men which were supposed to be swept away by science and technology and political revolution are destructive as ever." The nation-state is no longer viewed as the ultimate community, nor is it even the primary source of loyalty in many instances.

Ethnicity Versus Assimilation

There is a tenacious persistence of core cultural values that reject absorption into a higher level of identification. This is not to deny the role of conflict in retribalization. Awareness of one's ethnicity may well be, to a great degree, a function of coercive assimilation. Thus, when social groups are mobilized, it does not necessarily follow that congeniality and cooperation will occur. Increased contact, exposure, and communication may exaggerate one's self-image, magnify cultural differences, produce conflict, and induce political dissociation. Additionally, economic development, an increase in material goods and services, does not immunize a society from ethnic conflict. The concomitants of economic growth, urbanization-secularization-industrialization, may lead to competition over limited opportunities and resources. Previously stable interethnic differences have fit patterns of comparative advantage or coexistence while the industrial-technical society tends to have a commonizing effect on economic behavior and produces competitive channels of achievement.

Critics of ethnicism assert that it is dysfunctional, uneconomical, and irrational. Such criticism is hardly substantiated. Ethnic distinctions may in effect serve useful functions in cross-cultural relations. Larger states do not necessarily develop more rapidly than smaller ones. Smaller states have developed at least as rapidly as larger states since World War II (Taiwan, Lebanon, Cyprus, Hong Kong as opposed to India, Indonesia, Pakistan). In some instances, these may be diseconomies of scale. Finally, conflict is not necessarily irrational but the roots of cultural expression that produce conflict are psychosociological. Cultures and ethnic groups have an inner logic that determines behavior, values, and attitudes that confound objective description or absolutism. The complexity of cultures necessitates a multidimensional appreciation of the intertwining institutions and people that synthesize a political, cultural, and collective consciousness. Concurrently, one must be sensitive to heterogeneity between and among ethnic groups.

Claude Lévi-Strauss defines culture as "the complex whole which includes knowledge, belief, art, morals, custom, and other capabilities and habits by man as a member of society." He urges the social scientist to understand the dynamics operating in the macro and micro levels of human behavior, and to relate the "synchronic to the diachronic, the individual to the culture, the physiological to the psychological, the objective analysis of institutions to the subjective experience of individuals." Structural anthropology aims not so much at the compartmentalization and universalization of culture and its institutions, but at the relationships between the institutions and social behavior.

Ethnicity reveals a structure analogous to that of culture. Fredrik Barth sees atomic groups "biologically self-perpetuating, their members share fundamental cultural values, realized in overt unity in cultural form; they make up a field of communication and interaction and their membership identifies itself and is indentified by others." An ethnic group is a culture and yet may belong to a larger culture. A static concept of ethnic groups conceives their cultural differentiation as a function of social isolation, ecological factors, adaptive measures, invention, and selective borrowing. Such an approach negates the high import of cultural interaction.

A complex hierarchy of potential indentification exists in ethnic consciousness, but Barth stresses that "ethnic identity is superordinate to most other statuses, and defines a way an individual operationalizes and externalizes his reference group's norms." Adherence thus entails the channeling of social life, and "implies a recognition of limitations or shared understanding, differences in criteria for judgement of value and performance, and a restriction of interaction to sectors of assumed common understanding and mutual interest."

As structural anthropology accentuates the dynamic relationship between man and culture and its divergent consequences, social anthropology concentrates on the dynamic relationship of ethnic groups as they define social-psychological boundaries between and among themselves. Barth's insights are particularly useful here; "Boundaries persist despite a flow of personnel across them. . . .categorical ethnic distinctions do not depend on an absence of mobility, contact, and information." On the other hand, adds Barth, "stable interethnic relations presuppose a structure of interaction: a set of prescriptions governing situations of contact, and allowing for articulation in some sectors or domains of activity, and a set of proscriptions or social situations preventing interethnic interaction in other sectors, and thus insulating parts of the cultures from confrontation and modification."

Thus begin to emerge the anthropological roots of ethnic conflict: the fluid relationships existing between ethnic groups catalyze sociopsychological identification and boundaries, and do not necessarily induce conflict. Shared values are sometimes a component but not a sufficient condition of mutual understanding; the sectors of mutual activity entail competition as well as cooperation. Conflict and cooperation alike are indicators that man is living on the same plane; communication is thus predicated on a certain degree of community as illustrated in structural anthropology.

Psychological anthropology plays an important role in the configurations and matrices of ethnic interaction that result in conflict. It focuses on the teleological roots of ethnic conflict and the fundamental difference between ethnic groups, and explores the relationship of human beings, their levels of interaction, and such crosscurrents as social change and economic development. Such currents infuse change and substance into cultural adaptation and contribute to the friction within and between cultures. Using the ascriptive-contractual typology of Maine, the Gemeinshaft-Gesellschaft of Töennis, the mechanistic-organic of Durkheim, the traditional-transitional-modern of Lerner, it seems that all indexes of fluidity and degrees of receptivity between cultures delineate the diffusion of exposure.

Predictability of ethnic conflict appears to be contingent upon those levels of articulation between cultures that are effective and those that are decreasingly utilitarian, and their varying intensities. One might not expect ethnic conflict even if ethnic group A has a predominant advantage in political representation if ethnic group B is not politicized. Internecine behavior is as much a function of commonality of values as of a multiplicity of values. Thus, viewed from an ecological perspective, ethnic transactions are dependent on a (1) minimal competition for scarce resources (be they natural, occupational) where the area of articulation will be in trade; (2) territorial claims (in which articulation is politicized); (3) symbiosis and interdependence where articulation is multiple; and (4) partial competition for the same niche—where conflict is most likely.

Ethnicism and Development

Is it conflict that causes tribalism or tribalism that causes conflict? We hope to demonstrate that the biases of our Western ideologies and methodologies have consistently led us to accept the former while treating the latter as a casualty for the trash heap of history. Our religious faith in progress has prevented us from recognizing that while there is nothing inevitable about ethnic conflict, neither is it inevitable that nation builders will discover the precise formula to absorb so formidable an antagonist. Thus we are compelled to posit the ethnic nation as an irreducible dilemma for the state—one which under the proper (or dysfunctional) conditions can emerge as a destructive divisive force. Conflict, such as economic scarcity or political or cultural repression, can exacerbate these tendencies, but it is not demonstrable that an absence of these conflicts (were it possible) would mean the withering away of the ethnic nation.

Professor Milton Gordon has reminded us that the term ethnic group has been used to embrace the unities of race, religion, and national origin. However, the common denominator of these categories is a common social-psychological referent that acts to create a consciousness of peoplehood. Thus the term ethnic is invested with a broader significance than it has been given by some sociologists who use the term ethnic group as a typology of national origin. Obviously, the raising of such a consciousness has direct implications in social, economic, and of course political behavior. How difficult it must be, for example, to persuade an ethnic group to reweave the values, attitudes, and norms that characterize a group's authority patterns since, as Milton Gordon puts it:

> Common to all these objective bases, however, is the social-psychological element of a special sense of both ancestral and future-oriented identification with the group. These are the "people" of my ancestors, therefore they are my people, and they will be the people of my children and their children. . .in a very special way which history has decreed. I share a sense of indissolvable and intimate identity with *this group* and *not that one* within the larger society and the world.

Clifford Geertz has elaborated upon the contrast inherent in such a definition, which he refers to as communalism. In India, it is based on religious contrasts, in Malaya we are primarily attracted to racial differences and in the Congo by tribal affiliations. Divisions based on economic, class, or political disaffection may be the harbinger for civil strife but alienation based on culture, language, race, and nationality are elements that comprise what Professor Shils has called the primordial ties and are foci of authority and patriotism within the state, which it often seeks to replace or from which it seeks to disassociate. Geertz identifies several ascriptive characteristics around which much ethnic conflict has revolved: assumed blood ties—such as those that characterize the hill tribes of Southeast Asia and the Kurds; race—a volatile element in the transactions between the excolonial powers and the excolonial states; language—such as that which served as the basis for the political crisis that toppled the Belgian government and threatens the Canadian unity; religion—of which Indian partition is an outstanding example of these divisive passions and the turmoil in Ireland a disturbing reminder; and custom—examples of which are the Bengalis in India and the Javanese in Indonesia.

Whether we are dealing with the extermination of Brazilian Indians or the contemporary ethnic conflict in Uganda, Ireland, or Pakistan, we are naturally attracted to the anomaly of the twentieth century—the impulse for Western modernization and the accelerating consciousness for self-determination among varieties of linguistic, religious, and geographical ethnic groups. The questions that such a conflict pose for a normative political scientist may be: "Although I believe that states must assimilate ethnic nations Y and Z in order to provide the modern economic, health, and social services that they deserve as citizens of the twenty-first century—what about the possibility that nations X and Y resist the devaluation of sovereignty? What rights if any do they have under my scheme for modernization? What limitations, if any, should be placed on the central authority in their attempts to force secessionist ethnic nations to adapt to the political economy of the State?"

Each of us can pose a different question that places more or less emphasis on the fruits of modernization or the political or cultural exhilaration of ethnic sovereignty but finally we must confront the root question of how we shall balance our commitment to human rights with the contemporary experience of nation-building—often a bitter by-product of civil war. Then again, as we are rediscovering in the social sciences, our view of the controversy may be considerably influenced by the state we are living in at a particular point in history. States wracked by ethnic conflicts are probably less inclined to view secession and civil war as expressions of some transcendent human struggle than states that experience an acceptable level of ethnic conflict that does not approach dissociation. Another problem is posed when a state or international agency, attempting to intervene in behalf of a national minority confronts the dilemma posed by Conor Cruise O'Brien:

> We tell, let us say, the Tutsi that the right he fancies he possesses to dominate the Hutu is not a real right. He replies in effect that as far as his culture is concerned it *is* a right. We tell him it is not a right, because it is contrary to democracy, an ideology to which our ancestors became converted in the nineteenth century. He says his ancestors did not become so converted; are we claiming that our ancestors were superior to his? Now, that is a forked question, and we have to very careful how we answer it. If we say, "No, no, of course not my dear fellow," he can say in reply: By what right then are we telling him that he must act according to the acquired conviction of our ancestors who are admittedly no better than his own. If, on the other hand, we say, yes, our people represent a more advanced stage of civilization than his do, he may reply that this is exactly his own position in relation to the Hutu.

The response of the state to disaffected ethnic minorities has not been generous by most Western standards. The Tibetans with the Chinese, the Montagnards in South Vietnam and the examples of Iraq, Cyprus, Rwanda, and the Sudan are indispensable reference points for predicting the state response to ethnic conflict and the politics of dissociation. Self-determination movements are invariably viewed as threats to the survival of the state. States threatened by such acts of dissociation have treated the leaders of these movements as traitors and have interned them without even the causal regard for their own concepts of due process. In Guyana, for example, a Security Bill was passed in 1966 by the black-controlled government to restrict the activities of East Indians. The terms of the act call for the prime minister to intern without trial for 18 months anyone he believes has or will act in a manner that threatens public order. The Sixteenth Amendment to the Indian Constitution, passed in response to the Pravidistan movement, seeks to "prevent the fissiparous, secessionist tendencies in the country engendered by regional and linguistic loyalties, and to preserve the sovereignty and territorial integrity" of the Indian state.

States can usually expect to lend covert or overt assistance to other states confronting ethnic dissidents unless, of course, the dissident ethnic elements are perceived as instrumentalities in the foreign policy armamentarium of one state to disrupt the internal affairs of another state.

Basque nationalism furnishes a good example of the former; Chinese foreign policy in Burma, the latter. The Basque region is on the border of Spain and France. Although the French deny providing assistance to the Spanish government, since 1970 France has increased the expulsion of Basque political refugees. Basques on either side of the border note that improved French-Spanish relations that culminated in the French sale of armaments to Spain, have contributed to growing collaboration of the governments on the Basque problem.

Neoethnic Behavior

A politics of neoethnicism is investing itself in the styles, politics, and social organization in America, which will impact widely on theories of national development and integration. Neoethnicism as a system is a transition from the national consciousness of the nation-state to more communal forms of identity and organization characterized by cultural patriotism, ethnic nationalism, and a revolt against anxiety. A primary agent of this transformation is the primacy of communication in the process of mobilizing unassimilated minorities and subcultures, the growth of particularistic and minority nationalism, in a redefinition of national consciousness. It has been described at its farthest points by a process of retribalization, the philosophical concession to communal imperatives characterized by the interdependence of fate, and a proliferation of related life-styles. In its paramount expression, it is the apostasy of the nation-state, an exhaustion with the cumulative preoccupations of national and world institutions, and the preference for the pursuit and study of personal and parochial problems. It is expressed in a variety of ideologies, among a variety of classes. It has assumed both subtle and overt expressions and is stimulated by structural changes in the function of the state.

Neoethnicism is not an exercise in the apocalyptic. It is an articulation of the crisis in the expectation and promise of national institutions. It confutes the viability of state institutions to respond to the social-psychological needs of community, and it has found its expression on political and cultural themes and motifs as diverse as civil disobedience, the chants of La Raza, ethnic consciousness, youth ghettos, subcultures, decentralization, community control, rural and professional communes, and the growth of the modern university.

Privatism, ethnicism, the occult, community-oriented protest, consumer unionism, and communes testify to the decline of the nation-state ethic and the absence of the subscription of diverse national, ethnic, neoethnic preferences to the creation of state initiatives and ideology. The deauthorization of the symbols and the ideology of the nation-state is not a temporary phenomenon, nor is it primarily a casualty of the Vietnam war. It is bound up in, although not necessarily intrinsic to, the neoethnic rage. But public temperament is in transition, as well; decentralization, revenue-sharing, and community control are manifestations of this postponement of national gratification and a commitment to the development of smaller, more manageable administrative units. Some of the young have been among the first to grasp the significance of this transition and shape themes that accommodate their respective youth cultures. As such, these themes prefigure issues as seemingly diverse as revenue-sharing and freedom-of-choice school designs, youth ghettos, the new sex consciousness of women, and the competition among ethnic and neoethnic groups for political and economic rewards that had induced much of the current social conflict. One senses in the ugly sinews of distrust that gripped the United States in the past decade a crisis of expectation. No longer convinced that national or state administrative bodies were prepared or capable of developing efficient responses to local conflicts and the social-psychological needs of the individual, ethnicity and neoethnicity have become for many the prime foci of political and cultural concern and have eroded the foundations of the theories of national integration.

Part XII
Sociobiology: Back to Basics?

Over the years and despite the magnitude of national and international changes, anthropologists have continued to explore fundamental aspects of cultural diversity. In line with early studies in the discipline, the human ability to meet basic needs for survival, and transcending essential problems to create complex and enduring social institutions, has persisted as a central interest. As we've seen, the relationship of once-isolated people to the natural environment and to outside political and economic systems has undergone the greatest transformation. The disruption of primitive hunting-gathering and horticulture is global, as is the impetus to integrate individual members of tribe or village into national and urban contexts. So it is that the job of the contemporary ethnographer requires a sharp eye for behavioral discontinuities and social invention as well as sustained traditions.

At the same time that researchers of today's societies have had to confront the dynamics of rapid change, the investigations of archaeologists and physical anthropologists have broadened our perspective on the development of the species *homo sapiens* and the sources of civilization. On the one hand, discoveries at the Olduvai Gorge site in Tanzania, at Lake Rudolph in Kenya, and elsewhere, have proved a spectacular pay-off to the late L.S.B. Leakey's almost 40 years of research on the physical origins of man. In 1975 the discovery of a human skull dating back 1,500,000 years greatly extended our history as inhabitants of this planet and sustained Dr. Leakey's hypothesis that this region of the world was indeed a fertile "Eden" for hominid and eventually *homo sapiens* life. (Skulls now assigned to the genus *Homo* may be as old as 2.8 million years.)

At the same time, archaeologists working in the Middle East have been accumulating remarkable evidence on the origins of early high civilizations in ancient agricultural communities. Tracing the earliest developments of writing, manufacture, trade, urban conglomerations, and social classes from human and material remains has been aided by sophisticated techniques for dating and the increased use of statistics to organize data. Similar evidence has been found in Mesoamerica and Peru.

As with the biological evolution of man, the mysteries surrounding the emergence and decline of societies in the "Fertile Crescent" are far more abundant than any certain conclusions, a fact that mass media attention to "the first man" or "the first civilization" tends to obscure. The puzzles of human evolution and prehistory have more missing pieces, and, after the location of crucial points—biological or social revolutions in form—it is evidence of cultural diversity that is most striking and that defies the imposition of any one great scheme on human history. Even the work at Olduvai Gorge and elsewhere in East Africa has broadened our understanding of evolution to include several hominid branches, only one of which (*Homo erectus*) led to modern man.

Discoveries such as these are fascinating not simply as physical facts, but for what they have suggested about the cultural context of early *homo sapiens* who were hunters and gatherers, perhaps in wandering bands or in lakeside encampments. The stages of prehistory proposed by nineteenth-century writers had to be based on suppositions. Today, speculations on human social development can draw directly on a small but significant factual base. At the same time that we can compare our specifically human characteristics—bipedal locomotion, large cranial capacity, the generalized hand, extended pregnancy, and dependence of the young—with those of our nearest primate relatives, these same characteristics are best seen in their social dimensions, as they facilitate and shape relations between and among people.

Given anthropologists' concerns with the fundamentals of human organization, including its biological basis, it comes as no surprise that the recent phenomenon known as the "sociobiology controversy" should provoke significant reaction within this social science in particular.

In 1975 in the final chapter of his book, *Sociobiology: A New Synthesis,* Harvard University biologist Edward O. Wilson proposed a merger of the natural and social sciences to develop general laws concerning the evolution and biology of human behavior. Coming at the end of a volume devoted largely to insect colonies and some animal groups, this suggestion appeared a reasonable follow-through from the ongoing studies of social behavior in lower species. As author Wilson notes in the first article in this section, it should be possible to look at human organization as one among many socially organized life forms.

The proposal would probably not have become controversial if Wilson had not gone on to cite features of human behavior, most notably altruism, as characteristics shaped by our biological evolution and presumably still subject to change. The most vehement reaction to this link between a highly valued capacity of humankind and biological make-up came from natural scientists within the Harvard community, including leaders of the organization, Science for the People. Their criticism in general was that the proposed synthesis raised the specter of nineteenth-century Social Darwinism, an interpretation of social reality that bastardized the theory of natural selection to render judgment against the "less evolved": nonwhites, the poor, and women. As his critics saw it, Wilson was proposing a causal relationship between behavior and biology in the dangerous terms of evolutionary categories. To begin research on such a subject, it would have to be presumed that individual behavioral characteristics were fixed (in the same simplistic way that the breeding patterns of fruit flies are fixed) and changed only with some gross and/or long-term impact on the biological group. On the basis of such clinically oriented research, could there not emerge classifications of people by their biological predispositions for better or worse behavior? Would the natural sciences then provide a rationale for the biological determinism of every conceivable social evil and social good? And, most important of all, who would be judging good and bad behavior?

In part and in part only, the negative reactions to sociobiology have been a function of the general feeling that the limits of a disinterested science have long been reached. For example, coincidental with the publication of Dr. Wilson's book was a bitter protest against Harvard University plans to initiate laboratory experiments in advanced genetics without guaranteeing the highest level of protection for the public. As amazing advances are made in science, belief in the notion of scientific progress has diminished sharply because we do not know and have not fully considered the implications of our own technology. Genetic engineering and test-tube babies are becoming facts of science; how can we interpret them as social facts?

It is no wonder, then, that Wilson's seemingly innocent suggestion that aspects of human behavior should be seen as rooted in biology conjured up nightmarish programs for eliminating deficient populations, or as an alternate disaster, that human behavior might be reduced to a genetic factor that would become the basis for genetic engineering in the name of moral progress. Taken to their most horrible conclusion, the general laws sought by Wilson might become the justification for a Brave New World of clones and genetically planned castes.

Does the mixed marriage of the natural and social sciences necessarily have to be such a disasterous issue? Probably not, though even before the ethical goals of research are formulated and responsibility for the products of research is taken, something must be said about the theoretical and methodological differences between the natural and social sciences. To what extent can we use each other's techniques and information?

To begin, a view of human social life in some ways comparable to that of coral, termites, wolves, and chimpanzees has its advantages, provided we understand, as Wilson seems to, the eventual uselessness of pushing some analogies: leaders of wolf packs don't participate in political institutions as we know them; there is no division of labor among chimps because, properly speaking, they do not work; and communication among bees bears only the vaguest resemblance to human interaction.

In the second essay in this section, physical anthropologist S.H. Washburn distinguishes between entertaining man-animal comparisons and those that are serious and productive. The comparison of facial expressions among humans, chimpanzees, and lions, for example, reminds us how much we have in common with other complex species on a simple expressive level; the reminder should have the humbling effect of placing us in the context of the total biology of this planet.

On the level of science, however, how is biological and social research to be combined? Long before this problem came to the attention of anthropologists, a good many published works had accumulated that traced the variables of health care, nutrition, and ecology to basic cultural institutions such as the family and kinship organization. Yet the research cited by Wilson in his essay, research that meets the "exacting criteria of postulational-deductive science," has a much more technical tone to it. That social scientists should begin inquiry by limiting themselves to a single variable such as genetic fitness suggests that they know a good deal about the technical measurement of such a feature. It also suggests that some population or populations have been seized upon as limited "gene pools" on which to test propositions.

That the reductionism implied in such research cannot sit well with all anthropologists is brought out by Washburn in the conclusion to his essay, and then is presented by social anthropologist Marvin Harris in his debate (broadcast on Radio Smithsonian) with Edward Wilson. Unlike the controlled environment of the laboratory, the environment of human society is one of virtually unlimited interaction. The cultural meaning implied in any behavior is a powerful and yet not perfectly standard overlay on the physical reality of the people involved; whatever their blood-types or set of genes, humans can be understood and yet be not at all predictable in their behavior. Only one of the biological implications of this is that *homo sapiens* can devise elaborate mating proscriptions and then proceed to mate almost indiscriminately, across barriers of caste, class, religion, race, and language. Further, human beings are notorious for masking the transgressions of conventional mating by complex fictions or outright lies. Genetic fitness makes sense only as the most broad biological category, and the laboratory gene pool is impossible to find outside the laboratory. One might guess that even the relict populations such as the Yanomamö and Munduruců who have become the favorites of sociobiologists have led their researchers a merry chase on the subjects of parentage, warfare, homosexuality, and infanticide—on every subject but their obviously wretched condition as societies at the brink of destruction.

Other principal points of conflict between natural science methods and the reality of human social organization are raised in the Wilson-Harris debate. Foremost among these is the question of what we learn by reducing behavior to opaque descriptive categories, a feat that Skinnerian psychologists accomplished long ago and with no apparent benefit. We can, for example, contrast "the biological sense of altruism," as Wilson uses it, to centuries of philosophical insight on human sympathy in all its complex variations and add to this our own many volumes on social learning. Granting that we are each limited by our own biology and granting too that we cannot beat an intellectual retreat from the discoveries of the biological sciences, such reductionism actually distorts rather than illumines facets of human nature.

The proposal that we go even one step further and link the biological sense of altruism to a particular and as yet undiscovered gene meets with even more resistance. As British philosopher Mary Midgely has argued in her recent *Beast and Man,* more than any one trait, the overwhelming proneness of human beings to complex, expressive social interaction, so that from birth our humanity is contingent on the actions of others, may be what distinguishes us from other species with more limited repertoires. Certainly a glance at the "wolf-children" literature substantiates what we already know, that without other people we are less human, whatever our genetic composition. To specify any one aspect of interactive behavior and link it to a single gene may be as implausible as the proposition (as yet unmade) that language capacity—which relies on a complicated array of neck, throat, mouth, head, neurological, and brain characteristics—could also be reduced to one genetic component.

As social scientists we have the responsibility to ask the right questions, those that advance rather than muddle understanding and also those that reflect a moral approach to the human condition. A long time ago, Robert Lynd in his 1937 work *Knowledge For What?* cautioned members of all the social sciences that they should be accountable for the information generated by their research and that this accountability begins with the formulation of the research objective and the choice of a particular subject area. The ethics of the sciences are more than afterthoughts tacked on to pure (as opposed to applied) research, just as intellectual work does not consist of undirected, unplanned ventures. If concern for human dignity and survival is the right foundation for our study of culture and social organization, this should be reflected in our research priorities.

There is a great seriousness that has overtaken our ordering of research priorities, and the controversy surrounding sociobiology has demonstrated the urgency and concern with which natural and social scientists approach the subject of new directions in their fields. Wilson's initial proposal, no less than the reactions it aroused, intended to give a more enlightened perspective on human society. It also touched upon a fact of growing concern to everyone, but all too neglected by social scientists: the gap between technological advancement and reasonable social policy. We should be addressing the impact of scientific technology of all sorts, from medical experiments to agronomy and military hardware, with an eye towards understanding how to control what is, after all, our most blatantly unique and dangerous human characteristic—invention. The divide between the natural and social sciences is in many respects, an unfortunate one that leaves us bereft of expertise and our brethren in the laboratories bereft of insight.

The subject of sociobiology, as a controversy and the source of new research endeavors, is a fine lead-in to the concluding section of *Anthropological Realities* on the application and ethics of the discipline.

References

Ardrey, R. 1966. *The Territorial Imperative*. New York: Atheneum.
Ardrey, R. 1970. *The Social Contract*. New York: Atheneum.
Eibl-Eibesfeldt, I. 1975. *Ethology: The Biology of Behavior*. New York: Holt, Rinehart & Winston.
Eiseley, L. 1958. *Darwin's Century*. New York: Doubleday.
Fox, R. 1972. "Alliance and Constraint: Sexual Selection in the Evolution of Human Kinship Systems." In *Sexual Selection and the Descent of Man*, edited by B. Campbell. Chicago: Aldine.
Hamilton, W. D. 1975. "Innate Social Aptitudes of Man: An Approach from Evolutionary Genetics." In *Biosocial Anthropology*, edited by R. Fox, pp. 133-155. New York: Wiley.
Lorenz, K. Z. 1963. *On Aggression*. New York: Harcourt, Brace and World.
Lorenz, K. Z. 1974. "Analogy as a Source of Knowledge." *Science* 185:229-233.
Midgely, Mary. 1978. *Beast and Man*. Ithaca: Cornell University Press.
Simpson, G. G. 1949. *The Meaning of Evolution*. New Haven: Yale University Press.
Simpson, G. G. 1953. *The Major Features of Evolution*. New York: Columbia University Press.
Tiger, L., and R. Fox, 1966. "The Zoological Perspective in Social Science." *Man* 1:75-81.

Tinbergen, N. 1968. "On War and Peace in Animals and Man." *Science* 160:1411-18.
Van den Berghe, P. 1974. "Bringing Beasts Back In: Toward a Biosocial Theory of Aggression." *American Sociological Review* 39:778-88.
Van den Berghe, P. 1975. *Man in Society*. New York: Elsevier.
Van Lawick-Goodall, J. 1971. *In the Shadow of Man*. Boston: Houghton Mifflin.
Wilson, E. O. 1975. *Sociobiology: The New Synthesis*. Cambridge: Harvard University Press.

34.
What Is Sociobiology?
Edward O. Wilson

I was surprised—astonished—by the intitial reaction to *Sociobiology: The New Synthesis*. When the book was published in 1975, I expected a favorable reaction from other biologists. After all, my colleagues and I had merely been extending Neo-Darwinism into the study of social behavior and animal societies, and the underlying biological principles we employed were largely conventional. The response was in fact overwhelmingly favorable. From the social scientists, I expected not much of a reaction at all. I took it for granted that the human species is subject to sociobiological analysis no less than genetic or endocrinological analysis; the final chapter of my book simply completed the catalog of social species by the addition of *Homo sapiens*. I hoped to make a contribution to the social sciences and humanities by laying out in immediately accessible form the most relevant methods and principles of population biology, evolutionary theory, and sociobiology. I expected that many social scientists, already convinced of the necessity of a biological foundation of their subject, would be tempted to pick up the tools and try them out. This has occurred to a limited extent, but there has also been stiff resistance. I now understand that I entirely underestimated the Durkheim-Boas tradition of autonomy of the social sciences, as well as the strength and power of the antigenetic bias that has prevailed as virtual dogma since the fall of Social Darwinsim.

I did not even think about the Marxists. When the attacks on sociobiology came from Science for the People, the leading radical left group within American science, I was unprepared for a largely ideological argument. It is now clear to me that I was tampering with something fundamental: mythology. Evolutionary theory applied to social systems is an extension of the great Western traditions of scientific materialism. As such it threatens to transform the assumptions about human nature made by some Marxist philosophers into testable hypotheses. Its first line of evidence is not favorable to those assumptions, insofar as most traditional Marxists cling to a vision of human nature as a relatively unstructured phenomenon swept along by economic forces extraneous to human biology. Marxism and other secular ideologies previously rested secure as unchallenged satrapies of scientific materialism; now they were in danger of being displaced by other, less manageable biological explanations. The remarkably harsh response of Science for the People exemplifies what Hans Küng has called the fury of the theologians.

Sociobiology Misunderstood

But much of the confusion has come from a simple misunderstanding of the content of sociobiology. Sociobiology is defined as the systematic study of the biological basis of all forms of social behavior, including sexual and parental behavior, in all kinds of organisms, including man. As such it is a discipline—an inevitable discipline, since there has to be a systematic study of social behavior. Sociobiology consists mostly of zoology. About 90 percent of its current material concerns animals, even though over 90 percent of the attention given to sociobiology by nonscientists, and expecially journalists, is due to its possible applications to the study of human social behavior. There is nothing unusual about deriving principles and methods, and even terminology, from intensive examinations of lower organisms and applying them to the study of human beings. Most of the fundamental principles of genetics and biochemistry applied to human biology is based on colon bacteria, fruit flies, and white rats. To say that the same science can be applied to human beings is not to reduce humanity to the status of these simpler creatures.

Nor is there anything new or surprising about having such a discipline within the family of the biological sciences. The term sociobiology was used independently by John P. Scott in 1946 and by Charles F. Hockett in 1948, but the word was not picked up immediately by others. In 1950 Scott, who had been serving as the secretary of the small but influential Committee for the Study of Animal Behavior, suggested sociobiology more formally as a term for the "interdisciplinary science which lies between the fields of biology (particularly ecology and physiology) and psychology and sociology." From 1956 into 1964 Scott and others constituted a Section on Animal Behavior and Sociobiology of the Ecological Society of America, which became the present Animal Behavior Society. During 1950–1970 "sociobiology" was employed intermittently in technical articles, a usage evidently inspired by its now quasiofficial status. But other expressions, such as "biosociology" and "animal sociology," were also employed. When

I wrote the final chapter of *The Insect Societies* (1971), which was entitled "The prospect for a unified sociobiology," and *Sociobiology: The New Synthesis* (1975), where I suggested that a discrete discipline should now be built on a foundation of genetics and population biology, I selected the term sociobiology rather than some other, novel expression because I believed it would already be familiar to most students of animal behavior and hence more likely to be accepted.

Biological Capacity

Pure sociobiological theory, being independent of human biology, does not imply by itself that human social behavior is determined by genes. It allows for any one of three possibilities. One is that the human brain has evolved to the point that it has become an equipotential learning machine entirely determined by culture. The mind, in other words, has been freed from the genes. A second possibility is that human social behavior is under genetic constraint but that all of the genetic variability within the human species has been exhausted. Hence our behavior is to some extent influenced by genes, but we all have exactly the same potential. A third possibility, close to the second, is that the human species is prescribed to some extent but also displays some genetic differences among individuals. As a consequence, human populations retain the capacity to evolve still further in their biological capacity for social behavior.

I consider it virtually certain that the third alternative is the correct one. Because the evidence has been well reviewed in other recent works, most notable those by Napoleon Chagnon and William Irons, editors, I. Devore, editor, and Daniel G. Freedman, I will not undertake to exemplify it or review it in detail. Instead, let me outline its content.

Specificity of Human Social Behavior

Although the variation of cultures appears enormous to the anthropocentric observer, all human behavior together comprises only a tiny subset of the realized social systems of the thousands of social species on earth. Corals and other colonial invertebrates, the social insects, fish, birds, and nonhuman mammals display among themselves an array of arrangements which are difficult for human beings even to understand, much less imitate. Even if we were to attempt to duplicate some of these social behaviors by conscious design, it would be a charade likely to create emotional breakdown and a rapid reversal of the effort.

Phylogenetic Relationships

Our social arrangements most closely resemble those of the Old World monkeys and apes, which on anatomical and biochemical grounds are our closest living relatives. This is the result expected if we share a common ancestry with these primates, which appears to be an established fact, and if human social behavior is still constrained to some extent by genetic predispositions in behavioral development.

Conformity to Sociobiological Theory

In the case of the hypothesis of genetic constraints on human social behavior, it should be possible to select some of the best principles of population genetics and ecology, which form the foundations of sociobiology, and apply them in detail to the explanations of human social organization. The hypothesis should then not only account for many of the known facts in a more convincing manner than previous attempts, but also identify the need for new kinds of information not conceptualized by the unaided social sciences. The behavior thus explained should be the most general and least rational of the human repertory, the furthest removed from the influence of year-by-year shifts in fashion and convention. There are in fact a substantial number of anthropological studies completed or underway that meet these exacting criteria of postulational-deductive science. Among them can be cited the work of Joseph Shepher on the incest taboo and sexual roles; Mildred Dickeman on hypergamy and sex-biased infanticide; Irons on the relation between inclusive genetic fitness and the emic criteria of social success in a herding society; Chagnon on aggression and reproductive competition in the Yanomamö; William Durham on the relation between inclusive fitness and warfare in the Mundurucú and other primitive societies; Robin Fox on the relation of fitness to kinship rules; Melvin Konner and Freedman on the adaptive significance of infant development; James Weinrich on the relationship of genetic fitness and the details of sexual practice, including homosexuality; and others.

Genetic Variation within the Species

According to V.A. McKusick and F.H. Ruddle, by 1977 more than 1200 loci had been located on human chromosomes through the first analysis of biochemical and other mutations. Many of these point mutations, as well as a growing list of chromosomal aberrations, affect behavior. Most simply diminish mental capacity and motor ability, but at least two, the Lesch-Nyhan syndrome, based on a single gene, and Turner's syndrome, caused by the deletion of a sex chromosome, alter behavior in narrow ways that can be related to specific neuromuscular mechanisms. The adreno-genital syndrome, which is induced by a single recessive gene, appears to masculinize girls through an early induction of adrenocortical substances that mimic the male hormone.

More complex forms of human behavior are almost certainly under the control of polygenes (genes scattered on many chromosome loci), which in turn create their effects through the alteration of a wide array of mediating devices, from elementary neuronal wiring to muscular coordination and "mental set" induced by hormone levels. In most instances, the role of behavorial polygenes can be evaluated, but only qualitatively, by the careful application of twin and adoption studies. The most frequently used method is to compare the similarity between identical twins, which are known to be genetically identical, with the similarity between fraternal twins, which are no closer genetically than ordinary siblings. When the similarity between identical twins proves greater, this distinction between the two kinds of twins is ascribed to heredity. Using this and related techniques, geneticists have produced evidence of a substantial amount of hereditary influence on the development of a variety of traits that affect social behavior, including number ability, word fluency, memory, the timing of language acquisition, sentence construction, perceptual skill, psychomotor skill, extroversion-introversion, homosexuality, the timing of first heterosexual activity, and certain forms of neurosis and psychosis, including the manic-depressive syndrome and schizophrenia.

In published work there is a flaw in the results that render most of them less than definitive: identical twins are commonly treated more alike by their parents than are fraternal twins. They are instructed in a more nearly parallel manner, dressed more alike, and so forth. In the absence of better controls, it is possible that the greater similarity of identical twins could, after all, be due to environmental influences and not their genetic identity. However, new and more sophisticated studies have begun to take account of this additional factor. J.C. Loehlin and R.C. Nichols, for example, analyzed the many aspects of the environments and performances of 850 sets of twins who took the National Merit Scholarship test in 1962. The early histories of the subjects, as well as the attitudes and rearing practices of the parents, were taken into account. The results showed that the generally more similar treatment of the identical twins cannot account for their greater similarity in general abilities, personality traits, or even ideals, goals, and vocational interests. It is evident that either the similarities are based in substantial part on genetic identity, or else environmental agents were at work that remained hidden to Loehlin and Nichols.

My overall conclusion from the existing information is that *Homo sapiens* is a typical animal species with reference to the quality and magnitude of the genetic diversity affecting its behavior. I also believe that it will soon be within our ability to locate and characterize specific genes that alter the more complex forms of social behavior. Obviously the alleles discovered will not prescribe different dialects or modes of dress. They are more likely to work measurable changes through their effects on learning modes and timing, cognitive and neuromuscular ability, and the personality traits most sensitive to hormonal mediation. If social scientists and sociobiologists somehow choose to ignore this line of investigation, they will soon find human geneticists coming up on their blind side. The intense interest in medical genetics, fueled now by new methods such as the electrophoretic separation of proteins and rapid sequencing of amino acids, has resulted in an acceleration of discoveries in human heredity that is certain to have profound consequences for the genetics of social behavior.

Genes and Methodological Reductionism

I wish now to discuss in broad terms the ways in which the several intellectual traditions represented so well by the other contributors to this special issue might be reconciled with the relatively uncompromising biologistic approach I have taken to the present time.

The first area of conflict that can be resolved is the relation of genes to culture. Many social scientists see no value in sociobiology because they are persuaded that variation among cultures has no genetic basis. Their premise is right, their conclusion wrong. We can do well to remember Rousseau's dictum that those who wish to study men should stand close, while those who wish to study man should look from afar. The social scientist is interested in the often microscopic but important variations in behavior that almost everyone agrees are due to culture and the environment. The sociobiologist is interested in the more general features of human nature and the limitations that exist in the environmentally induced variation. He is especially interested in the fact that although all cultures taken together constitute a very great amount of variation, their summed content is far less than that displayed by the remaining species of social animals. By comparing the diagnostic features of human organization with those of other primate species, the sociobiologist aims to reconstruct the earliest evolutionary history of social organization and to discern its genetic residues in contemporary societies. The approach complements that of the social sciences and in no way diminishes their importance—quite the contrary.

Those immersed in the rich lore of the social sciences sometimes reject human sociobiology because it is reductionistic. But almost all of the great advances of science have been made by reduction, in the form of conjectures that are often bold and momentarily premature. Theoretical physics transformed chemistry, chemistry transformed cell biology and genetics, natural selection theory transformed ecology—all by stark reduction which at first seemed inadequate to the task. Reduction is a method by which new mechanisms and relational processes are discovered. In the most successful case histories of postulational-deductive science, propositions are expressed in forms that can be elaborated into precise, testable models. The other side of reduction, the antithema of the thema, is synthesis. As the new principles and equations are validated by repeated testing, they are used in an attempt to reconstitute the full array of the phenomena of the subject. Karl Popper has correctly suggested that philosophical reductionism is wrong but methodological reductionism is necessary for the advancement of science. Here is how I tried to summarize the role of sociobiological reduction in *Daedalus* (Fall 1977):

> The urge to be reductionistic is an understandable human trait. Ernst Mach captured it in the following definition: "Science may be regarded as a minimal problem consisting of the completest presentment of facts with the least possible expenditure of thought." This is a sentiment of a member of the antidiscipline, impatient to set aside complexity and get on with the search for more fundamental ideas. The laws of his subject are necessary to the discipline above, they challenge and force a mentally more efficient restructuring, but they are not sufficient for its purposes. Biology is the key to human nature, and social scientists cannot afford to ignore its emerging principles. But the social sciences are potentially far richer in content. Eventually they will absorb the relevant ideas of biology and go on to beggar them by comparison.

Physical Basis of Mind

The strongest redoubt of counterbiology appears to be mentalism. It is difficult—for some it is impossible—to envision the existence of the mind and the creation of symbolic thought by biological processes. The human mind, this argument often goes, is an emergent property of the brain that is no longer tied to genetic controls. All that the genes can prescribe is the construction of the liberated brain.

But the relation between genes, the brain, and the mind is only a practical difficulty, not a theoretical one. Models have already been produced in neurobiology and cognitive psychology that allow at least the possibility of mind as an epiphenomenon of complex but essentially conventional neuronal circuitry. Consciousness might well consist of large numbers of coded abstractions, some fed stepwise through a hierarchy of integrating centers whose lowest array consists of the primary sense cells, others originating internally to simulate these hierarchies. The brain—in Charles Sherrington's metaphor the "enchanted loom where millions of flashing shuttles weave a dissolving pattern"—not only experiences scenarios fed to it by the sensory channels; it creates them by recall and fantasy. In sustaining this activity, the brain depends substantially on the triggering effect of verbal symbols. It also relies on what have been called plans or schemata, configurations within the brain, either innate or experiential in origin, against which the input of the nerve cells is compared. The matching of the real or expected patterns can have one or more of several effects. It can contribute to mental "set," the favoring of certain kinds of sensory information over others. It can generate the remarkable phenomena of Gestalt perception, in which the mind supplies missing details from the actual sensory information in order to complete a pattern and make a classification. And it can serve as the physical basis of will: the mind can be guided in its actions by feedback loops that lead from the sense organs to the brain schemata to the neuromuscular machinery and sense organs and back again until the schemata "satisfy" themselves that the correct action has been taken. The mind could be a republic of alternative schemata, programmed to compete for control of the decision centers, individually waxing and waning in power according to the relative urgency of the body's needs being signalled through other nervous pathways passing upward through the lower brain centers. The mind might or might not work approximately in such a manner. My point is that it is entirely possible for all known components of the mind, including will, to have a neurophysiological basis subject to genetic evolution by natural selection. There is no a priori reason why any portion of the foundation of human social behavior must be excluded from the domain of sociobiological analysis.

Convergence

Some critics have objected to the drawing of analogies between animal and human behavior, especially as it entails the same terminology to describe phenomena across species. This reservation has always struck me as insubstantial. The definitions and limitations of the concepts of analogy and homology have been well worked out by evolutionary biologists, and it is difficult to imagine why the same reasoning cannot be extended with proper care to the human species. We already speak of the eye of the octopus and the eye of man, copulation in an insect and copulation in man, and learning in the earthworm and learning in man, even though in each of these cases the two species are in different superphyla and the traits listed were independently evolved. The questions of interest are in fact the degrees of convergence and the processes of natural selection that made the convergence so close. When biologists compare altruism in the honeybee worker with human altruism, no one seriously believes that they are based on homologous genes or that they are identical in detail. Slavery practiced by *Polyergus* and *Strongylognathus* ants resembles human slavery in some broad features and differs from it in others, as well as in most details of its execution. By using the same term for such comparisons, the biologist calls attention to the fact that some degree of convergence has occurred, and he invites an analysis of all the causes of similarity and difference. There is a hellenistic term for insect slavery—dulosis—but its usage outside entomology would not only complicate language but slow the very comparative analysis which is of greatest interest.

Speaking the Common Language

I am most puzzled by the occasional demurral that sociobiology distracts our attention from the real needs of the world. The question is raised: How can we worry about the origins of human nature when the nuclear sword hangs over us? When people are starving in the Sahel and Bangladesh, and political prisoners are rotting in Argentinian jails? In response one can answer: Do we want to know, in depth and with any degree of confidence, why we care? And after these problems have been solved, what then? The highest goals professed by governments everywhere are human fulfillment above the animal level and the realization of individual potential. But what is fulfillment, and to what ends can potential be expanded? I suggest that only a deeper understanding of human nature, which must be developed from neurobiological investigations of the brain and the phylogenetic reconstruction of the species-specific properties of human behavior, can provide humanity with the perspective it requires to formulate its highest social goals.

The excitement of sociobiology comes from the promise of the role it will play in this new humanistic investigation. Its potential importance beyond zoology lies in its logical position as the bridging discipline between the natural sciences on the one side and social sciences and humanities on the other. For years the chief spokesmen of the natural sciences to Western high culture have been physicists, astronomers, geneticists, and molecular biologists, articulate and persuasive scholars whose understanding of the evolution of the brain and of social behavior was unfortunately minimal. Their perception of values and the human condition was almost entirely intuitive, and hence scarcely better than that of other intelligent laymen. Biology has been employed as a science that accounts for the body of man; it concerns itself with technological manifestations such as the conquest of disease, the green revolution, energy flow in ecosystems and the cost-benefit analysis of gene splicing. Natural scientists have by and large conceded social behavior to be biologically unstructured, and therefore the undisputed domain of the social sciences. For their part, most social scientists have granted that human nature has a biological foundation, but they have regarded it as of marginal interest to the resplendent variations in culture that hold their professional attention.

In order for the fabled gap between the two cultures to be truly bridged, social theory must incorporate the natural sciences into its foundations, and for that to occur, biology must deal systematically with social behavior. This competence is now being approached through the two-pronged advance of neurobiology, which boldly hopes to explain the physical basis of mind, and sociobiology, which aims to reconstruct the evolutionary history of human nature. Sociobiology in particular is still a rudimentary science. Its relevance to human social systems is still largely unexplored. But in the gathering assembly of disciplines, it holds the greatest promise of speaking the common language.

35.
Animal Behavior and Social Anthropology

S.L. Washburn

Interest in animal behavior has increased sharply, as shown by the number of programs on television, the success of popular books, and the recent appearance of reviews and textbooks. This general interest has been further stimulated and canalized by Edward O. Wilson's *Sociobiology: The New Synthesis,* which calls for a new synthetic science of animal behavior. Wilson's popular view has taken on many of the qualities of an intellectual movement. Its adherents are enthusiastic and they do not welcome criticism.

From the point of view of social anthropology, it is essential to keep the very heterogeneous study of animal behavior separate from sociobiology as described by Wilson. Clearly the appeal of sociobiology is that it offers an evolutionary and genetic explanation for a remarkable diversity of animal behaviors, but equally clearly the theory leads to gross errors when applied to human behavior. The reasons for this are complex, and, I can see only a few of them. But what I will try to do here is to suggest that social anthropologists may gain many insights into human behaviors by considering the behavior of other animals, but sociobiology (as practiced at present) will only bring confusion to anthropological problems.

As I read anthropology, I see a long history of biology confusing and retarding the development of the social sciences. The belief in nineteenth-century evolution theory, orthogenesis, reductionism, biological analogies, homeostasis, racial dominance, IQ superiority, eugenics, and the ever-present confusion of genetic and environmental causes—all have been major liabilities to social science. History cannot be changed, but a strong case can be made that the founders of social science would have been far better off if they had never heard of biology or evolution. But at the very time that biology was a liability to the social sciences, major progress was being made in the biological understanding of human behaviors.

At present a great deal is known about the biology of our species, information essential for the practice of medicine. Information on a very wide variety of behavorial topics (sleeping, dreaming, thinking, speaking, etc.) is available for social scientists. Using this kind of knowledge in trying to understand human biology in no way contradicts Durkheim and the idea that social facts must be explained by social facts. Attempts to discern the biology of the human actors, of the social systems, and of their interrelations comprise three supplementary kinds of information. Problems arise when the distinctions separating the differing kinds of information are blurred. In shaping their argument, sociobiologists must attack Durkheim and the logic of social facts, minimize the distinction of heredity and environment, and postulate genes to account for behaviors—a repetition of the errors of previous biological confusions.

The fundamental way sociobiology creates confusion may be illustrated by a quotation from W.D. Hamilton, whose papers on genetics form the foundation of sociobiological thinking. The following paragraph from Hamilton's article, "Innate Social Aptitudes of Man" illustrates what may happen when a person who has made major contributions to the theory of natural selection (inclusive fitness) discusses human evolution. The following nonsense belongs in the era of laissez-faire capitalism and Spencerian social evolution.

> The incursions of barbaric pastoralists seem to do civilizations less harm in the long run than one might expect. Indeed, two dark ages and renaissances in Europe suggest a recurring pattern in which a renaissance follows an incursion by about 800 years. It may even be suggested that certain genes or traditions of the pastoralists revitalize the conquered people with an ingredient of progess which tends to die out in a large panmictic population for the reasons already discussed. I have in mind altruism itself, or the part of the altruism which is perhaps better described as self-sacrificial daring. By the time of the renaissance it may be that the mixing of genes and cultures (or of cultures alone if these are the only vehicles, which I doubt) has continued long enough to bring the old mercantile thoughtfulness and the infused daring into conjunction in a few individuals who then find courage for all kinds of inventive innovation against the resistance of established thought and practice. Often, however, the cost in fitness of such altruism and sublimated pugnacity to the individuals concerned is by no means metaphorical, and the benefits to fitness, such as they are, go to a mass of individuals whose genetic correlation with the innovator must be slight indeed. Thus civilization probably slowly reduces its altruism of all kinds, including the kinds needed for cultural creativity.

This absurdity has been highly praised, and this kind of writing does not seem to disturb sociobiologists.

Obviously, the importance of this particular passage lies in the kind of thinking it represents. It precisely repeats the errors of the early evolutionists who thought that their theory was so powerful that facts could just be arranged in order *without* doing the necessary research. Stone tools were arranged in evolutionary orders without archeological information. The orders proved to be wrong. The mistaken notion that evolution necessarily moves from the simple to the complex led to countless hypothetical reconstructions. Close to a hundred years of mistakes were justified by the belief in the power of evolutionary theory. Though the general theory of evolution is correct, a theory does not give conclusions; it directs the nature of the research, but each application of the theory demands careful research.

This is the fundamental weakness in Hamilton's passage and in the majority of sociobiological thinking as applied to human behavior. Writers are so confident in the power of the theory (selection, adaptation, inclusive fitness) that a minimum effort is made to learn the facts of human behavior and of human history.

In analyzing the whole Hamilton paper, I find the basic form is (1) useful genetic theory, briefly presented and clearly discussed; (2) practically no effort to uncover the facts of human evolution, of recent human history, or of animal behavior; (3) conclusions which are personal biases, stemming from neither facts nor theories. This is the general form through which sociobiology is applied to the interpretation of human behavior—and it is for this reason that it is repeating the mistakes of many years ago. There is no way for a scientist to leap directly from genetic or evolutionary theory to conclusions about human behavior. The principal task for the scientist is the research which links theory and conclusion. Lacking this link, sociobiology may be useful and illuminating, or reductionist, racially biased, and absurd.

For example, although sociobiologists speak of human evolution, practically no attention is paid to the archeological record. The record shows that, starting a little before agriculture, there was a very rapid change in technology which spread across the world in a very few thousands of years. The conditions that had dominated human evolution for some millions of years changed, and the nature of the change, the speed of the change, and the rate of diffusion all show that the changes were the result of learning, not biological evolution. Inclusive fitness theory states that an individual's social actions should lead to the perpetuation of the person's genes, either through descendants or through the survival of relatives. But in the previously cited quotation from Hamilton, it should be noted that, with civilization, benefits to fitness will no longer go to closely related individuals. In like manner, worried by increased mobility, Ilan Eshel thinks that evolution may no longer favor altruistic genes. To generalize the problem, the more people there are, the more mobility, the more variety of selective pressures, and the shorter the time span, the less will inclusive fitness theory be useful. And what the archeological record shows is a great increase in all these factors, beginning with late paleolithic and mesolithic times and accelerating to the present. Today an individual's actions are mostly with nonrelatives, and millions of people are deliberately reducing the number of their offspring. The conditions that dominated the evolution of *Homo sapiens* no longer exist, and a theory of evolution cannot be indiscriminately applied to human evolution as if the contemporary situation were similar to that of thousands of years ago.

The very rapid increase in population in the last 200 years is certainly the result of technology, not of changing gene frequencies. As earlier and earlier times are considered, it becomes increasingly difficult to prove that the basic changes were due entirely to learning, not genes. My belief is that there has been no important change in human abilities in the last 30,000 years. If this is even in large part the case, biological evolution cannot account for the social conditions of the modern world. This is certainly not a new idea, but it is the historical reason for stressing the importance of learned social facts rather than genes.

It has become fashionable to minimize the nature-nurture argument by stressing that both are important, that animal behavior is more plastic than it had been previously considered, and that human behavior may be more determined by genes. For example, S.T. Emlen suggests that the importance of the distinction has been exaggerated. Sociobiologists must take this position because they want to emphasize the importance of genetics in accounting for human social behaviors. As far as the interpretation of human social behavior is concerned, social anthropology will regress at least 50 years by allowing the distinction to become blurred. Given populations of *Homo sapiens*, social behavorial differences are to be understood as the results of history, of different groups of human beings learning different languages and ways of life.

The essential confusion in the comparison of human behavior with that of other animals is in the nature of learning. Confusion at this level lies behind most of the problems of comparing the social behaviors of man, and will constantly appear and reappear in a wide variety of forms when biologists and social anthropologists discuss behavior.

In these discussions, the term "culture" is not too helpful a word, partially because there are so many definitions and usages, and also because there is more learning in animal behavior than had been initially believed. Therefore, it is useful to regard language, and all the complexity of behaviors which language makes possible, as the basic difference between human and nonhuman. Language (the complex of brain-speaking with a phonetic code-perception of verbal patterns), unique to man, a product of singularly human evolution, is a behavior not found in any other animal. Language is the ability which makes the nature-nurture problem in the human species special and almost totally different from the comparable problem in other species. Without language, human behavior might be interpreted along rules similar to those governing the behavior of other animals. With language, the rules change, and human social behaviors cease to be under genetic control.

Human language is basic to environmental reference and social reference. Technology, economics, social relations, political systems, religions, arts—all human activities—depend on language, and it is language that makes it possible for humans to learn complex systems of behaviors. It is my belief that only very minimal technical progress is possible without at least some simple form of language, and, of course, no complex technology or science would be possible without this special form of communication. From an evolutionary point of view, it is not only that the human brain has evolved, but that the brain can easily learn to manage quantities and varieties of information without parallel in the animal world. The communication of this information depends on language. When considering human behaviors, it is language that gives the nature-nurture problem a major new dimension, vastly increasing the realities and possibilities of learning. When comparing human and nonhuman behaviors, any theory that minimizes the importance of distinguishing between linguistically mediated learned behaviors and other behaviors, in which learning may be much less important, is bound to cause confusion.

Comparative Behavior

Though the comparative study of behavior has been a very important element in the rise of biosocial science, there is no agreement on how comparisions are to be made. For example, a recent book on the biological bases of human social behavior includes nothing on the brain, little on hormones, a scrap (misleading) on language, and the author apparently considers the study of behavior to mean looking at the outsides of animals. Comparisons frequently take a pesudo-evolutionary form, although this method has been criticized for many years, and the sort of comparison usually made cannot possibly deal adequately with human behavior.

Comparisons Are Fun

Quite aside from any practical benefits, it is interesting to learn of the language of the bees, pheromones, factors guiding migrations in fish or birds, life of the penguin, or world of the herring gull. Just as the discovery of the gorilla or okapi stirred former generations, so the analysis of animal behavior excites many today. The success of myriad television programs and popular books shows the interest in behavior, and topics such as ant navigation by polarized light demonstrate a very sophisticated science, a far cry from traditional natural history. If one aim of education is to learn about the world, then, an appreciation of the world should include some understanding of the diversity of life and the extraordinary variety of behaviors. Typically, in this kind of comparison enormously diversified groups of vertebrates—even insects—are compared to a single group of human beings, and no attempt is made to prove that there is a common biological basis for the behaviors being compared.

Comparisons may alert us to new thoughts, new points of view. Experiments on monkeys direct attention to the possible importance of early experience in man. We are alerted to the existence of whole new sensory worlds and social systems that work with almost mechanical precision. But neither comparisons nor alerting are proof. They offer suggestions, and a very different sort of information is needed if the information is to be seriously used in the solution of human problems.

Serious Comparisons

It is natural to want to apply the understanding that comes from animal behavior to the behavior of human animals. To do this it is crucial to decide when such comparisions are useful and when they are not. For example, Konrad Lorenz's *King Solomon's Ring,* a great book, especially considering when it was written, belongs to the "fun" stage in the development of animal behavior. It interested many people in animal behavior, and was instrumental in the establishment of ethology as a distinctive science. Lorenz's *On Aggression* is not a helpful book, mainly because it uses bits of behaviors from oddly selected animals to suggest causes for important human social problems. It closes with advice that does not come from the data and can only be characterized as irrational: "The main function of sport today lies in the cathartic discharge of aggressive urge . . . ."

Lorenz has been criticized for *On Aggression,* but the issue is not the author; it is the method. For example, in one argument Richard Alexander mixes information about insects, birds, and Tibetan peasants—a discussion meaningless in serious comparison. The final chapter in Wilson's *Sociobiology: The New Synthesis* is an extreme example of the misuse of comparative information. The point can be illustrated by comparing Wilson's treatment of insect behavior with human behavior. When discussing insects (where he has facts), he does not bring human beings into the discussion. But when discussing man (where facts are minimal) insects are used to make critical points. And in passing, it might be pointed out that, in spite of countless references, the castes of India are not genetically determined and bear no resemblance to castes of insects.

Serious comparisons require careful, detailed analysis and experiments whenever possible. For example, the facial expressions of man and monkey have often been compared. But it has been shown that massive removal of the cortex of the brain in monkeys affects facial expression minimally; comparable damage in man would result in total facial paralysis. The experiment demonstrates that human facial expression is far more under cortical control, far more amenable to learning, than is the case in nonhuman primates. In monkeys, both sounds and facial expression are primarily under control of the primitive, emotion-controlling parts of the brain (limbic system). Just comparing monkey and human expressions and sounds cannot reveal the major structural differences underlying both facial expression and sound control.

In comparing the biological bases for human social activities (such as being social, speaking, gesturing, feeling various emotions), differences in the brain are always involved, and comparisons are necessarily complex. For example, the human family is a remarkably varied institution, serves many functions, and cannot be usefully described in any simple way. But, if the family is described as a "pair bond" (R.R. Larsen), then all the variety stemming from the uniquely human brain, language, history, and complex function is lost. One may then look for other creatures that pair bond, and end up with the notion that the human family may be better understood by studying herring gulls. This example illustrates two common mistakes in the comparative study of behavior. First, any chance to understand the human condition is lost by reducing the understanding of the family to the expression "pair bond." Second, it is a useless exercise, because pair bonding, where it does occur, can only be understood by analysis, not by uncontrolled comparisons. As Washburn, Hamburg, and Bishop have shown, gibbons do pair bond, but to understand this behavior it is necessary to appreciate a way of life in which locomotion, diet, and territorial behavior are all interrelated. Lorenz points out that comparisons between closely related forms are the most likely to be useful. This wide advice is almost never followed when human behaviors are compared with those of other animals.

Ethology has been so important in the rise of animal behavior that it merits a special word. The genius of ethology has been in its employment of experiments, and not the study of natural behavior, as is well illustrated in Niko Tinbergen's classic, *The Herring Gull's World*. Interpretations were constantly checked by experiments, and the world of this bird is revealed as being something very different from what it appeared to the observing human. While the results of ethological investigation are fascinating, and while Irenäus Eibl-Eibesfeldt's *Ethology: the Biology of Behavior* is well worth careful consideration, the chapter on the ethology of man shows how misleading the ethological approach can be. By investigating human behavior with the questions and techniques suitable for animals with very simple nervous systems, the whole nature of human behavior is lost. Human behavior cannot be understood by observation alone, and even when considering infants who cannot yet talk, the mother is part of a way of life based on speech, complex social behavior, and technology. The notion of cataloging behavior in an ethogram or biogram comes from the study of the behavior of a few animals—largely in captivity—and is completely inappropriate when applied to man. In terms of anthropological history, biograms and ethograms belong with prefunctional anthropology, and functioning systems do not lend themselves to that kind of cataloging. Whether the concern is biological mechanisms, biosocial functional complexes, or the elaboration of symbolic systems, the notion of the ethogram (behavior catalog) is misleading and provides no useful guide to research.

From a practical point of view, the easiest way to avoid gross reductionism is to start comparisons from the position of human behavior. Our heritage from evolutionary thinking leads to almost all comparisons being made in the opposite direction. The problem ethologists have with human social behavior is that in their whole strategy of research there is no place for the critical importance of language and learning, nor for the biology of cognition and language as being the facilitating mechanisms for uniquely human behaviors. Human ethology might be defined as the science which plays the game that humans can't speak. No one who starts with an understanding of human behavior will speak of pair bonds or compare the complex social and technical hunting patterns of man with those of the biologically based hunting patterns of carnivores (unaided by weapons, performed by both sexes, sometimes at speeds of more than twice human Olympic records).

If the "fun" kind of comparisons (aggression in fish, birds, and Yanomamö) are replaced with serious comparisons, then research reveals differences rather than similarity, and uniquely human behavior is based upon, and facilitated by, uniquely human biology. In summary, animal behavior is a fascinating study in its own right. It is pleasurable and basically liberating in the best traditions of a free and basic science. But at the present time most comparisons are far more likely to be misleading than helpful to social anthropologists.

The methods of ethology have been defended, by Blurton Jones, as being similar to those of comparative anatomy. But the methods referred to are the very part of comparative anatomy that worked only to a very limited extent, or in some instances not at all. Specifically in the case of man, no one reconstructed a fossil ancestor that looked like *Australopithecus*. The lesson from comparative anatomy is that generally there must be fossils, an actual evolutionary sequence. Even in anatomy, there is no way to traingulate back from present forms to reconstruct ancestral populations, and the case is even worse for behavior.

Examining the conclusions of some of the leaders in the field of evolutionary biology, one can see the problems generated by the mixture of evolutionary theory with social anthropology: Alexander concludes that society is based on lies; Hamilton thinks infusions of pastoral genes are necessary to keep creativity; Wilson thinks neurobiology is necessary for ethics. In addition to technical disagreements, especially over group selection, these authors read like a mixture of Herbert Spencer and science fiction.

There is a variety of reasons that lie behind the confusions of evolutionary theory when it is applied to man. Perhaps the most fundamental is the belief that, if the theory is correct, the application of the theory is easy and routine. But some general theories, the notion of selection leading to adaptation for one, are only guides for research. If human locomotion is the area of interest, then the structure of the pelvis and the lower limbs must be interpreted according to the way they function. This adaptation is unique to man and there is no way that the form can be predicted by the theory. Nor is the form resulting from the evolutionary process necessarily efficient or ideal. It is just what, as a part of a complex process, succeeded in competition with others. In the female, adaptations for locomotion and easy childbirth are in conflict. In both sexes the lower back is too weak. The ligaments of the knees should be stronger. The mechanics of the ankle and foot could easily be improved. Perhaps in a few million years the adaptation might have become more efficient, but in the short run the defects may have to be remedied by the surgeon. Even in behaviors that are largely genetically determined, there is no reason to suppose that the behaviors are necessary, ideal, or more than the compromise that survived in evolutionary competition.

The application of the general theory of evolution (selection, adaptation, inclusive fitness) requires that the facts used in fitting the theory be correct, and that the theory itself only suggests where to look for facts and which ones may be relevant. This is the fundamental weakness of the authors I have cited. They know theory, but very little about human behavior or the few known facts of evolution. The power of the theory gives them confidence that their personal opinions are correct and should be adopted.

The theory that biology is adaptive is very similar to Bronislaw Malinowski's theory of functionalism. Both are useful as guides to research, and I have often pointed out that Malinowski's *Scientific Theory of Culture* is a better guide to the behavior of the nonhuman primates than to language-based human behavior. But in neither biology nor human behavior may one simply assume that the fact one is dealing with is adaptive—or even a fact. Consider the nose, which is obviously adapted for respiration. Its function is to admit and warm air; so a great many papers have been written attempting to correlate the external form of the bony nose with climate and temperature. But the nose is also the middle of the face and the incisor teeth form in the bone just below the nasal opening. As can be seen in growth patterns or by comparison with other primates, the nasal width is, in part, a function of the size of the teeth, and the center of the face must be seen as a complex involving several factors.

One may not look at a structure or a behavior and simply assume an adaptation. For example, Alexander postulates that the menopause may have evolved because women reach an age at which it is advantageous for them to take care of the already present offspring rather than to have more—suggesting positive selection for menopause, a genetic explanation. But an alternative theory is that the increasing efficiency of the human way of life (culture) made it possible for people to live longer and longer. With no genetic change, women would live past their reproductive period, a process still going on. There is no doubt that the length of human life has increased greatly over the last century and the process is continuing. One explanation is highly speculative and genetic; the other is environmental and can at least in part be directly verified.

Just as postulating positive selection of genes for menopause blocks consideration of the increase in length of life, so postulating genes for homosexuality assumes our cultural values and avoids analysis of very diverse behaviors in many cultural settings. Sociobiologists must postulate genes for behaviors because they would not have a science if they did not do so. Postulating genes for behaviors has been so prevalent in European thinking (eugenics, racially biased theories, genes for crime, genes for historical change) that is deserves a special name. I suggest genitis (gene-itis, the genetic disease). This disease consists of postulating genes to account for behaviors without making any major effort to see if the suggestions are reasonable. Most sociobiologists seem to have bad cases of genitis. Sociogiologists postulate genes for altruism and others for cheating, but it would be far more adaptive to possess genes for intelligence and be able to cheat or be altruistic as occasion demanded. Genitis leads to futile uncontrolled speculation.

Evolution and Semantics

The basic problem with postulating genes for social behaviors is that it shifts the nature of explanation from the logic of social facts to the logic of genetics. Even though the environment may be important in both cases, it makes a great deal of practical difference if the cause of crime is in large part genetic, or if crime is a word standing for a wide variety of behaviors learned under varying circumstances and defined differently in different cultures. At the present time, the word "evolution" has no clearly defined meaning, and it may be used in a way to confuse biologiocal and social explanations. For example, Donald Campbell in his presidential address to the American Psychological Association defined both biological and social evolution as "blind variation and systematic selective retention." But Lenski and Lenski define sociocultural evolution as "technical advance and its consequences." The best evidence for sociocultural evolution comes from the part of human behavior which is least appropriately labeled "blind." Raoul Naroll and William T. Divale define evolution as moving "in the direction of increasing functional complexity," and state that this is the case in biology, giving George Simpson as a reference. But Simpson stated that "evolution has so often and so misleadingly been generalized as just a succession from simple to more complex forms of life." Evolution from complex to simple is not just associated with loss (as in cave fish) but the human skull is far simpler than the skull of the ancestral fishes and the human brain is more complex. The ordering of human historical and social facts cannot be justified by appeals to biological evolution, nor can the use of the word "blind" do more than confuse genetic change with social change.

I have used recent references because these old problems are still very much with us. If it is desired to use words which stand for similar operations, then the following mean the same: "evolution," "biological evolution," "biological history," and the methods of study are "genetic," "biological," and change requires a long period of time. Another series of comparable words are: "evolution," "social evolution," "sociocultural evolution," "history," and the methods of study are concerned with the record of human learned behaviors. The two kinds of evolution may be in a feedback relation, but the processes involved, methods of study, and implications for social science, are radically different. When people resort to the word "evolution," even when qualified by "social" or "sociocultural," they believe that something has been said which is more important than referring to the same chronological events as "history." Evolution is a magic word, and it is used to predispose the reader to certain kinds of conclusions. However that may be, to avoid confusion it is necessary to consider evolution (genetic change), and history (cultural change) separately before the interrelations between the two are considered.

Evolution

If there are problems in the comparison of behaviors, these are compounded in the study of evolution. To the difficulties of comparison are added the complications of the fossil record, time, and constantly changing theories. Obviously the challenge is that with enough facts and the right theories, evolution, and only evolution, will give the overall synthesis. Evolution provides the master view of what happened and why it happened. But in spite of the technical power and intellectual magnificence of the evolutionary perspective, it is by no means clear how it can be applied in ways helpful to social anthropology. Clearly, the problem is that both biology and social anthropology are changing, and, from the social anthropological point of view, the question is whether people are more likely to be effective social anthropologists if they know some biology.

Just as in the case of comparisons, the study of human evolution must start with facts about human beings. It is only known that human beings are bipeds, have large brains, and great cognitive abilities, have language, religion, the arts, and complex social life—by studying humans. There is almost infinitely more information about humans than there is about monkeys or apes. The problems cannot be usefully framed by starting with animal behavior, particularly the behavior of forms in which behavior is largely genetically determined and stereotyped. Most human behavior has no close counterpart in any nonhuman animal, and this is the most important conclusion of the study of human evolution. For this reason the application of general theories, which apply to very different forms of life, must be applied to man only with the greatest caution. For example, the nature-nurture dichotomy was unfortunate, and it is a fact that most behaviors have genetic bases modified by environment. But the relative contribution of genes and environmental influence may vary from almost nothing to 100 percent. There is no evidence that there is any genetic component determining the differences in human languages or social systems.

Evolution is a master theory, accounting for the origin and diversity of life. It is the great materialistic theory taking the place of the idea of creation and helping in the understanding of the biological nature of the world and of man. But the existence of varying societies and cultures is made possible by human brains, language, and learning, and the rules of social learning are fundamentally different from those of evolutionary genetics.

Genetics

Sociobiology is in part a renewal of interest in natural selection, evolution, and adaptation. To the traditional formulation of these problems has been added the concept of kin selection. In *Sociobiology and Behavior,* David P. Barash gives a very clear account of the history of the concept and its consequences. According to traditional selection theory, there was no way of accounting for acts which appeared to reduce the fitness of the individual performing the acts (altruistic acts). Kin selection shows that there may be selection for altruistic acts, if they benefit the relatives of the altruist. Relationship is measured by the coefficient of relationship, which gives a measure of the proportion of genes which two individuals share because of common descent. For identical twins the coefficient will be one. For entirely unrelated individuals the coefficient will be zero. Between parent and offspring the coefficient is one-half, between full siblings, one-half; between aunts and uncles and nieces and nephews, one-quarter; between cousins, one-eighth.

According to sociobiologists, social structure should follow this genetic calculus. The patterns of actions between human beings should follow the same pattern as the genetic relations. Marshall Sahlins has shown that this is not the case, but it is too soon to tell whether his analysis will exert any influence on sociobiology. In modern mobile societies, most interactions will be with unrelated individuals (coefficient zero), and this is why Hamilton thinks that altruism and creativity must be reduced in civilizations, although all the historic evidence suggests that precisely the opposite is the case.

There is a fundamental complication in the analysis of kin selection. Although an individual receives half the genes from each parent, a person shares half the genes in which the parents differ and all the genes shared by both parents. Within a species the majority of genes are shared, and it has been estimated that two human beings, selected at random, will share something on the order of 90 percent of their genes. The similarity is much greater if it is based on estimates in the order of DNA. For example, M.C. King and A.C. Wilson estimate that human beings and chimpanzees share 99 percent of their genetic material, and that human races are 50 times closer. This should not be surprising if the anatomical similarities shared by all human beings are considered. But it means that individuals who would be considered unrelated (coefficient zero, as normally calculated) share almost all their genetic material.

There are three consequences of stressing shared genes and common biology, as opposed to stressing differences. First, traditional genetics could only find differences. If there were no contrasting alleles, a gene could not be defined. To a large extent traditional genetics had to be a science of difference, often of trivial difference. But with the understanding of DNA came the possibility of seeing similarity in the genetic substance, and the study of DNA shows that there is an enormous amount of duplication. It is no accident that sociobiologists pay no attention to DNA, or species-wide similarities that determine behaviors.

Second, if behaviors that are important to the basic adaptations and survival of the species are based in large part (not completely) on homozygous genes, then as far as these adaptations are concerned, random mating will have nearly the same results as the mating of close relatives.

Third, if in the case of human beings, we are concerned with the behaviors that form the base of the success of the species (bipedalism, hand skill, cognition, language, ease of learning, social complexity), these are all highly complex and, with rare exceptions, common to the whole species. Therefore, there is no reason to suppose that customs favoring close relatives would have great effects on the evolution of the biology which is important to human social behaviors.

One of the fundamental controversies in genetics is group selection, and this is of particular importance to social anthropologists. In general, sociobiologists deny the importance of group selection. Wilson, however, strongly supports it, and Alexander states that "human social groups represent an almost ideal model for potent selection at the group level." What Alexander means is what anthropologists would call culture, and what in this paper I have viewed as the results of language. Shared social knowledge may be adaptive, but not because of genes.

The issues may be simply stated as follows. It is individuals that leave offspring. If the life, or death, of individuals change gene frequencies, then there is evolutionary change. The gene frequencies in populations influence the phenotypes in the next generation, and are affected by the differential survival of individuals. But the survival of individuals may be determined by the group in which they live. The more knowledge, technology, social organization (culture), the more important the group is in determining survival.

If we use Theodosius Dobzhansky's definition of evolution as the changing gene frequencies in populations, and the changes are due to differential survival, and the survival may be strongly influenced by the group, then some important consequences follow. Contrary to much sociobiology, war may not have any effect on evolution at all. It is only if the gene frequencies of survivors are different from the vanquished that there is any effect on evolution, on changing the frequencies of genes. If most wars through most of human history have been with close neighbors, the effect on evolution was probably minimal. Further, it makes no difference if some people have many offspring and some none, unless this changed the gene frequencies of populations. For example, if celibate monks (taken as a group) and the males leaving most offspring (taken as a group) have the same gene frequencies, the evolutionary process is unaffected. There may be social change, demographic change, but evolutionary change can only be demonstrated if it can be shown that differential reproduction was accompanied by genetic change.

In summary, there is no clearly defined, universally accepted evolutionary theory that social anthropologists must accept. There has been great progress in the understanding of genetic mechanisms, but, naturally, there are still major controversies. The most fundamental problem comes from postulating genes to account for behaviors.

36.
Heredity Versus Culture: A Debate
Edward O. Wilson and Marvin Harris, with Ann Carroll

Carroll: Sociobiology has been called one of the most inflammatory doctrines to emerge from the campus in decades, and I think it's true that whenever you have such a controversial, issue, one that affects all of us so much, that misconceptions arise in the popular imagination.

To begin with, Dr. Wilson, would you define sociobiology for us?

Wilson: It's a discipline, and a well-established discipline within biology and has been for some 25 years. My book just helped synthesize it and organize it as an on-going subject. It's a study of all aspects of social behavior in all kinds of organisms up to—and, of course, this is the difficult part—human beings. It's been concentrated to the present time on animals, and the principles and basic mechanisms in the organization of animal societies. It is not a specific theory about human behavior. It allows for any of a wide array of possibilities concerning human behavior.

Carroll: But as far as basic tenets, would you say it's fair to say that social behavior is controlled by genes?

Wilson: It emphatically is in lower organisms. As to whether it is in human beings, this is now a matter under heated discussion.

I think most zoologists who work in the area of sociobiology see human behavior as constituting only a tiny subset of all of the realized social systems among thousands of species of social animals. And in that sense, they see human behavior constrained.

They also believe that—and I include myself among them—that human nature, that is, the predispositions, emotional constraints, hormonal feedback loops affecting social behavior in human beings, is quite structured; more so than many social scientists have appreciated or at least emphasized in their textbooks. And this structuring is consistent with evolutionary theory.

Carroll: As an anthropologist, Dr. Harris, how do you react to this?

Harris: My reaction is that we've already set up a false dichotomy which will inevitably confuse everyone concerning what the significance of sociobiology is from the point of view of anthropology.

For the last hundred years, anthropologists have been concerned with demonstrating the continuity between infrahuman animals and the human animal. And no anthropologist would deny that there is a human nature. On that level, the quarrel between us would come down to specifics of what do you put into human nature.

There's another dimension to sociobiology, however, which is concerned with the explanation of how particular populations vary with respect to their social response repertoires. And here, Dr. Wilson may be in disagreement with many of his colleagues, because he himself has stated that he thinks that the most important factor in determining the human social life is culture rather than genes. And we have to separate out these two kinds of sociobiology, and then we also have to see that anthropologists are very much in agreement that there is a human nature. But I think that Dr. Wilson and I would disagree as to what is in human nature.

Wilson: I'm sure that when we get down to the specifics of what constitutes human nature and how much constraints there are, there would be an area of disagreement.

Now, I am taken by Professor Harris' cultural evolutionism, and I find his approach to some of those complex problems in religion and social hierarchy in developing civilizations courageous and original, particularly in the context of present day anthropology. I know that he views this as exclusively a process of cultural evolution. I would find that difficult to dispute, and what I am most interested in is really the complementary aspect of the study which is the biological basis of the predispositions in human behavior, such as, say, the proneness to eat meat; the proneness to form hierarchy; xenophobia; territorialism; incest; taboos; and so on.

Harris: I'd like to separate those two things: what we share with primates in general and what is distinctive in the human biogram—which is that aspect of human life controlled by the distinctive complement of genes which humans have.

Wilson: It appears to me that there is a long list of such human traits and that a large percentage of them are shared with primates. For example, the facial expressions of human beings really appear to be hard wired and in many instances comparable to those found in the chimpanzee.

Harris: Okay, let's just take facial expressions. There's no doubt that as a result of the evolution of the facial musculature primates, and humans have an unusual degree of facial mobility and ability to express emotions on the face.

Granted that there is a genetic basis for the range of facial expressions, isn't it true that with very little social training, individuals are capable—in particular cultural traditions—of completely masking—overcoming—whatever genetic predisposition there might be. Isn't it true that so many different cultures use these facial expressions in contrary ways? Can't we learn so readily to mask our emotions, to control our facial expressions? And if that's the case, then the genetic component would seem to be—in this instance—less significant than the cultural components.

Wilson: The range of expressions I think is nevertheless quite narrow. There's no doubt that it's modifiable to the extent that it becomes a very important part of the communication repertory and that one can even reverse meaning with some difficulty. And yet studies have shown that you can get communication across cultures—say from literate European-American cultures to preliterate New Guinea cultures—with 80 percent accuracy on the basic emotions, including disgust, happiness, surprise, fear, and one or two others.

So that although flexibility no doubt exists, nevertheless, it is limited and there are basic patterns which tend to emerge. So that I think we now can use this to contrast the different perspectives of the biologist and the anthropologist.

The anthropologist, of course, is properly interested in these nuances and the changes that are possible through cultural training. The biologist tends to try to reduce that or look for the common patterns and thereby identify the origins of these in terms of genetic evolution. I think that the two approaches are complementary in the sense that the biologist compares the human species with all other species, where it fits, by a comparative approach, overlooking a great deal of that important cultural variation. The anthropologist is concerned with the origin and significance of that variation.

Carroll: Another one of the central tenets of sociobiology that interests me is the way of explaining altruism and saying that it is genetic selfishness, that of protecting your own kind. Could you explain this more?

Wilson: We've hit here on a subject in which I think biological sociobiology —general sociobiology—might make a contribution to anthropology at the theoretical level by helping to define what I've referred to as hard-core as opposed to soft-core altruism: hard-core based upon very special kinds of genetic chains through the helping of kin and soft-core being reciprocal —the familiar social contract that dominates so much of human behavior.

Carroll: You do for me and I'll do for you?

Wilson: Yes. It's clear that the mystery of the evolution of hard-core altruism—unilaternal altruism—is solved in theory. And population biologists have defined—with increasing precision—the conditions under which it can arise: how many kin you have to benefit and to what extent; how many groups have to go extinct to benefit other groups which have altruism within them and therefore are more cohesive and the like. So that a theoretical structure has been built up which I think eventually can be applied to the study of human populations to help tease apart these various components of altruism—unilaternal hard-cord versus the social contract.

Carroll: I know that you received a letter from a very troubled young man who had received a Carnegie gold medal for saving a drowning victim, and he was very concerned that you or other sociobiologists were feeling that his action was something that was genetically predetermined. How did you respond to him?

Wilson: By explaining that altruism is based upon impulses, upon emotional rewards in human beings even though it involves conscious decisions.

To qualify as altruism—at least in a biological sense—one needs only to engage in self-sacrificing behavior for the benefit of others. In lower animals, this may be an automatic response without any kind of associative conscious reflection on it. In human beings, as in most of our behavior, we are aware of the consequences, and calculate it, and yet we make decisions on the basis of moral precepts which themselves are to a large extent guided by our own emotional reactions.

Harris: I think that when sociobiological principles are applied in the fashion which corresponds to the calculus of the selfish gene in order to explain various aspects of human life, such explanations are redundant with respect to much more simple explanations on a sociocultural level. Technically what has just been done here is called reductionism. We reduced a phenomenon which is perfectly intelligible and explicable on a cultural level to a genetic level. And although there may be a correspondence between the two, it seems to me that if you're capable of giving an explanation for behavior such as saving a drowning person, or helping old people, or any of the behaviors which correspond to our moral codes, in purely cultural terms, you have a much more efficient system for explaining why people behave the way they do, than by this very cumbersome reduction to the genetic level.

Wilson: I would contend that both explanations are necessary in the same way that where the physiologist might be able to explain fully the sensation of sweetness in terms of sensory physiology and the circuit in the central nervous system that takes that information, the evolutionist, or the geneticist, is required to explain why sugar tastes sweet in the first place. In other words, why we have a predisposition to eat sugar, say, instead of ammonium salts.

In the same way, you may very well be able to account for the nuances of moral behavior in the origins of precepts in the behavioral development of individuals. On the other hand, the predispositions that human beings have to learn one thing as opposed to another, and the emotional constraints that go with this—do lead, indeed, to a certain amount of convergence in moral codes in cultures around the world—I think require a genetic explanation.

So I would argue for a dual explanation—what the biologists call the proximate explanation, the immediate mechanisms, as opposed to the ultimate, which is the genetic origin. Reductionism in this case—trying to adduce the genetic basis—is the method by which great advances in science have been made, but admittedly, it is only half of the process of science. Reductionism, in order to be truly effective, has to be accompanied by synthesis and by then an attempt to account for the full richness of the phenomena.

Harris: I think we've been skirting around the central issue of what is human nature and from an anthropological point of view we—I think most anthropologists would agree—have to take the genetic basis into consideration. But we have something as a species which no other species has, and that's genetically determined—as you, yourself say—and that's our capacity to develop symbol languages which have the property of semantic universality.

We can talk about anything, whether it's past, present, or future, or in any place in the world, having been there or not having been there. And as a result of that capacity we, as a species, have built up repertories of learned responses in social systems which are not equaled in any other species. And this ability for us to have culture is genetically determined—and from my point of view, genetic determination is the most important characteristic of the human species.

And during all of the thousands and millions of years during which selection took place for the capacity to have cultural repertories, it seems to me that the other genetic programming—that's specifically related to social response repertories—must have been selected again to the extent that it interfered with the capacity of humans to acquire cultural response repertories, rather than those that are specifically programmed by particular genes.

Wilson: I agree with you to this extent: that the human being is unique; that culture is overriding, and that therefore with reference to sociobiological theory the human species is a wild card. And I think that the extent to which these impulses have been overridden is an open empirical question. The sociobiologist is persuaded that there is enough hard under-structure in the form of emotional predisposition to learning rules that channel cultural evolution to make the biological investigation well worthwhile, but concedes that this hypertrophy that has resulted—you know, excessive development of many human uniquely human traits as a consequence of the unique position of a culture—is going to be very difficult to manage by sociobiological theory.

Yet I have a feeling myself that human beings are on a dual track of evolution: that their fastest track is cultural evolution and yet, they have gotten up to this point by conventional genetic evolution. And that no matter how far culture may take us, yet, the genes have culture on a leash. That is, that there are certain limits to the direction and distance that cultural evolution can proceed before the genetic imperatives will pull it short. And I think the length and the span of direction is the question of empirical interest.

Harris: When you phrase it that way, it's unobjectionable because we all would have to agree that we have a definite primate heritage, we have bipedalism, we have a mammalian heritage, and all of this goes into making the human organism. So I think when you state the fact that our behavior is on a leash—a genetic leash—I have to agree with you, when it's put in that general form. I wish we had more time to talk about the specifics because in general, it's not objectionable.

Carroll: That is one point that I did want to bring up because there have been a lot of fears arising out of sociobiology. You mention one—the male dominance fear—and also fear to show that the races—some races—are inferior, that social progress is impossible because of the pull of the gene. I understand from your explanation of sociobiology that you are not of that more radical end that sees those possibilities.

Wilson: No. That's not my reading of the evidence at all. My reading of the evidence—for example, in sex differences—is that there is a slight average difference in the predisposition in early development between very young girls and boys. When one looks over the full span of evidence [it] seems to me to be fairly strong for a slight predisposition with boys more prone toward individualistic behavior: wandering further away, being more prone to engage in rough and tumble play from the early stages of the social play onward.

So, one could say that the twig is slightly bent.

Carroll: But you're leaving lots of room.

Wilson: But only slightly, and I think the evidence is overwhelming that that slight bending can be bent back without a great deal of cultural pressure, so that it is possible to do something that would approach genuinely sexually equivalent societies.

Harris: I like the analogy you just made about bending the twig. The twig is bent slightly one way or another, but in this instance it could be bent back without any trouble whatsoever. I think that almost every one of those specific instances that you've mentioned in your book, *Sociobiology*, and your more recent articles—every one of those is of the same order. In other words, there might be some slight bending in one direction, but it's no trouble at all for cultures to bend them back completely the other way if there is sufficient ecological and material, practical reasons for the twig to be bent back the other way.

By the way, on this particular issue of the infant characteristics of the sexes, there's some very interesting material coming out now having to do with the effect that the males are more active and show greater aggression in infancy than females.

I think the emphasis—the strategic emphasis—has to be not on trying to find the genetic determinations, but on isolating the cultural, behavorial ones before we go to the genetic level.

Wilson: Why not both simultaneously?

Harris: Because there are limited resources. And once you begin to deflect the study of human beings away from this infinitely complex world of cultural creations to the genetic level, you are, I think, in a sense putting obstacles in the path of our unraveling the causes of cultural differences and similarities, which I think should be our main objective at this point.

Wilson: I think we have found the point of disagreement. And I also want to register a note of disagreement when you say that these predispositions can be erased with no trouble at all.

Harris: How about polygyny?

Wilson: That, I think, is one that's easily bendable. But I think, you see, this is an empirical question. And I think it would be premature to say that these things are easily adjusted. For example, the experience in the kibbutzim indicates that they may not be quite so easily overcome. In this case, you know, the tendency toward ...

Harris: Incest?

Wilson: No, I was thinking of the sex role differentiation.

Harris: Yes, well, there is also a tendency not to mate within those who would be exogamous.

Wilson: That is very powerful. I think you've just brought up a case where you could not bend the twig without its ...

Harris: It's being bent all the time.

Wilson: Yes, but with catastrophic consequences.

Harris: Well, of course, there is a deleterious biological feedback there if incest is practiced continually.

Wilson: And a psychological one also.

Harris: But to have that under genetic control flies in the face of an awful lot of evidence concerning the very high rate of incest social workers are reporting—estimating—as many as two million cases a year. The question is why has there been no society that has developed rules which would have promoted incest. And this, I think, would get us into a cultural reason, rather than into a genetic one. If there was reason to pass a law—some cultural reason for passing a law to make incest compulsory, I think the twig would be bent back all the other way.

Wilson: I doubt it. I think there are compelling genetic reasons to avoid it. And I believe that there is a very strong predisposition in early development so that it is automatically avoided. And even if you attempted to overcome it culturally, you would probably run into this very strong resistance in the early developmental trend in human beings, plus reap quite a wreckage in terms of genetic defects.

Harris: Yes, I would agree with that. But the wreckage that would occur would be fed back to the cultural level, not on the genetic level.

In other words, the first thing that would happen would be that ...

Wilson: They'd change their minds.

Harris: They would change their minds. In other words, this would be a predisposition which might be there, but could be bent totally the other way; but then would have very deleterious consequences on the cultural level. So that presumably the reason why we don't have societies which insist on a rule of incest mating is because when it was tried it had very deleterious consequences—some of which would be genetic but many of which would be psychological.

So that the adaptation would take place on the cultural level. And I wouldn't see a necessity for having a gene that controlled whether or not you were going to have incest.

Wilson: Except that there are apparently programmed learning rules, what the psychologists call prepared learning. The incest inhibition rule of avoidance of incest of people you've grown up with intimately for the first six years of your life appears to be an example of such a learning rule. Whenever you have an irrational strong predisposition to learn one thing as opposed to another, it suggests that evolution has built in a safeguard beyond mere rational calculation at the fully cultural level.

Harris: If that safeguard is there, it would seem to me quite weak, because it has to be backed up by very strong penalties and sanctions that cultures impose. I find it hard to believe that there is a set of genes that defines the limits of mating for humans, given the fact that we have such tremendous variety of sexual behavior and of mating activities and marriage forms. I just find it very difficult to accept that much more complex hypothesis that there is this set of genes. One of the difficulties with the sociobiological approach to these matters is that we have to talk about hypothetical genes. It's not the kind of genes we know about in dealing with blood groups. The question that we're dealing with here is whether things like mating and incest and social organization, types of political systems and all that, can be reasonably thought to be controlled by a set of genes whose frequency would have to differ within populations.

Part XIII
Anthropology: Ethics and Prospects

The scientific goal of anthropology—to describe human social organization with accuracy—has remained unchanged over the years, but the larger world within which the work of anthropology is done has altered greatly. Since the first professional societies and academic departments were formed, the changing role of Western powers in world affairs, the rise of Third World nationalism, and a new sense of social conscience in the university have multiplied the professional and ethical dilemmas that anthropologists have had to face and overcome.

Most of these dilemmas have had their sources in changing relationships with governments, domestic and foreign, and with informant populations. In the days of colonial empires, fieldworkers took a certain joy in opposing themselves to the "practical man" bureaucrat and "mucking it up with the natives." During the 1930s, when there was a closer and more serious collaboration between anthropologists and administrators, neither those involved with the U.S. Bureau of Indian Affairs nor the British African Institute ventured far from their roles as scholars and educators. Their responsibility was interpreted as the enlightenment of government officials who, armed with the right information, would then make humane and intelligent decisions. Questioning the fundamental justice of Western government having jurisdiction over non-Western communities was as unthinkable to anthropologists as to any other patriotic citizen of Great Britain or the United States.

In this country, the defeat of Indian tribes was a foregone historical conclusion to colonial settlement, and even American jurisdiction over trust territories in the Pacific, Central America, and the Caribbean provoked no political outrage among professional anthropologists. In the same way, British anthropologists saw the presence of white colonial officials in foreign lands as an unfortunate but undeniable fact of Western expansion. Nor were British or American officials perceived, on the whole, as malicious or punitive in carrying out their tasks; they were much more likely to be typified as ignorant and narrow-minded bumblers who could use a good dose of cultural relativity. Some, like Sir Andrew Cohen, once colonial governor of Uganda, had what we consider the good sense to seek out the company of anthropologists. Others, like the District Commissioner in Chinua Achebe's African classic, *Things Fall Apart*, could never see beyond their own roles to the reality of the people they ruled.

What anthropologists of former times never denied was the basic value of Western democratic institutions. They held fast even when poorly represented by their administrations, and even when the government was caught in the compromising position of abusing political power.

The hope of these government-affiliated anthropologists was that by convincing officials of the fundamental rationality of colonized people, the distance between democratic ideals and political practice would be closed and a greater autonomy of self-rule would fall to the natives. Hope, however, was not enough. Colonial administrators in Africa made little use of anthropological information on language and culture to improve communication with native groups. And, beyond the general doctrine of cultural relativity, American anthropologists actually had little to say in the formulation of Indian Affairs policy or policy pertaining to overseas trust territories.

As a touch of irony, the great period of financial support for British anthropology, the 1950s, coincided with Britain's rapid withdrawal from colonial responsibilities. Research information was never better, but the officials of new governments have been more interested in the advice of economists and rural development experts than in treaties on tribal organization. For American anthropologists, even after Indian Affairs reform was demolished during World War II, optimism remained undaunted that the discipline could contribute to government programs. In 1941, the Society for Applied Anthropology was incorporated with an eye towards emphasizing the consulting role of the anthropologist. But at home as abroad, anthropologists have been much less sought after than their academic colleagues in the hard sciences and quantitatively-oriented areas of economics, psychology, and sociology. For at least another 20 years, this position of minimal government work and an innocence about the goals and methods of U.S. international strategies continued. Along with many others, anthropologists in the postwar years assumed that the American way represented the freedom of people everywhere.

In this positive and rather quiet atmosphere, two break-through experiments in the combination of pure and applied anthropological research were initiated. Starting in 1948, University of Chicago graduate students, under the direction of Professor Sol Tax, started research among the Fox Indians living in the central Iowa town of Tama. The students requested that they be allowed to take an active role in helping the Indian community to achieve political autonomy. Permission for this innovation being granted, the researchers then moved past the participant-observer role to the techniques of "action anthropology." Their goal was to do nothing that would disrupt traditional Fox culture, but to offer opportunities in education and political discussion that were otherwise unavailable. Education courses were introduced that covered the history of Indian-white relations and gave particular attention to treaty negotiations. A forum for discussion of the problems and aims of the community and its difficulties with the dominant white society was instituted. Out of it emerged a more politically motivated Fox leadership and plans for a progressive community organization.

The effect of anthropological intervention was not to make a community Horatio Alger story out of the Fox project. The prejudices and economic depression faced by the tribe were only somewhat alleviated by open discussion and educational assistance. But the transformation of the fieldworker from a student of culture to a catalyst of social change was a radical one. Instead of accepting the total situation of the Fox tribe as the result of perfect cultural adaptation, the anthropologists involved in the project admitted that the small traditional community was hardly a match for larger political and economic forces unless it consciously manned its defenses in self-protection. Even then, its prospects remained uncertain.

The same reasoning motivated a second innovation in applied anthropology, this time in an overseas project sponsored jointly by the Peruvian Institute of Indigenous Affairs and Cornell University. The goal of the program was to convert one of Peru's thousands of feudal manors, populated by around 2,000 people, most of them peasant serfs bound to serve their patron, into a productive, self-governing community. Anthropologist Allan Holmberg, who served as project director later wrote:

> In 1952, quite by design, although unexpectedly and suddenly, I found myself in the delicate position of having assumed the role of patron (in the name of Cornell University) of a Peruvian hacienda, called Vicos, for a period of five years, for the purpose of conducting a research and development program on the modernization process.

Unlike the Fox project workers, the anthropologists working under Holmberg sought to locate and implement solutions to the specific problems of an agrarian community literally stuck in the European Middle Ages with all that era's worst aspects. Status differences and lack of cooperation between *mestizos* and Indians, as well as the changing technology of farming, the organization of work, and the distribution of economic resources troubled the local population, and these difficulties were met head-on by project planners. The most vehement resistance to changes in the community's social and economic organization came from the local property-owning elites whose positions were threatened by the emancipation of the peasants of Vicos. Despite their heavy opposition, the goal of the project was realized in 1962 when the manor passed by direct sale into the hands of the peasant community; but this was done with considerable strong-arming at the national level. As we know from William Foote Whyte's article on Peruvian peasants, the complexities of feudal traditions and national development are not open to easy solutions. The Vicos project represented a small practical victory for the community and, in retrospect, a truly innovative use of anthropology.

The turning point for anthropologists and other scientists doing research overseas came in 1965 with the outbreak of the controversy surrounding Project Camelot. In our first selection, this controversy is detailed and discussed by its principal chronicler, Irving Louis Horowitz, who took it upon himself to interview the major figures in the project and to research classified and unclassified documents relating to the case. The crux of the matter was that this U.S. Army enterprise implicated social science researchers in strategies to monitor and control the internal affairs of other nations, especially those of the Third World. Conceived by the Defense Department in 1963, the project was aimed at uncovering the sources of social revolution on the presumption that the United States would aid its allies in quelling insurgency. It seemed never to occur to Army administrators that government stability in itself is no measure of the just representation afforded citizens of the state, any more than a political revolution, if we consider our own national history, is necessarily a social evil. When the designs of the program became public knowledge, the scholars involved appeared to be uncritically accepting of the Army's presumptions, motives, and goals.

Furthermore, the disclosure in 1968 of the Defense Department's sponsorship of the University of California Himalayan Borders Project provoked an international incident and added fuel to the fire of anthropologists' complicity in government undercover activities. Subsequent revelations of the presence of Army-employed anthropologists in Vietnam and Thailand gave added weight to the criticisms of the discipline.

To a large degree, criticism and reevaluation of the anthropologist's relation to his own government resulted from the growing unpopularity of the Vietnam War, which affected nearly everyone's sense of political conscience. As a second influence, the civil rights movement of the 1960s underscored social injustices affecting racial and ethnic minorities and led to more articulate and vocal criticisms of social science experts as the lackeys of the power establishment. Here in the United States, resistance to being the objects of social science research took hold and still persists on the grounds that research only furthers the careers of academics without helping informants. This criticism was echoed in Third World countries where, in addition to political subversion, anthropologists began to be generally dismissed as holdovers from the days of colonial oppression.

In the second article in this section, Nancy Oestreich Lurie takes issue with the contention that anthropologists lack ethical concern. The specific criticism being addressed comes from Native American spokesman, lawyer Vine Deloria, former president of the National Congress of American Indians and the author of many books and articles on Indian-white relations. Perhaps his best-known book, *Custer Died for Your Sins*, contains a biting and yet very witty critique of the anthropologists who every summer inundate Indian reservations, gather information, and retreat to write specialized monographs that mean nothing to the Indian informants whose time they have arrogantly taken up. The specific criticism is well-founded, but does it represent the general tenor of relations between anthropologists and tribal informants? There is hardly a more qualified researcher than Lurie to muster the counterargument that successful and constructive cooperation has been much more typical than the anthropologist's callous disregard for the Indian situation. A good part of her own professional career has been devoted to court testimony in support of Indian treaty rights and to the mobilization of conferences that are by and about Native Americans.

The response of the profession to its own bad press and the bad press of the United States in foreign countries was to draft a formal code outlining the ethical responsibilities of anthropologists. Adopted by the American Anthropological Association in 1970, the code of ethics cites the primary responsibility of researchers to avoid clandestine or secret research that conflicts with the interests—physical, psychological, or social— of informants.

With the current expansion of opportunities for anthropologists to do applied research and the simultaneous shrinkage of academic openings, the same ethical and scientific problems raised by Project Camelot persist in causing dilemmas. More often than not, public and private clients define their own program goals, involve social scientists as suppliers of information, and then, independent of the researchers, make decisions or formulate policy. In recent years the tendency of the federal government has been to offer contract funding to teams of social scientists who are judged best equipped to handle the problem-solving entailed, as opposed to financing grant proposals for "pure" research. In the same way, foreign governments are most likely to employ anthropologists who are pragmatically oriented to speed up economic development and who are most interested in how research will serve that end. When the fieldworker becomes an employee, he or she is just as likely to suffer a loss of critical faculties as any other worker whose paycheck depends on taking orders. The best means of avoiding this compromising position lies in using the experience of those who have already met the dilemmas to educate graduate students in a "forewarned is forearmed" approach to nonacademic employment. This is already being done in some university departments, and is more and more discussed at national and regional meetings of the discipline. Training for applied anthropology and interdisciplinary problem-solving is almost certain to become an integral part of graduate programs, if anthropology is to meet the changing conditions of research opportunities.

In a related arena of ethical concern, the present era of Third World development has precipitated what can only be called a restaging of the most disastrous effects of European colonialism. Instead of centuries of bridging global distances and causing at each stage of expansion the death and cultural disorganization of non-Western societies, the sequence of contact between so-called civilized and primitive people has been speeded up and, at the same time, been narrowed to the confines of national boundaries. The destructive consequences remain the same; the breathing space for cultural reorganization and biological renewal does not. In addition, developing states tend to take the most expedient routes, as we did in our own history of industrialization, and to shunt aside more remote groups while increasing the burdens of lower classes.

The extinction of remote bands and the oppression of national subgroups diminishes our own humanity. In searching out other cultures, we have lost as much as they the innocence of isolation and ignorance. It is no longer possible to claim that we did not know of or that we are not affected by injustices that occur in other parts of the world. To discover, as Europeans did in the course of colonial conquests, that there are other people in the world is very disquieting, for it requires that the difficult problems of responsibilities, rights, and boundaries somehow be worked out through complicated, indirect, and otherwise frustrating means. We know that we share the common bonds of humanity, but it is difficult to know how to act on that fact.

The 1970 Code of Ethics included an appropriate reminder of another responsibility: that, in addition to informants' interests, we should be committed to the welfare and learning of students. Institutions of higher education have long been the principal supporters of anthropology, and the typical anthropologist spends more time as an educator than as a field researcher. The university and college system in the United States, and generally in Western countries, bears little resemblance to the ivy-covered citadels where the canons of method and theory were first debated among a handful of earnest professors and their equally earnest disciples. Now the undergraduate audience for anthropology is immense and the popularity of the subject increases yearly. A better public could hardly be imagined, for it is students who prove most open to considering other cultures and are most receptive to the humanistic ideals on which the discipline is based.

References

Clifton, James A. 1970. *Applied Anthropology: Readings in the Uses of the Science of Man.* Boston: Houghton-Mifflin.
Deloria, Vine. 1969. *Custer Died for Your Sins; An Indian Manifesto.* New York: Macmillan.
Foster, George M. 1969. *Applied Anthropology.* Boston: Little, Brown.
Gearing, Frederick Osmond et al., editors. 1960. *Documentary History of the Fox Project: 1948-1959: A Program in Action Anthropology, directed by Sol Tax.* Chicago: Dept. of Anthropology, University of Chicago.
Goodenough, Ward. 1963. *Cooperation in Change.* New York: Russell Sage Foundation.
Holmberg, A. 1958. "The Research and Development Approach to the Study of Change." *Human Organization* 17: 12-16
Horowitz, Irving Louis, editor. 1967. *The Rise and Fall of Project Camelot: Studies in the Relationship between Social Science and Practical Politics.* Cambridge, Mass.: M.I.T. Press.
Hymes, Dell, editor. 1969. *Reinventing Anthropology.* New York: Random House.
Sjoberg, Gideon. 1967. *Ethics, Politics, and Social Research.* Cambridge, Mass.: Schenkman.
Weaver, T., editor. 1973. *To See Ourselves: Anthropology and Modern Social Issues.* Glenview, Ill.: Scott, Foresman.

37.
The Life and Death of Project Camelot
Irving Louis Horowitz

In June of this year—in the midst of the crisis over the Dominican Republic—the United States Ambassador to Chile sent an urgent and angry cable to the State Department. Ambassador Ralph Dungan was confronted with a growing outburst of anti-Americanism from Chilean newspapers and intellectuals. Further, left-wing members of the Chilean Senate had accused the United States of espionage.

The anti-American attacks that agitated Dungan had no direct connection with sending US troops to Santo Domingo. Their target was a mysterious and cloudy American research program called Project Camelot.

Dungan wanted to know from the State Department what Project Camelot was all about. Further, whatever Camelot was, he wanted it stopped because it was fast becoming a *cause célèbre* in Chile (as it soon would throughout capitals of Latin America and in Washington) and Dungan had not been told anything about it—even though it was sponsored by the US Army and involved the tinderbox subjects of counter-revolution and counter-insurgency in Latin America.

Within a few weeks Project Camelot created repercussions from Capitol Hill to the White House. Senator J. William Fulbright, then chairman of the Foreign Relations Committee, registered his personal concern about such projects as Camelot because of their "reactionary, backward-looking policy opposed to change. Implicit in Camelot, as in the concept of 'counter-insurgency,' is an assumption that revolutionary movements are dangerous to the interests of the United States and that the United States must be prepared to assist, if not actually to participate in, measures to repress them."

By mid-June the State Department and Defense Department—which had created and funded Camelot—were in open contention over the project and the jurisdiction each department should have over certain foreign policy operations.

On July 8, Project Camelot was killed by Defense Secretary Robert McNamara's office which has a veto power over the military budget. The decision had been made under the President's direction.

On that same day, the director of Camelot's parent body, the Special Operations Research Organization, told a Congressional committee that the research project on revolution and counter-insurgency had taken its name from King Arthur's mythical domain because "It connotes the right sort of things—development of a stable society with peace and justice for all." Whatever Camelot's outcome, there should be no mistaking the deep sincerity behind this appeal for an applied social science pertinent to current policy.

However, Camelot left a horizon of disarray in its wake: an open dispute between State and Defense; fuel for the anti-American fires in Latin America; a cut in US Army research appropriations. In addition, serious and perhaps ominous implications for social science research, bordering on censorship, have been raised by the heated reaction of the executive branch of government.

Global Counter-Insurgency

What was Project Camelot? Basically, it was a project for measuring and forecasting the causes of revolutions and insurgency in underdeveloped areas of the world. It also aimed to find ways of eliminating the causes, or coping with the revolutions and insurgencies. Camelot was sponsored by the US Army on a four to six million dollar contract, spaced out over three to four years, with the Special Operations Research Organization (SORO). This agency is nominally under the aegis of American University in Washington, D.C., and does a variety of research for the Army. This includes making analytical surveys of foreign areas; keeping up-to-date information on the military, political, and social complexes of those areas; and maintaining a "rapid response" file for getting immediate information, upon Army request, on any situation deemed militarily important.

Latin America was the first area chosen for concentrated study, but countries on Camelot's four-year list included some in Asia, Africa, and Europe. In a working paper issued on December 5, 1964, at the request of the Office of the Chief of Research and Development, Department of the

Army, it was recommended that "comparative historical studies" be made in these countries:

- (Latin America) Argentina, Bolivia, Brazil, Colombia, Cuba, Domican Republic, El Salvador, Guatemala, Mexico, Paraguay, Peru, Venezuela.
- (Middle East) Egypt, Iran, Turkey.
- (Far East) Korea, Indonesia, Malaysia, Thailand.
- (Others) France, Greece, Nigeria.

"Survey research and other field studies" were recommended for Bolivia, Colombia, Ecuador, Paraguay, Peru, Venezuela, Iran, Thailand. Preliminary consideration was also being given to a study of the separatist movement in French Canada. It, too, had a code name: Project Revolt.

In a recruiting letter sent to selected scholars all over the world at the end of 1964, Project Camelot's aims were defined as a study to "make it possible to predict and influence politically significant aspects of social change in the developing nations of the world." This would include devising procedures for "assessing the potential for internal war within national societies" and "identify(ing) with increased degrees of confidence, those actions which a government might take to relieve conditions which are assessed as giving rise to a potential for internal war." The letter further stated:

> The US Army has an important mission in the positive and constructive aspects of nation-building in less developed countries as well as responsibility to assist friendly governments in dealing with active insurgency problems.

Such activities by the US Army were described as "insurgency prophylaxis" rather than the "sometimes misleading label of counter-insurgency."

Project Camelot was conceived in late 1963 by a group of high-ranking Army officers connected with the Army Research Office of the Department of Defense. They were concerned about new types of warfare springing up around the world. Revolutions in Cuba and Yemen and insurgency movements in Vietnam and the Congo were a far cry from the battles of World War II and also different from the envisioned—and planned for—apocalypse of nuclear war. For the first time in modern warfare, military establishments were not in a position to use the immense arsenals at their disposal—but were, instead, compelled by force of a geopolitical stalemate to increasingly engage in primitive forms of armed combat. The questions of moment for the Army were: Why can't the "hardware" be used? And what alternatives can social science "software" provide?

A well-known Latin American area specialist, Rex Hopper, was chosen

The Insiders Report

Were the men on Camelot critical of any aspects of the project?

Some had doubts from the outset about the character of the work they would be doing, and about the conditions under which it would be done. It was pointed out, for example, that the US Army tends to exercise a far more stringent intellectual control of research findings than does the US Air Force. As evidence for this, it was stated that SORO generally had fewer "free-wheeling" aspects to its research designs than did RAND (the Air Force-supported research organization). One critic inside SORO went so far as to say that he knew of no SORO research which had a "playful" or unregimented quality, such as one finds at RAND (where for example, computers are used to plan invasions but also to play chess). One staff member said that "the self-conscious seriousness gets to you after a while." "It was all grim stuff," said another.

Another line of criticism was that pressures on the "reformers" (as the men engaged in Camelot research spoke of themselves) to come up with ideas were much stronger than the pressures on the military to actually bring off any policy changes recommended. The social scientists were expected to be social reformers, while the military adjutants were expected to be conservative. It was further felt that the relationship between sponsors and researchers was not one of equals, but rather one of superordinate military needs and subordinate academic roles. On the other hand, some officials were impressed by the disinterestedness of the military, and thought that far from exercising undue influence, the Army personnel were loath to offer opinions.

Another objection was that if one had to work on policy matters—if research is to have international ramifications—it might better be conducted under conventional State Department sponsorship. "After all," one man said, "they are at least nominally committed to civilian political norms." In other words, there was a considerable reluctance to believe that the Defense Department, despite its superior organization, greater financial affluence, and executive influence, would actually improve upon State Department styles of work, or accept recommendations at variance with Pentagon policies.

There seemed to be few, if any, expressions of disrespect for the intrinsic merit of the work contemplated by Camelot, or of disdain for policy-oriented work in general. The scholars engaged in the Camelot effort used two distinct vocabularies. The various Camelot documents reveal a military vocabulary provided with an array of military justifications; often followed (within the same document) by a social science vocabulary offering social science justifications and rationalizations. The dilemma in the Camelot literature from the preliminary report issued in August 1964 until the more advanced document issued in April 1965, is the same: an incomplete amalgamation of the military and sociological vocabularies. (At an early date the project had the code name SPEARPOINT.)

Policy Conflicts Over Camelot

The directors of SORO are concerned that the cancellation of Camelot might mean the end of SORO as well in a wholesale slash of research funds. For while over $1,000,000 was allotted to Camelot each year, the annual budget of SORO, its parent organization, is a good deal less. Although no such action has taken place, SORO's future is being examined. For example, the Senate and House Appropriations Committee blocked a move by the Army to transfer unused Camelot funds to SORO.

However, the end of Project Camelot does not necessarily imply the end of the Special Operations Research Office, nor does it imply an end to research designs which are similar in character to Project Camelot. In fact, the termination of the contract does not even imply an intellectual change of heart on the part of the originating sponsors of key figures of the project.

One of the characteristics of Project Camelot was the number of antagonistic forces it set in motion on grounds of strategy and timing rather than from what may be called considerations of scientific principles.

- The State Department grounded its opposition to Camelot on the basis of the ultimate authority it has in the area of foreign affairs. There is no published report showing serious criticism of the projected research itself.
- Congressional opposition seemed to be generated by a concern not to rock any foreign alliances, especially in Latin America. Again, there was no statement about the project's scientific or intellectual grounds.
- A third group of skeptics, academic social scientists, generally thought that Project Camelot, and studies of the processes of revolution and war in general, were better left in the control of major university centers, and in this way, kept free of direct military supervision.
- The Army, creator of the project, did nothing to contradict McNamara's order cancelling Project Camelot. Army influentials did not only feel that they had to execute the Defense Department's orders, but they are traditionally dubious of the value of "software" research to support "hardware" systems.

Let us take a closer look at each of these groups which voiced opposition to Project Camelot. A number of issues did not so much hinge upon, as swim about, Project Camelot. In particular, the "jurisdictional" dispute between Defense and State loomed largest.

State vs. Defense

In substance, the debate between the Defense Department and the State Department is not unlike that between electricians and bricklayers in the construction of a new apartment house. What union is responsible for which processes? Less generously, the issue is: who controls what? At the policy level, Camelot was a tool tossed about in a larger power struggle which has been going on in government circles since the end of World War II, when the Defense Department emerged as a competitor for honors as the most powerful bureau of the administrative branch of government.

In some sense, the divisions between Defense and State are outcomes of the rise of ambiguous conflicts such as Korea and Vietnam, in contrast to the more precise and diplomatically controlled "classical" world wars. What are the lines dividing political policy from military posture? Who is the most important representative of the United States abroad: the ambassador or the military attaché in charge of the military mission? When soldiers from foreign lands are sent to the United States for political orientation, should such orientation be within the province of the State Department or of the Defense Department? When undercover activities are conducted, should the direction of such activities belong to military or political authorities? Each of these is a strategic question with little pragmatic or historic precedent. Each of these was entwined in the Project Camelot explosion.

It should be plain therefore that the State Department was not simply responding to the recommendations of Chilean left-wingers in urging the cancellation of Camelot. It merely employed the Chilean hostility to "interventionist" projects as an opportunity to redefine the balance of forces and power with the Defense Department. What is clear from this resistance to such projects is not so much a defense of the sovereignty of the nations where ambassadors are stationed, as it is a contention that conventional political channels are suffcient to yield the information desired or deemed necessary.

Congress

In the main, congressional reaction seems to be that Project Camelot was bad because it rocked the diplomatic boat in a sensitive area. Underlying most congressional criticisms is the plain fact that most congressmen are more sympathetic to State Department control of foreign affairs than they are to Defense Department control. In other words, despite military sponsored world junkets, National Guard and State Guard pressures from the home State, and military training in the backgrounds of many congressmen, the sentiment for political rather than military control is greater. In addition, there is a mounting suspicion in Congress of varying kinds of behavioral science research stemming from hearings into such matters as wire-tapping, uses of lie detectors, and truth-in-packaging.

Social Scientists

One reason for the violent response to Project Camelot, especially among Latin American scholars, is its sponsorship by the Department of Defense. The fact is that Latin Americans have become quite accustomed to State Department involvements in the internal affairs of various nations. The Defense Department is a newcomer, a dangerous one, inside the Latin American orbit. The train of thought connected to its activities is in terms of international warfare, spying missions, military manipulations, etc. The State Department, for its part, is often a consultative party to shifts in government, and has played an enormous part in either fending off or bringing about *coups d'état*. This State Department role has by now been accepted and even taken for granted. Not so the Defense Department's role. But it is interesting to conjecture on how matter-of-factly Camelot might have been accepted if it had State Department sponsorship.

Social scientists in the United States have, for the most part, been publicly silent on the matter of Camelot. The reasons for this are not hard to find. First, many "giants of the field" are involved in government contract work in one capacity or another. And few souls are in a position to tamper with the gods. Second, most information on Project Camelot has thus far been of a newspaper variety; and professional men are not in a habit of criticizing colleagues on the basis of such information. Third, many social scientists doubtless see nothing wrong or immoral in the Project Camelot designs. And they are therefore more likely to be either confused or angered at the Latin American response than at the directors of Project Camelot. (At the time of the blowup, Camelot people spoke about the "Chilean mess" rather than the "Camelot mess.")

The directors of Project Camelot did not "classify" research materials, so that there would be no stigma of secrecy. And they also tried to hire, and even hired away from academic positions, people well known and respected for their independence of mind. The difficulty is that even though the stigma of secrecy was formally erased, it remained in the attitudes of many of the employees and would-be employees of Project Camelot. They unfortunately thought in terms of secrecy, clearance, missions, and the rest of the professional nonsense that so powerfully afflicts the Washington scientific as well as political ambience.

Further, it is apparent that Project Camelot had much greater difficulty hiring a full-time staff of high professional competence, than in getting part-time, summertime, weekend, and sundry assistance. Few established figures in academic life were willing to surrender the advantages of their positions for the risks of the project.

One of the cloudiest aspects to Project Camelot is the role of American University. Its actual supervision of the contract appears to have begun and ended with the 25 percent overhead on those parts of the contract that a university receives on most federal grants. Thus, while there can be no question as to the "concern and disappointment" of President Hurst R. Anderson of the American University over the demise of Project Camelot, the reasons for this regret do not seem to extend beyond the formal and the financial. No official at American University appears to have been willing to make any statement of responsibility, support, chagrin, opposition, or anything else related to the project. The issues are indeed momentous, and must be faced by all universities at which government sponsored research is conducted: the amount of control a university has over contract work; the role of university officials in the distribution of funds from grants; the relationships that ought to be established once a grant is issued. There is also a major question concerning project directors: are they members of the faculty, and if so, do they have necessary teaching responsibilities and opportunities for tenure as do other faculty members.

The difficulty with American University is that it seems to be remarkably unlike other universities in its permissiveness. The Special Operations Research Office received neither guidance nor support from university officials. From the outset, there seems to have been a "gentleman's agreement" not to inquire or interfere in Project Camelot, but simply to serve as some sort of camouflage. If American University were genuinely autonomous it might have been able to lend highly supportive aid to Project Camelot during the crisis months. As it is, American University maintained an official silence which preserved it from more congressional or executive criticism. This points up some serious flaws in its administrative and financial policies.

The relationship of Camelot to SORO represented a similarly muddled organizational picture. The director of Project Camelot was nominally autonomous and in charge of an organization surpassing in size and importance the overall SORO operaton. Yet at the critical point the organizational blueprint served to protect SORO and sacrifice what nominally was its limb. That Camelot happened to be a vital organ may have hurt, especially when Congress blocked the transfer of unused Camelot funds to SORO.

Military

Military reaction to the cancellation of Camelot varied. It should be borne in mind that expenditures on Camelot were minimal in the Army's overall budget and most military leaders are skeptical, to begin with, about the worth of social science research. So there was no open protest about the demise of Camelot. Those officers who have a positive attitude toward social science materials, or are themselves trained in the social sciences, were dismayed. Some had hoped to find "software" alternatives to the "hardware systems" approach applied by the Secretary of Defense to every military-political contingency. These officers saw the attack on Camelot as a double attack—on their role as officers and on their professional standards. But the Army was so clearly treading in new waters that it could scarcely jeopardize the entire structure of military research to preserve one project. This very inability or impotence to preserve Camelot—a situation threatening to other governmental contracts with social scientists—no doubt impressed many armed forces officers.

The claim is made by the Camelot staff (and various military aides) that the critics of the project played into the hands of those sections of the military predisposed to veto any social science recommendations. Then why did the military offer such a huge support to a social science project to begin with? Because $6,000,000 is actually a trifling sum for the Army in an age of multi-billion dollar military establishment. The amount is significantly more important for the social sciences, where such contract awards remain scarce. Thus, there were differing perspectives of the importance of Camelot: an Army view which considered the contract as one of several forms of "software" investment; a social science perception of Project Camelot as the equivalent of the Manhattan Project.

Was Project Camelot Workable?

While most public opposition to Project Camelot focused on its strategy and timing, a considerable amount of private opposition centered on more basic, though theoretical, questions: was Camelot scientifically feasible and ethically correct? No public document or statement contested the possibility that, given the successful completion of the data gathering, Camelot could have, indeed, established basic criteria for measuring the level and potential for internal war in a given nation. Thus, by never challenging the feasibility of the work, the political critics of Project Camelot were providing back-handed compliments to the efficacy of the project.

But much more than political considerations are involved. It is clear that some of the most critical problems presented by Project Camelot are scientific. Although for an extensive analysis of Camelot, the reader would, in fairness, have to be familiar with all of its documents, salient general criticisms can be made without a full reading.

The research design of Camelot was from the outset plagued by ambiguities. It was never quite settled whether the purpose was to study counter-insurgency possibilities, or the revolutionary process. Similarly, it was difficult to determine whether it was to be a study of comparative social structures, a set of case studies of single nations "in depth," or a study of social structure with particular emphasis on the military. In addition, there was a lack of treatment of what indicators were to be used, and whether a given social system in Nation A could be as stable in Nation B.

In one Camelot document there is a general critique of social science for failing to deal with social conflict and social control. While this in itself is admirable, the tenor and context of Camelot's documents make it plain that a "stable society" is considered the norm no less than the desired outcome. The "breakdown of social order" is spoken of accusatively. Stabilizing agencies in developing areas are presumed to be absent. There is no critique of US Army policy in developing areas because the Army is presumed to be a stabilizing agency. The research formulations always assume the legitimacy of Army tasks—"if the US Army is to perform effectively its parts in the US mission of counter-insurgency it must recognize that insurgency represents a breakdown of social order. . . ." But such a proposition has never been doubted—by Army officials or anyone else. The issue is whether such breakdowns are in the nature of the existing system or a product of conspiratorial movements.

The use of hygienic language disguises the anti-revolutionary assumptions under a cloud of powder puff declarations. For example, studies of Paraguay are recommended "because trends in this situation (the Stroessner regime) may also render it 'unique' when analyzed in terms of the transition from 'dictatorship' to political stability." But to speak about changes from dictatorship to stability is an obvious ruse. In this case, it is a tactic to disguise the fact that Paraguay is one of the most vicious, undemocratic (and like most dictatorships, stable) societies in the Western Hemisphere.

These typify the sort of hygienic sociological premises that do not have scientific purposes. They illustrate the confusion of commitments within Project Camelot. Indeed the very absence of emotive words such as revolutionary masses, communism, socialism, and capitalism only serves to intensify the discomfort one must feel on examination of the documents —since the abstract vocabulary disguises, rather than resolves, the problems of international revolution. To have used clearly political rather than military language would not "justify" governmental support. Furthermore, shabby assumptions of academic conventionalism replaced innovative orientations. By adopting a systems approach, the problematic, open-ended aspects of the study of revolutions were largely omitted; and the design of the study became an oppressive curb on the study of the problems inspected.

This points up a critical implication for Camelot (as well as other projects). The importance of the subject being researched does not per se determine the importance of the project. A sociology of large-scale relevance and reference is all to the good. It is important that scholars be willing to risk something of their shaky reputations in helping resolve major world social problems. But it is no less urgent that in the process of addressing major problems, the autonomous character of the social science disciplines—their own criteria of worthwhile scholarship—should not be abandoned. Project Camelot lost sight of this "autonomous" social science character.

It never seemed to occur to its personnel to inquire into the desirability for successful revolution. This is just as solid a line of inquiry as the one stressed—the conditions under which revolutionary movements will be able to overthrow a government. Furthermore, they seem not to have thought about inquiring into the role of the United States in these countries. This points up the lack of symmetry. The problem should have been phrased to include the study of "us" as well as "them." It is not possible to make a decent analysis of a situation unless one takes into account the role of all the different people and groups involved in it; and there was no room in the design for such contingency analysis.

In discussing the policy impact on a social science research project, we should not overlook the difference between "contract" work and "grants." Project Camelot commenced with the U.S. Army; that is to say, it was initiated for a practical purpose determined by the client. This differs markedly from the typical academic grant in that its sponsorship had "built-in" ends. The scholar usually *seeks* a grant; in this case the donor, the Army, promoted its own aims. In some measure, the hostility for Project Camelot may be an unconscious reflection of this distinction—a dim feeling that there was something "non-academic," and certainly not disinterested, about Project Camelot, irrespective of the quality of the scholars associated with it.

The Ethics of Policy Research

The issue of "scientific rights" versus "social myths" is perennial. Some maintain that the scientist ought not penetrate beyond legally or morally sanctioned limits and others argue that such limits cannot exist for science. In treading on the sensitive issue of national sovereignty, Project Camelot reflects the generalized dilemma. In deference to intelligent researchers, in recognition of them as scholars, they should have been invited by Camelot to air their misgivings and qualms about government (and especially Army sponsored) research—to declare their moral conscience. Instead, they were mistakenly approached as skillful, useful potential employees of a higher body, subject to an authority higher than their scientific calling.

What is central is not the political motives of the sponsor. For social scientists were not being enlisted in an intelligence system for "spying" purposes. But given their professional standing, their great sense of intellectual honor and pride, they could not be "employed" without proper deference for their stature. Professional authority should have prevailed from beginning to end with complete command of the right to thrash out the moral and political dilemmas as researchers saw them. The Army, however respectful and protective of free expression, was "hiring help" and not openly and honestly submitting a problem to the higher professional and scientific authority of social science.

The propriety of the Army to define and delimit all questions, which Camelot should have had a right to examine, was never placed in doubt. This is a tragic precedent; it reflects the arrogance of a consumer of intellectual merchandise. And this relationship of inequality corrupted the lines of authority, and profoundly limited the autonomy of the social scientists involved. It became clear that the social scientist savant was not so much functioning as an applied social scientist as he was supplying information to a powerful client.

The question of who sponsors research is not nearly so decisive as the question of ultimate use of such information. The sponsorship of a project, whether by the United States Army or by the Boy Scouts of America, is by itself neither good nor bad. Sponsorship is good or bad only insofar as the intended outcomes can be pre-determined and the parameters of those intended outcomes tailored to the sponsor's expectations. Those social scientists critical of the project never really denied its freedom and independence, but questioned instead the purpose and character of its intended results.

It would be a gross oversimplification, if not an outright error, to assume that the theoretical problems of Project Camelot derive from any reactionary character of the project designers. The director went far and wide to select a group of men for the advisory board, the core planning group, and the various conference groupings, who in fact were more liberal in their orientations than any random sampling of the sociological profession would likely turn up.

However, in nearly every page of the various working papers, there are assertions which clearly derive from American military policy objectives rather than scientific method. The steady assumption that internal warfare is damaging disregards the possibility that a government may not be in a position to take actions either to relieve or improve mass conditions, or that such actions as are contemplated may be more concerned with reducing conflict than with improving conditions. The added statements about the United States Army and its "important mission in the positive and constructive aspects of nation building . . . " assumes the reality of such a function in an utterly unquestioning and unconvincing form. The first rule of the scientific game is not to make assumptions about friends and enemies in such a way as to promote the use of different criteria for the former and the latter.

The story of Project Camelot was not a confrontation of good versus evil. Obviously, not all men behaved with equal fidelity or with equal civility. Some men were weaker than others, some more callous, and some more stupid. But all of this is extrinsic to the heart of the problem of Camelot: what are and are not the legitimate functions of a scientist?

In conclusion, two important points must be clearly kept in mind and clearly apart. First, Project Camelot was intellectually, and from my own perspective, ideologically unsound. However, and more significantly, Camelot was not cancelled because of its faulty intellectual approaches. Instead, its cancellation came as an act of government censorship, and an expression of the contempt for social science so prevalent among those who need it most. Thus it was political expedience, rather than its lack of scientific merit, that led to the demise of Camelot because it threatened to rock State Department relations with Latin America.

Second, giving the State Department the right to screen and approve government-funded social science research projects on other countries, as the President has ordered, is a supreme act of censorship. Among the agencies that grant funds for such research are the National Institutes of Mental Health, the National Science Foundation, the National Aeronautics and Space Agency, and the Office of Education. Why should the State Department have veto power over the scientific pursuits of men and projects funded by these and other agencies in order to satisfy the policy needs—or policy failures—of the moment? President Johnson's directive is a gross violation of the autonomous nature of science.

We must be careful not to allow social science projects with which we may vociferously disagree on political and ideological grounds to be decimated or dismantled by government fiat. Across the ideological divide is a common social science understanding that the contemporary expression of reason in politics today is applied social science, and that the cancellation of Camelot, however pleasing it may be on political grounds to advocates of a civilian solution to Latin American affairs, represents a decisive setback for social science research.

38.
As Others See Us

Nancy Oestreich Lurie

The August, 1969, issue of *Playboy* magazine carried an article, "Custer Died for Your Sins," excerpted from the then forthcoming book of the same title by Vine Deloria, Jr. The book covers the nature of federal Indian administration, aspects of the contemporary Indian scene, Deloria's ideas of needed policy reform, and a chapter each on the alleged eccentricities and iniquities of missionaries, officials of government and anthropologists. For still unexplained reasons, it was Deloria's excoriation of anthropologists which was featured in *Playboy,* thus giving the widespread impression for the many who will not read the book that the biggest thorn in the Indian side is anthropologists.

Particularly distressing is that among the supposedly factional American Indians, to date not only has no one come forth to defend anthropologists, but even some of Deloria's critics among Indian activists, with whom he deals harshly in the book by implication if not by name, have applauded his stand on anthropologists (personal communications). If we are hurt and indignant about the specific charges Deloria makes, we should not be surprised at his bitterness or the fact that he has evoked a strong kindred response from other Indian people. It would be easy to refute everything Deloria says about us point for point, but in so doing we would miss the really important things he and other Indians are trying to tell us (Deloria, 1969).

First, it is worth noting that Deloria considers us one of three similar targets for Indians to shoot at. Although at the very end of the book he relents, saying he is hardest on the very groups in which he has the greatest hope for the Indians' future, it is curious that anthropologists are mentioned in the same breath with church and state. We always thought we were *different!* We always agreed with Indians that their difficulties derived from pious and political knuckleheadedness. Our peculiar distinction was that we came to learn from Indians on their terms, not lean on them like those other fellows. But Indian people have become wise to the fact that we always really worked in our own interests, which were those of science, and if we did not lean on Indians we also had little inclination to lean on people who *were* leaning on Indians. No matter how self-serving the individual clergyman or bureaucrat, their concern, institutionally speaking, was the Indians' interests, at least as they defined it.

Through the years, neat categories have become blurred. Religious groups and occasionally government agencies have sought enlightenment from anthropology, and anthropologists have put their skills at the disposal of these agencies for change. There is real potential for good in these relationships, and there may be potential for harm. It is worth noting that Americanists have always been proud that they were never resented by Indians in contrast to Africanists who have had to live down the fact that many of their founding fathers began their careers in colonial service. Applied anthropology in the service of American government and religion may smack of the same kind of colonialism the Africanists have outgrown and it evokes understandable suspicions from any administered people. Obviously Deloria does not believe his own conclusion that the only difference between applied anthropologists and pure anthropologists is that the latter use footnotes and the former do not. Deloria still thinks Indians can use our help, and ridicule is at least a disarming tactic to make us reveal our intentions.

Over the last decade or so, a few anthropologists have engaged in programs of the kind Deloria suggests as acceptable to Indians, that is, getting wherewithall, power, and any necessary empathic expertise into Indians' hands and letting them decide what their interests are and go after them in their own way with whatever support they can use from the anthropological sidelines. Deloria does not credit anthroplogists with any actual cases, but after all his negative ranting he must have some positive evidence to consider anthropologists significant to the Indians' future. I am inclined to believe that it is such relatively recent evidence rather than our old reputation as the Indians' long time friend which inspires any grudging respect for us today.

Anthropologists are faced with a problem of impression management and ought to begin analyzing how they really appear from the Indian point of view. The American Indian population is weighted on the young side and certainly youth characterizes the activists who are influential whether we want to admit it or not. Their views of the Indian-anthropologist relationship go back no more than twenty years. Our views go back much further because they are perpetuated in the traditions of the discipline and for some of us the old relationship persists if only in regard to particular informants cultivated years ago.

The anthropologist's impression of himself is strongly influenced by the period of field work from roughly the First World War to the early 1950s. At the time there were not many anthropologists. They were about the only "establishment" whites with whom any rank and file Indians dealt as equals; and the wise old Indians often held the stronger cards. Anthropologists were sympathetic if not very effectual allies in regard to Indians' interaction with other whites. Field research was usually an enterprise of mutual intellectual interest to both Indian and anthroplogist. Furthermore, the anthropologist was perceived as unique, an individual guest to the tribe which happened to harbor him. Some tribes did not even know of the existence of anthropologists. Psychically, at least, the anthropologist had certain utility for the Indian people he worked with in regard to their own self-esteem. Although most anthropologists did not get into the field until they began data gathering for the doctorate, they had the benefit of knowing their professor's experiences, what to expect generally, what was expected of them, and what horrible examples of bad field technique of the more distant past to avoid. Each trip was expected to be a revelation and usually was. There was not a great deal of grant money; the anthropologist was lucky to get a grub-stake. Thus he had to give generously of himself in time and effort as reciprocation for cooperation in his research. Money was seldom paid directly in informants' fees, but the anthropologist observed local etiquette of gift exchange in goods, services, and sometimes even cash. His novelty value was also an asset the anthropologist traded on in still quite isolated Indian communities, albeit this was often done unconsciously, and considered evidence of achieving empathy and good rapport.

If an anthropologist proved a nuisance or an insufferable bore, the Indians lost nothing in withdrawing from him. A real menace could be driven out by enlisting the power of the mission or the Bureau in devious ways, since Indian people sensed that these institutions were by nature antithetical to anthropology. While there were hazards and some real psychic agonies for a person to begin serious research while also learning field techniques, the Ph.D. candidate was at least deeply committed to his chosen field and motivated by the fact that his professional future depended on his success. It was the Indians who held the power whether he would survive intellectually in the field and be able to return. They knew it and he knew it. Everyone enjoyed the game.

We can mark the beginning of deteriorating relationships between Indians and anthropologists when, about twenty years ago, a joke came out of the Southwest which had already become a mecca for a great many anthropologists. The average Navajo family, it was said, consisted of father, mother, three children, and an anthropologist. In the last few years the joke has been repeated by Indians all over the country to describe any average Indian family. Furthermore, while more anthropologists have sometimes begun to mean more money for the Indian community, they do not necessarily mean more fun and sometimes they are no fun at all but a source of hurt. They are not so easily gotten rid of today as in the past as there are always fresh reinforcements from our growing ranks. A lone stranger can be dealt with but when the ratio approaches 1:100 as I am told it does in some places, e.g., Hopi and Pine Ridge in the summer of 1969, Indians are hard put to decide what to do about such an invasion. It is also hard to just withdraw when working for the anthropologist helps put bread on the table.

Of course Deloria and others overstate the case of the anthropologist as economic asset, but economics certainly plays an important part in Indian grievances. Where the rest of the country got out of the Depression during the Second World War and stayed out, wartime prosperity for Indian communities was short-lived. The war had been a tremendous educational experience for Indians in giving them new skills and knowledge of economic alternatives to survive and prosper. However, policies set in motion after the war were completely inimical to using their new knowledge to improve the lot of their communities. Meanwhile, not only anthropologists but scholars in general enjoyed more federal support for research than at any time in our history. The ethnographer was no longer hard up and he could use cash and probably did so quite benevolently, to pay informants or pay them more than was previously possible. This was not bad in itself and continued the tradition of reciprocating as one is able, but it gave the ethnographer the upper hand. He can hire people who produce and fire those who do not. Much of the really esoteric information has been collected and either the old timers are now dead or remaining esoterica may be uncollectable as the folks on old age assistance can still withdraw from anthropologists they do not like. We have turned our attention to more relevant, contemporary problems where any hard up sample of Indians will do to answer questions on alcoholism, suicide, juvenile delinquency, educational problems and the like. I do not deny the value of such research, I merely point out how it has contributed to our changed image.

I would also like to point out that people who are hungry and frustrated in efforts to carry out the kinds of community development they desire find it hard to appreciate the value of grant supported research when the same money could be used to alleviate the problems whose symptoms are being so assiduously studied.

Other things happened as younger scholars found the advice conveyed by their professional mentors ever less realistic and useful. Indians could be hired for cash more easily than cultivated sincerely as friends. Other data collecting methods became more appropriate to our new interests than participant observation and direct or hidden interview. We also reacted against the sink or swim method of learning to do field work and tried to teach our students the techniques with texts, role playing sessions, methods courses, and, above all, team research and field schools where students work under supervision. These are not simply doctoral students but include beginning graduate students who may never make it through their "comps" and even, heaven help us, undergraduates with no more serious commitment to anthropology than the cost of tuition for a summer's lark that will also provide credits toward fulfilling their majors. Some team projects and field schools have serious objectives—maybe all of them can be justified as ultimate contributions to knowledge. But it is hard to avoid the fact that Indians are more conveniently and economically at hand for field schools than other still unstudied peoples. The team student does not have to be terribly interested in the substantive data he gathers. He only has to be sure he gets it right. He seeks evidence of his success from the professor in charge and finds social outlets among his peers rather than having to depend on the community for psychic and social support. If people identified as anthropologists or even students of anthropology do not appear to take seriously what Indians have to tell them, seeing their words as so much cash on the line and their persons as mere challenges to practice methods and techniques, why should Indians take anthropologists seriously and accord them respect?

There are other problems not exactly of our own making but which contribute to the impression of anthropologists. Once we only had to worry about the aggressive Indian buff who collected relics and palmed himself off as an anthropologist. Today, there is a huge host of outsiders from academic and professional disciplines who have discovered Indians for their own purposes. We could easily unmask the buff and keep our own role pure but what are we going to do about these others who come armed with tape recorders, cameras, notebooks, questionnaires, and projective texts; who have research credentials from universities or government and private foundations; and who use methods and techniques we also employ? Indians find it hard to tell them from the new breeds of anthropologists of all ages. It does no good to tell Indians that no matter how much our behavior resembles that of the others there is a *tradition* that Indians should like anthropologists. We can rail all we wish about the scholar's sacred right to freedom of inquiry, but we should understand why Deloria proposes that "Anthropologists and Other Friends" (the actual title of his chapter in the book) should register their projects with tribal governing bodies and justify them in terms of benefits to the people studied.

Of course, I am pointing up the very worst situations. However, just at the time when we are mass producing field training on a commercial basis across the country and paying small attention to all the duplication of work being done with Indians by both anthropologists and non-anthropologists, Indians themselves are developing widespread networks of communications to promote widespread inter-tribal fellow feeling. The anthropologist's role is no longer that of unique visitor who always had to justify his presence if not his practical relevance to the tribe he worked with. The anthropologist is now known to all Indians as the representative of a class of people who, like missionaries and Indian Bureau personnel, come and stay unbidden and who exploit Indians and can be exploited for Indian purposes. We are resented as a category for what we are allegedly doing to Indians, even by members of tribes which have not been studied or where a resident anthropologist still enjoys good, old fashioned relationships with the people.

Deloria may have done us a real favor in publicizing the bad impression we now make, whether it is of our own or others' doing. Others may not be so eager to trade on our formerly good reputations and we can stand forth as the real anthropologists, only having to put our own house in order.

Nor do I think all anthropologists have to confine themselves to action programs to be acceptable to Indian people, despite all the Indian grumbling about using them only to get our PhDs or engaging in costly, pointless research in order to publish to avoid perishing. Indians can figure out as well as anyone else that if we were motivated solely by considerations of income and having the equivalent of academics' hours, we would have gone into journeyman trades and spared ourselves inconveniences of field work and all the paperwork. We need have no embarrassment in admitting to Indians that we are motivated by intellectual curiosity and a desire to further our understanding of the nature of man. This outlook is probably more acceptable to Indian people than it is to much of the non-Indian public which finds it downright suspect. Indian people understand the concept of knowledge for its own sake if one pursues questions that really capture one's own curiosity. They do not even have to be obviously practical questions as long as one is polite and respectful and assumes Indians can still teach us things rather than simply be used to test or train students in methods in regard to questions to which we already think we have the answers.

What really rankles Indians is our fetish of scientific purity as being above considerations of the practical Indian interest, while at the same time we have little difficulty in finding ways to benefit our own practical interests without compromising our purity. We obtain data and publish our results, and if these are marketable we collect royalties, serve as paid consultants, hit the lecture trail, or simply move on to ever more prestigious academic institutions at higher pay. In this regard we are no different from any other scholars. But let us not go on saying we thus fulfill any obligation we may owe Indians because we have preserved their history and culture for posterity or are performing a public relations function for them with accurate data as opposed to popular sterotypes. These are not only feeble rationalizations, they are insulting. Indians can speak for themselves and we do not even listen. When Indians really can use our informed clout to avoid threats to their social life or property or to get programs they feel would really help them, we sit on our hands and raise our eyes to the pure scientific clouds. Since 1951, untold numbers of anthropologists have acted as expert witness in Indian Claims cases, taking pious pride in serving the interests of justice and the Indians as impartial scientists—for a fee. During this same period the Menominee and Klamath were terminated by outrageous legal and political tactics and their problems continue to mount. The waters of Kinzua dam rise over a good part of the Allegheny Seneca Reservation. Northwest Coast tribes fight a running battle against the interests of sportsfishing in order to preserve their rights to salmon runs which they depend upon for their livelihood. Recently, a supposedly liberal senator, Gaylord Nelson of Wisconsin, has pushed strenuously to wrest the Apostle Islands and surrounding shoreline on Lake Superior from their Ojibwa owners to create a national park on the arguments of conservation and benefiting the region economically. There is no concern for the obvious facts that this scheme will work to the direct detriment of the Ojibwa who have conserved the land very well thus far and really will only benefit whites. Oil and other mineral interests, with governmental cooperation, threaten to run roughshod over the social and property rights of Eskimos and northern Indians in Alaska and Canada. Canada is trying to move down the road to termination with the same misguided liberal rationalizations of "desegregation" and total lack of understanding of Indians' problems as were shown in the 1950s in the United States.

If we respond to these and a host of similar cases which could be cited with the view that these problems are not the business of anthropologists, that there is nothing we can do, that these problems do not concern "my tribe" or "my theoretical orientation," then we must be prepared to take the consequences in our relationships with Indians in the future. It is as simple as that.

Let us find out what Indian people think anthropologists can do, whether to donate money, write to appropriate senators or congressmen, volunteer as expert consultants, engage in research or set our students on research Indian people desire which could still provide valuable learning experience for the students.

39.
Science: Forever Incomplete

Claude Lévi-Strauss

Some 35 years ago I spent several years in the United States. And I hope—this is only a hope that I entertain—I may have helped to build a bridge between an American intellectual tradition deeply embedded in the empiricist and positivist character of the Anglo-Saxon world stemming from Bacon through Locke and Hume, and the French rationalist tradition which is usually associated with the name of Descartes.

Out of this attempt, out of this mixture, if I may say so, a very strange offspring has appeared, bearing the name structuralism, a creation in which I fear neither America nor France would be willing to recognize herself. In my view, structuralism is trying at one and the same time to make the social sciences a little bit more scientific, even while its practitioners are quite aware that the social sciences are limited as sciences, and that we will probably never be able to reach the levels to which we aspire. I would like to offer a few reflections on this paradox.

I have said that we are trying to make the social sciences a little more scientific. Why and how can be summarized, I believe, in terms of three principal concepts. First, we need to recall an old lesson, one first taught in history by Marx, then in linguistics by Ferdinand de Saussure and, at about the same time, in psychology by Freud. That is, that what we perceive, what we believe, what appears at the level of consciousness, does not consist of the really important phenomena, which can only be reached at a hidden level. This insight, of course, was made possible when Descartes made his fundamental distinction between sensory data—smelling, touching, hearing, seeing and the like, which are always misleading—and the true primary qualities that physical science should solely consider, that is, what Descartes considers extension and movement.

Second, we take note that this is also what Kant told us, in a different way, when he asserted that what made knowledge possible was neither percepts nor ideas, but what he called categories of understanding, entities which are not of the same nature as the things that we believe we perceive. For if these deep structures which are hidden beneath the surface structures were to possess the same nature as the surface structures, then we would be led toward a regression *ad infinitum;* we would be imprisoned in a kind of vicious circle.

Third, we have tried to introduce into the social sciences the fundamental idea that we are looking at things which are extremely complicated and difficult, sometimes even impossible to describe because of their complexity. Yet if instead of looking at the things themselves we look at the relations which prevail between them, then we will discover that these relations are altogether more simple and less numerous than the things themselves, and that they can give us a firmer basis for investigation.

I am perfectly aware that, in opposition to this kind of approach to the social sciences and to social phenomena, several critiques may be raised, and have been raised. The first is that our hypotheses, or our interpretations, cannot be refuted, whereas in a true science it is possible to demonstrate the falsity of a hypothesis. To this assertion I will answer: This is true for a science which has reached an advanced stage of development, but it would have proved impossible for a science in its incipient state. If such a condition had been imposed upon physics at the outset, or upon chemistry, or upon biology, then these sciences would never have existed. As a matter of fact, even within the modern, advanced stages of these sciences, there are hypotheses and interpretations which cannot be refuted. (I am referring, of course, to the criterion of prediction.) Yet it is Popper himself who says of Darwinism that it is the best explanation we have. Similarly, what we as social scientists are trying to do is only to offer better explanations—which cannot be said to be true or false—than those accepted before. This certainly does not mean that our explanations will remain good forever. Indeed, quite the opposite: Later on, better explanations will prevail, and later, even better explanations, and so on. There is a progression, not an end which we can claim to reach.

The second criticism rests on the impossiblity of experimenting in the social sciences. The great superiority of the physical or biological sciences inheres in the fact that any hypothesis set forth anywhere in the world can be immediately subject to an experiment, or to numerous experiments, which can verify or refute the hypothesis. Obviously, for moral and practical reasons, we cannot experiment with human societies; and even if we had the power to do so, it would take too much time. All we can do—and this is the strength, the value of anthropology—is to go throughout the world in order to seek ready-made experiments. Those ready-made experiments are embodied in the four or five thousand societies which exist or have existed on the surface of the earth, and of which we have some records, during the documented portions of human history.

It is by virtue of the existence of these societies that I believe that it is possible for the social sciences to become somewhat more rigorous and to make some progress toward joining the more advanced sciences—let us call them the "true sciences." Nevertheless, between the "true sciences" and the so-called social or (as we perfer to say in French) "human sciences," there is a difference which we should not overlook. Whenever some great discovery is made in physics, chemistry, or biology, there is an immediate general agreement on a common frame of reference, which much simplifies the forward advance of that science. If you take, for instance, the theory of relativity some years ago, you will find that everybody agreed it was from this theoretical perspective that one should try to work. For quantum mechanics, the same consensus held. In biology, as soon as the subfield of molecular biology took shape, there was general agreement that this was the more fruitful approach. One need only look at the proceedings of the National Academy of Science in this country to see that practically all biologists are currently working with the same assumptions.

Why, then, in our case—the anthropological case—is it not at all the same situation? It is very striking that, whenever one of us anthropologists advances an interpretation or an hypothesis, hardly anyone is prepared to discuss the case and to say "you are right" or "you are wrong," for such and such a reason. Instead, the kind of response we are likely to receive is that this interpretation is of no interest because reality ought to be studied at a completely different level. It is this inability—provisional, I hope, but all the same an inability—to achieve a common frame of reference in our discipline, which reveals our weakness in relation to "true science."

We may try to go a little farther, and to ask why the situation is as I've described. The reason, in my opinion, is that in the long run what we are trying to do—whether as historians, anthropologists, sociologists, psychologists or whatever—is to fathom, at diverse levels of interpretation, what is going on in the human mind. Our difficulty is that it is impossible to prove anything about the mind, because the mind is not something we may plumb; and it is always possible (indeed, essential) to postulate that, when we uncover a deep structure, there will be another structure even deeper, and then another deeper yet. The mind is not of the same order as the things we are able to study, and this is because the "mind" is not a thing: It represents the way we apprehend things, and this discrepancy confronts us with a contradiction which may be forever impossible to overcome.

Now the question is—and this will be my final observation—whether this unhappy situation is specific to the social sciences or whether it exists to some extent in all the sciences, even the more advanced ones. It has been very heartening for us in the past years to see that the more advanced sciences are increasingly borrowing models from the social sciences. It is, for instance, striking that in trying to describe the genetic code, biology borrows heavily from linguistics; and that biologists are also borrowing from sociologists when they speak, for instance, of cell sociology—looking at communication between cells as a phenomenon comparable to social process. And it seems to me that, in a different way and perhaps to a more limited extent, the advanced sciences are now confronting those same antinomies and contradictions that we ourselves have confronted for so long. Thus for instance, molecular biologists have pointed out over and over again that the components that translate the genetic code are themselves coded in DNA. It follows that in order to make a code, a code is accordingly needed. There appears to be a kind of vicious circle here; in the long run it may be as impossible to explain what is life, as it will probably prove impossible for us in the social sciences to explain what is the mind and what is consciousness. It is striking, moreover, that the historical approach has of late been invading biology, physics, and chemistry. Biology, for instance, since it has now completely abandoned the old idea of a unilinear evolution from elementary life forms to more complex, and from complex to even more complex, and so on, is now viewing evolution rather as historians consider history. That is, biology is now concerned with showing that while there is progress and movement, at the same time there is also regression; that rather than unidirectionality, there is a multiplicity of directions; that instead of an "evolutionary tree" (which was the illustration fashionable in the last century), there is a branching pattern more like an intricate bush, the growth pattern of which can be described but not accounted for by a simple law. The same case may be made in regard to the attempt to reduce chemistry to physics, a great problem of the more advanced sciences and, in the long run, a problem in the history of the cosmos—a history which is obviously a unique event, one which cannot be explained, cannot be proved, cannot be refuted or falsified.

Of course, a great difference remains between the hard sciences, if I may call them that, and our own. This difference is that these problems, these antinomies, these difficulties which are logically impossible to solve, confront the more advanced sciences only when they engage the ultimate problems, and there are a great many problems they can solve before confronting the ultimate questions. Yet we social scientists are confronted with these difficulties at every step. This is one of the fundamental weaknesses—and perhaps also the fundamental greatness—of the humane sciences: that all problems pertaining *to* humankind are ultimate problems *for* humankind. There is no problem, however small, that does not concern each of us, because our life interests, our personal histories, our temperaments, our prejudices are immediately implicated in every problem. This is probably why the social sciences should not pretend to reach truth, which may be impossible to attain, but (more modestly) should strive for some measure of wisdom—the achievement of which is supremely difficult, as a matter of fact. But if we are able to make even some limited progress towards wisdom, then we may be—and this is perhaps our advantage—we may be more ready to resign ourselves to the general truth that science will remain forever incomplete.

Contributors

ROGER D. ABRAHAMS is professor of anthropology and humanities at Pitzer College and a folklorist and folksinger who has recorded on the Prestige and Folkways labels. He is the author of *Deep Down in the Jungle: Negro Narrative Folklore from the Streets of Philadelphia* and *Talking Black.*

FREDRIK BARTH is professor of anthropology at the University of Bergen in Norway, and is the author of numerous publications on Southeast Asian tribes, notably *Political Leadership among Swat Pathans* and *Nomads of South Persia.* He is also editor of the volume, *Ethnic Groups and Boundaries.*

JOHN W. BENNETT is professor of anthropology at Washington University in St. Louis. Among his numerous published works are *Hutterian Brethren: The Agricultural Economy and Social Organization of a Communal People* and *The Ecological Transition.*

RUTH BLUMENFELD teaches in the department of psychiatry, Children's Hospital, in Washington, D.C., and also in the department of anthropology at George Washington University. Her major fields of interest are the psychological aspects of cultural change and the development of social science courses for medical students.

JEAN L. BRIGGS is professor of anthropology at Memorial University of Newfoundland, and is the author of *Never in Anger: Portrait of an Eskimo Family.* Her principal research area is Eskimo ethnopsychology and values.

LUCY M. COHEN is professor of anthropology at Catholic University and president of the Society for Medical Anthropology. Her research interests combine community action efforts and minority issues—particularly those affecting migrant women.

RONALD COHEN is professor of anthropology and political science at Northwestern University. He has done research in Nigeria and in Arctic Canada, and is the coeditor (with Elman R. Service) of *Origins of the State: The Anthropology of Political Evolution*.

RICHARD W. FRANKE teaches anthropology at Montclair State College in New Jersey, and is the coauthor (with Barbara Chasin) of a volume on West Africa, *The Political Economy of Ecological Destruction*.

NATHAN L. GERRARD is professor of sociology at Morris Harvey College in West Virginia. His research interests are the cultural and social patterns of the "hollows"—the communities of the nonfarming poor in West Virginia.

GEORGE GMELCH teaches anthropology at the State University of New York at Albany. In addition to playing minor league and professional baseball, he has done research in Mexico and in Ireland, and is the author of *The Irish Tinkers: The Urbanization of an Itinerant People*.

JEANNE GUILLEMIN is associate professor of sociology at Boston College, and is former Congressional Fellow of the American Anthropological Association (1978-79). She is the author of *Urban Renegades: The Cultural Strategy of American Indians*. Dr. Guillemin's research interest is medical ethics and health care policy.

MARVIN HARRIS is professor of anthropology at Columbia University, and is the author of numerous publications on anthropological theory, including *The Nature of Cultural Things, The Rise of Anthropological Theory*, and *Culture, People, Nature: An Introduction to General Anthropology*.

JULES HENRY was professor of anthropology at Washington University in St. Louis, and is the author of the classic, *Culture Against Man*. He was consultant to the National Institute of Mental Health study of the Pruitt-Igoe housing project, and also consulted for the U.S. Office of Education, the Joint Commission on Mental Illness and Health, and the World Health Organization.

IRVING LOUIS HOROWITZ is Hannah Arendt distinguished professor of sociology and political science at Rutgers University. His numerous works include *Three Worlds of Development: Theory and Practice of*

International Stratification and *Taking Lives: Genocide and State Power.* He is editor-in-chief of *Society* magazine.

THOMAS KOCHMAN teaches in the department of speech theatre at the University of Illinois. His research interest is the ethnography of minority speech behavior. He is the author of *Rappin' and Stylin' Out: Communication in Urban Black America.*

CONRAD KOTTAK is professor of anthropology at the University of Michigan. In addition to writing on his fieldwork, he is the author of *Anthropology: The Exploration of Human Diversity* and *Cultural Anthropology.*

CLAUDE LÉVI-STRAUSS is the director of the Laboratory of Social Anthropology at the University of Paris and holds the chair in social anthropology at the College de France. He is a leader in the development of structuralism in anthropology, and has written many books, his best known being *The Savage Mind, The Elementary Structures of Kinship,* and four volumes on primitive mythology. His article included here was originally presented at the Johns Hopkins centennial celebration in 1978.

CHARLES J. LEVY has worked in the Laboratory of Community Psychiatry at Harvard Medical School on the problems of Vietnam veterans. His book, *Spoils of War,* is based on this research.

OSCAR LEWIS was professor of anthropology at the University of Illinois at Urbana. He wrote numerous books on the culture of poverty. Among them are *La Vida, A Puerto Rican Family in the Culture of Poverty, The Children of Sanchez,* and *Five Families.*

NANCY OESTREICH LURIE is professor of anthropology at the University of Wisconsin at Milwaukee. Her major field research has been with the Winnebago and Dogrib Indian tribes. She is the author of *Mountain Wolf Woman, Sister of Crashing Thunder: The Autobiography of a Winnebago Indian.* With Stuart Levine, she edited *The American Indian Today.* Her other activities include extensive involvement in Indian legal cases.

DAVID G. MANDELBAUM is professor of anthropology at the University of California at Berkeley. He is the author of the two-volume work, *Society in India,* and *Human Fertility in India: Social Components and Policy Perspectives.*

MARGARET MEAD was curator emeritus at the American Museum of Natural History, and was the leading exponent of anthropology in America. Among her many published works is *Culture and Commitment:*

A Study of the Generation Gap (with Rhoda Metraux). The article included in this volume is an edited transcript of an address to Barnard College students and their parents in 1970.

JOHN MIDDLETON is professor of anthropology at University College in London. He has done fieldwork in Uganda, Zanzibar and Nigeria, and is the author of *Lugbara Religion* and *The Central Tribes of the North-Eastern Bantu.*

CHARLES MOSKOS is professor of sociology at Northwestern University. He was program chairman of the National Bicentennial Symposium on the Greek Experience in America, and is the author of *Greek Americans: The Urban Conservatives.*

LEONARD PLOTNICOV is professor of anthropology at the University of Pittsburgh. He has done extensive field research in Nigeria, and is the author of *Strangers to the City: Urban Man in Jos, Nigeria.* With Arthur Tuden, he edited the volume, *Social Stratification in Africa.*

PAUL RIESMAN teaches anthropology at Carleton College. His research interests are dreams, myths, and individualism in traditional societies.

LAWRENCE ROSEN is professor of anthropology at Princeton University and a member of the New York State Bar Association. In addition to publications on Moroccan law and culture, he has edited *American Indians and the Law.*

DONALD ROTHCHILD is professor of political science at the University of California at Davis. He has conducted extensive research on ethnicity and Third World development in Africa. He has been visiting professor at the University of Ghana in Legon.

ABDUL A. SAID is professor of international relations at American University. His research interests are ethnicity, terrorism, and human rights. He is the coeditor (with Luiz R. Simmons) of *The Ethnic Factor in World Politics.*

LUIZ R. SIMMONS is the coeditor (with Abdul Said) of *The Ethnic Factor in World Politics.* He is editor of the *International Yearbook on Drug Addiction* and coeditor (with Martin Gold) of *Discrimination and the Addict.*

HEATHER STRANGE teaches anthropology at University College at Rutgers University. Her field research has included a study of the socioeconomic roles of village women in Malaysia.

Contributors

ANNE SUTHERLAND teaches anthropology at the University of Durham in England. She is the author of *Gypsies: The Hidden Americans.*

GERALD D. SUTTLES is professor of sociology at the State University of New York at Stony Brook. He is the author of *The Social Order of the Slum: Ethnicity and Territoriality in the Inner City* and *The Social Construction of Communities.*

ROBERT K. THOMAS teaches at Wayne State University, and has done field research in several American Indian communities. With Sol Tax, he codirected the Carnegie Cross-Cultural Education Project that was based primarily on the situation of the Oklahoma Cherokee.

ARTHUR TUDEN is professor of anthropology at the University of Pittsburgh. He has done extensive fieldwork in Rhodesia, and his main research interest has been on social stratification in African societies. He is the coeditor (with Vera Rubin) of *Comparative Perspectives on Slavery in New World Plantation Societies* and (with Leonard Plotnicov) of *Social Stratification in Africa.*

ALBERT WAHRHAFTIG teaches anthropology at Sonoma State College, and is a former research associate with the Carnegie Cross-Cultural Education Project, which was codirected by Robert K. Thomas and Sol Tax and focussed primarily on the Oklahoma Cherokee.

S. L. WASHBURN is university professor in the department of anthropology at the University of California at Berkeley. He is author of numerous works in physical anthropology and is the coauthor (with Elizabeth McCown) of *Human Evolution: Biosocial Perspectives.*

ROSALIE WAX is professor of anthropology at the University of Washington in St. Louis, and is the author of *Doing Fieldwork: Warnings and Advice,* as well as numerous publications on American Indian education.

MELFORD S. WEISS teaches sociology at California State University in Sacramento. His research interests include community development and Chinese society. He is the author of *Valley City: A Chinese Community in America.*

LIBRARY OF DAVIDSON COLLEGE